Creative Writing

FICTION, DRAMA, POETRY and THE ESSAY

Creative Writing

FICTION, DRAMA, POETRY and THE ESSAY

Howard C. Brashers
UNIVERSITY OF MICHIGAN

 D. VAN NOSTRAND COMPANY

New York   Cincinnati   Toronto   London   Melbourne

D. Van Nostrand Company Regional Offices:
NEW YORK   CINCINNATI   MILLBRAE

D. Van Nostrand Company International Offices:
LONDON   TORONTO   MELBOURNE

Copyright © 1968 by LITTON EDUCATIONAL PUBLISHING, INC.

ISBN: 0-442-20740-9

Published by D. Van Nostrand Company
450 West 33rd Street, New York, N.Y. 10001

5   4   3

Copyright Acknowledgments

ALBERT J. GUERARD: For his scansion of seven lines of "Wintry Delights" by Robert Bridges. Reprinted by permission.

HARCOURT, BRACE & WORLD, INC.: For "anyone lived in a pretty how town" by E. E. Cummings. Copyright, 1940, by E. E. Cummings. Reprinted from his volume *Poems 1923–1954* by permission of Harcourt, Brace & World, Inc.

HOLT, RINEHART AND WINSTON, INC.: For "Teaching Poems in Pairs" by H. C. Brashers; first printed in *Exercise Exchange*. For two brief excerpts from *Linguistics and English Grammar* by H. A. Gleason, Jr. Copyright © 1965 by Holt, Rinehart and Winston, Inc., Publishers.

KENNETH JOHNSON: For "Remedies" and "Travelers" by Kenneth Johnson. "Travelers" appeared first in *Verb* Magazine.

THE KENYON REVIEW: "Fiction and the 'Matrix of Analogy'" by Mark Schorer. First published in *The Kenyon Review*. Reprinted by permission of *The Kenyon Review* and Mark Schorer.

ALFRED A. KNOPF, INC.: For "The Glass of Water" by Wallace Stevens. Copyright 1942 by Wallace Stevens. For "The Snow Man" by Wallace Stevens. Copyright 1923 and renewed 1951 by Wallace Stevens. Both the above reprinted from *The Collected Poems of Wallace Stevens* by permission of Alfred A. Knopf, Inc.

LITTLE, BROWN AND COMPANY: For "After Great Pain, a Formal Feeling Comes" by Emily Dickinson. Copyright, 1929, © 1957, by Mary L. Hampson. From *The Complete Poems of Emily Dickinson*, edited by Thomas H. Johnson, by permission of Little, Brown and Company.

THE MACMILLAN COMPANY: For "The Ruined Maid" by Thomas Hardy. Reprinted with permission of The Macmillan Company from *Collected Poems* by Thomas Hardy. Copyright 1925 by The Macmillan Company. For "Critics and Connoisseurs" and "The Fish" by Marianne Moore. Reprinted with permission of The Macmillan Company from *Collected Poems* by Marianne Moore. Copyright 1935 by Marianne Moore; renewed 1963 by Marianne Moore and T. S. Eliot. For "Eros Turannos" by Edwin Arlington Robinson. Reprinted with permission of The Macmillan Company from *Collected Poems* by Edwin Arlington Robinson. Copyright 1916 by The Macmillan Company; renewed 1944 by Ruth Nivison.

THE MARVELL PRESS: For "Poetry of Departures" by Philip Larkin, reprinted from *The Less Deceived* by permission of The Marvell Press, Hessle, Yorkshire, England.

ELLEN C. MASTERS: For "Lucinda Matlock" by Edgar Lee Masters. Reprinted from *Spoon River Anthology* by Edgar Lee Masters (Macmillan 1914, 1942) by permission.

NEW DIRECTIONS PUBLISHING CORPORATION: For "In a Station of the Metro" by Ezra Pound. From Ezra Pound, *Personae*. Copyright 1926, 1954 by Ezra Pound. For "Poem in October" by Dylan Thomas. From *The Collected Poems of Dylan Thomas*. Copyright 1946 by New Directions. For "To Waken an Old Lady" by William Carlos Williams. Copyright 1938, 1951 by William

Carlos Williams. The above three items reprinted by permission of New Directions Publishing Corporation.

W. W. NORTON & COMPANY, INC.: For two excerpts from *Madame Bovary,* A Norton Critical Edition, by Gustave Flaubert. Edited with a substantially new translation by Paul De Man. By permission of W. W. Norton & Company, Inc.

PRINCETON UNIVERSITY PRESS: For "Specific Continuous Forms (Prose Fiction)" by Northrop Frye. From *Anatomy of Criticism* by Northrop Frye. For "Huswifery" by Edward Taylor. From *The Poetical Works of Edward Taylor,* T. H. Johnson (ed.), copyright 1939 Rockland Editions, 1943 Princeton University Press. Both the above reprinted by permission of Princeton University Press.

RANDOM HOUSE, INC.: For "O Where Are You Going" by W. H. Auden. Copyright 1934 and renewed 1961 by W. H. Auden. For "The Unknown Citizen" by W. H. Auden. Copyright 1940 by W. H. Auden. Both reprinted from *The Collected Poetry of W. H. Auden* by permission of Random House, Inc. For "Barn Burning" by William Faulkner. Copyright 1939 by William Faulkner. Reprinted from *Collected Stories of William Faulkner* by permission of Random House, Inc.

CHARLES SCRIBNER'S SONS: For "Soldier's Home," reprinted with the permission of Charles Scribner's Sons from *In Our Time* by Ernest Hemingway. Copyright 1925 Charles Scribner's Sons; renewal copyright 1953 Ernest Hemingway. For the following material, reprinted with the permission of Charles Scribner's Sons: Epigraph from *Look Homeward Angel* by Thomas Wolfe (copyright 1929 Charles Scribner's Sons; renewal copyright © 1957 Edward C. Aswell, Administrator C. T. A. and/or Fred Wolfe); excerpt from *The Great Gatsby* by F. Scott Fitzgerald (copyright 1925 Charles Scribner's Sons; renewal copyright 1953 Frances Scott Fitzgerald Lanahan); and "Luke Havergal" from *The Children of the Night* by Edwin Arlington Robinson.

HERBERT J. SPINDEN: For "Song of the Sky Loom." Reprinted from *Songs of the Tewa.* Copyright Herbert J. Spinden. By permission.

ESTATE OF ALAN SWALLOW: For Yvor Winters' scansion of "To Waken an Old Lady" by William Carlos Williams.

THE VIKING PRESS, INC.: For excerpt from "The Horse Dealer's Daughter." From *The Complete Short Stories of D. H. Lawrence,* Volume II. Copyright 1922 by Thomas B. Seltzer, Inc., 1950 by Frieda Lawrence. Reprinted by permission of The Viking Press, Inc.

Preface

Creative Writing is an attempt to isolate, define, and illustrate the gamut of techniques available to the creative writer and to provide exercises in the more important of these techniques. The isolation and definition of technique is, of course, what we usually mean when we speak of theoretical criticism; the illustrations amount to a short anthology; the exercises, because they usually present new material, are a sort of textbook. I have tried to integrate these several aspects, so that the book can serve both as a handbook of writing concepts and terminology and as a textbook in creative writing.

The basic assumption throughout this text is that writing can be taught. Though the prospective writer has to supply creativity and ideas from some source other than a course in creative writing, the creative writing course *can* present technique, encourage practice, and evaluate specific efforts. Every writer has to learn technique somewhere, since none is born with it and none writes successfully without it. In a creative writing course, we can teach the techniques that it might take a writer many years to learn by accident. This book is an attempt to obviate accident by presenting a programmed tour through possibilities.

Creative Writing is built around a four-stage learning process that every writer, whether consciously or not, goes through in learning to write. First, he analyzes the technique and potential of at least one of the forms—fiction, drama, poetry, or essay. He learns by impression or discipline how the form allows or encourages the use of certain qualities of language and discourages other uses; how the form deals in a characteristic mode of thought and resists other modes; how the form can achieve one aesthetic effect and not another. This analysis may be conscious and, thus, usable in the creative process. Or it may remain at the level of impression, where it operates more or less as a taste for a particular kind of thing in a particular genre; then the writer will compose through the spontaneous overflow of inspiration, and success will come, if at all, by accident.

Second, he compares what he knows with every bit of new information that he learns. He compares his analysis of the effect of a certain technique with every new use of that technique, compares it with similar techniques; contrasts it with different ones. He compares the forms of writing, one with the other. He compares every new story or poem he reads with what he has learned or thought about stories and poems. Slowly, he builds up a critical or historical or aesthetic background in the forms of writing, and he begins to use this background in his writing.

Third, he begins to imitate. If he is lucky or conscious, he won't imitate any specific writer's style or subject matter, but will imitate a technique here, a pattern there, an effect that would enhance his own thought, a use of language that wakes the reader. It is inevitable that we learn writing, as we learn language, partly by imitating the patterns we perceive in our culture, though imitation will not take a writer beyond the repetition of what has already been said or written.

Fourth, he creates. As a child learns oral language, he learns to put what he has analyzed, compared, imitated into meaningful patterns, such as have never occurred before. He finds, invents, creates those linguistic and literary patterns that communicate his thought. The more conscious he is about linguistic and literary patterns, the more likely he is to create something of value.

Creative Writing, by offering these four kinds of projects at every stage, allows a scope at once specific and broad, a scope that might be called an introduction to—or the fundamental techniques of—creative writing.

The book has grown out of my own study, out of notes and suggestions I started collecting when I was a student of Walter Van Tilburg Clark at San Francisco State College. I expanded these materials considerably while I was studying with John Williams at Denver University and talking often with Alan Swallow. I have added to it, over the years, as I have discovered new things in the process of teaching creative writing and in connection with my own writing. Moreover, there are innumerable sources in the process of my education to which I owe a debt of idea. If I present as my own what someone before me invented, it is my ignorance that causes me not to acknowledge his invention. We two have arrived at the same place by different routes.

Exuberant thanks for help while writing go to Robert L. Stilwell, my University of Michigan office mate, who was often an initial sounding board for new ideas; to Robert K. Johnson, now of the University of Bridgeport; and to Jay L. Robinson, of the University of Michigan. But the *sine qua non* of the book is my patient wife, Kerstin, who tolerated the loneliness and irascibility of a man in the act of writing.

H. C. B.

Contents

Introductory Note

Western man has traditionally valued five modes of aesthetic perception—the experiential, the dynamic, the meditative, the factual, and the mythic. These modes lie behind and distinguish our literary forms. Each of these forms deals with experience, but the process of aesthetic perception in each is different from the process in the others. The experiential mode, characterized by the illusion in the mind of an experience, whether familiar or fantastic, has usually taken the form of narrative. The writer of narrative prose fiction depends upon the capacity of the human mind to ignore the paper, ink, binding, etc., and to *see*, as it were, what the author has only written. The aesthetic process of perception is one of imaginative creation of image and idea, in which the function of the imagination is essential. This has unfortunately and one-sidedly been called the illusion of reality, but *that* illusion is only one side of experience. Very unreal symbols can communicate very real experiences. There is even a point where what we ordinarily call reality ceases to be of importance and what we can understand becomes primary. Here, the function of imagination is the mode of knowing.

The dynamic mode, characterized by the "movement," growth, or competition of ideas and images, has usually taken the form of drama. Works in mere language, for which our imaginations must supply the visual and conceptual details, can be made dynamic only with difficulty. This is not because of a failure of the imagination, but a limit of language. Language, usually, must take up one image-idea at a time, and no matter how rapidly it shifts subject, it must lay down the first before it can pick up the next. The techniques of the theater allow us to see several image-ideas in process, simultaneously. When these symbols on stage interact, compete, intertwine, we in the audience have the sense of ideas in motion. The aesthetic process of perception is direct and immediate and approaches the aesthetic conditions and processes of our own, private experience, not imagined experience. Perceiving the dynamism of idea-images is a mode of knowing; it is to emotional thought what the ostensible definition is to everyday life.

The meditative mode, characterized by a conceptual recognition of the relationships between the particular and the universal, has usually taken the form of the lyric. The lyric is, by definition, concerned with "expressing the poet's personal or inner feelings," but such particular meanings become art, become of interest to us, only when the poet manipulates enough patterns or symbols or experiences that the meaning takes on a degree of universality, takes on a quality of being abstracted from the particular experience and thus becomes applicable to the experiences of others. The lyric "I" has to become the reader, and what happens to it must be not only what happened to the poet, but also what could happen to you or me. The aesthetic process by which this transfer takes place is one of evaluation or meditation.

The factual mode, characterized by assertion and proof, is used widely in science, history, and such, but, in literature, usually takes the form of the essay. From the beginning, the essay has been an attempt to discover, establish, and defend the factuality of an idea in relation to other facts of the world. (Even the defense of an opinion is an attempt to establish its factuality.) In establishing such relationships, logic, the manipulation of facts and potential facts, whether used for persuasion, instruction, or entertainment, is instrumental; or, to put it another way, the process of perception is intellectual. (This does not eliminate emotion nor emotional content from essays, for emotions and emotional content are also aesthetic facts.)

The mythic mode, characterized by the use of symbolic characters and settings and the use of ritual, or symbolic action, has usually taken the form of religions, but in recent times has been treated a little less sacredly, as in Faulkner's *The Bear*. Myth works best (perhaps only) when we are unconscious of it—when we have a sense, not of myth, but of importance transcended and become essence, of understanding surpassed and become knowing. We usually indicate the great value we place on this mode of thought by saying that it is *above* reality and involves the *deepest* concerns of the human mind. Myth is to ordinary reality what emotional conviction is to understanding.

Each of these forms can make use of all the modes of thought, but will subordinate the other modes to its characteristic one. Religion obviously uses narrative, drama, lyric, oratory, and what variations on them can be invented, but it uses them in the service of, uses them in the production of, symbol and ritual. The essay, though usually and primarily factual, can use lyric, dramatic, anecdotal, or epic materials, without ceasing to be an essay, that is, without changing its basic aesthetic strategy of assertion, proof, logic, and factuality. The lyric can, within the limits of its usual mode, present its subject through assertion, or metaphor, or narrative, and, within these and other techniques, can be speculative or didactic or what have you. Drama can (and does) deal with social problems, ideas, propaganda, clichés, dreams, stereotypes, and whatever, without ceasing to be aesthetically dramatic. Prose fiction can deal with all of these—subject only to the limits of language and the imagination.

Each of these forms exists because it can communicate meanings which man finds important and which the other forms cannot communicate. This is to say that the language of fact communicates something different from, say, the language of myth. If the language of fact *could* express whatever man finds important in myth, the language of myth would not exist. Each of the literary forms exists because its aesthetic perceptions are unique and valuable. Whoever would write literature should be as familiar as possible with the immensely complicated issues of and variety in knowing and communicating.

To the Reader

An asterisk in this text, after the name of an author and/or title, indicates the presence of the asterisked item elsewhere in this text and in a special index immediately following the general index at the back of the book. The special index will facilitate quick location of cross-referenced items.

FICTION

E VERY subject is material for fiction; every subject is potential as art. Just as Edward Steichen and other photographers showed at the turn of the century that anything is potential subject for pictorial art, even a broken bottleneck, depending for its aesthetic effect upon technical treatment —the angle, the lighting, the focus, the development—so fiction writers have shown that every subject is available to fiction. The treatment is all.

Given, then, subject matter or experience out of which subject can be fashioned, technique is the most important thing for a young writer to learn. One does not expect to sing beautifully, or play the violin, without first having learned and practiced the elementals of those arts. One should not expect to write fiction well until he has, in some degree, mastered technique.

But which techniques? There are, after all, many different ways of looking at fictional techniques. We can, for instance, try to define fiction and try to distinguish it from the various forms of thought and writing that it resembles but is not to be identified with. We can look at its parts, the way Aristotle looked at poetic drama in his time, and discuss the range, distribution, and manipulability of such things as character, place, action. We can discuss fiction with regard to its rhetorical maneuvers—description, narration, exposition, and argument—which at various times take the form of various of the parts. Or we can discuss fictions as long, short, or of medium length; as realistic, fantastic, symbolic, imaginative; in verse, prose, or dialog. Novels, short stories, novellas, epics, short expository poems, long lyric poems, tragedies, comedies, satires, tales—almost all literary products—are fictions in one sense: they are artificial, created, "untrue." The house of fiction has many windows, said Henry James, and they look out upon many vistas.

All such approaches to the subject illuminate when they are opened. Here, a chapter on "The Materials and Forms of Fiction" evokes and discusses very briefly a few of these approaches in the hope that the brief treatment will be enough to keep the reader aware of the issues as matters quite different are discussed. The approach to fiction in this book is a combination of the general framework of style, as discussed in chapter 2, and what are essentially the Aristotelian parts of poetic drama. There are separate, detailed chapters on Style, Character, Setting, Point-of-View, Plot, Structure, and Theme, but hopefully the reader will be aware of these continually in relation to the style that is everything—be aware that point-of-view and choices of language are what define such audible elements of fiction as seriousness, rhythm, tone, mood; be aware that the vocabulary of fiction, the vehicles which carry the communication (as words carry the communication of language), consists of character, scene, and incident; be aware that the grammar of fiction, the means by which it communicates, is the imitation of experience, either rendered fully in scene or dialog, or summarized; be aware that plot and strategy in revelation account for the organization of fiction; and finally be aware that structure, which is described in terms of design and pattern, is the means of heightening the communication, of achieving aesthetic effect, of focusing theme.

For most of us, fiction exists, first and finally, for its theme. Much comes between the first and the finally—character, style, and such—and theme is not merely the meaning or ideas treated. A fiction is a created thing; it is created by a certain intelligence; that intelligence injects its perceptions, values, its totems and taboos, into the fiction it creates. For the author, the first existence of fiction is as a vehicle for expressing and communicating such themes; every fiction is thus a maneuver in persuasion and every writer is a teacher— he is trying to get the reader to accept a whole nexus. The value of fiction to the reader, finally, is in the perception of this nexus. None of us can live all experience, but a writer can show us what it is like to live beyond our limitations, can communicate to us potential feelings and values. Such "themes" are inevitable to fiction. Thus, while any subject is material for fiction, fiction exists for the theme in the subject.

1

An Introduction to The Materials and Forms of Fiction

There are at least four—and these are by no means all—ways of analyzing the materials and forms of fiction—the perceptual materials of fiction: character, action, setting, and such; the rhetorical modes in fiction: description, narration, exposition, and argument; the traditional distinctions of genres: sketch, short story, novella, and novel; and Northrop Frye's four forms of fiction: novel, romance, confession, and anatomy. These ways of analyzing are mutually exclusive, but every fiction will involve all the perceptual materials and all the rhetorical modes. All the forms use all the materials, inescapably.

The Aristotelian Materials of Fiction

Fiction is an imitation and communication, usually in prose, of experience, as expressed in character, scene, and action. Character, scene, and action are unavoidable in practical experience, for they make up our everyday world; it is no surprise that fiction should depend heavily and primarily upon them. Fiction, as literature, usually involves also several elements of aesthetic experience—style, point-of-view, structure, theme. Except for point-of-view, these are Aristotle's six "parts" of the drama, which most of us agree are closely related to fiction today. The techniques associated with each of these "parts"

5

involve certain conventions which are the main subject of this book and which deserve some short mention here.

Imitation is what we have traditionally referred to as *mimesis,* the depiction of possible experience. In one sense, this sets fiction in contrast to fact, though not necessarily in contrast to truth. "Truth is stranger than Fiction," says Mark Twain, "but that is because Fiction is obliged to stick to possibilities; Truth isn't." There have been many fictions that violated possible fact. One need only look at adventure literature with all its escape and romance to find fiction that is inimical to fact. But this is not to say that such fantasy is non-reality, for even these kinds of imitations are realities of human experience. Indeed, some of these experiences, in different periods of history, have seemed more real than life, as Aristotle suggested literature is. Productions of the imagination are very real, too, and can be imitated with truth. Imitation, in this sense, is the reproduction or re-creation, through description, narration, exposition, and argument, of imaginative reality.

Communication in literature depends on such a truth of the imagination. Each fiction is a kind of re-created country in which happen, as if anew, all the experiences that the writer is trying to communicate; a nexus of character, scene, and action; a "world." Each happening in that world is a perception for the reader. Each perception is an understanding, an evaluation, a mastering of knowledge about experience. What more is living? The writer, by controlling and shaping the happenings in a fiction, communicates his vision of life and living.

Prose is the usual form of such communication, though there is no reason that it should not be in verse or in speech. Indeed, there have been many fictions in verse (see, for example, "My Last Duchess," *), and fiction is related historically and temperamentally to the oral narrative, the tale told around the campfire. Though the confusions of modern civilization and the complexities of living have encouraged larger audiences than campfire circles and have created complex forms of distribution, most fiction retains the quality of being told. The voice, the oral quality persists. And though early fictions (as well as the history and biography that went into epic) were usually in verse, we have tended to prefer prose for our modern fictions. Verse focuses a little too much upon the felicity and perception of words; fiction depends more upon the re-imagined world, which is re-created most easily in prose. Indeed, one of the basic conventions of fiction is our aesthetic ignoring of the print on the page and the prose in the language. Our attention must fall away from these realities to allow the imagination to do the actual re-creating. The language, whether in verse, prose, or dialog, is merely a medium of imagination. One can say truthfully, then, that fiction is not in prose, but in the language of the imagination. What gets said, what gets communicated in a fiction, is simply what is made real in the imagination.

Experience in fiction is simply what is made real to the imagination. Fiction has often been tied to realism and "realism" has usually meant a kind of factual reproduction of the practical aspects of experience—character, scene, and action. But experience is more than practical, and what the imagination dwells upon is as real as the stone one kicks. The imagination may dwell upon the physically and scientifically impossible, as it often does in Romance, but it will always focus upon what Hawthorne calls the truth of the human heart. The very fact that the imagination produces an image makes the image real and makes it satisfactory material for fiction.

Character in fiction is always human, since that is all we can imagine. Even our inhuman ogres are products of the human imagination and are defined in the good and evil terms that the imagination perceives in experience. Al Kapp's "schmoo's" may seem non-human, but they are, in fact, extremely human. They reproduce prolifically, are marvellously eatable; they love to provide themselves for dinner; they are at once masochistic and protective. But all these qualities are very human in conception. So far as we know, only the human *thinks* about reproducing, about eating, about provision and protectiveness. "Schmoo's" are unusual manifestations of human characteristics, but they are human nonetheless. Trustworthy, loyal, brave Lassie is as good a boy scout as any human counterpart. In fiction, these characters may range from a costumed stick to a haunting threat, depending upon the experience the writer wishes to communicate. In our time, we have thought that these levels of character are primary in fiction, though such has not always been the case; Aristotle, for example, thought action, not character, was primary, but that was because the Classic concept of man reduced character to types.

Scene in fiction is the representation of space and the objects that occur in it, what Aristotle called spectacle. It is wholly visual because the human thinking process is probably pictorial. Thinking, for babies, is probably a process of perceiving images in the mind. "Mother" does not mean a responsible relationship, but a configuration of teeth, hair, and milk glands. Later, abstraction becomes possible, and we begin to think in the concepts that abstract words denote. But it is quite possible that abstract thinking is really only a "picturing" of abstract words. Such thinking has too few aspects to be used very successfully in fiction. To picture a word is not to make it memorable in the same way as to perceive an image with its thousand interrelationships worth ten thousand words. Further, the image is constant in our experience, even in dreams. Such images make up the scenes of fiction.

Action, too, is an integral part of experience, an inevitable fact of existence. Even non-action, or the absence of action is, in this case, a kind of action; this is expressed fictionally in the irresolution of plot. Incident is the movement of character in relation to other characters and to the scene. As Aristotle pointed out long ago, such action is the way we know what a man stands for, for his actions reveal his motivations. All this is practical and inescapable, even in daily life. In fictions, the incidents are arranged so as to reveal and illuminate such motivations. The conventions of plotting are ways in which we reduce the confusion of incident to the unity of action.

Style has both its practical and aesthetic aspects. At the practical level, its primary job is to evoke the experience which is to be communicated. If it fails to evoke the experience, though the experience may be mentioned, the experience is simply not there. On the other hand, everything that the style evokes becomes a part of the experience. Here style is content. But style also has an aesthetic dimension suggested by such terms as "felicity of expression." Fiction lives upon a certain amount of felicitous expression, but cannot live on too much. Excessive attention to words or expressions puts style back in the concerns of poetry; too little makes it mundane. Somewhere between these extremes is a point where style not only communicates practical details, but entertains us with the beauty of presentation as well.

Point-of-view, too, has its practical and aesthetic aspects. In practical life, point-of-view is limited to our own minds, our own perceptions; it limits out all other possible perceptions. The drama, of course, is limited to this point-of-view and to a fixed perceptual distance. That physical point-of-view is unvarying in drama probably accounts for the analytically-minded Aristotle's failure to isolate it as one of the "parts," though he does discuss briefly the effect of summarizing past and off-stage actions, as opposed to rendering them in character, scene, and action. Aesthetically, point-of-view allows a much broader potential of experience in fiction than in drama. It allows our imagination to take on the personas of a dozen other imaginations. Thus, it enriches the experience possible in fiction. It very much broadens the range of experience which can be communicated to us.

Structure is an almost wholly artificial matter in fiction; it deals with harmonies, with thematic variations, with totality, with what Aristotle called melody, though Aristotle was also concerned literally with music and song. In life, actions do not end, do not have structure, but blend with, and continue in, other experiences. Yet the mind has the ability to abstract meaning from experience and can see a number of actions as cohering and making a point, can see them as structures. The convention of plotting leads to a similar convention of structuring, of shaping imaginary experience for aesthetic effect. Such structure is very valuable for it allows us the illusion of mastering experience. It puts the experience in a package that can be seen at once as various and unified. Structure is a way of satisfying our aesthetic need for variety and unity.

Theme is equated with meaning in fiction. Experiences in life may not, in fact, mean anything, but in fiction we ask that they do. The art of rendering

experiences for art's sake is probably impossible, for we do not perceive experience until it is made relevant to human life. This relevance does not have to
be practical, but may be imaginative or aesthetic. A purely hedonistic theme,
art for itself, for pure pleasure, is probably impossible. On the other hand, the
purely didactic theme, art for instruction, for improvement, seems equally impossible. Neither kind of theme can exist except in imaginative reality. Literature, and especially fiction, is a way in which we can extend the practical limits
of the fact that each of us cannot do all things. The real dimension of theme is
its ability to make imagined experience vicariously potential. The imagined
practicalities represent for us ideas, summations, judgments, in short, meaning. We go to literature, not to life, for such a dimension of meaning. The
slice of life, say thirty minutes in front of the corner drugstore, cannot satisfy
our need for theme unless it becomes like an imagined experience with its
ideas, summations, and judgments. Such a dimension of theme allows us to
participate in experience without the practical results and threats of doing so.
Thus literature is a way of knowing, a way of learning by doing aesthetically.

All these elements make up the art of fiction from one point of view. They
are all subject to certain conventions which identify them as art, not life. For
example: we accept by convention the compression and segmenting of time
in ways which contradict life. We accept radical changes of pace and distant
shifts of place without confusion. We put our trust explicitly in everything
that the author tells us in his own voice, though we know that he is "just
making this up." In one sense, we go to fiction, rather than biography or
history, because it is unreal, and we go to it, rather than philosophy, because
it is less abstract. Fiction is at once all these things—tale, biography, history,
philosophy—but it is imaginative representation of their possibilities, not their
manifestations.

The Rhetorical Modes in Fiction

Another way of looking at fiction, and approaching a definition of it, is to
consider the rhetorical modes in which the basic elements—character, action,
scene—are manifested. The Classic modes of rhetoric are description, narration,
exposition, and argument. Obviously, in fiction a character and his environment must be described, his actions narrated, his motives explained, and (in
fiction as art) his story be made to advance a thesis.

The word *description* is derived from the Latin *de* and *scribere* "to write
down"; thus it is limited to the world of fact. Especially in fiction, it focuses on
visual fact. Descriptive writing is writing that depicts, writing that creates
verbal pictures, writing that evokes the existing details of material fact, in

person and place. Description, as a mode of communication, presents the image to the reader and allows the image to communicate its meaning. The static image *is* the communication.

In fiction, description is almost always static. It aims to re-create a picture, an emblem, the parts and interrelationships of which are the point. The most common example, of course, and perhaps an overuse of the technique, is the tableau. In the tableau, as for example in Hawthorne's work, persons are treated as more of the furniture, and action is essentially eliminated. But, like the emblems of the seventeenth century, such a picture can have symbolic meaning in its relationships. Its organization is necessarily spatial. When time and movement enter, we get narration.

Fiction is fairly clearly not a "slice of life," for the "slice of life" is merely descriptive. Mere description cannot satisfy our aesthetic demand for meaning. If it could, standing in front of the corner drugstore for a half hour would have as aesthetic an effect as a good short story. Of course, standing there, we may begin to impose meaning upon what we see and come to a conclusion that "life is like that," but until we begin to analyze character and suppose cause for action, a description of a passing parade is quite other than fictional.

The word *narration* means "the act of telling or narrating, as to tell or relate a story." A story is an account of a series of actions, real or fictitious, usually involving people in a physical environment and existing in time. Stories tend to be unique in their detail; they focus upon particular persons, places, events, not upon generalized or typal detail, though particulars intensely perceived tend to become concrete universals. Stories tend to take place in the past; though the present and future are possible, stories are always other than here and now; they are not temporally immediate and direct experience. Therefore, the narrator of a story finds it necessary to re-evoke details for his audience's imagination. This quality of narration usually suggests that the narrator knows the conclusion of the story he tells before it is begun, suggests, possibly, that he has told the story before. Traditionally, the principle of organization in narration has been temporal, with permissible pauses for exposition.

Fiction, however, is not merely narration. Fiction is not anecdote, though it may contain anecdote, just as it certainly contains description. Anecdote involves character, place, and action, but usually lacks the point that we expect in fiction. Newspaper stories are usually a bit more fully developed, but fiction is not merely news either. News usually does not tell why an event happened, and we ask that our fiction do so. Nor is fiction the oral tale—the primitive ancestor of the anecdote and news story—which usually narrates character and event, and describes place. There are cases where such oral tales do in fact satisfy our concept of fiction, but they do so because they have qualities other than those ordinarily belonging to the oral tale. The story, the narration, is only the skeleton on which the flesh of fiction grows.

Yet fiction depends upon narration. Two of our principal conventions derive from it, that of telling and that of temporal organization. There has been a great deal of criticism of telling, but no story ever exists upon mere showing. There has to be the sense of action, of development, of time passing and things changing. There have also been attempts to break up temporal organization and substitute some other form, such as concatenation or ideational progression. But, usually, non-temporal stories strike us as illogical gibberish or something more resembling the poem or the essay than fiction.

Exposition means "the act of presenting, explaining, or expounding facts or ideas." The word is also related to *expose,* to *exposé,* to *exposition.* All these suggest a technique of showing as in expositions of paintings or world fairs. It is contrasted to telling. As a rhetorical mode, it depends upon the showing as a means of explaining, as a means of establishing cause. It usually focuses upon process, rather than picture or story.

Fiction, of course, makes much use of exposition of process. We, as readers, want to be shown how a character got into his environment, how he acted in relation to others and that environment, and we always want to know why he came and why he acted. We want not only knowledge of what the character did, but also an explanation. Exposition in fiction, thus, focuses upon particularization of detail and the establishment of cause. The explanation of a causal string of detail does more than anything else to bring a fictional subject into imaginative existence. It convinces us aesthetically. It gives us the illusion of the fiction's being. Thus, fiction, in explaining persons and places, resembles both biography and history.

But fiction is not biography or history, though its literary form grew out of imitations of them. The biographer is always limited to what he knows to be external fact, as is the historian. In both cases the primary virtue is fidelity to mere fact. But fiction has the power to explain facts, to illuminate the poetic truth in fact. It was this that led Aristotle to assert that poetry was superior to history, for history merely records what has happened, poetry records what may. When the biographer or historian try to suggest such a dimension, they violate our sense of their job, which is to stick to fact. But the exposition of possible lives suggests philosophy and makes literature richer and of higher value than history.

Argument is the rhetorical mode that deals with such points, such philosophy. An argument is, of course, a quarrel, a debate, a disputation, but it is also "discourse intended to persuade or convince"; it is evidence or proof. The argument of a fiction is that part which advances the main idea, the thesis, or the author's opinion. It deals not only in the usual logic of persuasion, as in assertion and proof, but also in such psychological factors as tone and mood. Even the most casual fiction presents such an argument, whether the author is conscious of it or not. Argument, then, deals in abstraction, rather than in space, time, or process.

Fiction, of course, contains philosophy. The depiction of character, place, and event is the author's means of convincing his readers of his view of experience, of his view of what ought to be, what ought not to be, of what is right and wrong. Every nexus of character, place, and event produces such a world, which has a point and a moral system. Even when the author is unaware of his arguments, his unconscious choice of materials will delineate such philosophical points.

But fiction is not merely philosophy either. It is true that we ask a dimension of meaning in it, a dimension of argument that wholly distinguishes it from the anecdote or the history, but to focus merely upon this dimension is to work in the terms of the speculative essay, not in the terms of fiction. Fiction contains speculation, but we ask the speculation to be integrated with the other qualities. Fiction is a re-creation of experience in which the reader perceives, in their life-like balance, abstraction, process, time, and space.

Fiction, in fact, is all these things, description, narration, exposition, and argument. We object when any one of these modes is eliminated. These modes fairly completely explain the structure of the human mind and its understanding of experience. Fiction attempts to re-create a totality of experience through all of our modes of knowing. To leave one out is to cripple it.

Four Forms of Novelistic Fiction

Novelistic fiction has usually been divided into four loosely defined species —the sketch, the short story, the novella or novelette, and the novel. These are not merely distinctions in length; the four form a continuum that can be imperfectly described as follows:

A *sketch* is a passage of fiction that stresses, often in a brief glimpse, a single part of a larger fiction that may or may not exist. It usually uses only one technique, or image, or view, and ignores the other parts of fiction. We respond to it as to a fragment, though it is not without its genuine and independent effect. Most familiar, perhaps, is the character sketch, in which a character is described, usually independently of other characters. Many authors use the sketch as a means of getting acquainted with their characters, settings, themes, and so forth. One can easily imagine how the following very, very brief sketch might be used:

"Do you believe in God, young man?"

"No, ma'am."

"No! No! Tell the truth!" she cried, near tears. "Do you believe in God?"

"No, ma'am."

This passage has no beginning in the literary sense, no complication, no crisis or climax, no consequences, no close, little characterization and little action, but it is not without its effect. Like the painter's sketch, the writer's sketch is a figure, a flourish, an effect, that he may want to use in a larger context. It may be an action, a scene, a mood, for which the author does not reveal the motive. When he begins to reveal motive and depict change, he begins to tell a story.

A *short story* is a fiction that deals with characters, actions, settings, meanings, which are arranged for climax (that is, leading to a crisis and a critical choice of alternatives), and which leaves us with a sense of change and completeness. The causes of the climax and the sense of change that results from it constitute the beginning-middle-completion, or conflict-resolution, sequence we call plot; they distinguish the story from the sketch. However, the short story does not have the facilities for describing character very fully nor action very deeply, so it is usually limited to dealing with types, and even stereotypes. Further (and because of this limitation), the story is primarily concerned with *revealing* conditions which existed in the characters before the story began. If an author includes full character descriptions, thus lengthening his story, but does not manage to increase his effect, the reader will find the story one-sided, too much given to character sketches, too long for its substance. If the writer includes a character trait or action that was not inherent in the beginning, the reader will be struck with inconsistency and aesthetic failure. If the writer *develops* such new material, such changes, successfully, he has moved into one of the other types of fiction, for the primary distinction between the short story and the novel is in *revelation vs. development.*

A *novella,* or novelette, or short novel, is a fiction that deals with development of character, action, theme, and so on, but is usually limited in scope to developing a single character and theme. Thus, the novella is less ambitious than the novel. Many novellas deal with the development of a central character and ignore the concomitant development of other characters. This means that minor characters, and even the deuteragonist and the tritagonist, are usually conceived and presented in static and revelatory techniques, while the protagonist is presented in developmental terms. In a sense, the novella is a form that holds the environment steady and permits an intricate and intense perception of the development of a segment of experience.

A *novel,* then, is a story that deals with the full flux of time, place, and

action, among a group of developing characters; it is an imitation of experience in its natural and usual complexity. It generally presents two or more
developing characters, each forming a part of the other's environment, so that
both the back-drop and the characters are changing. This is not to say that all
elements in a novel are in flux; the type and even the stereotype are useful and
necessary as fixed points against which we can perceive and judge the movement of the others.

A word of caution! Like all such schemes, this oversimplifies the matter.
According to these criteria, *The Odyssey* is a very, very long short story, for
Ulysses never displays a trait that was not in the conception of him as ideal
Greek man before the story began, and the trials of the odyssey are only con-
strued to reveal these traits. At the other extreme, Chekhov in a story like "The
New Villa" manages to convey the development of several characters over an
extended period by focusing intensely, as his dramatic technique will allow
him, on several stages of their development; he wrote, in other words, a ten-
page novel. By these standards, too, most of what we call novels are long
novellas.

Northrop Frye's Four Genres

The short story, novella, and novel share an attitude toward experience;
they deal with it directly, logically, common-sensically. But the tale and the
romance have a different attitude; they bend experience, even into fantasy and
magic, in their attempt to make it communicate (in Hawthorne's famous
phrase) "the truth of the human heart." And other genres, "autobiographical"
confessions, for example, or such encyclopedic fictions as *The Anatomy of
Melancholy,* have still different attitudes. The following extended passage, by
Northrop Frye,[1] is the best clarification so far of the principles that distinguish
one genre of fiction from another. Frye is addressing himself to the critic, but
his insights are useful for the writer to keep in mind.

SPECIFIC CONTINUOUS FORMS

In assigning the term fiction to the genre of the written word, in which prose
tends to become the predominating rhythm, we collide with the view that the
real meaning of fiction is falsehood or unreality. Thus an autobiography coming
into a library would be classified as non-fiction if the librarian believed the
author, and as fiction if she thought he was lying. It is difficult to see what use

[1] From *Anatomy of Criticism.*

such a distinction can be to a literary critic. Surely the word fiction, which, like poetry, means etymologically something made for its own sake, could be applied in criticism to any work of literary art in a radically continuous form, which almost always means a work of art in prose. Or, if that is too much to ask, at least some protest can be entered against the sloppy habit of identifying fiction with the one genuine form of fiction which we know as the novel.

Let us look at a few of the unclassified books lying on the boundary of "non-fiction" and "literature." Is *Tristram Shandy* a novel? Nearly everyone would say yes, in spite of its easygoing disregard for "story values." Is *Gulliver's Travels* a novel? Here most would demur, including the Dewey decimal system, which puts it under "Satire and Humor." But surely everyone would call it fiction, and if it is fiction, a distinction appears between fiction as a genus and the novel as a species of that genus. Shifting the ground to fiction, then, is *Sartor Resartus* fiction? If not, why not? If it is, is *The Anatomy of Melancholy* fiction? Is it a literary form or only a work of "non-fiction" written with "style"? Is Borrow's *Lavengro* fiction? Everyman's Library says yes; the World's Classics puts it under "Travel and Topography."

The literary historian who identifies fiction with the novel is greatly embarrassed by the length of time that the world managed to get along without the novel, and until he reaches his great deliverance in Defoe, his perspective is intolerably cramped. He is compelled to reduce Tudor fiction to a series of tentative essays in the novel form, which works well enough for Deloney but makes nonsense of Sidney. He postulates a great fictional gap in the seventeenth century which exactly covers the golden age of rhetorical prose. He finally discovers that the word novel, which up to about 1900 was still the name of a more or less recognizable form, has since expanded into a catchall term which can be applied to practically any prose book that is not "on" something. Clearly, this novel-centered view of prose fiction is a Ptolemaic perspective which is now too complicated to be any longer workable, and some more relative and Copernican view must take its place.

When we start to think seriously about the novel, not as fiction, but as a form of fiction, we feel that its characteristics, whatever they are, are such as make, say, Defoe, Fielding, Austen, and James central in its tradition, and Borrow, Peacock, Melville, and Emily Bronte somehow peripheral. This is not an estimate of merit: we may think *Moby Dick* "greater" than *The Egoist* and yet feel that Meredith's book is closer to being a typical novel. Fielding's conception of the novel as a comic epic in prose seems fundamental to the tradition he did so much to establish. In novels that we think of as typical, like those of Jane Austen, plot and dialogue are closely linked to the conventions of the comedy of manners. The conventions of *Wuthering Heights* are linked rather with the tale and the ballad. They seem to have more affinity with tragedy, and the tragic emotions of passion and fury, which would shatter the balance of tone in Jane Austen, can be safely accommodated here. So can the supernatural, or the suggestion of it, which is difficult to get into a novel. The shape of the plot is different: instead

of manoeuvering around a central situation, as Jane Austen does, Emily Bronte
tells her story with linear accents, and she seems to need the help of a narrator,
who would be absurdly out of place in Jane Austen. Conventions so different
justify us in regarding *Wuthering Heights* as a different form of prose fiction from
the novel, a form which we shall here call the romance. Here again we have to
use the same word in several different contexts, but romance seems on the whole
better than tale, which appears to fit a somewhat shorter form.

The essential difference between novel and romance lies in the conception of
characterization. The romancer does not attempt to create "real people" so much
as stylized figures which expand into psychological archetypes. It is in the romance
that we find Jung's libido, anima, and shadow reflected in the hero, heroine, and
villain respectively. That is why the romance so often radiates a glow of subjective
intensity that the novel lacks, and why a suggestion of allegory is constantly
creeping in around its fringes. Certain elements of character are released in the
romance which make it naturally a more revolutionary form than the novel. The
novelist deals with personality, with characters wearing their *personae* or social
masks. He needs the framework of a stable society, and many of our best novelists
have been conventional to the verge of fussiness. The romancer deals with individuality, with characters *in vacuo* idealized by revery, and, however conservative
he may be, something nihilistic and untamable is likely to keep breaking out of
his pages.

The prose romance, then, is an independent form of fiction to be distinguished
from the novel and extracted from the miscellaneous heap of prose works now
covered by that term. Even in the other heap known as short stories one can
isolate the tale form used by Poe, which bears the same relation to the full romance that the stories of Chekhov or Katherine Mansfield do to the novel. "Pure"
examples of either form are never found; there is hardly any modern romance
that could not be made out to be a novel, and vice versa. The forms of prose
fiction are mixed, like racial strains in human beings, not separable like the sexes.
In fact the popular demand in fiction is always for a mixed form, a romantic
novel just romantic enough for the reader to project his libido on the hero and
his anima on the heroine, and just novel enough to keep these projections in a
familiar world. It may be asked, therefore, what is the use of making the above
distinction, especially when, though undeveloped in criticism, it is by no means
unrealized. It is no surprise to hear that Trollope wrote novels and William
Morris romances.

The reason is that a great romancer should be examined in terms of the conventions he chose. William Morris should not be left on the side lines of prose
fiction merely because the critic has not learned to take the romance form seriously.
Nor, in view of what has been said about the revolutionary nature of the romance,
should his choice of that form be regarded as an "escape" from his social attitude.
If Scott has any claims to be a romancer, it is not good criticism to deal only
with his defects as a novelist. The romantic qualities of *The Pilgrim's Progress*,
too, its archetypal characterization and its revolutionary approach to religious

experience, make it a well-rounded example of a literary form: it is not merely a book swallowed by English literature to get some religious bulk in its diet. Finally, when Hawthorne, in the preface to *The House of the Seven Gables,* insists that his story should be read as romance and not as novel, it is possible that he meant what he said, even though he indicates that the prestige of the rival form has induced the romancer to apologize for not using it.

Romance is older than the novel, a fact which has developed the historical illusion that it is something to be outgrown, a juvenile and undeveloped form. The social affinities of the romance, with its grave idealizing of heroism and purity, are the aristocracy (for the apparent inconsistency of this with the revolutionary nature of the form just mentioned, see the introductory comment on the *mythos* of romance in the previous essay[2]). It revived in the period we call Romantic as part of the Romantic tendency to archaic feudalism and a cult of the hero, or idealized libido. In England the romances of Scott and, in less degree, the Brontes, are part of a mysterious Northumbrian renaissance, a Romantic reaction against the new industrialism in the Midlands, which also produced the poetry of Wordsworth and Burns and the philosophy of Carlyle. It is not surprising, therefore, that an important theme in the more bourgeois novel should be the parody of the romance and its ideals. The tradition established by *Don Quixote* continues in a type of novel which looks at a romantic situation from its own point of view, so that the conventions of the two forms make up an ironic compound instead of a sentimental mixture. Examples range from *Northanger Abbey* to *Madame Bovary* and *Lord Jim.*

The tendency to allegory in the romance may be conscious, as in *The Pilgrim's Progress,* or unconscious, as in the very obvious sexual mythopoeia in William Morris. The romance, which deals with heroes, is intermediate between the novel, which deals with men, and the myth, which deals with gods. Prose romance first appears as a late development of Classical mythology, and the prose Sagas of Iceland follow close on the mythical Eddas. The novel tends rather to expand into a fictional approach to history. The soundness of Fielding's instinct in calling *Tom Jones* a history is confirmed by the general rule that the larger the scheme of a novel becomes, the more obviously its historical nature appears. As it is creative history, however, the novelist usually prefers his material in a plastic, or roughly contemporary state, and feels cramped by a fixed historical pattern. *Waverley* is dated about sixty years back from the time of writing and *Little Dorrit* about forty years, but the historical pattern is fixed in the romance and plastic in the novel, suggesting the general principle that most "historical novels" are romances. Similarly a novel becomes more romantic in its appeal when the life it reflects has passed away: thus the novels of Trollope were read primarily as romances during the Second World War. It is perhaps the link with history and a sense of temporal context that has confined the novel, in striking contrast to the worldwide romance, to the alliance of time and Western man.

---

[2] That is, in *The Anatomy of Criticism.* [*Editor's note*]

Autobiography is another form which merges with the novel by a series of insensible gradations. Most autobiographies are inspired by a creative, and therefore fictional, impulse to select only those events and experiences in the writer's life that go to build up an integrated pattern. This pattern may be something larger than himself with which he has come to identify himself, or simply the coherence of his character and attitudes. We may call this very important form of prose fiction the confession form, following St. Augustine, who appears to have invented it, and Rousseau, who established a modern type of it. The earlier tradition gave *Religio Medici, Grace Abounding,* and Newman's *Apologia* to English literature, besides the related but subtly different type of confession favored by the mystics.

Here again, as with the romance, there is some value in recognizing a distinct prose form in the confession. It gives several of our best prose works a definable place in fiction instead of keeping them in a vague limbo of books which are not quite literature because they are "thought," and not quite religion or philosophy because they are Examples of Prose Style. The confession, too, like the novel and the romance, has its own short form, the familiar essay, and Montaigne's *livre de bonne foy* is a confession made up of essays in which only the continuous narrative of the longer form is missing. Montaigne's scheme is to the confession what a work of fiction made up of short stories, such as Joyce's *Dubliners* or Boccaccio's *Decameron,* is to the novel or romance.

After Rousseau—in fact in Rousseau—the confession flows into the novel, and the mixture produces the fictional autobiography, the *Künstler-roman,* and kindred types. There is no literary reason why the subject of a confession should always be the author himself, and dramatic confessions have been used in the novel at least since *Moll Flanders.* The "stream of consciousness" technique permits of a much more concentrated fusion of the two forms, but even here the characteristics peculiar to the confession form show up clearly. Nearly always some theoretical and intellectual interest in religion, politics, or art plays a leading role in the confession. It is his success in integrating his mind on such subjects that makes the author of a confession feel that his life is worth writing about. But this interest in ideas and theoretical statements is alien to the genius of the novel proper, where the technical problem is to dissolve all theory into personal relationships. In Jane Austen, to take a familiar instance, church, state, and culture are never examined except as social data, and Henry James has been described as having a mind so fine that no idea could violate it. The novelist who cannot get along without ideas, or has not the patience to digest them in the way that James did, instinctively resorts to what Mill calls a "mental history" of a single character. And when we find that a technical discussion of a theory of aesthetics forms the climax of Joyce's *Portrait,* we realize that what makes this possible is the presence in that novel of another tradition of prose fiction.

The novel tends to be extroverted and personal; its chief interest is in human character as it manifests itself in society. The romance tends to be introverted and personal: it also deals with characters, but in a more subjective way. (Subjective here refers to treatment, not subject-matter. The characters are heroic and therefore inscrutable; the novelist is freer to enter his characters' minds because he is more objective.) The confession is also introverted, but intellectualized in content. Our next step is evidently to discover a fourth form of fiction which is extroverted and intellectual.

We remarked earlier that most people would call *Gulliver's Travels* fiction but not a novel. It must then be another form of fiction, as it certainly has a form, and we feel that we are turning from the novel to this form, whatever it is, when we turn from Rousseau's *Emile* to Voltaire's *Candide,* or from Butler's *The Way of All Flesh* to the Erewhon books, or from Huxley's *Point Counterpoint* to *Brave New World.* The form thus has its own traditions, and, as the examples of Butler and Huxley show, has preserved some integrity even under the ascendancy of the novel. Its existence is easy enough to demonstrate, and no one will challenge the statement that the literary ancestry of *Gulliver's Travels* and *Candide* runs through Rabelais and Erasmus to Lucian. But while much has been said about the style and thought of Rabelais, Swift, and Voltaire, very little has been made of them as craftsmen working in a specific medium, a point no one dealing with a novelist would ignore. Another great writer in this tradition, Huxley's master Peacock, has fared even worse, for, his form not being understood, a general impression has grown up that his status in the development of prose fiction is that of a slapdash eccentric. Actually, he is as exquisite and precise an artist in his medium as Jane Austen is in hers.

The form used by these authors is the Menippean satire, also more rarely called the Varronian satire, allegedly invented by a Greek cynic named Menippus. His works are lost, but he had two great disciples, the Greek Lucian and the Roman Varro, and the tradition of Varro, who has not survived either except in fragments, was carried on by Petronius and Apuleius. The Menippean satire appears to have developed out of verse satire through the practice of adding prose interludes, but we know it only as a prose form, though one of its recurrent features (seen in Peacock) is the use of incidental verse.

The Menippean satire deals less with people as such than with mental attitudes. Pedants, bigots, cranks, parvenus, virtuosi, enthusiasts, rapacious and incompetent professional men of all kinds, are handled in terms of their occupational approach to life as distinct from their social behavior. The Menippean satire thus resembles the confession in its ability to handle abstract ideas and theories, and differs from the novel in its characterization, which is stylized rather than naturalistic, and presents people as mouthpieces of the ideas they represent. Here again no sharp boundary lines can or should be drawn, but if we compare a character in Jane Austen with a similar character in Peacock we can immediately feel the difference between the two forms. Squire Western belongs to the novel, but Thwackum and Square have Menippean blood in them. A constant theme in the tradition is the ridicule of the *philosophus gloriosus,* already discussed. The novelist sees evil and folly as social diseases, but the

Menippean satirist sees them as diseases of the intellect, as a kind of maddened pedantry which the *philosophus gloriosus* at once symbolizes and defines.

Petronius, Apuleius, Rabelais, Swift, and Voltaire all use a loose-jointed narrative form often confused with the romance. It differs from the romance, however (though there is a strong admixture of romance in Rabelais), as it is not primarily concerned with the exploits of heroes, but relies on the free play of intellectual fancy and the kind of humorous observation that produces caricature. It differs also from the picaresque form, which has the novel's interest in the actual structure of society. At its most concentrated the Menippean satire presents us with a vision of the world in terms of a single intellectual pattern. The intellectual structure built up from the story makes for violent dislocations in the customary logic of narrative, though the appearance of carelessness that results reflects only the carelessness of the reader or his tendency to judge by a novel-centered conception of fiction.

The word "satire," in Roman and Renaissance times, meant either of two specific literary forms of that name, one (this one) prose and the other verse. Now it means a structural principle or attitude, what we have called a *mythos*. In the Menippean satires we have been discussing, the name of the form also applies to the attitude. As the name of an attitude, satire is, we have seen, a combination of fantasy and morality. But as the name of a form, the term satire, though confined to literature (for as a *mythos* it may appear in any art, a cartoon, for example), is more flexible, and can be either entirely fantastic or entirely moral. The Menippean adventure story may thus be pure fantasy, as it is in the literary fairy tale. The Alice books are perfect Menippean satires, and so is *The Water-Babies,* which has been influenced by Rabelais. The purely moral type is a serious vision of society as a single intellectual pattern, in other words a Utopia.

The short form of the Menippean satire is usually a dialogue or colloquy, in which the dramatic interest is in a conflict of ideas rather than of character. This is the favorite form of Erasmus, and is common in Voltaire. Here again the form is not invariably satiric in attitude, but shades off into more purely fanciful or moral discussions, like the *Imaginary Conversations* of Landor or the "dialogue of the dead." Sometimes this form expands to full length, and more than two speakers are used: the setting then is usually a *cena* or symposium, like the one that looms so large in Petronius. Plato, though much earlier in the field than Menippus, is a strong influence on this type, which stretches in an unbroken tradition down through those urbane and leisurely conversations which define the ideal courtier in Castiglione or the doctrine and discipline of angling in Walton. A modern development produces the country-house weekends in Peacock, Huxley, and their imitators in which the opinions and ideas and cultural interests expressed are as important as the love-making.

The novelist shows his exuberance either by an exhaustive analysis of human relationships, as in Henry James, or of social phenomena, as in Tolstoy. The Menippean satirist, dealing with intellectual themes and attitudes, shows his exuberance in intellectual ways, by piling up an enormous mass of erudition about his theme or in overwhelming his pedantic targets with an avalanche of their own jargon. A species, or rather sub-species, of the form is the kind of encyclopaedic farrago represented by Athenaeus' *Deipnosophists* and Macrobius' *Saturnalia*, where people sit at a banquet and pour out a vast mass of erudition on every subject that might conceivably come up in a conversation. The display of erudition had probably been associated with the Menippean tradition by Varro, who was enough of a polymath to make Quintilian, if not stare and gasp, at any rate call him *vir Romanorum eruditissimus*.[3] The tendency to expand into an encyclopaedic farrago is clearly marked in Rabelais, notably in the great catalogues of torcheculs and epithets of codpieces and methods of divination. The encyclopaedic compilations produced in the line of duty by Erasmus and Voltaire suggest that a magpie instinct to collect facts is not unrelated to the type of ability that has made them famous as artists. Flaubert's encyclopaedic approach to the construction of *Bouvard et Pecuchet* is quite comprehensible if we explain it as marking an affinity with the Menippean tradition.

This creative treatment of exhaustive erudition is the organizing principle of the greatest Menippean satire in English before Swift, Burton's *Anatomy of Melancholy*. Here human society is studied in terms of the intellectual pattern provided by the conception of melancholy, a symposium of books replaces dialogue, and the result is the most comprehensive survey of human life in one book that English literature had seen since Chaucer, one of Burton's favorite authors. We may note in passing the Utopia in his introduction and his "digressions," which when examined turn out to be scholarly distillations of Menippean forms: the digression of air, of the marvellous journey; the digression of spirits, of the ironic use of erudition; the digression of the miseries of scholars, of the satire on the *philosophus gloriosus*. The word "anatomy" in Burton's title means a dissection or analysis, and expresses very accurately the intellectualized approach of his form. We may as well adopt it as a convenient name to replace the cumbersome and in modern times rather misleading "Menippean satire."

The anatomy, of course, eventually begins to merge with the novel, producing various hybrids including the *roman à these* [4] and novels in which the characters are symbols of social or other ideas, like the proletarian novels of the thirties in this century. It was Sterne, however, the disciple of Burton and Rabelais, who combined them with greatest success. *Tristram Shandy* may be, as was said at the beginning, a novel, but the digressing narrative, the catalogues, the stylizing of character along "humor" lines, the marvellous journey of the great nose, the symposium discussions, and the constant ridicule of philosophers and pedantic critics are all features that belong to the anatomy.

A clearer understanding of the form and traditions of the anatomy would make a good many elements in the history of literature come into focus. Boethius'

---

[3] The most erudite man of the Romans. [*Editor's note*]
[4] Thesis novel. [*Editor's note*]

Consolation of Philosophy, with its dialogue form, its verse interludes and its pervading tone of contemplative irony, is a pure anatomy, a fact of considerable importance for the understanding of its vast influence. *The Compleat Angler* is an anatomy because of its mixture of prose and verse, its rural *cena* setting, its dialogue form, its deipnosophistical interest in food, and its gentle Menippean raillery of a society which considers everything more important than fishing and yet has discovered very few better things to do. In nearly every period of literature there are many romances, confessions, and anatomies that are neglected only because the categories to which they belong are unrecognized. In the period between Sterne and Peacock, for example, we have, among romances, *Melmoth the Wanderer;* among confessions, Hogg's *Confessions of a Justified Sinner;* among anatomies, Southey's *Doctor,* Amory's *John Buncle,* and the *Noctes Ambrosianae.*

To sum up then: when we examine fiction from the point of view of form, we can see four chief strands binding it together, novel, confession, anatomy, and romance. The six possible combinations of these forms all exist, and we have shown how the novel has combined with each of the other three. Exclusive concentration on one form is rare: the early novels of George Eliot, for instance, are influenced by the romance, and the later ones by the anatomy. The romance-confession hybrid is found, naturally, in the autobiography of a romantic temperament, and is represented in English by the extroverted George Borrow and the introverted De Quincy. The romance-anatomy one we have noticed in Rabelais; a later example is *Moby Dick,* where the romantic theme of the wild hunt expands into an encyclopaedic anatomy of the whale. Confession and anatomy are united in *Sartor Resartus* and in some of Kierkegaard's strikingly original experiments in prose fiction form, including *Either/Or.* More comprehensive fictional schemes usually employ at least three forms: we can see strains of novel, romance, and confession in *Pamela,* of novel, romance, and anatomy in *Don Quixote,* of novel, confession, and anatomy in Proust, and of romance, confession, and anatomy in Apuleius.

I deliberately make this sound schematic in order to suggest the advantage of having a simple and logical explanation for the form of, say, *Moby Dick* or *Tristram Shandy.* The usual critical approach to the form of such works resembles that of the doctors in Brobdingnag, who after great wrangling finally pronounced Gulliver a *lusus naturae.* It is the anatomy in particular that has baffled critics, and there is hardly any fiction writer deeply influenced by it who has not been accused of disorderly conduct. The reader may be reminded here of Joyce, for describing Joyce's books as monstrous has become a nervous tic. I find "demogorgon," "behemoth," and "white elephant" in good critics; the bad ones could probably do much better. The care that Joyce took to organize *Ulysses* and *Finnegans Wake* amounted nearly to obsession, but as they are not organized on familiar principles of prose fiction, the impression of shapelessness remains. Let us try our formulas on him.

If a reader were asked to set down a list of the things that had most impressed him about *Ulysses,* it might reasonably be somewhat as follows. First, the clarity with which the sights and sounds and smells of Dublin come to life, the rotundity of the character-drawing, and the naturalness of the dialogue. Second, the elaborate way that the story and characters are parodied by being set against archetypal heroic patterns, notably the one provided by the *Odyssey.* Third, the revelation of character and incident through the searching use of the stream-of-consciousness technique. Fourth, the constant tendency to be encyclopaedic and exhaustive both in technique and in subject matter, and to see both in highly intellectualized terms. It should not be too hard for us by now to see that these four points describe elements in the book which relate to the novel, romance, confession, and anatomy respectively. *Ulysses,* then, is a complete prose epic with all four forms employed in it, all of practically equal importance, and all essential to one another, so that the book is a unity and not an aggregate.

This unity is built up from an intricate scheme of parallel contrasts. The romantic archetypes of Hamlet and Ulysses are like remote stars in a literary heaven looking down quizzically on the shabby creatures of Dublin obediently intertwining themselves in the patterns set by their influences. In the "Cyclops" and "Circe" episodes particularly there is a continuous parody of realistic patterns by romantic ones which reminds us, though the irony leans in the opposite direction, of *Madame Bovary.* The relation of novel and confession techniques is similar; the author jumps into his characters' minds to follow their stream of consciousness, and out again to describe them externally. In the novel-anatomy combination, too, found in the "Ithaca" chapter, the sense of lurking antagonism between the personal and intellectual aspects of the scene accounts for much of its pathos. The same principle of parallel contrast holds good for the other three combinations: of romance and confession in "Nausicaa" and "Penelope," of confession and anatomy in "Proteus" and "The Lotos-Eaters," of romance and anatomy (a rare and fitful combination) in "Sirens" and parts of "Circe."

In *Finnegans Wake* the unity of design goes far beyond this. The dingy story of the sodden HCE and his pinched wife is not contrasted with the archetypes of Tristram and the divine king: HCE is himself Tristram and the divine king. As the setting is a dream, no contrast is possible between confession and novel, between a stream of consciousness inside the mind and the appearances of other people outside it. Nor is the experiential world of the novel to be separated from the intelligible world of the anatomy. The forms we have been isolating in fiction, and which depend for their existence on the commonsense dichotomies of the daylight consciousness, vanish in *Finnegans Wake* into a fifth and quintessential form. This form is the one traditionally associated with scriptures and sacred books, and treats life in terms of the fall and awakening of the human soul and the creation and apocalypse of nature. The Bible is the definitive example of it; the Egyptian Book of the Dead and the Icelandic Prose Edda, both of which have left deep imprints on *Finnegans Wake,* also belong to it.

Where, Then, Does One Begin?

In such a short space, we cannot (nor do we want to) exhaust the possibilities of the materials and forms of fiction, but hope to suggest the variety and complexity of them. Fiction deals first with experience, but abstraction and meditation are also experience; so fiction must contain the life of the mind, as well as the life of the world. It deals with experience, but it can deal with it in many ways—dynamically, as does the drama; discursively, as does the essay; meditatively, as does the lyric poem; experientially, as is its most common mode. Fiction deals with experience, but the experience can be real or imagined, and either of these can be fact or truth. It deals with experience through description, narrative, exposition, and argument; and all of these in myriad forms—sketch, short story, novella, or novel; romance or tale; confession or personal essay; anatomy or colloquy. Because of its variety, complexity, and flexibility, fiction can contain all the materials and forms of the other literary arts.

Where, then, does one begin, when he begins a study of fiction? With the language. Language is the one thing common to all forms of fiction, as to all forms of literature. Language brings us to style, style to choice, choice to the variety and complexity of technique, technique finally to meaning and theme. Meaning and theme, we may not prescribe nor proscribe, if we are to preserve intellectual and moral freedom. We are at liberty, of course, to reject what an author says, but not to control it. The author's burden, then, is one of persuasion. Persuasion is largely a matter of technique; technique, a matter of choice.

The variety and complexity of choice among techniques is the most we can teach; indeed, it is all. Let us turn, then, to the details of the technical considerations of fiction—style, character, setting, point-of-view, plot, structure, and theme.

2

A Framework
for Developing
Style

Style has been defined often, and usually aphoristically, by many different sorts of writers, critics, and philosophers, but the definitions fall into relatively few, fairly definable camps. Buffon ("Style is the man"), Croce ("A good thought cannot be badly expressed"), and Yeats ("Style is that which corresponds to the moral element in a man of action") represent the camp which believes that the thing expressed and the manner of expressing it are organic and inseparable. At the opposite extreme, Lord Chesterfield ("Style is the dress of thoughts"), Stendhal ("Style is this: to add to a given thought all the circumstances fitted to produce the whole effect that the thought ought to produce"), and Wilde ("A sure way to ruin is to come to London and express yourself with elegance") hold the opinion that, for a given idea, there are several manners of expression, and one of these manners will be better than the rest; indeed, one manner may even be Ideal, or Sublime. The definitions of one group—Pater ("Style is beauty"), James ("Style is all, quite simply") —are so general, so large and inclusive, as to obscure important detail; those of another group—Stevens ("Style is perception" and "Style is a technique of discovery")—are so delimiting as to afford little or no view of larger issues; it's the old familiar problem of the forest and the trees, seen from different extremes. Swift ("Proper words in proper places make the true definition of style") and Whitehead ("the direct attainment of a foreseen end, simply and without waste") hold that there is an intimate relationship

25

between the thing said and the act of saying it, but that the relationship is neither wholly organic nor separable, being mutable within a certain range.

The definition that most of us assume when talking about style goes something like this: "Style is the quality or sum of qualities [1] resulting from an author's choices among (or exploitation of) the resources of his language." Whenever a writer uses language, he makes myriad choices. These choices result in words, figures, maneuvers on the page, which can be isolated and described in relation to a framework of analysis. These elements, these resources of the language, fall into five broad groups—choices of pronunciation, choices of vocabulary, grammatical maneuvers, sequence or organization of ideas, and the patterning or heightening for effect of any or all of the choices. Each of these categories contains a great variety of usage, and each reveals wide potential that a conscious writer can deliberately manipulate.

Varieties of Pronunciation

Pronunciation is always and inevitably involved in style. Words on the page are only symbols of sounds, which in turn have experiential meanings. These sounds—whether they are casual, conversational, dialectal, formal, stilted, or whatever—are represented by the letters in the words and the arrangements of the words into syntactic patterns. These symbols are controlled by manipulable devices of style.

The first, and perhaps the most important, device for indicating in writing the use of ordinary speech is the contraction. Writers add to the reader's illusion of experience by writing *should've* (please, please, not *should of*) for *should have*. Depending upon his sophistication and education, a writer can use this device to indicate many character traits; for example, national origin: an English speaker in a certain situation will habitually say "I've not been well, lately" but an American will say "I haven't been well, lately." Though this is not simply a difference in the contraction, the phrasing will indicate to many readers that the intonation and the vowels in *not* and *been* are different in the normal voices of the two people. Regional origin or social level can be indicated by speech; in some parts of the American South, for example, medial *d* and *t* are often dropped, but in other parts, terminal *d* and *t* (as well as

---

[1] The quality or qualities we describe with such words as *tone* and *mood*. Tone briefly defined, is the attitude the author takes toward his material—comic, satirical, serious, earnest, playful. Mood, briefly, is the attitude the material makes the reader take toward it—gloomy, skeptical, helpless, and so forth. There is a great deal of overlap, of course, between the two; a playful tone may create a playful mood. These qualities involve such matters as judgment and taste; we will be returning to them at almost every stage of our discussion.

many other letters) are attenuated. Thus, a contraction like *didn't* may be rendered differently in different situations: a man from one area will say "He dint do hit," but a man from another area may say, "He didn' do-it." A major difference in rhythm of life is caught and revealed in the intonation of these two versions of the same words.

This brings us close to the problem of respelling, which is another popular device for indicating actual speech. Spelling to indicate pronunciation (or, more accurately, mispronunciation, which characterizes the speaker) is one of the most easily and most commonly manipulated of linguistic forms. When a writer gives us a character who reduces the three syllables of *moccasin* to two: *mox-kin,* he is telling us about the character's dialect, social background, education, attitudes, and possibly more. Respelling, then, along with vocabulary and grammar, can reveal national origins, social class, and so forth, and a satirical or ironic attitude toward any of these. The respellings *cahn't* or *bahth,* for example, could hardly be used today in English, unless the writer means to satirize speech in Back-bay Britain or Boston, or to reveal an almost incredibly pretentious pomposity in the character.

Respelling is surely the easiest device to misuse, too. "Vot-chu tink I yam, Chee-I? Street-girl?" and "Iz ziss zee vay to zee men'z room, pleez?" are over-done and dishonest caricatures if presented with no qualification. There are people who talk that way, but the reader needs more evidence of it than their mere speech. Respelling must be used with restraint—as one uses salt and pepper—to impart a flavor only. Otherwise, as in many of the dialect works of American Local Colorists of the nineteenth century, the very puzzles on the page may completely absorb the reader's attention, so that he misses the communication altogether. With this, as with all techniques, there remains the question of whether or not the information revealed is worth the cost of revealing it. (Printer's devices, like *italics,* CAPITALS, and **bold-face type,** function similarly; see J. D. Salinger's sel*ec*ted use of italics in particular *syl*lables to indicate Manhattan*ese,* for example. Here, again, the mere puzzle may divert the reader disastrously.)

Respelling and printer's devices cause difficulty because they are hard to read. The customary signals are changed so much that an accurate phonetic representation may turn into a caricature of the speaker. Good dialect men, like Twain and Faulkner, render a few carefully selected phrases in dialect and spell most words normally. They rely more on idiom and word choice, which, even in ordinary spelling, are at least as important as pronunciation in revealing dialect.

Discursive writers often try to eliminate qualities of pronunciation, as far as possible. Professor Dryasdust is always trying and managing to efface the personal voice in his writing, in the interest of being scholarly and scientifically objective. (Unfortunately, he often effaces with that voice whatever is of interest in his message.) But, try as he will, he cannot completely erase the oral qualities of pitch, stress, tone, and so on, which are permanently imbedded in language itself. Pitch is, at least partly, inherent in punctuation: we pronounce a period with the falling pitch that indicates the end of a sentence. Don't we pronounce the question mark on a direct question as a rising pitch? When we see commas in a series, or a comma after an introductory clause, or a comma after a long phrase at the beginning of a sentence, or a colon after an assertion, we pronounce them with the rising suspension of voice which promises that more is to follow. Exclamation marks indicate both pitch and stress, as does the arrangement of words. Parenthetical insertions, qualifying clauses or phrases, appositives, hesitations, and so on, help to define the tone of a piece of writing, whether it be guarded, assertive, equivocal, belligerent, ironic, or whatever. All of this [2] should indicate that no single choice can ever exist in isolation; every word is involved in pronunciation, vocabulary, grammar, sequence, and pattern. Escape this doom, a writer cannot; all he can do is choose well or badly.

In modern times, there has been a tendency to ignore pronunciation as a part of writing. Speed-reading is one of the most blatant of the attempts, but one sees the tendency also in the increase of silent reading and the decline of recitative habits. The attempt to ignore what cannot be ignored can cause problems; for example, the famous problem of Henry James's later style arises because critics refuse to *listen* to what is on the page. Try reading James aloud, and his appositions, qualifications, contrasts, time-wasters, all fall into place as the voice of a cultured, sensitive gentleman, dictating a novel. Understanding is easy; obscurity and the problem usually disappear.

The writer can deliberately use pronunciation to achieve particular results. Mark Twain's use of the colloquial is now well known; Huck's speech is so much a part of his characterization that it becomes a part of the pattern of his discoveries and, thus, influences the theme of the novel. Since Twain's time, more and more writers have tried to capture the living voice to serve them in their imitations of experience. Robert Frost came close to stating the ideal when he said, "The only living sentence is one with the living voice somehow caught in the syllables." And Ezra Pound enjoined in a letter to Harriet Monroe in 1915, "There must be no ... hindside-beforehandness, no straddled adjectives (as 'addled mosses dank'), no Tennysonianness of speech; nothing —nothing that you couldn't, in some circumstance, in the stress of some emotion, actually say." The influences of these and other men have produced

---

[2] See the section on Hebraic prosody in English in chapter 13 for a more detailed discussion of the audible effects of pitch, stress, and intonation.

in every nation today many a writer whose ear is keenly tuned, as Hemingway's was, to spoken language.

To record pronunciation accurately is, of course, difficult and requires a "good ear," but variant pronunciation can be one of the writer's most powerful weapons. He should learn to use it well.

Dialog

Here is a list of practical do's and don't's of dialog:

1) Dialog should always promote rather than retard the illusion of experience—that is to say, the primary purpose of dialog is not the communication of information but of experience. The literary work is a re-created scene, a re-created reality, in which a reader can perceive, as if anew, the meaning in original experience. Dialog should help him in this perceptual illusion.

2) Dialog should be part of a scene, but should be reserved for moments of significance within that scene. This means that the speaker should have a consciousness of the place he is in, of the other people, of action—of the total scene—and any bit of dialog should suggest place, person, and action in its own right.

3) Dialog should intensify elements already present in the scene—that is, it should be arranged for dramatic effectiveness. There are many facts about character and action which must go into a fiction but which are not important enough to be dramatized. These should be put in summary narrative. But because dialog attracts attention, it can be used to heighten and dramatize important detail.

4) Dialog should characterize the speaker by revealing his interests, his attitudes, and his unique rhythm of living, speaking, acting. An energetic, decisive person should speak in short, snappy, energetic, decisive sentences, or fragments. A wishy-washy person may grope for vocabulary and leave half his sentences unfinished. Ford Madox Ford once advised that whenever a character first appeared, he should "strike his own special note." For Ford, this special note was a kind of shorthand symbolism to the most important characteristic of the speaker.

5) Dialog should never be used to impart information to the reader which other characters already know. To tell a mother "Your son, John, is coming to our house for dinner on Sunday" conveys such information. Certainly she would know that her son's name was John, or, if she has more than one son, that John is one of them. The writer would here be trying to give the reader some exposition of relationships that all the speakers in the scene already know. To use dialog merely to inform the audience always sounds a false note and is an aesthetic mistake. On the other hand, dialog must always

be informative in the "special note" sense of character. It must always give the reader information about the scene.

6) Dialog should not be used for the random exchange of ideas or for formal debate. There is a form—the Platonic dialog—which uses dialog in this way, but it does not pretend to be an imitation of experience. Fiction must certainly contain ideas, but when dialog exists for the ideas or for formal debate, the fiction goes dead.

7) Beware of real conversations; court transcripts, tape-recorded speeches, and so on are often the flattest, loosest, most repetitious forms of language. They commonly contain many audible pauses, wandering, rambling "sentences," linked together by "and." The common responses are monosyllables and grunts. This is true even of the speech of obviously educated persons. Literature cannot live on such looseness. On the other hand, dialog should not become oratory. To have characters blasting prepared speeches or argumentative demonstrations at one another would violate our sense of experience. There are cases, of course, in which the writer could set the scene and the character for a formal speech and allow the character to become oratorical. Even then the writer needs to break up the oratory with descriptions of manner, tone, gesture, response in the audience. Oratory, if it is used, must be made a part of the scene, character, and action.[3]

Varieties of Vocabulary

The effect of vocabulary choice on style is commonly understood. Different words often say approximately the same thing, but the trick is to choose the one that conveys exactly that shade of meaning the writer wants, or has the right tone, or is appropriate to the situation or the speaker. Whether a character calls it a *thermostat* or *that-thing-a-ma-jig-on-the-wall-that-makes-the-heater-go-off-and-on,* the writer is revealing backgrounds, attitudes, value systems, education, social level, any number of things. Benjamin Franklin in his *Autobiography* tells us a great deal through vocabulary at the end of the passage that deals with the itinerant Presbyterian preacher, the Rev. Mr. Whitfield:

I happened soon after to attend one of his sermons, in the course of which I perceived he intended to finish with a collection, and I silently resolved he should

---

[3] The pronunciation of verse lies at the opposite extreme from dialog. It is usually intended to cast an artificial patina on experience for purposes of heightening. Indeed, we have accepted a rhetoric of verse traditionally, and this rhetoric has, at times, even been high-flown. But the pronunciation of verse is immensely complicated and will be treated in some detail in the chapter on verse.

get nothing from me. I had in my pocket a handful of copper money, three or four silver dollars, and five pistoles in gold. As he proceeded, I began to soften and concluded to give the coppers. Another stroke of his oratory made me ashamed of that and determined me to give the silver; and he finished so admirably that I emptied my pocket wholly into the collector's dish, gold and all. At this sermon there was also one of our club, who being of my sentiments . . . and suspecting a collection might be intended, had by precaution emptied his pockets before he came from home; towards the conclusion of the discourse, however, he felt a strong desire to give and applied to a neighbour who stood near him to borrow some money for the purpose. The application was unfortunately made to perhaps the only man in the company who had the firmness not to be affected by the preacher. His answer was, "At any other time, Friend Hopkinson, I would lend to thee freely, but not now; for thee seems to be out of thy right senses." [4]

The Quaker's answer is like an iceberg; only a fraction of its content is visible. Ask yourself what qualities, dramatic and personal, are revealed in his speech.

There has been a great deal of concern for such things as getting the right word in the right place, keeping the informal word out of formal writing, keeping slang in its province, and so forth. Consider the following triplets of words, sometimes said to be synonymous at the popular, literary, and learned levels. What is the stylistic result of choosing, say, the middle word, rather than either of the other two?

> rise—mount—ascend
> ask—question—interrogate
> goodness—virtue—probity
> fast—firm—secure
> fire—flame—conflagration
> fear—terror—trepidation
> holy—sacred—consecrated
> time—age—epoch [5]

Professor Albert C. Baugh, who wrote these series, notes that the first item in each case is English, the second French, and the last Latin. Each of these words makes a unique contribution to tone and mood; though the differences between the English and the French may be slight, the Latin tends to be bookish. Each word has its characteristic uses. The cowboy *mounts* his horse, the TV detective *interrogates* his suspect, *virtue,* not goodness or probity, is its own reward. These are matters of convention (and even of cliché), but, rather than make a judgment on the desirability of any of the words, the writer should learn to manipulate the distinctive qualities of each.

[4] Signet edition, p. 118.
[5] Albert C. Baugh, *History of the English Language,* Second Edition (New York: Appleton-Century-Croft, 1957), pp. 225–26.

The great danger in manipulating words is that one can get "cute." In the seventeenth century, "cute" words became a vice, and writers used such conceits as "the furniture of the mouth" when they meant teeth, "the memory of the day" when they meant a clock, and so on. This style is called *préciosité* and is the subject of Molière's satire in *The Precious Damsels,* in which he has Mascarille say,

Would you wish, menials, that I should expose the prolixity of my plumes to the inclemencies of the pluvious season, and that I should inscribe my shoe prints in mud? [6]

which means, approximately, "Do you think I want to get my hat wet and my shoes muddy?"

Nineteenth century journalism suffered from this affliction (as does this sentence), as the following excerpt from the Central City (Colorado) *Register-Call* of 1886 indicates:

Suddenly the young barrister was seen to step back in a very dramatic manner and expectorate on his open slender hands. He then threw himself back upon his pastern joints like Slade or Jim Mace (prize fighters) would do if they were in the squared circle. Then his bunches of fives (fists) cut circlets in the air, and those who viewed the approaching carnage from afar, knew that blood must flow. It must flow in rivulets, too, and the beautiful and spotless snow embanked in the street must change its color for that of the life current which courses through the veins and furnishes the pumps of the body with material to work. [7]

If you think we have fully recovered from this vice, just consider current sports-page jargon like "He belted the bean out of the plantation."

This attitude toward vocabulary is, of course, closely related to hyperbole, exaggeration for effect, and is the opposite of litotes, deliberate underplaying for effect, usually in negative form, as when "not bad" means "pretty good." Exaggeration is said to be an American habit and the primary feature of American humor. Only in America, I think, will one hear, seriously, the idiom, "over-exaggerated." The idiom implies that a certain degree of exaggeration is normal and permissible; thus the American meaning of "excessive" is different from the European. The Frenchman may think a rapier adequate for a given job; the American may want a broad-axe. The problem of political gobbledygook may well be related to this American penchant for exaggeration.

Gobbledygook, the proliferation of verbiage perpetrated by many bureaucrats, is the use of two, three, or ten syllables where one would do and five technical terms for one plain word. For example, instead of the once vivid

---

[6] Molière, *Eight Plays,* Trans. Morris Bishop (New York: Modern Library), p. 12.
[7] Reprinted in the Denver *Post,* "Empire Magazine," September 3, 1961, p. 23.

"Don't count your chickens before they're hatched," one gets "Never calculate your juvenile poultry prior to the satisfactory completion of the proper process of incubation." Or, as Stuart Chase notes, had Franklin D. Roosevelt's famous "I see one-third of a nation ill-housed, ill-clad, ill-nourished" been translated into standard bureaucratic gobbledygook, it might have read something like:

It has come to the attention of the proper authorities that substantial numbers of citizens within the continental limits of the United States are inadequately sheltered, that a considerably large segment of the indigenous population are without the benefits of decent and satisfactory products of the clothing industry, and that possibly as many as 33.3333% are inadequately supplied with edible agricultural products, as meat, vegetables, etc.[8]

And a footnote would state that 33.3333 was not computed beyond four places.

Among Chase's less involved examples are "give consideration to" instead of "consider"; "is of the opinion that" instead of "believes"; and "information which is of a confidential nature" instead of "confidential information." Of course, a novelist may make a character speak gobbledygook, but then he communicates more the pompous personality of the character than what the character has to say.

Any word is appropriate in its time and place, otherwise it would not be in our language. But some of the best advice for a young writer is still Ezra Pound's injunction, "Go in fear of abstraction!" One has to balance this advice, immediately, with a note about the effectiveness of Emily Dickinson's personifications of abstractions. Choose concrete language rather than abstraction, but, on the other hand, do not use concrete when abstract terms are demanded. Similarly, do not fail to give the Quaker his Quaker vocabulary, or the cowboy and railroad engineer their jargons, or the teen-age hippies their slang. Such failures would be aesthetic mistakes.

In choosing his vocabulary, the writer needs to be highly conscious, so conscious that, when his lexicon fails him, he can invent a figurative substitute. Metaphors, similes, metonymies, personifications, symbols, and so on, are constantly occurring in prose and are almost obligatory in poetry. Such figurative devices, in which the meaning is something other than the direct, denotative meanings of the words used, furnish the writer his richest opportunities—indeed, they offer him the possibility to say something that mere language cannot say. Our urge and need to say more is precisely the reason we have literature at all. It is in the margin beyond denotation that our great-

[8] Paraphrased from the opening of the chapter on "Gobbledygook" in Stuart Chase's *Power of Words* (New York: Harcourt, 1954), a passage which Mr. Chase had, in turn, paraphrased from a National Security Agency report.

est potential awaits us. It is also there that our worst enemy lurks, the cliché.

The cliché has always been a plague to writers. It often results when we think in phrases; we gather a phrase here, a phrase there, paste them together in the handiest fashion (note this very sentence), until our language resembles what George Orwell in his excellent essay "Politics and the English Language" called a prefabricated henhouse. Such groups of words reflect a writer's laziness of mind, for in allowing someone else to choose his word-groups, his vocabulary, he is essentially allowing someone else to do his thinking. And because it is borrowed, that thinking is stale, Oh, stale.

Another common source of the cliché is the worn-out metaphor or comparison, such as "the pounding surf" and "stuck out like a sore thumb." When such a word-group loses its original startle, it is said to be dead. Of course, some dead metaphors make their way into the lexicon where they assume a more or less specific meaning and function as compound words or idioms, as Dark Ages, full-blown, and overwhelm. Of these, no danger. But be careful of the dying metaphor; create your own comparisons rather than rob someone else's henhouse.

A third source of the cliché is the common adjective-noun combination. Mark Twain is said to have gone through his manuscripts and categorically blue-penciled every adjective. Then he went back through and restored only those which changed the meaning—which is to say that many of our adjectives don't really mean anything at all. Here, again, certain constructions, for example, "the little red schoolhouse," come to have fixed, lexical meanings. But during the time that "little red schoolhouse" was used as a nostalgic sentimentality, it was a cliché. It was the connotation that made it a cliché then, for an accurate description of a schoolhouse that happened to be small and red cannot be a cliché, though it might be useless. An absolutely precise vocabulary is the writer's best antidote to triteness.[9] Compare "the distant rumble of artillery" with "the ground quivered from the sound of cannons three miles away." Indeed, an absolutely precise vocabulary is one of the writer's primary tools for saying what he chooses.

Varieties of Grammar

As with respelling and vocabulary, "bad" grammar reveals dialect, social level, personality, and so forth. But good grammar (that is, what is accepted

[9] If you choose to use a cliché (and this is possible), you should be aware of the consequences. The purpose should justify the effect; a character with a cliché habit of mind would be falsely rendered in fresh language. But you should also remember that, no matter how justified, you still have a cliché.

as normal, correct usage) also lends itself to a great variety of possibilities and effects. Commonly, the young writer fails to use the variety of possibilities open to him and thus produces either run-on or choppy writing. As H. A. Gleason, Jr., says in *Linguistics and English Grammar:*

One variety of the run-on-sentence disease shows in compositions consisting of long sequences of quite unvaried clauses, all joined into one long chain by "and." Its polar opposite seems to be "short choppy sentences," where a similar sequence of clauses is made into an equal number of sentences, all of the same pattern. Actually, the two are but different symptoms of the same fundamental difficulty. Each is the invariant use of a single technique of joining clauses. The stylistic failing is monotony.[10]

Variety is the antidote to monotony. One simple way to improve a boring passage is to mix the kinds of juncture and sentence length at random. But it is much better if the writer can have a purpose in his mixing, so that the rhetoric of the sentence is matched to the message he wishes to convey—subordinate ideas in subordinate clauses, primary ideas in main clauses, simple ideas in simple sentences. And it is better yet if the writer can contrive to make the mixing itself an element of the rhetoric, so that expansive ideas are developed in a series of sentences, each one larger than the last until a climax is reached and the sentences become shorter again. In other words, the writer controls the unity and dynamics—the dramatic effect—of a complicated idea by mixing his structures. Unity and effect, of course, are the antidotes to chaos (uncontrolled variety) and confusion.

One can overdo variety, especially pointless variety. Is the rhetoric of the last paragraph with its sentences of six, twenty, forty-four, forty-seven, twenty-one, and fourteen words justified? The problem is, of course, to match the motive to the rhetoric, as Macaulay does in his praise of Bacon, so that an expansive quality of lengthening involvement is reflected in the lengthening sentences, and one begins to kind of roll with the rhetoric. A related problem is illustrated by the juxtaposition of this paragraph and the preceding one. The expansion-contraction movement itself becomes a unit in our aesthetic response and generates its own monotony. Over-used, the technique can be boring.

There is another serious failing in style in the last two paragraphs, in spite of the involved strategy: almost every sentence is in the structural pattern of a subject-object assertion, followed by a number of noun clauses and phrases. Sentence structure, too, can generate failings. An unbroken series of periodic

[10] New York: Holt, Rinehart & Winston, 1965, p. 432.

sentences, for example, will impress the reader with its artificial suspense, just as a series of loose sentences will impress him with its casualness, which may or may not be detrimental. Young writers who have just overcome the problems of the choppy-run-on and simple assertive styles typically write in monotonous complex structures in which the dependent clause always comes at the beginning of the sentence. Such a structure is called left-branching. The dependent clause, if the writer wishes to vary his effect, can be imbedded between some of the ordinary elements of the sentence. And, of course, the writer can use right-branching sentences, can tack such a clause on at the end, when he wants to. To avoid monotony, the writer has at his disposal all the grammatical resources of the language—parenthetical insertions, appositive phrases, clauses, and even appositive sentences. Even fragments. His problem is to choose those structures that will best communicate the qualities of tone and mood he wants.

The process of choice is not merely a mechanical one. It may be possible to avoid monotony by a deliberate manipulation of sentence elements, but it is not likely that any real interest can be generated by such a means. It is almost a truism now that it takes greatness of happening to create real interest. But once the writer has managed this magnitude, he will find choice reopened to him on a higher, mechanical level. He will find that a given idea can be worded one way or another, with a difference in effect.

In addition to sentence structure, word-ordering can indicate relatively simple things, like national background: "Is it happy you'll be with Paddy Evans?" The German, the Spaniard, the Negro, the Jew, and many others all have their vaudeville caricatures. They are part of the curse of cliché that every writer has to deal with, sooner or later.

But word-ordering can be more ambitious. It can emphasize a point, or heighten the reader's reaction to a part or a section of the writing. If the writer wants to communicate the idea that "the writer cannot avoid using style," he can word it several ways: "Style, the writer cannot avoid." "Avoid using style, the writer cannot." "Avoid style? The writer cannot." "How can a writer avoid using style?" (This last one has to have a context that supplies the incredulous tone.) Or again, a mother says to her wayward son, "You will not get one dollar from me!" and the writer has to add the exclamation mark to indicate the tone. Rearranging those very words can make the exclamation point superfluous, though it is still grammatically appropriate: "Not one dollar will you get from me!" The rearrangement can hardly be spoken or understood as anything but angry refusal. If even simple sentences have so much potential, how much has the language! Word-order and grammar can be immensely complicated and difficult to handle, but they contain also some of the writer's best opportunities to control the responses of his readers. At the ambitious end of their spectrum, they merge with a topic that is slightly larger in scope, the arrangement of ideas themselves.

Organization or Sequence of Ideas

The arrangement a writer gives his ideas is a part of what he says. At the level of the sentence, the paragraph, and the whole composition, a change in the sequence of presenting ideas can change the effect and effectiveness of the ideas. Organization, then, determines what idea or part of an idea is noticeable, and influences, consequently, the total communication. If an idea is placed so that it is not noticeable, it might as well not be placed at all. Placement *is* predication.

We should all be familiar with how one makes sentences and paragraphs effective and sensible. Our schoolteachers have surely told us often enough that the middle of a sentence is the least effective part of it, that if we want an idea or a word to have prominence, we should place it at the beginning or at the end. For example, such a bland sentence as,

> Mary's shoes were red,

can be arranged to:

> Red were Mary's shoes.

The message and the meter in the two sentences are the same, but not the rhythm—pitch, stress, and juncture have changed. Nor the effect! Such a poetic effect, of course, might be detrimental, if used without reason. The same general rules, as well as some related to logic and articulation, apply to paragraphs. Whole compositions are a bit more difficult.

The great problem for the writer is that there are almost as many kinds of arrangements as there are groups of ideas. Arrangement may consist simply of giving the reader the background, but the background may be simple or complicated. Thus Benjamin Franklin uses his own resistance to Rev. Whitfield and his own somewhat comic conversion as a preparation for his friend's resistance, conversion, and application for a loan. It is significant that Franklin has summarized the events of considerable time in these few sentences, because what he is interested in showing is Whitfield's effectiveness as a preacher. Thus he focuses our attention on the changes wrought in selected members of the audience and highlights the friend's conversion for us by the Quaker's refusal. Note that I, in introducing the passage, felt the need to mention that Whitfield was an itinerant Presbyterian (this prepares for the Quaker) but assumed that the reader would know that Franklin's resistance grew out of his

Deism. It would be quite instructive for the young writer to try to decide just how much of Franklin's anecdote needs to be quoted to illustrate a point. Does the Quaker's refusal alone make a point? Do the refusal and the friend's conversion do it? Do the refusal, the friend's conversion, and Franklin's conversion all have to be included? What role does placement play in each of these parts? These are all matters which critics discuss under the heading of organic form. Arrangements in which an idea grows out of all that has gone before and prepares us for all that comes after are so numerous, individual, and complicated that we can only try here to make the young stylist aware that they exist.

The logic of articulation, as revealed in such words as *then, therefore, because, however, in spite of* establishes organic relationships between sentences and, thus, between ideas. When we see *but* used as a conjunction, we expect the following idea to contrast to the preceding one. When we see *thus* or *therefore,* we expect a logical progression of idea. The writer uses *for example, consequently, in conclusion,* and any number of other expressions, including *and so forth,* to keep his reader out of chaos. This articulation also appears in repetition of the subject, in parallel grammatical forms, in synonyms and contrasts, in anything that communicates to the reader that a group of ideas belong together. These can be simple or complicated—a word or a pattern of expectations aroused by a skeleton sentence.

Fiction, the illusion of experience, is often held together by the logic of articulation. When John awoke, he realized that he was thirsty. *So* he got up, went to the kitchen, and made himself a cup of coffee. *Then* he went to the living room. *Last night's* newspapers were scattered on the floor. He moved quietly, *because* his wife was *not yet* awake . . .

Such articulation is also the organizing principle of the essay that a composition teacher might illustrate on the blackboard as an inclined plane. The writer starts with an idea, stated simply. Then he restates the idea in much wider terms, drawing in implication from different areas of experience. Then he restates the idea a third time, perhaps now expanding into philosophical implications. This technique of restatement, of course, can go on as long as the idea will tolerate expansion. The arrangement for expansion keeps it clear in the reader's mind.

However, there are a number of conventional arrangements which have a more or less definable form. One of these is the "Greek temple" form of most expository essays. Teachers of elementary composition perennially draw a scheme of a Greek temple on their blackboards and explain to their students that the foundation (the introduction of their essays) must be broad enough to support the whole thing and especially broad enough to support (contain in general form) each of the columns (these are the parts of the body) and that the triangular roof (this is the conclusion) "covers" all the main ideas in the body and "gives them a point" (chalk pointing at or encircling the point of the roof). The puns in this maneuver are actually a part of its effectiveness. This is the form of this essay on style. It is the form of most discursive essays and can be used in fiction if the writer is subtle enough, as was demonstrated by Ford in *The Good Soldier,* and Conrad in *Lord Jim, Nostromo* and other works.

The great value of the "Greek temple" arrangement is that it organizes the reader's response to the writer's ideas. The skeleton sentence in the introduction offers the reader a *modus operandi*—the way the writer intends to discuss the subject. Indeed, this "M.O." sentence sets up certain expectations in the reader's mind and gives him the signposts that guide him through the message. It makes possible shiftings of thought or subject that might otherwise have struck the readers as mere chaos, but are now accepted without hesitation, because they have been prepared for.[11] Indeed, there is probably some little aesthetic pleasure when the reader sees the writer fulfilling the expected arrangement.

Another kind of arrangement is illustrated by deductive and inductive strategy. Consider the following paragraph:

Style is a terrifying thing. Style makes the young writer quail before the immense task of choosing the proper words for the proper places, so that his writing will have the effect he wants. Style makes the sophomoric writer hesitate at the choice, because he is aware that the words on the page have become a revelation and a judgment of the attitudes and connotations in the imitated experience, is aware that style imposes moral judgment upon both the material and the reader. Style makes the experienced writer labor at the choice, for he knows that style is his only technique for controlling what the reader will discover. Style makes the psychoanalyst chuckle, for he knows that the choices, the judgments, the discoveries in style reveal the ultimate personality of the man. Few people will deny that an awareness of style awakens terrifying anxieties which no one can quell all of the time.

The paragraph begins with deductive and ends with inductive strategy. The opening sentence is a generalization and an assertion, which is exemplified and supported by the four sentences following. If one reads the paragraph without

---

[11] Consider, in this connection, the aesthetics of the footnote. What is the effect of arranging material, as I have earlier, so that something other than documentation is given in a note? The material on clichés (footnote 9 of this chapter), though slightly different in subject from the text (this makes it possible for it to appear in a note), *could* have been rephrased and worked into the text. What is the effect on the reader's sense of organization, when he is directed to look at a note? Similarly, what is the effect of a parenthetical passage?

the last sentence, it is wholly deductive in method. But if one reads the paragraph without the *first* sentence, the four medial sentences function as observed phenomena in the world, and the last sentence functions both as the inductive conclusion and as the topic sentence in the paragraph. Deductive strategy involves a tone of assertive and perhaps irrefutable proof; it may irritate the reader precisely because of this tone. Many writers prefer inductive strategy because, in a sense, the reader is invited into the process of discovery. Both can be used, and both can be used together. And the uses are not by any means restricted to expository writing; J. D. Salinger makes very effective use of Holden Caulfield's inductive leaps from a single incident to a generalization.

There are other conventional arrangements—temporal sequence, the reverse of temporal sequence, flashback, and so on. One so obvious as hardly to need mention is the series arranged for climax. The writer can choose to put his most important ideas first or last; his choice will influence the relative heft that each idea has. Any climactic series heightens the reader's attention, thus the technique brings up the larger problem of heightening in general.

Converging Patterns for Heightening of Effect

Each of the techniques discussed above—choice of pronunciation, choice of vocabulary, grammatical maneuvers, and idea sequence—falls naturally into some pattern when we use it. In the ordinary course of writing, we may use any and all of these patterns, one here, another there, a third in another place, so that they become interwoven in the general background fabric of the tone; for example, a persistent selection of words with gloomy connotations will create a gloomy mood. Often, we work to keep such devices from showing, to make style—as was Hawthorne's ideal—melt into meaning. But it is also possible to manipulate patterns in a way that makes the material at hand stand out, that heightens the reader's attention and sharpens his memory.

The sequence or organization of ideas establishes an elementary sort of pattern. Something happens as a result of something else and presupposes a third element to follow. The anecdote from Benjamin Franklin's *Autobiography* is, on the one hand, an excellent illustration of elementary, sequential pattern, and, at the same time, a good illustration of more ambitious patterning. In fact, there are several, simple patterns operating in the passage: there is first the narrative thread of what happened first, second, third; then there is the pattern and conflict of religious convictions; third, there is the pattern of friendships—Franklin with Whitfield, Franklin with Hopkinson, Hopkinson with the Quaker; fourth, there is the pattern of humorous irony;

fifth, there are the patterns of pronunciations, word-choice, and grammar; and there may be other patterns involving the passage within the chapter, the chapter within the book, the book within the man's philosophy. Such multiplicity of pattern is common in all but the most barren of prose. Often, these patterns do not work together: one climaxes while another is building, one dissipates while two others coalesce, and the several patterns melt into the background. But when two or more of these patterns converge, an unusual prominence is given to the language and ideas at the convergence. Franklin's Quaker's refusal to lend Hopkinson money climaxes the narrative thread of the anecdote, points up the pattern of religious differences, establishes the limits of friendship, contradicts the ironic pattern with its dead seriousness, and involves a sharp change in linguistic pattern—that is, in pronunciation, vocabulary, and grammar. All of these patterns converging simultaneously make the passage so memorable that readers can often quote the Quaker's line accurately after a single reading and can do so even after a considerable lapse of time. Franklin converges patterns of anecdote, irony, seriousness, and linguistic choice over and over again in his *Autobiography*. (Remember the "speckled axe" anecdote? Franklin's struggles with virtue? And in a quite different vein, his treatment of General Braddock?) This mark of his style establishes the tone of the book, exhibits his philosophy, and leaves us with ideas of Franklin's life that have to be corrected by other biographical means. (The Franklin of the book is, in a sense, Franklin's best fictional creation.) Unless unusual prominence is desired, the writer must keep his multiple patterns out of phase with one another, but when prominence is desired, he must make his patterns reinforce each other, for only then can he reinforce his point.

What are some of the techniques with which the writer can manipulate his patterns? One of the simplest is to change tone abruptly. The change in tone, resulting from different linguistic elements, in the Quaker's line in the Franklin anecdote would solicit our attention even without the other devices. Some public speakers—university recruiters speaking at high schools are particularly numerous among them—simply insert a few words of slang, or tell a joke, or shift their ground momentarily to make their points. How many high-sounding speeches have each of us heard about how education is good and how the future lies before us, in which the speaker breaks his tone with something like "You better b'lieve it!" Since this use of the device calls attention to the fact that the writer is using a device (no melting into meaning here), it is detrimental to good effect, not constructive. The same thing can happen when patterns are out of phase: earlier in this chapter, you read the words "an expansive quality of lengthening involvement is reflected in the lengthening sentences, and one begins to kind of roll with the rhetoric," in which the expression "kind of roll" is disparate with the general tone of the paragraph, a fairly sophisticated tone illustrated in the quoted sentence by the balance imposed through the repetition of the word "lengthening." The words "kind of roll" in the context of the paragraph, and even the sentence, are a sour note that should not be allowed to sound, except as an illustration.[12] The ideal, of course, is to make the break in tone reveal something significant, so that the reader's attention is directed to what is revealed, not to the device for revealing it.

The use of "roll with the rhetoric" may suggest a cluster of devices: alliteration, assonance, consonance, onomatopoeia, dissonance, puns, anything in which pronunciation would call attention to the words. We all know, as did the Anglo-Saxons, how pronounceable alliteration makes a line, and how easy to remember; it heightens attention. Emily Dickinson influences the reader's attention in her poem, "A Route of Evanescence," through a careful control of assonance, consonance, and dissonance.

> A route of evanescence
> With a revolving wheel;
> A resonance of emerald;
> A rush of cochineal.
> And every blossom on the bush
> Adjusts its tumbled head;—
> The mail from Tunis, probably,
> An easy morning's ride.[13]

In the first four lines, the poet imitates the smooth whirring of the hummingbird by eliminating all but two or three of the plosives and stops; in the last four lines, she puts in as many as she can to suggest explosive violence. The contrast enhances the subject of the poem, is a part of the poet's strategy of patterning. Onomatopoeia, dissonance, puns can be used in some of the same ways; in fact, Tennyson's line, "The moan of doves in immemorial elms" makes use of most of these devices. Usually, of course, this principle of patterning operates subconsciously when we write; a word doesn't "sound right," so we change it. At every point in writing, we can change it, deliberately, to heighten or attenuate the effect.

---

[12] One might consider, also the effects of making a written discussion self-illustrative, as this one is. Leaving such "errors" as "kind of roll" in the text must create a tension in the sensitive reader, especially in an essay on style. To create this tension, as well as others (the quotations in the chapter's first paragraph, the promises of coming discussion in the second), and then to deal with it later in the chapter may itself be an act of patterning, an act that makes the parts cohere in a way they otherwise would not.

[13] As recorded by Thomas Wentworth Higginson in "The Letters of Emily Dickinson," *Atlantic Monthly,* 58 (October, 1891).

Diction can also be used for prominence. An unusual precision in word-choice can demand a reader's special attention. Earlier in this chapter, you read the words "placement is predication." The reader is expected to see (if he doesn't know the Latin derivation) that "predication" is the same word as "predicate" in our grammar books and to understand that the sentence means "placement functions like the predicate in a sentence; it is a way of saying something." (Note, too, that the sentence comes at the end of a paragraph in which the idea in the sentence is developed; the unusual diction, then, is intended to emphasize the meaning.)

Unusual diction can even make clichés useful, as Red Fenwick's review of *The Fifty-Niners* in the Denver *Post* indicates.

Once upon a bloody chapter in history there were three frontier hell holes where holsters were slicker, gunmen quicker and thieves thicker than any place else in the lusty west.

The rimes, of course, also function to heighten the pattern, as does the deliberate over-use of clichés. The satirical tone points up the cliché-ness and divorces the writer from it.

Word-ordering is another manipulable device. The example on page 36, "Not one dollar will you get from me," shows use of the device for emphasis. The most important words in the sentence are *not* and *one;* the rearrangement from "you will not get one dollar from me" takes them out of weak positions in the sentence and gives them prominence.

Sentence structure, length, rhythm, and flow of idea are very important devices for heightening attention. John Donne is extremely sensitive to these matters in this passage from "Meditation XVII":

... No man is an island, entire of itself; every man is a piece of the continent, a part of the main. If a clod be washed away by the sea, Europe is the less, as well as if a promontory were, as well as if a manor of thy friend's or of thine own were. Any man's death diminishes me because I am involved in mankind, and therefore never send to know for whom the bell tolls; it tolls for thee ...

Length of sentence is, perhaps, the most important part of Donne's rhetoric. The word-count in the independent clauses is 8 in the first, 13 in the second, 34 in the third, 22 in the fourth, and 4 in the last. This lengthening and contracting process focuses our attention on the last clause, for the growth of sentence length leads us to invest a certain aesthetic "weight" in each of the clauses. Donne's pattern of heightening forces us to give the same aesthetic weight to "it tolls for thee" as we give to the other lengthy sentence—four, strong, tense stresses. This rhythmic pattern coincides with the pattern of contrast—"never send to know . . . it tolls for thee," and with the completion of the syllogism. Thus, at least three patterns converge here for effect. Donne is manipulating our aesthetic responses. Paragraph structure, strategy, speed, placement can all be made to participate in such patterns.

Patterns of metaphor, alliteration, rime, rhythm, and so forth, are not the exclusive materials of poetry but are also used in prose. Poetry adds a few abstract patterns, such as the poetic foot, line length, stanza forms, and so on; thus, poetry offers more opportunity in a given space for patterns to converge. A high number of convergences of pattern is a prime characteristic of poetry, while prose has relatively fewer, though that prose is dead which has none. Poetry can make accent, line-end, phrase-end, rime, and possibly more converge on a single syllable. This process is so critical, aesthetically, that it is deadly *not* to use multiplicity of pattern in poetry; one of the poet's worst sins is to make a rime for the sake of the chime. Abstract patterns make poetry pregnant, as Yvor Winters was well aware when he decided that the heroic couplet is the form with the most potential. Any and all of those same patterns are available to the prose writer; whether or not he uses them judiciously is another matter.

Style, Then, Is a Quality

Style, then, is a quality or a cluster of qualities that result from an author's choices among the entire resources of his language. If he is unconscious of it, it will exist anyway, though any effects it achieves will be ascribable only to his "instincts," not to his intentions. The writer's product is doomed to have some kind of style. To be aware of the stylistic effects of pronunciation, vocabulary, grammar, organization, and patterning is the author's only means for dealing effectively with his own and with others' styles.

We have not tried to be exhaustive here. Indeed, anyone, with a bit of thought, can come up with uses of pronunciation that this discussion has not touched on. Almost anyone, too, would immediately think of temporal sequence, the reverse of temporal sequence, and flashback as possible organizations of ideas. We have, rather, tried to maintain a balance among the parts of this discussion (that's another device) and to offer a framework of five parts that can be used in approaching any style, anywhere. We offer a method; the student will have to expand its detail in the application.

We have been concerned, too, with heightening the young writer's attention to the act of writing as an act of many choices. Too often, beginning writers seem to think that writing is an irrational accident; they have this feeling here (hand on heart) and they want to get it there (gesture of pouring toward paper), and if they get anything down on paper, they think it's got to be good because it's theirs. Instead, the choices in writing should be understood as conscious and deliberate acts, if only so that style can, with extended usage, becomes unconscious again.

PROJECTS FOR WRITING AND DISCUSSION

There are four distinct and valuable kinds of exercises for the writer who is trying to develop his styles. (Styles, not style, for the writer needs as many styles as he has things to say.) These exercises fall into a four-stage conceptual progression, from the easy to the difficult, based, in turn, upon analysis, comparison, imitation, and original creation.

A. *ANALYSIS*

1. Analyze selected passages of at least three common styles of today, as the Hemingway style, the Faulkner style, the *New Yorker* style, and so on. For each selection, make a list of its characteristics of pronunciation, vocabulary, grammar, organization, and patterning. *Time* magazine, for example, might be described as having a style characterized by: (a) cleverer-than-thou tone, especially in the condescension of phrases like "it was assumed," and "of all things"; flair and, usually, sophisticated sarcasm; penchant for alliteration; (b) vocabulary that tends to search for the cute and witty, often in variations on dying metaphors and puns; propensity for piling up, in adjective form, ideas that might more commonly be subordinate clauses; coinage of words; use of professions or descriptions as adjectives; (c) grammatical variations from "correctness" occurring to embarrass the subject under discussion and participial openings and archaic inversions of subject and verb (as in "to Hollywood came cinemactress Monroe..."); (d) organization along deductive or inductive logical lines and commonly unfinished, so that the reader has to draw the prepared conclusion; (e) patterning usually toward some "clincher," which has to be prepared by an underplayed passage; the clincher is often a clever and revealing quote or pun, or some rhetorical maneuver.

2. Collect and study closely typical examples of some of the more important historical styles, such as, for example, the style of Bacon, Sir Thomas Browne, Joseph Addison, William Hazlitt, Thomas Carlyle, Macaulay, Hawthorne, Melville, James, Mark Twain, James Joyce, Hemingway, Faulkner, and any other writer, including poets, you think important. You might make an album of these samples and append to each a list of its characteristics. In any case, it would be very valuable to write out your observations, rather than leave them in the form of vague impressions.

3. Analyze, if you can, three of the more important "period" styles, as the Rococo, Baroque, Neo-Classical, Romantic, Victorian, and the "Plain" style of the Puritans. Decide, if you can, what the characteristics of prose are in our own time.

4. Analyze your own style in a passage you wrote a few months ago. Rewrite the passage in a different style.

B. *COMPARISON*

1. Vardis Fisher suggested a worthwhile exercise in comparing styles in his *God or Caesar?* He gave several pairs of sentences that were supposed to be fairly close to one another lexically as, for example, (a) "She heard birds and a toad singing in the trees and bees humming all around and she felt happy," and (b) "The first flute of birds in the branches, the early hum of bees, the tree-toad's bell, spoke to her heart, lonely and loving." [14] The first sentence he wrote himself; the second he quoted from Robert Nathan, but did not identify the source. He invited the young writer to ask himself such questions as: What does each sentence communicate? What does each communicate that its "equivalent" doesn't? What accounts for the differences?

A comparison of these two might begin by noting that, although the lexical meanings are very nearly the same in both sentences, the tones and thus the effects are quite different. The first sentence is matter-of-fact and plodding; the second is romantic and lyrical. These qualities result from several aspects of style. For example, the pronunciation and grammar contrast sharply. The first is a loose sentence; it could be punctuated and ended after "birds," "singing," "trees," "humming," "around," and at the end. Each of these points in the sentence has at least a bit of the dying fall of a matter-of-fact declarative statement. By contrast, the second sentence is periodic; each element of the series forces us into a rising pitch which indicates that the sentence is incomplete. This lift at several points and the suspense of the periodic grammar get incorporated into the lyric quality and account for some of the effect. What does Nathan gain or lose by using a vocabulary of metaphors ("flute," instead of "song" of birds) and by the sentiment of "her heart, lonely and loving"?

In a similar manner, analyze and compare the following groups of passages.

Group I:

a.   [Pearl's] was a look so intelligent, yet inexplicable, so perverse, sometimes so malicious, but generally accompanied by a wild flow of spirits, that Hester could not help questioning, at such moments, whether Pearl was a human child. (Nathaniel Hawthorne in *The Scarlet Letter*)

b.   Hester sometimes thought that Pearl might be an inhuman child, for her

---

[14] Caldwell, Idaho: Caxton, 1953, p. 143.

looks, though usually full of spirit, were often perverse, malicious, inexplicable, even as they were intelligent.

c.   Pearl's glance seemed to *know*. Hester sometimes saw a glint there that seemed to say, perversely, "I'm not like you. I'm not merely human. I have an intelligence and a maliciousness that is beyond the human."

d.   "Well, you know; she looks odd."
"You mean..."
"Oh, I don't know, really. She seems intelligent; that I'll say. And she..."
"She's inexplicable."
"That's it! And perverse. She's perverse, too."
"Would you go so far as to say 'malicious'?"
"Malicious? Well, yes, though she's usually pleasant enough—has a wild flow of good spirit."
"But you think she's odd."
"Well, odd's not strong enough a word. I'd almost say—Sometimes—Have you ever thought..."
"Thought what?"
"That—That, maybe, she's—Maybe she's not human?"

Group II:

a.   After a wobbly start, he took up again the unfinished work of becoming life's American, the completely affirmative man, and plunged headlong into plans for composing an epic poem based on American history. (Ross Lockridge, Jr., in *Raintree County*)

b.   He had had a wobbly start. But he recovered and began it all again. He was planning an epic poem. The epic of American History. He wanted to be a famous and positive American.

c.   After a start made wobbly not only by his own infirmities and the demands of an exacting family but by the old avatars of the subject itself, he took up again plans for his epic of American history—*plans,* for that was all he had to show for all his long and hard work and false starts, all he had on paper, though his skull had already been the fields untold times where his ancestors stalked, angry and acusing, playing out the old inevitable story of lust and pain and privation and forgiveness, pointing out at *him* with blunt, Uncle-Sam-poster fingers, saying *You! You! We want you! You are to be life's American, the completely affirmative man.*

Group III:

a.   [May Bartram says] "Of the way you did feel? Well, it was very simple. You said you had had from your earliest time, as the deepest thing within you, the sense of being kept for something rare and strange, possibly prodigious and terrible, that was sooner or later to happen to you, that you had in your bones the foreboding and conviction of, and that would perhaps overwhelm you." (Henry James in "The Beast in the Jungle")

b.   He had a feeling that something—he knew not what, but suspected it was to be terrible—was going to happen to him.

c.   Well, y'know, I was just standing there and all of a sudden I had this creepy feeling that *some* thing was about to happen. To me, I mean. I felt like it had always been about to happen, y'know, from the time when I was just a little kid, and it was just waiting for me to stand right or turn my back or something. And it was going to be something big, like a goddam beast in the jungle, or something, that was going to spring at me.

Group IV:

a.   Talk not to me of blasphemy, man; I'd strike the sun if it insulted me. For could the sun do that, then could I do the other. (Herman Melville in *Moby Dick*)

b.   For in all human hearts, there is a sympathy and an urge that demands equality with the universe. Every man wants to stand on the sun, as it were, and not wait till the resurrection to become as the gods.

Group V:

a.   Sweet is the swamp with its secrets
     Until we meet a snake.
                    (Emily Dickinson in "Sweet is the Swamp with its Secrets")

b.   The swamp is sweet with secrets
     Until we meet a snake.

c.   The secret swamp is sweet and lovely,
     Except when we encounter a snake.

Group VI:

a.   Lives of great men all remind us
        We can make our lives sublime,
     And, departing, leave behind us
        Footprints on the sands of time.
                    (Henry Wadsworth Longfellow in "Psalm of Life")

b.   Biographies of prominent persons indicate
        That fame is available to you and me,
     That death need not be the end of reputation,
        That our memorials can persist through eons.

Group VII:

a.   from *The Adventures of Tom Sawyer,* by Mark Twain

     When Tom awoke in the morning, he wondered where he was. He sat up and rubbed his eyes and looked around. Then he comprehended. It was the cool gray dawn, and there was a delicious sense of repose and peace in the deep pervading calm and silence of the woods. Not a leaf stirred; not a sound obtruded upon great Nature's meditation. Beaded dewdrops stood upon the leaves and grasses. A white layer of ashes covered the fire, and a thin blue breath of smoke rose straight into the air. Joe and Huck still slept.

Now, far away in the woods a bird called; another answered; presently the hammering of a woodpecker was heard. Gradually the cool dim gray of the morning whitened, and as gradually sounds multiplied and life manifested itself. The marvel of Nature shaking off sleep and going to work unfolded itself to the musing boy. A little green worm came crawling over a dewy leaf, lifting two-thirds of his body into the air from time to time and "sniffing around," then proceeding again—for he was measuring, Tom said; and when the worm approached him, of its own accord, he sat as still as a stone, with his hopes rising and falling, by turns, as the creature still came toward him or seemed inclined to go elsewhere; and when at last it considered a painful moment with its curved body in the air and then came decisively down upon Tom's leg and began a journey over him, his whole heart was glad—for that meant that he was going to have a new suit of clothes—without the shadow of a doubt a gaudy piratical uniform. Now a procession of ants appeared, from nowhere in particular, and went about their labors; one struggled manfully by with a dead spider five times as big as itself in its arms, and lugged it straight up a tree-trunk. A brown spotted lady-bug climbed the dizzy height of a grass-blade, and Tom bent down close to it and said, "Lady-bug, lady-bug, fly away home, your house is on fire, your children's alone," and she took wing and went off to see about it— which did not surprise the boy, for he knew of old that this insect was credulous about conflagrations, and he had practised upon its simplicity more than once. A tumblebug came next, heaving sturdily at its ball, and Tom touched the creature, to see it shut its legs against its body and pretend to be dead. The birds were fairly rioting by this time. A catbird, the Northern mocker, lit in a tree over Tom's head, and trilled out her imitations of her neighbors in a rapture of enjoyment; then a shrill jay swept down, a flash of blue flame, and stopped on a twig almost within the boy's reach, cocked his head to one side and eyed the strangers with a consuming curiosity; a gray squirrel and a big fellow of the "fox" kind came scurrying along, sitting up at intervals to inspect and chatter at the boys, for the wild things had probably never seen a human before and scarcely knew whether to be afraid or not. All Nature was wide awake and stirring, now; long lances of sunlight pierced down through the dense foliage far and near, and a few butterflies came fluttering upon the scene. (Chapter XIV)

b.   from *The Adventures of Huckleberry Finn,* by Mark Twain

Two or three days and nights went by; I reckon I might say they swum by, they slid along so quiet and smooth and lovely. Here is the way we put in the time. It was a monstrous big river down there—sometimes a mile and a half wide; we run nights, and laid up and hid daytimes; soon as night was most gone we stopped navigating and tied up—nearly always in the dead water under a towhead; and then cut young cottonwoods and willows, and hid the raft with them. Then we set out the lines. Next we slid into the river and had a swim, so as to freshen up and cool off; then we set down on the sandy bottom where the water was about knee-deep, and watched the daylight come. Not a sound anywhere—perfectly still—just like the whole world was asleep, only sometimes the bullfrogs a-cluttering, maybe. The first thing to see, looking away over the water, was a kind of dull line—that was the woods on t'other side; you couldn't make nothing else out; then a pale place in the sky; then more paleness spreading around; then the river softened up away off, and warn't black any more, but gray; you could see little dark spots drifting along ever so far away—trading-scows, and such things; and long black streaks—rafts; sometimes you could hear a sweep screaking; or jumbled-up voices, it was so still, and sounds came so far; and by and by you could see a streak on the water which you know by the look of the streak that there's a snag there in a swift current which breaks on it and makes that streak look that way, and you see the mist curl up off of the water, and the east reddens up, and the river, and you make out a log cabin in the edge of the woods, away on the bank on t'other side of the river, being a wood-yard, likely, and piled by them cheats so you can throw a dog through it anywheres; then the nice breeze springs up, and comes fanning you from over there, so cool and fresh and sweet to smell on account of the woods and the flowers; but sometimes not that way, because they've left dead fish laying around, gars and such, and they do get pretty rank; and next you've got the full day, and everything smiling in the sun, and the song-birds just going it!

A little smoke couldn't be noticed now, so we would take some fish off of the lines and cook up a hot breakfast. And afterwards we would watch the lonesomeness of the river, and kind of lazy along, and by and by lazy off to sleep. Wake up by and by, and look to see what done it, and maybe see a steamboat coughing along up-stream, so far off towards the other side you couldn't tell nothing about her only whether she was stern-wheel or side-wheel, then for about an hour there wouldn't be nothing to hear nor nothing to see—just solid lonesomeness. Next you'd see a raft sliding by, away off yonder, and maybe a galoot on it chopping, because they're most always doing it on a raft; you'd see the ax flash and come down—you don't hear nothing; you see that ax go up again, and by the time it's above the man's head then you hear the *k'chunk!*—it had took all that time to come over the water. So we would put in the day, lazying around, listening to the stillness. Once there was a thick fog, and the rafts and things that went by was beating tin pans so the steamboats wouldn't run over them. A scow or a raft went by so close we could hear them talking and cussing and laughing— heard them plain; but we couldn't see no sign of them; it make you feel crawly; it was like spirits carrying on that way in the air. Jim said he believed it was spirits; but I says: "No; spirits wouldn't say, 'Dern the dern fog.'" (Chapter **XIX**)

c.   from *Life on the Mississippi,* by Mark Twain

I had myself called with the four-o'clock watch, mornings, for one cannot see too many summer sunrises on the Mississippi. They are enchanting. First, there is the eloquence of silence; for a deep hush broods everywhere. Next, there is the haunting sense of loneliness, isolation, remoteness from the worry and bustle of the world. The dawn creeps in stealthily; the solid walls of black forest soften to gray, and vast stretches of the river open up and reveal themselves; the water is glass-smooth, gives off spectral little wreaths of white mist, there is not the faintest breath of wind, nor stir of leaf; the tranquility is profound and infinitely satisfying. Then a bird pipes up, another follows, and soon the pipings develop into a jubilant riot of music. You see none of the birds; you simply move through an atmosphere of song which seems to sing itself. When the light has become a little stronger, you have one of the fairest and softest pictures imaginable. You have the intense green of the massed and crowded foliage near by; you see it paling shade by shade in front of you; upon the next projecting cape, a mile off or more, the tint has lightened to the tender young green of spring; the cape beyond that one has almost lost color, and the furthest one, miles away under the horizon, sleeps upon the water a mere dim vapor, and hardly separable from the sky above it and about it. And all this stretch of river is a mirror, and you have the shadowy reflections of the leafage and the curving shores and the receding capes pictured in it. Well, that is all beautiful; soft and rich and beautiful; and when the sun gets well up, and distributes a pink flush here and a powder of gold yonder and a purple haze where it will yield the best effect, you grant that you have seen something that is worth remembering.

C. IMITATION

1. Analyze and imitate the style of your favorite author; then, for balance, analyze and imitate a style that you do not especially like.

2. Select a scene from a story by a well-known author and try to render it in the style of some other author. Then render it in your own style.

3. The stories by Hemingway * and Faulkner,* printed in chapter 3, each show a young person in conflict with his environment, which, in the form of an older generation, is making certain demands upon the young ones. In each case, the youth soon realizes that he will have to lie if he is to remain in that environment. Rewrite the beginnings of these stories—say, the first page or so; up to the point where they realize they must lie or get out—doing "Barn Burning" as if it were by Hemingway, "Soldiers Home" as if it were by Faulkner. You may, of course, delete detail, or invent it, according to the needs of the style.

D. CREATION

1. Write a description of a given house for as many different effects as you can achieve. For example, a Victorian mansion, the White House, the Parthenon in Athens can all be seen as ludicrous misfits or as epitomes of culture, depending upon the style, the choice and tone of detail, with which one describes them.

2. Try writing a given line with as many different pronunciations as you can.

For example, John DosPassos used the line, "Waiter I want a gin fizz please" in *Manhattan Transfer*. This line can be transformed into:

"Waiter, I want a gin fizz, please."
"Waiter! I want a gin fizz!"
"Waiter, *I* want a gin fizz, please."
"Waiter! . . . Please, I want a gin fizz."
"Waiter, I want a *gin* fizz, please."
"Waiter, Uh . . . I want . . . uh . . . a gin fizz."
"Please, waiter? I want a gin fizz; please?"

Many more transformations of such a line are possible. Write your own line, then begin to transform it. Remember that sometimes a good effect can be achieved by letting your character grope for words.

3. Write a particular scene in three or four different styles, emphasizing dialog and using only such minimal narrative tags as "he said" and "she said" and such minimal stage directions as "he opened the door, walked across the room, and sat down." Take, say, the following situation—a male and a female enter a public establishment, sit down, and order a drink; through their styles, reveal their ages, their sophistication, their economic stature, their level of education, and such, and help the reader to infer the kind and class of the place in which they are drinking; but do *not* describe the people or the place directly.

4. Write the same scene as in the above exercise in three or four different styles, using only description and indirect, summarized, or generalized conversation.

5. Write the same scene again—or invent a new one—using description, dialog, summary, indirection, all the devices you want, and paying particular attention to heightening for effect.

Two Essays on the "Use" of Style

Such is a framework for analyzing and practicing style. But what of the application of these theories to the actual task of writing? What is the relationship between the choices a writer makes and the meanings he communicates? How does one "use" style? Let's invite first a critic and then a writer to comment upon some specific uses of style. In the following essay, the critic, Mark Schorer, emphasizes the effect of vocabulary (and vocabulary substitutes) on meaning.[15]

[15] The writer's essay appears on pp. 67–73.

FICTION AND THE
"MATRIX OF ANALOGY"

1. If the novel, as R. P. Blackmur recently proposed, is now to enjoy the kind of attention from criticism that for the past twenty years has been the privilege of poetry, criticism must begin with the simplest assertion: fiction is a literary art. It must begin with the base of language, with the word, with figurative structures, with rhetoric as skeleton and style as body of meaning. A beginning as simple as this must overcome corrupted reading habits of long standing; for the novel, written in prose, bears an apparently closer resemblance to discursive forms than it does to poetry, thus easily opening itself to first questions about philosophy or politics, and, traditionally a middle-class vehicle with a reflective social function, it bears an apparently more immediate relation to life than it does to art, thus easily opening itself to first questions about conduct. Yet a novel, like a poem, is not life, it is an image of life; and the critical problem is first of all to analyse the structure of the image. Thus criticism must approach the vast and endlessly ornamented house of fiction with a willingness to do a little at a time and none of it finally, in order to suggest experiences of meaning and of feeling that may be involved in novels, and responsibilities for their style which novelists themselves may forget.

To choose, more or less at random and without premeditated end, one novel by each of only three novelists, and to examine in each only one element in the language, the dominant metaphorical quality—this, positively, is to work piecemeal, and merely to suggest. I emphasize not *metaphor* but *quality,* intending not only the explicit but the buried and the dead metaphors, and some related traits of diction generally, that whole habit of value association suggested in Scott Buchanan's phrase, the "matrix of analogy." The novels are *Persuasion, Wuthering Heights,* and *Middlemarch.*

2. *Persuasion* is a novel of courtship and marriage with a patina of sentimental scruple and moral punctilio and a stylistic base derived from commerce and property, the counting house and the inherited estate. The first is the expression of the characters, the second is the perception of the author. And whether we should decide that a persistent reliance on commerce and property for concepts of value is the habit of Jane Austen's mind, the very grain of her imagination, or that it is a special novelistic intention, is for the moment irrelevant. It is probable that the essence of her comedy resides, in either case, in the discrepancy between social sentiment and social fact, and the social fact is to be discovered not so much in the professions of her characters as in the texture of her style.

We are told at once that the mother of the three Elliot girls felt in dying that in them she left "an awful *legacy* . . . an awful *charge* rather"; that Sir Walter Elliot is devoted to his eldest daughter, Elizabeth (who opens "every ball of *credit*" and is waiting to be "properly *solicited* by baronet-blood"), but feels that his two younger daughters, Mary and Anne, are "of very inferior *value*"—indeed, "Anne's word had no *weight.*" Anne is befriended by Lady Russell, who "had a *value* for rank and consequence," and even though it was Lady Russell no less than Sir Walter who discouraged Anne's marriage, seven years before, to the propertyless Captain Wentworth, Anne *"rated* Lady Russell's influence highly." "Consequence," we are told, "has its *tax,"* and for seven years Anne has been paying it. The problem of the novel is to relieve her of the necessity of paying it and at the same time to increase her value.

We are in a world of substance, a peculiarly material world. Here, indeed, changes are usually named *"material* alterings"—for example, in "style of living" and "degree of consequence." Perhaps the word is used most tellingly in the phrases "a face not materially *disfigured"* and "a material difference in the *discredit* of it"; for *figure* and *credit* suggest the two large areas of metaphorical interest—arithmetic and business.

Time is *divided,* troubles *multiply,* weeks are *calculated,* and even a woman's prettiness is *reckoned.* Thus, one's independence is *purchased;* one is *rendered* happy or unhappy; one is on *terms,* friendly or unfriendly, with others. Young Mr. Elliot has "nothing to *gain* by being on *terms* with Sir Walter," but Lady Russell is convinced that he hopes "to *gain* Anne" even though Anne cannot "know herself to be so *highly rated."* We are asked to "take all the charms and perfections of Edward's wife upon *credit,"* and "to judge of the general *credit due."* Captain Wentworth thought that he had *earned* "every blessing." "I have *valued* myself on honourable toils and just *rewards."* So Mary is in the habit of *claiming* Anne's energies, and Anne does not feel herself *"entitled* to reward." Young ladies have a *"stock* of accomplishments." "Here were *funds* of enjoyment!" Anne does not wish "for the possibility of *exchange."* Experience is thought of as *venture, reversal, prospect, fortune,* and *allowance.* Anne *"ventured* to recommend a larger *allowance* of prose in" Captain Benwick's "daily study." The death of a wife leaves a man with *"prospects* . . . blighted,"* and Anne contemplates "the *prospect* of *spending"* two months at Uppercross. In this metaphorical context, even the landscape takes on a special shimmer: "all the *precious* rooms and furniture, groves, and *prospects."* An "arrangement" is *prudent* or *imprudent,* and feelings must be *arranged* as prudently as accounts: no one's "feelings could *interest* her, till she had a little better *arranged* her own." One *pays* addresses, of course, but one is also *repaid* for the "trouble of exertion." "It had *cost* her something to encounter Lady Russell's surprise." A town has *worth,* a song is not *worth* staying for, and Anne "had the full *worth* of" tenderness in "Captain Wentworth's affection." Captain Wentworth's account of Captain Benwick ("whom he had always *valued highly"*) *"stamped* him well in the esteem of every listener." "Ten minutes were enough *to certify that"* Mr. Elliot was a sensible man. Stamped, certified; and at last Anne's character is *"fixed* on his mind as perfection itself," which is to say that, like a currency, it has been stabilized.

Moral qualities are persistently put in economic figures: Mary "had no *resources* for solitude" and she had *inherited* "a considerable *share* of the Elliot self-importance." Love, likewise: if Elizabeth is hoping to be *solicited* by baronet-blood, Anne has had to reject the "declarations and proposals" of an improvident

sailor. "Alliance" is a peculiarly appropriate word for such prudential arrangements as these, and at the end of the novel, when "the engagement" is *"renewed,"*
one sees bonded documents. Anne need no longer suffer those fits of dejection in
which she contemplates others' *"prosperous* love," for hers at last has prospered,
too.

In this context certain colorless words, words of the lightest intention, take on
a special weight. The words *account* and *interest* are used hundreds of times in
their homeliest sense, yet when we begin to observe that every narration is an
account, and at least once "an *account . . .* of the *negotiation,"* we are reminded
that they have more special meanings. When Anne's blighted romance is called
"this little history of sorrowful *interest,"* we hardly forget that a lack of money
was the blight. Is "a man of principle" by any chance a man of substance?

The significance of this metaphorical substructure is clearest perhaps, not when
Jane Austen substitutes material for moral or sentimental values, but when she
juxtaposes them. "He had . . . been nothing better than a thick-headed, *unfeeling,
unprofitable* Dick Musgrove, who had never done anything to entitle himself to
more than the abbreviation of his name, living or dead." More simply, these three
from a single paragraph: "a *fund* of good *sense,"* *"leisure* to *bestow,"* "something that is *entertaining* and *profitable."* "I must endeavour," says Captain
Wentworth, in another such juxtaposition near the end of the novel, "I must endeavour to subdue my *mind* to my *fortune." Persuasion* is a novel in which sensibility—and I am not now raising the question whether it is the sensibility of the
author or of her characters or of her characters except for her heroes—a novel
in which sensibility is subdued to property.

The novel explicitly asks, what is "the value of an Anne Elliot" and where is
the man who will "understand" it? Anne herself feels that her value has sunk:

> A few months hence, and the room now so deserted, occupied by her silent,
> pensive self, might be filled again with all that was happy and gay, all that
> was *glowing and bright* in *prosperous love,* all that was most unlike Anne
> Elliot!

> . . . Anne felt her spirits not likely to be benefited by an increasing acquaint-
> ance among his brother-officers. "These would have been all my friends," was
> her thought; and she had to struggle against a great tendency to lowness.

"A great *tendency to lowness."* The phrase clarifies her situation, for Anne's is
finally the problem of a stock that has a debased value, and when she thinks of
doing good in such a further phrase as "good of a lower standard," we can
hardly escape the recognition that this is a novel about marriage as a market,
and about the female as marketable, and that the novel makes the observation
that to sentimental scruple and moral fastidiousness, as they are revealed to us
in the drama, much property is not necessary but *some* is essential—and this is
shown us primarily in the style. The basis of the comedy lies in the difference
between the two orders of value which the metaphors, like the characters, are all

the while busily equating. At the end, in the last sentence, a prosperous sailor's wife, Anne has been relieved of "the tax of consequence," but now "she must *pay the tax* of quick alarm for belonging to that profession which is, if possible, more distinguished in its domestic virtues than in its national importance."

3. The style of Jane Austen is so entirely without flamboyance or gesture, the cited illustrations are so commonplace, so perfectly within the order of English idiom, that, unless we remind ourselves that our own habits of speech are even more intimately involved in the life of cash than Jane Austen's, no case at all may appear. Yet the inevitability of individual imaginative habit, the impressive fact that every mind selects its creative gamut from the whole range of possible language, and in thus selecting determines its insights and their scope, in short, its character and the character of its creations, is at once apparent when we open some other novel. Emily Brontë is very different from Jane Austen, yet both were unmarried provincial women, living in the same half of the same century, speaking the same language, both daughters of clergymen, and one might reasonably expect to encounter, even in *Wuthering Heights,* some of those perfectly normal figures with which *Persuasion* abounds. There are, I think, none of the same kind. Emily Brontë does not "divide the time" but, on the first page, "the desolation"; "time," when she mentions it, "stagnates," and "prudence" is "diabolical." If there are any figures of the same kind, they are so few, and in their own metaphorical context, function so differently, that the total quality owes nothing to them. Where Wentworth speaks of the "crown' of "all my other success," Lockwood speaks of the "copestone on my rage and humiliation." Both *crown* and *copestone on* mean climax, but "crown" is drawn from rank and money, "copestone" from earth and building. If Nelly Dean's phrase, "the crown of all my wishes," suggests a kingdom at all, it is a heavenly kingdom, quite different from "all my other successes." The difference signifies. *Wuthering Heights* has its own sphere of significant experience, and its metaphors, like its epithets and verbs, tell us different things. They tell us, too, of a special problem.

Wuthering Heights, as I understand it, means to be a work of edification: Emily Brontë begins by wishing to instruct her narrator, the dandy, Lockwood, in the nature of a grand passion; she ends by instructing herself in the vanity of human wishes. She means to dramatize with something like approval—the phrase that follows is from *Middlemarch*—"the sense of a stupendous self and an insignificant world." What her metaphors signify is the impermanence of self and the permanence of something larger.

To exalt the power of human feeling, Emily Brontë roots her analogies in the fierce life of animals and in the relentless life of the elements—fire, wind, water. "Wuthering," we are told, is "a significant provincial adjective, descriptive of the atmospheric tumult to which its station is exposed in stormy weather," and, immediately after, that "one may guess the power of the north wind blowing over the edge, by the excessive slant of a few stunted firs at the end of the house; and by a range of gaunt thorns all stretching their limbs one way, as if craving alms of the sun." The application of this landscape to the characters is made explicit in the second half of the novel, when Heathcliff says, "Now, my bonny lad, you are *mine!* And we'll see if one tree won't grow as crooked as another, with the same wind to twist it!" This analogy provides at least half of the metaphorical base of the novel.

Human conditions are like the activities of the landscape, where rains *flood*, blasts *wail*, and the snow and wind *whirl wildly* and *blow* out lights. A serving woman *heaves* "like a sea after a high wind"; a preacher *"poured* forth his zeal in a *shower"*; Mrs. Dean *rushes* to welcome Lockwood, "exclaiming *tumultuously"*; spirits are "at high-water mark"; Linton's soul is as different from Heathcliff's "as a moonbeam from lightning, or frost from fire"; abuse is *lavished* in a *torrent*, or *pours forth* in a *deluge*; illnesses are *"weathered* ... through"; "sensations" are felt in a *gush*; "your veins are *full of ice water*; but mine are *boiling"*; hair *flies*, bodies *toss* or *tremble* like reeds, tears *stream* or *rain down* among ashes; discord and distress arise in a *tumult*; Catherine Linton "was *struck* during a *tempest* of passion with a kind of fit" and *"flew off* in the *height* of it."

Faces, too, are like landscapes: "a *cloud* of meditation" hangs over Nelly Dean's *"ruddy* countenance"; Catherine had "a suddenly *clouded* brow; her humor was a mere *vane* for constantly varying caprices"; "the surface of" the boy Heathcliff's "face and hands was dismally *beclouded"* with dirt; later, his face *"brightened* for a moment; then it was *overcast* afresh." "His forehead ... *shaded* over with a heavy *cloud"*; and "the *clouded* windows of hell," his eyes, *"flashed."* Hareton, likewise, grows "black as a *thundercloud"*; or *darkens* with a frown. The older Catherine experienced whole *"seasons* of gloom," and the younger Catherine's "heart was *clouded* ... in double *darkness."* Her "face was just like the *landscape—shadows* and *sunshine* flitting over it in rapid succession; but the *shadows* rested longer, and the *sunshine* was more transient." Sometimes "her eyes are *radiant* with *cloudless* pleasure," and at the end, Hareton shakes off "the *clouds* of ignorance and degradation," and his *"brightening* mind *brightened* his features."

Quite as important as the imagery of wind and cloud and water is the imagery of fire. In every interior, the fire on the hearth is the center of pictorial interest, and the characters sit *"burning* their eyes out before the fire." Eyes *burn* with anguish but do not *melt*; they always *flash* and *sparkle*. Fury *kindles*, temper *kindles*, a *"spark* of spirit" *kindles*. Catherine has a *fiery* disposition, but so do objects and states: words *brand*, shame is *burning*, merriment *expires* quickly, fevers *consume* life; hot coffee and basins *smoke*, they do not steam; and Isabella shrieks "as if witches were running *red-hot* needles into her." Sometimes fire is identified with other elements, as when a servant urges *"flakes* of *flame* up the chimney," or when Isabella complains that the fire causes the wound on her neck, first stopped by the icy cold, to stream and smart.

Metaphors of earth—earth takes more solid and durable forms than the other elements—are interestingly few. Twice Heathcliff is likened to "an arid wilderness of *furze* and *whinstone"*; there is a reference to his *"flinty* gratification"; and

once he speaks scornfully of "the *soil* of" Linton's "shallow cares." Earth and
vegetation sometimes result in a happy juxtaposition of the vast or the violent
and the little or the homely, as when Heathcliff says of Linton that "He might
as well plant *an oak in a flowerpot,*" or when he threatens to "crush his ribs in
like *a rotten hazelnut,*" which is like his saying that Catherine's passion could be
as readily encompassed by Linton as *"the sea* could be . . . contained in that
horse-trough."

Most of the animals are wild. Hareton's "whiskers encroached *bearishly* over
his cheeks," and Heathcliff denies the paternity of "that bear." Hareton had been
"cast out like an unfledged *dunnock,*" and Heathcliff is a "fierce, pitiless, *wolfish*
man." He is also "a *bird* of bad omen" and "an evil *beast*" prowling between
a "stray *sheep*" "and the fold, waiting his time to spring and destroy." He has a
"ferocious gaze" and a *savage* utterance; he *growls* and *howls* "like a beast," and
is many times named "a brute," "a beast," "a brute beast." He struggles like a
bear, he has *sharp cannibal teeth* which *gleam* "through the dark," and *"basilisk*
eyes . . . *quenched* by sleeplessness." He *gnashes* his teeth and *foams* like a *mad
dog.* He is "like a *bull*" to Linton's *"lamb,"* and only at the very end, the exhausted end, "he breathed as fast as a *cat."*

For the domestic and the gentler animals are generally used for purposes of
harsh satire or vilification. Edgar, "the soft thing," "possessed the power to depart,
as much as a *cat* possesses the power to leave a *mouse* half killed, or a *bird* half
eaten." He is "not a *lamb*" but "a sucking *leveret,*" and his sister is a "pitiful,
slavish, mean-minded *brach,*" she is among those *worms,* who, "the more they
writhe, the more" Heathcliff yearns "to crush out their entrails." Hindley dies in
a stupor, "snorting like a *horse*"; "flaying and scalping" would not have roused
him, and when the doctor arrives, "the *beast* has changed to *carrion.*" Hareton is
"an infernal *calf,*" and young Linton is a *"puling chicken*" and a *"whelp."* Like
a dying dog, he "slowly *trailed* himself off, and lay down," or, like a cold one, he
"shrank closer to the fire." He "had *shrunk* into a corner of the settle, as quiet as
a *mouse*"; he is called "a little perishing *monkey*"; and he "achieved his exit
exactly as a *spaniel* might." He is also "an abject *reptile*" and "a *cockatrice.*"
Hareton, who is capable on occasion of gathering *"venom* with reflection," is once
called a *"magpie,"* and once said to be "obstinate as a *mule*"—one of the few
kindly animal references in the novel. To be sure, Isabella describes herself as
though she were a deer: "I *bounded, leaped* and *flew* down the steep road; then
. . . *shot* direct across the moor, *rolling* over the banks, and *wading through*
marshes." And Catherine, on the whole, is not abused. She is a "cunning little *fox*"
and she runs "like a *mouse,*" but chiefly she is "soft and mild as a *dove."*

Emily Brontë's metaphors color all her diction. As her epithets are charged
with passion—"jealous guardianship," "vexatious phlegm," "importunate branch"
—so her verbs are verbs of violent movement and conflict, both contributing to a
rhetorical texture where everything is at a pitch from which it can only subside.
The verbs *demand* exhaustion, just as the metaphors *demand* rest. And there is
an antithetical chorus in this rhetoric, a contrapuntal warning, which, usually

but not only in the voice of Nelly Dean, says, "Hush! Hush!" all through the novel, at the beginning of paragraph after paragraph. At the end, everything *is* hushed. And the moths *fluttering* over Heathcliff's grave and "the soft wind *breathing* through the grass" that grows on it have at last more power than he, for all his passion. These soft and fragile things paradoxically endure.

The passions of animals, if we may speak of them as passions, have meaning in that they are presumably necessary to survival; Heathcliff's passion destroys others, himself, and at last, itself. The tumult of the elements alternates with periods of peace, and the seasons are not only autumn and winter. The *fact* of alternation enables nature to endure. The singleness of Heathcliff's tempestuous and wintry emotional life dooms it. Thus there is a curious and ironic contrast between the condition and the destiny of Heathcliff, and the full facts of those areas of metaphor. When, at the end of the novel, Nelly remarks that "the same moon shone through the window; and the same autumn landscape lay outside" as eighteen years before, she is speaking with metaphorical accuracy; but Heathcliff is *not* the same. He has not indeed come into a "sober, disenchanted maturity"— that will be the privilege of Hareton and the second Cathy; but he has completely changed in the fashion that Joseph described much earlier—"so as by fire." "... there is a strange change approaching: I'm in its shadow at present," he declares when he has found that nothing is worth the feeling of it. At last, after all the windy tumult and the tempests, he says, "I have to remind myself to breathe. . . ."

If his life, exhausted at the end, has not been, as he once said of it, "a moral teething," and the novel, therefore, no tragedy, the story of his life has been a moral teething for the author. Lockwood is instructed in the nature of a grand passion, but he and Emily Brontë together are instructed in its final fruits: even roaring fires end in a bed of ashes. Her metaphors instruct her, and her verbs. That besides these rhetorical means (which in their functioning make tolerable the almost impossibly inflated style), she should have found structural means as well which give her whole narrative the remote quality of a twice-told tale, the property of an old wife (and so make its melodrama endurable), should reinforce the point. At the end, the voice that drones on is the perdurable voice of the country, Nelly Dean's. No more than Heathcliff did Emily Brontë quite intend that homespun finality. Like the older Catherine, Emily Brontë could have said of her book, "I've dreamed in my life dreams that have stayed with me ever after, and changed my ideas: they've gone through and through me, like wine through water, and altered the color of my mind." Her rhetoric altered the form of her intention. It is her education; it shapes her insight.

4. *Middlemarch* is a novel written on a much grander scale than either of these others, with many points of narrative interest, a much more complex structural pattern, and an important difference in its metaphorical language. Jane Austen's metaphors are generally of the "buried" kind, submerged, woven deep in the ordinary, idiomatic fabric of the language; Emily Brontë's are generally epithet-

ical. George Eliot's tend always to be, or to become, explicit symbols of psychological or moral conditions, and they actually function in such a way as to give
symbolical value to much action, as Dorothea's pleasure in planning buildings ("a
kind of work which she delighted in") and Casaubon's desire to construct a
"Key to all Mythologies." Their significance lies, then, not so much in the choice
of area (as, "commerce," or "natural elements" and "animals") as in the choice
of function, and one tests them not by their field, their content, but by their conceptual portent. I should like to suggest a set of metaphorical qualities in *Middlemarch* which actually represents a series apparent in the thinking that underlies
the dramatic structure. First of all, there are metaphors of unification; then, of
antithesis; next, there are metaphors which conceive things as progressive, and
then, metaphors of shaping and making, of structure and creative purpose; finally,
there are metaphors of what I should call a "muted" apocalypse.

George Eliot's metaphors of unification pivot on her most characteristic verbs
—these are of conciliation and reconciliation, of unification, of course, and of
inclusion, of mingling, of associating, of merging and mixing, of embracing and
comprehending, of connecting, allying, binding together and making room for. The
elements to be brought together are as various as the universe—they may be merely
"mingled pleasures" or "associated facts which . . . show a mysterious electricity
if you touched them," or the relation of urban and rural areas, which "made fresh
threads of connection"; again, they may be attitudes—"criticism" and "awe"
mixing, or qualities *uniting,* as, presumably, "the glories of doctor and saint" in
dreary Casaubon, or men themselves making more *energetic alliances* "with im-
partial nature"; or they may be those yearnings of one individual for another
which find completion in love, the institution of marriage, and the literal embrace;
or, most important, they may be "lofty conceptions" which embrace multitudi-
nousness—for example, the daily life of Tipton parish and Dorothea Brooke's
own "rule of conduct." If only we knew more and felt more, these metaphors insist; for there *is,* we are told, "a knowledge which . . . traces out the suppressed
transitions which unite all contrasts." This is religious yearning, and it finds occasional pseudo-religious fulfillment, as after Lydgate's successful cogitations on
morphology: he finds himself "in that agreeable after-glow of excitement when
thought lapses from examination of a specific object into a suffusive sense of its
connections with all the rest of our existence," and one can "float with the repose
of unexhausted strength."

The metaphors of unification imply the metaphors of antithesis; the first represent yearnings, the second a recognition of fact. Thus we have metaphors of
reality vs. appearance, as: "the large vistas and wide fresh air which she had
dreamed of finding in her husband's mind were replaced by anterooms and winding passages which seemed to lead no-whither"; or of chaos vs. order (humorously dramatized by Mr. Brooke's "documents," which need arranging but get
mixed up in pigeon-holes) as Mary Garth's "red fire," which "seemed like a
solemn existence calmly independent of the petty passions, the imbecile desires,
the straining after worthless uncertainties, which were daily moving her con-

tempt"; or of shapelessness *vs.* shape, as "a kind Providence furnishes the limpest personality with a little gum or starch in the form of tradition." There are other kinds, of outer *vs.* inner, for example: "so much subtler is a human mind than the outside tissues which make a sort of blazonry or clock-face for it." It is this, the outer-inner antithesis, which underscores one of George Eliot's favorite words —"inward" or "inwardly," a usage which is frequently annoying because it is tautological, applied to states which can *only* be inward under the circumstances of the fiction, but, for that reason, all the more symptomatic. There are metaphorical antitheses of fact to wish, imbalance to balance, restlessness to repose, and many other opposites. Most important, and perhaps most frequent, are the figures which oppose freedom to various forms of restraint—burdens, ties, bonds, and so on: "he replies by calling himself Pegasus, and every form of prescribed work 'harness,' " to which the answer is, "I shall let him be *tried* by the *test* of freedom." Another example of the restraint-freedom opposition illustrates the way that reported action, when conjoined with these metaphors, pushes both on to explicit symbolism: near the end, Dorothea observes on the road outside her window "a man with a bundle on his back and a woman carrying her baby," and, still nearer the end, when Lydgate has "accepted his narrowed lot," that is, the values of his child-bride, he thinks, "He had chosen this fragile creature, and had taken the burden of her life upon his arms. He must walk as he could, carrying that burden pitifully."

The oppositions in these metaphors of antithesis are the classic oppositions between Things as They Are and Things as They Should Be, between the daily realities of a community like Middlemarch and the "higher" realities of that "New Jerusalem" toward which Dorothea and others are "on the road."

Everyone and everything in this novel is moving on a "way." Life is a *progress,* and it is variously and inevitably described as road, stream, channel, avenue, way, journey, voyage, ride (either on horse or by carriage), vista, chain, line, course, path, and process. To these terms one should add the terms of *growth,* usually biological growth, which carry much the same value. There must be at least a thousand and possibly there are more metaphorical variations on the general idea of life as progress, and this progress is illimitable. At the end of the novel we are told, in words somewhat suggestive of a more orthodox religious spirit than George Eliot, that "Every limit is a beginning as well as an ending."

Everything strains forward. Consciousness is a stream. "In Dorothea's mind there was a current into which all thought and feeling were apt sooner or later to flow—the reaching forward of the whole consciousness toward the fullest truth, the least partial good." "Character, too," we are told, "is a process," and it is a process which we recognize by achievement—"the niceties of inward balance, by which man swims and makes his point or else is carried headlong." Like Leopold Bloom, George Eliot's characters think of their existence as "the stream of life in which the stream of life we trace," but with a difference: the personal life finally flows into the "gulf of death," but the general stream flows on, through vistas of endlessly unfolding good, and that good consists of individual achievements of "the fullest truth, the least partial good," of Lydgate's individually *made points.* This is a progressive, in no sense a cyclical view of human history.

These metaphors of progress, like the restraint-freedom antithesis, involve George Eliot in her many complementary metaphors of hindrance to progress. The individual purpose is sometimes confused by "a social life which seemed nothing but a labyrinth of petty courses, a walled-in maze"; sometimes by the inadequacy of the purpose itself, as Casaubon, who "was lost among small closets and winding stairs"; experience and circumstance over and over become "yokes," which slow the progress, for there are those always "who carry a weight of trials"; one may *toil* "under the fetters of a promise" or move, like Lydgate, more haltingly than one had hoped under the *burden* of a responsibility.

These hindrances are, generally speaking, social, not moral. One submits to them in the interests of the whole procession, and when one does not submit— as Dorothea, refusing to devote herself to Casaubon's scholarship after his death— it is because one has discovered that they are not in the interests of the whole procession. The particular interests of the procession are indicated by the extended metaphors drawn from nearly every known field of physical and medical science. It is by the "serene light of science" that we glimpse "a presentiment of endless processes filling the vast spaces planked out of" our "sight by that wordy ignorance which," in the past, we "had supposed to be knowledge." It is by the same light that we are able to recognize our social obligations, according to the Religion of Humanity.

Thus, quite smoothly, we come to that fourth group of prevailing metaphors, those having to do with purpose. They are of shaping, of forming, of making, of framing; they pivot on notions of pattern or rule, measure or structure. They are all words used in metaphors which, explicitly or by implication, reveal the individual directing his destiny by conscious, creative purpose toward the end of absolute human order. Opposed to them are the many metaphors of derogation of the unorganized, notably the human mind, which, at worst, like Mr. Brooke's, availing nothing perceptible in the body politic, is a *mass.*

At the end of this grand vista are the metaphors of what I have called the "muted" apocalypse. The frequency with which George Eliot uses the words *up, high,* and *higher* in metaphorical contexts is equalled only, perhaps, by her use of the word *light,* until one feels a special significance in "giving *up*" and in all the faces that *beam,* all the ideas that *flash* across the mind, and all the things that are all the time being "taken" in *that light* or *this light.* Fire plays a perhaps predictably important metaphorical role, and, together with light, or alternating with it, usually accompanies or is implied by those frequent metaphors in which things are *gloriously* transformed, transfused, or transfigured. Treating this complex of figures as I do, as a kind of apocalyptic drama which of course does not exist in the novel as such, but surely does in the imagination of George Eliot, we are, now, at the moment before climax, all those metaphors involving ideas of veneration and adoration, or worshipful awe; these, in my factitious series, are immediately followed by the climax itself, which is contained in endless use of the word "revelation" and figurative developments from it. Perception, in this novel, is indeed thought of as revelation, and minds and souls are always "opening" to the influx. Things are many times "manifested" or "made manifest," as if life were a perpetual epiphany. If perception is not a "revelation," it is a "divination," and for the ordinary verb, "to recognize," George Eliot usually prefers to use "to divine." It is here that we come upon her unquestionably favorite word, and the center of her most persistent metaphors. For the word "sight" or "feeling" she almost always substitutes the more portentous word "vision." Visions are of every possible kind, from *dim* to *bright* to *blinding,* from *testing* to *guiding.* The simplest sight of the physical detail may be a vision; every insight is of course a vision, usually an *inward* vision.

The experience now subsides. If perception is revelation, then it is, secondarily, nourishment, and the recurrence of metaphors in which perception is conceived as spiritual food and drink, and of all the metaphors of *fullness, filling,* and *fulfilment,* is perhaps predictable. It is likewise energizing, in various figurative ways, and in moments of climactic understanding, significantly, a charge of electricity flows through the human organism.

Illumination, revelation, fulfilment. One step remains in this pattern of a classic religious experience; that is expectation. Metaphors of expectation are everywhere; I will represent them in their most frequent form, a phrase so rubbed by usage that it hardly seems metaphorical at all. It is "to look forward," and it appears on nearly every page of *Middlemarch,* a commonplace there too, yet more than that: it is the clue to the whole system of metaphor I have sketched out; it is the clue to a novel, the clue to a mind.

I have separated into a series a metaphorical habit which of course always appears in conflux, and it is only because these metaphors do constantly associate themselves in the novel, that one may justifiably hit upon them as representing George Eliot's selectivity. One of many such elaborate confluences is as follows:

> ... Mr. Casaubon's talk about his great book was *full* of *new vistas;* and this sense of *revelation,* this *surprise of a nearer introduction* to Stoics and Alexandrians, as people who had ideas not totally unlike her own, kept in abeyance for the time her usual eagerness for a *binding theory* which could bring her own life and doctrine into *strict connection* with that amazing past, and give the remotest *sources* of knowledge some *bearing* on her actions ... she was *looking forward* to *higher initiation* in ideas, as she was *looking forward* to marriage, and *blending* her *dim* conceptions of both. ... All her eagerness for acquirement lay within that *full current of sympathetic* motive in which her ideas and impulses were habitually *swept along.* She did not want to deck herself with knowledge—to wear it loose from the *nerves and blood that fed her action;* and if she had written a book she must have done it as St. Theresa did, under the *command of an authority that constrained her conscience.* But something she yearned for by which her *life might be filled* with action at once rational and ardent: and since the time was gone by *for guiding visions* and spiritual directors, since prayer *heightened* yearning, but not instruction, *what lamp* was there but knowledge?

Here are nearly all of them: metaphors of unification, of antithesis (restraint-freedom), of progress, of the apocalypse: height, light, revelation, vision, nourishment, and, of course, the forward look. The passage is not in the least exceptional. In my analytical sketch of such persistent confluences, I separated the elements into a series to demonstrate how completely, step by step, they embody a pseudo-religious philosophy, how absolutely expressive is metaphor, even in fiction, and how systematic it can become. This is a novel of religious yearning without religious object. The unification it desires is the unification of human knowledge in the service of social ends; the antitheses that trouble it (and I observe in this otherwise classic series no antitheses either of Permanence and Change, or of Sin and Grace) are the antitheses between man as he is and man as he could be in this world; the hindrances to life as progress are man's social not his moral flaws; the purposive dedication of individuals will overcome those flaws; we see the fulfilment of all truly intellectual passions, for the greater glory of Man.

Our first observation on the function of metaphor in this novel should, then, be of its *absolutely* expressive character. The second is perhaps less evident, and we may call it the interpretive function of metaphor, the extent to which metaphor comments on subject. The subject of this novel may be Middlemarch, a community, but, as even the title metaphorically suggests, the theme is the nature of progress in what is probably meant to be the typical British community in the 19th Century. (Observe, too, these names: Brooke, a running course, and Lydgate, his progress blocked by his wife, twice-blocked by his name.) Or we can select subjects within the subject, as the clerical subject interpreted by the pseudo-religious theme: the true "religious" dedication of a Dorothea Brooke, and the characters around her falling into various "religious" postures: Casaubon as the false prophet, Bulstrode as the parody-prophet, Lydgate as the nearly true prophet—a "scientific Phoenix," he is called—somehow deflected from his prophecy; and Ladislaw as the true prophet. Indeed, given the metaphorical texture, one cannot escape the nearly systematic Christ analogy which George Eliot weaves around Ladislaw, omitting from her figure only the supremely important element of Christ's sacrifice, and the reason for which He made it. This is to be expected in a novel which is about progress without guilt. Here, even the heroic characters cannot be said to have inner struggles, for all their "inward visions." Here there is much illumination and nearly no self-doubt; much science, and never a sin. One recognizes from the metaphorical structure that this novel represents a decay of the full religious experience into that part of it which aspires alone: Christian optimism divorced from the basic human tragedy.

The metaphorical complex provides a third, and a more interesting function: a structural function. *Middlemarch* is concerned with nearly every important activity in community life—political, clerical, agricultural, industrial, professional, domestic, of course, even scholarly. It involves many different characters and groups of characters. The relations between some of these characters and even between some of these groups are often extremely tenuous, often merely accidental. The dramatic structure, in short, is not very taut, yet one feels, on finishing the book, that this is a superbly constructed work, that, indeed, as foolish Mr. Brooke observes, "We're all one family, you know—it's all one cupboard." What makes it so is thematic rather than dramatic unity.

The measure of Middlemarch is Dorothea's *sublimity,* the interpretive height from which she judges. From her sublimity, everything shades off, all the way down to garrulous Mrs. Cadwallader and villainous Mr. Bulstrode. The metaphors of unification which George Eliot enjoyed to use, those images of intermingling and embracing, are important in a double sense: they express Dorothea's ethical sentiments, and, actually, they and the others, bind the material together. They tell us *how to take* each Middlemarcher, *in what light.* They do this chiefly through the creation of symbolic echoes of the major situations in the minor ones, echoes often ironic, sometimes parodies.

Thus, in the imagery of vision, Dorothea's remark, made so early as in Chapter III, has a special ring: "I am rather shortsighted." In the imagery of human progress, Mr. Garth's question about Bulstrode, the pious fraud,—"whether he shall settle somewhere else, as a lasting thing"—has such symbolic value. Mr. Garth's own attitude toward agriculture is a thematic parody of the exaltation of Dorothea, Lydgate, and Ladislaw: "the peculiar tone of fervid veneration, of religious regard in which he wrapped it, as a consecrated symbol is wrapped in its gold-fringed linen." In the imagery of structure, a special meaning seems to attach to the word "dwell," when it refers to characters experiencing some state of mind. Lydgate's morphological research is another such symbolic extension of the metaphors of structure. Dorothea's avenue of limes outside her window, leading toward the sunset, becomes, finally, a representation in the landscape of the idea of progress. The political newspapers, notably unenlightened, are called *The Pioneer* and *The Trumpet,* and these are surely parodies, one of the progress metaphors, the other of the apocalyptic. Even that humble rural tavern, the *Weights and Scales,* reminds us of more exalted concern, in this novel, with justice and with metaphors of balance. And so that wretched farm called Freeman's End, which has nearly destroyed its tenant and his family, is an eloquent little drama of the freedom-restraint metaphors.

"We all of us," says George Eliot, "grave or light, get our thoughts entangled in metaphors, and act fatally on the strength of them." If the writing of a novel is a deed, as Conrad liked to think, she spoke truer than she knew.

5. Four tentative proposals seem relevant:

1. Metaphorical language gives any style its special quality, and one may even suggest—only a little humorously—that this quality derives in part from the content of the metaphors, that quantity shapes quality. Certainly the particular "dryness" of Jane Austen's style is generated in part by the content of her images of the counting house, and certainly the inflatedness of Emily Brontë's is generated in large part by the prominence of wind and of atmospheric tumult in her metaphors. I cannot, unfortunately, suggest that George Eliot's pleasure in "light" has any notable effect on the quality of her style, but we can say that the content of her

conceptions as her metaphors express it predicts a style solemn always, heavy probably, and sodden perhaps.

2. Metaphorical language expresses, defines, and evaluates theme, and thereby demonstrates the limits and the special poise within those limits of a given imagination. We have seen three novels in which metaphors in effect answered questions that the novels themselves neglected to ask.

3. Metaphorical language, because it constantly strains toward symbolism, can be in novels as in poems the basis of structure, and it can even be counterposed to dramatic structure. We have observed the structural function in *Middlemarch*. In *Wuthering Heights* we may observe the more complicated contrapuntal function of metaphor in structure. Gerard Manley Hopkins, writing of Greek tragedy, spoke of "two strains of thought running together and counterpointed," the paraphrasable "overthought," and the "underthought"

> conveyed chiefly in the choice of metaphors etc. used, and often only half realized by the poet himself, not necessarily having any connection with the subject in hand but usually having a connection and suggested by some circumstance of the scene or of the story.

The metaphors of *Wuthering Heights* comprise such an "underthought," for although they are equated in the work, the work itself yet somehow develops a stronger and stronger contrast between the obligations of the human and the non-human creation.

4. Finally, metaphorical language reveals to us the character of any imaginative work in that, more tellingly perhaps than any other elements, it shows us what conceptions the imagination behind that work is able to entertain, how fully and how happily. I mean to say that style *is* conception, and that, for this reason, rhetoric must be considered as existing within—importantly within, and, sometimes, fatally within—what we call poetic. It is really style, and style primarily, that first conceives, then expresses, and finally tests these themes, these subjects, even these "kinds"—Jane Austen's manners, Emily Brontë's passions, George Eliot's morals. "Symbolization," said Susanne Langer (and I could not comfortably close these observations without mentioning her excellent name), "Symbolization is both an end and an instrument." "The right word," said George Eliot, "is always a power, and communicates its definiteness to our action." And, "The Eye," said William Blake, "sees more than the heart knows."

In the essay printed below, Walter Van Tilburg Clark focuses upon structuring for aesthetic effect, which involves not only all the choices of language, but considerations of character, scene, and incident, as well.

The story discussed is his little masterpiece, "The Portable Phonograph."

THE GHOST OF AN APPREHENSION

Since the story took place in my mind somewhat as a play might, the intention producing the scene, the scene and the intention selecting the cast, and all three, by means of certain guiding principles which developed with them, dictating the action, and since its approach has occurred often with me, in novels as well as in stories, it will help both to shape the discussion to follow and in a measure to widen its application, if we put the synopsis itself into something like dramatic form. To brief the brief, then (the story is only eight pages long):

THE SCENE. Interior of a dugout above a creek thinly lined with alders. A small, smoky, peat fire in the center. In one wall a niche containing a few battered cooking utensils. In the opposite wall an earth bunk with two old army blankets on it. Above the entrance, a rolled canvas, which is the door. Outside (the backdrop, so to speak) a desolate prairie, pitted by craters and grooved by the frozen ruts of huge wheels and caterpillar treads. Here and there a remnant of highway pavement, a spidery entanglement of barbed wire, and, in the depressions, a few small, shadowy trees. On the far horizon, a red sunset with bars of black cloud across it. Overhead, changing clouds gliding rapidly south before a high, booming wind. A single wedge of wild geese passes over, going southward more swiftly than the clouds and conversing faintly among themselves. A prairie wolf yaps in the distance. There is no other sound or motion. The air near the ground is still and full of the cold promise of winter.

THE CAST. Four men, all dirty, ragged, and bearded: Dr. Jenkins, a former professor and the host, and three visitors: a powerful, sardonic man, once a writer; a polite, conciliatory soul, whose past is not revealed; and a very thin, nervous young man with a bad cough, who has been a musician. The writer and the conciliatory soul have evidently been here before, though not often, but the musician is making his first call.

THE ACTION. Dr. Jenkins has just finished reading *The Tempest* aloud, and while he wraps up his library, Shakespeare, the Bible, *The Divine Comedy,* and *Moby Dick,* is discussing with the writer and the anonymous one, the present, and possibly future, worth of the books. When he has put the books into the niche with the pots, there is a brief, coercive silence, after which he reluctantly produces an old portable phonograph and twelve records. They may hear one record; one record, once a week, is his rule. He reads the titles. A Gershwin named by the writer is rejected as too sharp a reminder. The musician is given the choice, and after hearing the titles again, and complaining that there are parts he can't remember, he selects a Debussy nocturne. Dr. Jenkins, in a sudden, penitent gesture, takes out one of his three remaining steel needles, though he has been using thorns himself. The visitors rise to their knees in a reverent semicircle to watch him insert the needle and set the record on. At the first note of the piano, however, the musician shrinks back against the wall, where he struggles silently against his cough and the agony of hearing music again.

When the record is finished, the visitors rise. The musician is the last to rise, but then he goes out at once, without a word. The other two leave more slowly and formally. Dr. Jenkins lingers in the doorway, peering down into the dusk and listening. At last, just as a cloud erases one of four visible stars, he hears a faint cough from down among the alders. He lowers the canvas and pegs it down, and puts the phonograph and records, and then the books too, into a hole above the bunk and seals them in. After changing his blankets around so that he will lie facing the door, and putting more fuel on the fire, he stands watching the canvas again. Still only the wind, which has at last come down to earth, moves it. He prays and gets under his blankets, where, "On the inside of the bed, next to the wall, he could feel with his hand the comfortable piece of lead pipe."

Even so brief a retelling, when we remember that the story first appeared in the fall of 1941, suggests fully enough all we need to know about the apprehension which was the source of the idea. It also brings us at once to the crux of the writing problem, for it was just the very universality of that apprehension which placed the severest strictures upon the design of the story, and so compelled me, in the first stage, to formulate the guiding principles already mentioned.

Clearly I could justify the use of such a theme only by bringing that universal apprehension into sharp focus, by so heightening the reader's reaction to what he already knew and feared as to make the vaguely possible into the concretely probable. Gradually it became evident that the means to such a concentration and heightening must be three. First, if I were to avoid the flavor of Wellsian prophecy, the great apprehension itself must be touched upon lightly and indirectly, must be little more than a taken-for-granted backdrop. Secondly, the incident played against that backdrop, and the characters engaged in it, had to be highly credible, not in terms of their situation, but in terms of an everyday American life. In short, it didn't seem to me that the desired tone could be achieved in the key of either the incident or the scene alone, but that it must arise out of the dissonant juxtaposition of the two. And finally, the manner of the story had to convey the same contrast, had to be fiddle light on the surface and bass viol deep beneath, which is to say, it had to be satirical. One cannot afford to speak seriously of the end of the world. All of these necessities, the minor and credible activity, presented against a background of doom, in a manner calculated to sustain the dissonance, added up, of course, to a very short story. One does not strain a joke about the end of the world, either.

I didn't, naturally, start with a notion of saying something about the finality of modern war, and out of that melancholy fog evolve a set of rules, and out of them a story. The process was not that orderly. First, I just began to write. I can't remember exactly what set me off. Probably it was some intensifying item of the day's news, stirring me when I had time to sit and brood on it until I had to get rid of the emotion it built up, and the first, suggestive images began to appear. Almost always, whatever may have been working up to it in my mind, recognized and unrecognized, it is some image suddenly coming alive and suggesting more to follow, or to precede, that makes me reach for a pencil. In this case it was the prairie, the vast, desolated backdrop of the dugout, which first appeared, accompanied by a feeling that such a scene implied in itself all that one could afford to say directly about a final war. In short, the critical process began with the creative, and by the time I had completed the introductory description (a slow procedure, involving much cutting, rewriting, and rearranging) the controlling principles, more or less as I have stated them, were already in full operation, the cast had appeared and been approved, and the incident had arisen out of their gathering. The story was finished, except for putting it down, which meant little more than keeping an ear open for that desirable dissonance.

The prairie first appeared blackened by old fires, full of shell craters, deeply scored everywhere by the tracks of enormous tank battles and the vestiges of hopeless entrenchment, and devoid of all present signs of human life. There were no houses, or even shells of houses, no barn, no windmills, no fences, no recognizable fields or even stubs of groves or orchards. It was bare as the moon. It suggested a warfare of almost cosmic proportions (since Hiroshima, we can delete the "almost") which was what I wanted, and it suggested also, that a good deal of time had passed since the battle. That hint of time softening the edges of all detail, but unable to restore anything, made the destruction even more final, and sufficiently indicated, it seemed to me, that the survivors necessary to the story must be so few, and so far set back, as to be without hope or use. But then I saw that the mooniness was too complete, and could just as well mean a region that had always been desert as it could the ruin of a productive region. Yet it seemed wrong to name the place, and I still didn't want any skeletons of buildings against the sky. I preferred that tundralike emptiness stretching away to the western horizon. (I was looking west, perhaps because Americans have that habit, perhaps because the war we most dreaded was raging in Europe, and so, in the story, would have gone across America westward, but probably just because the scene had first appeared in an end-of-day light, and one would naturally be looking toward the sunset.) So there appeared the broken remnants of a highway as unobtrusive tokens of the past. Clearer signs of time elapsed since the fighting were also needed, yet signs which would not too much relieve the sterility of the earth, so there grew up the sparse lines of willows and alders in the trenches and creek beds, and the stunted, new trees in the craters.

Sometime during the first viewing, though I avoided the narrowing effect of a name (the nature of the land, and the fact that the four men were unquestionably American, seemed enough in the way of location) the region became definitely the American Middle West, because it spread the devastation over the whole world to show the heart of the most isolated major power swept over, and the grain lands gone in a warfare which concentrated on cities. It made the place not only a field of the final war, but the final field as well.

Late autumn became the necessary time of year, the last season before the complete death and the somehow healing secrecy of winter, just as sunset, the last hour of vision before the secrecy of night, was the proper time of day. To begin with, the sky had been cloudless, the sunset one of those infinitely penetrable, green-gold fadings that come with cold, but now such a horizon seemed too peaceful, and even suggestive of hope. There had to be some motion in that inert landscape, some threat in the sky. So the clouds formed, moving in a wintry wind, and the sunset turned red, and then, although that came as an afterthought, in part because the professor had to hear that last faint cough down in the alders, the unmoving lower air settled in. The chief intent was that the dissonance of the two regions of air should furnish a physical lead into the moral dissonance of the action, and also that it should reinforce the threat of the black clouds across the sunset, suggest apprehension by ear and skin as well as by eye. Finally, for by now the story was fully in view, some touch of conscious life was needed, by which to move from the backdrop into the play. Hence, as also maintaining the mood, the far-off yapping of the wolf, unheard in those parts for generations, and the brief, almost invisible passage of the geese, unconcerned with the land except as a distance to get over.

The action of the story, prepared all during the arranging and rearranging of this backdrop, moved forward so swiftly, almost automatically, in its details, as to be now largely beyond recall. I do remember the vital factors of the preparation, however. I remember that the cast first appeared to me as three in number, the three who became the professor, the writer, and the musician; that they were all men because even one woman might imply a future; and that they became men of highly mental pasts because that rendered them more nearly helpless, increased their recession, and made it more likely that they would retain the necessary surface of polite conduct. I remember also that the three men first came together in the open, around a wood fire down by the creek, but that somehow nothing would happen among them there. The size and finality of the setting shrank them and paralyzed them with futility. I could not even seem to discover any reasons for their bothering to get together, save an animal loneliness which had no dramatic potential except through a much longer development than I could afford. When at last it became clear that it was the scene which rendered them so unusable, the dugout, as in keeping with the tank tracks and the barbed wire, appeared in the bank behind me, and we moved into it. That was all it took. The men not only came alive, but swelled to more than life-size, filling the little cave enormously, assuming the importance for me that they had for each other, and setting the lifeless prairie away into its proper backdrop perspective. The vestigial touches of home-making effort became possible: the few and battered utensils, kept in a niche, like a saint; the peat fire and the earthen bunk, hinting of a nearly woodless world; the army blankets and the canvas. Also, the home made necessary the host, and the professor, as likely to be the most provident and the most chairmanly, at once assumed that role, and with it his manner and his more numerous years. Indeed it was only then that he certainly became a professor, a kind of epitome of civilized man in his most familiar form, suggesting thereby a great deal through his mere presence in a cave.

When the fragments of possible conversation among the three men, the professor, the writer, and a third who was for a time alternately a painter and a musician, began to occur in the midst of the backdrop details, I shortly felt the need of a fourth man, not only because I sensed that the musician-painter was going to be nearly inarticulate, and, for the sake of variety and interplay, three speakers were preferable to two, but also because the trio was a bit too patly symbolic, and so likely to resist the individualism without which they couldn't convince. (The writer was first seen as a sculptor—which has something to do with the physical characteristics he retained—but changed his profession, partly for the same reason, to break up the rigid one-two-three alignment by drawing nearer to the professor's interests, making a one-two grouping, and partly because it better suited the intent of the tale that he should be thwarted by an absence of that so-common commodity, paper. Of clay there would still be a plenty.) So the fourth man joined the group, the man with the unknown past, the representative of the great, departed audience whose need had produced the specialists. He was a real help, for not only did he relieve the stiffness of the allegory, but he also furnished a constrasting attitude, a second psychological level, being a trifle deferential in the presence of the more specific abilities of the others, but also more resigned because his individual needs were less acute. He was, in short, different in kind, whereas the other three, all upon one level of bolder individuality, were different only in particulars: the harsh cynicism of the frustrated writer; the advanced tuberculosis which makes time so important to the musician; the grave, reluctant, orderly air of the professor. Furthermore, I believe that I had found in him another sufficiently concealed means to irony, for his deference was, of course, wholly pointless in that time, a mere hang-over from an irrecoverable social pattern, and yet it was just that trace of deference, that touch of the conciliatory, that held together, by its remnant of drawing-room conduct, a group that otherwise would almost certainly have broken into an undesirable violence.

Once we were in the dugout, and the anonymous fourth had entered, there seemed to be only one thing lacking, that precipitating agent which would settle the whole narrative out in visible form, the reason for the gathering. I cannot remember how many reasons I fleetingly considered off the top of my mind while I completed the backdrop and caught unusable but suggestive glimpses of the civilized pasts of the men. (The professor, for instance, had taught English in a Midwestern college, specializing in Victorian Literature, but had a wide range of interests beyond that. He had lived in a small, white, frame house, with vines on the front porch, and a dark, somewhat stuffy study in it, with heavy rugs, too much furniture, and the walls lined with books, mostly old and worn, but here and there in bright, new bindings or dust jackets. He had two children, but both were grown and away from home, and he was rather lonely, because he had retired just a couple of years before the war, and his wife, a plump, bespectacled woman, although a fine mother and housekeeper, did not share any of his intellectual interests.) I remember very clearly, however, that the happiest moment of the whole preliminary came with the discovery of the portable phonograph. Beyond question it was the very object, the key symbol, for which I'd been hunting ever since my first dusky glimpse of the prairie. It was portable, which was important. It would seem valuable enough to such a man as the professor, to be worth carrying off in a crisis. It was a universally familiar object, and so would derive its dramatic virtue entirely from its present rarity. In its combined material inconsequence—for certainly it was one of the lesser gadgets of our abundantly gadgeted civilization— and spiritual consequence, as the only remaining vehicle of perhaps the highest achievement of mind and emotion of that same civilization, it became the very centerpiece of the desired dissonance, the touchstone for action and language. The title arrived with it, of course. In its presence, the relationships of the cast were rapidly established. It became evident that the small, suppressed element of con- flict that was needed must spring from it and from the music it produced. As a result, the musician at once assumed the brief future that would make him des- perate, and become certainly a musician rather than a painter, and also the new- comer, the stranger in the group, the man in whom the restraint of association would play the smallest part and the hunger for music the greatest. At once, also, the professor, as the owner of the treasure, became the antagonist. To all intents the story was complete.

There remained only to discover a valid and contributory means of prolonging, though backwards, into the hours before the tale opens, a meeting which would otherwise be incredibly brief, and which could not, obviously, be extended by eat- ing and drinking. Books were beyond question the means, and certainly, in this context, the reasons for selecting the four the professor had brought with him are equally clear, at least by the time the writer has spoken of *Moby Dick* as some- thing they can all understand now (he might usefully have dropped a word about Ishmael's coffin-boat) and added that Shelley had too much soul, and was "no earthly good." Nor is there any mystery about his selecting *The Tempest* for the reading, once we realize that Caliban and Ariel are at it again over the portable phonograph. The act of reading and the reverence accorded the books serve also as a kind of induction to the high sacrament of the music, in which the professor becomes the priest of a doomed faith and the visitors literally assume kneeling positions around the phonograph.

It is intended that the conclusion should leave with the reader a sense of unity, of the opening dissonance resolved, though not into peace, but rather by means, gently, gently, of almost entirely reducing the professor to the cave man, blending him, as it were, into the terrible landscape. As he stands suspiciously in the door- way, after the guests have departed, he sees, at the very instant he hears the cough- ing down in the alders, one of four bright stars suddenly hidden by a cloud. It is a sufficient sign to the primitive credulity revived in him, and indirectly, we hope, in the reader. Then also, as he stands watching the canvas he has pegged down, it is moved by "the first gusts of a lowering wind." The opening dissonance between the wuthering upper air and the still ground air is also resolved, and again, as in the case of the human dissonance, by suggesting an end, by bringing winter to the door. Yet, in the last line, as the professor lies on the earth bench, facing the billowing canvas, "On the inside of the bed, next the wall, he could feel with his hand the comfortable piece of lead pipe." His weapon still comes from that lost world of gadgets. He cannot bring even violence to the level of the new—the very old—world in which he now lives. And of course futility, in any but the meanest and most temporary sense, attends the defense for which he is prepared.

It seemed to me that sentence plucked the proper closing note, one that might linger for a time with a tenuous but moving reminder of the whole intention. If so, it was so, happily, by means of the very last phrase, and particularly by means of the one word "comfortable." Nothing in the phrase was considered, not "comfortable" any more than the rest, but even as it came, that "comfortable" tickled me, not so much because of its immediate implication, in which the paradox was clear enough, as for some more remote, redoubling connotation which I could not, at the moment, catch hold of. Then, a few seconds after I had poked home the final period, it came to me. I had done a bit of lucky thieving from Bill of Avon. (Perhaps the professor's volume of Shakespeare had put it out handy for the borrowing.) Remember how Juliet, waking in the tomb, and not yet aware that Romeo is dead, murmurs drowsily to the gentle Friar Lawrence, "Oh, comfortable Friar—"? Oh, poor professor, with only his lead pipe. And I was sure that at least the ghost of that old, warm, trusting "comfortable" would lurk to trouble the reader as it had troubled me. Nor could I feel, considering the grim little twist I had given it, that Bill would begrudge me his word. After all, he was no mean shakes of a borrower himself.

3

Character and
Characterization: I

Through history, two kinds of stories have competed with each other—the story of action and the story of character.[1] The story of action is the sort that appeals to men because it represents man's *doings;*[2] the story of character appeals because it represents man's thoughts and mental states.[3] Both are meaningful to the human mind. Which basis an age chooses depends to a great extent upon its concept of the relation of character and action to meaning. In the Neo-Classical age, stories of action were considered more artful, because propriety—proper actions—and form were considered more important than people. The Romantic age preferred matters of character and personality. In our own time, we have tended to think character, especially as it reveals theme, is more important. This sense of importance we derived from Freud and Jung, which is to say that our interest in character is primarily neither ethical nor moral, but psychoanalytical and psychomythical. The psychoanalytical interest leads us toward studies in *character;* the psychomythical interest, toward symbolic *action;* so both kinds of stories are still open to us. It is even possible for us to fuse the two kinds.

Fusion of character and action, in fact, is finally not only possible, but necessary. Like Henry James, we today cannot imagine, in a really successful fiction,

---

[1] Incidentally, other bases for stories have generally failed. Stories based on theme and style, for example, have tended to be indistinguishable from poetry and verse. Stories based on form or structure have seemed mere tricks or puzzles. But experiment and experience may yet make these bases usable.

[2] See, for example, Mark Twain's "The Hat Island Crossing." *

[3] See, for example, Hemingway's "Soldier's Home" * or Faulkner's "Barn Burning." *

a passage of description that is not in its intention narrative, a passage of dialogue that is not in its intention descriptive, a touch of truth of any sort that does not partake of the nature of incident, or an incident that derives its interest from any other source than the general and only source of the success of a work of art— that of being illustrative. . . . What is character but the determination of incident? What is incident but the illustration of character? [4]

But, like the professor who knows that style and content are not separable, but must act as if they were, we must often act as if character and action are isolated phenomena. Thus, if we approach the subject of character and characterization broadly and analytically, we will find that there are such things as "characters of action" and "characters of character (or thought)," that there is a range of defensible ideas about how character and action should be related in a narration, and that there are discernible techniques for revealing either or both of these matters. Specifically, there are some six kinds of character, at least three concepts of character, nine techniques of characterization that every writer needs to know about, and several common faults we should all be on guard against.

Six Kinds and Three Concepts of Character

Six major kinds of characters in our fictions form a continuous circle of relationships in our fictional possibilities—the pawn or non-character, the type, the profile or half-round, the round, the fragrant, and the heroic. There are, in some of these, several sub-divisions, and there are many gradations between the divisions; so it is equally true that there are as many kinds of character as there are fictional creations: we are talking about a continuum, not a string of nodules. If, at certain key points, we make a triangle of the circle, we will also discover the three, primary concepts of character—the Classic, the Romantic, and the Mythic.

The Pawn, or Non-character

If we begin at the action extreme of the action-character argument, we get the pawn, the non-character, the post without personality, the integer, the costumed stick, whose only purpose and existence is in the actions it performs. Anecdotes usually contain such non-persons: "one fellow says to the other fellow—" and the point has nothing to do with personality or character, but only with the fact that one fellow is the performer of action, the other the

[4] Henry James, "The Art of Fiction," in *Selected Fiction,* ed. Leon Edel (New York: Dutton, Everyman's Library, 1953), p. 597.

observer. Much children's literature contains such characters. So does much detective literature and possibly science-fiction, though it is certainly possible for any or all of these to contain real characters. One of the most notable literary uses of the pawn is in such adventure literature as *The Arabian Nights,* and in poetry, which, when it uses character, usually depicts the pawn or the heroic.

Consider this anecdote:

Student cafeteria
24 April 1957, 6:30 p.m.

Three ladies are sitting at a table in a college cafeteria, each with a finger held in a text book. One of them reads from a library book: "The stanza, not the line, is the 'unit.'" All three write this in the margins of their textbooks.

The first one reads again: "The form is a matter of the progression of emotions that make the general thematic statement." They all write again in the margins of their textbooks.

The first one reads: "Sometimes a meaningless phrase will be repeated until, through association, it gains a particular meaning in the poem."

"D'ya think that's what this is?" says the second lady.

The first one reads mechanically from her textbook. " 'In the room the women come and go, talking of Michelangelo.' Yeah," she says, "that sure sounds like a meaningless phrase to me."

"The whole thing sounds meaningless to me," says the second, and she laughs, ha ha ha.

The first one reads again: "Do I dare to eat a peach?' "

Both of them explode in giggles, and keep giggling while the first tries to continue reading: " 'I shall wear white flannel trousers, and walk upon the beach.'

" 'Shall I part my hair behind?' " says the third lady. " 'Bald spot at the back of my head ...' "

ha, ha, ha, ha, ha, ha.

"Do you guess this is just a sort of a dream?" says the first, composing herself and speaking seriously.

The second lady shrugs her shoulders.

"A sort of a philosophy?" continues the first. "What does it mean by 'The Love Song'? Why is it a Love Song?"

"I don't know," says the second lady.

"You mean you don't understand this poem?" says the first, apparently parodying some professor.

"I don't have to understand it," says the second; "I just have to teach it."

"I don't like this class," says the third. "I'm probably going to get a 'D.' "

"I don't like the teacher," says the second. "He never talks about anything in the text. He just rambles on and on about anything that comes to his mind."

"I don't like this class," agrees the first lady.

To what extent are the three speakers "characters of pure action"? The point or points of the anecdote reside in the verbal ironies, and these exist whether the speakers have personalities, or "characters," or not. It could have been three men, or three fat women, or three paranoids, as easily as it was, in fact, two middle-aged women—one heavy, the other thin—and one, very young, very shy undergraduate. Some qualities of personality do in fact begin to emerge by the time the anecdote is over, but they are irrelevant to the "theme"—if one can call it that—of the sketch.

The Type

The type character is known by the actions he performs, too, but he also has a modicum of character, usually a cluster of *typical* human reactions or traits. The ladies in the anecdote above have to be students in order to perform their action; to the extent that they embody such typical student actions as the reliance on libraries and ponies, their resistance to the course, the young one's shyness, and such, they become type characters. This kind of statistical summary of our experience is the usual and first thing we mean when we speak of types.

This kind of type is probably necessary in life and literature. Without some method of summarizing, and categorizing, some organizing principle, experience is chaos. We rely on the corner policeman, the salesgirl, the newspaper boy to have certain qualities and to perform their typical actions; it is a great convenience to be able to deal with them in their typical, essential, and invariable capacities. Of course, each one is an individual, capable of human complexity, and presses that complexity upon us when we look very close or talk to him very long. We know that it is a falsification of life to typify such human beings. We know that when we do typify them, we are making them into elementary symbols for experience; we are thinking of them as ideas, not people. We know that our literary representations of them are once further removed, so that we get ideas about ideas. (Incidentally, when our ideas-about-ideas get simplified or distorted, we get certain variations on type: flat characters, stereotypes, caricatures, and the like.) But, because we do not have time or energy to deal with every one we meet as an individual personality, we find ourselves necessarily typifying people, categorizing them, organizing our experience so it will make sense. We accept types in life so that we can focus meaning and action. And we accept types in books for the same reason. This is the practical meaning of type.

But there is a much more important and subtle meaning of types, which has to do with our perception of them. *Type* here is meant in the sense of "representative form," those marks or symbols which distinguish the members of one group from members of other groups, but focus upon the qualities of the individual, not the group. These marks or symbols identify the character as a certain human being, not as a certain kind of human being. The dramatist relies upon this kind of type, because he must make his audience immediately and fairly fully apprehend the humanness of his characters—and do it with very brief evidence. This is not to say that he tells us a man is a plumber, and we then infer that he sits watching TV and drinking beer all evening; that's stereotype; that's a generalization, an idea, right or wrong, about human beings. What the dramatist does rely on is a kind of Gestalt sketch in words that allows us to perceive in our own minds the individual referred to. In a line drawing of a cat, tufted ears, slanted eyes, radiating whiskers, and a white space are all that are needed to make us "see" a complete cat. We supply what is missing from our common knowledge of cats and a psychological propensity for completing forms. When stoop-shouldered Willy Loman shuffles on in dim light and remarks that he's "tired to the death," we don't have to be told that he's getting old, that he has dressed dumpily for some years, that his life and job have not been going well. All that, and more, is contained in the completion that those first sketched details imply. This type, this perceptual gestalt that is actually incomplete, these forms that represent a certain individual, serve us as a character until the details are corroborated or corrected. Miller, of course, goes on to show Willy as a rather complete and specific man, with passions and a past. But sometimes a writer wants or needs no more than a Gestalt illusion of a character. Then his task is to discover and present those details that will cause us to recognize, to perceive, from our common experience, a potential individual. That the recognition depends upon our experience makes him a type, rather than an individual. This concept of recognition is what aestheticians mean when they say *type*.

These two kinds of type form a sort of dual backbone in the Classic concept of character, which is oriented toward representativeness, inclusiveness, and universality, rather than uniqueness. In Classic Greek concepts, Ulysses, Oedipus, and such, are qualified *typical* men, who represent some ideal in the culture. Ulysses is, as far as his character is concerned, a kind of composite of ideal Greek virtues, and his odyssey is a series of tests to see whether or not those virtues can survive corruption. They do, and the fact that they do makes the whole action mythic. Oedipus, as a character, is an embodiment of the idea that the good of the state is more important than the good of any individual, even oneself. Such characters have private lives, too, but the emphasis and meaning reside in their public lives. This concept of the *typal* function of character is what led Aristotle, apparently, to assert that plot was the soul and source of any imitation of action that is serious, complete, and of a certain magnitude. For the Classicist, through history and today, type is primary in characterization.

SOME SUB-DIVISIONS OF TYPE

The least characterized of the type characters is what E. M. Forster called the *flat* character,[5] an unfortunate name, really, because it suggests a certain pasteboard dimension of inhumanity. The pure flat character is the embodiment of a single idea, or set of traits, or quality; when the writer puts more than one set of traits in a character, he begins to curve toward the round (or at least, toward what we, here, will call the half-round, or profile). This one dimension of the flat character, which can usually be expressed in a single phrase or sentence, is the formula for the character's thought and action and a description of him.

There are two great advantages to using flat characters, says Forster. First, the reader easily recognizes them emotionally. What Forster apparently means is that such characters supply a kind of "instant" scene and situation, in which the main business can proceed without delay. We don't have to bother with explanations, but can focus on action. Russian novels typically include too much explanation, thinks Forster, or to put it another way, too few flat characters. One does remember how, in Tolstoi, for instance, even the passing peasant, whose only function is to deliver a message or bow to a nobleman, is described in some detail, though a pawn could (perhaps, should) have performed his role. This characterization, this curving toward the round, often seems to us a digression, seems unrelated to the themes of the book (though the Russians have a way of getting the whole universe, even the way a peasant bows, into their themes). The novel in English has tended to get to its themes more directly. It is often convenient for an author, says Forster, to focus his full force upon the primary issues at once; flat characters allow such focus because the reader so easily and so quickly recognizes them for what they are and the functions they fill.

A second advantage, says Forster, is that the reader easily remembers them afterwards. He fixes them in his mind as unchanging and, therefore, dependable in memory. They become the still points by which we can measure the progress of primary characters. Indeed, virtually all short stories and novellas, and most novels, find this function of the flat character not only advantageous, but indispensable.

A good example of a flat character, and one often pointed out, is Emma Woodhouse's father in Jane Austen's *Emma*. Mr. Woodhouse refers every-

[5] See *Aspects of the Novel* (New York: Harcourt, Brace, Harvest Books ed., 1956), pp. 67–69.

thing, whether it is a problem in the estate, a proposal for a party, an act of God, or an invasion—refers everything to, subordinates everything to, the preservation of health and equanimity. As Lionel Trilling points out,[6] Mr. Woodhouse is the image of *stasis,* an embodiment of the principle of inertia. And there are several delightfully comic scenes in which the other people, fully aware of his Johnny-one-note character, manipulate his moods and moves to their own purposes.

A third advantage, which Forster does not mention, is that flat characters, like Mr. Woodhouse, participate in the creation of round characters, through the author's juxtaposition of them in comparison or contrast to the round character. Nothing defines Emma Woodhouse's vivacious, energetic, adventuresome personality quite so well as her father's *stasis.* Mrs. Weston, the ideal female character in *Emma,* does not, can not, make us notice Emma's energy, because she is so much like Emma herself. But when Emma is juxtaposed against her stick-in-the-mud father, we remark the effervescent qualities that are at the center of her personality. An author can, if he chooses, do most of his characterization in this way. Jane Austen points out Emma's judicious speech and thought by showing us Miss Bates, who is possessed of continuous speech and uncontrollable flow of idea; points out Emma's rationality by showing us Harriet, who is a silly sentimental feather in the wind of emotion and whim; points out several things by showing us Mrs. Elton, who is vulgar, pretentious, forward, ignorant, and snobbish, among other things (which is to say, Mrs. Elton is a profile).

A special case of the type character is what Henry James called the *ficelle* (from *ficelles du théâtre:* stage tricks). The *ficelle* is a character whose only function is to reveal something about a main character. In discussing the problem of revealing certain kinds of information about Strether in *The Ambassadors,* James remarks that

a pounce is made on Maria Gostrey—without even the pretext, either, of *her* being, in essence, Strether's friend. She is the reader's friend much rather—in consequence of dispositions that make him so eminently require one; and she acts in that capacity, and *really* in that capacity alone, with exemplary devotion, from beginning to end of the book. She is an enrolled, a direct, aid to lucidity; she is in fine, to tear off her mask, the most unmitigated and abandoned of *ficelles.*[7]

Maria Gostrey is a type character, but ficelles can also be pawns or profiles.

---

[6] See his "Introduction" to *Emma* (New York: Houghton Mifflin, Riverside ed., 1957).

[7] From James's Preface to *The Ambassadors* (New York ed., 1907–1909).

One thinks of the little old man in James's "The Beast in the Jungle," whose only qualities are a face and a hunched back of grief, but whose presence causes the epiphany to pounce at Marcher as surely as if it were a beast. And one thinks of Henrietta Stackpole in James's *Portrait of a Lady,* who has an occupation, leisure time, a certain set of personality traits, and a value system, and who is used over and over as a means of dramatizing the thoughts and values of the important characters.

The stereotype is another variation on the type character. Stereotypes come about when those qualities considered typical become fixed, become codified, solidified, and simplified, as in the idea of the absent-minded professor, the dumb blonde, and such. These are abstractions from reality, concepts about experience, rather than reality or experience. Thus, one can say that, by defini-tion, they are always falsifications of reality. They never represent individuals, but always ideas. They are a common pitfall of even experienced writers, and the only time they have enjoyed artistic respect in English was in seventeenth-century "character" writing about such ideas as the good man, the fair milk-maid, the dastard, and a child. See also, however, the characters of Theophrastus and the Greek and Latin traditions derived from him.

The caricature is a common and sometimes useful variation on the type character, in which certain traits have been exaggerated, usually to ludicrous or comic proportions. The caricature most usually comes about when a writer begins not by drawing upon what he has observed as typical, but by assigning a character a certain set of identifying traits or marks. Too often, one of these traits or marks—a propensity to flirt with members of the opposite sex, for instance, or a physical detail, like flashing blue eyes—gets emphasized until other qualities pale and we are left with a cartoon, rather than a picture. Of course, this kind of character is very useful in burlesque and satire and in magazines like *Playboy.*

The Profile

With the profile, we are a bit past the mid-way point of the action-character continuum, where personality and thought are as important as action. A profile is a character who is "half-round," who has more than typical traits, but who has not yet acquired the complexities we experience when we come to know a person intimately. Mrs. Elton in Jane Austen's *Emma* is an example, already mentioned. No doubt, many of her qualities, such as her snobbish condescen-sion, are merely typical of resort-life at Bath, from which she comes; but there are also things about her that are purely personal, that would make her a boor, even at Bath—her propensity to meddle in other people's affairs, her obtuseness, her forwardness. Another example is any of those "Profiles" in *The New Yorker* and other magazines, in which some of the public and private, typical and peculiar, remarkable and mundane actions and thoughts of an individual are summarized in a form that can be used almost equally well for a eulogy or an obituary. A third example is any of John F. Kennedy's *Profiles in Courage,* partial portraits of men, meant to emphasize a limited set of traits, especially patriotism. Profiles themselves form a continuum—some may be near types, some near roundness.

Whereas types are derived from ideas, profiles are derived from observation of a particular individual, thus from life. Indeed, they may pass for life, as they quite frequently do in our experience. We may live next door to a man for several years, know his family, his job, his voice, his style of doing many things, and never know that he hates cats, until one day a cat comes into the neighborhood, or never know that he has been seducing his wife's cousin for many years.

Profiles rarely deal with the hidden life, for, when they do, the character tends to take on the complexities of roundness. This is not to say that a profile cannot be vivid; they are often quite vivid in history and biography, where they are inevitable because historians and biographers must limit themselves to revealed thought and known action. (Note, in passing, that the historian emphasizes the action end of the continuum; the biographer, the character end, though there is always overlap.) This limitation is what led Aristotle to assert that art is more real than life. Life, the record of life, is only what *has* happened; art is also what *can* happen. But what *has* happened is often very interesting and sometimes allows us to infer those things which cannot be known. Because of this, the profile is also fairly common in literature, and sometimes quite vivid. Much of our literature takes the form of pseudo-history or pseudo-biography, and, as long as it maintains an effaced or external view, as long as it avoids the hidden life, the writer is dealing in profiles.

The literary use of profiles varies, however, with the treatment or conception of them. The simpler profile may serve to set a scene more ambitiously than a type would, or may participate in the action as more than a simple supporting actor. More ambitious profiles may perform secondary roles, or even primary. Some writers, notably Hemingway, like to use profiles as central characters and thus allow the reader the aesthetic pleasure of seeming to discover something about the character. This drawing of inference is not the same as "each person interprets a character the way he wants to." Insofar as the writer is successful, and Hemingway was generally successful with his profiles, the only interpretation, the only inference that is relevant, is the one that follows logically (or psychologically) from the data that is presented. Handled well, a profile can be a rich and acute vehicle of communication.

The Round Character

The character "in the round" is one who convinces us of his capacity to be human, which is to say, he approaches the internal and external complexities that we perceive in ourselves. He is usually found in fiction, rarely in life.

E. M. Forster suggests [8] that a novelist's characters most often resemble himself; he makes up a series of traits that he thinks might be himself if he were, say, female, fat, and forty, gives them a voice, gestures, values that he can imagine himself using, and describes the whole business in words. They are not creations at all, in one sense; they *are* human; they are the author. This capacity for being human seems a much better test of a round character than Forster's more famous one: the character's ability to surprise convincingly.

Round characters, being capable of life, are capable of growth, and thus are inevitably changed, are *educated* in the strictest sense of the word, by every one of their significant experiences. They may astonish us with a new kind of action, or a change of heart or mind—astonish us until we perceive the development of the change—at which point it becomes not a change at all, but a part of a unified progress. Real change, real surprise, would be aesthetically fatal, since it would be a contradiction to possibility for that particular imagined individual.

The common, practical, three-part, rule-of-thumb for making a change convincing is that the change must be possible to the character, it must be motivated, and it must be given time to happen. By being possible to a character, we mean the change must be logically "in character," must follow from what Aristotle called the "laws of probability or necessity," what we today are likely to call the laws of psychology and human nature. It is possible, of course, for a character to be consistently inconsistent, at least on the surface, but in a fully known character, motivation would dissolve the inconsistency, by making the erratic behavior the logical result of some cause. Motivating an action or a change is usually a much simpler matter—of giving the character a plausible desire, which the action or change will satisfy. At a more difficult level, the writer might have to make the reader aware of motives that the character is unconscious of—which might, in turn, dictate the point-of-view that is necessary. The time needed for a change to happen is more a matter of aesthetics than of psychology, for a change may happen instantaneously in a character, yet take several minutes for us to comprehend. But if the reader does not have time to *see* all the stages of a change, they are aesthetically simply not there.

This focus on the feelings and motives of an individual is, of course, central to the Romantic concept of character, which emphasizes uniqueness, exclusiveness, and particularity, at the expense of the general. Jane Austen's Emma

[8] *Aspects of the Novel,* p. 44.

Woodhouse and James Joyce's Stephen Dedalus, for example, are conceived as peculiar individuals (though they also have universal dimensions). Emma, as a character, is a collection of unique values and emotions, and the point of her story is that she develops from immature folly to mature rationality. After she has developed, we see that she has been moving toward Jane Austen's ideal of behavior for bright young women, but all through the book, our focus is upon Emma as an individual, not as an object lesson. Stephen Dedalus's reactions are presented to us as not only individual, but peculiar; when in an emotional and religious crisis at the end of Chapter III of *Portrait of the Artist as a Young Man,* Stephen perceives the order and rightness of life in the arrangement of white pudding, sausages, and eggs on the shelf, we are to believe that this perception and this emotion in just this form are impossible for any other individual in the universe. And, of course, Joyce's stream-of-consciousness technique emphasizes the uniqueness of the experience. There is no universality at all in this view of Stephen, though again, at the end we see typal significance in his whole action: his education has been—as his name implies—a trying on of the wings of his parent culture. Freudian and other psychologies, of course, have been profoundly influential upon this concept of character. The emphasis and meaning of such characters reside in their private lives, not their public roles.

But it is probably impossible for us to see a character very long without seeing him in some typal pattern; so Romantically conceived characters have a way of blossoming into more than peculiar significance. This may happen through our comparisons of the character with other people we have known or read about. It may happen through an author's deliberately blurring out the individual into representativeness—usually an awkward and unsuccessful technique. Or it may happen when an individual's uniqueness is discovered to us in such clarity and completeness that we begin to perceive an essence of being human. Total, willed introspection is a classic device of self-discovery; if the self exhibited by such complete, clear, and internal detail partakes deeply and essentially of human nature, then we have not only a person, but an archetype.

The Fragrant Character

A fragrant character, as Lionel Trilling called some of Forster's people,[9] is one whose influence or "character" is infused through the rest of the work as the fragrance of a flower through a room. Mrs. Wilcox, in Forster's *Howards End,* is a certain moral force acting upon her husband and sons; after she has

[9] In his monograph, *E. M. Forster* (New York: New Directions, 1943).

died, that force, her "presence," continues to act upon them. Similarly, in *A Passage to India,* the memory of Mrs. Moore haunts the Indian scene she has left; when the Indians chant her name, the value-system she represented is reinvoked in Adela, clears Adela's confused mind, causes her to confess and bring about justice. Thus, we have passed that point of the action-character continuum which is the epitome of personality and have entered the segment where social function is dominant.

One of the best examples of a fragrant character is the awesome Mrs. Newsome in Henry James's *The Ambassadors.* Mrs. Newsome does not appear at all in the action of the book; she is back in Wollett, Massachusetts, as pure and crusty as any New England dowager could be. But all the characters in the book, Chad and Strether, especially, are continually making choices, performing actions, keeping secrets, in accordance with what Mrs. Newsome would or would not approve of. She is a mighty force to contend with, though she does not appear. This was exactly James's intention, "that Mrs. Newsome, away off with her finger on the pulse of Massachusetts, should yet be no less intensely than circuitously present through the whole thing, should be no less felt as to be reckoned with than the most direct exhibition, the finest portrayal at first hand could make her." [10]

Fragrant characters occur also in life—a crusty old grandfather, a hell-fire-and-brimstone preacher, a calf-eyed girl that a boy is in love with. Such an adage as "Don't do anything your grandmother wouldn't approve of" presupposes the grandmother's fragrance.

We can see, also, in the examples above, a certain affinity of the fragrant character with the type character, though fragrant characters are more likely to be profiles or in the round, if they function with a very effective "fragrance." Indeed, the reaction of other people to them tends to give them added dimension.

The Heroic Character

If we extend the social function of a character until it becomes important to the tribe or the nation, we get the heroic character. Then we have an epic world in which Melville's Ahab, for example, can ask some of man's ultimate questions, or in which the fate of the hero (take Attila the Hun, for an example from life) is bound up with the fate of the people. Villains, like Satan or Hitler, can also be heroic in this sense. Consider the monumental representations of human possibilities in the following example: [11]

10 From James's Preface.
11 Ahab's Black Mass, from Chapter XXXVI, "The Quarter-Deck," of Herman Melville's *Moby Dick.*

It drew near the close of day. Suddenly [Ahab] came to a halt by the bulwarks, and inserting his bone leg into the auger-hole there, and with one hand grasping a shroud, he ordered Starbuck to send everybody aft.

"Sir!" said the mate, astonished at an order seldom or never given on shipboard except in some extraordinary case.

"Send everybody aft," repeated Ahab. "Mast-heads, there! come down!"

When the entire ship's company were assembled, and with curious and not wholly unapprehensive faces, were eyeing him, for he looked not unlike the weather horizon when a storm is coming up, Ahab, after rapidly glancing over the bulwarks, and then darting his eyes among the crew, started from his standpoint; and as though not a soul were nigh him resumed his heavy turns upon the deck. With bent head and half-slouched hat he continued to pace, unmindful of the wondering whispering among the men; till Stubb cautiously whispered to Flask, that Ahab must have summoned them there for the purpose of witnessing a pedestrian feat. But this did not last long. Vehemently pausing, he cried:—

"What do ye do when ye see a whale, men?"

"Sing out for him!" was the impulsive rejoinder from a score of clubbed voices.

"Good!" cried Ahab, with a wild approval in his tones; observing the hearty animation into which his unexpected question had so magnetically thrown them.

"And what do ye next, men?"

"Lower away, and after him!"

"And what tune is it ye pull to, men?"

"A dead whale or a stove boat!"

More and more strangely and fiercely glad and approving, grew the countenance of the old man at every shout; while the mariners began to gaze curiously at each other, as if marvelling how it was that they themselves became so excited at such seemingly purposeless questions.

But, they were all eagerness again, as Ahab, now half-revolving in his pivot-hole, with one hand reaching high up a shroud, and tightly, almost convulsively grasping it, addressed them thus:—

"All ye mast-headers have before now heard me give orders about a white whale. Look ye! d'ye see this Spanish ounce of gold?"—holding up a broad bright coin to the sun—"it is a sixteen dollar piece, men. D'ye see it? Mr. Starbuck, hand me yon top-maul."

While the mate was getting the hammer, Ahab, without speaking, was slowly rubbing the gold piece against the skirts of his jacket, as if to heighten its lustre, and without using any words, was meanwhile lowly humming to himself, producing a sound so strangely muffled and inarticulate that it seemed the mechanical humming of the wheels of his vitality in him.

Receiving the top-maul from Starbuck, he advanced towards the main-mast with the hammer uplifted in one hand, exhibiting the gold with the other, and with a high raised voice exclaiming: "Whosoever of ye raises me a white-headed whale with a wrinkled brow and a crooked jaw; whosoever of ye raises me that white-headed whale, with three holes punctured in his starboard fluke—look ye, whosoever of ye raises me that same white whale, he shall have this gold ounce, my boys!"

"Huzza! Huzza!" cried the seamen, as with swinging tarpaulins they hailed the act of nailing the gold to the mast.

"It's a white whale, I say," resumed Ahab, as he threw down the top-maul; "a white whale. Skin your eyes for him, men; look sharp for white water; if ye see but a bubble, sing out."

All this while Tashtego, Daggoo, and Queequeg had looked on with even more intense interest and surprise than the rest, and at the mention of the wrinkled brow and crooked jaw they had started as if each was separately touched by some specific recollection.

"Captain Ahab," said Tashtego, "that white whale must be the same that some call Moby Dick."

"Moby Dick?" shouted Ahab. "Do ye know the white whale then, Tash?"

"Does he fan-tail a little curious, sir, before he goes down?" said the Gay-Header deliberately.

"And has a curious spout, too," said Daggoo, "very bushy, even for a parmacetty, and mighty quick, Captain Ahab?"

"And he have one two, tree—oh! good many iron in him hide, too, Captain," cried Queequeg disjointedly, "all twisketee betwisk, like him—him" faltering hard for a word, and screwing his hand round and round as though uncorking a bottle—"like him—him—"

"Corkscrew!" cried Ahab, "aye, Queequeg, the harpoons lie all twisted and wrenched in him; aye, Daggoo, his spout is a big one, like a whole shock of wheat, and white as a pile of our Nantucket wool after the great annual sheep-shearing; aye, Tashtego, and he fan-tails like a split jib in a squall. Death and devils! men, it is Moby Dick ye have seen—Moby Dick—Moby Dick!"

"Captain Ahab," said Starbuck, who, with Stubb and Flask, had thus far been eyeing his superior with increasing surprise, but at last seemed struck with a thought which somewhat explained all the wonder. "Captain Ahab, I have heard of Moby Dick—but it was not Moby Dick that took off thy leg?"

"Who told thee that?" cried Ahab; then pausing, "Aye, Starbuck; aye, my hearties all round; it was Moby Dick that dismasted me; Moby Dick that brought me to this dead stump I stand on now. Aye, Aye," he shouted with a terrific, loud, animal sob, like that of a heart-stricken moose; "Aye, aye! it was that accursed white whale that razeed me; made a poor pegging lubber of me for ever and a day!" Then tossing both arms, with measureless imprecations he shouted out: "Aye, aye! and I'll chase him round Good Hope, and round the Horn, and round the Norway Maelstrom, and round perdition's flames before I give him up. And this is what ye have shipped for, men! to chase that white whale on both sides of land, and over all sides of earth, till he spouts black blood and rolls fin out. What say ye, men, will ye splice hands on it, now? I think ye do look brave."

"Aye, aye!" shouted the harpooners and seamen, running closer to the excited old man: "A sharp eye for the White Whale; a sharp lance for Moby Dick!"

"God bless ye," he seemed to half sob and half shout. "God bless ye, men. Steward! go draw the great measure of grog. But what's this long face about, Mr. Starbuck; wilt thou not chase the white whale? art not game for Moby Dick?"

"I am game for his crooked jaw, and for the jaws of Death too, Captain Ahab, if it fairly comes in the way of the business we follow; but I came here to hunt whales, not my commander's vengeance. How many barrels will thy vengeance yield thee even if thou gettest it, Captain Ahab? it will not fetch thee much in our Nantucket market."

"Nantucket market! Hoot! But come closer, Starbuck; thou requirest a little lower layer. If money's to be the measurer, man, and the accountants have computed their great counting-house the globe, by girdling it with guineas, one to every three parts of an inch; then, let me tell thee, that my vengeance will fetch a great premium *here!*"

"He smites his chest," whispered Stubb, "what's that for? methinks it rings most vast, but hollow."

"Vengeance on a dumb brute!" cried Starbuck, "that simply smote thee from blindest instinct! Madness! To be enraged with a dumb thing, Captain Ahab, seems blasphemous."

"Hark ye yet again,—the little lower layer. All visible objects, man, are but as pasteboard masks. But in each event—in the living act, the undoubted deed—there, some unknown but still reasoning thing puts forth the mouldings of its features from behind the unreasoning mask. If man will strike, strike through the mask! How can the prisoner reach outside except by thrusting through the wall? To me, the white whale is that wall, shoved near to me. Sometimes I think there's naught beyond. But 'tis enough. He tasks me; he heaps me; I see in him outrageous strength, with an inscrutable malice sinewing it. That inscrutable thing is chiefly what I hate; and be the white whale agent, or be the white whale principal, I will wreak that hate upon him. Talk not to me of blasphemy, man; I'd strike the sun if it insulted me. For could the sun do that, then could I do the other; since there is ever a sort of fair play herein, jealously presiding over all creations. But not my master, man, is even that fair play. Who's over me? Truth hath no confines. Take off thine eye! more intolerable than fiends' glarings is a doltish stare! So, so; thou reddenest and palest; my heat has melted thee to anger-glow. But look ye, Starbuck, what is said in heat, that thing unsays itself. There are men from whom warm words are small indignity. I meant not to incense thee. Let it go. Look! see yonder Turkish cheeks of spotted tawn—living, breathing pictures painted by the sun. The Pagan leopards—the unrecking and unworshipping things, that live; and seek, and give no reasons for the torrid life they feel! The crew, man, the crew! Are they not one and all with Ahab, in this matter of the whale? See Stubb! he laughs! See yonder Chilian! he snorts to think of it. Stand up amid the general hurricane, thy one tost sapling cannot, Starbuck! And what is it? Reckon it. 'Tis but to help strike a fin; no wondrous feat for Starbuck. What is it more? From this one poor hunt, then, the best lance out of all Nantucket, surely he will not hang back, when every formast-hand has clutched a whetstone? Ah! constrainings seize thee; I see! the billow lifts thee! Speak, but speak!—Aye, aye! thy silence, then, *that* voices thee. (*Aside*) Something shot from my dilated nostrils, he has inhaled it in his lungs. Starbuck now is mine; cannot oppose me now, without rebellion."

"God keep me!—keep us all!" murmured Starbuck, lowly.

But in his joy at the enchanted, tacit acquiescence of the mate, Ahab did not hear his foreboding invocation; nor yet the low laugh from the hold; nor yet the presaging vibrations of the winds in the cordage nor yet the hollow flap of the sails against the masts as for a moment their hearts sank in. For again Starbuck's downcast eyes lighted up with the stubbornness of life; the subterranean laugh died away; the winds blew on; the sails filled out; the ship heaved and rolled as before. Ah, ye admonitions and warnings! why stay ye not when ye come? But rather are ye predictions than warnings, ye shadows! Yet not so much predictions from without, as verifications of the foregoing things within. For with little external to constrain us, the innermost necessities in our being, these still drive us on.

"The measure! the measure!" cried Ahab.

Receiving the brimming pewter, and turning to the harpooneers, he ordered them to produce their weapons. Then ranging them before him near the capstan, with their harpoons in their hands, while his three mates stood at his side with their lances, and the rest of the ship's company formed a circle round the group; he stood for an instant searchingly eyeing every man of his crew. But those wild eyes met his, as the bloodshot eyes of the prairie wolves meet the eye of their leader, ere he rushes on at their head in the trail of the bison; but, alas! only to fall into the hidden snare of the Indian.

"Drink and pass!" he cried, handing the heavy charged flagon to the nearest seaman. "The crew alone now drink. Round with it, round! Short draughts—long swallows, men; 'tis hot as Satan's hoof. So, so; it goes round excellently. It spiralizes in ye; forks out at the serpent-snapping eye. Well done; almost drained. That way it went, this way it comes. Hand it me—here's a hollow; Men, ye seem the years; so brimming life is gulped and gone. Steward, refill!

"Attend now, my braves. I have mustered ye all round this capstan; and ye mates, flank me with your lances; and ye harpooneers, stand there with your irons; and ye, stout mariners, ring me in, that I may in some sort revive a noble custom of my fisherman fathers before me. O men, you will yet see that—Ha! boy, come back? bad pennies come not sooner. Hand it me. Why, now, this pewter had run brimming again, wer't not thou St. Vitus' imp—away, thou ague!

"Advance, ye mates! Cross your lances full before me. Well done! Let me touch the axis." So saying, with extended arm, he grasped the three level, radiating lances at their crossed centre; while so doing, suddenly and nervously twitched them; meanwhile, glancing intently from Starbuck to Stubb; from Stubb to Flask. It seemed as though, by some nameless, interior volition, he would fain have shocked into them the same fiery emotion accumulated within the Leyden jar of his own magnetic life. The three mates quailed before his strong, sustained, and mystic aspect. Stubb and Flask looked sideways from him; the honest eye of Starbuck fell downright.

"In vain!" cried Ahab; "but, maybe, 'tis well. For did ye three but once take the full-forced shock, then mine own electric thing, *that* had perhaps expired from out me. Perchance, too, it would have dropped ye dead. Perchance ye need it not. Down lances! And now, ye mates, I do appoint ye three cupbearers to my three pagan kinsmen there—yon three most honorable gentlemen and noblemen, my valiant harpooneers. Disdain the task? What, when the great Pope washes the feet of beggars, using his tiara for ewer? Oh, my sweet cardinals! your own condescension, *that* shall bend ye to it. I do not order ye; ye will it. Cut your seizings and draw the poles, ye harpooneers!"

Silently obeying the order, the three harpooneers now stood with the detached iron part of their harpoons, some three feet long, held, barbs up, before him.

"Stab me not with that keen steel! Cant them; cant them over! know ye not the goblet end? Turn up the socket! So, so; now, ye cup-bearers, advance. The irons! take them; hold them while I fill!" Forthwith, slowly going from one officer to the other, he brimmed the harpoon sockets with the fiery waters from the pewter.

"Now, three to three, ye stand. Commend the murderous chalices! Bestow them, ye who are now made parties to this indissoluble league. Ha! Starbuck! but the deed is done! Yon ratifying sun now waits to sit upon it. Drink, ye harpooneers! drink and swear, ye men that man the deathful whaleboat's bow—Death to Moby Dick! God hunt us all, if we do not hunt Moby Dick to his death!" The long, barbed steel goblets were lifted; and to cries and maledictions against the white whale, the spirits were simultaneously quaffed down with a hiss. Starbuck paled, and turned, and shivered. Once more, and finally, the replenished pewter went the rounds among the frantic crew; when, waving his free hand to them, they all dispersed; and Ahab retired within his cabin.

There are several factors in this passage that help elevate Ahab into heroic proportions. Ahab's own demonic intensity alone makes him larger than life, for he exhibits much more than the usual capacity for intensity. The philosophical extent to which he is willing to carry his chase after the whale, his hypnotic control of his fellow men, his consecration to his concept of his own needs—all operate in a similar way.

There are, also, many devices of juxtaposition and imagery that give this scene the power of a religious ceremony and Ahab the dimensions of a high priest who is challenging God. The crew is the congregation; the mast and the coin are altar and ikon (the trinity on the coin is described in detail in another chapter); there are the elements of a service—invocation, testimonial, discipline for the errant, communion, musical chanting, and benediction. The symbolism of the drink is especially important, though no less important, perhaps, than the symbolism of the spears—Ahab demands and receives perfect submission to his will, submission to his religion, when he forces the primitive harpooners to turn the points of their weapons down, a universal sign of submission among primitives; that the spears become the goblets in the communion that seals the maneuver is a stroke of pure genius. By such devices, Melville makes his characters participate in very important human myths.

In such a mythic concept of character, Jungian psychologists say, we sit back and let the heroic figures act for us. We create them in such ways that they come to represent us, but represent us in such depth and detail that the patterns of their experience are the patterns of our potential experience, made heroic, charged with great emotion, and presented in a way that allows us to see meaning and discovery in ourselves. Because these larger-than-life characters embody human experience in concentrated proportions, they also concentrate meaning. They live their lives with an intensity that is not possible for the usual run of being, but embody in that intensity, for exhibition and understanding through vicarious experience, the widest potential of all beings, in a form that the common man cannot possibly achieve. Jungian psychologists have recalled our attention to and helped us understand a wide variety of patterns into which our heroic figures fit. These figures have an affinity to types, but are so large and so inclusive that we call them archetypes.[12]

The main thing about a heroic figure playing a public (or depth-psychology) role is that he plays the role. That is, he is known primarily by the action he performs, not by the personality he carries. Thus, the continuum of character comes full circle (or full spiral)—from the character of pure action, through the types, through the character of pure personality, through the social and public functions of character, and back to the character's role as action, but action which embodies psychomythical thought. Remove that, and you have a pawn again.

Whenever we meet a fictional character, we begin inevitably at the beginning of this continuum. He is first a pawn, a mere stick or a blob that occupies space, perhaps performs some action. If the author makes us see him a little longer, we will surely see him as a type, which, with further information, may develop into a profile. From profiles, or from interior data, we may infer or perceive round characters, who, when they come to dominate other people, can become fragrant characters, and that is only a short

[12] Jung and Kerényi have isolated and described a number of archetypal patterns. Erich Neumann, Joseph Campbell, and Northrop Frye, among many others, each in his own way, have also written interesting and revealing analyses. See, for example, C. G. Jung, *Archetypes and the Collective Unconscious* (Bollingen, 1959); Jung and C. Kerényi, *Essays on a Science of Mythology* (Harper, n.d.); Erich Neumann, *The Origins and History of Consciousness* (Bollingen, 1954; Harper Torchbooks, 2 vols. 1962); Joseph Campbell, *The Hero with a Thousand Faces* (Pantheon, 1954; Meridian, n.d.).

way from the heroic. If we ever see a heroic character, it is probable that we have also seen him as all the other kinds.

Indeed, any character that is "human," that convinces us of his reality, is capable of being any and all of these kinds of characters at different moments. The quality of being human probably encompasses all of them simultaneously. But, because our perception is limited to a sequence of single details, perceived sequentially and funded by the memory of prior detail, our view of a character is doomed to be fragmentary and incomplete. It is only *because* our view is fragmentary and incomplete that we can partition a unity into kinds and concepts of character, as here. And authors, aware of our limitations, make use of these concepts, as when they refuse to give us the private and mythic lives of flat characters, on the grounds that some detail may be aesthetically irrelevant to their intentions.

Two Stories for Study and Reference

SOLDIER'S HOME [13]

Krebs went to the war from a Methodist college in Kansas. There is a picture which shows him among his fraternity brothers, all of them wearing exactly the same height and style collar. He enlisted in the Marines in 1917 and did not return to the United States until the second division returned from the Rhine in the summer of 1919.

There is a picture which shows him on the Rhine with two German girls and another corporal. Krebs and the corporal look too big for their uniforms. The German girls are not beautiful. The Rhine does not show in the picture.

By the time Krebs returned to his home town in Oklahoma the greeting of heroes was over. He came back much too late. The men from the town who had been drafted had all been welcomed elaborately on their return. There had been a great deal of hysteria. Now the reaction had set in. People seemed to think it was rather ridiculous for Krebs to be getting back so late, years after the war was over.

At first, Krebs, who had been at Belleau Wood, Soissons, the Champagne, St. Mihiel and in the Argonne did not want to talk about the war at all. Later he felt the need to talk but no one wanted to hear about it. His town had heard too many atrocity stories to be thrilled by actualities. Krebs found that to be listened to at all he had to lie, and after he had done this twice he, too, had a reaction against the war and against talking about it. A distaste for everything that had happened to him in the war set in because of the lies he had told. All of the times that had been able to make him feel cool and clear inside himself when

[13] By Ernest Hemingway.

he thought of them; the times so long back when he had done the one thing, the only thing for a man to do, easily and naturally, when he might have done something else, now lost their cool, valuable quality and then were lost themselves.

His lies were quite unimportant lies and consisted in attributing to himself things other men had seen, done or heard of, and stating as facts certain apocryphal incidents familiar to all soldiers. Even his lies were not sensational at the pool room. His acquaintances, who had heard detailed accounts of German women found chained to machine guns in the Argonne forest and who could not comprehend, or were barred by their patriotism from interest in, any German machine gunners who were not chained, were not thrilled by his stories.

Krebs acquired the nausea in regard to experience that is the result of untruth or exaggeration, and when he occasionally met another man who had really been a soldier and they talked a few minutes in the dressing room at a dance he fell into the easy pose of the old soldier among other soldiers: that he had been badly, sickeningly frightened all the time. In this way he lost everything.

During this time, it was late summer, he was sleeping late in bed, getting up to walk down town to the library to get a book, eating lunch at home, reading on the front porch until he became bored and then walking down through the town to spend the hottest hours of the day in the cool dark of the pool room. He loved to play pool.

In the evening he practiced on his clarinet, strolled down town, read and went to bed. He was still a hero to his two young sisters. His mother would have given him breakfast in bed if he had wanted it. She often came in when he was in bed and asked him to tell her about the war, but her attention always wandered. His father was non-committal.

Before Krebs went away to the war he had never been allowed to drive the family motor car. His father was in the real estate business and always wanted the car to be at his command when he required it to take clients out into the country to show them a piece of farm property. The car always stood outside the First National Bank building where his father had an office on the second floor. Now, after the war, it was still the same car.

Nothing was changed in the town except that the young girls had grown up. But they lived in such a complicated world of already defined alliances and shifting feuds that Krebs did not feel the energy or the courage to break into it. He liked to look at them, though. There were so many good-looking young girls. Most of them had their hair cut short. When he went away only little girls wore their hair like that or girls that were fast. They all wore sweaters and shirt waists with round Dutch collars. It was a pattern. He liked to look at them from the front porch as they walked on the other side of the street. He liked to watch them walking under the shade of the trees. He liked the round Dutch collars above their sweaters. He liked their silk stockings and flat shoes. He liked their bobbed hair and the way they walked.

When he was in town their appeal to him was not very strong. He did not like them when he saw them in the Greek's ice cream parlor. He did not want them themselves really. They were too complicated. There was something else.

Vaguely he wanted a girl but he did not want to have to work to get her. He would have liked to have a girl but he did not want to have to spend a long time getting her. He did not want to get into the intrigue and the politics. He did not want to have to do any courting. He did not want to tell any more lies. It wasn't worth it.

He did not want any consequences. He did not want any consequences ever again. He wanted to live along without consequences. Besides he did not really need a girl. The army had taught him that. It was all right to pose as though you had to have a girl. Nearly everybody did that. But it wasn't true. You did not need a girl. That was the funny thing. First a fellow boasted how girls mean nothing to him, that he never thought of them, that they could not touch him. Then a fellow boasted that he could not get along without girls, that he had to have them all the time, that he could not go to sleep without them.

That was all a lie. It was all a lie both ways. You did not need a girl unless you thought about them. He learned that in the army. Then sooner or later you always got one. When you were really ripe for a girl you always got one. You did not have to think about it. Sooner or later it would come. He had learned that in the army.

Now he would have liked a girl if she had come to him and not wanted to talk. But here at home it was all too complicated. He knew he could never get through it all again. It was not worth the trouble. That was the thing about French girls and German girls. There was not all this talking. You couldn't talk much and you did not need to talk. It was simple and you were friends. He thought about France and then he began to think about Germany. On the whole he had liked Germany better. He did not want to leave Germany. He did not want to come home. Still, he had come home. He sat on the front porch.

He liked the girls that were walking along the other side of the street. He liked the look of them much better than the French girls or the German girls. But the world they were in was not the world he was in. He would like to have one of them. But it was not worth it. They were such a nice pattern. He liked the pattern. It was exciting. But he would not go through all the talking. He did not want one badly enough. He liked to look at them all, though. It was not worth it. Not now when things were getting good again.

He sat there on the porch reading a book on the war. It was a history and he was reading about all the engagements he had been in. It was the most interesting reading he had ever done. He wished there were more maps. He looked forward with a good feeling to reading all the really good histories when they would come out with good detail maps. Now he was really learning about the war. He had been a good soldier. That made a difference.

One morning after he had been home about a month his mother came into his bedroom and sat on the bed. She smoothed her apron.

"I had a talk with your father last night Harold," she said, "and he is willing for you to take the car out in the evenings."

"Yeah?" said Krebs, who was not fully awake. "Take the car out? Yeah?"

"Yes. Your father has felt for some time that you should be able to take the car out in the evenings whenever you wished but we only talked it over last night."

"I'll bet you made him," Krebs said.

"No. It was your father's suggestion that we talk the matter over."

"Yeah. I'll bet you made him," Krebs sat up in bed.

"Will you come down to breakfast, Harold?" his mother said.

"As soon as I get my clothes on," Krebs said.

His mother went out of the room and he could hear her frying something downstairs while he washed, shaved and dressed to go down into the dining-room for breakfast. While he was eating breakfast his sister brought in the mail.

"Well, Hare," she said. "You old sleepyhead. What do you ever get up for?"

Krebs looked at her. He liked her. She was his best sister.

"Have you got the paper?" he asked.

She handed him the Kansas City *Star* and he shucked off its brown wrapper and opened it to the sporting page. He folded the *Star* open and propped it against the water pitcher with his cereal dish to steady it, so he could read while he ate.

"Harold," his mother stood in the kitchen doorway, "Harold, please don't muss up the paper. Your father can't read his *Star* if it's been mussed."

"I won't muss it," Krebs said.

His sister sat down at the table and watched him while he read.

"We're playing indoor over at school this afternoon," she said. "I'm going to pitch."

"Good," said Krebs. "How's the old wing?"

"I can pitch better than lots of the boys. I tell them all you taught me. The other girls aren't much good."

"Yeah?" said Krebs.

"I tell them all you're my beau. Aren't you my beau, Hare?"

"You bet."

"Couldn't your brother really be your beau just because he's your brother?"

"I don't know."

"Sure you know. Couldn't you be my beau, Hare, if I was old enough and if you wanted to?"

"Sure. You're my girl now."

"Am I really your girl?"

"Sure."

"Do you love me?"

"Uh, huh."

"Will you love me always?"

"Sure."

"Will you come over and watch me play indoor?"

"Maybe."

"Aw, Hare, you don't love me. If you loved me, you'd want to come over and watch me play indoor."

Kreb's mother came into the dining-room from the kitchen. She carried a plate with two fried eggs and some crisp bacon on it and a plate of buckwheat cakes.

"You run along, Helen," she said. "I want to talk to Harold."

She put the eggs and bacon down in front of him and brought in a jug of maple syrup for the buckwheat cakes. Then she sat down across the table from Krebs.

"I wish you'd put down the paper a minute, Harold," she said.

Krebs took down the paper and folded it.

"Have you decided what you are going to do yet, Harold?" his mother said, taking off her glasses.

"No," said Krebs.

"Don't you think it's about time?" His mother did not say this in a mean way. She seemed worried.

"I hadn't thought about it," Krebs said.

"God has some work for everyone to do," his mother said. "There can be no idle hands in His Kingdom."

"I'm not in His Kingdom," Krebs said.

"We are all of us in His Kingdom."

Krebs felt embarrassed and resentful as always.

"I've worried about you so much, Harold," his mother went on. "I know the temptations you must have been exposed to. I know how weak men are. I know what your own dear grandfather, my own father, told us about the Civil War and I have prayed for you. I pray for you all day long, Harold."

Krebs looked at the bacon fat hardening on his plate.

"Your father is worried, too," his mother went on. "He thinks you have lost your ambition, that you haven't got a definite aim in life. Charley Simmons, who is just your age, has a good job and is going to be married. The boys are all settling down; they're all determined to get somewhere; you can see that boys like Charley Simmons are on their way to being really a credit to the community."

Krebs said nothing.

"Don't look that way, Harold," his mother said. "You know we love you and I want to tell you for your own good how matters stand. Your father does not want to hamper your freedom. He thinks you should be allowed to drive the car. If you want to take some of the nice girls out riding with you, we are only too pleased. We want you to enjoy yourself. But you are going to have to settle down to work, Harold. Your father doesn't care what you start in at. All work is honorable as he says. But you've got to make a start at something. He asked me to speak to you this morning and then you can stop in and see him at his office."

"Is that all?" Krebs said.

"Yes. Don't you love your mother, dear boy?"

"No," Krebs said.

His mother looked at him across the table. Her eyes were shiny. She started crying.

"I don't love anybody," Krebs said.

It wasn't any good. He couldn't tell her, he couldn't make her see it. It was silly to have said it. He had only hurt her. He went over and took hold of her arm. She was crying with her head in her hands.

"I didn't mean it," he said. "I was just angry at something. I didn't mean I
didn't love you."

His mother went on crying. Krebs put his arm on her shoulder.

"Can't you believe me, mother?"

His mother shook her head.

"Please, please, mother. Please believe me."

"All right," his mother said chokily. She looked up at him. "I believe you,
Harold."

Krebs kissed her hair. She put her face up to him.

"I'm your mother," she said. "I held you next to my heart when you were a
tiny baby."

Krebs felt sick and vaguely nauseated.

"I know, Mummy," he said. "I'll try and be a good boy for you."

"Would you kneel and pray with me, Harold?" his mother asked.

They knelt down beside the dining-room table and Krebs's mother prayed.

"Now, you pray, Harold," she said.

"I can't," Krebs said.

"Try, Harold."

"I can't."

"Do you want me to pray for you?"

"Yes."

So his mother prayed for him and then they stood up and Krebs kissed his
mother and went out of the house. He had tried so to keep his life from being
complicated. Still, none of it had touched him. He had felt sorry for his mother
and she had made him lie. He would go to Kansas City and get a job and she
would feel all right about it. There would be one more scene maybe before he got
away. He would not go down to his father's office. He would miss that one. He
wanted his life to go smoothly. It had just gotten going that way. Well, that was
all over now, anyway. He would go over to the schoolyard and watch Helen play
indoor baseball.

BARN BURNING [14]

The store in which the Justice of the Peace's court was sitting smelled of cheese.
The boy, crouched on his nail keg at the back of the crowded room, knew he
smelled cheese, and more: from where he sat he could see the ranked shelves
close-packed with the solid, squat, dynamic shapes of tin cans whose labels his
stomach read, not from the lettering which meant nothing to his mind but from
the scarlet devils and the silver curve of fish—this, the cheese which he knew he
smelled and the hermetic meat which his intestines believed he smelled coming in
intermittent gusts momentary and brief between the other constant one, the smell
and sense just a little of fear because mostly of despair and grief, the old fierce

[14] By William Faulkner.

pull of blood. He could not see the table where the Justice sat and before which his father and his father's enemy (*our enemy* he thought in that despair; *ourn! mine and hisn both! He's my father!*) stood, but he could hear them, the two of them that is, because his father had said no word yet:

"But what proof have you, Mr. Harris?"

"I told you. The hog got into my corn. I caught it up and sent it back to him. He had no fence that would hold it. I told him so, warned him. The next time I put the hog in my pen. When he came to get it I gave him enough wire to patch up his pen. The next time I put the hog up and kept it. I rode down to his house and saw the wire I gave him still rolled on to the spool in his yard. I told him he could have the hog when he paid me a dollar pound fee. That evening a nigger came with the dollar and got the hog. He was a strange nigger. He said, 'He say to tell you wood and hay kin burn,' I said, 'What?' 'That whut he say to tell you,' the nigger said. 'Wood and hay kin burn.' That night my barn burned. I got the stock out but I lost the barn."

"Where is the nigger? Have you got him?"

"He was a strange nigger, I tell you. I don't know what became of him."

"But that's not proof. Don't you see that's not proof?"

"Get that boy up here. He knows." For a moment the boy thought too that the man meant his older brother until Harris said, "Not him. The little one. The boy," and, crouching, small for his age, small and wiry like his father, in patched and faded jeans even too small for him, with straight, uncombed, brown hair and eyes gray and wild as storm scud, he saw the men between himself and the table part and become a lane of grim faces, at the end of which he saw the Justice, a shabby, collarless, graying man in spectacles, beckoning him. He felt no floor under his bare feet; he seemed to walk beneath the palpable weight of the grim turning faces. His father, stiff in his black Sunday coat donned not for the trial but for the moving, did not even look at him. *He aims for me to lie,* he thought, again with that frantic grief and despair. *And I will have to do hit.*

"What's your name, boy?" the Justice said.

"Colonel Sartoris Snopes," the boy whispered.

"Hey?" the Justice said. "Talk louder. Colonel Sartoris? I reckon anybody named for Colonel Sartoris in this country can't help but tell the truth, can they?" The boy said nothing. *Enemy! Enemy!* he thought; for a moment he could not even see, could not see that the Justice's face was kindly nor discern that his voice was troubled when he spoke to the man named Harris: "Do you want me to question this boy?" But he could hear, and during those subsequent long seconds while there was absolutely no sound in the crowded little room save that of quiet and intent breathing it was as if he had swung outward at the end of a grape vine, over a ravine, and at the top of the swing had been caught in a prolonged instant of mesmerized gravity, weightless in time.

"No!" Harris said violently, explosively. "Damnation! Send him out of here!" Now time, the fluid world, rushed beneath him again, the voices coming to him again through the smell of cheese and sealed meat, the fear and despair and the old grief of blood:

"This case is closed. I can't find against you, Snopes, but I can give you advice. Leave this county and don't come back to it."

His father spoke for the first time, his voice cold and harsh, level, without emphasis: "I aim to. I don't figure to stay in a country among people who . . ." he said something unprintable and vile, addressed to no one.

"That'll do," the Justice said. "Take your wagon and get out of this country before dark. Case dismissed."

His father turned, and he followed the stiff black coat, the wiry figure walking a little stiffly from where a Confederate provost's man's musket ball had taken him in the heel on a stolen horse thirty years ago, followed the two backs now, since his older brother had appeared from somewhere in the crowd, no taller than the father but thicker, chewing tobacco steadily, between the two lines of grim-faced men and out of the store and across the worn gallery and down the sagging steps and among the dogs and half-grown boys in the mild May dust, where as he passed a voice hissed:

"Barn burner!"

Again he could not see, whirling; there was a face in a red haze, moonlike, bigger than the full moon, the owner of it half again his size, he leaping in the red haze toward the face, feeling no blow, feeling no shock when his head struck the earth, scrabbling up and leaping again, feeling no blow this time either and tasting no blood, scrabbling up to see the other boy in full flight and himself already leaping into pursuit as his father's hand jerked him back, the harsh, cold voice speaking above him: "Go get in the wagon."

It stood in a grove of locusts and mulberries across the road. His two hulking sisters in their Sunday dresses and his mother and her sister in calico and sun-bonnets were already in it, sitting on and among the sorry residue of the dozen and more movings which even the boy could remember—the battered stove, the broken beds and chairs, the clock inlaid with mother-of-pearl, which would not run, stopped at some fourteen minutes past two o'clock of a dead and forgotten day and time, which had been his mother's dowry. She was crying, though when she saw him she drew her sleeve across her face and began to descend from the wagon. "Get back," the father said.

"He's hurt. I got to get some water and wash his . . ."

"Get back in the wagon," his father said. He got in too, over the tail-gate. His father mounted to the seat where the older brother already sat and struck the gaunt mules two savage blows with the peeled willow, but without heat. It was not even sadistic; it was exactly that same quality which in later years would cause his descendants to over-run the engine before putting a motor car into motion, striking and reining back in the same movement. The wagon went on, the store with its quiet crowd of grimly watching men dropped behind; a curve in the road hid it. *Forever* he thought. *Maybe he's done satisfied now, now that he has* . . . stopping himself, not to say it aloud even to himself. His mother's hand touched his shoulder.

"Does hit hurt?" she said.

"Naw," he said. "Hit don't hurt. Lemme be."

"Can't you wipe some of the blood off before hit dries?"

"I'll wash to-night," he said. "Lemme be, I tell you."

The wagon went on. He did not know where they were going. None of them ever did or ever asked, because it was always somewhere, always a house of sorts waiting for them a day or two days or even three days away. Likely his father had already arranged to make a crop on another farm before he . . . Again he had to stop himself. He (the father) always did. There was something about his wolflike independence and even courage when the advantage was at least neutral which impressed strangers, as if they got from his latent ravening ferocity not so much a sense of dependability as a feeling that his ferocious conviction in the rightness of his own actions would be of advantage to all whose interest lay with his.

That night they camped, in a grove of oaks and beeches where a spring ran. The nights were still cool and they had a fire against it, of a rail lifted from a nearby fence and cut into lengths—a small fire, neat, niggard almost, a shrewd fire; such fires were his father's habit and custom always, even in freezing weather. Older, the boy might have remarked this and wondered why not a big one; why should not a man who had not only seen the waste and extravagance of war, but who had in his blood an inherent voracious prodigality with material not his own, have burned everything in sight? Then he might have gone a step farther and thought that that was the reason: that niggard blaze was the living fruit of nights passed during those four years in the woods hiding from all men, blue or gray, with his strings of horses (captured horses, he called them). And older still, he might have divined the true reason: that the element of fire spoke to some deep mainspring of his father's being, as the element of steel or of powder spoke to other men, as the one weapon for the preservation of integrity, else breath were not worth the breathing, and hence to be regarded with respect and used with discretion.

But he did not think this now and he had seen those same niggard blazes all his life. He merely ate his supper beside it and was already half asleep over his iron plate when his father called him, and once more he followed the stiff back and ruthless limp, up the slope and on to the starlit road where, turning, he could see his father against the stars but without face or depth—a shape black, flat, and bloodless as though cut from tin in the iron folds of the frockcoat which had not been made for him, the voice harsh like tin and without heat like tin:

"You were fixing to tell them. You would have told him." He didn't answer. His father struck him with the flat of his hand on the side of the head, hard but without heat, exactly as he had struck the two mules at the store, exactly as he would strike either of them with any stick in order to kill a horse fly, his voice still without heat or anger: "You're getting to be a man. You got to learn. You got to learn to stick to your own blood or you ain't going to have any blood to stick to you. Do you think either of them, any man there this morning, would? Don't you know all they wanted was a chance to get at me because they knew I had them beat? Eh?" Later, twenty years later, he was to tell himself, "If I had said they wanted only truth, justice, he would have hit me again." But now he said nothing. He was not crying. He just stood there. "Answer me," his father said.

"Yes," he whispered. His father turned.

"Get on to bed. We'll be there tomorrow."

Tomorrow they were there. In the early afternoon the wagon stopped before a paintless two-room house identical almost with the dozen others it had stopped before even in the boy's ten years, and again, as on the other dozen occasions, his mother and aunt got down and began to unload the wagon, although his two sisters and his father and brother had not moved.

"Likely hit ain't fitten for hawgs," one of the sisters said.

"Nevertheless, fit it will and you'll hog it and like it," his father said. "Get out of them chairs and help your Ma unload."

The two sisters got down, big, bovine, in a flutter of cheap ribbons; one of them drew from the jumbled wagon bed a battered lantern, the other a worn broom. His father handed the reins to the older son and began to climb stiffly over the wheel. "When they get unloaded, take the team to the barn and feed them." Then he said, and at first the boy thought he was still speaking to his brother: "Come with me."

"Me?" he said.

"Yes," his father said. "You."

"Abner," his mother said. His father paused and looked back—the harsh level stare beneath the shaggy, graying, irascible brows.

"I reckon I'll have a word with the man that aims to begin tomorrow owning me body and soul for the next eight months."

They went back up the road. A week ago—or before last night, that is—he would have asked where they were going, but not now. His father had struck him before last night but never before had he paused afterward to explain why; it was as if the blow and the following calm, outrageous voice still rang, repercussed, divulging nothing to him save the terrible handicap of being young, the light weight of his few years, just heavy enough to prevent his soaring free of the world as it seemed to be ordered but not heavy enough to keep him footed solid in it, to resist it and try to change the course of its events.

Presently he could see the grove of oaks and cedars and the other flowering trees and shrubs where the house would be, though not the house yet. They walked beside a fence massed with honeysuckle and Cherokee roses and came to a gate swinging open between two brick pillars, and now, beyond a sweep of drive, he saw the house for the first time and at that instant he forgot his father and the terror and despair both, and even when he remembered his father again (who had not stopped) the terror and despair did not return. Because, for all the twelve movings, they had sojourned until now in a poor country, a land of small farms and fields and houses, and he had never seen a house like this before. *Hit's big as a courthouse* he thought quietly, with a surge of peace and joy whose reason he could not have thought into words, being too young for that: *They are safe from him. People whose lives are a part of this peace and dignity are beyond his touch,*

he no more to them than a buzzing wasp: capable of stinging for a little moment
but that's all; the spell of this peace and dignity rendering even the barns and
stable and cribs which belong to it impervious to the puny flames he might con-
trive . . . this, the peace and joy, ebbing for an instant as he looked again at the
stiff black back, the stiff and implacable limp of the figure which was not dwarfed
by the house, for the reason that it had never looked big anywhere and which now,
against the serene columned backdrop, had more than ever that impervious quality
of something cut ruthlessly from tin, depthless, as though, sidewise to the sun, it
would cast no shadow. Watching him, the boy remarked the absolutely undeviat-
ing course which his father held and saw the stiff foot come squarely down in a
pile of fresh droppings where a horse had stood in the drive and which his father
could have avoided by a simple change of stride. But it ebbed only for a moment,
though he could not have thought this into words either, walking on in the spell
of the house, which he could even want but without envy, without sorrow, certainly never with that ravening and jealous rage which unknown to him walked
in the ironlike black coat before him: *Maybe he will feel it too. Maybe it will even*
change him now from what maybe he couldn't help but be.

They crossed the portico. Now he could hear his father's stiff foot as it came
down on the boards with clocklike finality, a sound out of all proportion to the
displacement of the body it bore and which was not dwarfed either by the white
door before it, as though it had attained to a sort of vicious and ravening minimum not to be dwarfed by anything—the flat, wide, black hat, the formal coat of
broadcloth which had once been black but which had now that friction-glazed
greenish cast of the bodies of old house flies, the lifted sleeve which was too large,
the lifted hand like a curled claw. The door opened so promptly that the boy knew
the Negro must have been watching them all the time, an old man with neat
grizzled hair, in a linen jacket, who stood barring the door with his body, saying,
"Wipe yo foots, white man, fo you come in here. Major ain't home nohow."

"Get out of my way, nigger," his father said, without heat too, flinging the door
back and the Negro also and entering, his hat still on his head. And now the boy
saw the prints of the stiff foot on the door jamb and saw them appear on the pale
rug behind the machinelike deliberation of the foot which seemed to bear (or
transmit) twice the weight which the body compassed. The Negro was shouting
"Miss Lula! Miss Lula!" somewhere behind them, then the boy, deluged as though
by a warm wave by a suave turn of carpeted stair and a pendant glitter of chan-
deliers and a mute gleam of gold frames, heard the swift feet and saw her too,
a lady—perhaps he had never seen her like before either—in a gray, smooth gown
with lace at the throat and an apron tied at the waist and the sleeves turned back,
wiping cake or biscuit dough from her hands with a towel as she came up the hall,
looking not at his father at all but at the tracks on the blond rug with an expression of incredulous amazement.

"I tried," the Negro cried. "I tole him to . . ."

"Will you please go away?" she said in a shaking voice. "Major de Spain is not
at home. Will you please go away?"

His father had not spoken again. He did not speak again. He did not even look at her. He just stood stiff in the center of the rug, in his hat, the shaggy iron-gray brows twitching slightly above the pebble-colored eyes as he appeared to examine the house with brief deliberation. Then with the same deliberation he turned; the boy watched him pivot on the good leg and saw the stiff foot drag round the arc of the turning, leaving a final long and fading smear. His father never looked at it, he never once looked down at the rug. The Negro held the door. It closed behind them, upon the hysteric and indistinguishable woman-wail. His father stopped at the top of the steps and scraped his boot clean on the edge of it. At the gate he stopped again. He stood for a moment, planted stiffly on the stiff foot, looking back at the house. "Pretty and white, ain't it?" he said. "That's sweat. Nigger sweat. Maybe it ain't white enough yet to suit him. Maybe he wants to mix some white sweat with it."

Two hours later the boy was chopping wood behind the house within which his mother and aunt and the two sisters (the mother and aunt, not the two girls, he knew that; even at this distance and muffled by walls the flat loud voices of the two girls emanated an incorrigible idle inertia) were setting up the stove to prepare a meal, when he heard the hooves and saw the linen-clad man on a fine sorrel mare, whom he recognized even before he saw the rolled rug in front of the Negro youth following on a fat bay carriage horse—a suffused, angry face vanished, still at full gallop, beyond the corner of the house where his father and brother were sitting in the two tilted chairs; and a moment later, almost before he could have put the axe down, he heard the hooves again and watched the sorrel mare go back out of the yard, already galloping again. Then his father began to shout one of the sisters' names, who presently emerged backward from the kitchen door dragging the rolled rug along the ground by one end while the other sister walked behind it.

"If you ain't going to tote, go on and set up the wash pot," the first said.

"You, Sarty!" the second shouted. "Set up the wash pot!" His father appeared at the door, framed against that shabbiness, as he had been against that other bland perfection, impervious to either, the mother's anxious face at his shoulder.

"Go on," the father said. "Pick it up." The two sisters stooped, broad, lethargic; stooping, they presented an incredible expanse of pale cloth and a flutter of tawdry ribbons.

"If I thought enough of a rug to have to git hit all the way from France I wouldn't keep hit where folks coming in would have to tromp on hit," the first said. They raised the rug.

"Abner," the mother said. "Let me do it."

"You go back and git dinner," his father said. "I'll tend to this."

From the woodpile through the rest of the afternoon the boy watched them, the rug spread flat in the dust beside the bubbling washpot, the two sisters stooping over it with that profound and lethargic reluctance, while the father stood over them in turn, implacable and grim, driving them though never raising his voice again. He could smell the harsh homemade lye they were using; he saw his mother come to the door once and look toward them with an expression not anxious now but very like despair; he saw his father turn, and he fell to with the axe and saw from the corner of his eye his father raise from the ground a flattish fragment of field stone and examine it and return to the pot, and this time his mother actually spoke: "Abner. Abner. Please don't. Please, Abner."

Then he was done too. It was dusk; the whippoorwills had already begun. He could smell coffee from the room where they would presently eat the cold food remaining from the mid-afternoon meal, though when he entered the house he realized they were having coffee again probably because there was a fire on the hearth, before which the rug now lay spread over the backs of two chairs. The tracks of his father's foot were gone. Where they had been were now long, water-cloudy scoriations resembling the sporadic course of a lilliputin mowing machine.

It still hung there while they ate the cold food and then went to bed, scattered without order or claim up and down the two rooms, his mother in one bed, where his father would later lie, the older brother in the other, himself, the aunt, and the two sisters on pallets on the floor. But his father was not in bed yet. The last thing the boy remembered was the depthless, harsh silhouette of the hat and coat bending over the rug and it seemed to him that he had not even closed his eyes when the silhouette was standing over him, the fire almost dead behind it, the stiff foot prodding him awake. "Catch up the mule," his father said.

When he returned with the mule his father was standing in the black door, the rolled rug over his shoulder. "Ain't you going to ride?" he said.

"No. Give me your foot."

He bent his knee into his father's hand, the wiry, surprising power flowed smoothly, rising, he rising with it, on to the mule's bare back (they had owned a saddle once; the boy could remember it though not when or where) and with the same effortlessness his father swung the rug up in front of him. Now in the star-light they retraced the afternoon's path, up the dusty road rife with honeysuckle, through the gate and up the black tunnel of the drive to the lightless house, where he sat on the mule and felt the rough warp of the rug drag across his thighs and vanish.

"Don't you want me to help?" he whispered. His father did not answer and now he heard again that stiff foot striking the hollow portico with that wooden and clocklike deliberation, that outrageous overstatement of the weight it carried. The rug, hunched, not flung (the boy could tell that even in the darkness) from his father's shoulder struck the angle of wall and floor with a sound unbelievably loud, thunderous, then the foot again, unhurried and enormous; a light came on in the house and the boy sat, tense, breathing steadily and quietly and just a little fast, though the foot itself did not increase its beat at all, descending the steps now; now the boy could see him.

"Don't you want to ride now?" he whispered. "We kin both ride now," the light within the house altering now, flaring up and sinking. *He's coming down the stairs now,* he thought. He had already ridden the mule up beside the horse block; presently his father was up behind him and he doubled the reins over and slashed the mule across the neck, but before the animal could begin to trot the hard, thin arm came round him, the hard, knotted hand jerking the mule back to a walk.

In the first red rays of the sun they were in the lot, putting plow gear on the mules. This time the sorrel mare was in the lot before he heard it at all, the rider collarless and even bareheaded, trembling, speaking in a shaking voice as the woman in the house had done, his father merely looking up once before stooping again to the hame he was buckling, so that the man on the mare spoke to his stooping back:

"You must realize you have ruined that rug. Wasn't there anybody here, any of your women . . ." he ceased, shaking, the boy watching him, the older brother leaning now in the stable door, chewing, blinking slowly and steadily at nothing apparently. "It cost a hundred dollars. But you never had a hundred dollars. You never will. So I'm going to charge you twenty bushels of corn against your crop. I'll add it in your contract and when you come to the commissary you can sign it. That won't keep Mrs. de Spain quiet but maybe it will teach you to wipe your feet off before you enter her house again."

Then he was gone. The boy looked at his father, who still had not spoken or even looked up again, who was now adjusting the loggerhead in the hame.

"Pap," he said. His father looked at him—the inscrutable face, the shaggy brows beneath which the gray eyes glinted coldly. Suddenly the boy went toward him, fast, stopping as suddenly. "You done the best you could!" he cried. "If he wanted hit done different why didn't he wait and tell you how? He won't git no twenty bushels! He won't git none! We'll gether hit and hide hit! I kin watch . . ."

"Did you put the cutter back in that straight stock like I told you?"

"No, sir," he said.

"Then go do it."

That was Wednesday. During the rest of that week he worked steadily, at what was within his scope and some which was beyond it, with an industry that did not need to be driven nor even commanded twice; he had this from his mother, with the difference that some at least of what he did he liked to do, such as splitting wood with the half-size axe which his mother and aunt had earned, or saved money somehow, to present him with at Christmas. In company with the two older women (and on one afternoon, even one of the sisters), he built pens for the shoat and the cow which were a part of his father's contract with the landlord, and one afternoon, his father being absent, gone somewhere on one of the mules, he went to the field.

They were running a middle buster now, his brother holding the plow straight while he handled the reins, and walking beside the straining mule, the rich black soil shearing cool and damp against his bare ankles, he thought *Maybe this is the end of it. Maybe even that twenty bushels that seems hard to have to pay for just a rug will be a cheap price for him to stop forever and always from being what he used to be;* thinking, dreaming now, so that his brother had to speak sharply to him to mind the mule: *Maybe he even won't collect the twenty bushels. Maybe it will all add up and balance and vanish—corn, rug, fire; the terror and grief, the being pulled two ways like between two teams of horses—gone, done with for ever and ever.*

Then it was Saturday; he looked up from beneath the mule he was harnessing and saw his father in the black coat and hat. "Not that," his father said. "The wagon gear." And then, two hours later, sitting in the wagon bed behind his father and brother on the seat, the wagon accomplished a final curve, and he saw the weathered paintless store with its tattered tobacco- and patent-medicine posters and the tethered wagons and saddle animals below the gallery. He mounted the gnawed steps behind his father and brother, and there again was the lane of quiet, watching faces for the three of them to walk through. He saw the man in spectacles sitting at the plank table and he did not need to be told this was a Justice of the Peace; he sent one glare of fierce, exultant, partisan defiance at the man in collar and cravat now, whom he had seen but twice before in his life, and that on a galloping horse, who now wore on his face an expression not of rage but of amazed unbelief which the boy could not have known was at the incredible circumstance of being sued by one of his own tenants, and came and stood against his father and cried at the Justice: "He ain't done it! He ain't burnt . . ."

"Go back to the wagon," his father said.

"Burnt?" the Justice said. "Do I understand this rug was burned too?"

"Does anybody here claim it was?" his father said. "Go back to the wagon." But he did not, he merely retreated to the rear of the room, crowded as that other had been, but not to sit down this time, instead, to stand pressing among the motionless bodies, listening to the voices:

"And you claim twenty bushels of corn is too high for the damage you did to the rug?"

"He brought the rug to me and said he wanted the tracks washed out of it. I washed the tracks out and took the rug back to him."

"But you didn't carry the rug back to him in the same condition it was in before you made the tracks on it."

His father did not answer, and now for perhaps half a minute there was no sound at all save that of breathing, the faint, steady suspiration of complete and intent listening.

"You decline to answer that, Mr. Snopes?" Again his father did not answer. "I'm going to find against you, Mr. Snopes. I'm going to find that you were responsible for the injury to Major de Spain's rug and hold you liable for it. But twenty bushels of corn seems a little high for a man in your circumstances to have to pay. Major de Spain claims it cost a hundred dollars. October corn will be worth about fifty cents. I figure that if Major de Spain can stand a ninety-five dollar loss on something he paid cash for, you can stand a five-dollar loss you haven't earned yet. I hold you in damages to Major de Spain to the amount of ten bushels of corn over and above your contract with him, to be paid to him out of your crop at gathering time. Court adjourned."

It had taken no time hardly, the morning was but half begun. He thought they would return home and perhaps back to the field, since they were late, far behind all other farmers. But instead his father passed on behind the wagon, merely indicating with his hand for the older brother to follow with it, and crossed the road toward the blacksmith shop opposite, pressing on after his father, overtaking him, speaking, whispering up at the harsh, calm face beneath the weathered hat: "He won't git no ten bushels neither. He won't git one. We'll . . ." until his father glanced for an instant down at him, the face absolutely calm, the grizzled eyebrows tangled above the cold eyes, the voice almost pleasant, almost gentle:

"You think so? Well, we'll wait till October anyway."

The matter of the wagon—the setting of a spoke or two and the tightening of the tires—did not take long either, the business of the tires accomplished by driving the wagon into the spring branch behind the shop and letting it stand there, the mules nuzzling into the water from time to time, and the boy on the seat with the idle reins, looking up the slope and through the sooty tunnel of the shed where the slow hammer rang and where his father sat on an upended cypress bolt, easily, either talking or listening, still sitting there when the boy brought the dripping wagon up out of the branch and halted it before the door.

"Take them on to the shade and hitch," his father said. He did so and returned. His father and the smith and a third man squatting on his heels inside the door were talking, about crops and animals; the boy, squatting too in the ammoniac dust and hoof-parings and scales of rust, heard his father tell a long and unhurried story out of the time before the birth of the older brother even when he had been a professional horsetrader. And then his father came up beside him where he stood before a tattered last year's circus poster on the other side of the store, gazing rapt and quiet at the scarlet horses, the incredible poisings and convolutions of tulle and tights and the painted leers of comedians, and said, "It's time to eat."

But not at home. Squatting beside his brother against the front wall, he watched his father emerge from the store and produce from a paper sack a segment of cheese and divide it carefully and deliberately into three with his pocket knife and produce crackers from the same sack. They all three squatted on the gallery and ate, slowly, without talking; then in the store again, they drank from a tin dipper tepid water smelling of the cedar bucket and of living beech trees. And still they did not go home. It was a horse lot this time, a tall rail fence upon and along which men stood and sat and out of which one by one horses were led, to be walked and trotted and then cantered back and forth along the road while the slow swapping and buying went on and the sun began to slant westward, they—the three of them—watching and listening, the older brother with his muddy eyes and his steady, inevitable tobacco, the father commenting now and then on certain of the animals, to no one in particular.

It was after sundown when they reached home. They ate supper by lamplight, then, sitting on the doorstep, the boy watched the night fully accomplish, listening to the whippoorwills and the frogs, when he heard his mother's voice: "Abner! No! No! Oh, God. Oh, God. Abner!" and he rose, whirled, and saw the altered light through the door where a candle stub now burned in a bottle neck on the table and his father, still in the hat and coat, at once formal and burlesque as though dressed carefully for some shabby and ceremonial violence, emptying the reservoir of the lamp back into the five-gallon kerosene can from which it had been filled, while the mother tugged at his arm until he shifted the lamp to the other hand and flung her back, not savagely or viciously, just hard, into the wall, her hands flung out against the wall for balance, her mouth open and in her face the same quality of hopeless despair as had been in her voice. Then his father saw him standing in the door.

"Go to the barn and get that can of oil we were oiling the wagon with," he said. The boy did not move. Then he could speak.

"What . . ." he cried. "What are you . . ."

"Go get that oil," his father said. "Go."

Then he was moving, running, outside the house, toward the stable: this the old habit, the old blood which he had not been permitted to choose for himself, which had been bequeathed him willy nilly and which had run for so long (and who knew where, battening on what of outrage and savagery and lust) before it came to him. *I could keep on*, he thought. *I could run on and on and never look back, never need to see his face again. Only I can't. I can't,* the rusted can in his hand now, the liquid sploshing in it as he ran back to the house and into it, into the sound of his mother's weeping in the next room, and handed the can to his father.

"Ain't you going to even send a nigger?" he cried "At least you sent a nigger before!"

This time his father didn't strike him. The hand came even faster than the blow had, the same hand which had set the can on the table with almost excruciating care flashing from the can toward him too quick for him to follow it, gripping him by the back of his shirt and on to tiptoe before he had seen it quit the can, the face stooping at him in breathless and frozen ferocity, the cold, dead voice speaking over him to the older brother who leaned against the table, chewing with that steady, curious, sidewise motion of cows:

"Empty the can into the big one and go on. I'll catch up with you."

"Better tie him up to the bedpost," the brother said.

"Do like I told you," the father said. Then the boy was moving, his bunched shirt and the hard, bony hand between his shoulder-blades, his toes just touching the floor, across the room and into the other one, past the sisters sitting with spread heavy thighs in the two chairs over the cold hearth, and to where his mother and aunt sat side by side on the bed, the aunt's arms about his mother's shoulders.

"Hold him," the father said. The aunt made a startled movement. "Not you," the father said. "Lennie. Take hold of him. I want to see you do it." His mother took him by the wrist. "You'll hold him better than that. If he gets loose don't you know what he is going to do? He will go up yonder." He jerked his head toward the road. "Maybe I'd better tie him."

"I'll hold him," his mother whispered.

"See you do then." Then his father was gone, the stiff foot heavy and measured upon the boards, ceasing at last.

Then he began to struggle. His mother caught him in both arms, he jerking and wrenching at them. He would be stronger in the end, he knew that. But he had no time to wait for it. "Lemme go!" he cried. "I don't want to have to hit you!"

"Let him go!" the aunt said. "If he don't go, before God, I am going up there myself!"

"Don't you see I can't?" his mother cried. "Sarty! Sarty! No! No! Help me Lizzie!"

Then he was free. His aunt grasped at him but it was too late. He whirled, running, his mother stumbled forward on to her knees behind him, crying to the nearer sister: "Catch him, Net! Catch him!" But that was too late too, the sister (the sisters were twins, born at the same time, yet either of them now gave the impression of being, encompassing as much living meat and volume and weight as any other two of the family) not yet having begun to rise from the chair, her head, face, alone merely turned, presenting to him in the flying instant an astonishing expanse of young female features untroubled by any surprise even, wearing only an expression of bovine interest. Then he was out of the room, out of the house, in the mild dust of the starlit road and the heavy rifeness of honeysuckle, the pale ribbon unspooling with terrific slowness under his running feet, reaching the gate at last and turning in, running, his heart and lungs drumming, on up the drive toward the lighted door. He did not knock, he burst in, sobbing for breath, incapable for the moment of speech; he saw the astonished face of the Negro in the linen jacket without knowing when the Negro had appeared.

"De Spain!" he cried, panted. "Where's . . ." then he saw the white man too emerging from a white door down the hall. "Barn!" he cried. "Barn!"

"What?" the white man said. "Barn?"

"Yes!" the boy cried. "Barn!"

"Catch him!" the white man shouted.

But it was too late this time too. The Negro grasped his shirt, but the entire sleeve, rotten with washing, carried away, and he was out that door too and in the drive again, and had actually never ceased to run even while he was screaming into the white man's face.

Behind him the white man was shouting, "My horse! Fetch my horse!" and he thought for an instant of cutting across the park and climbing the fence into the road, but he did not know the park nor how high the vine-massed fence might be and he dared not risk it. So he ran on down the drive, blood and breath roaring; presently he was in the road again though he could not see it. He could not hear either: the galloping mare was almost upon him before he heard her, and even then he held his course, as if the very urgency of his wild grief and need must in a moment more find him wings, waiting until the ultimate instant to hurl himself aside and into the weed-choked roadside ditch as the horse thundered past and on, for an instant in furious silhouette against the stars, the tranquil early summer night sky which, even before the shape of the horse and rider vanished, stained abruptly and violently upward: a long, swirling roar incredible and soundless, blotting the stars, and he springing up and into the road again, running again, knowing it was too late yet still running even after he heard the shot and, an instant later, two shots, pausing now without knowing he had ceased to run, crying "Pap! Pap!" running again before he knew he had begun to run, stumbling, tripping over something and scrabbling up again without ceasing to run, looking backward over his shoulder at the glare as he got up, running on among the invisible trees, panting, sobbing, "Father! Father!"

At midnight he was sitting on the crest of a hill. He did not know it was mid-night and he did not know how far he had come. But there was no glare behind him now and he sat now, his back toward what he had called home for four days anyhow, his face toward the dark woods which he would enter when breath was strong again, small, shaking steadily in the chill darkness, hugging himself into the remainder of his thin, rotten shirt, the grief and despair now no longer terror and fear but just grief and despair. *Father. My father*, he thought. "He was brave!" he cried suddenly, aloud but not loud, no more than a whisper: "He was! He was in the war! He was in Colonel Sartoris' cav'ry!" not knowing that his father had gone to that war a private in the fine old European sense, wearing no uniform, admitting the authority of and giving fidelity to no man or army or flag, going to war as Malbrouck himself did: for booty—it meant nothing and less than nothing to him if it were enemy booty or his own.

The slow constellations wheeled on. It would be dawn and then sun-up after a while and he would be hungry. But that would be tomorrow and now he was only cold, and walking would cure that. His breathing was easier now and he decided to get up and go on, and then he found that he had been asleep because he knew it was almost dawn, the night almost over. He could tell that from the whippoor-wills. They were everywhere now among the dark trees below him, constant and inflectioned and ceaseless, so that, as the instant for giving over to the day birds drew nearer and nearer, there was no interval at all between them. He got up. He was a little stiff, but walking would cure that too as it would the cold, and soon there would be the sun. He went on down the hill, toward the dark woods within which the liquid silver voices of the birds called unceasing—the rapid and urgent beating of the urgent and quiring heart of the late spring night. He did not look back.

4

Character and
Characterization: II

The Nine Ways to Reveal Character

With respect to any single character, there are only three people who can
reveal anything to the reader: that character himself, any other character in
the action, and the author. (These three voices, incidentally, correspond to a
traditional scheme of point-of-view: first-person-singular, third-person-limited,
and third-person-omniscient. More about this subject in chapter 6.) Each of
these voices has only three generic ways he can "tell" the reader anything:
through his thoughts, through his speech, and through his actions. Therefore,
though there are thousands of specific tricks, there are only nine generic ways
to reveal character. Some of them are thought to be out of fashion nowadays,
but it is only certain ways of using them that are eschewed. All the ways, in
many variations, are still used. Every young writer needs to be introduced to
the range of possibility in characterization before he selects and develops a
limited few methods—before solidified habit patterns cripple his conceptions.

Through Main Character's Thoughts

In the twentieth century, we have preferred to have authors reveal their
characters through dramatic embodiment, so that we have the illusion that the
characters are revealing themselves. One of the ways in which they reveal
themselves is by telling us what their thought processes are, whether these
are self-analysis, analysis of the action, or statements that reveal the level of
their perceptions, their intentions, their blind spots, and so on.

The simplest way for a character to reveal his own thoughts is, of course, to have him relate them directly to the reader. We have tended to dislike this technique when done badly, but accept it readily when done well. Here, for example, is F. Scott Fitzgerald's Nick Carraway analyzing himself directly:

The abnormal mind is quick to detect and attach itself to this quality when it appears in a normal person, and so it came about in college that I was unjustly accused of being a politician because I was privy to the secret griefs of wild, unknown men. Most of the confidences were unsought—frequently I have feigned sleep, preoccupation, or a hostile levity when I realized by some unmistakable sign that an intimate revelation was on the horizon. . . . Reserving judgements is a matter of infinite hope. I am still afraid of missing something, if I forget that, as my father rather snobbishly suggested, and I snobbishly repeat, a sense of the fundamental decencies is parcelled out unequally at birth.[1]

Huckleberry Finn is a good example of a character whose moral dimension is revealed almost exclusively through self-analysis, but indirectly, so that the reader has to draw the conclusions as to character traits. Three times in the novel, Huck struggles with his conscience,[2] trying to convince himself that he should turn Jim in, as any "proper" St. Petersburg citizen would, but knowing in his heart of hearts that he cannot betray his friend. His thoughts at these times not only reveal Huck's moral character, they create the moral dimension of the book. In Chapter XVI, for example, Huck has just saved Jim from the bounty hunters with his story of smallpox on the raft:

I got aboard the raft, feeling bad and low, because I knowed very well I had done wrong, and I see it warn't no use for me to try to learn to do right; . . . Then I thought a minute, and says to myself, hold on,—s'pose you'd a done right and give Jim up; would you felt better than what you do now? No, says I, I'd feel bad—I'd feel just the same way I do now. Well, then, says I, what's the use you learning to do right, when it's troublesome to do right and ain't no trouble to do wrong, and the wages is just the same?

Later, in Chapter XXXI, Huck is having his final and most significant bout with conscience. He has written a letter to Miss Watson, telling her where Jim is, and he is trying to convince himself that he has done "right."

It was a close place. I took [the letter] up, and held it in my hand. I was a trembling, because I'd got to decide, forever, betwixt two things, and I knowed it. I studied a minute, sort of holding my breath, and then says to myself:

[1] *The Great Gatsby* (New York: Scribner's, 1925, 1933), p. 1.
[2] See Richard P. Adams, "The Unity and Coherence of *Huckleberry Finn,*" *Tulane Studies in English,* 6 (1956): 87–103.

"All right, then, I'll *go* to hell"—and tore it up.

It was awful thoughts, and awful words, but they was said. And I let them stay said; and never thought no more about reforming.

In both these cases, as elsewhere, Huck's thoughts reveal to us that he has what Henry Nash Smith so accurately called "A Sound Heart and a Deformed Conscience." [3] The conflict between these two aspects of Huck is the basic plot dilemma in the book.

There are two very serious dangers in the technique; it can easily slip into braggadocio or sentimentality. It is very easy for a character to assume a holier-than-thou (or worse-than-thou) tone, and this tone alienates us in books, as well as in life. And it is also easy for a character to "beg" the reader to respond with more sentiment than the situation warrants. Twain solved both of these problems with Huck's naïveté and his earnest tone. The earnest tone convinces us that these thoughts did actually occur and that Huck is now a mere reporter; the naïveté permits the reader the dramatic irony of knowing more about Huck's mind than Huck himself knows, and this knowledge gives the reader the aesthetically luxurious illusion of being in the position of Huck's creator.

Some reader evaluation of the quality of Huck's thought is implicit in what has been said so far, but it is also possible to make the quality of thought the primary characteristic of a person. In Eudora Welty's "A Piece of News," for example, the simplistic quality of the backwoods characters is revealed through Ruby Fisher's credulous assumption that a woman of the same name, who is mentioned in a newspaper article, is Ruby herself. The reverie this assumption prompts, and the fantasy of wish-fulfillment that follows, are by no means backwoodsy. But the credulous quality of character they reveal allows Mrs. Welty to increase her aesthetic and thematic intensity considerably, without at the same time including an ambitious and possibly distracting character development.

It is, of course, possible to reveal character by calling attention to what a character *does not* think, that is, by pointing out his blind-spots. In William Golding's *Lord of the Flies,* there are several parallels between Robinson Crusoe on his deserted island and the school boys on theirs. Crusoe immediately builds a shelter that passes for a house, sets about to domesticate some animals and plants on the island, and ingeniously constructs a number of simple machines that will help him in coping with his environment. In short, he "invents" materialistic, industrial civilization in miniature. Golding's boys are desultory and inept at building shelter, are wild and primitive in their methods

---

[3] See the essay of that name in Smith's *Mark Twain: The Development of a Writer* (Cambridge, Mass.: Harvard U. Press, 1962). The essay has also been widely reprinted.

of gathering food, and are more concerned with frittering away time in play than in anything industrious or productive. Ralph thinks enough about these things and exerts enough influence to remind us at every stage of what these boys ought to be thinking and doing, if they were good Crusoes. That these are all blind-spots of the boys redoubles at every stage our horror at their advancing savagery.

Through Main Character's Speech

Every character has his own style—his own value system, his own morality, his own vocabulary, his own tone, his own rhythm and way of doing things. Whenever we see him in thought, speech, or action, he reveals this style; he strikes, as Ford Madox Ford remarked, his own special note. This aspect of character is revealed most clearly and effectively in speech.

As has been mentioned earlier, and as Huck's voice illustrates, a character's pronunciation, intonation, rhythm, level of vocabulary, good or bad grammar, in fact all the qualities of his speech, reveal many things about that character's backgrounds, values, sentiments—in short, his life. Consider, for example, the couple that emerges in the following dialog:

A SATURDAY MORNING

"Hey, where you goin'?" he yelled, as his son went out the front door. "Come back here and say where you're goin'! Sonuvabitchin' kid. Where's he goin', Mary?"

"I don't know. D'ya think I keep up with your kid all th' time? And Jesus Christ, do you have to start screaming so early in the morning? and drinking?"

He crumpled his newspaper, reached over, and turned the dial on the TV, muttering about the Saturday morning kiddie-shows on all the channels. He grunted disgustedly about Saturday morning in general. At last, he stood up and yelled, "I'm goin' outside 'n' mow the lawn."

"I know."

"What?'

"I said, good. Now I can clean the front room. But don't decide to go someplace this afternoon; I want to go to the hospital and visit Willie."

"D'ya hafta go every day? He's gonna be in there two months. I'm not gonna be a chauffeur."

"If he was your kid, maybe you'd think a little different."

"I told you before—that don't matter. I raised him like my own kid. I'm payin' the bills. What d'ya want from me? I been drivin' you there every day for two weeks."

"He almo—"

"I know, I know, but he's okay now. I'm tired of hangin' 'round that place all th' time. I got a right to live a little. Take a bus, or sumpthin', 'n' get off o' my back."

"Yeah, you got it so hard. Maybe you should get the sympathy. Maybe you should've been there instead. Maybe they should've jumped you in the alley."

"He was lookin' for it. He was lookin' for trouble. What th' hell was he doin' on Taylor Street, anyway? Nothin' there but hillbillies and niggers."

"Willie wasn't looking for trouble. He told you that. The cops told you that. Those punks would've jumped anybody. They had the knives. Willie just went to the dance at the church. What kind o' trouble was he looking for at the church?"

"We got a church here; what's he hangin' 'round over there for? We moved out o' there a long time ago."

"Maybe he's still got friends there. There's plenty of people we used to know still living there."

"Aw, I'm goin' out 'n' mow the sonuvabitchin' lawn."

These are type characters, perhaps even stereotypes, easily identified and placed in our socioeconomic structure—and this fact illustrates the limits of revealing character through speech: one is limited, especially in short pieces, to evoking what the reader is already familiar with and can place easily. The writer of dialog is probably limited to types; roundness usually requires much longer development or added use of other techniques.

A good example in which carefully constructed ways for the reader to judge what happened objectively and a longer development reveal a slightly more ambitious character is Ring Lardner's "Haircut." The barber babbles on, telling the story that he thinks is a hunting accident, revealing his own sensibility—or should we say insensibility—revealing not only the horror of the murder, but also the horror of his ignorance.

Consider, for another example, a fiction in verse:

My Last Duchess

Robert Browning

Ferrara:
That's my last Duchess painted on the wall,
Looking as if she were alive. I call
That piece a wonder, now; Fra Pandolf's hands
Worked busily a day, and there she stands.
Will 't please you sit and look at her? I said
'Fra Pandolf' by design, for never read
Strangers like you that pictured countenance,
The depth and passion of its earnest glance,

But to myself they turned (since none puts by
The curtain I have drawn for you, but I)
And seemed as they would ask me, if they durst,
How such a glance came there; so, not the first
Are you to turn and ask thus. Sir, 'twas not
Her husband's presence only, called that spot
Of joy into the Duchess' cheek; perhaps
Fra Pandolf chanced to say, 'Her mantle laps
Over my lady's wrist too much,' or 'Paint
Must never hope to reproduce the faint
Half-flush that dies along her throat.' Such stuff
Was courtesy, she thought, and cause enough
For calling up that spot of joy. She had
A heart—how shall I say?—too soon made glad,
Too easily impressed; she liked whate'er
She looked on, and her looks went everywhere.
Sir, 'twas all one! My favor at her breast,
The dropping of the daylight in the West,
The bough of cherries some officious fool
Broke in the orchard for her, the white mule
She rode with round the terrace—all and each
Would draw from her alike the approving speech,
Or blush, at least. She thanked men,—good! but thanked
Somehow—I know not how—as if she ranked
My gift of a nine-hundred-years-old name
With anybody's gift. Who'd stoop to blame
This sort of trifling? Even had you skill
In speech—which I have not—to make your will
Quite clear to such an one, and say, 'Just this
Or that in you disgusts me; here you miss,
Or there exceed the mark'—and if she let
Herself be lessoned so, nor plainly set
Her wits to yours, forsooth, and made excuse—
E'en then would be some stooping; and I choose
Never to stoop. Oh, sir, she smiled, no doubt,
Whene'er I passed her; but who passed without
Much the same smile? This grew; I gave commands;
Then all smiles stopped together. There she stands
As if alive. Will 't please you rise? We'll meet
The company below, then. I repeat,
The Count your master's known munificence
Is ample warrant that no just pretense
Of mine for dowry will be disallowed;
Though his fair daughter's self, as I avowed

At starting, is my object. Nay, we'll go
Together down, sir. Notice Neptune, though,
Taming a sea-horse, thought a rarity,
Which Claus of Innsbruck cast in bronze for me?

Each line the Duke speaks progressively reveals his character, as well as the scene and his visitor's reactions. With each grandiose heraldic virtue he claims —his position, his wealth, his name—he reveals to us his pettiness, his insensitivity, his ignorance. And he does it all himself, with his own voice.

A still more ambitious example of the same technique is Chekhov's "On the Road." We see Liharev in his long harangue about women; we see him captivating Mlle. Ilovaisky; we see her offer herself, symbolically, bodily, to him; and we see his blindness, his inability to understand his own harangue or perceive its effect—he is living a life entirely of illusion.

The quality of style in a given character depends, of course, upon the quality of mind the writer gives him. This may range from the lowest to the highest—from the man who speaks only in clichés and obscenities, to such a man as Henry Adams (see *The Education of Henry Adams*), whose analogical habit of mind produced an abundance of rich metaphors. The great thing is to convince the reader that the character could speak that way. Very often, setting, dress, subject matter, and other things external to the character himself play a large role in convincing the reader to accept a certain speech style.

There have been times in history when acceptance of speech style was not an important matter. In the nineteenth century before Twain, dialog was a vehicle, not of realism, but of the author's literary pose. Thus the dialog in even such a good book as *The Scarlet Letter* is often abysmally bad, by our standards, and dialog in the dime novels of then and now is worse. Still, these works tell their stories, communicate their themes, and not without some aesthetic power. It is always possible that a new age will not value realistic speech as our does.

Through Main Character's Actions

A man reveals his character most finally and most fully in his actions. Thoughts he can keep to himself; speech is no more than mere promise; but what's done is done; there's no undoing it. And it's only when it's done that it has consequences and meaning. Of course, the fact that a character thinks is an act, and that act of thinking reveals something. And speech, too, is an act and is revealing, even when it is a lie; but when we want to know the *real* man behind the thought and speech, we say "put your money where your mouth is," or "put up or shut up," or "actions speak louder than words."

Actions seem more important in life, too, than mere words or thoughts. People often remember a man by the job he has, or the way he cut his lawn, or the way he stood with his pot-belly sticking out below his belt, longer than they remember his name. It is a familiar scene in a courtroom that people having lost objects they have owned and used for years are unable to describe them accurately, because they have thought of them so long only in relation to the functions they perform. This is more true of adults than of children, who often have not lost their sense of wonder at things and can discover straight pins in sidewalk cracks and other such minutiae.

In fiction, as in life, the best way to know a man is to see him acting his part, to see him acting upon choices that reveal his value system. Actions do reveal motives; it was this connection that caused James to assert that there was no essential difference between characterization and action. As we have seen earlier, he could not conceive of characters that did not cause action, nor of action that did not reveal character. To show a man doing is to show the essential man.

In such a story as Hemingway's "Indian Camp," we are not told that the father is protective toward Nick, but we see him acting protectively. He wakes Nick to take him on a trip, as a father would. In the boat, he puts his arm around Nick and, in general, plays the role of the father initiating his son into the mysteries of life. He also reveals by his actions the shortcomings in his role. He is evasive about the causes of their trip, presumably out of protectiveness toward Nick. He begins instructing Nick in the medical aspects of caesarean section, but shows himself woefully unprepared as a medical doctor —he has brought neither anaesthetic nor scalpel. We infer from his incompetence as a medical man his incompetence as a humane man and, thus, an incompetence to guide Nick successfully through an initiation to life. Hemingway tells us none of this. He merely shows his characters acting and those actions tell us, if we are sensitive to the language of fiction.

Another fine example of characterization by action is in Walter Van Tilburg Clark's story "The Portable Phonograph." The professor is shown to be a professor through the books, the phonograph, the records, and more importantly, in the intelligent foresight he showed in salvaging these items. His role as host, his gesture in using a steel needle in the phonograph, the reverent position of prayer which all four men assume to watch the starting of the phonograph, the ironic amenities of social leave-taking when the music is done, the suspicious housekeeping the professor does, and his making ready of his weapon, all reveal the character and even the theme.

More extreme examples can be found in most any psychiatric case history or in the curiously psychiatric tales of Hawthorne. Father Hooper's assumption of the black veil is almost all the characterization we ever get. His action is his character. Similarly, Wakefield's desertion of his home is almost all the characterization we get of him. In these cases, more than in most, the action is the man.

Here is D. H. Lawrence, showing us how people reveal through their actions a deeper, more important, and truer dimension than is usual for them: In "The Horse Dealer's Daughter," just after the Doctor has pulled the girl from the pond and is reviving her beside the fire:

"I'll go and shift these wet things," he said. But still he had not the power to move out of her presence, until she sent him. It was as if she had the life of his body in her hands, and he could not extricate himself. Or perhaps he did not want to.

Suddenly she sat up. Then she became aware of her own immediate condition. She felt the blankets about her, she knew her own limbs. For a moment it seemed as if her reason were going. She looked round with wild eye, as if seeking something. He stood still with fear. She saw her clothing lying scattered.

"Who undressed me?" she asked, her eyes resting full and inevitable on his face.

"I did," he replied, "to bring you round."

For some moments she sat and gazed at him awfully, her lips parted.

"Do you love me, then?" she asked.

He only stood and stared at her, fascinated. His soul seemed to melt.

She shuffled forward on her knees, and put her arms round him, round his legs, as he stood there, pressing her breasts against his knees and thighs, clutching him with strange, convulsive certainty, pressing his thigh against her, drawing him to her face, her throat, as she looked up at him with flaring, humble eyes of trans-figuration, triumphant in first possession.

"You love me," she murmured, in strange transport, yearning and triumphant and confident. "You love me. I know you love me, I know."

And she was passionately kissing his knees, through the wet clothing, passion-ately and indiscriminately kissing his knees, his legs, as if unaware of everything.[4]

For Lawrence, of course, this Freudian level of almost hypnotic action was the most important; it is there that people reveal character that they are some-times themselves unaware of.

Not only do actions reveal the man, but reactions as well. In a sense, we could say that actions never occur independently in life, but only in a context of interactions. The revelation of action and reaction is the literary counter-part:

So in the second dog watch one day the Red Whiskers, in the presence of the others, under the pretense of showing Billy where a sirloin steak was cut—for

[4] In *The Complete Short Stories,* Vol. II (New York: Viking, 1961).

the fellow had once been a butcher—insultingly gave him a dig under the ribs. Quick as lightning Billy let fly his arm. I dare say he never meant to do quite as much as he did.

Herman Melville, Billy Budd

Melville, of course, is making use of Red Whiskers as a ficelle, to bring out Billy's quick temper and violent reactions, which play a crucial role in the story.

In Melville's "Bartleby, the Scrivener," Bartleby's repeated line: "I prefer not to," reveals the morality that Bartleby stands for; he refuses to act or react in all cases bearing upon the Wall Street activities of the "snug business man."

These are all reactions to people. Reactions to environment, both physical and social, can also be used to reveal a great deal about character. In *Giants in the Earth,* Ole Rölvaag reveals a great deal by showing his people reacting to the bleakness of the northern prairies. They go mad, or fight back with renewed and increased efforts, or submit with the dull taciturnity of people who have a hard life. These are all reactions normally directed at other people, and, indeed, the prairie by its vastness and its importance to prairie-farmers takes on many of the qualities of being a person.

A slightly different reaction to a slightly different environment can be illustrated by Jay Gatsby's reaction to opulence in F. Scott Fitzgerald's *The Great Gatsby.* Gatsby's character is formed by his response to the financial and social structure of the country. Before his experience with the financier on the yacht, he was rather a *tabula rasa,* a blank tablet, upon which is later inscribed the value system of his character. His reactions are the primary revelations of those values.

The same system of reaction is expanded to a naturalistic vision in Theodore Dreiser's *An American Tragedy.* Clyde Griffith's social and economic environment instill in him a desire for glitter and power and transform forever after his reactions to experience. Again, these reactions are the primary revelation of his value system. That the transformation is seen as an expression of sociological and economic determinism makes the story Naturalistic.

A somewhat more complicated depiction of action and interaction is in Chekhov's "The New Villa." The Kucherovs perform an action by building the new villa and moving to the area. The peasants of the village, especially Rodion and Stepanida react in ambiguous ways. These reactions, in turn, cause the Kucherovs and especially Elena Ivanovna, the wife, to perform certain new acts. These new acts cause new reactions among the peasants. These reactions again cause new acts on the part of the Kucherovs. Finally, the patience of the Kucherovs, who merely wanted to be left alone, is exhausted and they sell their villa and go back to Moscow. The fairly complicated pattern of action and reaction is one of the things which make "The New Villa" a very small novel, rather than a short story. The action and reaction not only creates character, but reveals a history of a nation's social structure.

Through Another Character's Thoughts

The second person in the fiction who can tell us characterizing detail is generically any character other than the one being characterized, and, again, he has three ways of telling us his information—by thinking, by speaking, and by acting.

The other character's thoughts are likely to be a very limited means of characterizing the primary character in short fictions, principally because to reveal a subordinate character's thoughts shifts the focus away from the primary character and tends to make the supporting character more important. Usually this would violate the writer's purpose. However, one could conceive of the other character's thoughts playing an important role in a fairly extensive fiction, as is the case of the awesome Mrs. Newsome in Henry James's *Ambassadors* (see p. 85). There, however, the focus is not upon the thoughts themselves, but upon the reaction to them.

Because of the problem in focus, it is common to have the other character's thoughts revealed indirectly, rather than directly. An example is in Faulkner's "Barn Burning." * We are lodged firmly in Sarty's point of view, but his father, Ab Snopes, has attitudes and thoughts toward him that are important in Sarty's motivations. We never see his father's thoughts directly. We infer them only from his actions.

However, if we consider the characterization of the father, Ab Snopes, as primary, we do get a case in which another character's thoughts characterize the focal character. Sarty's fear and respect of his father and his accurate prediction of what his father will think or do next, are very important in revealing Ab to us. Through Sarty's understanding of Major and Mrs. de Spain's thoughts, we get more of the same kind of detail.

Through Another Character's Speech

What the other character says, either directly to the focal character or about him when he is absent, also gives us considerable information about the focal character. What he says to him, of course, comes in the nature of an action and a reaction. Whether he answers militantly or meekly, he characterizes the focal character. Krebs's response to his mother in "Soldier's Home" * has a particular tone. The fact that Krebs assumes this tone toward his mother, tells us that his mother is the kind of woman who demands that particular tone. Krebs's direct dialog characterizes not only himself, but the person he speaks to.

Perhaps it is more common to convey information about the focal character through gossip or discussions at which he is not present. Discounting the characterization which the speakers do of themselves, consider the focal character that emerges from this little sketch titled "Yeah, That's Living":

> "Well, you know them. They never go out anywhere, and when they do she spreads it around afterwards like God Almighty herself. 'Oh, yes, Charles and I did see you at one of those places, didn't we? Let's see. Which one was it? I forget them so easily.' She said something like that to me once, and I gave her the name of a restaurant that doesn't exist, and you know what she said? She said, 'Well, then, it must have been Thursday. Because Friday, we were at the L'Anglais.'"
>
> 'You don't mean it!"
>
> "Yes, I do. Swear to it. Stack of Bibles, and all."
>
> "Well, I didn't think she ever went that far."
>
> "D'you doubt it? I could tell—"
>
> "Oh, no. I don't doubt it. I know for a solid fact that she has them so far in debt that they even have their installments on the installment plan. And what does he do? For a living, I mean? Adds up figures in some office for eight hours a day."
>
> "That's living."
>
> "Yeah, that's living."

Through Another Character's Actions

The most important and most dramatic characterizing which the other character can do is his action and reaction in relation to the focal character. We have already touched upon this, to some extent, in our discussion of kinds of characters. A fragrant character is almost inevitably revealed by other characters' reactions to him. This is, for example, how Mark Twain's character Captain Sellers, is revealed in the following sketch:

> We had some talk about Captain Isaiah Sellers, now many years dead. He was a fine man, a high-minded man, and greatly respected both ashore and on the river. He was very tall, well built, and handsome; and . . . his brethren held him in the sort of awe in which illustrious survivors of a bygone age are always held by their associates. . . .
>
> Whenever Captain Sellers approached a body of gossiping pilots, a chill fell there, and talking ceased. For this reason: whenever six pilots were gathered together, there would always be one or two newly fledged ones in the lot, and the elder ones would be always "showing off" before these poor fellows; making them sorrowfully feel how callow they were, how recent their nobility, and how humble

their degree, by talking largely and vaporously of old-time experiences on the river; always making it a point to date everything back as far as they could, so as to make the new men feel their newness to the sharpest degree possible, and envy the old stagers in the like degree. And how these complacent baldheads *would* swell, and brag, and lie, and date back—ten, fifteen, twenty years, and how they did enjoy the effect produced upon the marveling and envying youngsters!

And perhaps just at this happy stage of the proceedings, the stately figure of Captain Isaiah Sellers, that real and only genuine Son of Antiquity, would drift solemnly into the midst. Imagine the size of the silence that would result on the instant! And imagine the feelings of those baldheads, and the exultation of their recent audience, when the ancient captain would begin to drop casual and indifferent remarks of a reminiscent nature—about islands that had disappeared, and cut-offs that had been made, a generation before the oldest baldhead in the company had ever set his foot in a pilot-house!

Many and many a time did this ancient mariner appear on the scene in the above fashion, and spread disaster and humiliation around him. If one might believe the pilots, he always dated his islands back to the misty dawn of river history; and he never used the same island twice; and never did he employ an island that still existed, or give one a name which anybody present was old enough to have heard of before. If you might believe the pilots, he was always conscientiously particular about little details; "When the state of Mississippi was where Arkansas now is"; and would never speak of Louisiana or Missouri in a general way, and leave an incorrect impression on your mind—no, he would say, "When Louisiana was up the river farther," or "When Missouri was on the Illinois side."

Through Author's Thoughts—Direct Analysis

In the early part of the twentieth century, a general prejudice against the use of the author's analysis in characterizing people grew up. The reaction was against gossipy, moralizing confidences about character by Victorian novelists and had been encouraged by the impetus toward realism and "scientific objectivity" in Literary Naturalism, which had their most influential extension in the effaced point-of-view of Hemingway. Generally speaking, we today prefer to be shown character, not to be told about it. But the technique of telling, through direct author analysis, is time honored and still common—much more common than some would think.

A good example of a somewhat old-fashioned use of the technique is in Washington Irving's "Adventure of the German Student."

On a stormy night, in the tempestuous times of the French revolution, a young German was returning to his lodgings, at a late hour, across the old part of Paris. The lightning gleamed, and the loud claps of thunder rattled through the lofty streets—but I should first tell you something about this young German.

Gottfried Wolfgang was a young man of good family. He had studied for some time at Göttingen, but being of a visionary and enthusiastic character, he had wandered into those wild and speculative doctrines which have so often bewildered German students. His secluded life, his intense application, and the singular nature of his studies, had an effect on both mind and body. His health was impaired; his imagination diseased. He had been indulging in fanciful speculations on spiritual essense, until, like Swedenborg, he had an ideal world of his own around him. He took up a notion, I do not know from what cause, that there was an evil influence hanging over him; an evil genius of spirit seeking to ensnare him and ensure his perdition. Such an idea working on his melancholy temperament, produced the most gloomy effects. He became haggard and desponding. His friends discovered the mental malady preying upon him, and determined that the best cure was a change of scene; he was sent, therefore, to finish his studies amid the splendors and gayeties of Paris.

And here is an example from Nathaniel Hawthorne's *The Scarlet Letter:*

As is apt to be the case when a person stands out in any experience before the community, and at the same time, interferes neither with public nor individual interests and convenience, a species of general regard had ultimately grown up in reference to Hester Prynne. It is to the credit of human nature, that, except where its selfishness is brought into play, it loves more readily than it hates. Hatred, by a gradual and quiet process, will even be transformed to love, unless the change be impeded by a hostility.

For a contemporary example, here is William Golding, explaining a character's inhibition in *Lord of the Flies:*

Here, invisible yet strong, was the taboo of the old life. Round the squatting child was the protection of parents and school and policemen and the law. Roger's arm was conditioned by a civilization that knew nothing of him and was in ruins.

In general, Hemingway is the champion of showing, not telling, but he is also a master of direct analysis. We have already examined his care in *showing* character in "Indian Camp"; we can now look at his similar care in *telling* about character in "Soldier's Home." As we all knew, before Wayne Booth said it, every telling is a showing. The details that we are told about exhibit character, action, scene, for our inspection. In "Soldier's Home," Hemingway tells us about Krebs for about the first half of the story, and he tells us not only what Krebs thinks, but also why he thinks it; that is, Hemingway characterizes Krebs, via direct analysis.

Hemingway tells us directly that Krebs "found that to be listened to at all he had to lie, and . . . [he] had a reaction to war and talking about it. A distaste for everything that had happened to him in the war set in because of the lies he had told." And again, "Krebs acquired the nausea in regard to experience that is the result of untruth or exaggeration, . . . In this way he lost everything." Hemingway's method here is no different from the method of Victorian novelists. The information is important to Krebs's character, and Hemingway simply tells us what has caused Krebs to be the way he is.

In the same story, Hemingway also uses indirect analysis—which is closer to showing than it is to telling. He opens the story, for example, with a simple juxtaposition of two photographs, one showing Krebs in a situation, from which we must infer one value system, the other showing Krebs in a situation that reveals a contrasting value system. The contrast between the two foreshadows the dramatic contrast between Krebs and his mother in the second half of the story. There Hemingway shows us the details of a conflict which, once again, are a kind of indirect analysis of character. This indirect analysis, or showing, is nowadays much, much more important in characterizing than the direct, but the direct reveals no less importantly the author's thoughts about his character.

Through Author's Style

When Wallace Stevens defined style as a technique of discovery, he was asserting an evaluative role for the writer's choice and use of words. We have already noted how choice of such details as a character's pronunciation, vocabulary, and grammar will reveal a great deal about that character. No less importantly, the things a character owns or is associated with reveal his character. In Faulkner's "Barn Burning," for example, a great deal is revealed in the shabby poverty of the Snopeses—"the battered stove, the broken beds and chairs, the clock inlaid with mother-of-pearl, which would not run, stopped at some fourteen minutes past two o'clock of a dead and forgotten day and time, which had been his mother's dowry." (Faulkner's deliberate misplacing of certain modifiers here is also an evaluating device of style.) By contrast, the huge, white house of Major de Spain, the fine rug, the well-clothed servant, the polished bannister, reveal a quite different character and segment of the world.

The writer's choice of detail in even simpler description is also of prime importance. Consider, for example, the evaluating function of detail in the following student sample:

Maggie stands tapping her foot on the pavement. The neon sign, GUY'S BAR —GRILL, flickering above, makes steadily alternating orange, blue, and green reflections on the dark grey pavement, on Maggie, on the dirty grey brick, and the garish red door of the bar. She takes a long drag on her cigarette, shifts her weight, and begins tapping again with the other foot. She drops the cigarette, rubs it out with her shoe, fixes a falling shoulder strap of her lowcut, shiny, bottlegreen dress, then leans back with only her upper back and shoulders against the wall and waits.

Consider the effect of removing or changing such details as the name of the bar, the dirt that seems to be everywhere, or of describing her dress as décolleté and jade-green. With these changes the passage might achieve, instead of the suggestions of a prostitute, the suggestions of a social lioness, waiting in the gala red and blue flashing lights of a theater's marquee.

By careful choice of such evaluative detail, an author can secure sympathy or antipathy for his character. If he shows a young woman, trying to live in honesty and honor toward herself and others, in spite of all immoral pressures, he will secure our sympathy to the extent that our culture values the virtues in the evaluative detail. If he shows us an absent-minded professor with tobacco crumbs on his soiled and wrinkled vest, we find it very difficult to sympathize with him when he slips on a banana peel and falls on his shiny pants. The choice of detail can be detrimental to a positive response, but a negative response may be the essential characterization that the writer wants. Such use of detail is so common among popular writers and is so suspect that it is sometimes called the "Catty School of Writing." [5]

The technique does not differ in more artistic literature, though authors have usually tried to use it more subtly and more honestly. Here, for example, in *Great Expectations,* Dickens shows us Estella evaluating with the same sort of detail as above, but the fact that he shows her using the technique removes it from him and characterizes her:

"He calls the knaves, Jacks, this boy!" said Estella with disdain, before our first game was out. "And what coarse hands he has! And what thick boots!"

Dickens more often uses detail that develops its own evaluation in the process and situation of being presented. For example, in the same novel:

It was then I began to understand that everything in the room had stopped, like the watch and the clock, a long time ago. I noticed that Miss Havisham put down the jewel exactly on the spot from which she had taken it up. As Estella dealt the cards, I glanced at the dressing table again, and saw that the shoe on it, once white, now yellow, had never been worn. I glanced down at the foot from which

---

[5] See Ernest Earnest, "The Catty School of Writing," *Saturday Review,* 40 (June 29, 1957): pp. 9ff.

the shoe was absent, and saw that the silk stocking on it, once white, now yellow, had been trodden ragged. Without this arrest of everything, this standing still of all the pale decayed objects, not even the withered bridal dress on the collapsed form could have looked so like grave-clothes, or the long silk veil like a shroud.

So she sat, corpse-like, as we played at cards, the frillings and trimmings on her bridal dress looking like earthy paper.

Conrad, in *Heart of Darkness,* uses detail to suggest Marlow's groping for words and for an accurate description:

His eyes, of the usual blue, were perhaps remarkably cold, and he certainly could make his glance fall on one as trenchant and heavy as an ax. But even at these times the rest of his person seemed to disclaim the intention. Otherwise, there was only an indefinable, faint expression on his lips, something stealthy—a smile—not a smile—I remember it but can't explain.

And, of course, detail in Conrad is most often symbolically suggestive:

Marlow sat cross-legged right aft, leaning against the mizzen-mast. He had sunken cheeks, a yellow complexion, a straight back, an ascetic aspect, and with his arms dropped, the palms of hands outwards, resembled an idol.

In *The Sun Also Rises,* Hemingway reveals a considerable complexity of character by subtle mixtures of the kinds of detail he reveals about his people. This is not quite the same as the Dickensian habit of putting "a little bit of good in the worst of us," but much more subtle, and, finally, much more life-like. Lady Brett, for example, is described in contradictory terms. Her sexy body is, "built like the hull of a racing yacht," yet she has "hair brushed back like a boy." She is an English woman of title. In fact, the detail invites a thought about the stereotype of the English aristocrat, including such qualities as reserve, propriety, decorum, coldness, class-consciousness, but Brett is anything but these. She is certainly anti-decorous and her chief characteristic is uncontrollable sexual promiscuity. Her internal contradictions help to convince us that she is real. Impotent Jake Barnes is the only character in the book that shows any potential for growth. Most of the other characters in *The Sun Also Rises* are revealed by similar methods.

Lionel Trilling's central character in "Of This Time, Of That Place," is revealed through a similar juxtaposition of opposing details. On the one hand, we are told that Howe is 26 years old, which suggests youth. On the other hand, we are told that he has a Ph.D. from Harvard, which suggests thorough, mature preparation. His life as a poet—he has published two volumes and is ready with a third—suggests a life of intellectuality, but his life on Cape Cod, his use of his legacy, and his social life suggest a dilettante. Howe's problem in the story is revealed through this detail. His dilemma is that he has two concepts of himself, two roles that he cannot choose between—the role of the uncompromising intellectual and the role of the opportune socialite. Howe is thus an excellent example of character precipitating action and action revealing character.

Through Author's Selectivity

Each word on the page represents a choice of the author. Each image the words create; each character, scene, or action the images create; each theme the characters, scenes, and actions create—all are choices of the author. His selection to reveal one word, one image, one detail about a character, rather than to choose among the myriad of other possible details, is the most characterizing action that he can perform.

Such choice is inevitable and usually unconscious, but it is good for the writer to know that it is always functioning in his communication with the reader. The very fact that a writer chooses to write about a given character at all reveals his sensibility, some of his values, and his sense of what is important; it is then his task to make those sensibilities, values, and imports viable. The ways he chooses to make them viable, the ways he chooses for the re-creation of his vision—which characteristics he makes a character take on, what kinds of settings he moves him in, what kinds of incidents he involves him in, and so on—give his character the particular cast and qualities that make it possible for him to perform at all. And within each of these technical choices, the writer's selections of which scenes to dramatize, which to summarize, what point-of-view to use, what focus and emphasis to direct on each given detail further reveal the poise, limits, and finally the theme of the fiction. Different selection among these choices would reveal different people in different concerns. In addition to all this, the writer's selections among the possibilities of structure and theme reveal and govern what is there on the page and what is not. All these choices bear heavily on the character that emerges.

For example, Hemingway's choice to write about Fred Henry in the context of the First World War in Italy was important to what he wanted to say. The choice of environment does a great deal in characterizing Fred Henry. In the first section of the book, Fred and we are often asked why he, an American, is in the Italian army, why he is fighting. His misleading answers reveal his modesty and suggest his idealism.

Hemingway's choice of other characters with whom Fred Henry is involved also reveals a great deal about Fred. In fact, Fred's entire character is revealed through juxtapositions with other characters and in the actions he performs. One comparison shows us that Rinaldi, the scientist, is oriented almost wholly toward physical experience, but that Fred is not. Another comparison shows us that the priest is interested only in spiritual experience, but that Fred is not. Further juxtapositions compare Fred with various soldiers and civilians—he is neither a professional soldier, as is Ettore, nor a coward, as is the hernia victim from Pittsburgh. His sense of responsibility is revealed to us on the one hand by comparison with the peasant attitudes of his ambulance drivers and, on the other, by comparison with the tourist attitudes of Simmons and the other Americans he meets in Milan. All these comparisons reveal important information about Fred's character and help to fix the limitations of his values in relation to experience.

From all of Hemingway's careful juxtapositions, we gradually discover what Fred's character is. The total effect of the comparison is that Fred embodies the syndrome of a pre-World War I idealist. His motives, which we infer from his reactions to other people, fix and define the most important aspects of his character. He is on the good side, fighting a war to end all wars, making the world safe for democracy. Hemingway's selectivity creates him as a Wilsonian idealist before the disillusionment that causes his farewell to arms.

Writing and Using Character Sketches

Balancing Between the Typical and the Unique

The amount and kind of characterizing detail a writer chooses to include in a story will vary with his purposes. But sometimes these purposes are not in harmony with detail actually included. The problem is most often one of finding that particular balance between the typical and the unique that will make each character assume the life-likeness he needs in order to perform his function well. Writers use various forms of character sketches in trying to solve the problem before and during writing.

Minor characters may need very little thought and advance planning. A character who is merely to perform an action and disappear needs no personality; a character who is to fill in background in a scene may need no more than a few characteristics—as: girl, fifteen, pretty, smiles a lot. Such a brief list of characteristics is, in fact, the simplest of character sketches; the real person it represents tends to be some person we know or a personification of our concepts of the typical pretty fifteen-year-old; that is, a lot of this sketch is actually not written down, but carried in our head. This kind of character can stand in the background with little danger, but if and when she begins to act, she needs a few individualizing characteristics—glasses, dirty Levi's, a boy friend, or something. When such detail constitutes a kind of statistical summary of a familiar class, the character is almost certain to be fictionally dead. When some unique characteristic is added, maybe a crooked tooth or a liking for sour grapes, there is a much better chance that an aesthetic type will emerge and be sufficiently life-like for its purpose.

Such a sketch before writing is inevitable, even when the writer is unconscious of it. Many writers make a practice of writing down the list and even of extending it to some length, trying to get a fix on the character, trying to get the personality settled so that it will be consistent. If such a list includes some details about actions in the character's past, or some analysis of his thought processes, the list may amount to a profile.

Some writers recommend a "collage" approach to this kind of sketch—take a few physical details from one person you know or have seen, take an action from another, take a thought from a third, and so on. Since the collage is copied from life, the great danger is that, if the writer puts his character in a situation not copied from life, the character may fail to act at all. However, the collage method has a very strong advantage, especially for the beginning writer: qualities from life, such as a gesture, a tone, a uniqueness that the writer is unaware of, often get incorporated into the character and give it the life-likeness that is needed. Some writers have claimed that they could not begin until they had a collage in mind.

It is a good idea to write down, in extended paragraphs, the more important characterizing actions and thoughts of each major character and to record a bit of his conversation. This would produce a combination list and discussion, a slightly more ambitious sketch. Such a sketch is a good aid in objectifying the character. An extended profile can help free the character from the writer's memory, may give him a bit of independence. This is a first step toward individualizing the character.

Aristotle suggested that, to individualize a character, an author first conceive him in his typicality and, later, add those qualities that made him unique as an individual. Henry Fielding claimed he was following this advice in creating the several inn-keepers in *Tom Jones;* each one has the qualities of his class, but each in his own way. This is, of course, the Classic method of characterization; it aims to make a character simultaneously consistent with a *class* and inconsistent with the *members* of the class. This is probably a habit of mind and, thus, a common procedure with most of us.

Locke implies something quite different—that the writer should begin with his character as a *tabula rasa,* a blank tablet, upon which experience inscribes its lessons. Experience is not only the best teacher, it is the only. And the cumulative responses to experience *are* the items of the character sketch. In a way, the writer is condemned to this method in practice, because he has to begin writing when the reader knows no details at all and build up, step by step, experience by experience, the characteristics he wants. Even direct analysis is an item in such a process. The logical result and full extension of this method would be the environmental determinism and conditioned responses of Literary Naturalism. Environmental determinism and conditioned responses do exist, of course, but most of us resist the notion that they account wholly for experience, Freudian psychology notwithstanding. The use of Freudian Naturalism on a *tabula rasa* is, however, a good way to create a living caricature.

The passage of time and recording of experience suggest a third way of individualizing character—writing the thumbnail biography. Begin with birth and background and record sequentially important incidents, some in scene, some in summary. Unlike Aristotle's and Locke's, this approach allows the recording of irrelevant details. Not all detail that goes into a sketch is likely to get used in a story, but the extra detail often gives the writer the self assurance that supports the character as the reader actually sees him. This sort of character would be comparable to an iceberg; only a part of him would be showing, but the rest would be felt and inferred. Aesthetically, it is very important for a reader to have the feeling that the writer could, if he chose, tell much, much more about his character than he does. If the reader feels that he knows as much about the character as the writer does—and this kind of information is very, very difficult to hide—he will feel that the writer has reached his limits, that he can do no more, that he was straining to achieve what he did. (This is why many beginners' efforts seemed strained.) But, if the writer has detail in reserve—and the reader will know this, too—he communicates the impression that he is in perfect control of everything, that he could do more if he wished, that he has yet more power than the reader imagines.

All these qualities are probably discernible in a good, life-like character in a fiction; an extended character sketch can help the writer to create, objectify, and control them. A good sketch can give life to an imagined character, perhaps even enough that the character—hopefully—will run away with the story. Some of the greatest characters of the greatest artists happily did that.

A Sample Sketch

DAVID AND ALICE GROPER

David Groper was an honest, clean, rather ordinary farm boy with a lot of loose hair and a quick mind, but no especial values, no passionate convictions or dedications. To be sure, he had received a value system from his parents in the thousand little unconscious ways that parents use to transfer their value systems to their children—in church, in school, even in the home, in various forms of approval, disapproval, and emotional blackmail. All this amounted to what anthropologists would call a culture, a set of mentifacts, if not artifacts, that cohere as a studiable group. But no matter. David lost values and parent culture both, suddenly and completely, during his second year at State University.

He was standing in line to see a counselor—not because he needed counsel, but because he had to have a counselor's rubber stamp imprint on his list of courses—when he noticed that Alice, the girl in front of him, had a crooked tooth. He noticed it because he felt very ordinary, and this was out of the ordinary. It was an upper incisor and slanted back toward the base of her tongue. He was fascinated by it and came to notice the rest of the girl; she had a well-formed face, a good complexion, and high, hard, pointed breasts. She was a beauty queen, spoiled by a bad tooth which could have been straightened at age 12, but hadn't been. She was self-conscious about it. She wore a wooden amulet on a leather thong around her neck, Roman sandals, and long stringy hair. He rushed out of the counselor's office to start a conversation with her. They went for coffee, then to dinner, then to a movie, and that night in his room, where women were not allowed, she ruined him by asking "What did your parents ever do for you? I mean, really. What did they ever give you that was of value?"

The following term, they moved to an apartment where they could live together. He let his hair and beard grow; he bought a suede coat, and they began attending student activist meetings. Courses in political science and ethical philosophy rapidly became interesting to David and slowly he became what his professor called brilliant. With a penetrating mind unhampered by inherited pre-conceptions, he cut through arguments to essential issues. In the apartment, they settled down to connubial happiness—supported by money their unsuspecting parents sent—and came to love each other profoundly. In apartment and classroom, David was both conventional and rebellious, and he graduated with honors and a beard.

They married and went on a Peace Corps mission. For two years, they taught tropical Indians fair play, pig raising, elementary reading, cooking, carpentry, and cooperation. When they left, the Indians caught them and beat them, thinking they were trying to escape, and they returned to their homeland to discover that they had worked for eleven cents a day and no thanks. The eleven cents didn't matter, but the no thanks did. Their activist ideals were shaken. To complicate matters, they had run out of birth control pills, and Alice was pregnant.

David went to graduate school and, for more years than it ought to have taken, persisted toward a Ph.D. A frugal life of chip-in-edge dinnerware, diapers, and enforced quiet for study hours wore their love too thin, and in the seventh year of their marriage, each went his bitter way—Alice getting fat and feeling that she had been ill-used, David with alimony and child-support payments he could not make. Part-time and full-time work prolonged his years in graduate school, but he finally took his Ph.D., saying to a friend, "Man, I'm going to take everything I can get. I mean, really. Everything of value I see is fair game to me." He was never again so naïve as to say that aloud.

In time, David became a professor at State University. He published his dissertation and two text-books, and then began writing a continuing series of rather brilliant little monographs on a variety of subjects. They were short, incisive, novel contributions to learning, and, when graduate students began having to buy them, he became moderately and miserlily wealthy. His secretary was the only unbitter person who knew that when a bright young graduate student came to David with a good idea, he invariably said it was worthless and began writing it up himself. David Groper was a cold, hard, bitter man who would pound the desk and shout that his experiences with his parent culture had given him nothing, nothing, nothing at all.

Faults of the Amateur (and Professional)

The use of mere detail is likely to be the first problem that arises whenever anyone tries to "put together" a character. The advice is to use a list, but a list is not a discussion, nor is the accumulation of a list of details necessarily capable of evoking a living character—as you can clearly see from reading the details of character on a crime poster in the local Post Office. All the information is there, but it is all dead. It is mere detail. The writer's task is to make the detail take on a quality of being more than denotation; the detail must be made to tell something about thought process or value system; it must be made to *mean*. Mere detail cannot satisfy readers for long; significant detail can and does.

A hundred, and even fifty, years ago, the use of ordinary detail was not so damaging, was, in fact, quite useful. There was a time when society was so settled that to say that a man went riding in the park on Sunday and smoked cigars was to say a great deal about his social, economic, personal, moral, and political make-up. To show a woman lighting a cigarette in a novel of 1860 was quite a different thing from showing the same scene in 1960. Edith Wharton, at the turn of the century, was perhaps the last great "interior decorator" of fiction, who could make such detail come off. But in our time, we have had few established indexes we could rely upon, and writers have had to find ways of revealing directly, imaginatively, social, economic, moral details about their characters.

Sub-orbiting (shooting high, falling short) is another common failing. It comes of trying too hard to make detail take on the kind of significance mentioned above. In trying to elevate the character, the writer chooses detail that reveals his attempt but does not accomplish his design. The reader feels the high intensity of the attempt, but perceives the low intensity of what is actually on the page; he sees that the symbols are pasted on, so to speak. The writer's reach exceeds his grasp. The antidote to the failing is, of course, the choice of more powerful detail, more intense and perceptive images, more intellectual power, more revealing meanings. Such may be impossible for a poor writer, but even competent writers can improve their attempts, often, by long and hard meditation. The writer should not settle for the first thing that crosses his mind, but make the thing prove its worth; make it show that it is the *mot juste*, just exactly the right and only thing to do the job.

Inconsistency often creeps in during the search for exactly the right and only image that will orbit a meaning. When the writer is looking for the right thing, several surely come to mind; he may tentatively adopt a number of these, expanding his product; but some of these may be inconsistent with others; the impressive volume of the product and the highly personal nature of it encourage the writer to retain everything, with little regard for its perceptiveness or its harmony with the rest and with the intention. A writer may, for example, establish an ordinary character in an early scene; then later comes a scene in which the writer has great personal and emotional interest; he makes his character take on his own personality and gives the character brilliant lines, incisive perceptions, handsome gestures. The inconsistency comes in trying to tell himself and his reader that the two are the same character, or, to put it another way, that the second scene is "in character." His antidotes may be to eliminate one or the other of the offending scenes, or to transform one of them, or to describe in some detail how the early character could and did develop into the later character. Inconsistency often results when the author, not the character, runs away with the story. Fully imagined, life-like characters usually cannot be made to act inconsistently.

Improbability is a related problem; it has more to do with actions than with the other qualities of character. It most often occurs when a conceivable character, delineated in terms we are familiar with and understand, is made to perform some action that is not predictable, even in afterthought. The action is improbable or inconsistent with what we know about the character. The action is unmotivated. The writer's task is to give the reader the detail that will make the action possible, and even probable; he has to explain the motivation. This may mean changing the conception of the character, or it may mean modifying the action to conform with the already established character. It is always possible, in such expanded treatment, to make the improbable probable and the inconsistent consistent, by the power of the explaining detail.

Credibility is largely the same thing, seen from a slightly different point of view. There may be a gap between what the reader sees and what he believes. He may feel that the action or trait or thought in the fiction is quite possible and even probable, but that it didn't happen in this situation or to this character. This may arise from a writer's attributing an inappropriate thought or action to a character. The reader reacts, not by saying that what he sees is impossible, but that, for this character in this situation, it is not life-like.

"But it really happened!" is the young writer's most common defense. The

problem is, however, that whether or not it happened in life, it has not yet *happened,* aesthetically, in the fiction. The imagination has not yet impregnated it with those details, those gestures, those qualities that make it happen, as if anew, in the reader's mind. Although it may have been an experience, it is not yet an experience of the reader's. In this connection, young writers often wonder if they should write from their experience or from imagination. And the answer is both. Until an experience has been fully imagined, it is dangerous to use it in a fiction. It is always dangerous for young writers to write about *places* they have had no experience with, because the lack of experience usually prevents imaginative reality. A possible exception to this lies in research. It is less dangerous for writers to write about *actions* they have not experienced, for the very act of conceiving the act gives it some power from the imagination. There is no guarantee that actions so conceived will be alive, however, for it is possible to merely report action, just as it is possible to merely record detail.

PROJECTS FOR WRITING AND DISCUSSION

A. *ANALYSIS*

1. Reread the scene in the college cafeteria. * What devices of characterization are operating in the sketch? Make a list of these devices. Would you suggest any additional detail that might make the scene more imaginatively real? Try rewriting it, along the expanded lines you conceive.

2. Reread Franklin's anecdote about Rev. Whitfield * and determine what characterizing devices Franklin used. Would you suggest any additional devices or details? Would you suggest any economies that might tighten and increase the effect of the anecdote?

3. What kind of character would you say Captain Isaiah Sellers is? * What makes him so? Make a list of the kinds of detail that Twain uses in creating the character and a parallel list of the techniques he uses to convey each detail. Would you like to add any detail? If so, what technique would you suggest using? Would you like to delete any detail? Why? Are there any details rendered in one technique that you think should be rendered in another? Why?

4. Analyze the sketch of David and Alice Groper.* What kinds of characters are they? What details and techniques make them so? In which moments is each a flat or type character? In which moments, if any, is each round? E. M. Forster thought it quite possible for a flat character to blossom into temporary roundness for a scene, a speech, a gesture; are there any scenes or moments where Alice or David change from flat to round, or from round to flat?

5. Analyze the techniques of revelation in "Soldier's Home" * and "Barn Burning."*

B. *COMPARISON*

1. Compare and contrast the sketch "Yeah, That's Living" * with Washington Irving's sketch of the German student.* What kinds of details are rendered? What kinds of techniques are used in rendering them? What does each accomplish that the other doesn't? What does each do that the other would benefit from? Try doing one in the style of both at once.

2. Compare Twain's scenes of Huck in the boat * with Browning's "My Last Duchess." * Both are sketches designed to render a moral dimension in a character; what are the similarities between them? The differences? Can you imagine one done in the style of the other? Why or why not? Can you imagine either of them done in the style and techniques of Irving's German student? * Why or why not?

3. Compare and contrast the techniques used for rendering David and Alice Groper.* What are the similarities? What are the differences? Try writing an extended sketch of Alice, using the techniques and kinds of details used presently for David, and including David in an ancillary role, similar to Alice's present one.

4. Compare and contrast Harold Krebs ("Soldier's Home" *) and Colonel Sartoris Snopes ("Barn Burning" *).

5. Compare and contrast Captain Isaiah Sellers * and Ahab.*

C. *IMITATION*

1. Reread "A Saturday Morning." * Try writing a scene that you are familiar with in the same techniques. Notice that there is very little narrative or scenic detail, but primarily conversation. You may, if you wish, set the sketch up as a dramatic skit. This will be a kind of Lockean sketch.

2. Write a sketch about your grandfather, or a village character, in the manner of Twain's "Captain Isaiah Sellers." * Pay considerable attention to details that would make the character fragrant. Use the Aristotelian approach to character.

3. Write a sketch in the manner of "David Groper," * paying particular attention to the individualizing influence of experience. This, of course, is the biographical approach, with details from both the Lockean and Aristotelian approaches.

D. *CREATION*

1. Write a sketch of a character with a Freudian trauma. Extend him to caricature dimensions, if you wish.

2. It is a very common literary practice to embody the various facets of a given personality in more than one character. For example, Robert Louis Stevenson wrote of *Dr. Jekyl and Mr. Hyde,* a man with two personalities, one appearing when the other drinks a chemical. These two represent the dark and light sides of a single man, sides that are in us all. Similarly, Dostoyevsky in "The Double," Melville in "Bartleby, the Scrivener," and "Benito Cereno," Conrad in "The Secret Sharer," and so on. Write sketches of doubles that you are familiar with. These need not have great psychological significance, but might be merely social or personal relationships, as, for example, a man and wife as one, a grandfather and a boy as complements, or co-workers, each unable to do a job they can do together.

3. It is also possible, though not common, to embody both sides of a personality in characters separate from the focal character. In Lionel Trilling's "Of This Time, Of That Place," for example, the two sides of Joseph Howe are embodied in students: Tertan is the uncompromising intellectual; Blackburn is the social opportunist. Write three related sketches in which two characters are embodiments of the sides of the one character's dilemma; for example, a young boy may be torn between his genuine desires to be aesthetic, like his mother, and his equally genuine desires to be practical, like his father.

4. It is also common for a writer to let a range of characters represent a range of attitudes. Walter Van Tilburg Clark touched on this in his discussion of the men in "The Portable Phonograph" (see "The Ghost of an Apprehension" *). This kind of maneuver, of course, produces characters who have allegorical significance. Write sketches of a series of allegorical characters, making them human as well as symbolic. Let three soldiers in basic training represent, say, the social, economic, and political points of view in relation to a war they are about to enter. Or let three girls whom a boy is trying to seduce represent the moral, ethical, and practical aspects of courtship and marriage. This last, of course, is not far from the effect that D. H. Lawrence achieved in *Sons and Lovers* with the mother, Miriam, and Clara.

5

Setting

It is very difficult, if not impossible, to imagine anything happening no-where. A necessary part of the vocabulary of our imagination is the time and place in which things happen; we cannot perceive nor understand without some image of time and place. This necessity always results in *things*—land-scapes, furniture, houses, stage props—and the *passage* of time. The nearest exception to this mundanity is probably the later work of Henry James, in which characters move in furnitureless white vacuums, absorbed by their own and others' personalities; but even there, there is setting: the *things* the char-acters handle are their personalities, and their manipulations of them take time. James's settings become highly non-corporeal and subjective contexts, but contexts nonetheless. Setting in fiction is the context, both temporal and spatial, of the images, experiences, causes, and thoughts in which characters interact. These four qualities correspond to the four modes of rhetoric: description, narration, explanation, and argument.

The Roles of Setting

Setting as Description

Because setting is most obviously the main avenue of description in fiction, it is often thought of as the enumeration of the physical and temporal details. And so it is—at its simplest. But here, as in the creation of character, mere detail is likely to be perfectly dead. The writer must choose the particular details that will evoke for the reader the whole image—the details themselves, the implications of detail, the tone and mood that evaluate detail—that is the setting. A mere list of physical and temporal details will not do that.

Anton Chekhov, in a letter to his brother, Alexander (May 10, 1886), suggested that the more common the detail, the less likely it is to evoke anything at all. Men are so used to seeing golden sunsets, that to describe a sunset as golden does not demand their attention—and until attention is demanded and secured, no evocation of image, no description, has taken place. Chekhov's formula was to choose a detail so unusual or so dramatic that it would capture the necessary attention; the grand example, of course, is his splinter of broken glass glittering on the moonlit mill-dam.

The idea behind and the efficacy in such description is that detail can and should imply more than itself. When Chekhov opens "The Lady with the Dog" with the sentence, "It was reported that a new face had been seen on the quay; a lady with a little dog," he is including a great deal of detail by implication.[1] We infer that the scene is a coastal city, that it is a resort rather than a commercial port, that it is the sort of place where ladies with little dogs may walk for their pleasure, without need of large dogs for protection, that the resort is a bit lazy since the lady's presence *is reported,* that it is fine strolling weather, probably summer, and that this lady's arrival is going to precipitate the story. The recorded details imply many other details. Detail that suggests other detail has the power of coming alive imaginatively.

Stephen Crane's sentence at the end of Chapter 9 of *The Red Badge of Courage,* "The red sun was pasted in the sky like a wafer," may carry the dependence upon implication too far. Certainly the image works; battle-smoke and dust filter reduce the mid-day sun to a wafer pasted in the sky, but the implications come through only after a great deal of thought. The smoke and dust are neither recorded nor suggested in the scene, and the reader has to supply them from his own thought. The writer is asking the reader to do a good part of the *actual* writing, that is, the imaginative evocation of detail.

The reader must have something to do, of course; otherwise his interest and imagination are lost. What gets into the reader's mind is the index of success for descriptive writing. The writer, then, must build upon what the reader is already capable of, or familiar with, and then suggest and imply the rest. Daniel Defoe used suggestive detail so well in *A Journal of the Plague Year*— using a historical detail here, a real person there, enumerating the names of streets and buildings, inventing personalities, facial expression, conversations, incidents, and so on—that people thought it was an eye-witness account, until someone noticed that Defoe was a boy of five or less at the time of the plague. William Dean Howells, too, was so good at describing minutiae that it is often difficult to distinguish between his factual travel books and his imagined fic-

---

[1] Sean O'Faolain pointed this out at some length in *The Short Story* in a section often reprinted as "On Convention."

tions. At evoking credible scenes in a million details more or less, Defoe and Howells are the great masters; the young writer could study their works with profit.

The mood that detail implies is especially important when a quality, rather than a physical detail, is being described. Here is Mark Twain's Huckleberry Finn, describing his first perception of Phelps Farm:

> When I got there it was all still and Sunday-like, and hot and sunshiny—the hands was gone to the fields; and there was them kind of faint dronings of bugs and flies in the air that makes it seem so lonesome and like everybody's dead and gone; and if a breeze fans along and quivers the leaves, it makes you feel mournful, because you feel like it's spirits whispering—spirits that's been dead ever so many years—and you always think they're talking about *you*. As a general thing it makes a body wish *he* was dead, too, and done with it all.
>
> Phelps's was one of these little one-horse cotton plantations; and they all look alike. A rail fence round a two-acre yard; a stile, made out of logs sawed off and up-ended, in steps, like barrels of a different length, to climb over the fence with, and for the women to stand on when they are going to jump onto a horse; some sickly grass-patches in the big yard, but mostly it was bare and smooth, like an old hat with the nap rubbed off; big double log house for the white folks—hewed logs, with the chinks stopped up with mud or mortar, and these mud-stripes been whitewashed some time or another; round-log kitchen, with a big broad, open but roofed passage joining it to the house; log smoke-house back of the kitchen; three little log nigger-cabins in a row t'other side the smokehouse; one little hut all by itself away down against the back fence, and some outbuildings down a piece the other side; ash-hopper, and big kettle to bile soap in, by the little hut; bench by the kitchen door, with bucket of water and a gourd; hound asleep there, in the sun; more hounds asleep, round about; about three shade-trees away off in a corner; some currant bushes and gooseberry bushes in one place by the fence; outside of the fence a garden and a water-melon patch; then the cotton fields begins; and after the fields, the woods.
>
> I went around and clumb over the back stile by the ash-hopper, and started for the kitchen. When I got a little ways, I heard the dim hum of a spinning-wheel wailing along up and sinking along down again; and then I knowed for certain I wished I was dead—for that is the lonesomest sound in the whole world.[2]

In the first paragraph, the pre-Romantic distinction between the outer and the inner is once again broken down, and the inner evaluation changes the outer detail. The moribund mood comes through strongly, not only because of the details like "dronings of bugs and flies," but also because of the similes

[2] Opening of Chapter XXXII.

that Huck uses to specify the qualities attached to those details, as in "like everybody's dead and gone." Consider the same kinds of details in a different evaluating context, as "the industrial machines droning happily, like bugs and flies at work." Evaluating detail is indispensable where the setting is not merely a place, but an emotional attitude toward a place.

There is a sharp contrast when the tone of Twain's second paragraph takes over. Tone, we must remember, is the attitude the writer takes toward his materials and is to be distinguished from mood, the attitude the reader is invited to take. As is well known, the details of Phelps Farm are the details of Twain's uncle John Quarles's farm near Hannibal. Twain's nostalgia for his uncle's farm comes through in his enumeration of the details of Phelps Farm, in the feeling that the author, not the character, has had the experiences that evaluate the descriptive details. Twain, not Huck, is the one that knows about stiles, and women riding horses, and the differences between log houses and "nigger-cabins." These were details from Twain's boyhood, and there is a certain loving nostalgia in his enumerating them again. It is only this nostalgia that keeps the list from going dead with the second or third item, and, indeed, if you do not perceive to nostalgia, the description is probably very bad to you. None of the moribund mood of the first and third paragraphs comes through in the second, but instead a positive, optimistic mood. Twain's description is qualitatively inconsistent.

So-called historical settings and settings in other cultures usually suffer from a misapplication of tone and mood. A certain writer, say, goes to the seventeenth or eighteenth centuries because it gives him opportunity to use a lot of low-cut, bosom-freeing dresses and a lot of swishing swords. Or another goes to Classical times so that he can show men standing around in togas, one end draped over a free arm, the hand of which holds a half-unrolled scroll. The tone and mood that evaluates such imagery is almost invariably from today's world of Romanteroticism and pseudo-and-anti-intellectualism. The detail can show, and the showing may be realistic or caricatured, but what the detail tells is dishonest.

The ability to control both the detail and the evaluative implications of description is among the most valuable techniques a writer can learn. It can make it possible for him to evoke just those qualities of imaginative reality he needs in the reader's mind and make them have the resonance of genuine experience. When the writer does this, he is not only controlling physical and temporal scene, but theme as well. Description can make all the difference between a flat page of print and a scene. Here, as in so many other cases, the writer must maintain a delicate balance between undesirable extremes: mere detail *shows;* implicating detail *tells;* good description does both at once.

Setting as Narration

Scenes are not merely static, but have a way of shifting, growing, changing with the characters, so that they participate in the actual telling of the story. People, after all, are living in time, and they carry *things* with them through time. The things of a moment can indicate what kinds of actions have just taken place, what are taking place, and even what may take place in the future. This ability was behind Chekhov's famous injunction to young playwriters about the aesthetic promises they make with a scene. If you put a firearm on the mantel in Act I in such a way that attention is called to it, you had better fire it in Act III or use it in some other way. You arouse the audience's *narrative* expectations by focusing upon scenic detail; to disappoint that expectation would be an aesthetic mistake. In foreshadowing action, setting participates in narration.

It is also well known that setting can act as a character in a story, when the reactions of the real characters give it that dimension. Admiral Byrd, writing of his six months alone near the South Pole, described the palpability that loneliness took on for him; it sat across from him at dinner, it followed him when he went to check his weather instruments, it snuggled into the sleeping bag with him at night.[3] E. E. Cummings described, in *The Enormous Room,* how the prison room took on the qualities of his persecutors and tortured him. Characters in Ole Rölvaag's and Hamlin Garland's prairie stories come to think of place as a malignant being, after winds blow crops away, torrential rains wash them away, long drouths shrivel them, and the sun dances about them in heat waves; after loneliness creeps up like a thief and steals their sanity, and mortgages come due six months before they can pay. This is inner experience, of course, but fiction often deals, most importantly with inner experience. Setting is capable of becoming part of a character's story.

Setting can also act as the author's voice in his narration. Nathaniel Hawthorne begins *The Scarlet Letter* with a descriptive context of

A throng of bearded men, in sad-colored garments and gray, steeple-crowned hats, intermixed with women, some wearing hoods, and others bareheaded, . . . assembled in front of a wooden edifice, the door of which was heavily timbered with oak, and studded with iron spikes.

and contrasts it with his description of Hester:

The young woman was tall, with a figure of perfect elegance, on a large scale. She had dark and abundant hair, so glossy that it threw off the sunshine

---

[3] Richard E. Byrd, *Alone* (New York: Putnam, 1938).

with a gleam, and a face which, besides being beautiful from regularity of
feature and richness of complexion, had the impressiveness belonging to a marked
brow and deep black eyes.[4]

These descriptions are almost wholly evaluative and the contrast between them
is patent. Hawthorne is juxtaposing one against the other as a means of focusing the reader on the primary action of the story, for the prime-mover of the
plot is the conflict between the Puritan's and Hester's value systems. The scene,
thus described, begins to tell the story. Similarly, the juxtaposition [5] of the
bleak image of "the black flower of civilized society, the prison," with the
bright red "wild rose-bush" that grows at its door, suggesting "that the deep
heart of Nature could pity and be kind" introduces the themes that Hawthorne
is most interested in exploring—the relationships between man-made law,
natural law, moral law, and the truth of the human heart. Both juxtapositions
recur in a variety of situations and images. Both tell a part of the story.

Hawthorne is famous for his tableau style, in which static description pre-
dominates, with very little action occurring. Like symbolic emblems, his settings
reveal actions that have occurred and prefigure actions yet to come. The reader's
mind then assembles the Gestalt of action. When we look closely at the story,
we find that we have primarily an illusion of action, based upon observed
nodules of inaction, but the illusion is, after all, very real and quite powerful—
so we must conclude that Hawthorne's descriptions narrate. His settings tell
the story.

More active description that functions in much the same way is, perhaps,
more common. D. H. Lawrence's descriptions of Bestwood and the surrounding countryside in *Sons and Lovers,* for example, are related more as a kind of
experience than as set tableaux. The coal pits that pock the farmlands, the
patina of coal-dust and ash that covers everything, the colliers made grey-
faced by their long-dark work, their minds made ash, their houses jammed
together in narrow, squalid, amiable poverty which even the sweet-williams
and pinks cannot relieve—all this and more comes to us slowly, as the experience of the people. It is social protest, of course, and very pointed; it tells a
story that Lawrence thought one of the terrible crimes of all time—the slow
dehumanization of feeling man and the despoiling of nature. In the midst of
process, before their awakening, his characters have little sense of what is
happening to them; until they learn to verbalize it convincingly, Lawrence
makes his settings tell that part of the story.

Setting always narrates, though many writers choose not (or, perhaps, are
unable) to make it narrate anything of significance. Even the ordinary weekly
magazine story that uses familiar detail has a telling setting; though the writer

[4] Chapter II, paragraph 11.
[5] In Chapter I, paragraphs 2 and 3.

may think it merely incidental to the story, such a setting usually appeals to
stock responses and thus typically functions to corroborate and engrain the
clichés of the reader's mind. It tells him that his world is right and that he is
with it; the tale such a setting tells is soporific. To use setting in this way is an
aesthetic mistake.

Description that narrates is a valuable technique, and the serious writer
should go to some pains to become able to write it well.

Setting as Explanation

Setting can explain character, action, and the meanings attached to them by
making clear the causes of characteristics or of actions, by showing the results
of them, or by operating as an analog to them. The first of these is very important. Here, for example, is Henry Adams, great-grandson of John Adams
and grandson of John Quincy Adams, explaining the effect of milieu upon
his formative years (he speaks of himself in the third person):

Nothing stuck in the mind except home impressions, and the sharpest were those
of kindred children; but as influences that warped a mind, none compared with
the mere effect of the back of the President's bald head, as he sat in his pew on
Sundays, in line with that of President Quincy, who, though some ten years
younger, seemed to children about the same age. Before railways entered the
New England town, every parish church showed half-a-dozen of these leading
citizens, with grey hair, who sat on the main aisle in the best pews, and had sat
there, or in some equivalent dignity, since the time of St. Augustine, if not since
the glacial epoch. It was unusual for boys to sit behind a President grandfather,
and to read over his head the tablet in memory of a President great-grandfather,
who had "pledged his life, his fortune, and his sacred honor" to secure the independence of his country and so forth; but boys naturally supposed, without much
reasoning, that other boys had the equivalent of President grandfathers, and that
churches would always go on, with the bald-headed leading citizens on the main
aisle, and Presidents or their equivalents on the walls. The Irish gardener once
said to the child: "You'll be thinkin' you'll be President too!" The casualty of
the remark made so strong an impression on his mind that he never forgot it.
He could not remember ever to have thought of the subject; to him, that there
should be a doubt of his being President was a new idea. What had been would
continue to be. He doubted neither about Presidents nor about Churches, and
no one suggested at that time a doubt whether a system of society which had
lasted since Adam would outlast one Adams more.[6]

We are familiar enough with similar causal influences of milieu in fiction
that a few examples should be enough to focus the technique in our minds.

[6] *The Education of Henry Adams* (New York: Modern Library), pp. 15–16.

Gustave Flaubert's Madame Bovary is made the way she is by her sense of contrast between the Romantic glitter of Paris and the despicable, moribund countryside. Stephen Crane's Maggie is undone by the social, economic, and moral environment of the Bowery. Conrad's Kurtz in *Heart of Darkness* is found out for what he is through the introspection that the interior of the jungle forces one into. Ole Rölvaag's people in *Giants in the Earth* are the victims of loneliness, weather, mortgage-holders, markets, and such. Steinbeck's Joad family in *Grapes of Wrath* are caught up in a milieu of the social, economic, and political upheavals of a particular time and place. In all these and other cases, the milieu causes the characters to react; from such reactions, we derive meaning. Setting helps to explain that meaning.

There are even cases where the explaining power of setting is so important that the novel would collapse without it. Such a case is Walter Van Tilburg Clark's *The Ox-Bow Incident*. It takes place in Bridger's Wells, Nevada, shortly after a spring thaw and round-up in the 1880's. More than 600 cattle are missing from the several herds of the valley. The characters are depicted as essentially honest and kind men, but now the mistrust that comes with rustling and the "edge" of irritability after a hard winter complicate their characters. The atmosphere is charged for violence and revenge. Rumor becomes electric. When three men are accused of stealing forty cattle, no amount of reason, good sense, or hesitation can save them from being lynched. Irrationality, authoritarianism, injustice, an unspecified and undirected need for release, are in control. Without the electric atmosphere, none of these qualities would have emerged; the men are all quiet, home-loving, settled types; without the causal factors in the setting, no story would have happened.

Settings that explain by showing the results of character and action are also possible and common in fiction. People's motives and accomplishments get incorporated into the milieu and cause it to take on describable characteristics, which reveal some of the meanings that fictional situations exist for. Indeed, a common theme in fiction is based upon giving a set of characters a particular initial situation and seeing what they will make of it. The characters cause the setting to become what it becomes; and it reveals their efforts. Examples range from Thoreau's *Walden* to Knut Hamsun's *Growth of the Soil*.

E. M. Forster devotes his entire first chapter to this kind of setting in *A Passage to India,* though it is not fashionable nor often successful nowadays to do so. Chandrapore, inhabited by Hindus and Moslems, lies in the lowest level of the scene, along the muddy river, from which it is hardly distinguishable. On slightly higher ground is the Maidan and the railway station, an area inhabited by Eurasians and showing more comfort and less ugliness than the lower level. Then comes a dip and another rise leading up to the Civil Station, where the Europeans' bungalows are nestled nicely into tropical abundance. This setting reveals the levels of caste and class which furnish the novel with its primary problem. But there is nothing inherent in the setting that it should do so; the Europeans have made the setting take on the qualities it has by the exercise of their value system for more than a century. The setting reveals what they are by revealing what they have done.

Whenever a writer uses an already existing setting, it is usually of this kind. Settings of wars and historical events can only be used successfully if the writer takes into account the fact that the men he is depicting have been partially responsible for the milieu. Men made the Napoleonic Wars, for example, and the American Civil War, and the colonies in Africa, Asia, and wherever. To use one of these scenes is to use, inevitably, the motives and actions of men that brought about these scenes. Merely to set the scene in a recognizable place at a recognizable time is to do a low-powered version of the same thing. Time and place explain what has happened and imply what may happen.

Cause and effect can operate circularly in setting, the effect becoming a second cause and producing a new effect, which then has causal power, and so on. In Sherwood Anderson's *Winesburg, Ohio,* for example, the characters have a tremendous need for contact with other people, need to communicate, need to share the warmth of humanity. But their small-town environment dictates certain *mores* which prevent what Anderson called the "fruition of the spirit." They are stifled by conventions, by the forces of opinion, by limitations of language and action. The terrifying irony is, however, that the characters themselves make up the social vice in which they are clamped; they are not only victims of their lonely fates, but perpetrators of them. Caught in their vicious circle, they become grotesque—Alice Hindeman runs naked in the rain, searching for contact with any human being; Enoch Robinson moves to New York where he rents a room which he populates with imaginary people whose only function is to communicate with him.

Setting can also explain by offering analogies which are not involved with cause or effect, but which reveal or suggest some meaning about character, action, or theme. The first chapter of *A Passage to India* has something of this quality in it, for the extent of the revelation is in excess of what we could be expected to know about character or action at that point; in fact, the juxtapositions seem almost symbolic in their import. James Fenimore Cooper's forest-versus-civilization settings are analogs of the Rousseauistic ideas that are a part of his theme. Such analogies make relationships clearer, sometimes make it possible for us to grasp them.

Nathaniel Hawthorne's *The House of the Seven Gables* is one of the simplest and most famous examples of setting used as analog. The Pyncheon family has been cursed and has gradually decayed morally over the generations; but such decay is, after all, not so visible—Clifford is pale and scrawny; the Judge is fat and selfish; but these are not qualities that would distinguish them from other people who live in the same street. Hawthorne shows the old house of the seven gables in analogous decay; its gloom parallels the debilitation of its inhabitants; its yard reveals their corruption; even the chickens are depicted as morally depraved. The setting suggests meanings which another setting would not; in fact, setting here becomes symbol and explains through analogy.

Setting as Argument

When setting becomes symbol, it becomes part of the argument of the fiction; it exists quite apart from the images, experiences, and causes depicted in the scene, and, while a different set of characters and actions would change the overall product, a change in character and action would not change that part of the setting that sets forth symbol as thought. The thought, the argument, would continue to be itself, even in new trappings. Such settings have been called *moralized landscapes,* and they take a variety of forms.

Perhaps the simplest form of the moralized landscape is the sort found in sentimental novels. Never a maiden's heart can break, but the very heavens must storm. Never a villain rob a man or rape a maid, but it be done in the dark. And in Hollywood movies, the music goes somber, or dainty, or raucously tense in accord with the action. In such cases, the writer's situation will not support the emotion that he wants the scene to evoke and he begs for additional response, as it were, by infusing the setting with qualities outside the situation. The use of this technique by novelists of sentiment gave us the literary term, *sentimental.* The trouble in such a case is that the symbolic detail has no referent, nothing that it can symbolize.

There are, however, many artistic uses of the technique, cases in which the thing symbolized is worthy of the symbol. Conrad's Axel Heyst in *Victory,* for example, is a man who wants to live on a mountain-top, separated and aloof from the rest of humanity. He opts out of civilization and goes to live on an island, for an island, from the vantage point of the ocean floor, is but a mountain, and Heyst there finds the kind of life that his symbolic nature demands. Or, to take another example, Hemingway's famous first chapter of *A Farewell to Arms* traces the symbolic and real changes that transform the vacation atmosphere of the landscape into the disintegrated mess of a war-spoiled land. Or, take Hemingway's equally famous, careful development of the correlations between rain and impending disaster. In such cases, the setting reveals to us how we are to interpret the motive in the fiction.

One of the most interesting variations of the moralized landscape is the idyll. The idyll, as a genre, says Friedrich Schiller,[7] "presents the idea and description of an innocent and happy humanity," whose innocence and happiness imply remoteness from the "artificial refinements of fashionable society." Thus, idylls are traditionally set in remote, pastoral places and times, as if before civilization, and, there, the greatest hardship people have to endure is the weather. Amien's song in Shakespeare's Forest of Arden describes such a place:

> Under the greenwood tree
> Who loves to lie with me,
> And turn his merry note
> Unto the sweet bird's throat,
> Come hither, come hither, come hither:
>   Here shall he see
>   No enemy
> But winter and rough weather.

> Who doth ambition shun,
> And loves to live i' the sun,
> Seeking the food he eats,
> And pleased with what he gets,
> Come hither, come hither, come hither:
>   Here shall he see
>   No enemy
> But winter and rough weather.[8]

But these *usual* trappings of remote time and place are accidental, says Schiller; they "do not form the object of the idyll, but are only to be regarded as the most natural means to attain this end. The end is to portray man in a state of innocence, which means a state of harmony and peace with himself and the external world.... A state such as this is not merely met with before the dawn of civilization; it is also the state to which civilization aspires, as to its last end, if only it obeys a determined tendency in

---

[7] In "On Simple and Sentimental Poetry," (1795), from *Essays Aesthetical and Philosophical* (London: George Bell, 1884). I am indebted to Lionel Trilling's "Introduction to *Emma*" for bringing the essay to my attention, though it is now widely reprinted.

[8] *As You Like It,* Act I, Scene v.

its progress. The idea of a similar state, and the belief in the possible reality of this state, is the only thing that can reconcile man with all the evils to which he is exposed in the path of civilization."

One notes a heavily Romantic insistence upon the concept of perfectability and an interpretation of history as progress toward perfection. Schiller admits, "We can only seek [idylls] and love them in moments in which we need calm, and not when our faculties aspire after movement and exercise. A morbid mind will find its *cure* in them, a sound soul will not find its *food* in them. They cannot vivify, they can only soften." Thus, the traditional idea of idylls is that they are Romantic escapism. But Schiller thinks this is not the necessary form for idylls to take; he envisions a kind of idyll in which the calm we seek is "the calm that follows accomplishment, not the calm of indolence—the calm that comes from equilibrium re-established between the faculties not from the suspending of their exercise."

In such a genre, the setting would be part of the argument. Samurai settings in Japanese literature function similarly as argument, though with a quite different theme. Primitive settings, civilized settings, surrealistic settings—they all make a point, though it is sometimes difficult to summarize and specify their argument because fiction argues subliminally and intends to communicate with "original" experience, not summary.

A Use of Setting

Settings, then, can describe, narrate, explain, and argue, but none of these in isolation. Descriptions argue; explanations narrate; arguments explain, narrate, and describe. All the modes function simultaneously in good fiction. Let us look at a story in which setting plays an important role.

THE BRIDE COMES TO YELLOW SKY [9]

1

The great Pullman was whirling onward with such dignity of motion that a glance from the window seemed simply to prove that the plains of Texas were pouring eastward. Vast flats of green grass, dull-hued spaces of mesquit and cactus, little groups of frame houses, woods of light and tender trees, all were sweeping into the east, sweeping over the horizon, a precipice.

A newly married pair had boarded this coach at San Antonio. The man's face

[9] By Stephen Crane.

was reddened from many days in the wind and sun, and a direct result of his
new black clothes was that his brick-coloured hands were constantly performing
in a most conscious fashion. From time to time he looked down respectfully at
his attire. He sat with a hand on each knee, like a man waiting in a barber's
shop. The glances he devoted to other passengers were furtive and shy.

The bride was not pretty, nor was she very young. She wore a dress of blue
cashmere, with small reservations of velvet here and there, and with steel buttons
abounding. She continually twisted her head to regard her puff sleeves, very stiff,
straight, and high. They embarrassed her. It was quite apparent that she had
cooked, and that she expected to cook, dutifully. The blushes caused by the careless scrutiny of some passengers as she had entered the car were strange to see
upon this plain, under-class countenance, which was drawn in placid, almost
emotionless lines.

They were evidently very happy. "Ever been in a parlour-car before?" he asked,
smiling with delight.

"No," she answered: "I never was. It's fine, ain't it?"

"Great! And then after a while we'll go forward to the diner, and get a big
lay-out. Finest meal in the world. Charge a dollar."

"Oh, do they?" cried the bride. "Charge a dollar? Why, that's too much—for
us—ain't it, Jack?"

"Not this trip, anyhow," he answered bravely. "We're going to go the whole
thing."

Later he explained to her about the trains. "You see, it's a thousand miles
from one end of Texas to the other; and this train runs right across it, and never
stops but four times." He had the pride of an owner. He pointed out to her the
dazzling fittings of the coach; and in truth her eyes opened wider as she con-
templated the sea-green figured velvet, the shining brass, silver, and glass, the
wood that gleamed as darkly brilliant as the surface of a pool of oil. At one end
a bronze figure sturdily held a support for a separated chamber, and at convenient
places on the ceiling were frescoes in olive and silver.

To the minds of the pair, their surroundings reflected the glory of their marriage
that morning in San Antonio; this was the environment of their new estate; and
the man's face in particular beamed with an elation that made him appear
ridiculous to the negro porter. This individual at times surveyed them from afar
with an amused and superior grin. On other occasions he bullied them with skill
in ways that did not make it exactly plain to them that they were being bullied.
He subtly used all the manners of the most unconquerable kind of snobbery. He
oppressed them; but of this oppression they had small knowledge, and they speedily
forgot that infrequently a number of travellers covered them with stares of derisive
enjoyment. Historically there was supposed to be something infinitely humorous
in their situation.

"We are due in Yellow Sky at 3:42," he said, looking tenderly into her eyes.

"Oh, are we?" she said, as if she had not been aware of it. To evince surprise at
her husband's statement was part of her wifely amiability. She took from a pocket
a little silver watch; and as she held it before her, and stared at it with a frown
of attention, the new husband's face shone.

"I bought it in San Anton' from a friend of mine," he told her gleefully.

"It's seventeen minutes past twelve," she said, looking up at him with a kind of shy and clumsy coquetry. A passenger, noting this play, grew excessively sardonic, and winked at himself in one of the numerous mirrors.

At last they went to the dining-car. Two rows of negro waiters, in glowing white suits, surveyed their entrance with the interest, and also the equanimity, of men who had been forewarned. The pair fell to the lot of a waiter who happened to feel pleasure in steering them through their meal. He viewed them with the manner of a fatherly pilot, his countenance radiant with benevolence. The patronage, entwined with the ordinary deference, was not plain to them. And yet, as they returned to their coach, they showed in their faces a sense of escape.

To the left, miles down a long purple slope, was a little ribbon of mist where moved the keening Rio Grande. The train was approaching it at an angle, and the apex was Yellow Sky. Presently it was apparent that, as the distance from Yellow Sky grew shorter, the husband became commensurately restless. His brick-red hands were more insistent in their prominence. Occasionally he was even rather absent-minded and far-away when the bride leaned forward and addressed him.

As a matter of truth, Jack Potter was beginning to find the shadow of a deed weigh upon him like a leaden slab. He, the town marshal of Yellow Sky, a man known, liked, and feared in his corner, a prominent person, had gone to San Antonio to meet a girl he believed he loved, and there, after the usual prayers, had actually induced her to marry him, without consulting Yellow Sky for any part of the transaction. He was now bringing his bride before an innocent and unsuspecting community.

Of course people in Yellow Sky married as it pleased them, in accordance with a general custom; but such was Potter's thought of his duty to his friends, or of their idea of his duty, or of an unspoken form which does not control men in these matters, that he felt he was heinous. He had committed an extraordinary crime. Face to face with this girl in San Antonio, and spurred by his sharp impulse, he had gone headlong over all the social hedges. At San Antonio he was like a man hidden in the dark. A knife to sever any friendly duty, any form, was easy to his hand in that remote city. But the hour of Yellow Sky—the hour of daylight —was approaching.

He knew full well that his marriage was an important thing to his town. It could only be exceeded by the burning of the new hotel. His friends could not forgive him. Frequently he had reflected on the advisability of telling them by telegraph, but a new cowardice had been upon him. He feared to do it. And now the train was hurrying him toward a scene of amazement, glee, and reproach. He glanced out of the window at the line of haze swinging slowly in toward the train.

Yellow Sky had a kind of brass band, which played painfully, to the delight of the populace. He laughed without heart as he thought of it. If the citizens could dream of his prospective arrival with his bride, they would parade the band at the station and escort them, amid cheers and laughing congratulations, to his adobe home.

He resolved that he would use all the devices of speed and plainscraft in making the journey from the station to his house. Once within that safe citadel, he could issue some sort of vocal bulletin, and then not go among the citizens until they had time to wear off a little of their enthusiasm.

The bride looked anxiously at him. "What's worrying you, Jack?"

He laughed again. "I'm not worrying, girl; I'm only thinking of Yellow Sky." She flushed in comprehension.

A sense of mutual guilt invaded their minds and developed a finer tenderness. They looked at each other with eyes softly aglow. But Potter often laughed the same nervous laugh; the flush upon the bride's face seemed quite permanent.

The traitor to the feelings of Yellow Sky narrowly watched the speeding landscape. "We're nearly there," he said.

Presently the porter came and announced the proximity of Potter's home. He held a brush in his hand, and, with all his airy superiority gone, he brushed Potter's new clothes as the latter slowly turned this way and that way. Potter fumbled out a coin and gave it to the porter, as he had seen others do. It was a heavy and muscle-bound business, as that of a man shoeing his first horse.

The porter took their bag, and as the train began to slow they moved forward to the hooded platform of the car. Presently the two engines and their long string of coaches rushed into the station of Yellow Sky.

"They have to take water here," said Potter, from a constricted throat and in mournful cadence, as one announcing death. Before the train stopped his eye had swept the length of the platform, and he was glad and astonished to see there was none upon it but the station-agent, who, with a slightly hurried and anxious air, was walking toward the water-tanks. When the train had halted, the porter alighted first, and placed in position a little temporary step.

"Come on, girl," said Potter, hoarsely. As he helped her down they each laughed on a false note. He took the bag from the negro, and bade his wife cling to his arm. As they slunk rapidly away, his hangdog glance perceived that they were unloading the two trunks, and also that the station-agent, far ahead near the baggage-car, had turned and was running toward him, making gestures. He laughed, and groaned as he laughed, when he noted the first effect of his marital bliss upon Yellow Sky. He gripped his wife's arm firmly to his side, and they fled. Behind them the porter stood, chuckling fatuously.

2

The California express on the Southern Railway was due at Yellow Sky in twenty-one minutes. There were six men at the bar of the Weary Gentleman saloon. One was a drummer who talked a great deal and rapidly; three were Texans who did not care to talk at that time; and two were Mexican sheepherders, who did not talk as a general practice in the Weary Gentleman saloon. The barkeeper's dog lay on the boardwalk that crossed in front of the door. His head was on his paws, and he glanced drowsily here and there with the constant vigilance of a dog that is kicked on occasion. Across the sandy street were some vivid green grass-plots, so wonderful in appearance, amid the sands that burned near them in a blazing sun, that they caused a doubt in the mind. They exactly resembled the grass mats used to represent lawns on the stage. At the cooler end of the railway station, a man without a coat sat in a tilted chair and smoked his pipe. The fresh-cut bank of the Rio Grande circled near the town, and there could be seen beyond it a great plum-coloured plain of mesquit.

Save for the busy drummer and his companions in the saloon, Yellow Sky was dozing. The new-comer leaned gracefully upon the bar, and recited many tales with the confidence of a bard who has come upon a new field.

"—and at the moment that the old man fell downstairs with the bureau in his arms, the old woman was coming up with two scuttles of coal, and of course—"

The drummer's tale was interrupted by a young man who suddenly appeared in the open door. He cried: "Scratchy Wilson's drunk, and has turned loose with both hands." The two Mexicans at once set down their glasses and faded out of the rear entrance of the saloon.

The drummer, innocent and jocular, answered: "All right, old man. S'pose he has? Come in and have a drink, anyhow."

But the information had made such an obvious cleft in every skull in the room that the drummer was obliged to see its importance. All had become instantly solemn. "Say," said he, mystified, "what is this?" His three companions made the introductory gesture of eloquent speech; but the young man at the door forestalled them.

"It means, my friend," he answered, as he came into the saloon, "that for the next two hours this town won't be a health resort."

The barkeeper went to the door, and locked and barred it; reaching out of the window, he pulled in heavy wooden shutters, and barred them. Immediately a solemn, chapel-like gloom was upon the place. The drummer was looking from one to another.

"But say," he cried, "what is this, anyhow? You don't mean there is going to be a gun-fight?"

"Don't know whether there'll be a fight or not," answered one man, grimly; "but there'll be some shootin'—some good shootin'."

The young man who had warned them waved his hand. "Oh, there'll be a fight fast enough, if any one wants it. Anybody can get a fight out there in the street. There's a fight just waiting."

The drummer seemed to be swayed between the interest of a foreigner and a perception of personal danger.

"What did you say his name was?" he asked.

"Scratchy Wilson," they answered in chorus.

"And will he kill anybody? What are you going to do? Does this happen often? Does he rampage around like this once a week or so? Can he break in that door?"

"No; he can't break down that door," replied the barkeeper. "He's tried it three times. But when he comes you'd better lay down on the floor, stranger. He's dead sure to shoot at it, and a bullet may come through."

Thereafter the drummer kept a strict eye upon the door. The time had not yet been called for him to hug the floor, but, as a minor precaution, he sidled near to the wall. "Will he kill anybody?" he said again.

The men laughed low and scornfully at the question.

"He's out to shoot, and he's out for trouble. Don't see any good in experimentin' with him."

"But what do you do in a case like this? What do you do?"

A man responded: "Why, he and Jack Potter—"

"But," in chorus the other men interrupted, "Jack Potter's in San Anton'."

"Well, who is he? What's he got to do with it?"

"Oh, he's the town marshall. He goes out and fights Scratchy when he gets on one of these tears."

"Wow!" said the drummer, mopping his brow. "Nice job he's got."

The voices had toned away to mere whisperings. The drummer wished to ask further questions, which were born of an increasing anxiety and bewilderment; but when he attempted them, the men merely looked at him in irritation and motioned him to remain silent. A tense waiting hush was upon them. In the deep shadows of the room their eyes shone as they listened for sounds from the street. One man made three gestures at the barkeeper; and the latter, moving like a ghost, handed him a glass and a bottle. The man poured a full glass of whisky, and set down the bottle noiselessly. He gulped the whisky in a swallow, and turned again toward the door in immovable silence. The drummer saw that the barkeeper, without a sound, had taken a Winchester from beneath the bar. Later he saw this individual beckoning to him, so he tiptoed across the room.

"You better come with me back of the bar."

"No, thanks," said the drummer, perspiring; "I'd rather be where I can make a break for the back door."

Whereupon the man of bottles made a kindly but peremptory gesture. The drummer obeyed it, and, finding himself seated on a box with his head below the level of the bar, balm was laid upon his soul at sight of various zinc and copper fittings that bore a resemblance to armour-plate. The barkeeper took a seat comfortably upon an adjacent box.

"You see," he whispered, "this here Scratchy Wilson is a wonder with a gun— a perfect wonder; and when he goes on the war-trail, we hunt our holes—naturally. He's about the last one of the old gang that used to hang out along the river here. He's a terror when he's drunk. When he's sober he's all right—kind of simple—wouldn't hurt a fly—nicest fellow in town. But when he's drunk—whoo!"

There were periods of stillness. "I wish Jack Potter was back from San Anton'," said the barkeeper. "He shot Wilson up once—in the leg—and he would sail in and pull out the kinks in this thing."

Presently they heard from a distance the sound of a shot, followed by three wild yowls. It instantly removed a bond from the men in the darkened saloon. There was a shuffling of feet. They looked at each other. "Here he comes," they said.

3

A man in a maroon-coloured flannel shirt, which had been purchased for purposes of decoration, and made principally by some Jewish women on the East Side of New York, rounded a corner and walked into the middle of the main street of Yellow Sky. In either hand the man held a long heavy, blue-black revolver. Often he yelled, and these cries rang through a semblance of a deserted village, shrilly flying over the roofs in a volume that seemed to have no relation to the ordinary vocal strength of a man. It was as if the surrounding stillness formed the arch of a tomb over him. These cries of ferocious challenge rang against walls of silence. And his boots had red tops with gilded imprints, of the kind beloved in winter by little sledding boys on the hillsides of New England.

The man's face flamed in a rage begot of whisky. His eyes, rolling, and yet keen for ambush, hunted the still doorways and windows. He walked with the creeping movement of the midnight cat. As it occurred to him, he roared menacing information. The long revolvers in his hands were as easy as straws; they were moved with an electric swiftness. The little fingers of each hand played sometimes in a musician's way. Plain from the low collar of the shirt the cords of his neck straightened and sank, straightened and sank, as passion moved him. The only sounds were his terrible invitations. The calm adobes preserved their demeanour at the passing of this small thing in the middle of the street.

There was no offer of fight—no offer of fight. The man called to the sky. There were no attractions. He bellowed and fumed and swayed his revolvers here and everywhere.

The dog of the barkeeper of the Weary Gentleman saloon had not appreciated the advance of events. He yet lay dozing in front of his master's door. At sight of the dog, the man paused and raised his revolver humorously. At sight of the man, the dog sprang up and walked diagonally away, with a sullen head, and growling. The man yelled, and the dog broke into a gallop. As it was about to enter an alley, there was a loud noise, a whistling, and something spat the ground directly before it. The dog screamed, and, wheeling in terror, galloped headlong in a new direction. Again there was a noise, a whistling, and sand was kicked viciously before it. Fear-stricken, the dog turned and flurried like an animal in a pen. The man stood laughing, his weapons at his hips.

Ultimately the man was attracted by the closed door of the Weary Gentleman saloon. He went to it and, hammering with a revolver, demanded drink.

The door remaining imperturbable, he picked a bit of paper from the walk, and nailed it to the framework with a knife. He then turned his back contemptuously upon this popular resort and, walking to the opposite side of the street and spinning there on his heel quickly and lithely, fired at the bit of paper. He missed it by a half-inch. He swore at himself, and went away. Later he comfortably fusilladed the windows of his most intimate friend. The man was playing with this town; it was a toy for him.

But still there was no offer of fight. The name of Jack Potter, his ancient antagonist, entered his mind, and he concluded that it would be a glad thing if he should go to Potter's house, and by bombardment induce him to come out and fight. He moved in the direction of his desire, chanting Apache scalp-music.

When he arrived at it, Potter's house presented the same still front as had the other adobes. Taking up a strategic position, the man howled a challenge. But this house regarded him as might a great stone god. It gave no sign. After a decent wait, the man howled further challenges, mingling with them wonderful epithets.

Presently there came the spectacle of a man churning himself into deepest rage over the immobility of a house. He fumed at it as the winter wind attacks a prairie cabin in the North. To the distance there should have gone the sound of a tumult like the fighting of two hundred Mexicans. As necessity bade him, he paused for breath or to reload his revolvers.

4

Potter and his bride walked sheepishly and with speed. Sometimes they laughed together shamefacedly and low.

"Next corner, dear," he said finally.

They put forth the efforts of a pair walking bowed against a strong wind. Potter was about to raise a finger to point the first appearance of the new home when, as they circled the corner, they came face to face with a man in a maroon-coloured shirt, who was feverishly pushing cartridges into a large revolver. Upon the instant the man dropped his revolver to the ground and, like lightning, whipped another from its holster. The second weapon was aimed at the bridegroom's chest.

There was a silence. Potter's mouth seemed to be merely a grave for his tongue. He exhibited an instinct to at once loosen his arm from the woman's grip, and he dropped the bag to the sand. As for the bride, her face had gone as yellow as old cloth. She was a slave to hideous rites, gazing at the apparitional snake.

The two men faced each other at a distance of three paces. He of the revolver smiled with a new and quiet ferocity.

"Tried to sneak up on me," he said. "Tried to sneak up on me!" His eyes grew more baleful. As Potter made a slight movement, the man thrust his revolver venomously forward. "No! don't you do it, Jack Potter. Don't you move a finger toward a gun just yet. Don't you move an eyelash. The time has come for me to settle with you, and I'm goin' to do it my own way, and loaf along with no interferin'. So if you don't want a gun bent on you, just mind what I tell you."

Potter looked at his enemy. "I ain't got a gun on me, Scratchy," he said. "Honest, I ain't." He was stiffening and steadying, but yet somewhere at the back of his mind a vision of the Pullman floated: the sea-green figured velvet, the shining brass, silver, and glass, the wood that gleamed as darkly brilliant as the surface of a pool of oil—all the glory of the marriage, the environment of the new estate. "You know I fight when it comes to fighting, Scratchy Wilson; but I ain't got a gun on me. You'll have to do all the shootin' yourself."

His enemy's face went livid. He stepped forward, and lashed his weapon to and fro before Potter's chest. "Don't you tell me you ain't got no gun on you, you whelp. Don't tell me no lie like that. There ain't a man in Texas ever seen you without no gun. Don't take me for no kid." His eyes blazed with light, and his throat worked like a pump.

"I ain't takin you for no kid," answered Potter. His heels had not moved an inch backward. "I'm takin' you for a damn fool. I tell you I ain't got a gun, and I ain't. If you're goin' to shoot me up, you better begin now; you'll never get a chance like this again."

So much enforced reasoning had told on Wilson's rage; he was calmer. "If you ain't got a gun, why ain't you got a gun?" he sneered. "Been to Sunday-school?"

"I ain't got a gun because I've just come from San Anton' with my wife. I'm married," said Potter. "And if I'd thought there was going to be any galoots like you prowling around when I brought my wife home, I'd had a gun, and don't you forget it."

"Married!" said Scratchy, not at all comprehending.

"Yes, married. I'm married," said Potter, distinctly.

"Married?" said Scratchy. Seemingly for the first time, he saw the drooping, drowning woman at the other man's side. "No!" he said. He was like a creature allowed a glimpse of another world. He moved a pace backward, and his arm, with the revolver, dropped to his side. "Is this the lady?" he asked.

"Yes; this is the lady," answered Potter.

There was another period of silence.

"Well," said Wilson at last, slowly, "I s'pose it's all off now."

"It's all off if you say so, Scratchy. You know I didn't make the trouble." Potter lifted his valise.

"Well, I low it's off, Jack," said Wilson. He was looking at the ground. "Married!" He was not a student of chivalry; it was merely that in the presence of this foreign condition he was a simple child of the earlier plains. He picked up his starboard revolver, and, placing both weapons in their holsters, he went away. His feet made funnel-shaped tracks in the heavy sand.

Commentary

Setting operates at two levels in "The Bride Comes to Yellow Sky." The first is fairly simple and almost ruins the story; the second is symbolic and makes the story the classic that it is.

At the first, most obvious level, the story moves by a series of contrasts. The opening scene of the Pullman speeding through Texas is the first stroke of several that call our attention to the bumptious quality of Jack Potter and his bride. Their simple amazement at the silver and olive elegance of the railway car is contrasted to their own frontier crudeness of brick-red hands, clothes they are unaccustomed to, and the simpler life they use as their index of comparison. The scene in the Weary Gentleman saloon continues this note by means of the drummer who is entertaining the hicks with a few stories.

The setting is an important aspect of the several contrasts. In describing sets, it defines them and helps to characterize the people who move in them. When people begin to react to them in one way or another—as in the contrast of the newly-weds' view of the elegance and the porter's view of them —the setting begins to tell part of the story, and, indeed, it tells us a great deal. It tells us so much that the setting begins to explain much of the obvious situation. When the humorous element enters, the setting even argues: there is supposed to be something infinitely humorous in the situation of newly-married bumpkins amid elegance.

This strain of the story is almost ruinous, for it is dealing in stereotypes that become simpler and simpler as the story progresses. If it were all, it would reduce the resonance of the story to comic slapstick.

What, then, saves the story? First, the characters take on some human complexity. Jack Potter is not merely the town marshall of Yellow Sky, but reveals a fair capacity for feeling in his concept of his duty to Yellow Sky and his notion of their expectation of him. He is wrestling with a dilemma that is quite real for him. His bride comes momentarily into the round when she blushes in comprehension of what is bothering Jack. Scratchy Wilson, too, becomes complex and human when confronted with the situation the bride represents. These qualities are quite in contrast to the bumpkins that the first level of setting creates. But they gain much of their liveliness from their context of the symbolic time and place.

The symbolic setting allows the characters to become representative of much more than country bumpkins. The fact that the bride is coming from civilized San Antonio to frontier Yellow Sky precipitates character, action, and theme, for it imitates, in small, the rather large scene that was America at a particular time and place. This is late nineteenth century, after transcontinental railroads, but before the completion of the "taming of the West." The bride comes to represent the American woman, whose presence in the Yellow Sky's of the American frontier did much to reform the rowdy, crude Scratchy Wilson's of an earlier epoch. Jack Potter is the crude man of decency whose needs made the woman (and law and order) necessary. The characters, in taking on the power of representation, make the setting generalized and symbolic. In fact, setting and character in "The Bride Comes to Yellow Sky" come very close to the Classic ideals of representation of the typical; this story reveals in a small and particular situation what happened during the large and general impact of settled society on the frontier. It is a symbolic picture of a country in the process of transformation. The overtones that resonate from this action in this setting give the story its aesthetic richness and even explain why Scratchy Wilson, who had never given up "believing" in women and what they represented in his time, but had never had experiences that would show him how to deal with them, can only react with bafflement. The setting *is* a large part of the story's theme.

PROJECTS FOR WRITING AND DISCUSSION

A. ANALYSIS

1. In his essay, "Fiction and the 'Matrix of Analogy,' " * Mark Schorer pointed out the importance of metaphorical detail in scene and theme. Ordinary detail can work in the same way. Analyze, for example, the matrix of detail in "The Bride Comes to Yellow Sky." * What is the function of such details as the little green plots of grass across from the Weary Gentleman saloon? of the content of the story the drummer is telling? of Scratchy Wilson's sneered "why ain't you got a gun? . . . Been to Sunday-school?" Point out as many cases as you can of double-duty details like these.

2. Analyze the setting and the function of it in the segment from Melville, "Ahab's Black Mass." * How does the detail operate? Which details could you leave out? Can you think of any that might have improved the scene, without making it too patently obvious?

3. What significance, if any, do time and place have in "Soldier's Home"? *

4. Bring to class and be prepared to tell about a setting that you think serves its story especially well.

B. COMPARISON

1. The two photographs at the beginning of "Soldier's Home" * are really two, small settings, frozen. Analyze each and compare their effects. What is left to suggestion and implication? What details support the meanings you find in the photos? Discuss the role of these two photographs in the story as a whole.

2. Compare the use of details in Huck's description of Phelps farm * and Henry Adams's description of church-going. * What similarities can you find? What differences? How can you account for the different tones and moods?

3. Compare the tones in "Ahab's Black Mass" * and "Barn Burning." * What details account for these tones? Would you suggest any changes to either author, assuming he could improve his work.

4. Compare the settings in "The Bride Comes to Yellow Sky" * and "Soldier's Home." * Can you see what might be called a literary influence in the two stories? Discuss similar uses of details and point out differences. What finally is the significance of the differences?

C. *IMITATION*

1. Describe your grandfather's home in the tone and mood that Twain uses toward Phelps Farm.* Then describe it in a contrary mood and tone—say, one suggesting fertility and productiveness, instead of moribund laziness.

2. Describe the effect of a milieu that has shaped your mind, as the childhood habits and assumptions shaped Henry Adams's mind. Try, like Adams, to place the milieu and yourself in a historical process.

3. Project a possible story setting that would elevate meaning in the way that Crane and Hemingway sometimes elevate meaning.

D. *CREATION*

1. Describe a photograph or a tableau situation that you think is resonant with meaning. It might be, for example, a professor shuffling down a hallway, with his wife two steps behind him, or a child of two or three years breaking away from his mother in a park or a railway station or a department store.

2. Write a sketch in which a historical scene is made to reflect part of your thematic intention. A Civil War scene might be too easy, but suggests the kind of thing possible.

3. Write a scene in a setting you know well, in such a way that time and place are essential to the scene.

6

Point-of-View

Stories, fictions, are not dead things; they tend to have a life of their own. Since they are in language, and since such qualities of language as intonation, stress, pause, rhythm, have a way of insisting upon being said, an oral quality persists in stories. This quality of being said posits the existence of a sayer, a sayer who has existence only within the language of the work itself. He is distinct from the author, though he may be—indeed, is—one of the author's personae. This sayer is in the position of being the apparent teller of the story,[1] though we all know that the author is the actual teller. We sometimes call him the implied author, or the narrator.

This narrator, whose presence is unavoidable, has long presented serious aesthetic problems, which are generally lumped together under the heading "point-of-view." Point-of-view is generally defined as the position, the vantage point, the spatial placement (which can be internal or external), which the narrator takes in relation to the story he tells. Sometimes it is defined instead as the position the *author* takes in relation to the story, and there have been many schemes which attempt to catalog and characterize the variety of positions possible.

There are several weaknesses and conventions involved in these definitions and schemes of point-of-view. The primary weakness is that they do not account for the aesthetic response of the reader. The reader, not the writer, is the one who is put in a particular *aesthetic* position by way of his perception of the narrator. The writer presumably knows *all,* and thus such authorial position and identification as point-of-view imply are irrelevant to the reader's perception of the story. The reader's perceptions of the author,

---

[1] This is true even in epistolary technique, telling by way of letters, which is only a rhetorical variation of "first-person-singular."

especially if he knows a few biographical details or has read some commentary on the author's intentions, are irrelevant to and outside the literary work. Only the reader's perceptions of the apparent narrator, whether he approximates the author or not, are aesthetically significant in point-of-view.

Another weakness is that most of these schemes have concentrated upon a physical and spatial concept of point-of-view. They conceive it as the *place* from which the action is seen. But the word, point-of-view, has another common meaning, that of *opinion,* or *attitude.* This kind of point-of-view is also involved in the reader's perception of the narrator and of the action he narrates. Such attitudes identify the personality of the apparent narrator and, thus, function as an index of choice in style and content.

The aesthetic definition of point-of-view is this: the person apparent, the perceiving consciousness, through which the reader perceives the action, scene, character, and thoughts that make up the story. This person apparent may be paranoid or stupid or sensitive. He may be located inside one character's brain, in his eyes, on his shoulder, three feet away from him, thirty feet away, removed in time and distance so that the action is only conceptual, not immediate, in a hundred other physical and a thousand emotional positions. Wherever point-of-view is lodged, it is a person apparent, with a personality and a value system, which become part of the process of the reader's perception. (This is even true of effaced narrators, as in Hemingway's "The Killers." There the perceiving consciousness approaches the personality of the ideal scientist—observing, recording, maintaining equanimity and objectivity—though there is a lot of uneffaced juxtaposition going on in that story.) The personality calls attention to certain aesthetic problems: Authority, for example—how does he know what he tells? How much are we to believe? Is he sensitive enough or aware enough to see and understand what is important? Is he in a positon to know?

Most point-of-view schemes deal, at least by implication, with Authority. One of the primary conventions of fictions is that we accept whatever the *author* says. If the author tells us that a character went to a window and looked out, we accept fully and by convention that the character did go to the window and look out. If a narrator, however, tells us the same thing, we are necessarily left in doubt. There is no reason for us to trust the narrator's authority to tell us this, until he has been shown to be trustworthy and reliable. The inherent unreliability of the narrator makes careful reading necessary and opens up wide possibilities for aesthetic complexity in his perception and narration. Thus the problem of authority is a primary aesthetic concern in point-of-view.

Another convention which we seldom notice is our acceptance of the narrator's past knowledge of the events he relates. He is almost always put in the conventional position of looking back upon an action that is already complete. Presumably he knows everything he can about that action, including its outcome. By convention, he speaks in the grammatical past tense, which we accept as the narrative present. We generally ignore all this when we are reading and allow the narrator to pretend that he is ignorant and in the midst of experience. This convention allows him to develop considerable aesthetic immediacy in relation to us as readers. The techniques of point-of-view permit the author to manipulate these conventions.

The rhetoric and aesthetics of point-of-view are so immensely complicated that almost any scheme which focuses upon *placement* is doomed to fail to explain it. Not only the physical, but also the mental relationships of several people are involved, for example, in such complicated points-of-view as Conrad uses in *Heart of Darkness* and *Lord Jim*. In *Heart of Darkness,* the author, Conrad, tells us what a narrator on the deck of the Nellie tells us about Charlie Marlow who is telling us about his relations with Kurtz and sometimes about Kurtz's own attitudes toward the natives. In *Lord Jim,* Conrad tells us what Marlow, the narrator, learns from several subordinate narrators about Jim. At every stage of each of these narrations within narrations, we are confronted with both the physical and mental relationships between a narrator and his narration. In a real sense, point-of-view is a process of aesthetic identification with a person; therefore, there are virtually as many kinds of points-of-view as there are stories.

Aesthetically, the writer cannot have any point-of-view other than total omniscience. He may choose to tell the story in the vocabulary and perceptions of a narrator, as Sherwood Anderson does in "I Want to Know Why," but it is absurd to suppose that he is limited to the vocabulary and perceptions of his narrator. Every choice of juxtaposition, every choice of scene and character, every choice of weakness or naïveté in the narrator, are all acts of knowledge and are all perfectly known to the writer. He chooses to limit the method so that he can limit the reader's perception, which may be important in the rhetoric or aesthetic of the story. It is only if the writer assumes the pose of a reader, as he does no doubt repeatedly while in the act of writing, that the conventions and limitations of the narrator become important to him.

A Matrix of Points-of-View

There are innumerable points-of-view, but let us attempt a matrix which would account for all the possibilities, *as seen by the reader*. There are only four primary dimensions of point-of-view, but the matrix these four dimensions create allows for development of all the known possibilities of point-of-view.

The objective-subjective continuum

Ranging through all possible points-of-view is a conceptual dimension with pure objectivity at one end and pure subjectivity at the other. Along this dimension, we have traditionally marked three spots: the purely omniscient (perfectly factual), the third-person-limited, and the first-person. These spots, of course, correspond to the three speakers in fiction. Variations in the personalities of these speakers and in the control of the reader's aesthetic identification with them expand the three nodules into many other possibilities. A petty, selfish third-person-limited can sound almost like a first-person; a sensitive, intelligent, and unthreatened third-person-limited can approach omniscience. And there are varieties of omniscience, too, from that which relies completely on facts and which is therefore objective, to that which contains an element of judgment or argument and which is therefore slightly less objective. At the other extreme, one can easily imagine pure subjectivity and subjectivity slightly less pure.

Along this continuum, too, lie the grammatical possibilities in point-of-view. There are really only two significant grammatical points-of-view, the first-person and the third-person, the familiar "I" and "he." "We" becomes a variation upon "I," because the spoken quality that persists in language resists the plural with its single voice; "we" points-of-view degenerate aesthetically into the "I" who is summarizing what several people experienced. Similarly, stories written in the "you" point-of-view, once we become used to the curiosity of the grammar, become indistinguishable from third-person stories. Similarly with "thou" and "ye." It makes no difference, aesthetically, if the reader identifies with and perceives the story through a person called "you" or one called "he." Conceptually, the point-of-view is simply *another* person.

The impulse, however, to separate the plural side of the grammatical possibilities conceptually soon asserts itself and we get three significant nodules on the continuum. In addition to the "I," we have the "he" who is a participant in the action, whose knowledge of the action is limited, and the "he" who is the author, who knows all and tells what he chooses. These three points-of-view are the traditional points mentioned above and the three persons who can reveal information to the reader, mentioned in the section on character.

The continuum accounts for grammatical possibilities and the possible speakers, and it contains a component of distance, since obviously the reader cannot be as close to an objective omniscience as he can to a subjective consciousness. The distance here, however, is largely conceptual or intellectual.

The fact that it is conceptual actually eliminates, from the reader's point-of-view, one often discussed quality—the limited narrator as observer vs. the limited narrator as actor in the story. To the reader, the limited narrator is always and necessarily acting, and, though he may be telling about someone else, what is actually and aesthetically dramatized is his own consciousness during the act of telling. In a real sense, this means that all first-person-singular stories are first and most importantly about the mind of the narrator. If an author fails to take this into consideration and writes a story which the narrator has nothing to do with, we perceive the narrator as mere gimmick, as a mere means of telling the story and, thus, an aesthetic mistake. Aesthetically, whenever an author uses a narrator who is outside the action, he subordinates what he thought was his primary action to a depiction of a character.

The dramatized-summarized continuum

A second dimension that crosses every point of the first dimension is concerned with the technique of revelation, which may range from absolute telling to absolute showing, from the perfectly undramatized to the perfectly dramatized. Descriptive techniques which are static and pictorial lie at the one extreme; dialog and thought, which are pure actions, lie at the other extreme. This is the dimension that is traditionally spoken of as dramatized-undramatized, scene-summary, showing-telling.

If we lay this continuum of the technique of telling across the continuum of the personality of the teller, we get a two-dimensional matrix on which can be plotted incomplete versions of most traditional points-of-view. They will be incomplete because they still lack two other important dimensions.

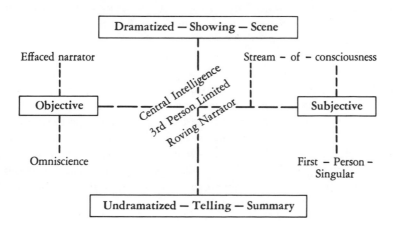

Objectivity, perfectly dramatized, limited to showing in scene what happens, is the effaced narrator which Hemingway made famous. He is omniscient in that, though we do not hear his voice, we get the result of his choices as to what to show, and those choices are everything. This narrator contrasts with the traditional sense of the omniscient narrator (objectivity, perfectly summarized), who has the privilege of dramatizing or summarizing whichever parts of the story he chooses, but compares with him in that both are at the objective end of the first continuum.

At the other end of the objective-subjective continuum, there are also two contrasting points-of-view. Subjectivity, perfectly dramatized, is stream-of-consciousness, in which we are shown only the thoughts of the perceiving consciousness and nothing that is not a thought. Action and scene can be revealed only as they become part of the flow of thought in the view-point character's mind. The consequent elimination of a measure of objectivity is the greatest weakness of the stream-of-consciousness technique. Subjectivity, perfectly summarized, is the old first-person-singular. The first-person-singular is limited to telling of action that has happened in his past. His repeating the story is his way of summarizing, choosing what he will tell and compressing the rest. He can, of course, narrate actual conversations and describe the scenes of those conversations; he thus can enter a kind of middle ground between the subjective extremes.

Near the middle ground of both continua are three of the traditional third-person-limited points-of-view. Squarely in the middle is the third-person-limited itself. If the author chooses to dramatize that third-person's perceptions and thoughts in language more objective than the character himself actually has done, one gets the technique of the central intelligence, which Henry James thought the best of all possible points-of-view because the reader gets both a measure of subjectivity and objectivity in the process of perception and has the range of the dramatized-undramatized continuum. If we move from the center slightly toward subjectivity and summary, we find the roving narrator, or shifting third-person. In this point-of-view, the author takes the liberty of entering in turn more than one mind. Generally, he has limited himself to rendering that mind in its own language, that is, with a considerable measure of subjectivity. If this subjectivity is pushed to the extreme of the dramatization continuum, we get the third-person stream-of-consciousness which was typical of Virginia Woolf in *To the Lighthouse*. Third-person-limited, perfectly dramatized, tends to become either the effaced narrator or the stream-of-consciousness. Third-person-limited, perfectly undramatized, becomes slightly essayistic and drifts toward total omniscience or toward first-person-singular.

Authority and Distance

Let us now imagine a third dimension perpendicular to the two continua. At one end of this axis is the action of the story itself; at the other end is the reader. The reader can be moved along this continuum in degrees of perceptual, conceptual, and psychic distance from the action. The authority of the perceiving consciousness, through which the reader perceives the story, varies with these distances.

The simplest of the distances is, of course, perceptual distance, which is analogous to the relation between a movie camera and the subject it photographs. We can be told what the perceiving consciousness sees at the top of a hill three miles away, or of his feeling of a twitch in his smile; the *place* from which we perceive can be manipulated from the perfectly internal to the perfectly external. The dramatist is, of course, limited to a single point of perceptual distance, which he supplements with empathic identification and psychic distance, but the fiction writer has a total range at his disposal. This dimension is governed by the author's descriptive language.

Across this range of perceptual distance, authority is always perfect. As we have already mentioned, it is one of the conventions of fiction that we accept absolutely whatever perceptions occur in a work. The interpretations characters put upon perceptions are, of course, suspect and present a problem in authority, but that is another matter from perceptual distance. It has rather to do with conceptual distance.

Conceptual distance involves the character of the perceiving consciousness—his sensitivity, his blind spots and repressions, his ability to understand what he perceives, and so on. Examples are Flaubert's *Madame Bovary,* James's *Portrait of a Lady,* and virtually every first-person-singular point-of-view. We necessarily distrust the concepts of the perceiving consciousness and accept what he says as mere opinions lacking proof. In practice, this gulf between *our* conceptions and the conceptions of the perceiving consciousness, this distance which exists, must be bridged by corroborating evidence for his perceptions. We have to be shown by other characters, by juxtapositions, by author's commentary, or by some other authoritative means, that the point-of-view figure was reliable or unreliable. It is along this dimension of distance that irony becomes possible, because it is here that we have the possible juxtaposition of two conceptions of action. The point-of-view character can have one conception and the corroborating evidence show us another, which contrasts to it. The comparison that results from such juxtaposition is necessary to irony as a technique.

Psychic distance, in a sense, has to do with an excess of authority. If the writer creates the action with too much authority, with too much psychic realism, the reader may be unable to distinguish the action from reality. The grand example is Orson Welles's "Invasion from Mars" broadcast, which had people calling up the police and jumping out windows. Welles spoke with such vivid authority that his listeners were unable to perceive any psychic distance between a real invasion from Mars and his fictional one. In print, too, the reader's psychic distance from the action may be diminished to the point that the action becomes as painful to him as real experience could be. On the other hand, if the psychic distance is long, the reader may find the action unreal and uninteresting. Then he will feel that the question of authority, the question of whether the represented action occurred or not, is irrelevant, because he will truthfully assert that aesthetically it has not occurred.

These three kinds of distance make up a single dimension which puts the reader's total perceptual matrix at one end and the action represented at the other. This continuum of perception can occur in any and all of the traditional points-of-view though it is shortest in the subjective side. Stream-of-consciousness and first-person-singular have the most trouble with conceptual distance —the disparities between the conceptions in the story and those within the reader's mind sometimes affect the authority of the simple perception itself; depending upon the extent of empathic identification, the subjective can also become too close psychically. On the objective side, perceptual distance is little problem, because we accept what the narrator objectively presents. But if he presents it with vivid descriptive and psychic realism, he can violate a desirable psychic distance. Conceptual distance is little problem where subjectivity is removed. Thus, this dimension of point-of-view has to do with the reader's imagined physical, logical, and psychological distance from the action.

The Dimension of Time

Now imagine the three dimensional matrix of personality, technique, and perception, moving through a fourth dimension—time. Fiction, we all know, deals with people acting in time, as well as in place. The perception of time is therefore as much an element of point-of-view as any other quality of experience. There is a continuum of ways to treat time, ranging from exact imitation at the one extreme, to near extinction at the other.

The most obvious way of treating time in fiction is to imitate it directly, to render the experience in the fiction in the exact time it would take the action to occur in life. This possibility is seldom used for very large blocks of writing, for we all know that experience has its high points and its low. To render the low parts of experience in literal time, as contemporary French novelists attempt in their "durational realism," is to render irrelevancies as if they were important. Aristotle advised playwriters to use messengers to narrate and summarize some actions as happenings off-stage, rather than to render the events in the form of action, because the elapsed time of an event is not always commensurate with the event's importance. Effaced narrators often have trouble with this aspect of time, because to summarize or fragment would be to break point-of-view by implying a different consciousness than the effaced narrator.

Time can also be imitated conceptually. This kind of imitation is involved with relativity. Relatively simple actions can be perceived in relatively small amounts of time, that is, with a short representation. But more complex actions require relatively longer to perceive. The progress of time in a fiction can be made to imitate the necessities of conceptualization; in fact, fiction which fails to allow for conceptual time is usually quite disappointing.

This suggests pace as a technique for representing time. Pace in fiction has to do with the expansion or contraction of literal time into conceptual time. The action can be speeded up at one place, slowed down in another, made to move fastest or slowest at the climactic point, and so on. Some authors adopt a general use of pace. Thomas Mann, for example, almost always slows down the action of his fiction, so that things move relatively slowly in relation to the actual time the action would take. This allows Mann considerable opportunity for conceptualizing theme. On the other hand, some authors make it a practice of contracting time, so that their work is filled with actions and little else. Done badly, this produces the pulp adventure story. Done well, it can produce artistic fiction.

Another way to treat time is to fragment it in various ways. One can, for example, rearrange the sequence of events if he wishes. Flashback technique is the most famous and, perhaps, simplest rearrangement of time. Time can also be fragmented by allowing lapses of consciousness between segments of the represented action. Thus, we may see what happened this morning, then get a white space, then see what is happening now. As a rule of thumb, it is a good idea not to let anything happen in those white spaces, except time pass or scene change. Another possible fragmentation of time is Ford Madox Ford's concept of "time-shift." Essentially, the time-shift involves moving back and forth in time on the principle of word and event association. A character acting in the present thinks of something that happened in the past and that something becomes an image-bridge, through which the events of the past are evoked, sometimes at considerable length. This technique of the character remembering is to be distinguished from the simple flashback. The flashback is a literal transportation in time; the character remembering involves two sequences of time simultaneously, *then* as a part of *now*.

The conceptual treatment of time, whether in pace or rearrangements, culminates in summary and generalization of time. Actions can be conceived of as having happened in no particular time; the memory can almost perceive them outside of time. This kind of summary and generalization of experience enters into fiction, of course. But it is impossible to think of an action as happening (as opposed to having happened) without the passage of time. Since fiction is a representation of scene and character in action, some passage of time remains necessary to fiction. One can almost extinguish it, but not quite.

Any use an author makes of time is necessarily a part of our perception of the material he presents—is a part of point-of-view. The author's manipulations of the time techniques, indeed, can govern what we see in fiction. It can focus and manipulate our attention in such a way as to determine what is dramatically and aesthetically part of our perception. Thus, time is an extremely important part of point-of-view.

A Use of Point-of-View

It is surely obvious that manipulations of time intimate structure and form, as do personality, technique, and distance. Point-of-view, then, is integrally bound up, not only with style, character, and scene, but with plot and structure as well. Let us look at an example in which all these things are operating:

WITHIN A MAGIC PRISON [2]

Tom turned on the light where he was reading the newspaper, and Lizzie turned on her light where she was playing cribbage. Tom settled down, unconsciously brushing his fingers up and down the chair's fabric as he read, making the very faintest rasping sound. Lizzie sat near the window; she enjoyed feeling the dark breeze brush past her skin, and the breeze made the cards cool to the touch. Each was isolated in a little round cell of light, which did not touch the other, and most of the living room was lost in the shadows of evening. Slowly, the warm summer evening slid into a warm summer night. Tom turned a page.

God, what a dull way to spend an evening, Tom thought. He crinkled his newspaper to annoy his wife, but she didn't look up. Everyone else we know has dinner out once in a while, or goes dancing, or takes in a show, or plays bridge. Or visits friends. God, would they laugh if they ever knew that evening after evening my wife plays cribbage with herself. Not even solitaire, but cribbage. God. How they'd laugh if they knew how absurdly you occupy yourself, my dear.

[2] By Evelyn Dysarz, assisted by H. C. Brashers.

Lizzie finished a game and put the pegs back into the starting position. That's the third game I've played, Tom, and you lost them all. Lost as surely as if you fell overboard in the middle of the Atlantic Ocean. It just goes to show what a dull person you are, Tom. We've been married 27 years and the only thing I can show for it is, I can shuffle cards good. And it's all your fault.

I know she thinks more of that cribbage board than she does of me. She had a dedicated glow in her eyes as she came in here this evening, and she passed by my chair without a word, except for that damned superior look in her eyes, superior and dedicated. If ever all the cribbage factories in the whole world went bankrupt, and her own little board suddenly disappeared completely and absolutely and positively, I wonder what she would do. You made quite a scene that time when you wanted Peter to join the church choir and he didn't want to, and he was crying and you were yelling, and you sent him to bed immediately after dinner. You had your way that time, but if suddenly all the cribbage boards in the whole world disappeared, there would be absolutely nothing you could do about it. Ha! That would be a good one. Then you'd *have* to talk to me, and we'd go out sometimes and have fun. And I could casually mention to the boys at work, "Oh, I just remembered the *funniest* joke that Liz and I heard when we were at Charlie's last night . . ." and everyone would gather around, and they'd all laugh at the joke. No, Liz, not at me, at the joke. "Yes," I'd say, "we go to Charlie's once in a while because they have such droll entertainment, but their food really is under par." It's too bad you spoil it all, Liz. You must have a guilty conscience . . . Oh, bury m-e-e-e on the lone prairie . . . We'll play that at your funeral, and everyone will think it's a tremendous joke, Liz. You know I won't laugh, but I know everybody else will. Your grave will be on some desolate, windblown plain, and anyone that passes can read that "here lies a person that wasted her life playing cribbage with herself." God!

Jack o' diamonds, Jack o' diamonds, Oh, good ol' Jack o' diamonds. That Jack o' diamonds is a good ol' man, Tom. Yo, ho, blow the man down. You ain't helpin' me here, but you're still a pretty fine ol' man, Jack o' diamonds, pretty fine, yo, ho, blow the man down. Now, if you want to see a *really* fine man, just take a gander at the man sittin' right over there. Real fine. He sits at home all evening, reading a newspaper. Read, read, read. "Oh, look!" says he, "an article on the tax system of Lower Slobovia. I must read this. Wait. Don't turn the page. I haven't read that square inch down in the right hand corner." But there isn't anything there. "I must read it, anyway." Oh, We'll be reading in the old town tonight. Swing your partner, allemand left. "Sorry, sir, my partner seems to be reading the newspaper." "Well, throw him out, and *on* with the show." I'm so tired of your damned paper, dear Tom, dear boy. You wouldn't remember, of course, but we used to do things together, you and I . . . 3 . . . 6 . . . 12 . . . 21. 4 . . . 11 . . . 18. I'm still beating you, Tom. But then, you *never* were any good. And now you're as good as dead. You never talk to me any more, not like you used to; you're too wrapped up in your newspaper. No, *embalmed* is the word. There's no life in you anymore, Tom; you just sit there reading. Reading. The change happened slow and easy, but one day you was lively, and then all of a sudden you just sit there all evening. Like you was dead. Lord help you Tom, like you was dead.

Before he turned the page, he looked once again at the article on sandlot baseball. The young boy's picture on the left looked like his paperboy. His paperboy was a friendly young kid, who always had enough change to change five dollar bills, but Tom hadn't realized that he played baseball, also. That was very interesting to know, and Tom added it to his detailed outline of the world. He couldn't afford to let details like that get away from him. All the boys looked active and sturdy. Tom tried to guess their names. The second boy on the right looked like a Herman, but all the rest looked like Mikes and Joes. The name a boy had would reflect his character and, therefore, Tom had to know the prevalent names, in order to revise his comprehensive outline of the world when these boys grew up. He looked at the picture again. He must remember that, of seven boys of the character type that would get their pictures in the paper for playing baseball, only three looked ambitious. Tom turned the page.

Liz gathered the cards again and glanced, worried and mad, at Tom. Tom's team had rallied and surged forward. Come along now, men, she said to her own team; you can't let a bunch of brutes get away with this sort of thing. Here's a new set of cards; let's see if you can't do better now. Ho! Jack o' Diamonds again! Yo, Ho, You're a good one. I'll appoint you commander. Now, get in there and rally your men. Over the top! Charge! Make my time worthwhile. 12 . . . 18 . . . 21. . . . That's a good boy, Jack o' Diamonds! That's a good boy! We'll show those—those—newspaper readers! Now, let's try it again; push them like they was dead.

Tom watched his wife cautiously from behind his newspaper. She was dealing another hand, and the cards were brightly glossy as they flew beneath the lamp's glare. The cribbage board was directly in front of her, and the two piles of cards grew on either side of the board. She thinks I don't know, thought Tom, but the pile by her side is me, and that's the side that always loses. I watch you, Lizzie, my dear.

Liz looked at Tom with a critical eye. Reddened fingers encircled the newspaper. His shoes were unlaced, and his left ankle rested on his right knee. The newspaper blocked her view; he seemed to shrink behind its formidable mass, making a dull white wall between her and him. I can't see your eyes, Tom, but I know they're systematically traveling across every line. Somewhere in your forgotten childhood, your mother must have commanded you with a wagging finger to read every line. God, Tom, you're methodical.

Tom finished a story and stared out the dark window. It's dark already, he thought. Another evening wasted. And it's all your fault, Liz. John and Dinky and their wives were going to play bridge tonight. They never even asked me if you and I wanted to play because they know what a bore you are. And I bet they laugh about it.

I wonder what Anthony M. Glint is doing tonight. And to think I almost married him. He sent me chocolates every week and all my girl friends were so jealous. How he could dance! And that night we came home early and made fudge together! We had the kitchen window open and I stirred the fudge and he held a towel over the doorway so no one could smell it, and then we ate every single piece, and I got sick. Did we ever have fun that night . . .

You know, Liz, of all the people I have ever, ever met, you are the dullest, d-u-l-e-s-t.

You probably don't know that people like Anthony M. Glint exists, you clod.

Well, no, I've met *one* person duller than you, but my God, you wouldn't believe that person existed, she was so—so—dormant. Everyone laughed at her behind her back. In front of her back, beside her back—she couldn't tell the difference. Maybe she was one of your friends, because you certainly act like her.

Tony Glint and you are as unlike as night and day. He knew how to have fun.

Possibly she was your mother. But then, I can't imagine anyone that could possibly be old enough to be your mother.

Lizzie's chair squeaked as she bent forward and shuffled the cards with a snap, but the sound was buffered in the silence and did not disturb it.

Tom crackled the newspaper, turning a page, but the silence rushed in and settled on everything as soon as he was still again.

From outside, they heard a car driving up the street. The motor stopped in front of their house. They heard footsteps, and then the doorbell rang. Tom cocked his head like a hunted man, listened, then carefully folded his newspaper and put it on the table. He asked Lizzie, who was running her fingers through her hair to straighten it, if she was expecting any visitors. Liz said no and quickly gathered her cards up into a neat pile. Tom laced his shoes and went to answer the door. I'll wait til it rings again, Tom thought, maybe it was just some neighborhood kids playing a joke; and he stood by the door with his hand on the knob, in the gloom.

The doorbell rang again. Tom turned on the hall light and swung open the door.

"Peter! Liz, Peter's here. Come on in. How are you, son? My, but you're looking well." Tom peered out the door. "Is your wife out there in the car?"

"Yes, Judy and I were just passing by, Dad. Hi Mom. Anyway, we just dropped in to see if you want to go to a movie with us. We're going downtown to the Victoria theater—it starts in twenty minutes—and then out to a late dinner somewhere. Want to grab a sweater and come? It would be fun with the four of us."

Tom looked at Liz and said cautiously, "You're looking fine, Pete. Looks like you're still growing. Ha. Ha," he laughed nervously.

"How about the movie?" said Peter.

"Well, I don't know. Your mother may not want to go. It sure is getting late. It got dark a long time ago, and I was just about ready to go to bed. What about you, Liz?"

"Your dad may be right, Peter. You look a little tired tonight, Tom. Maybe you should go to bed early. It's too bad you didn't phone a little earlier, Peter, and we could have gotten ready. It's nice seeing you again, though. Is your wife in the car? Say hello to her for me, will you?"

"Yes, do say hello to her for us. Too bad you didn't phone."

"Well, O.K. You get out of it this time," said Peter. "Gotta go. Starts in 20 minutes. Love and kisses. See you later." He ran down the porch steps and out to his car.

They stood at the door and watched him drive away, watched until the red tail lights disappeared, then they walked back to their separate cells of light in the living room. Liz said she thought Peter was gaining weight and Tom answered, jocularly, playing a game, that he hadn't noticed. Each said it was good to see their son again; each said he was looking well. Both agreed he should have phoned.

A boy ran by outside, his footsteps pounding on the sidewalk, and he shouted to some vanished companion, "Hey, wait for me." His voice floated down the street. Liz looked out the dark window for ten or fifteen seconds with a blank, staring expression, then roused herself and began to finish the game with vigor. Tom sat down and propped up his newspaper.

He quickly found his place in the newspaper. He looked irately at his wife to see what she was doing, but she was already absorbed in her game; Tom's scowl melted into a look of eagerness as he lifted his newspaper to conceal his face.

Two piles of cards lay on either side of the wooden cribbage board. The four pegs on the cribbage board marched along the no-man's land; they were hostages, and neither side dared shoot in fear of hitting one of their own. The hostile troops were encamped on either side of the forbidding wooden wall. A few soldiers tried to hop as high as they could to see what the enemy was doing. Liz scolded these men: you mustn't look. That is part of the rules. Control your men, Captain! My Aunt Mary used to cheat and look, and soon no one wanted to play with her. *Control* your men, Captain. A faint reply surged up to Liz's ear: Yes, General. I've tried, Sir, but the men are becoming anxious. Don't fret, my Captain. The game is almost over. I'll deal you a new regiment, and we'll see how well *they* do. Line them up in their strongest formations. All 15's group together! Now, let's try again. Liz was hard at work preparing the men, while the four captives watched helplessly from their high position. They were anxious, too. Things hadn't gone well that evening, and they had almost been stranded high up on their wall all night, but Liz had returned to save them. The Right Hand men forged ahead amidst rallying battle cries. The Left Hand captain, a brutish, nasty fellow called Tom, pushed his men into battle unmercifully and almost succeeded in ruining the game. Tom had called for a truce because of the approaching night, in order to go into town for something. But the Right Hand captain had outwitted Tom; he remembered that there was a full moon shining on him and ordered the battle to continue. Don't give up an inch, he cried. The captives on the wall separated. Two captives stayed to watch the camp activity, while the other two raced ahead, yelling "Hey, wait for me!" running side by side, to watch the raging battle beneath them and to see the charging men who threw themselves bodily into the fight. The tiny insects bombarding the window screen to reach the lamp's fire were actually dangerous enemy aircraft, hoping to invade the room and destroy the men indiscriminately. Liz had to hurry.

The classified advertisements! Peter had wrecked his schedule, but Tom *couldn't* skip the classified ads. Help wanted: male. Part time trucker wanted.

Previous experience helpful. Must be reliable. . . . Night dishwasher wanted. One meal included. . . . On and on they went. Tom pictured a broad-shouldered man with a baseball cap in his hand answering the first ad, and the manager giving him the weekly run to Columbus and back, and if Tom ever drove along the highway to Columbus, and if ever a big transport truck passed him, it might be this exact same fellow, and he had read the very same ad the truckdriver had read when he applied for the job. They practically knew each other! There was the dishwasher, and all the others, and Tom always followed the ad until it disappeared. Tom had always been told that the world was complex, but he had discovered that sooner or later everything was revealed in the pages of his newspaper. Tom felt a secret power and almost chuckled out loud, until he remembered Lizzie. He knew the action of a hundred different men tomorrow, because they would be applying for these jobs, and he'd known the actions of a hundred men yesterday, and a hundred the day before, and the day before. They added up.

Liz snapped the cards out into two piles. Those brutish Left Hand men had surged ahead, and she had to marshall all her power to overtake them, before she could turn in for the night. Come, my captain, you can't let a thing like a Left Hand win spoil my whole evening. Get up there! Work! Those fellows have just had a run of freakish luck. It's incredible. But luck is nothing to pit against our skill. Get in there now and catch up with those fellows. Get ahead. Capture the brutes; throw them in prison; give them newspapers to read.

Those people are still looking for their lost dog; it's been two weeks now: Male pointer, black with a white spot on its back. . . . Found: male dog, black. If it was the same one, then Tom could add to his Outline two more groups of people that were linked together! Tom would have seen them linked. Sometimes people were brought together by even such a small thing as a lost gold watch, or a walking cane. A man had power if he could just keep track of all this! He was an overseer; a god! Tom bent closer and sucked one of his knuckles. God. It was too complicated. Cars for Sale. Wanted to Buy. Female Help. And the Deaths. They disrupted everything. All his calculations had to be in constant flux, because these stupid people died. Why couldn't they just be like Liz? She was dead, but she never got in the newspaper. How could he tell if a new job had been created, or just an old one refilled after someone had died? How to keep the two apart?

Look! Look! The same phone number! God, the same phone number! One in Cars for Sale and the other in Female Positions Desired. God. What could have happened? A '55 Chevy, 2 door, low mileage, 154 cc., blue, must sell. . . . Secretarial, efficient, typing speed 75 wpm, some shorthand, experienced. Tom squinted his eyes and bit his lip, trying to squeeze the last drop of meaning out of the phrases. God . . .

Liz picked up her men and integrated them for the last time. She was breathing hard. It had been a tough chase, but it was worth it. She got up to go to bed; Tom was still hidden behind his newspaper. I didn't want to *force* Tom to go, she thought. It would probably have been real boring. I just hate going anywhere with him because he's absolutely no fun at all. I'll just have to live with him somehow, though, and make the best of it.

"Tom, I think I'll go on up to bed, now," said Liz. "Still reading your news-paper, I see."

"Oh, this?" said Tom, quickly turning pages as if to scan the newspaper. "Just a force of habit. I'll be up in a minute. How did the *game* go tonight?"

"Um . . . Red won again tonight, I think."

Engrossed, she moved a vase on the end table half an inch, murmuring, "There. That's better." Her words trailed behind her as she left the room.

"Don't wait up for me," said Tom softly, as she went up the stairs.

He waited for the light, the footsteps, the creaking stairs, and then, faintly, the door opening, a few steps, the dresser drawer rasping. Soon the house was still, except for the occasional creak. He sat up straight and, quickly, turned back the pages. He was on to something here, but, God, what trouble would the lady be in to have to sell her car and find a new job? Tom started checking the Houses for Sale. No, she didn't have to sell her house. If she was short of cash, though, she would have to sell something. He looked at the For Sale column. Baby crib. No. . . . Pair of skis, No. . . . Two couches, table, lamp. No. . . .

Commentary on Choosing a Point-of-View

The theme and aesthetic effect of "Within a Magic Prison" depend upon the dramatization of the real, internal values of Tom and Lizzie; this dependence dictated the choice of point-of-view.

Neither Tom nor Lizzie understand very clearly, nor wish to admit, the reasons that they spend their evenings at home, and both are involved in rationalizing their apparent frustrations. There is a good deal of irony, in other words, between their perceptions of themselves, of each other, and our perceptions of them; the point-of-view, therefore, had to allow for the dual (in this case, triple) vision of irony. This need suggested the use of a nar-rator who was external to the action itself and at some distance from the reader. But the purely internal nature of the material suggests the possibility of stream-of-consciousness, which has the power of dramatizing thought processes and value systems with considerable reader identity and empathy and thus of enhancing the imaginative reality of the experiences narrated, but the lack of a context by which irony could be perceived or by which any values can be finally evaluated, ruled out the possibility of a pure stream-of-consciousness.[3]

---

[3] This limitation of stream-of-consciousness is its most serious weakness. When Stephen Dedalus, at the end of part III of James Joyce's *Portrait of the Artist as a Young Man* (see the Viking Portable, p. 404) has been absolved of his sin of frequent-ing prostitutes and goes home to perceive in eggs on the shelf and in a plate of sausages and white pudding that all is right with the world, it is impossible for us to know which way to take his purely internal epiphany. We could easily see the juxtaposition of the church and white pudding as satirical; but the intensity of the internal perception makes

Conventional first-person-singular, lodged in one of the characters, would allow the immediacy and perhaps the identity of stream-of-consciousness, but would make it difficult or impossible to get the internal views of the other character. Irony in such a point-of-view would also necessitate so much corroborating scene that the story would be swelled far beyond its proper length. Any very subjective point-of-view, then, seemed unusable, but considerable subjectivity was needed.

The purely objective points-of-view seemed equally unusable. The effaced narrator would not be very satisfactory, even if we included in his perceptions the thought processes of Tom and Lizzie, for there would then be the problem of a lengthy development in which juxtapositions could lead the reader to the point. A commenting omniscient narrator would also be undesirable, since, if he commented, there could be no excuse for his not *revealing* the whole point of the story—which depends instead upon dramatization for its effect. Nor did the medial points-of-view offer much. The central intelligence focuses somewhat too much on the *process* of perception and its corroboration for this story and besides, often includes a slightly embarrassing voice of the author. A roving narrator might make the whole thing a bit like a slapstick essay. Yet, some objectivity was needed; we had to be told how to take what we were being shown.

The necessity of getting the perceptions of both Tom's and Lizzie's minds suggested the possibility of alternating between two streams-of-consciousness. The alternation posited an omniscient narrator, even though he was effaced to the point where all he did was perform the alternation. This same narrator could profitably be used for describing setting, relating movement, and for revealing the climactic and final scenes which involve almost purely external actions and dialog. If this narrator could be given, convincingly, *selective* omniscience, that is no knowledge of things that would damage the effect but some knowledge of why Tom and Lizzie think the way they do, he could be used as the fixer of tone and mood—the indexes against which the rest of the

---

us think that Joyce wanted us to take the scene seriously. There is simply no index by which we can evaluate the tone and mood of the scene.

The lack of an index results from eliminating most of the usual "vocabulary" of fiction. Scene and incident are eliminated, except as they become thought, and action and speech are eliminated from characterization. All we have left is the dramatized thought of a mind, and we can't tell when that mind is fooling itself or not. There is no context of character, scene, and incident to establish a definition of fooling. Joyce's *Ulysses*, perhaps the most successful use of the stream-of-consciousness, solves the problem of context by borrowing, *en masse*, the scenes, incidents, and even characters of *The Odyssey*. Virginia Woolf's *To The Lighthouse* gets its context from the author's biography. Solving the puzzle of its context—which may mean that we have to invent one—is prior to the understanding of any stream-of-consciousness work.

material would be evaluated. It could, in other words, establish a very objective tone, but a highly subjective mood.

Selective omniscience, then, became the point-of-view in "Within a Magic Prison" because it solved several important problems. In addition to satisfactorily straddling the objective-subjective dilemma, it introduced consistency into what was otherwise very inconsistent material. There are long honored injunctions against breaking point-of-view and against inconsistency. Essentially, these injunctions have been honored because they involve certain matters of aesthetic importance—unity and form. Aesthetically, to break point-of-view or to make it inconsistent is the same as to put a pike's head on a donkey; the unity and form of the thing are made illogical, absurd, dichotomized, and, perhaps, finally unknowable. But certain points-of-view can make us accept a donkey's head on a man, or antlers on a dupe; and selective omniscience can make two people's quite different stories part of the same unity, by subordinating them to the story told by the omniscience. One of the great advantages of omniscient points-of-view is that they can contain in short, fragmented, balanced forms all the other points-of-view. This story established on its first page a convention of using several varieties of perception and started a structural pattern which was to keep those conventions from getting out of hand. These conventions allowed us to use stream-of-consciousness when it was most effective or necessary, effaced presentation when that was needed, and to evaluate the contents of Tom's and Lizzie's minds when that evaluation would give the reader a suggestion for measuring their most private thoughts. The aesthetic promises that these early shifts made became very important to the point-of-view and the structure of the story.

PROJECTS FOR WRITING AND DISCUSSION

A. ANALYSIS

1. Analyze the first-person-singular points-of-view in the two selections by Mark Twain, Huck in the boat * and the Hat Island Crossing.* What does one do that the other doesn't? Discuss ways in which one could create and use *selective* first-person-singular points-of-view.

2. Analyze the point-of-view in Ambrose Bierce's "An Occurrence at Owl Creek Bridge." * Is it consistent? Is it effective? Outline first the problems that the story's point-of-view must accomplish, then see how Bierce solved these problems, then suggest improvements if you see any.

3. Read a story by Henry James, say "The Beast in the Jungle" or "The Pupil,"

or read Lionel Trilling's "Of This Time, Of That Place" and analyze the technique of the central intelligence.

4. Make a list of the advantages and disadvantages of each of the traditional points-of-view. Suggest, if you can, ways to overcome each disadvantage.

5. Analyze the pattern of points-of-view in a fairly complicated story you are familiar with. If you can think of none, try Katherine Anne Porter's "The Jilting of Granny Weatherall."

B. *COMPARISON*

1. Analyze and compare the points of view in the three Twain passages * used in the chapter on style. What are the differences, apart from stylistic differences? What does point-of-view contribute to each? Would you suggest any improvements, through improved point-of-view, for any of the passages?

2. Both Melville's "Ahab's Black Mass" * and Crane's "The Bride Comes to Yellow Sky" * are in omniscient point-of-view. What similarities and differences do you see in them? What role do tone and mood play in the differences? What role does effaced description play?

3. Compare the points-of-view in the Hemingway * and Faulkner * stories.

4. Compare the points-of-view in the two sketches, "A Saturday Morning" * and "David and Alice Groper." * Discuss the relative potentialities of such different points-of-view and the situations to which each is best suited.

C. *IMITATION*

1. Write a sketch, in which you use the effaced narrator, such as is used in "A Saturday Morning" * or the last part of Hemingway's "Soldier's Home." *

2. Analyze the source and techniques of irony in Browning's dramatic monologue, "My Last Duchess." * Write a monologue in which you try to get the same qualities of characterization and irony through point-of-view's stylistic selections.

3. Write a group of related sketches, using the stream-of-consciousness as your point-of-view. Use "Within a Magic Prison" * as your model, or Eugene O'Neill's "More Stately Mansions," which puts stream-of-consciousness techniques on stage.

4. Many writers attempt to control conceptual distance by reporting the perceptions of their point-of-view character in language more sophisticated than the character. Faulkner's "Barn Burning" * contains such a technique. Analyze it; then write a sketch in which you experiment with the technique.

5. Related to this last technique, but more ambitious is the technique of the central intelligence, which renders everything—character, scene, incident—from a

particular conceptual limitation. Write a sketch in which you imitate the technique of Henry James's *The Ambassadors* or Lionel Trilling's "Of This Time, Of That Place."

6. Examine Thomas Mann's manipulation of time and omniscience in "Disorder and Early Sorrow." Write a sketch in imitation of Mann, but be careful that you do not become essayistic.

D. *CREATION*

1. Write sketches in which you experiment with the points-of-view that are not already involved in the imitative projects.

2. Write sketches in which you invent characters—a blasé iconoclast, a nostalgic alumnus, a country boy, and so on—who become your point-of-view *and* your index of choices in style.

3. Set yourself some "impossible" tasks in point-of-view manipulations, as James did in "Maude Evelyn," which is a story about a girl that does not exist.

7

Plot
and
Plotting

A plot is a *purposeful* arrangement of incidents. The purpose of the arrangement is to reveal an action that is "serious, complete, and of a certain magnitude" (to use a phrase from Aristotle's *Poetics*). The word *action* is used in a somewhat larger than usual sense, as a collection of smaller actions or incidents which belong together in our thinking process and which make up what we call a story. The arrangements in plot focus our attention upon the themes in the action. They tell us what the story is about and lead us to the resolutions of thematic questions. However, we need to distinguish between the structure of a plot and the structure of an action in life which plot can reveal. Actions in life and in concept are always temporal, sequential, and causally arranged, but they are by no means so orderly in plots, which may involve many manipulations of time and motive as in flashbacks, progression for effect, stream of consciousness, and so on.

The Classical Analysis of Plots and Actions in Life

If we reduce a meaningful and complete action or story in life to its component parts, we can discover analytically and philosophically that it is made up of five major stages. It has its beginnings or causes out of which it arises; a development or growth sequence; a climax, which involves a critical and decisive choice or turning point; a second developmental sequence, which reveals the implication of climax; and, finally, the close, the denouement, the unravelling. These five stages correspond to the five acts of Classical dramatic theory.

Every story in life that is larger than an anecdote, whether it is Aunt Susie's divorce or Angelica's becoming a nun, will incorporate these five elements. Even when a literary plot employs some other organization than time, we can still discover these elements in the action the story reveals to us. It is therefore of considerable value to reduce the story to a significant and unified outline before arranging and expanding it for meaning. A conceptual outline of a causal and sequential action includes the following:

Induction to the problem, conflict, or tension

In life and in art no beginning exists without the presence of a problem, or conflict, or tension-begetting situation. The posing of a problem posits and demands a continuation of a string of incidents. It transforms random events into the beginning of an action; it suggests a story which looks forward to a decision or a resolution of the generating problem. The existence of that problem implies the existence of characters to embody it and motives that cause the characters to act. When character, motive, and conflict are clear to an audience, a story has begun.

GETTING STARTED

Beginnings in logic and in literature usually contain journalism's five W's: who, what, where, when, why. Even anecdotes commonly begin with these elements: "On the way to school the other day, I met a fellow who was riding a horse." The characters, the action, the place, the time, and even the cause (habitual action) are all implied in this opening. The human mind needs these bits of information for an illusion of clarity. They are the links of logic. It is surprising how many of our stories also begin with this information.

It is, perhaps, obvious that character, action, and place should be involved in any telling; time and cause are no less important. Time, as well as place, helps us to identify experience. Not only does an action occur in a particular moment ("When he spoke to me, I answered"), it occurs also in a general sequence of time ("On my way to school last week"). A plot must have time to occur, both in general and in particular. Cause plays a primary role in convincing us of both general and particular time. Actions in life may, in fact, occur instantaneously, but they cannot be related so quickly. To communicate the impact of experience, one has to explain the causes of that experience— not only the causes here and now, but also the general long-range motivations. Aesthetically, what causes us to perceive the beginning of an action is the delineation of one cause against another, one set of motivations against another, one character against an adversary. The induction is ended when this major question is clear to the reader. The point at which this occurs is sometimes called the point of attack.

The process of beginning may take considerably more space than an opening paragraph; in novels it often takes two or three chapters. However, the opening paragraph that does not suggest character, motive, or conflict is aesthetically irrelevant to the story. Hemingway's "Soldier's Home" begins without apparent conflict, but the juxtaposition of the two photographs, one which shows Krebs in the old, complacent, middle-class, pre-war value system and the other which shows him in a situation where all his old values have been destroyed, promises the very confrontation with his mother which is the main action and climax of the story. Symbolically, the total story is present in that juxtaposition. The conflict is present in being promised.

FOUR KINDS OF CONFLICTS

The multiplicity of experience has been reduced analytically to simpler terms—for whatever those terms are worth: It is now a truism that there are only four types of conflicts: man against society—that is, another man or a group of men or women; man against God, or his conception of the supernatural; man against nature—that is, weather, mountains, forest; and man against himself—that is, two parts of a single personality in an internal psychological conflict. It is rare for any of these to occur alone and, indeed, most experience has three dimensions, the psychological, the social, and the physical.

Complications—Rising Action

Once the induction to a story is clear in our minds, our response undergoes a qualitative change; we begin to look for evidence on either and both sides of the conflict or problem. The characters cannot be left in their initial simplicity but must be given more depth. Their motivations must be expanded and fulfilled, their foibles qualified, their strengths emphasized. The complexity of experience must be given to both sides so that there is a little good in the bad side, a little bad in the good side, to parody the old saw. We must be shown that there is no easy choice between the two, or else the choice is made immediately and the conflict resolved. If this happens, we have an anecdote rather than a story.

This growth stage of a plot usually proceeds in a series of secondary crises and their resolutions. Each ancillary problem of the major conflict (or tension-begetting situation) presents itself in a miniature induction, through some generating circumstance, rises to a crisis, and is resolved. Sometimes a new crisis will present itself before an old one is resolved, and several may be resolved at once. Generally, however, each of these secondary crises and resolutions is dramatically more tense and more important than those preceding it, so that the usual "curve" of dramatic action is an ascending series of waves, each wave representing a secondary crisis and resolution, and the series culminating in the major climax of the story.

THE PROBLEM OF MELODRAMA

Melodrama typically skips the growth stage of a conflict. It conceives of character as revelation of conflicting motives and dramatically opposed sides. The Good Guy is All Good, the Bad Guy, All Bad. Character and action are reduced to stereotype. Because of this alignment, a melodrama needs no growth or complications, only obstacles to the resolution. The resolution itself is obvious and foregone in the morally aligned beginning.

THE PROBLEM OF SUSPENSE

The complications which enter a problem also introduce suspense. There are two kinds of suspense: one based on the outcome of action ("Who did it?" and "What will happen?") and the other based on the cause or manner of action ("How will it be done?" and "Why was it done?"). Who-did-it suspense is, of course, typical of detective fiction. What-will-happen suspense is typical of adventure fiction (and of melodrama, if the resolution can be effectively delayed). The how-and-why suspense is typical of psychological fiction. The first kind of suspense, that based on the outcome of action, is the least effective, because it has least opportunity to gain thematic significance. The second kind, that based on the cause or manner of action, is by far more useful in serious literature.

Climax—Choice—Turning Point

The problem or conflict or tension can go on for some time, becoming more complicated, so that choosing between the antagonists may become a real, difficult, and important problem. But, sooner or later, all the evidence will be in, and the confrontation between the antagonists will occur. The third stage of plot focuses upon this crisis. The complication stage leading up to a climax may, in fact, be characterized by a whole series of crises, each one presenting obstacles to be overcome, each one leaving the original conflict intact but more complicated. The fundamental problem, conflict, or tension will remain unresolved until the major crisis or climax. The climax is a moment of choice—the turning point of the problem, as Aristotle called it— in which the hero through action or choice becomes irrevocably committed to one side or the other of the problem. Everything that goes before anticipates this moment of critical choice, and everything that comes after results from it. The climax is thus the focal point of a plot. In graphic illustrations of dramatic intensity, it is the highest point—the apex of the pyramid—the point where rising action turns to falling action. It need not be the most violent incident (and usually isn't), but it is the most critical. It is the point of no return to other possibilities entertained during the complication stage. The decision has been made.

POSSIBILITIES IN OUTCOME

There are several possibilities for the outcome of the conflict, problem, or tension in the moment of climax. Most obviously, the protagonist can "win," can successfully achieve his designs, accomplish his desires, "save the day." Or, he can apparently win, only to be outwitted in the end. He can be "destroyed," his antagonist "winning," or he can be destroyed, his antagonist not winning. In any of the latter three cases we are close to tragedy. The protagonist can make a firm decision which, when acted upon, becomes the irrevocable turning point, or he can be changed by events for better or worse without "winning." This is the usual outcome in literary naturalism. Finally there is a possibility that nothing happens; the situation returns to its original stasis or to a stasis with a difference. This outcome is typical of Chekhovian plots, which usually depend upon tension and dissipation, rather than conflict and resolution, for their effect.

Consequence—Falling Action

Every act is the cause of some effect. Every choice has its consequence. The fourth stage of plot is concerned with the results of the turning point or climactic choice. A climax that is meaningful enough to support a literary work will involve important consequences. To the extent that an author dodges the consequences or skips over them quickly, our interest in the work and its magnitude of meaning are diminished, for the consequences of an action are the most philosophical and meaningful stage of it. The consequences, like the complications, are usually thought of in a developmental sequence, though possibly in reverse order. Exploring the implications of action is not easy, but it is of high thematic importance. It accounts for the success or failure of a theme.

PERIPETEIA AND DISCOVERY

The falling action of a plot may include those two elements so dear to Aristotle—peripeteia and discovery—though they are by no means obligatory. Peripeteia is the ironic reversal of expectation. For example, in Arthur Miller's *The Crucible,* John Proctor tells the court of his and Abigail's adultery in order to discredit *her* testimony, but the act has the effect of discrediting *his.* The discovery may be as simple as the revelation of identities, or as complicated as a character's recognition of his own true psychological condition. Both these devices can be blended into the consequences and given a thematic dimension.

DRAMATIC IRONY

It is always possible, of course, for a character in a story to be unaware of the turning point even after the audience perceives it. The hero may still think it possible to escape the consequence of his choice or action; Macbeth, for example, wades through more and more blood and murder, trying to undo what he has done. Dramatic irony occurs when the audience is aware of something present or inevitable which the character has not yet perceived. The character's ignorance, especially if it leads to recognition or discovery, can also be important in the consequences stages.

Denouement—Resolution

The closing stage of the plot, the denouement, is the final resolution of the problem, conflict, or tension that originally gave rise to the story; it is the fulfillment of the consequences which follow from the climax. It is the final and usually most important of those consequences. It is often the most violent and most noticeable incident and is, therefore, often mistaken for the climax, which it resembles in that both come at the end of an anticipatory series.

SIGNIFICANCE

The word *dénouement,* means unravelling, or literally in French and in Aristotle's terms, "untying the knot," of the problem. It may be as explicit as the moral at the end of a fable. In fact, the fable's end is the simplest and most forward of denouements. It *is* the point. In most contemporary fiction, the point is not so explicitly stated, but only implied. Hemingway, at the end of "Soldier's Home," merely indicates his resolution and leaves us to draw its significance. Similarly, most contemporary authors prefer to draw clearly the first several stages in a logical sequence and leave the reader to make the final insight. They end the story with an image or an incident which controls the possible interpretation the reader can make. Such a denouement has the power of controlling the theme by controlling the reader's inductive leap.

Because of its importance, and because of its conceptual power, the denouement is often thought to have an affinity with symbolism. It is, in a sense, the essence and the evaluation of the whole action. Thus, the outcome tends to represent the whole story in our memories.

Needless to say, a coincidence, an accident, a surprise, or a *deus ex machina* —an unexpected aid from outside the limits and implications of the generating problem—will be aesthetically fatal as a denouement, unless it is a part of the philosophy in the consequences.

THE PROBLEM OF THE SURPRISE ENDING

The surprise ending has long been a bug-a-boo in serious fiction, but we will generally accept it if it is functional and essential to the story. To surprise for the sake of the surprise is not enough. Nor is it enough that the surprise be merely psychologically explicable. In addition to the shock and the reality of the situation, the surprise ending must contribute significantly to the plot, character, or theme of the story. The following example includes a successful surprise ending which offers us profitable study.

AN OCCURRENCE AT OWL CREEK BRIDGE [1]

A man stood upon a railroad bridge in northern Alabama, looking down into the swift water twenty feet below. The man's hands were behind his back, the wrists bound with a cord. A rope closely encircled his neck. It was attached to a stout cross-timber above his head and the slack fell to the level of his knees. Some loose boards laid upon the sleepers supporting the metals of the railway supplied a footing for him and his executioners—two private soldiers of the Federal army, directed by a sergeant who in civil life may have been a deputy sheriff. At a short remove upon the same temporary platform was an officer in the uniform of his rank, armed. He was a captain. A sentinel at each end of the bridge stood with his rifle in the position known as "support," that is to say,

[1] By Ambrose Bierce.

vertical in front of the left shoulder, the hammer resting on the forearm thrown straight across the chest—a formal and unnatural position, enforcing an erect carriage of the body. It did not appear to be the duty of these two men to know what was occurring at the center of the bridge; they merely blockaded the two ends of the foot planking that traversed it.

Beyond one of the sentinels nobody was in sight; the railroad ran straight away into a forest for a hundred yards, then, curving, was lost to view. Doubtless there was an outpost farther along. The other bank of the stream was open ground—a gentle acclivity topped with a stockade of vertical tree trunks, loopholed for rifles, with a single embrasure through which protruded the muzzle of a brass cannon commanding the bridge. Midway of the slope between the bridge and fort were the spectators—a single company of infantry in line, at "parade rest," the butts of the rifles on the ground, the barrels inclining slightly backward against the right shoulder, the hands crossed upon the stock. A lieutenant stood at the right of the line, the point of his sword upon the ground, his left hand resting upon his right. Excepting the group of four at the center of the bridge, not a man moved. The company faced the bridge, staring stonily, motionless. The sentinels, facing the banks of the stream, might have been statues to adorn the bridge. The captain stood with folded arms, silent, observing the work of his subordinates, but making no sign. Death is a dignitary who when he comes announced is to be received with formal manifestations of respect, even by those most familiar with him. In the code of military etiquette silence and fixity are forms of deference.

The man who was engaged in being hanged was apparently about thirty-five years of age. He was a civilian, if one might judge from his habit, which was that of a planter. His features were good—a straight nose, firm mouth, broad forehead, from which his long, dark hair was combed straight back, falling behind his ears to the collar of his well-fitting frock coat. He wore a mustache and pointed beard, but no whiskers; his eyes were large and dark gray, and had a kindly expression which one would hardly have expected in one whose neck was in the hemp. Evidently this was no vulgar assassin. The liberal military code makes provision for hanging many kinds of persons, and gentlemen are not excluded.

The preparations being complete, the two private soldiers stepped aside and each drew away the plank upon which he had been standing. The sergeant turned to the captain, saluted and placed himself immediately behind that officer, who in turn moved apart one pace. These movements left the condemned man and the sergeant standing on the two ends of the same plank, which spanned three of the crossties of the bridge. The end upon which the civilian stood almost, but not quite, reached a fourth. This plank had been held in place by the weight of the captain; it was now held by that of the sergeant. At a signal from the former the latter would step aside, the plank would tilt and the condemned man go down between two ties. The arrangement commended itself to his judgment as simple and effective. His face had not been covered nor his eyes bandaged. He looked a moment at his "unsteadfast footing," then let his gaze wander to the swirling water of the stream racing madly beneath his feet. A piece of dancing driftwood caught his attention and his eyes followed it down the current. How slowly it appeared to move! What a sluggish stream!

He closed his eyes in order to fix his last thoughts upon his wife and children. The water, touched to gold by the early sun, the brooding mists under the banks at some distance down the stream, the fort, the soldiers, the piece of drift—all had distracted him. And now he became conscious of a new disturbance. Striking through the thought of his dear ones was a sound which he could neither ignore nor understand, a sharp, distinct, metallic percussion like the stroke of a blacksmith's hammer upon the anvil; it had the same ringing quality. He wondered what it was, and whether immeasurably distant or near by—it seemed both. Its recurrence was regular, but as slow as the tolling of a death knell. He awaited each stroke with impatience and—he knew not why—apprehension. The intervals of silence grew progressively longer; the delays became maddening. With their greater infrequency the sounds increased in strength and sharpness. They hurt his ear like the thrust of a knife; he feared he would shriek. What he heard was the ticking of his watch.

He unclosed his eyes and saw again the water below him. "If I could free my hands," he thought, "I might throw off the noose and spring into the stream. By diving I could evade the bullets and, swimming vigorously, reach the bank, take to the woods and get away home. My home, thank God, is as yet outside their lines; my wife and little ones are still beyond the invader's farthest advance."

As these thoughts, which have here to be set down in words, were flashed into the doomed man's brain rather than evolved from it the captain nodded to the sergeant. The sergeant stepped aside.

Peyton Farquhar was a well-to-do planter, of an old and highly respected Alabama family. Being a slave owner and like other slave owners a politician, he was naturally an original secessionist and ardently devoted to the Southern cause. Circumstances of an imperious nature, which it is unnecessary to relate here, had prevented him from taking service with the gallant army that had fought the disastrous campaigns ending with the fall of Corinth, and he chafed under the inglorious restraint, longing for the release of his energies, the larger life of the soldier, the opportunity for distinction. That opportunity, he felt, would come, as it comes to all in war time. Meanwhile he did what he could. No service was too humble for him to perform in aid of the South, no adventure too perilous for him to undertake if consistent with the character of a civilian who was at heart a soldier, and who in good faith and without too much qualification assented to at least a part of the frankly villainous dictum that all is fair in love and war.

One evening while Farquhar and his wife were sitting on a rustic bench near the entrance to his grounds, a gray-clad soldier rode up to the gate and asked for a drink of water. Mrs. Farquhar was only too happy to serve him with her own white hands. While she was fetching the water her husband approached the dusty horseman and inquired eagerly for news from the front.

"The Yanks are repairing the railroads," said the man, "and are getting ready for another advance. They have reached the Owl Creek bridge, put it in order and built a stockade on the north bank. The commandant has issued an order, which is posted everywhere, declaring that any civilian caught interfering with the railroad, its bridges, tunnels or trains will be summarily hanged. I saw the order."

"How far is it to the Owl Creek bridge?" Farquhar asked.

"About thirty miles."

"Is there no force on this side of the creek?"

"Only a picket post half a mile out, on the railroad, and a single sentinel at this end of the bridge."

"Suppose a man—a civilian and student of hanging—should elude the picket post and perhaps get the better of the sentinel," said Farquhar, smiling, "what could he accomplish?"

The soldier reflected. "I was there a month ago," he replied. "I observed that the flood of last winter had lodged a great quantity of driftwood against the wooden pier at this end of the bridge. It is now dry and would burn like tow."

The lady had now brought the water, which the soldier drank. He thanked her ceremoniously, bowed to her husband and rode away. An hour later, after nightfall, he re-passed the plantation, going northward in the direction from which he had come. He was a Federal scout.

As Peyton Farquhar fell straight downward through the bridge he lost consciousness and was as one already dead. From this state he was awakened—ages later, it seemed to him—by the pain of a sharp pressure up in his throat, followed by a sense of suffocation. Keen, poignant agonies seemed to shoot from neck downward through every fiber of his body and limbs. These pains appeared to flash along well-defined lines of ramification and to beat with an inconceivably rapid periodicity. They seemed like streams of pulsating fire heating him to an intolerable temperature. As to his head, he was conscious of nothing but a feeling of fullness—of congestion. These sensations were unaccompanied by thought. The intellectual part of his nature was already effaced; he had power only to feel, and feeling was torment. He was conscious of motion. Encompassed in a luminous cloud, of which he was now merely the fiery heart, without material substance, he swung through unthinkable arcs of oscillation, like a vast pendulum. Then all at once, with terrible suddenness, the light about him shot upward with the noise of a loud plash; a frightful roaring was in his ears, and all was cold and dark. The power of thought was restored; he knew that the rope had broken and he had fallen into the stream. There was no additional strangulation; the noose about his neck was already suffocating him and kept the water from his lungs. To die of hanging at the bottom of a river! —the idea seemed to him ludicrous. He opened his eyes in the darkness and saw above him a gleam of light, but how distant, how inaccessible! He was still sinking, for the light became fainter and fainter until it was a mere glimmer. Then it began to grow and brighten, and he knew that he was rising toward the surface—knew it with reluctance, for he was now very comfortable. "To be hanged and drowned," he thought, "that is not so bad; but I do not wish to be shot. No; I will not be shot; that is not fair."

He was not conscious of an effort, but a sharp pain in his wrist apprised him that he was trying to free his hands. He gave the struggle his attention, as an idler might observe the feat of a juggler, without interest in the outcome. What splendid effort! What magnificent, what superhuman strength! Ah, that was a fine endeavor! Bravo! The cord fell away; his arms parted and floated upward, the hands dimly seen on each side in the growing light. He watched them with a new interest as first one and then the other pounced upon the noose at his neck. They tore it away and thrust it fiercely aside, its undulations resembling those of a water snake. "Put it back, put it back!" He thought he shouted these words to his hands, for the undoing of the noose had been succeeded by the direst pang that he had yet experienced. His neck ached horribly; his brain was on fire; his heart, which had been fluttering faintly, gave a great leap, trying to force itself out at his mouth. His whole body was racked and wrenched with an insupportable anguish! But his disobedient hands gave no heed to the command. They beat the water vigorously with quick, downward strokes, forcing him to the surface. He felt his head emerge; his eyes were blinded by the sunlight; his chest expanded convulsively, and with a supreme and crowning agony his lungs engulfed a great draught of air, which instantly he expelled in a shriek!

He was now in full possession of his physical senses. They were, indeed, preternaturally keen and alert. Something in the awful disturbance of his organic system had so exalted and refined them that they made record of things never before perceived. He felt the ripples upon his face and heard their separate sounds as they struck. He looked at the forest on the bank of the stream, saw the individual trees, the leaves and the veining of each leaf—saw the very insects upon them: the locusts, the brilliant-bodied flies, the gray spiders stretching their webs from twig to twig. He noted the prismatic colors in all the dewdrops upon a million blades of grass. The humming of the gnats that danced above the eddies of the stream, the beating of the dragonflies' wings, the strokes of the water spiders' legs, like oars which had lifted their boat—all these made audible music. A fish slid along beneath his eyes and he heard the rush of its body parting the water.

He had come to the surface down the stream; in a moment the visible world seemed to wheel slowly round, himself the pivotal point, and he saw the bridge, the fort, the soldiers upon the bridge, the captain, the sergeant, the two privates, his executioners. They were in silhouette against the blue sky. They shouted and gesticulated, pointing at him. The captain had drawn his pistol, but did not fire; the others were unarmed. Their movements were grotesque and horrible, their forms gigantic.

Suddenly he heard a sharp report and something struck the water smartly within a few inches of his head, spattering his face with spray. He heard a second report, and saw one of the sentinels with his rifle at his shoulder, a light cloud of blue smoke rising from the muzzle. The man in the water saw the eye of the man on the bridge gazing into his own through the sights of the rifle. He observed that it was a gray eye and remembered having read that gray eyes were keenest, and that all famous marksmen had them. Nevertheless, this one had missed.

A counter-swirl had caught Farquhar and turned him half round; he was again looking into the forest on the bank opposite the fort. The sound of a clear, high voice in a monotonous singsong now rang out behind him and came across the water with distinctness that pierced and subdued all other sounds, even the beating of the ripples in his ears. Although no soldier, he had frequented camps enough to know the dread significance of that deliberate, drawling, aspirated chant; the lieutenant on shore was taking a part in the morning's work. How coldly and pitilessly—with what an even, calm intonation, presaging, and enforcing tranquillity in the men—with what accurately measured intervals fell those cruel words:

"Attention, company! . . . Shoulder arms! . . . Ready! . . . Aim! . . . Fire!"

Farquhar dived—dived as deeply as he could. The water roared in his ears like the voice of Niagara, yet he heard the dulled thunder of the volley and, rising again toward the surface, met shining bits of metal, singularly flattened, oscillating slowly downward. Some of them touched him on the face and hands, then fell away, continuing their descent. One lodged between his collar and neck; it was uncomfortably warm and he snatched it out.

As he rose to the surface, gasping for breath, he saw that he had been a long time under water; he was perceptibly farther down stream—nearer to safety. The soldiers had almost finished reloading; the metal ramrods flashed all at once in the sunshine as they were drawn from the barrels, turned in the air, and thrust into their sockets. The two sentinels fired again, independently and ineffectually.

The hunted man saw all this over his shoulder; he was now swimming vigorously with the current. His brain was as energetic as his arms and legs; he thought with the rapidity of lightning.

"The officer," he reasoned, "will not make that martinet's error a second time. It is as easy to dodge a volley as a single shot. He has probably already given the command to fire at will. God help me, I cannot dodge them all!"

An appalling plash within two yards of him was followed by a loud, rushing sound, *diminuendo,* which seemed to travel back through the air to the fort and died in an explosion which stirred the very river to its deeps! A rising sheet of water curved over him, fell down upon him, blinded him, strangled him! The cannon had taken a hand in the game. As he shook his head free from the commotion of the smitten water he heard the deflected shot humming through the air ahead, and in an instant it was cracking and smashing the branches in the forest beyond.

"They will not do that again," he thought; "the next time they will use a charge of grape. I must keep my eye upon the gun; the smoke will apprise me—the report arrives too late; it lags behind the missile. That is a good gun."

Suddenly he felt himself whirled round and round—spinning like a top. The water, the banks, the forests, the now distant bridge, fort and men—all were commingled and blurred. Objects were represented by their colors only; circular horizontal streaks of color—that was all he saw. He had been caught in a vortex and was being whirled on with a velocity of advance and gyration that made him giddy and sick. In a few moments he was flung upon the gravel at the foot of the left bank of the stream—the southern bank—and behind a projecting point which concealed him from his enemies. The sudden arrest of his motion, the abrasion of one of his hands on the gravel, restored him, and he wept with delight. He dug his fingers into the sand, threw it over himself in handfuls and audibly blessed it. It looked like diamonds, rubies, emeralds; he could think of nothing beautiful which it did not resemble. The trees upon the bank were giant garden plants; he noted a definite order in their arrangement, inhaled the fragrance of their blooms. A strange, roseate light shone through the spaces among their trunks and the wind made in their branches the music of Aeolian harps. He had no wish to perfect his escape—was content to remain in that enchanting spot until retaken.

A whiz and rattle of grapeshot among the branches high above his head roused him from his dream. The baffled cannoneer had fired him a random farewell. He sprang to his feet, rushed up the sloping bank, and plunged into the forest.

All that day he traveled, laying his course by the rounding sun. The forest seemed interminable; nowhere did he discover a break in it, not even a woodman's road. He had not known that he lived in so wild a region. There was something uncanny in the revelation.

By nightfall he was fatigued, footsore, famishing. The thought of his wife and children urged him on. At last he found a road which led him in what he knew to be the right direction. It was as wide and straight as a city street, yet it seemed untraveled. No fields bordered it, no dwelling anywhere. Not so much as the barking of a dog suggested human habitation. The black bodies of the trees formed a straight wall on both sides, terminating on the horizon in a point, like a diagram in a lesson in perspective. Overhead, as he looked up through this rift in the wood, shone great golden stars looking unfamiliar and grouped in strange constellations. He was sure they were arranged in some order which had a secret and malign significance. The wood on either side was full of singular noises, among which—once, twice, and again—he distinctly heard whispers in an unknown tongue.

His neck was in pain and lifting his hand to it he found it horribly swollen. He knew that it had a circle of black where the rope had bruised it. His eyes felt congested; he could no longer close them. His tongue was swollen with thirst; he relieved its fever by thrusting it forward from between his teeth into the cold air. How softly the turf had carpeted the untraveled avenue—he could no longer feel the roadway beneath his feet!

Doubtless, despite his suffering, he had fallen asleep while walking, for now he sees another scene—perhaps he has merely recovered from a delirium. He stands at the gate of his own home. All is as he left it, and all bright and beautiful in the morning sunshine. He must have traveled the entire night. As he pushes open the gate and passes up the wide white walk, he sees a flutter of female garments; his wife, looking fresh and cool and sweet, steps down from the veranda to meet him. At the bottom of the steps she stands waiting, with a smile of ineffable joy, an attitude of matchless grace and dignity. Ah, how beautiful she is! He springs forward with extended arms. As he is about to clasp her he feels a stunning blow upon the back of the neck; a blinding white light blazes all about him with a sound like the shock of a cannon—then all is darkness and silence!

Peyton Farquhar was dead; his body, with a broken neck, swung gently from side to side beneath the timbers of the Owl Creek bridge.

Commentary

When we examine his character, Peyton Farquhar's long and involved vision of escape, which ends with his surprise death, is no strain on the reader's credulity. He was a well-to-do planter, a slave owner, "an original secessionist and ardently devoted to the Southern cause." Although he was unable to serve with the "gallant army," he longs for the "larger life of the soldier, the opportunity for distinction," and is ready to serve the South in any capacity, no matter how lowly. The reader senses that the distinction and larger life he wants is a grandiose, romantic spree, not unrelated to the spectacular adventures related in Scott and Dumas, who were so much a part of the Southern gentleman's education. There is no service too humble, no adventure too perilous for him. His vision of escape is merely the psychological fulfillment of his desires.

His unrealistic desire is so strong that he can be fooled by the Federal scout. He, unlike the reader, does not detect the trap the scout lays for him, precisely because he is too busy planning the perilous adventure. The scout tells him that he has seen the order warning civilians against summary hanging "posted everywhere." Peyton Farquhar does not reflect that only a person who had freely wandered on the Union side of the lines would have seen such a sign; certainly a man in a Confederate uniform could not have done so. Rather, Farquhar asks only about details: how far away is the bridge; is it guarded; could a civilian do any damage to the Federal cause? He is ripe for adventure, even if it has to be merely a psychological one. The element of surprise is necessary for bringing Peyton Farquhar into sharp focus; it evokes the last and most important detail of his characterization, for it shows the extent of his romantic folly.

It is this characterization of Peyton Farquhar as a complete romantic fool that makes the thematic statement of the story. Bierce wants us to accept him as a typical Southern planter. He is of an old and highly respected Alabama family, is quite like other gentlemen in the South, is a slave owner, thus a politician, thus a secessionist. His attitudes toward his wife, home, family are also typical. As death approaches him, they are the ideals on which he tries to fix his attention; as he approaches death, they are his visions of heaven. What nineteenth-century Southerner would not fight a duel for a lady's honor or against an insult to his home? What Southerner was not fighting to maintain, unviolated, that wide walk with the gate at its end, where his wife gave the water to the grey-clad soldier with "her own white hands"?

If we are to extend such a generalized Peyton Farquhar into a thematic statement, the Southern cause becomes a mess of romantic folly. The uncompromising Southern planters and politicians had created their "gallant army" to defend a hopeless cause, driven largely, as Peyton Farquhar is driven, by their emotions of honor and distinction. Even the surprise ending is a part of it when we reflect on the rude awakening that came to Southern gentlemen with their defeat. It is a theme not unlikely for a writer who went to war in the Union cause at the age of 19, was twice wounded, and was cited for bravery. Bierce wrote the story some twenty-five years later; it took Southern writers another forty years to discover the theme.

But our criterion for the validity of the surprise must be the same as in our first statement: that it be functional and essential to the story. Not only must the surprise serve the story, but that service must be such that nothing else would do the job. The surprise in "An Occurrence at Owl Creek Bridge" is so much a part of the theme and character that it is obliged to be a part of the plot. It not only shocks us, but shocks us into the realization of what the story is about.

It is worth noting also the very careful progression of illusory detail with which Bierce prepares the ending, so that the attentive reader, even if he does not extend Farquhar into the symbol of Southern Romanticism, should not be surprised. The escape is clearly imaginary, and the illusory details begin almost at once. There is not only the romantic agony of Farquhar's despairing, but a literally impossible heightening of the sense perceptions—fish heard, leaf veins and drops of dew seen at great distance, and such double-duty images as the grey eye of the rifleman on the bridge. Not only could the eye not be seen at that distance, it is also a completely romantic, traditional image of the "cold grey eye" of the infallible marksman of the stereotyped Western, who was also Southern by birth.

Psychological Form

The classical analysis of plot is very close to the psychological analysis of form. Both are oriented toward focus and unity of meaning. In both, elements that are not involved in focus and unity are aesthetically irrelevant.

The classical plot results in psychological unity of subject. The opening stage focuses on a conflict or a difference of attitude and presupposes an outcome of the conflict. This conflict—climax—resolution sequence satisfies our psychological need for completeness and unity. Kenneth Burke put it a little differently; "Form is the creation of an appetite in the mind of the auditor, and the adequate satisfying of that appetite." [2]

Consider the psychological form of the following adventure from Mark Twain's *Life on the Mississippi:*

THE HAT ISLAND CROSSING

Next morning I felt pretty rusty and low-spirited. We went booming along, taking a good many chances, for we were anxious to "get out of the river" (as getting out to Cairo was called) before night should overtake us. But Mr. Bixby's partner, the other pilot, presently grounded the boat and we lost so much time getting her off that it was plain the darkness would overtake us a good long way above the mouth. This was a great misfortune, especially to certain of our visiting pilots, whose boats would have to wait for their return, no matter how long that might be. It sobered the pilot-house talk a good deal. Coming up-stream, pilots did not mind low water or any kind of darkness; nothing stopped them but fog. But down-stream work was different; a boat was too nearly helpless with a stiff current pushing behind her, so it was not customary to run down-stream at night in low water.

There seemed to be one small hope, however; if we could get through the intricate and dangerous Hat Island crossing before night, we could venture the rest, for we would have plainer sailing and better water. But it would be insanity to attempt Hat Island at night. So there was a deal of looking at watches all the rest of the day and a constant ciphering upon the speed we were making; Hat Island was the eternal subject; sometimes hope was high and sometimes we were delayed in a bad crossing and down it went again. For hours all hands lay under the burden of this suppressed excitement; it was even communicated to me and I got to feeling so solicitous about Hat Island, and under such an awful pressure of responsibility, that I wished I might have five minutes on shore to draw a good, full, relieving breath and start over again. We were standing no regular watches. Each of our pilots ran such portions of the river as he had run when coming up-stream, because of his greater familiarity with it, but both remained in the pilot-house constantly.

An hour before sunset Mr. Bixby took the wheel and Mr. W. stepped aside. For the next thirty minutes every man held his watch in his hand and was restless, silent, and uneasy. At last somebody said, with a doomful sigh:

[2] *Counter-Statement* (Chicago: U. of Chicago Press, 1957), p. 31.

"Well, yonder's Hat Island—and we can't make it."

All the watches closed with a snap, everybody sighed and muttered something about its being "too bad, too bad—ah, if we would *only* have got here half an hour sooner!" and the place was thick with the atmosphere of disappointment. Some started to go out but loitered, hearing no bell-tap to land. The sun dipped behind the horizon, the boat went on. Inquiring looks passed from one guest to another, and one who had his hand on the door-knob and had turned it, waited, then presently took away his hand and let the knob turn back again. We bore steadily down the bend. More looks were exchanged and nods of surprised admiration—but no words. Insensibly the men drew together behind Mr. Bixby, as the sky darkened and one or two dim stars came out. The dead silence and sense of waiting became oppressive. Mr. Bixby pulled the cord and two deep, mellow notes from the big bell floated off on the night. Then a pause, and one more note was struck. The watchman's voice followed, from the hurricane-deck:

"Labboard lead, there! Stabboard lead!

The cries of the leadsmen began to rise out of the distance and were gruffly repeated by the word-passers on the hurricane-deck.

"M-a-r-k three! M-a-r-k three! Quarter-less-three! Half twain! Quarter twain! M-a-r-k twain! Quarter-less—"

Mr. Bixby pulled two bell-ropes and was answered by faint jinglings far below in the engine-room, and our speed slackened. The steam began to whistle through the gauge-cocks. The cries of the leadsmen went on—and it is a weird sound, always, in the night. Every pilot in the lot was watching now, with fixed eyes, and talking under his breath. Nobody was calm and easy but Mr. Bixby. He would put his wheel down and stand on a spoke, and as the steamer swung into her (to me) utterly invisible marks—for we seemed to be in the midst of a wide and gloomy sea—he would meet and fasten her there. Out of the murmur of half-audible talk one caught a coherent sentence now and then—such as:

"There; she's over the first reef all right!"

After a pause, another subdued voice:

"Her stern's coming down just *exactly* right, by *George!* Now she's in the marks; over she goes!"

Somebody else muttered:

"Oh, it was done beautiful—*beautiful!*"

Now the engines were stopped altogether and we drifted with the current. Not that I could see the boat drift, for I could not, the stars being all gone by this time. This drifting was the dismalest work; it held one's heart still. Presently I discovered a blacker gloom than that which surrounded us. It was the head of the island. We were closing right down upon it. We entered its deeper shadow, and so imminent seemed the peril that I was likely to suffocate, and I had the strongest impulse to do *something,* anything, to save the vessel. But still Mr. Bixby stood by his wheel, silent, intent as a cat, and all the pilots stood shoulder to shoulder at his back.

"She'll not make it!" somebody whispered.

The water grew shoaler and shoaler by the leadsman's cries, till it was down to: "Eight-and-a-half! E-i-g-h-t feet! E-i-g-h-t feet! Seven-and—"

Mr. Bixby said warningly through his speaking-tube to the engineer: "Stand by, now!"

"Ay, ay, sir!"

"Seven-and-a-half! Seven feet! *Six*-and—"

We touched bottom! Instantly Mr. Bixby set a lot of bells ringing, shouted through the tube, *"Now,* let her have it—every ounce you've got!" then to his partner, "Put her hard down! snatch her! snatch her!" The boat rasped and ground her way through the sand, hung upon the apex of disaster a single tremendous instant, and then over she went! And such a shout as went up at Mr. Bixby's back never loosened the roof of a pilothouse before!

There was no more trouble after that. Mr. Bixby was a hero that night, and it was some little time, too, before his exploit ceased to be talked about by river-men.

Commentary

Note how carefully Twain arouses our hopes, creates the expectation, gives the incident psychological form. The careful details of the grounded boat, which causes lost time, and the darkness which may overtake Mr. Bixby suggest the suspense of "Will he arrive in time to make the dangerous crossing." Mr. Bixby is pitted against nature.

The motivation of the visiting pilots and their pressing need to "get out of the river" complicates the matter. Twain describes in some detail the suppressed excitement as the afternoon passes. The suspension of regular procedures, the efforts of each pilot in running that part of the river he is most familiar with, the frequent glances at open watches—all increase our appetite to know what will happen. When some of the guests jump to a conclusion, close their watches, and start to leave, but Mr. Bixby presses on, our appetite is deepened and complicated. For now the question is no longer "Will he make it in time?" but "Will he make it in the dark?" A new kind of suppressed excitement enters at this point. Again, the careful details of the taking of the soundings, Mr. Bixby's manipulation of the wheel, the excitedly silent waiting of the visiting pilots sharpen and deepen our sense of expectation. The delays involved in crossing the series of reefs and the approach to the final, most dangerous crossing prepare us for the dramatic intensity of Mr. Bixby's manipulation of the boat in the crossing. The success of his maneuver resolves all our expectations and satisfies our suspense. The incident, psychologically, is unified. The classical approach to plot insures this unity of psychological form.

Some Kinds of Plots

Psychological form can be achieved in a variety of ways and for a variety of purposes. The classical progression of causality is only one of the ways. Because of the structure of an action in life, it is inevitable that time should offer the plot-maker his most important structural principle. The writer, especially in the twentieth century, is at liberty to treat time in quite a variety of ways—chop it up and rearrange it, stretch some of its parts into a different proportion, stress some and ignore other parts, look at it from unusual points of view, and so on. The perceptual aspects of time have already been discussed in the chapter on point-of-view; we now turn to the structural aspects of time, considering some six of the many kinds of plots—the chronological, the episodic, the classic (and popular) formula—flashback, the associated progression, the kaleidoscopic progression, and the *progression d'effet*, or progression for effect.

Chronological Plots

The five stages of action correspond quite often, though not always, to the five acts of classical drama and follow both causal sequence and the clock. The plot-maker can present an even sequence and give the parts equal space and proportion, as Hemingway does in *A Farewell to Arms,* or he may change the proportions and make the climactic incident occur very early in the presentation, as in *Oedipus Rex, King Lear,* and *The Scarlet Letter,* all of which are more interested in the consequences of action than in the morality and events that go into choices.

A Farewell to Arms is a very good example of an evenly paced and chronological treatment of action in the Classical mode. The opening chapter sets the scene; chapter two introduces Rinaldi; chapter three focuses on the priest; chapter four on Catherine, so that very quickly we have some knowledge of all the principal actors and the thematic attitudes they represent. As we have already pointed out, we learn rapidly and progressively what Fred Henry is and is *not.* He is not merely a physical man like the physician Rinaldi; he is not merely a spiritual man, like the priest; he is not cowardly, like the hernia victim from Pittsburgh; nor a soldier of fortune, like Ettore. He is not irresponsible like Passini and the other drivers; nor irresponsible like Simmons and the other singers. Against all of these foils, Fred Henry emerges as a kind of Wilsonian idealist, a man who is fighting a war, but chooses what he thinks is the Good side. He thinks, in the beginning, that wars can be won and that they are instruments of progress. He cannot express it directly, but he is fighting to make the world safe for democracy.

When he meets Catherine, his idealistic dedication to the war is juxtaposed against the traditional attitudes toward women and the family. Their courtship begins as a game of chess, gets serious when Catherine is unable to meet Fred after he had been to the front, progresses to a liaison in the hospital in Milan, becomes a "marriage" in all but law, and is "blessed with issue" when Catherine becomes pregnant. This progression of scenes is used to show us Fred Henry's progressive dedication to the value system of traditional family virtues.

The problem, the conflict, the dilemma in *A Farewell to Arms* lies in Fred Henry's dedication to these conflicting value systems. The scenes alternate between love and war, each scene making a statement which is a fragment of the whole theme. These alternating statements become almost a "conversation" of thematic material. Each new idea alters the preceding idea, so that, as Fred becomes increasingly dedicated to the fertile and productive values of the family, he slowly loses faith in the war as an instrument of progress.

The conflict between Fred's dedication to love and war undergoes many crises and changes substantially as time passes. These crises come to a climax when Fred is confronted by the kangaroo court on the banks of the Tagliamento River. When he runs from the guards and plunges into the river, he is exercising his choice to get out of the war. He is taking his farewell to arms. In a sense, one might say that Fred is pushed into this turning point by the circumstances, that he is acted upon, rather than acting on his own. But if we look closely at the progression leading up to this climax, we see that it is the accomplishment of a decision which Fred has been making all during the retreat from Caporetto: He is fed up with patriotic verbiage, extremely lonely for Catherine, and has come to think that ideals such as wars are fought for do not exist; all that exists are concrete things which names denote.[3] Fred emerges from his immersion in the river, which is described in the vocabulary of the baptism, a new man. All his dedication to the ideas of the war are washed away, and he is spiritually a philosophical pacifist.

There are several important consequences to this climactic turning point. At the simplest level, he must hide from the police on the train, at Milan, at Stressa, and everywhere. He seeks out Catherine and assumes the role of protector, or family man—which represents the side of his conflict that he has chosen to preserve. There are parts of the action in this consequence stage which strain credulity. The thirty-five kilometer trip across Lago Maggiore, in a rowboat, at night, during a storm, is enough to tax any Boy Scout, no matter

[3] See Ernest Hemingway, *A Farewell to Arms* (New York: Scribner's 1957), pp. 184–185.

how physically strong, clean-living, loyal, honest, and durable he is. And when Fred and Catherine are installed in their idyllic mountain hide-away, Fred is so far from any productive masculine role that he has to grow a beard to prop up his concept of his own masculinity. Hemingway intended these portions of the book to be taken seriously. The Boy Scout section does exhibit most of the virtues of the Hemingway code. The idyllic mountain section is apparently intended to support the pre-World War I ideals of the family and to prepare the reader for the tragedy.

The death of the child and the death of Catherine are the principal incidents in the denouement. Fred Henry's ruminations on the meaning of life, death, theology, and such, causes this tragic denouement to take on an expanded thematic significance. It demonstrates for us the extent of Hemingway's cosmic pessimism, the thematic meaning of his preoccupation with violence and death: A man's apparent conflicts, whether they be love or war, are finally reduced to being only a stage in the real problem of living. A man's choice is not whether he will be destroyed by war or love, for the world will destroy him inevitably; his only choice is the posture with which he will meet the violence of his own death. Thus, Hemingway posed the existential problem.

A Farewell to Arms is an almost symmetrical treatment of Classical action in an even-paced chronology. There is a prime advantage in this strategy of revealing a story: the power of the logical progression of a causal sequence gets incorporated into the theme. There is also the opportunity to match at every moment the rhetoric of the style to the motive of the action. Both of these possibilities play an important role in convincing a reader of the reality and importance of the imitated experience.

A writer is, however, at liberty to be asymmetrical if he wishes. *Oedipus Rex* and *King Lear* both get to the climax in their opening scene, and the major part of the action and theme are the downward curve to the denouement. *The Scarlet Letter* begins several months after the climactic action and traces, torturously, the effect of that climax upon four people. In such plots, the writer is not interested in the causes of action, but in its thematic consequences.

It is possible to slant one's symmetry in the opposite direction, as in the case of Ibsen's *Master Builder*. Ibsen is interested in the subtly changing psychology of the old architect, his apprentice, and the strange girl who precipitates the action. He is not at all interested in the consequences to self, family, or society, and crumbles up the last half of the material in a brief scene. We move from the climactic decision to climb the steeple, to the consequential fall, to the death and denouement of the Master Builder. Such a story still has the power of causal sequence and the opportunity to match rhetoric to motive, but it does not have the thematic power that a complete classical action would have.

Episodic Plots

Ordinarily, episodic progression of events is one of the least satisfactory forms of plot, but it can sometimes be made artistic and thematically functional. In a sense, episodic progression is no organization at all. One incident simply follows another, with no necessary connection either in time or causality. This is the typical structure of picaresque fiction. Each incident has a completeness and effect all its own. Such a string of incidents resemble beads along a string. The connection between them is, in fact, temporal, but temporal only because of the fact that language is temporal. We have to read one thing before another.

It is possible to make the technique thematically important, as Mark Twain did in the middle section of *Huckleberry Finn* (from chapter 17 to chapter 31). The progression of the story in this section is through episodes more or less complete in themselves and linked only by the presence of the river, Huck and Jim, and the King and the Duke. The Grangerford incident (chapters 17 and 18) was written at a different time from the other episodes and is often printed as a separate and reasonably complete short story. The same kind of completeness is characteristic of Twain's satirical sketches of the Pokeville camp meeting, the frontier Shakespearean performance, the Sherburn-Boggs incident, the Mary Jane Wilkes incident, and the Royal Nonesuch. One finds, of course, a similar strategy and structure in *Don Quixote*. In both novels, the subject and thematic dimension emerges from a huge cross-section of society. That cross-section is revealed as the cumulative effect of the individual episodes.

Hemingway used a somewhat similar strategy and structure in *In Our Time,* a book that appears to be a collection of short stories, but continually impresses readers as a fragmentary novel. Part of Hemingway's theme is the fragmentation of experience; the episodic technique, which makes rapid shifts in subject, scene, and character, contributes considerably to that theme.

William Faulkner also uses episodic technique in *The Unvanquished* and in *Go Down, Moses*. These, too, are fragmentary novels; the focus, however, is not on the fragmentation of experience, but upon the continuity of causality. Faulkner gives us episodes from the distant past, each complete as a short story or novella and each continuing the historical progression of his themes. His episodes are not so much like beads on a string as they are points in a perceptual Gestalt. In the pens of careful writers like Hemingway and Faulkner, episodic plot can be made very successful.

The Classical (and Popular) Formula—Flashback

The flashback plot is a very common, but sometimes problematical, principle of organization. Simply, this is the kind of story that begins *in medias res*, in the midst of things, during an incident of high excitement or intensity, then flashes back to earlier incidents which gave rise to the excitement and intensity, then proceeds to the climax and denouement. This is the structure of thousands of stories from *The Iliad* to the typical offering in last Saturday's *Post*.

The formula begins with action in the midst of things to secure the reader. The drama and the excitement of the opening are what slick writers call the narrative hook and is intended to catch and hold the reader's attention. The limitation, as far as artistic literature is concerned, is that the action is necessarily obscure, hence the rhetoric is excessive. We cannot know the motive for the intense action and, thus, the rhetoric of that action goes unmotivated. Done badly, this invites sentimentality.

The flashback section, of course, supplies the motivation for the opening excitement. It gives us the background of the characters and the string of incidents which gave rise to the present drama. It is thus a rather dead section as far as the reader's interest is concerned—which may be the reason that popular writers rely so much on stereotypical situations and characters; their exposition can be brief.

Often this flashback section occurs in the mind of a character, but we should distinguish between a character remembering and a flashback. In a flashback, the previous time is rendered fully, as if we and the character were actually transported back to that time and situation. The point-of-view transports us completely. But when a character is depicted as remembering previous incidents, we do not lose sight of the present time and situation. The point-of-view keeps these in focus, and part of the scene is the fact that a character existing here and now in this temporal environment is remembering, nostalgically or traumatically, another time. The flashback always interrupts the progress of a story; a character remembering always continues it.

The climax and denouement normally follow the flashback in the formula, but they are too often wadded up and disposed of quickly and together. This temptation to ignore the consequence, along with the inherent obscurity in the opening, are the greatest dangers of the formula. The advantage is in the aesthetic "frame" that a return to earlier images produces; the two segments of similar material can organize and evaluate the rest. If the writer can manage to make thematic use of the last section, the formula can produce artistic fiction. We have already discussed how Ambrose Bierce, in "An Occurrence at Owl Creek Bridge," achieved this significance, and it need not be repeated here.

Associational Progression—The Stream of Consciousness

The stream of consciousness, or the associational and emotional progression as a principle of organization, grew out of the associational philosophy of Locke, Berkeley, and others, and the associational psychology of Thorndike and others. Images in the mind do not always follow the clock nor the logic of causality. Indeed, the structure of experience in the mind seems to be merely episodic and the establishment of causal sequence seems to be a function of the mind's ability to reflect upon experience and logically organize material, which even involves ignoring irrelevancies. The stream of consciousness, as plot, is an attempt to render directly the associational structure of the mind.

The principle of association is not merely accidental, but highly meaningful. Freud and others have shown us that there is no accidental occurrence in the mind. Freud's first tenet was the materialistic and scientific notion that all action is caused, though the causes may be hidden from the performer of the action, as well as from his analyst. Thus, although the progression may be apparently accidental, each image, each incident has deep and important causes. Mental association does not occur in a vacuum.

The literary principle of the associational progression seeks to make cause clearer through apparently accidental juxtapositions. The stream of consciousness is a rhetorical device for recreating meanings. The juxtaposition of one thing against another appeals to our faculty of intuition for knowledge, rather than to our logic. This kind of knowledge, this dimension of meaning is, after all, very real in experience.

The technique has problems with motivation—because of the subjectivity of all of the matter and because of its brevity. Motivation tends to remain private and, hence, obscure. The whole intention of the technique, of course, is to clarify the motivations and thus the meaning, but the lack of objective reference in the communication and the continual distrust of the subjective point-of-view's authority hinder this clarity.

The technique tends to produce uni-level writing for the simple reason that fifteen minutes of a man's mind is likely to be uni-level. Variations tend to be merely rhetorical or stylistic. When this separation of subject and treatment occurs, our response is merely to the artificiality of it, not to the reality it imitates.

Kaleidoscopic Progression

The kaleidoscopic progression, as used by John DosPassos, is a combination of the episodic and associational structures. The rhetorical principle of communication is once again juxtaposition; here, however, the intention is not to reveal the structure of the mind, but the flavor of a total experience, perhaps even, of collective experience. As in a kaleidoscope, each time a scene becomes set, identifiable, describable, the instrument turns, and we see a new configuration. In *Manhattan Transfer,* DosPassos shifts from scene to scene within New York City—lovers in the park, snatches of popular songs, workmen at the wharves, incidents from his characters' lives, and so on. The immediate effect is confusion, but slowly a cumulative effect emerges and the city is shown, not so much in cross-section as in its total flavor. The technique is a kind of public transporation system on which we have been given a transfer ticket useable for all possible trips within the city. New York City has never come so close to being captured in literature. In a sense, the city is the main character.

DosPassos used the same kaleidoscopic technique in his trilogy, *U.S.A.* In the first part of the trilogy, *The 42nd Parallel,* he gives us glimpses of American life and history during the westward movement, along a line approximating the latitude of Boston, New York, Chicago, Salt Lake City, and the northern edge of California. His kaleidoscope includes the "Newsreel," by which he supplied historical perspective and context; the "Biography," in which he presented profiles of famous or typical men; the "novel," in which he presented illustrative narratives; and the "Camera Eye," in which he entered in his own person to comment on the progress. The second part, *1919,* treats American idealism before and after World War I in a similar way. The third part, *The Big Money,* relies less on kaleidoscopic techniques, often proceeding on ordinary chronological principles. The whole trilogy is intended to give us Dos-Passos's notion of the spirit of America.

Progression d'effet

The *progression d'effet* is a theoretical technique developed by Joseph Conrad and Ford Madox Ford, in response to many of the same problems that produced the stream-of-consciousness technique. Conrad and Ford were concerned with subjectivity and subjective meaning, but they felt that subjectivity and meaning are never divorced from objective detail. Like the French Impressionist painters, and unlike the Zolaesque school of Naturalistic writers, they were convinced that experience is inescapably moored in *things*. However, as the people who were working with stream-of-consciousness found, Conrad and Ford saw that external, sequential experience of the sort plotted so carefully in Victorian novels did not always or even often say what they wanted to say about the interior and spirit of man; so they chopped up time and incident and rearranged them according to the *effect* each bit of experience had upon the reader. Thus, the cumulative effect or impression that things made became the primary consideration in organization. As Ford later said, "We were, in short, producers who thought forever of the consumer." [4]

Conrad's *Lord Jim* is a good example of the technique in a major work. Our first glimpse of Jim is as "Tuan Jim"—in his last years of honor and responsibility; perhaps, he is even heroic. The effect on the reader, at any rate, is intended to be one of romantic heroism, whether the reader respects that or not. Then Conrad turns to Marlow's slow discovery of the nobility and courage that Jim shows during the trial scenes, in which we feel that Jim is unjustly persecuted, even though we do not know the crime he is accused of—unjustly in the sense that the captain and the other mates, by skipping out, have shown themselves to be more culpable than Jim and to deserve greater punishment. Jim's romantic heroism and uncompromising honesty at the trial secure our admiration for him and prepare us to forgive him all his motivations by understanding them. If Conrad had begun *Lord Jim* with Jim's leap from the *Patna's* deck (or had begun *Nostromo* with Nostromo's defection with the silver during the Civil War—to suggest another example), he would have lost the particular effect involved in our sympathy for his characters. This loss of sympathy would have precluded Conrad's psychological exploration in the second half of the book of romanticism and psychic illusions, which include even *our* admiration for the romantically heroic Jim during the trials. In other words, Conrad's ideational progression is an attempt to deal rationally with the non-rational structure of our minds.

There are three important technical concerns at every stage of such a work. The first is with the effect itself. This concern makes the novel impressionistic and forces upon it the necessity to "show, not tell." In fact, this critical dictum derives from impressionism and effect in fiction. The second concern is with ideas and the structures of themes, for the writer is concerned with effect only for the ideas that are put into the reader's mind. These ideas then have to be arranged in some rational, knowable order, which of course has to derive from the order of the effects. This rational order can be traditional cause and effect, expository, Naturalistic, or whatever.[5] The third concern is with the dramatic

---

[4] In "Techniques," *The Southern Review,* 1 (July, 1935). See pp. 20–25, 27–35.

[5] In his *tour de force, The Good Soldier,* Ford organized his *progression d'effet* on the principle of the expository essay. He preserved an extremely firm dating system but mixed up the parts of the story, so that they would reveal the themes of his real subject. The first effect asserts a thesis, as it were; the following effect explores it, point by point. With scissors and paste, we could, if we wished, rearrange *The Good Soldier* into a

progression of the incidents (and effects); Ford, especially, came to believe that the rhythm of incidents had to become faster and faster, more and more intense, as the progression got forward. Conrad's and Ford's considerable influence on contemporary fiction derive from the theories in these three technical concerns.

The Social Critic's Hangfire

There is a story that J. D. Salinger was long unable to finish *The Catcher in the Rye* and that, exasperated at last, he went to New York, locked himself in an apartment, and forced the book to its present conclusion. Whether fact or not, the story rings true. The book's forced ending cripples it; it dodges all the issues raised by Holden's revolt. Indeed, by returning to the beginning situation (or revising the beginning to fit his ending), Salinger effectively evaded the task of completing the aesthetic and structural components of the book at all. The dilemma of the social critic and the American either-or habit of mind caused his plot to hang fire.

The story is a picaresque odyssey, in which Holden Caulfield is conceived in such a way that he (and we) must find fault with every facet of his world. In other words, Holden's adventures are a vehicle for social criticism. The conflict that develops as soon as the book begins is between Holden's value system and the value system of his surrounding world, and we are left in no doubt as to where our sympathies are supposed to lie.

In the opening section, before Holden leaves Pencey, his character is established as deeply and traditionally American. He is a passionate democrat in the sense of being essentially a product of enlightened egalitarianism. He dislikes Mr. Haas at Elkton Hills because Mr. Haas is unfair and does not give the same treatment to handsome parents as he does to the fat or corny-looking ones. Holden dislikes Old Thurmer because Thurmer is class-conscious; he accepts Selma Thurmer because she is *not*. He dislikes Ackley because Ackley violates the Millsean principle that you can squeeze your pimples anywhere you want to, except where it will irritate a fellow citizen. He dislikes Stadtlater because Stadtlater is the individualist (and/or egoist) who ignores equality. At the same time, Holden is a Romantic Individualist, of the Emersonian mold, who puts a high premium on realizing the Self; all Holden wants is to be left alone so that he can become what he wants to be—genuine, honest, true—not

---

conventional, chronological narrative, but it would not then have the theme that Ford wants to attach to the narrator's experience. The accumulation of effects with a different arrangement of parts would say something different.

be forced into accepting false values. Since he is participating in such important post-Enlightenment myths, it is possible for readers in Boston and Berlin to sympathize with him. Since the vehicle of these myths is specifically American, American readers, especially the young revolutionaries that needed a voice, even sympathized with him at a craze level.

The society against which Holden is posed is shown to be perfectly rotten. For one thing, there is a complete decay of taste: Old Ernie plays the piano with such extra-musical showmanship devices and with such random musical flourishes that Holden (or anyone) can not even recognize the song he is playing, much less judge if he is playing well or poorly. But the audience accepts him and pours into the club, applauding loudly and stupidly. For them, the reputation of the performer has replaced taste and critical judgment. The same thing has happened to D. B. in Hollywood, as Lillian Simmons demonstrates. This crowd, like the one at the matinee, has come to the point where they can't tell the Lunts from angels. But Phoebe knows when a movie is bad; so did Allie; so does Holden.

Another rotten aspect of society is the pretense with which people try to cover up their inability, a pretense that reaches hypocritical proportions immediately, because people have no basis for the "opinions" they "hold." An alternate way of dealing with inability is to hide in conformity to convention, so Old Sallie wants to skate at Radio City because it's the thing to do. And the pressures are always on Holden to "apply himself and all" so that he can grub up enough money to buy a Cadillac, so that he can start worrying about scratches on it and can start talking about how many miles he gets to a gallon.

The question facing Holden at every turn is whether he is going to join the phonies and apply himself and all, or if he can realize the Self that is implicit in every fragment of his criticism. What being a phony means is fairly clear to us as we read the book, but Holden's alternative is less clear. Phoebe is there to help us see this other possibility. Together, she and Holden depict Salinger's belief in being militantly honest and genuine, in keeping taste and values uncorrupted, in avoiding acquisitiveness, in remaining uninvolved almost to the extent of renouncing the mundane. The first two of these are very close to the Romantic cult of the child, while the last two are somewhat Zen-y. Teddy and the precocious Glass children are, of course, further developments of this alternative.

Phoebe also presents Holden with the major and final crisis of the book, when she meets him at the Museum, suitcase in hand, and announces that she is going to run away to the idyllic and pristine West with him. (Loaded American symbols, those!) Holden gets dizzy and almost falls over. (He had passed out a few minutes before, but felt better afterward.) Then, he gets angry and repeats for us several times how upset he is. What he is unable to verbalize is that Phoebe has presented him with an insoluble dilemma: because of his loyalty to her, he can't leave her with the phonies; that would violate her Self. But he can't take her with him because she is too young; that, too, would violate her Self. Presented with alternatives that are equally impossible (not just untenable), Holden reacts by disintegrating. He changes his plans immediately; he is no longer going West, but will go home; and he holds onto himself only long enough to give us that last happy image of Phoebe on the carousel. But his inability to choose has brought on his breakdown.

Instead of climactic choice, we have refusal to choose. And the book ends where it began, with the question, "What am I going to do?" still perfectly intact. Since there is no climactic choice, there can be no consequences. What we have is half a novel, a magnificently developed problem and its complications, so true that it can be used as a supplementary textbook in sociology and adolescent psychology. But it stops, half way to its structural and aesthetic completion. Salinger worked himself into a dilemma where he had to stand Holden on a moral mountain and/or destroy the rest of society; he couldn't bring himself to make Holden do either. To put Holden—a disordered, adolescent mind—on a Utopian pedestal would be an aesthetic mistake; to kill society because of him is equally undesirable.

Similar hangfires are common enough in the works of Americans who have used literature as social criticism. The grand example, of course, is the book with which *Catcher in the Rye* is often compared, *Huckleberry Finn*. Huck, too, is in total conflict with a rotten society, and his alternative is defined for us in terms of Nigger Jim and life on the raft. But as Twain and Huck near the necessary climactic choice, Twain blanches, because he is not ready to accept the implications, the consequences, that he himself has prepared for. Twain had prepared Huck to recognize that Miss Watson and St. Petersburg are as rotten as the King and the Duke. Miss Watson *is* capable of selling slaves like Jim down the river away from their families, as Mary Jane Wilks actually permits the King to do. The evidence in Twain's complications prepares Huck for the judgment that "just plain folks" in St. Petersburg and otherwhere are rotten. But before the climax, Twain blanched. For reasons more sophisticated than the Brooks thesis, but similar to it, Twain could not put Huck on the moral mountain, even though *we* would accept him there. At the crucial point, of course, Twain brought back Tom Sawyer, made the end of the book a regression in his social philosophy, and presented Huck's defeat, as Leo Marx wrote, "in the guise of victory." [6] Huck, too, ends with the question with which he began.

[6] See his essay, "Mr. Eliot, Mr. Trilling, and *Huckleberry Finn*," *The American Scholar*, 22 (Autumn, 1953): 423–40, which has also been widely reprinted.

American literature is full of heroes that are GOOD, posed against social conditions that are BAD.[7] In a conflict between God and the Devil, no quarter can be given. Twain and Salinger are on the verge of saying that society is perfectly evil and has to be annihilated, when suddenly they realize that that is an impossibility. The critic, the hero, and all their sustenance would be destroyed too. Simple destruction does not solve the moral problem.

What the American social critic has done when faced with the dilemma that he can neither accept nor destroy society, has been to become either a misanthrope or a Utopian. Ambrose Bierce, Twain in his later works, Faulkner in some of his aspects, are examples of the first; they seldom tire of showing us how culpable man can be. Edward Bellamy and Howells in his later works are examples of the other; they present us with imaginary pictures which they wish represented man. But the trouble with both these views in a possible continuation of Holden's conflict is that they give up on society as criticized; they drop experiential novelistic thinking and detail and move into a mode that is not fiction in the same sense that Huck's and Holden's problems and complications are fiction. Aesthetically, they are part of a different action or plot and introduce disunity. As Chaucer says, "If a painter paint a pike with ass's feet and the head of an ape, it means nothing; it is only a joke."

And Salinger does not want to joke with his fiction; he is deadly serious. Perhaps this is why he has chosen such "ideal" characters since Holden; he seems aware that he must avoid heroes whose triumph would appear to us poetically unjust. So he gives us Franny and Zooey, who *are* trying to find ways in which they can live in the same world with "the fat lady." But his conception of the precocious Glass children as combining the best of the Romantic child-cult and the best of Zen removes them from our world and makes them Utopian. They are not like us at all. They solve our mundane problems by being so uncorrupted that the ills don't appear, or by being so full of renunciation that they are above them. They solve our problems by pretending that the problems don't exist. Aesthetically, they are looking at experience in a way quite different from ours. Thus we find ourselves preferring Salinger's half-novel to his later Utopian work, because Holden describes our dilemma truly, even if he cannot resolve it.

---

[7] The American either-or habit of mind is responsible for such dilemmas. From Puritans to Parrington, Americans have habitually conceived such problems in absolute terms; you are either with us or against us, as a judge in Arthur Miller's *Crucible* says, which is as contemporary as the Gospels, the Revelations, Salem Village, and *The Catcher in the Rye*. When an American conceives social criticism in such terms, there can be no compromise. Not so with the British: Dickens and others can write anti-social novels with the idea of reforming existing practices. But the American conception is usually so moralistic that reform is an impossibility.

Some Other Pitfalls

Autobiographical Hangfire

The dilemma the social critic finds himself in is, of course, a very personal one. He discovers that his criticism is directed against the very sources of his own emotional sustenance. Thus his theme can be said to hang fire for personal or autobiographical reasons. This seems to have been especially the case with Mark Twain who had prepared himself to hate the worlds of Hannibal, Hartford, and Howells, but found himself also courting their approval. He got caught up on a contradiction in his personal value system and tricked himself by presenting his own defeat in the guise of victory.

There is, however, a much more typical kind of autobiographical hangfire— a kind which young writers are especially prone to. The young writer writes out of the conflicts of his own life, as do we all, for there is no other source. He uses his own experience because it presents the thematic problems that are most important to him at this moment, problems which he needs to solve before he can grow. But, too often, the inexperienced writer copies life slavishly. He writes a segment of his emotional autobiography.

The hangfire comes with the necessity of focusing the material into a climax. Because the problem is still unresolved in the writer's life, it is doomed to remain unresolved in his story, so long as he remains closely autobiographical. He is not creating a story but recording one, and because it has not come to a climax and resolution in his life, it refuses to come to a climax and resolution in the story.

The antidotes to autobiographical hangfire are objectivity and perspective upon the material. Until the character and incidents of one's own emotional autobiography gain an independent existence, so that the writer can see them as divorced from his own life, the problem will persist. Considerations of theme in the abstract and in the concrete, as well as some disciplined exercise in sketching in his characters and scenes and in outlining his point-of-view and plot, will help the young writer objectify what is painfully subjective.

The Private Story

The private story is a very close relative to the autobiographical story. It is the kind of story in which the writer invests a private system of meaning, image, and vocabulary. The stimuli that do get on the page are adequate to remind the writer of the story he wishes he had written, but fail to evoke the story for his readers. His vocabulary and his story depend upon private signification. He shows such a story to his friends and is baffled when they fail to understand. After all, his bloody heart is on the page, to him at least—why can't they see it?

The antidotes to the private story are also objectivity and perspective. The writer must abandon his subjective vocabulary of image and meaning, abandon his private language and adopt the common language of us all. His problem is to make the private story public, and he must use public means.

Insulting the Man from Mongolia

The problem of using the public language is related also to a problem we can call insulting the Man from Mongolia. This is simply the failure to put everything that is necessary on the page. The student writer should try out his stories by reading them aloud to the Man from Mongolia, whom we define as an ideal listener, a man who responds to no cultural stimuli or assumptions, to no private language, who understands only language, but understands that perfectly. He is the man who comprehends everything that is on the page and nothing that is not.

This ideal listener may come in various degrees of sophistication depending upon the techniques and strategies of the writing itself. For the fairly obvious story, he will be a fairly obvious man; for the subtle story, he will be subtle— which is to say that we do not have to write our art so that the little old lady of Prairie Flats can understand it. We write it for an ideal auditor at a particular level. The techniques and the ambitions of a story define that level.

The writer's first task in any story is to make his story clear to the Man from Mongolia for his particular story. This is a problem of the creation of imagery, the realization of detail, the vivifying of incident. When these things are made clear, the story should be a success.

Bad Pace and Proportion

Another problem having to do with the presentation of the story material is the reader's sense of pace and proportion. Pace at its simplest is the rate at which the story takes place. There should be a fairly even progress of time or a gradual and motivated change. One cannot go too fast; he must allow time for the reader to absorb the incident, and this is not always the same as the time it takes the incident to happen. A writer can conceivably be forced to violate his own sense of proportion; the necessity of clarity to the reader may dictate that a situation or an attitude be repeated in more ways than one before he grasps it.

In satisfying the reader's demands for pace and proportion, however, the writer should avoid violating them in another sense. If the story invites a response of verisimilitude, it ought to stick fairly closely to the probabilities of experience. One incident that takes a given time to happen should be consistent in pace and proportion with similar incidents. One would not tack an arm by Bellini upon a reclining figure by Henry Moore, because it would violate our sense of proportion. The story that changes its techniques too abruptly can violate our sense of proportion in exactly the same way.

Abuse of the White Space

Proportion is also related to a misuse or abuse of the white space in stories. Too often a young writer will finish a scene on one note with a character at a particular stage of development, then start a new paragraph or section on a quite different note and stage of development. He allows, in other words, a great deal to happen in the white space between paragraphs. When he so abuses the white space, it is inevitable that the change, the story, and the theme will be unmotivated from the reader's point of view. The writer is, in fact, inviting the reader to "write" imaginatively a part of a private story. This may be successful in the soporifics of weekly magazines, but it is not successful artistically.

Writing a Scenario

In the *Poetics,* Aristotle advises, "Whether the story is an old one or whether you yourself are making it up, you should first reduce it to a significant and unified outline, then afterwards expand and interpolate your scheme." Writing a scenario is one way to accomplish the clarity of thought and structure that Aristotle had in mind.

One useful form is a double-column scenario of the story. In the left column should go the five principal headings: induction, complications, climax, consequences, and denouement, along with statements of what each character, scene, and incident is supposed to accomplish. This amounts to reduction to a significant and unified outline. In the right column should go notations about the concrete rendering of the intentions in the left, the kinds of scenes one will need, the kinds of characters, the kinds of images and incidents, and, certainly, some notation as to the order in which these elements will appear. Thus, a scenario maker can come out with two parallel outlines, one theoretical and conceptual, the other practical and fictional.

A plan for a story usually begins with a fairly simple statement of overall intention. "Within a Magic Prison," * for example, began with something like, "I want to show two old people, sitting at home every night, secretly blaming each other for their isolation, but secretly enjoying that isolation more than anything possible." Then followed a discussion of point-of-view, as has already been given at some length, and a first draft. The plan and scenario for the final draft, had they been written down, might have looked something like this:

Plans for a story: "Within a Magic Prison"

1. *Characters:* Tom, who reads newspapers; Lizzie, his wife, who plays cribbage; married 27 years; one son, Peter.
2. *Setting:* living room, one warm summer evening; habitual scene: Tom at
his newspaper, Liz at her cards.
3. *Point-of-view:* alternating stream-of-consciousness, tempered with omniscient p-o-v, limited, and with scene revealed in essentially effaced technique.
(Note: each of these three may be fairly long and fully developed as previous
examples have been; each should be as long as the writer needs for his particular story, longer than that when they are to be explained to someone else—
such as a teacher, or the Man from Mongolia.)
4. Scenario (can be more or less detailed than the following) :

SCENE I

Time: early one summer evening
Place: living room; Tom's chair and Liz's window
Characters: Tom and Liz

Plans and Analysis of Scene	Particulars of Embodiment
1. INDUCTION:	
Setting the scene, characters, isolation. Generating circumstance: habitual evening; establish suppressed irritation, not open conflict.	Tom takes up his newspaper as usual, and Liz begins her cribbage. Isolation. Tom thinks: "If it weren't for you, Liz, we could go out and have some fun."
Begin with omniscience; blend to stream-of-consciousness, alternating between Tom and Liz.	And Liz thinks: "If it weren't for you, Tom, we could go out and dance, or something."
Problem should be clear when each one has had one paragraph of thoughts.	
2. COMPLICATIONS:	
Alternate between Tom and Liz. Keep segments small at first, then let them get bigger, gradually. Bring back omniscience to put in a bit of objective description.	Tom has long, varied fantasy about Liz losing her cribbage board and the two of them going out.
	Liz has long, varied fantasy on Tom's newspaper reading and dancing.
	Summary of appearances.

Old experience-exposition, including mention of son, Peter, which prepares for his appearance later.

Tom finishes a news story and wonders what it would be like to go out.

Liz remembers fun with old boyfriend, Anthony M. Glint.

By shortening segments of thought given to each and paying attention to content, we can create illusion of conversation and the illusion of crisis, but actual silence is important.

Continued castigation of each other —building in intensity toward a crescendo to end the scene.

SCENE II

Time: a few minutes later, same night
Place: at the front door
Characters: Tom, Liz, and Peter

Plans and Analysis of Scene   Particulars of Embodiment

3. MAJOR CRISIS:

Peter's invitation, if accepted, would eliminate problem and apparent conflict.

Peter invites Tom and Liz to go out to a movie and a meal afterwards.

Chit-chat delays answer a moment, so Tom and Liz can react to invitation.

Point-of-view here should be essentially effaced, since causes of isolation are close to surface; omniscience of opening would have no reason for not revealing all.

Tom: "Your mother might not want to go out."
Liz: "Your father needs his rest."

CLIMAX:

Tom and Liz have chosen to stay at home.

Both: "You should have phoned."
Peter: "Well, I'll let you off this time. Gotta run. G'bye."

SCENE III

Time: A few minutes later, same night
Place: Living room, again; same as Scene I
Characters: Tom and Liz

Plans and Analysis of Scene   Particulars of Embodiment

4. FALLING ACTION:

Having chosen to stay at home, they consequently return to living room and further engrossment in their usual activities, which must now explain decision.

Boy's yell, ironic echo in the night, can be used to echo through scene.

They return to living room; hear a boy running past, shouting, "Hey, wait for me!" They settle down to newspaper and cribbage again.

Tom reads article on sandlot baseball. His Comprehensive Outline of the World is revealed. His sense of power in knowledge derived from newspaper revealed.

Repeat of blame of each other for isolation, but pleasant relaxed settling down. Emotional investment of both should build up and should be revealed through dramatization of subjective states, that is, stream-of-consciousness.

Liz plays cribbage. Her Famous Battle of the Cribbage Board revealed. Emotional investment revealed:

Tom reads Classified Ads, the *pièce de résistance* of his Outline of the World—the truck-driver, the dishwasher.

Liz's game gets more and more exciting; fantasy in military terms: Great Battles of the Cribbage Board.

Deepening intensity of both should dramatize the real *choice of each, that is, what they "wait" for: Tom substitutes the newspaper for life; Liz substitutes cribbage. "Hey, Wait for me" motif is fulfilled by isolation.*

Tom, at classified ads—sense of power and importance—lost dog, irritation with "Deaths"—discovery of same phone number in Cars for Sale and Positions Desired. Quickening interest.

Liz wins her battle, rationalizes again the refusal to go out.

5. CONCLUSION:

Evening ending, time for bed. Total absorption of each resolves original conflict by revealing new dimension in each. Both are happiest in their chosen isolation.

Liz: "I think I'll go to bed, now."
Tom: "Don't wait for me."
Liz goes. Tom returns to want-ads, experiences victory in newspaper, as Liz had in cribbage. Fade out on Tom, pursuing one more detail for his Outline.

Such was the scenario for the revised version of "Within a Magic Prison," which was the final version, except for one important detail. After the revision was completed, we noticed that the thoughts after the climax were substantively different from the thoughts before it; so we went back, moved Tom's news-paper article on sandlot baseball to an early, prominent position in scene I, and invented a new "battle" section for Lizzie. In this way, we foreshadowed the end by introducing Tom's Outline of the World and Lizzie's Battles of the Cribbage Board in a minor key, both of which complement and balance the minor key of accusation in the last scene.

There are several advantages to preparing a scenario carefully. Most impor-tant, perhaps, is that the writer becomes very familiar with his material. He gets to know his characters well, hopefully well enough that when he begins the actual writing the characters themselves eliminate any inconsistencies in characterization and supply much of the incidental gesture and detail that make for a convincing texture in the writing. He also gets to know his scene and discovers what he can depend on setting to do for him. And he clarifies for himself the major incidents. A good plan in advance can free the writer from being distracted from the writing by large, planning questions.

Secondly—and this is highly important, too—a scenario makes revisions possible, even before the writing begins. In fact, one may revise a story three or four times before he actually writes it; the writing, then, becomes like a fourth or fifth draft—in a fairly finished and somewhat polished version. To work in scenario makes revision easier, for you can see easier where revision is needed.

Another value of the scenario is that it disciplines the movement of the story and helps to eliminate irrelevant and misleading detail. Going through the thinking process lets the writer discover where he is going; he has a possible outcome. In an interview in *The Paris Review,* E. M. Forster stressed the value of knowing what is going to happen. The novelist needs a major event, loom-ing before him like a mountain, through which, toward which, around which, the story must go. "He may alter this event as he approaches it, indeed he probably will, indeed he probably had better, or the novel becomes tied up and tight." [8] But the direction-giving and form-giving presence of it in the beginning is invaluable and necessary.

Another great value of the scenario is that a writer can determine before he has done much of the actual writing whether he, in fact, has a story or not. If the scenes he has in mind do not lend themselves to revealing a unified action of some magnitude, he had better modify his ideas or give them up. One can test the drama and significance of proposed action before the pen actually gets on the page.

The scenario is especially useful to inexperienced writers in helping them

[8] From the *Paris Review* interview. See Malcom Cowley (ed.), *Writers at Work* (New York: Viking, Compass ed., 1960), pp. 26–27.

objectify what might otherwise be private experience. More experienced writers go through the same process, but they often do it subconsciously or half-consciously.

PROJECTS FOR WRITING AND DISCUSSION

A. ANALYSIS

1. Analyze and make a brief outline of the "actions in life" that "Barn Burning," * "The Bride Comes to Yellow Sky," * and "An Occurrence at Owl Creek Bridge" * imitate. Ask such questions as: What is the central, controlling problem in each action in life (not necessarily the same as the story)? When—in which incident—did that problem come into being? What stages of complication does it go through? When—in which incident—is a decision made in relation to the problem? What effects does the decision have? What incident, scene, or alignment of forces puts the final touches on the resolution of the problem?

2. Make a brief summary of the important developments in the three stories referred to in question 1 and note which developments forward which phases of classic plot. Is it always necessary to actually record the incidents which create and resolve problems? What compensations must one make in a story if he leaves out, say, the problem-generating scene? Can you imagine a problem-generating incident so simple or so obvious or so complicated as to effectively kill a story if it were recorded? Name or describe such an incident. Or one so damaging to the interest of the theme that it would have to be delayed or disguised in the story, or referred to only obliquely? Name or describe.

3. Analyze the psychological form of three of your favorite stories. Ask yourself such questions as: What aesthetic promises are made at the beginning? How do they affect and effect anticipation? How are the promises fulfilled? Are any left unsatisfied?

4. Discuss the relationships between an action in life and psychological form. What, for instance, is the relationship between the thematic seriousness of the one and the created anticipations of the other? between the completeness of one and the unity of the other? the magnitude of one and the satisfaction of the other? Under what conditions could the one *be* the other?

B. COMPARISON

1. Compare the plot elements of "The Hat Island Crossing" * "Ahab's Black Mass" * and "Soldier's Home." * Which are stories, and which are incomplete? What are the differences between an incident, an anecdote, and a story? How do each of the examples use incidents and anecdotes?

2. Compare the plot elements of "A Saturday Morning" * and "David and Alice Groper." * Are either reasonably complete as stories? What are the differences in plot, apart from the obvious differences in scenic and summary revelations? Are the differences similar to the differences between a short story and a novel? If so, how? If not, what are the major differences?

3. "Ahab's Black Mass" * and "The Hat Island Crossing" * are both parts of longer works, yet they have quite different effects in isolation. Can you account for the differences? If you are familiar with the works from which they come, analyze how each is related to the larger works. Can you make any generalizations about the relations of a part to the whole of a work?

4. Compare the surprise ending of a typical O'Henry story, say "The Gift of the Magi" or "The Furnished Room," with the surprise in "An Occurrence at Owl Creek Bridge."

C. IMITATION

1. Sarty Snopes's problem in "Barn Burning" * is something like: loyalty to the idea and practice of filial piety vs. loyalty to a developing, private notion of right and wrong. Write a scenario in which you embody the same problem. Use, say, the son of a wealthy Detroit industrialist as the central character, so that the terms of filial piety and morality have different specific social and economic expression from those dealt with in "Barn Burning."

2. Write a scene such as "A Saturday Morning," * including by intimation as many of the plot elements as you can. Again, translate the scene to another locale and level of society.

3. Try writing an extended sketch such as "David and Alice Groper." * Give the characters an overall problem and make each paragraph or incident embody a subsidiary problem with a partial solution. Try also to give the whole some unifying form.

4. Stephen Crane's *Maggie: a Girl of the Streets* is often said to be a "translation" of Flaubert's *Madame Bovary* to New York Bowery conditions. Try translating "Within a Magic Prison" * to teen-age conditions.

D. CREATION

1. Write a plan (character sketches, notes for setting and point-of-view, scenario) for a problem story—that is, one which like "The Hat Island Crossing" * shows characters attempting to solve a problem or overcome an obstacle or more. Keep the plot simple—with only one set of characters representing one approach to the problem.

2. Write a plan for a conflict story—that is, one in which two characters, each with his own designs, are set in conflict with each other. Be sure to give both sides real values, so that you do not come up with a melodrama.

3. Plan a dilemma story—that is, a story in which a character is torn between two equally undesirable possibilities, as is Sarty Snopes: he cannot bring himself to lie for his father; neither can he make himself run away (though this side finally gets the upper hand). Embody the characteristics of each possibility in secondary characters, as in Sarty's older brother and his mother, or as Lionel Trilling does with Tertan and Blackburn in "Of This Time, Of That Place."

4. Write a plan for an alter-ego, or double, story—one in which two sides of a personality are represented as competing for control of the self.

5. Write a plan for a tension-dissipation story—in which the tension-begetting situation creates crises but no solutions. Stephen Crane's "The Upturned Face" is a good example.

6. If you ever plan a novel, here is *one* way of going about it: Outline briefly the characters and the major elements of the plot: the induction, consequences, and so on. Then break the outline into its logical parts or scenes for treatment in individual chapters. Make for yourself a statement of what each chapter is to accomplish,[9] and then write a brief scenario for each chapter, in which you make notes about the theory and practice of accomplishing your objective. You can give each chapter some form and plot, but be sure to keep each accomplishment subordinate to the overall design. Read, for example, "Battle Royal," the first chapter of Ralph Ellison's *Invisible Man;* it has a certain integrity, in that it resolves some of the problems it poses, but it is a chapter in a novel, in that it raises more questions than it answers.

[9] Remember how Henry Fielding did it in *Joseph Andrews?* "Chapter VIII: in which, after some very fine writing, the history goes on, and relates the interview between the lady and Joseph; where the latter hath set an example, which we despair of seeing followed by his sex, in this vicious age. Chapter IX: what passed between the lady and Mrs. Slipslop, in which we prophesy there are some strokes which everyone will not truly comprehend at first reading." Fielding has his tongue in his cheek at least half the time; but his chapter headings *are* a kind of outline of the novel.

8

Structure: Design and Pattern

Structure we can define as the arrangement of the parts for aesthetic purpose. It differs thus from plot which is the arrangement of parts for thematic purpose. It differs also from form in that form is directly involved with logic and understanding, and thus with theme, while structure is concerned with the potential and limits of attention. Attention is very closely bound up with — indeed might be identical with—aesthetic perception. The continuum of attention ranges from boredom to chaos, and in between lies the world we call aesthetic. There are two sets of principles in structuring which have to do with our perceptions at either end of the attention continuum. Design, the first set of principles, is a way of avoiding boredom by injecting variety; pattern, at the other extreme, is a way of avoiding chaos or confusion by introducing unity. By avoiding boredom and confusion, the natural enemies of aesthetic perception, design and pattern become the writer's primary means of structuring for aesthetic effect.

The necessity for design grows out of the fact that our attention gets tired. Most people are already familiar with the fact that when the eye looks at a particular color or image for a while, the perceptors undergo fatigue and the eye simply quits seeing. The sense of smell also undergoes similar fatigue, as people who live near stockyards well know and appreciate. Attention undergoes a similar mutation when it is overused; then we are bored. The use of design counteracts boredom, for it introduces variety. One of the ways to make a fatigued eye see again is to show it a contrasting color or image, or to change in various and subtle ways the one that made it tired. Similarly, when the attention goes dead, we need to introduce variety to resuscitate it. If we introduce sufficient variety, we can not only maintain interest, but heighten attention.

On the other hand, pattern exists because we can get too much variety, which would be chaos or confusion. The necessity for pattern grows out of our urge to simplify, to reduce our experience to readily understandable configurations. If we see a random configuration of dots or colors which are more complex than the mind and perception can take in, we are faced with confusion. On the other hand, when these colors or dots are arranged in patterns, the chaos and confusion disappear, and perception is unified. Pattern reduces chaos to understanding. Our need for this reduction is so powerful that we very often project "subjective" patterns where none exists objectively. A random configuration of twelve dots is often perceived as three groups of four dots—that is, are seen in a comprehensible scheme, are seen in a single scheme. Thus, in preventing confusion, the principle of pattern not only maintains attention, but produces a sense of unity.

Design and pattern are thus intimately involved with the age-old aesthetic principle of unity in variety, variety in unity. Design introduces the variety that prevents dullness. Pattern organizes that variety into a unity. The one introduces interesting material; the other makes it understandable. Overuse of either set of principles will defeat the aesthetic purpose of both. Aesthetic structuring is always a delicate balancing act between aesthetic mistakes.

The Principles of Design

There are at least four important principles of design. They do not occur in isolation, though we isolate them for purposes of discussion. They very often combine with one another to produce what seems like additional principles. All are essentially ways of making aesthetic promises. The four principles are: contrast, gradation, theme and variation, and restraint.

Contrast

Contrast is the simplest of the principles of design. It staves off boredom by offering perception the opposite of what it may be bored with. It is very effective because of its extremity in the change offered, but its limitation is that it cannot be used too often without introducing confusion.

The foil in characterization is perhaps the most obvious use of contrast. We have already discussed at some length the principle of foils in connection with Jane Austen's *Emma* (see p. 80), Hemingway's *A Farewell to Arms* (see p. 129), and Salinger's *The Catcher in the Rye* (see p. 207). In each of these cases, the principle of characterization is the principle of contrast. We are simply shown what the main character is *not* and are left to infer what he is.

A somewhat more subtle use of the principle of contrast in creating character is in Flaubert's *Madame Bovary*. Consider the following passages for example:

Charles trotted over the country-roads in snow and rain. He ate omelettes on farmhouse tables, poked his arm into damp beds, received the tepid spurt of blood-letting in his face, listened to death-rattles, examined basins, turned over a good deal of dirty linen; but every evening he found a blazing fire, his dinner ready, easy-chairs, and a well-dressed woman, charming and so freshly scented that it was impossible to say where the perfume came from; it might have been her skin that communicated its fragrance to her blouse.

She delighted him by numerous attentions; now it was some new way of arranging paper sconces for the candles, a flounce that she altered on her gown, or an extraordinary name for some very simple dish that the servant had spoilt, but that Charles swallowed with pleasure to the last mouthful. At Rouen, she saw some ladies who wore a bundle of charms hanging from their watch-chains; she bought some. She wanted for her mantelpiece two large blue glass vases, and some time after an ivory nccessaire with silver-gilt thimble. The less Charles understood these refinements the more they seduced him. They added something to the pleasure of the senses and to the comfort of his fireside. It was like a golden dust sanding all along the narrow path of his life...

But it was above all the meal-times that were unbearable to her, in this small room on the ground-floor, with its smoking stove, its creaking door, the walls that sweated, the damp pavement; all the bitterness of life seemed served up on her plate, and with the smoke of the boiled beef there rose from her secret soul waves of nauseous disgust. Charles was a slow eater; she played with a few nuts, or, leaning on her elbow, amused herself drawing lines along the oilcloth table-cover with the point of her knife.[1]

The contrast between Emma and Charles is less direct than the contrasts we have seen earlier. Where those in Hemingway or Salinger suggest a theme of the moment, Flaubert's contrasts suggest long established habits of character. It is not so much that Emma is bored with Charles as that she has always been bored with Charles and has attempted cure after cure for her ennui. It is not so much that Charles does not understand what Emma is doing; it is almost that he has never really seen her. Such a line as "An extraordinary name for some simple dish that the servant had spoilt, but that Charles swallowed with pleasure to the last mouthful" suggests the ideal culinary world of Emma's notion of Paris and the peasant world of Charles's omelettes in farm houses. These images are not so much contrasts as they are alien worlds. The hopelessness that emerges from this juxtaposition is not only a principle of characterization here, but also a key to the theme.

The principle of contrast can operate also in the construction of action. The

[1] Norton Critical Edition, pp. 43, 47.

tragedy with a comic sub-plot is perhaps the most obvious example. Very often, the tragic action and the comic action will be concerned with the same theme but offer contrasting outcomes. In such a case, each contrasted member makes a comment on the other.

An ambitious use of the principle of contrast of action is Aldous Huxley's *Point Counterpoint.* Hardly does Huxley let one set of characters perform an action when he shifts to a new set of characters performing the action or to the same kinds of characters faced with a new problem. His novel is an elaborate system of contrast upon contrast, extending to theme and variation. His satirical theme depends upon the irony that emerges.

In all the cases mentioned, both sides of the contrast are present on the page. But contrast can exist by appealing to a stock response in the reader and presenting him with a contrast to it. The obtuse priest in *Madame Bovary* is an example. Because he is a priest, we expect certain qualities of him—spirituality, sensitivity to human suffering, comprehension of need, and so on. But when Flaubert shows Emma appealing to him for help, his only qualities are materialism, insensitivity, obtuseness, and such. The priest's character is created by the principle of contrast, though only one side of the contrast is actually presented. This dependence upon the reader's expectations can be aesthetically dangerous if it goes unprepared.

Gradation

Gradation is the occurrence of more than two similar but different items in a scheme, a hierarchy, an evenly spaced continuum. It introduces more subtle variety than the principle of contrast and is very good for relieving a one-to one patness in symbolic relationship or melodramatic contrasts. Its only limitation is that all items in the series, all elements of the scheme, must be perceived as belonging to a gradational series. This usually means that there must be an almost evenly spaced grouping of elements along the scheme. This can be done statically, in which case we call it hierarchy, or it can be done dynamically, in which case we call it an evolution.

Huckleberry Finn contains a good example of a gradational hierarchy of characters. If we begin at the "top" of river bank society, we find Colonel Grangerford and Colonel Sherburn, men who embody the approved ideals of that community. The hierarchy grades off one step when we come to Judge Thatcher, the widow Douglas, and Mary Jane Wilks; these are all leaders in the community and eminently respectable, but they are not in the same class as the Southern aristocracy of the colonels. One step further down, we discover Miss Watson and Silas and Sally Phelps, people still respectable but a little less admirable than those in the classes above them. Miss Watson and the Phelps are directly involved in the slave trade. Their superiors, while deriving their caste and class from the existence of slave trade, yet pretend to rise above it. Another step down we find Mrs. Judith Loftus, and a step below her the bounty hunters near Cairo. These people are less admirable than Miss Watson and the Phelpses, differing only in their degree of support of the whole system of caste and class. Mrs. Loftus is making ready to search for Jim in hopes of reward, while the bounty hunters are already active. Little more than opportunity separates the bounty hunters from Huck's Pap and old Boggs. These men are the dregs of Colonel Sherburn's civilization, but they share its value system about runaway "niggers" and the whole social and economic fabric of slave society hierarchy. The robbers on the sinking steamboat, *Sir Walter Scott,* differ only a very little from Pap, and the King and the Duke carry the gradation to its last step. Part of Twain's point is that all these people, in spite of their social and economic differences, are part of the same system. Indeed, in Twain's view it is finally impossible to distinguish between the thievery of Colonel Grangerford and that of the King and the Duke. Tom Sawyer is a kind of summation of this whole gradational hierarchy and, of course, Huck and Jim are in contrast to it. The complexity of the gradational structure of "the enemy" enriches the theme immeasurably beyond a simplistic or melodramatic juxtaposition.

Incidents in a plot can also form a gradational hierarchy: In *The Catcher in the Rye,* for example, there is a series of incidents whose relationship, one to the other, is very similar to the relationships between characters in *Huckleberry Finn* (and in *The Catcher in the Rye* for that matter). At the hotel, Maurice and the prostitute beat Holden and rob him of twice the real price, though ironically they have their ethical code—they will take no more than two times the price for nothing. The same incident occurs at least twice more in the gradational structure of the novel; the record store operator takes only two prices for the old record Holden buys; Holden's lawyer-father's business, Holden implies, is taking two prices for small service. Holden finds it difficult to distinguish between the value systems that this gradation reveals.

A thematic gradation of taste is also found in *The Catcher in the Rye.* It includes the Joe College types at the matinee who can't tell the Lunts from angels, the crowd at old Ernie's bar who have substituted reputation of the performer for aesthetic evaluation and can't judge whether Ernie is an angel or a Lunt, and old Sally who wants to go skating at Rockefeller Center, simply because it is the thing to do. For all the people in this gradation—and there are more—taste is derived from publicity. Holden, Phoebe, and their dead brother Allie, contrast to this gradation; they can tell good movies from bad movies.

Evolutionary gradation we have already discussed to some extent in connection with the development of Huck's moral stature in relation to his bouts with conscience. A similar development of character is the evolution of value and choice in Fred Henry in *A Farewell to Arms*. As we have noted earlier, Fred begins his story in support of the war and slowly changes to desertion from the army. Hemingway is careful to show us that this is no momentary or accidental change, but a slow evolution of value.

An evolutionary gradation of action can be found in Chekhov's "The New Villa." The peasants began with certain tentative demands upon the Kucherovs. Though they are rather unconscious of the evolution, their second set of demands are slightly increased, and their demands continue to increase gradationally, bit by bit, until the Kucherovs can simply no longer stand it. The Kucherovs embody a contrasting gradation in their progressive attempts to make friends with the peasants. Both the contrast and the gradation are primary avenues of theme.

Theme and Variation

Theme and variation is also a grouping of images, but images that are perceived as belonging to the same class, rather than as being different. Its only requirements are that the motif or image which is the theme be simple enough to comprehend at a glance, and that the variations upon this theme be perceived as variations, not as contrasts. Theme and variation is a powerful organizing device because there is almost no limit to the amount of material that can be unified by it. It offers both simplicity and complexity.

There are two principle kinds of theme and variation: repetition and modulation. Repetition is the relatively simple recurrence of the same image, action, character, incident, over and over again, usually in different contexts. Frank Baldanza points out that *Tom Sawyer* is organized largely upon this principle of repetition. We are told over and over again of Tom's "thirst for heroic grandeur," [2] which is expressed in incident after incident, context after context. More specifically, he says the repetition of such devices as the spying episodes, all of which follow essentially the same pattern, hold the book together more effectively than its loose plot.

A slightly more complex example of repetition occurs in *Madame Bovary*. When Emma and Charles are being married, they walk through heavy weeds, and Emma has to stop and pluck the burrs from her stockings. Later, a variant repetition of this incident occurs when Rodolphe and Emma are riding through the heavy ferns. Rodolphe's quick movement to help Emma untangle herself from the ferns both contrasts with and "repeats" the motif of Charles's

---

[2] *Mark Twain, An Introduction and Interpretation* (New York: Holt, 1961), p. 108.

insensitive failure to help Emma. The two scenes repeat each other by their structure of incident, but contrast in their thematic outcome.

Modulation is a more important form of theme and variation. It is repetition with a difference. It incorporates a gradation into the variations so that the terminal image is at once different from, modulated from, the original motif and still unified with it as a variation upon a developing theme. This is a common and important device for the writer.

Madame Bovary again offers us good examples of modulations of a motif. For example, consider Emma's response to the little plaster priest, the statue at the end of her garden. When Emma first sees the little statue, she is indifferent and objective in her perception of it; it is simply a little plaster priest reading his breviary. The next time she sees the little priest, she has undergone considerable development, so that her perception of it is modulated. She now notices for us that one of his feet has fallen off and that the plaster is white and scabby. The modulation in these perceptions are parallels to the modulations in Emma's hopes. When we see the little statue the third time, it is bounced out of the carriage and broken during the move from Tostes to Yonville. By this time, the little statue is almost symbolic of Emma's smashed life.

A slightly more complicated example of theme and variation is the development of Emma's sensation of vertigo from casual to causal to casualty. We are first introduced to the motif of whirling and concentric circles in the ball at Vaubyessard, where Emma enjoys dancing with the Viscount. Her memory of the whirling sensation of the dance the next morning is connected with the circles of widening hope that radiate around her, radiate toward Paris, like an aureole. The disappointments of her hopes are later described in terms of her illness, whose primary symptom is dizziness or vertigo. When her hopes are transformed into dreams, she draws upon the image of the dancing at Vaubyessard and the whirling sensation that transports her out of time and space. The earlier experiences get incorporated in her present development. Later, more of the imagery of that memory-dream world at Vaubyessard return and add to her consciousness. Her response to the Viscount on that long ago night gets incorporated in her response to Rodolphe and is an important step in her capitulation to him. Exactly this same sensation of whirling is reintroduced when Rodolphe rejects Emma. This times it has the added objective element of the whirring of Binet's lathe. Flaubert is very careful to make us see the whirring of the lathe as the objective correlative to Emma's sense of confusion and defeat. Later, Emma's defeat is described to us in the same images. She is unable to distinguish the whirling senses of her memories and her hopes from the phantoms of her disappointment. Her world is collapsing around her like a rising spiral that has suddenly gone limp. The motif of vertigo is thus one of the devices used to reveal to us every important variation in Emma's development.

Restraint

Restraint is a different order of principle. Instead of being involved with putting detail in, it is involved with taking detail out. It exists because of the impossibility of maintaining attention at a single high state without boredom or confusion resulting. As Henry James once noted, if you expect a scene to stand out intensely, you must precede it with a scene of lower intensity. Our perception of mountains depends upon our perception of valleys. The limits of our attention are such that we need this "undercutting" as James called it. The principle is one of economy in the expenditure of attention.

One side of the principle is concerned with the avoidance of excess. This, of course, is essentially the problem of sentimentality. The writer must be careful that the motive he supplies in the literary work is not in excess of the corresponding motive in life. He must not beg for excessive emotion, but restrain himself.

This principle is also related to the relationship between dreams and literature. Very often, the images of the dream when recorded literally are vastly inadequate as literature. Dreams probably involve the total electromagnetic capability of the brain, and thus any image in a dream is an adequate expression of the motives in the dream. When these images are translated to language, one loses the adequacy and invites sentimentality.

The other side of the principle is the arrangement for climax. The writer should pay some attention to the possibility of heightened response to important points in his work. The human mind habitually responds to such an arrangement and, indeed, almost demands it. The easy question that has an easy answer is seldom pleasing aesthetically, but the difficult question which rouses our anticipation, suspends a possible answer, frustrates our expected solutions, graduates toward a finally satisfactory answer, is highly pleasing. Such a maneuver would be economical in the expenditure of feeling; it avoids using up potential response.

These principles of design make important aesthetic promises. Each occurrence of an image used in design focuses our attention upon the potential of that image and makes us expect that something will be done with it in the course of the composition. This is the principle of Chekhov's "Firearm on the Wall"—that is, if you introduce a detail in the early stage of an action, you are asthetically promising that you will use it in a later stage. To fail to do so would be an aesthetic mistake.

Every aesthetic promise in an action enriches our potential for paying attention. It operates aesthetically in a way comparable to the psychology of form. The promise presupposes and looks forward to a fulfillment of the promise. The resulting expectation and fulfillment enrich and reward attention.

The total of the aesthetic promises a work makes creates, in a sense, the scope and scale of the work. The promises delineate and define the kind of material that can appear. They define it with respect to the ambition of its theme, the extent of application, the seriousness that is invited, the length that will be tolerated, and so on. They delineate the subject by making it possible for us to identify extraneous or irrelevant material. Every literary composition is a vehicle, a vessel, that occupies a certain conceptual space. The aesthetic promises and their fulfillment create this space; our judgment of a work's success is related to how well it fills its space.

Deliberate Use of Design

It is possible, of course, to use the principles of design deliberately in shaping a story. We have already touched on this issue very lightly in the notes on making the parts of "Within a Magic Prison" produce contrast, gradation, and growth. We will here look at a slightly more involved example:

CRACK, CRASH ORANGE FLARE [3]

Charles raced his stick-horse around the corner of the storage shack. Scout and hunter for the wagon train, he stopped when he saw his father, sitting on the stoop, with the twenty-two rifle in his hands. It was an ordinary Winchester pump-action rifle, which his father had bought when first married, but there was something magic about it to Charles. It was small enough for him to hold. He could lift it to his shoulder.

Charles dropped his stick-horse, holstered his cap-pistol, and went over to his father. "What cha doin', Daddy?"

"Sighting it in," said his father, as he lifted the gun to his shoulder.

Then Charles saw the row of kitchen matches, stuck in a clay crack about fifteen feet in front of the shack. Crack! went the rifle and sputt! went the clay, but the matches stood still. The clay-red wrinkles in his father's face smoothed as he lowered the rifle; he looked at the front sight, picked up the tap-hammer between his cowboy boots, and tapped the sight to move it a tiny amount. Then he raised the rifle again. Crack, sputt, and a match-tip crashed orange-flare, then flame.

"Let me do it, Daddy; let me shoot it."

3 By H. C. Brashers.

Unmoved, his father shucked out the spent cartridge and looked down the sights again. Crack-sputt, crash orange-flare-flame.

"C'n I shoot it, please, Daddy? Can I, hunh?" said Charles, rubbing one bare foot on the top of the other and squinting in the brutal, West-Texas summer.

"Think you're big enough, eh?" said his father, opening his arms and widening his knees to take Charles in.

"No, not in your lap. I'll sit here," said Charles. He sat on the step, beside his father.

He received the rifle, pointed outward. Of course, he was big enough. It seemed like hundreds of times he had sat in his father's lap and had shot out flivver windows at rabbits and, once, he had hit a tin-can they put up on a fence post. Still, with the rifle at his shoulder, now, and his eye squinting down the V and blade of the sights, his heart and breath were jigging like the match in the clay. Above, beside. Sputt, utter failure. He shucked out the spent cartridge and was ready to try again.

"Here, Son," said his father, turning him so that he could brace himself more steadily. "Rest your elbow on your knee, like this. Then try to hold it still. And squeeze the trigger; don't jerk."

Crack, sputt, and he cut a match an inch below the head.

"I hit it, Daddy! I hit it!"

"No, you didn't."

"Yes, I did." Charles ran to the match—swinging the rifle in his right hand, familiarly, grasping the balance. He grabbed the stub from the clay crack and ran back to his father. "See? I hit it!"

"Down! Point the gun down!"

Then Charles realized how careless he was, but he tried to make an excuse. "It's not loaded, anyway. I haven't pumped it yet."

"Guns are always loaded," said his father, taking the rifle from him.

Charles summarized to himself all the stories of careless men who had shot themselves, or friends, with unloaded guns, and shame reeled in his head, twisting him around, pushing him down into a rolling, lightless blackness, in which he could see no more than a white circle, like the end of a tunnel. Then he saw the match-stub in his hand and his excitement brought him back to soar in delight, before he could even mumble an apology for his carelessness.

"See? I hit it! I hit it," he cried, holding up the match.

"No, you didn't," said his father, taking the match. "You cut it more 'n an inch below the head."

"But I cut it! I hit it!"

"You was aiming at the head, weren't you? Well, you missed it. You missed it, the same as if you'd shot an inch to the side, or above it."

Stopped momentarily, then rebounding, Charles begged, "Let me try it again."

But his father was already standing up and turning toward the house, saying gratuitously, since the idea of quitting was already accomplished, "No. That's enough for today."

But Charles tagged after, speaking quickly to get it said, now that the time was ripe: "Daddy, when can I take the rifle and shoot some rabbits in the pasture? Hunh? When can I?"

"When you learn how to handle a gun safely," he said, the words drifting back over his shoulder.

Charles, alone on the clay ridge where the house overlooked the fields and the pasture, picked up his match-stub where his father had let it fall and went to compare its splinters with the charred matches in the clay-crack. He could just see himself—someday—faced with a row of matches. Crack, crash, orange-flare-flame. Crack, crash, orange-flare-flame....

Not long afterwards, Charles begged Owen, the big, pale hired-hand, to walk with him to the back of the pasture to fetch the milk cows.

"You c'n do it by yourself," said Owen. "You do it ever' day, don't chu?"

"Yes," said Charles. "But if you go with me, I can take the twenty-two and do a little hunting."

"Does George allow you to take the twenty-two?"

"It's okay when somebody big is along," said Charles, dodging the direct question. Owen was leaning against the horse-lot and looking vacantly at nothing in particular. His hands and head were too large for the rest of his body. When other men would be whittling or chewing a straw or looking for signs of weather, Owen just looked contentedly at anything.

"If you go with me, I could hunt rabbits," Charles pursued.

No response.

"We could go a half-hour early, so we wouldn't be late getting the cows up."

Still no response.

"Please, Owen, You're not doing anything special anyway, are you?"

"No," said Owen. "Nothin' special. Jist waitin' for George to come back." He looked around toward the house to see if Charles's father was coming, tho both of them knew they would have heard the flivver and trailer from a mile away, were George arriving.

"Okay," said Owen. "I'll go with you."

Charles sprang to the house and grabbed the twenty-two, yelling to his mother, "Owen and me 're going after the cows and we're goin' t' take the twenty-two," and not even waiting for the answer he heard anyway, "You-all be careful, now," as the screen door slammed.

Charles caught up with Owen on the lower side of the lot.

"Better let me carry the gun," said Owen.

"It's all right," said Charles, stepping out in front so the gun would not point toward Owen. "It ain't heavy."

"Well, you be careful."

They walked along a cow-trail on the rim of the quarter-mile swale, at the bottom of which were the dirt water-tanks. Opposite them, on the north rim of the swale, the squat, square, Mexican shack stood.

"D'ya think I could hit the Mex'can shack from here?" Charles asked.

"Nope," said Owen, looking across at it, too. "It's too far away; the bullet won't carry that far."

"Besides, there might be stock in the brush down there, hunh?" said Charles.

"Yep," said Owen, returning his attention to the ground.

"A person has to watch where he's shooting, doesn't he?"

"Yep."

"You oughtn't to ever shoot toward a house, or a barn, or anywhere where people or stock might be."

"That's right," said Owen. Then, after a moment, he stooped and pulled up a dust-green plant. "D'you know what loco weed looks like?"

"Nope."

"I about half suspect that this's loco weed." He turned it in his hand. "Let's look around and see if we find any more growing."

"What for?"

"We ought to pull up any we find. It makes the stock go crazy."

Owen began walking in ever-widening circles around the spot where he had found the dust-green plant.

Charles began walking in circles, too, but soon he found a terrapin in a hollow under a mesquite bush and prodded it out with the point of the gun. The terrapin extended his toothless, wizened, amazed old head and began extending his feet to regain the cool hollow. Charles shucked a shell into the barrel and the terrapin snapped his head and feet in. Charles turned him over and prodded the light-colored belly. He propped the terrapin up on a tuft of grass, so that he could shoot into the head-hole.

"Did you find any, yet?" called Owen.

"Any what?" asked Charles, looking up, hesitating.

Just then a cotton-tail sprang from hiding at Owen's feet and bounded off toward the barn and lot. Charles swung the loaded and cocked rifle thru the shape of Owen and Crack! Crack! twice into the grass around the rabbit before it was out of sight and before Owen was screaming:

"Stop! Be careful! Don't"

And before Charles sunk, swirling in a dark tunnel of shame, for he recognized the multiplicity of his carelessness—toward a man, toward a house, toward something huge and still unformed in his own mind—toward the idea of responsibility. So that, when Owen said:

"Here, you'd better let me carry the gun."

Charles relinquished the awkward, heavy weapon and walked away, behind Owen, in the cow-trail, his cowboy-boots pocking the Texas dust.

Farther out in the pasture, mesquite gave way to acorn brush and the wind had whipped the land into lumpy dunes and smooth round hollows with hardpan bottoms. A rabbit jumped up well ahead of them and Owen shot once at it but missed.

"Shoot again!" cried Charles. "Shoot again!"

But Owen did not shoot, although he had the rifle to his shoulder and followed the rabbit with the sights to where it disappeared in a hollow.

"Criminee! Why didn't you shoot again?"

"Couldn't get a good bead on him," said Owen.

"Why not? Why couldn'tchu?"

"I don't know. I just couldn't get the sights on his head again."

"Well, here. Let me take the gun," said Charles. "I could've shot again."

He took the rifle from Owen and went ahead of him in the cow-trail. He walked along, jauntily, holding the rifle in his right hand, by the balance. He walked up the rise of a dune and—intrepid, cold-eyed, courageous—surveyed the unknown land before him. Like a pictured pioneer in a school book, he stood on a bluff, overlooking the wide prairie, noticing the grazing grounds and migration routes of buffalo, keenly waiting for the wisp of signal smoke that would mean trouble ahead. But, with the gun in his hand, he was ready for anything. He stood outside himself, as it were, and measured himself and the gun against the bald Texas sky and the late afternoon sun, and he found his image adequate. He was a hunter. Tall and bold, he proceeded then was startled to a stop by a rabbit breaking cover almost at his feet.

"Shoot," said Owen, because Charles was hesitating too long. "Don't let him get away!"

Then Charles had the rifle to his shoulder and Crack! the bullet splashed thru the acorn brush. The rabbit leaped like a doe having fun or a sheep escaping. Crack! again, splash acorn brush.

"Let me have it," cried Owen, excited now, reaching to take the gun.

"No! I can do it!" The rabbit was nearly a hundred yards away now—and Charles could only see it in flashes above and thru the brush.

Crack! And Zump! The rabbit leaped higher than a man's head.

"I hit it!" cried Charles. "I hit it."

"No, you didn't," said Owen.

"Yes, I did! Didn't you see him jump when I hit him?"

"I wasn't looking at him. I was reaching for the gun."

"Well, didn't you hear that thump? I hit him!"

"Not in the head. If you hit him, it was just in the flesh and he's long gone by now."

"No! I hit him, I tell you. Come on! We'll go find him."

"You'll never find that rabbit!"

"I bet I will."

Charles ran on ahead to the spot where he thought the rabbit was when he hit it. Owen came slowly, listlessly after.

The rabbit was not where Charles thought it would be and he could see no signs of it. He began walking in ever-widening circles around the spot, while Owen climbed up a dune to look toward the back of the pasture, where the cows were.

"Come on," said Owen. "You'll never find that rabbit."

"Yes, I will. You just see."

But Charles looked and looked until he was ready to give up, because the rabbit had apparently gotten away. Then, crossing a hollow with a hard-pan bottom, he found it. His hind legs were a crumpled mess, but he was standing up on his front legs and staring at nothing at all. The bullet had cut his spine and he had tumbled helplessly to the open bottom of the hollow.

"Here he is!" cried Charles.

Owen came up to the rim of the hollow and glanced in. "Yeah. It was just a lucky shot. Hit him in the hind quarters, hunh?"

"What do I do now?" asked Charles.

"Leave him; can't you see he's in his death-trance?"

"You mean, just—just leave him like that?"

Owen did not answer. He was looking toward the cows again.

"Won't he get away?" asked Charles.

"Well, finish him off then and come on."

"Finish him off? How?"

Again Owen made no reply.

Charles looked again at the rabbit, who was still staring at nothing. He did not even seem to see, as Charles came up close and prodded him with the point of the gun. Charles walked in front of him and still there was only that vacant stare. Finish him off, Owen had said, so Charles put the end of the gun between the rabbit's eyes and Crack! nothing happened. There was a little red round hole and powder burns on the rabbit's forehead, but he had not moved, not even with the impact of the bullet. In his death-trance, the muscles had cramped. Charles shot again into the rabbit's head and still nothing happened.

Owen was waiting, not watching, on the rise of a dune.

"He won't die, Owen," said Charles. "What'll I do?"

"Knock his brains out and come on."

Charles did not ask how to knock his brains out, tho he did not know. The rabbit was still staring, but there was no expression there, no indication of feeling. Charles looked at the rabbit, fascinated, absorbed in the problem. Finally, he picked up a large, heavy clod and threw it down on the rabbit. The clod burst; the rabbit regained his forefeet and resumed staring.

Charles had another plan: He would kick the rabbit's brains out. He kicked the rabbit in the side of the head with his toe. The rabbit rolled over and over, made no sound nor sign of feeling, regained his forefeet, and stared. Charles kicked him again. The same thing happened.

Charles stared at the rabbit. He picked up a rock that he knew was not large enough and smashed it down on the rabbit. The rock broke one of the rabbit's front legs; he could not get up. But he was still staring—lying on his side and staring.

Charles lifted his foot and stamped on the rabbit, but the ball of his foot was inadequate. So he moved closer, obsessed, determined, now, balanced himself so that he could use his cowboy-boot heel. Stomp! once, and stomp! twice. Then Crack! the rabbit's skull burst like the shot of a rifle, and Crash orange flare, his brains squirted out on the red clay. At the same time, the rabbit made a small, desperate noise like the stretching of shoe-leather. Every muscle in him quivered. Then he was still and limp.

Charles was limp, too. He quivered uncontrollably in every muscle. A huge, impenetrable blackness covered him, leaving only one hole of brightness for his consciousness of himself and another for the crushed orange flare brain. He was about to cry, but Owen called:

"Haven't you finished with that yet?"

Then Charles recovered. He slipped, in trying to walk up the slope, and slid back on his knees. He looked behind him, quickly, to see if his foot was coming near the rabbit—seeing crash! the brain—and scrambled up the rise of the dune where Owen was waiting for him, cold-eyed. He handed Owen the rifle.

"You keep it," said Owen. "Maybe you can hit another one."

"No," said Charles. "You take it."

His heels crashed into the dust of the trail and Charles added deliberately, holding on to the light at the end of his consciousness, "You take it; it's your turn."

They walked away, toward where the cows waited, Owen first and Charles behind him. Deep in the bright end of an immense tunnel of black shame, Charles's boot heels came down crack in the cow-trail dust and his boot-leather made a ritching noise with every step. Crack! crash, orange-flare-brain, boot-leather ritch. Crack! crash, orange flare-brain, boot-leather ritch. . . .

Design in "Crack, Crash Orange Flare"

The originating impetus, the total effect, the reason for existence of the story grow out of the moment when the boy, having crushed the rabbit's skull, is reacting to his own act. For any writer, such a moment is inherently dangerous. There is always a great danger of merely telling about it—"Looking at the skull, he was more ashamed than he had ever been in his life. He wanted to run, to get away, to leave the rabbit's eyes behind." Or there is a danger that the writer will invite the reader to imagine the moment—"You can easily imagine how terrible he felt"—which is simple sentimentality. To make that moment carry the desired aesthetic effect, I knew I would have to supply it with a context, a context that would suggest to the reader (hopefully would even *give* him) the emotions and thus the theme I wanted. The imagery for that context I took from perhaps a dozen different scenes in my own childhood. These images I shuffled in accordance with the principles of design until I thought they did the job. These principles—theme and variation, contrast, gradation, and restraint—had to focus the observer's attention, draw unity out of a multiplicity of detail, and illustrate the variety in that unity.

Theme and variation played around the key moment suggested, almost musically, the primary motif of the story. The most intense quality of the boy's feeling was vertigo, which I fancied was not uncommon in the human being in such situations of stress. This vertigo gave me that series of concentric circles and spirals in the story—especially the image of the dark tunnel, closing in and leaving only that little hole of light at the end. This image offered problems; it was too literary, quite outside the vocabulary and possibly the experience of the boy. But I kept it, partly because it imitated the quality of the vertigo so well, almost too well, and partly because I could remember myself sitting inside culverts and being fascinated by the feeling of darkness closing down to a hole of light. At any rate, its literary quality dictated that I prepare the reader for it; hence the two repetitions in varied form of the identical image, the first time in a context of elation and therefore of slight duration, the second time more fully, with explicit linking to the shame and irresponsibility the boy must feel, the reader must feel for the boy, in the key moment. To relieve the patness of a one-to-one relationship between this image and the shame, I introduced people walking in circles, looking for things, and a number of spots or holes in the story—that bald Texas sun, the hole in the rabbit's forehead. I thought afterwards of the hole in the gun barrel, and that suggested an alternative to the tunnel—the spiral riflings and the almost painful shininess one sees in a gun barrel on a day like that. There was even a kind of grizzly appropriateness in putting the boy at the end of the gun barrel, in the firing line, as it were, but I rejected the idea on the grounds that it would have been too blatant, too much altogether. One has to restrain himself sometimes.

The key moment also gave me the other primary motif in the story—the crashing upon perception of the orange flare, which motivated the vertigo. Here, I could not afford to let the reader know or suspect the meanings in advance, yet the image had to be foreshadowed. The technique that suggested itself was contrast, especially in the form of irony. Since there was already a gun in the situation, my father appeared, shooting kitchen matches, sighting in his rifle, as I remember him doing when I was a boy. All this, in turn, suggested the feeling I remember in myself of looking forward to that great day when I, too, could shoot matches and watch the orange flare burst upon perception. The grand, impatient anticipation of that feeling contrasted in the right way with the disappointment and withdrawal from the orange flare in the key moment; so I used it. The image also attached itself to the aftermath of the vertigo, in the paradox of boot-heels crashing in the dust of the trail. This transfer of the boy's emotion was desirable. I therefore strengthened it with the ritching noise and with the simple, verbal repetition, then foreshadowed it by offering one earlier variation, at the end of part II.

This bursting-orange-flare image also gave me a good deal of the rhetoric. Not only the cracking of the rifle (rather than a pop or a bang); not only the splashing of bullets in acorn brush (rather than "ripping thru the shinnery"); not only the title and its variations; but especially the rhetoric of jamming accents together, as many as I could get in a string—"Crack! Crash! Orange-flare-brain, boot-leather ritch!" This rhetoric I played off against a kind of continuous, unrelenting, rolling (concentric, I fancied) narrative, delivered in sentences of varying degrees of involution. The idea was to jam my spirals with so much tension that they would burst at the punctual moment.

The only other important theme-and-variation concerned the theme of carelessness and responsibility. To focus the reader on the right issue in the key moment, I had to introduce the ideas to him early. Thus the miniature scenes of the boy, swinging the rifle around with the potential of shooting something or someone he shouldn't, his childish talk about this explicit issue in part II, and these culminating in his shooting something that—at this stage of his life, at least—he shouldn't have. This, being conceptual, was dangerous, so I tried to blend it with action, as such, and with some of the minor motifs that were playing, the relative heaviness of the gun and the like.

The principle of contrast entered into some of these concerns, as is already evident, but it also functioned on its own. The boy's role toward authority, for example, not only had to be varied, it had to be contrasted in its two most important moments. Otherwise, the whole fabric of tempting taboo, of challenging the adult establishment, upon which the debacle of the story depends, would not come into focus. The contrast worked out in the form of two scenes of begging, two of decision-making, two of ways of carrying a gun, and in some of the variations already mentioned.

The most important contrast of the story, however, focused once again upon the key moment. That moment had to be extremely *real,* almost palpable, not only to the boy but to the reader. The scene had to be gory, bloody, quite the opposite of romantic. So, since this was a hunting story, I rummaged in my mind for contrasting, romantic images of hunting. That's when the boy came riding in on his stick-horse, playing the role of a scout and hunter for the wagon train. I liked the irony of this image, because it is so characteristic of American boys who make mythic experience of their grandfather's real experiences. This image had to come first in the story, since the gory one came last. And, in a late revision, I expanded essentially the same image to some magnitude—"like a pictured pioneer in a school book"—to contrast with, and dramatically undercut, the last, focal scene. This contrast revealed, I thought, one of the thematic hinges of the story: the boy's inability to live up to the reality of the roles he was challenging.

The principle of gradation had two important effects on the story. First, it

introduced the second adult character, fairly early in the thinking process, long
before writing began. So long as the father in the story kept being as stern,
as unpermissive, as no-nonsensical, as my own father would have been in that
situation, nothing would happen. I couldn't make him change, either, because
this kind of image of authority was needed to make the challenging of it
meaningful and worthwhile. A hired hand we had when I was eight or nine
suggested himself, not so much as a contrast to the father but as a diluted
form of him. This man could be the father's deputy, representing the same
principles, but in a lower key, more permissively. His gradation in the hierarchy of authority let the story start moving, offered opportunity for a number
of contrasts (see, for example, the two adults' responses to the boy's cry, "I
hit it! I hit it!"), and made possible the second gradation which became the
"story line."

This second gradation is the evolution of roles the boy plays. In the first
part, he is an "apprentice," though he doesn't especially like it. He wants the
independence of *not* sitting between his father's knees (this detail entered in
one of the revisions) and is looking forward to that time when he, too, will
handle authoritatively the symbols of authority and can crash matches into
orange flares. In the second part, he assumes and plays the role of "companion." He assumes equality with Owen, takes turns, and dares to criticize.
In the third part, he actually assumes leadership and maintains it, until the
reversal in the key moment, when he becomes once again the child, surrenders
(actually pushes away) the symbol of authority, and takes up a following
position. Thus, the story tugged, as I had known from the beginning it would,
at the mythic pattern of initiation and especially at the failure of the young
challenger.

In our time, such a pattern can very easily be overdone, and I knew from
the beginning that I would have to refrain from direct reference to it. To
have called attention to it would have been excessive, just as to have used the
riflings in the gun barrel would have been. We have to leave something to
subtlety. We have to let the reader discover something by himself in the story.
So it's always a good idea to avoid becoming pat. The writer has to restrain
himself, too, in being careful not to use up all the reader's response, interests,
or attention too early. This means, usually, an arrangement of material for
climax and a deliberate use of suspense, thus the clod, the kicking, the ball
of the foot, and finally the heel in the boy's dispatch of the rabbit. The
various motifs and contrasts I was using would suggest, I hoped, the alignment
of forces, would pose the question, the challenge, that was the boy's primary
motivation, without my becoming explicit. I hoped, too, that the variations
I kept playing back and forth would keep the question alive and suspenseful
until the climactic, focal delivery.

As in so very much of the story, the key moment dictated again the primary use of a design principle. That moment is so intensely internal and deals so much in emotions and values, that to render it directly, to name the emotions, would have been a mistake. A description of such internal material, no matter how well foreshadowed, almost always becomes sentimental, because it is bound to ask some readers for more response than they deem appropriate, and others for less. This problem imposed a restraint upon point-of-view; indeed, it chose point-of-view. Since I could not afford to enter fully into the boy in that moment, I had to use a point-of-view that effaced certain matters by focusing only and wholly upon the perceptual components of those matters. This focus upon perceptual matters became essential to the story.

Such, then, were the considerations of design in the writing of "Crack, Crash Orange Flare." Most of this thinking was done before and during the writing of the first draft. Some of the details were added in revision. And some elements of the story simply and happily happened, as consequences of the others—the cap-pistol, the cowboy boots, the trance-like stare in the boy's eyes. Because my father and Owen kept insisting upon being themselves, even in this fiction, they may have injected other, unplanned elements. But most of the detail in the story is deliberately there.

I still hear the story somewhat as a musical composition—which pleases me, because it mitigates and enhances the theme. To me, the story swells and contracts in its progress, modulates, orchestrates, counterpoints melodies—and these qualities give the story its "size." Every idea, every story, in a sense creates its own "space" by the aesthetic promise it makes; I was trying, at every stage, to be at least as aware of my aesthetic promises as I was of the fulfillment of them, for real, aesthetic success can be measured only in these terms of promise and fulfillment. I can only hope that I have succeeded, even while the music of its design makes me love the story.

Abstract Patterns

Pattern is quite a different thing from design. Design operates to introduce complexity through its contrasts and variations; pattern operates to reduce a complex totality to a perceptual unity. It is any kind of mental connecting tissue that allows and forces us to perceive a complexity as a single thing. It thus reduces chaos and confusion and promotes unity in perception.

Pattern is usually spoken of in pictorial analogies, because visual analogies aid our understanding of conceptual manipulations. It is common, for example, to divide pattern into two opposing principles of organization and illustrate them with images: we speak of embracing patterns, that is, the kind that organize our perception in the same way that a frame around a picture organizes it; and we speak of skeletal patterns, that is, organization on the principle of successive subdivisions, as in the branches of a tree, or of connection, as in the animal skeleton. In either case, the pattern asserts analogically and specifically the mental connecting tissue which forces us to see that thing before us, not as a confusion of leaves, twigs, limbs, branches, trunk, and bark, but as a tree. Ideas lend themselves also to such patterns.

This is all to say that the organizing effect of pattern is extremely important in perception and, thus, in our aesthetic response to an action. It is also to suggest that patterns emerge primarily from organizing arrangements of action. As in music, this particular aesthetic aspect of perception is usually spoken of in spatial and visual terms; thus, critics often talk about the "curve" of the plot.

We can be much more specific about the shape of patterns than the critic who talks about "curves." There are three very different abstract patterns into which perception falls—element patterns, axis patterns, and radial patterns —and quite a number of organizing, mythic patterns. There are many literary uses and variations upon all these kinds of patterns, but all have the effect of reducing variety to unity.

Element Patterns

Element patterns consist of the repetition, over and over again, of the same motif; a string of beads and a picket fence are organized perpetually by element patterns. A picket fence is not a mass of boards, paint, nails, and what have you that go into a picket fence, but a picket fence. The arrangement of the parts includes certain mental connecting tissue which allows us to see it as a single thing.

An extension of simple element patterns in literature is, of course, possible and even common. It is the typical organizing principle of most picaresque fiction, especially those stories in which the episodes are fairly complete in themselves. What holds *Don Quixote* together aesthetically is our perception that his episodic adventures, different from one another as they are, are illustrative of a single, particular man.

A slightly more ambitious use of a simple element pattern is the French novel *La Ronde*. The line of action proceeds from one finite character to the next to the next and to the next only on the basis of a sexual liaison. The action is, indeed, a string of beads, but it leads us through several levels of society and returns at the end to its point of beginning. It thus links together elements in a cross-section of society—which linking is, of course, the thematic point.

Collections of related short stories are also organized upon this principle. Faulkner and Hemingway have caused simple element patterns to look to us rather like fragmentary novels of considerably more organizational complexity than they, in fact, have. As we have already noted, Faulkner's *The Unvanquished* and *Go Down, Moses* are series of stories, often separated by time and often involving different characters, but the individual stories are parts of the same grand design and what emerges is an aesthetic picture of an age. Similarly, Hemingway's *In Our Time* is a series of stories and scenes, usually not sequential, but suggesting nevertheless a complicated sequence.

Incremental extensions of element patterns are also possible. In E. M. Forster's *A Room with a View,* Lucy Honeychurch goes through certain repeated sequences of action. She is young, pretty, and naïve; the purpose of the novel is to show her development toward clear-headedness in relation to the demands of her head and heart. In the first part of the book, she is taken on an excursion, is separated from the group, tumbled into a bed of flowers, and kissed by a man she does not want to kiss her. She discovers, however, that she has submitted to the kissing in response to her heart and that it, therefore, to the reader, has a certain appropriateness which she is not wholly willing to admit intellectually. In the next section of the book, she is taken on a new excursion, is separated from the group, thrown accidentally into a natural, floral setting, and is kissed by her fiancé whom she does not love. She submits to the kissing in response to her head and her intellect and discovers a certain appropriateness in her disappointment that it was not exciting. In a third section of the book, Lucy is again taken through the same sequence of incidents—the excursion, separation, and so on—and this time discovers the proper balance between the demands of the head and the heart. The novel is thus organized upon the principle that each element in the pattern be an increment on the original pattern. It is organized in analogy to a stairway. Each increment of an element pattern brings Miss Honeychurch one step closer to the fulfillment of her potential. Delineating the terms of this fulfillment is Forster's thematic purpose.

One should be able to see that there are certain elements of design in such a use of pattern. The second excursion inevitably recalls to mind, by repetition and contrast, the first excursion. The repetition and contrast are complicating factors in our aesthetic perception, but the element patterns in which they are organized act to encourage a unified perception. This is a young lady with an internal split. The contrasts depict this split and convince us that both sides of the contradiction do, indeed, belong to Miss Honeychurch. The third excursion complicates Lucy's problem further by introducing a new attitude toward the material, but unifies it by fitting the incremental repetition into the pattern.

We have already discussed at some length another example of an incremental pattern. The themes and variations in *Madame Bovary* operate both as elements of design and as organizing patterns. Again, the analogy would be that of a stairway. Each step of Emma's development both repeats her problem and organizes our perception of it.

Flashbacks are generally variations of incremental pattern, but they need not be discussed further here.

Axis Patterns

Axis patterns also are arrangements of the parts in analogy to visual and spatial experience. Whenever we see a scene in the world, a sculpture, for example, we invariably project an axis vertically through its center. This imaginary line helps us organize the perceptual experience. It tells us what part of the statue is on the right, what part on the left, how much is in front, how much is behind, and so on. It defines, in short, the perceptual unity of a complex, three-dimensional perception. Similarly, whenever we look at a painting, we unconsciously organize its perceptual stimuli in relation to a vertical axis; some of the picture lies on the right of the middle, some on the left. Some psychologists have suggested that this projection of an axis is psychologically necessary because the human being is intimately involved with such an axis within his own body; it is the imaginary but very practical line against which he measures balance, movement, direction, almost all of his experience. And in literature, as in life, this quality of perception is an important part of aesthetic organization.

Symmetry is the simplest form of organization on an axis. In literature, this is a way of describing what critics have traditionally spoken of as rising and falling action. When we represent these qualities of perception graphically, we draw a pyramid to represent the two sides of the symmetry. We use the horizontal plane to represent the passage of time, and the axis occurs at some midpoint in time, which separates the rising curve of thought from the falling curve.

An example of pyramidal symmetry is Thomas Mann's "A Railway Accident." Methodically, Mann gives us the ironic references to the narrator and his precious attitude toward his manuscript; the old peasant woman in black who is trying to get into the second-class carriage; the guard who is the image of authority, the image of the STATE and who rebukes the old peasant woman; the dandy with the dog on a leash who defies rules and takes his dog into his sleeping compartment; and the sleeping car attendant who is businesslike, taciturn, and diplomatic, and who is cowed by the dandy with the dog. Having built up this cross-section of society, Mann then allows the accident to occur. Methodically, he then constructs an ironic mirror-image of the first half of the story—the dandy is shouting, "Help," "Great God," and "Almighty God," in perfect contrast to his earlier arrogance; the sleeping car attendant becomes friendly, voluble, neighborly, in contrast to his earlier character; the guard limps up relating his experience in the whining tones of newspaper clichés; the narrator is shown in a new attitude toward himself and his manuscript; and, finally, the little old peasant woman in black manages to get into a first-class carriage, along with all the others. The pattern of the story is almost symmetrical. The falling action is an almost perfect reversal of the rising action.

A second kind of symmetrical pattern is what E. M. Forster called the hour glass pattern of Henry James's *The Ambassadors*. Chad and Strether begin the novel in opposition to one another. As time passes, Strether modulates in the direction of Chad's position and Chad modulates in the direction of Strether's position. At the physical center of the book, their paths cross, and Strether goes on to occupy Chad's original position at the end and Chad takes up Strether's original position. If we illustrate the curve of this action graphically, we get an hour-glass, or a big X, the two arms of which represent the developments of the two men. The pattern is still perfectly symmetrical and efficiently organizes our perceptions.

Symmetry, of course, is a form of balance; there are other forms of balance. All stimuli are not of the same aesthetic weight. Some things are relatively more interesting than other things. This means that a relatively heavy incident or scene can balance, aesthetically, a relatively large amount of lighter material. The axis would thus be moved nearer to one side of a graphic representation than to the other.

Such an aesthetic balance is typical of the ordinary short story. The writer often saves until the last the most dramatic parts of his subject and invests these parts with the heavier part of theme. He can then afford to allow his turning point or climax to come rather late in the story. He may allow one page of delivery to effectively balance ten pages of preparation.

Failure of aesthetic balance is one of the most common faults of the amateur. Encouraged by the apparent imbalance of a successful story, the young writer may try to make a relatively small part of his story balance a relatively large part. In a sense, he puts a watermelon on one side of the scales and a green pea on the other. Such a balance will only work when the pea is extremely heavy, or extremely "explosive."

It is possible, however, that we may yet come to value imbalance as imbalance. One can discover some visual examples of deliberate imbalance which are aesthetically pleasing—the red rose in one side of the senorita's hair, for instance, or some of the deliberately unbalanced water colors of the Chinese. In some cases where symmetrical balance is excessive, we accept imbalance as relief. But, so far, our literary aesthetics have not permitted deliberate imbalance, though it may yet do so.

The most powerful resistance to aesthetic imbalance is our habitual empathic attempt to correct it. If one sees a statue leaning over, the imbalance is terrifically disturbing and one finds himself leaning, as it were, to restore the axis to the center of gravity. A slanted picture on the wall gets straightened because its crooked axis disturbs us. We seem to have a strong psychological need to see the world in the same stable terms that we wish to feel in ourselves. When we perceive imbalance, our internal balance is upset, and we empathically try to correct the imbalance by projecting our need upon the perceived object. If all is not right with the world, we try to right it.

Radial-Circular Patterns

Radial-circular patterns are a third kind of arrangement of parts in analogy to visual and spatial experience. In such patterns, we have a center around which the rest of the pattern revolves, analogous to the apex and circumference of a circle. There are two important positions on this "wheel" which offer us the two primary examples of radial pattern—the hub and the tire. If we stand at the center of such a pattern, the parts of it branch outward in all directions, but continually remind us of the conceptual center which makes all the rest understandable. On the other hand, if we follow the path of the tire, we surround the subject and return to our point of beginning, always aware of the center. The first of these is a skeletal pattern, the other an embracing.

One variety of the hub and spoke pattern can be illustrated by the Japanese movie *Rashomon.* The center of the subject, to which we keep returning, is the murder itself. But we branch out from this conceptual center successively on four different views of the center, four subjective tellings of the story. The point, finally, is that neither the central view nor any of the ancillary views is adequate by itself, but that an accurate depiction of the experience is a perceptual totality of all of them. The pattern is one in which the rays radiate *outward* from the center, but continually remind us of the center as an organizing index.

The converse of this radial pattern can be illustrated by *The Scarlet Letter* in which various motifs begin in ways apparently isolated from one another and gradually, as the novel progresses, *converge* upon the center. Leland Schubert has shown us [4] how Hawthorne deliberately made most of his

---

[4] See Leland Schubert, *Hawthorne, the Artist* (Chapel Hill: U. of North Carolina Press, 1944), pp. 141–150.

motifs and symbols converge on the final scaffold scene. He points out that the motif of the "A" is used some one hundred and fifty times, each time accruing more thematic content. The corollary motif is Dimmesdale's gesture of putting his hand over his heart—which Pearl keeps asking about. We discover in the final scaffold scene that these two motifs were intimately related, for Dimmesdale, too, has his scarlet letter. The motifs of the black and red roses converge similarly on the scaffold scene. Similarly, too, the motif of Pearl's repeated question about the earthly family, as when she invites Dimmesdale to stand with her and Hester on the scaffold, and the motif of Dimmesdale's answer about the heavenly family, converge at the scaffold scene. All these motifs are apparently isolated from one another at the beginning, but slowly move toward the apical point. The rays move from the circumference to the bright center.

There are three kinds of embracing circular patterns: the simple circumference, concentric circles, and the spiral. The circumferential pattern can be illustrated by Hemingway's *The Sun Also Rises*. The characters move from place to place performing "lost," futile, unavailing actions and return to their points of beginning. They move from place to place, but never get anywhere. They appear at the same bars, performing the same actions, again and again. The cyclic nature of this life is pointed up by the epigraph and title from Ecclesiastes. That nothing ever leads anywhere, except to the point of beginning, is a major part of Hemingway's theme.

The pattern of concentric circles can be illustrated by Henry James's *The Ambassadors*. According to Robert Spiller [5] the pattern of perception, the point-of-view, is organized on the principle of concentric circles. In the beginning, we have only Strether's point-of-view of the subject matter. Then when Chad's sister, Sarah, arrives we gain a new way of looking at the material, which now includes Strether's way of looking at the material, and as time passes, we infer other circles around these circles, the points of view of Maria Gostrey and Madame de Vionnet. It is the pattern that the pebble produces in the pond. The pattern could move either outward in ever-expanding circles, or inward toward a vibrant core. It would even be possible for such a pattern to expand a while and then contract.

The spiral pattern can be illustrated by Hawthorne's *The Scarlet Letter*. When the story opens, Hester Prynne is being punished for adultery on the scaffold in the market place. The plot and theme then revolves about the act in discursive, rather than dramatic, ways. The adultery and the scaffold are always in the center of conception, kept there by the scarlet "A," but our focus is kept on the periphery. We move in circles, as it were, around the

[5] *The Cycle of American Literature* (New York: Macmillan, 1955), p. 141.

subject and the four principal characters. In the middle chapter of the book, the action and characters return to the scaffold in the market-place and we are given a new view of the characters and their sins. We have returned to the point of beginning but with a difference. Then the action moves out once again, discursively circling the new matter and the old motifs, coming in the final scene a third time to the scaffold in the market-place. It is again the point of beginning but again with a difference. The pattern is moving upward and outward like a spiral. This structure was especially appropriate in revealing Hawthorne's real interest, for he was not interested in the linear effects of adultery, but in the psychological effects which revolve about sin.

Other kinds of spirals seem possible. Lucy Honeychurch's stairstep pattern of development is analogous to a spiral staircase. Each of her excursions is a round trip, but she is never the same for successive new beginnings; she is part way up to the landing. Her spiral rises but does not expand. One can also imagine spiral patterns that converge and descend, as in the last half of *War and Peace*.

The frame, or envelope, story—the story within the story—is also a common literary use of circular, organizing patterns.

Although we speak of these patterns in visual analogies, they are all conceptual. Literature is a temporal art depending on memory and conception for our perception of such "shapes." These patterns of visual analogies, however, are fairly easy to conceptualize; the conceptual patterns which themselves depend upon conceptions—that is, the mythic patterns—are more difficult.

Mythic Patterns

There are certain accretions of human experience which are so nearly common to all people that they can be depended upon as organizing patterns. These are the myths, the narratives of common experiences, of communal experiences, which are repeated in each person and in each culture in stage after stage, place after place. Jungian psychologists insist that these narratives are not intended, but are spontaneous productions of the psyche. We have already discussed certain of the archetypal character patterns; the patterns of actions in which these characters get involved are equally a part of man's vicarious celebration of his potential. Because they are common and collective, we can use them as literary patterns.

One of the simplest, oldest, and most common of these mythic patterns is the Journey. The road, the river, the path on which the journey takes place has long been used as a metaphor—the course of life. The finite incidents that happen along the road have been analogous to the stages of development in our lives. Thus, any journey is a kind of metaphorical extension of our own psychic experience. Because of this, we find it possible to identify with such different characters as Don Quixote, Huckleberry Finn, and Holden Caulfield. Because of this, too, we find it possible to see their variant experiences as unified. It is not so much that we see their experiences as aesthetically connected; rather we see them conceptually analogous to our own. The pattern of experience—the narrative—becomes the conceptual basis upon which we perceive unity.

Primitive and psychological mythology abound in journeys. Some of them take place at night, some must move across water, some take the hero to the mythic center of the earth. Virtually all of them include a quest. The details of such journeys are, of course, symbolic. But the symbols do not have an absolute existence. They undergo variations for particular individuals, but their basic outlines recur in many specific forms. One particular cluster of journey and quest myths is rather important in myth and literature. This is the pattern that Joseph Campbell [6] called the monomyth, the patterns of initiation, transformation, and return.

The pattern of initiation has been extremely important in American literature. Indeed, it is now almost a truism that American literature is a variation on the initiation myth. It is a myth involved with growth and growing, so it is not surprising that a young and growing nation should have been importantly concerned with it. Essentially, it is the introduction of a young person to the next higher stage of his development. Every child undergoes certain changes when he becomes an adult. These changes are ritualized and externalized in the myth. Because this has been a valuable psychological device and serves to take the threat out of change, it has also been an important literary device.

A good example of the initiation story is Hemingway's "Indian Camp." Nick is awakened at night and taken on a journey across water to the Indian camp, where his father wants to initiate him into the mysteries of birth. The imagery of the story suggests the most dangerous and the most primitive aspects of experience. When the caesarian surgery goes wrong, the initiation expands its focus from simple birth to blood, violence, and death. This is too much experience for Nick and he reverts to infantile ignorance and dependence upon the parent. His initiation fails. But hundreds of other American stories show the initiation succeeding. The child learns to cope with the material of the initiation.

The pattern of transformations has been less important in American litera-

---

[6] *The Hero with a Thousand Faces* (New York: Bollingen Foundation, 1949; Meridian, 1956).

ture, but appears in a few works. Here, the process of change is most important and, especially, the change in a mature direction. Hemingway's Nick Adams begins "Big Two-Hearted River" as a dessicated shell of a man. He has a bad case of war nerves and an overwhelming desire to reject his society, if not all experience. In the interior of Upper Michigan, he performs certain rituals which are designed to "get things right," to reconstruct his character and personality. By the end of the story, he has successfully transformed himself into a new man.

A much more ambitious attempt at a transformation is Frederick Manfred's *Lord Grizzly*. It is the story of Hugh Glass, who was a member of the Ashley expedition on the Upper Missouri in 1827. Hugh left the main party to hunt for game, encountered a grizzly bear, and was mangled to the point of death. The grizzly sunk her teeth into his skull, lacerated his back to the bone in some twenty scratches, and broke his left leg. He was left on the banks of a stream as dead. But he recovered, set his own leg and crawled most of the 240 miles to Fort Kiowa. During the crawl, Hugh conceived an immense hatred for the men who had left him as dead. His desire for revenge was a primary part of the motivation that kept him crawling. Once his wounds were healed, he set out to track down and kill the men who had deserted him. He finds them, but does not kill them. Manfred's intention seems to be to show how environment and the experience of tracking the men slowly transforms Hugh psychologically so that when he finds the men, he no longer needs the revenge that had motivated him. Like the crucifixion of Christ, his experience has transformed the god in him from wrathful to tolerant.

The myth of return has been less important literarily. Essentially, it is the myth of the old wise man, mother earth, and such other figures who produce sustenance, either physical or psychic, for man. It is the return of the young hero who has been successfully initiated, successfully transformed, and now returns to bestow upon his culture the secret gifts of his maturity. It is Prometheus stealing fire for mankind. Since our taste in literature has been oriented toward realism, a kind of photographic reproduction of external experience, we have not seen very many modern examples of the pattern of mythic return. We would tend to think of a returned hero as a man with a Messiah complex, one to be avoided. If we could expand our conception of realism to include psychic reality, which often is clothed in marvelous and fantastic symbols, the pattern of the return might be more usable, as it was in primitive mythology.

There are many other patterns of myths, and more are being created every year in response to cultural developments. The American Civil War, for example, seems to have activated quite a number of myths, not least the confrontation of brother against brother. There are so many aspects of the Civil

War with which Americans are not yet comfortable, that the mere evocation of it as subject, even without any literary merit in the work, will continue to commandeer large audiences for some time to come. The Great Depression, the Hollywood Star system, the assassination of President Kennedy, the Cold War, and other recent experiences have also created mythic patterns. The writer, having discovered these patterns, can use them to unify the chaos of his detail.

PROJECTS FOR WRITING AND DISCUSSION

The best exercises, by far, are those that a writer sets himself in the process of writing a story. Indeed, it seems rather foolish to even think of *practicing* the immensely complicated, aesthetic business that is structure. Nevertheless, there are certain little exercises that a beginner might put himself through; hopefully they would start him thinking in aesthetic terms, so that eventually he could forget all the conscious effort that this whole chapter has implied.

A. ANALYSIS

1. Analyze the structure of Hemingway's "Soldier's Home." * What is the relationship between the summary narrative of the first half and the dramatized scene of the second half? What contrasts do you find? What gradations? What variations on what themes? Can you find places where Hemingway restrained himself from telling or showing too much, or too much too quickly?

2. Analyze the structure of Faulkner's "Barn Burning." * How does Faulkner suggest the burden of the past? Point out examples of design. What is the function of Sarty's caricatured sisters? What is the pattern of the story? Is it the same as the pattern of Ab Snopes's series of barn burnings? or is it a different pattern which results from that?

3. Does Ambrose Bierce's "An Occurrence at Owl Creek Bridge" * have a structure? How could it have been improved?

4. Read Lionel Trilling's "Of This Time, Of That Place." What is its pattern? Note that Howe's interviews with the students follow certain parallels. What are they? What effect on structure do they have? Try to draw a diagram that represents the structure of the story.

5. Analyze the structure of your favorite novel. Then analyze the structure of a novel that fails, to see whether the failure is primarily one of structure or of some other element. Next time you have to write a paper for an English class, try writing on the structure of a story or a novel.

B. *COMPARISON*

1. Compare the structures of "Soldier's Home" * and "Barn Burning." * Why does Hemingway use a summary narrative before his dramatization, while Faulkner uses dramatization before summary narrative? Does the opening, dramatized scene of "Barn Burning" add anything? anything that "Soldier's Home" might have benefitted by?

2. Both "Of This Time, Of That Place" and "Within a Magic Prison" * proceed by alternation between two sides of a contrast. Compare and contrast their structures. Which is more effective? Does the notion of effectiveness have to be modified by the scope of the story? What effect do the relative number of crises and the amount of time passing in the stories have on structure and effectiveness?

3. Compare the strategies of withholding information in the "Hat Island Crossing" * by Mark Twain and "An Occurrence at Owl Creek Bridge" * by Ambrose Bierce. Why does one result in "surprise" and the other not? What has this to do with structure, or the arrangement of parts for aesthetic purpose?

C. *IMITATION AND CREATION*

1. Write a "symmetrical" story. Set your main character in conflict with and in contrast to a graded series of, say, three secondary characters. Arrange the encounters with these three in order of importance, so that the third of them will precipitate the climax and turning point. Then show the main character interacting with each of the three again, in reverse order. This structure would be similar to Thomas Mann's in "A Railway Accident." Its design is based on contrast and gradation, its pattern, on the pyramid.

2. Write a "stair-step" story. Take a main character and put him into similar situations, say, three different times. For example, take a boy (or girl) away to college for the first year; he (she) returns to his home-town at Christmas, spring vacation, and Easter. Each time, he visits an old high school girl-friend (or friend, or parent), but each time, he is different. The primary design principle here would be theme and variation; the pattern would be elemental. (There would also be an opportunity to work with a mythic pattern of Birth, Death, and Resurrection; indeed, if this pattern is not to be used, it might be advisable to change the times to Thanksgiving, semester break, and the next summer, lest one suggest patterns not intended.)

3. Write a "circular" story. Take a main character, a shoe salesman, say, and show his life going through its cycles, returning to its point of beginning. Here the point of climax and crisis would have to be that the man is unaffected. Theme and variation could be used to suggest the sameness of everything he does; memory of past events might extend the scene at hand into a picture of his whole life. Be careful not to overuse certain words in describing his actions; and be sure

that those actions have some variety. Otherwise you are in danger of becoming repetitive and boring.

4. Write an "episodic" story, in which the arrangement of incidents is based on the *progression d'effet.* You may, if you wish, write the material out as an expository essay first, then try to translate the ideas into scene, character, and action. Pay particular attention to such enriching and connecting devices as theme and variation.

An Essay on the "Use" of Structure

Structure, then, can be thought of as the combined defense of unity and variety against chaos and oversimplicity. But what of the application of these theories to an actual work or to the task of writing? How does one "use" structure? It seems to me extremely valuable for the prospective writer to explore, in considerable detail, an ambitious application of the principles of structure. Joseph Conrad's *Heart of Darkness* is a rewarding work for such a study, for it includes the mythic journey into darkness, an initiation, transformation, and return, as well as elaborate parallels to Buddhistic myth, and it is all knit together by contrasts, gradations, theme-and-variations, and even restraints. There is hardly a detail of style, character, scene, or incident that does not contribute to Conrad's structure and, thus, to his theme.

Structure and Theme in Heart of Darkness

Surely, we all notice the obvious connections between The Buddha and Charlie Marlow in Joseph Conrad's *Heart of Darkness,*[7] but the novel is far more intimately connected with Buddha than these superficial references indicate. In fact, the structure of Conrad's story is parallel, step by step, to Buddha's Noble Eight-Fold Path. This structure helps to embody and specify Conrad's theme.

The most obvious structure of the story is, of course, that of the journey, which is a complete monomyth: the journey to the interior of Africa becomes

---

[7] Parenthetical page notations in this discussion, unless it is otherwise stated, refer to Joseph Conrad, *Three Great Tales* (New York: Modern Library Paperback, n.d.). In the beginning, Marlow is described in the pose of a meditating Buddha: "Marlow sat cross-legged right aft, leaning against the mizzenmast. He had sunken cheeks, a yellow complexion, a straight back, an ascetic aspect, and, with his arms dropped, the palms of hands outwards, resembled an idol" (p. 200). Shortly, he lifts his hand and becomes "a Buddha preaching in European clothes and without a lotus flower," (p. 221), and, at the very end, he returns to "the pose of a meditating Buddha" (p. 307).

a metaphor for Marlow's journey to the interior of himself; there, he is
initiated and transformed; then he returns to the tribe to try to tell of the
secrets he has perceived in the darkness. But, within the journey, there is
another pattern, an element pattern of the episodes, each of which is more
or less discrete. There is, for instance, the cluster of scenes with Europeans
before Marlow embarks for the trip out; these scenes are variations upon or
contrasts to one another, so that they cohere as a cluster, as an episode.
Similarly, the incident of shelling the coast of Africa and the several incidents
at the Outer Station cohere, by parallel and contrast, as an episode. These
episodes are distinguished from one another, not only by the narrative summary that serves as transition, but also by changes in character, setting, action,
and—as we shall see later—theme.

There are eight distinct episodes in Marlow's story: in Europe before em-
barking, at the Outer Station, at the Central Station, on the upper reaches of
the river, at the Inner Station waiting for Kurtz to appear, the trip down-
river, visiting the Intended, and, finally, the scene on the deck of the *Nellie*.
These eight episodes reflect, in thematic concerns and in the matrix of terminology, the corresponding eight stages of the Noble Eight-Fold Path—
Right Views, Right Intentions, Right Speech, Right Action, Right Livelihood,
Right Effort, Right Mindfulness, and Right Concentration.[8]

RIGHT VIEWS

In the pose of a meditating Buddha, Marlow begins his story with a discussion of *Right Views*—which can be defined as "to be openminded; to face
facts; to accept the Four Noble Truths." [9] Marlow begins by expressing the
point of view that the Thames, England, the civilized world, has also been
one of the dark places of the earth and notes how far the Roman conquest
had been from filling the ideal of Right Views. Marlow's motives for the
Congo trip are nearly a "Right View"; he is going in a spirit of adventure, to
"lose myself in all the glories of exploration" (p. 222), as he tells us in
connection with the map in the Fleet Street window. On the continent, we get

---

[8] Buddha, "The Sermon at Benares." There have been, of course, hundreds of translations, from the middle ages on, and the Eight-Fold Path has been the most commonly
known detail about Buddhism. The translations used here are the ones used in "Buddha
and Buddhism," *Encyclopaedia Britannica* (1959 edition), Vol. IV, p. 326. See *The
Gospel of Buddha*, by Paul Carus (La Salle, Ill.: Open Court, 1897, 1912, and other
editions); *Wheel of the Law: Buddhism* (London: Trubner, 1871); and *A Survey of
Buddhism*, by Bhikshu Sangharakshita (Bangalore, India: Indian Institute of World
Culture, 1957); among others, for further information and different translations, some
of which are indicated in the present discussion.

[9] F. M. Fitch, *Their Search for God* (New York: Lothrop, Lee, and Shepard, 1947),
p. 114.

other views. Marlow's aunt's "glorious idea" of being "engaged in the noble cause" (pp. 223–24) is heavily ironic and contributes to the removal of Marlow's childish illusions. The director of companies and the clerk who "glorified the company's business" (p. 226), are as much "out of touch with truth" (p. 228) as Marlow's aunt. They accept Marlow as "one of the Workers, with a capital—you know. Something like an emissary of light, something like a lower sort of apostle" (p. 228). But Marlow is under no such illusion. He "ventured to hint that the company was run for profit" (p. 228), but he is put down with talk about "weaning those ignorant millions from their horrid ways" (p. 228). These Europeans have "wrong" views, and Marlow objects to being allied with them. Only the eccentric doctor who measures skulls shares some of the "right view" with Marlow. His interests are completely non-craving: "in the interests of science—the mere wealth I leave to others" (p. 227). (We shall find this sort of motif and variation, gradation, and contrast at every stage, for it is Conrad's method to work in alternations of images and of themes.) Marlow feels uneasy, "as though I had been let into some conspiracy" (p. 226); "a queer feeling came to me that I was an imposter" (p. 228). His mind is not closed; he is ready to face facts, even those about himself.

RIGHT INTENTIONS

Intention, Resolve, Aims form the matrix of concerns in the second episode. The man-of-war shelling the coast is described not only as ludicrous, but also as insane in its intention.

There was a touch of insanity in the proceeding, a sense of lugubrious drollery in the sight; and it was not dissipated by somebody on board assuring me earnestly there was a camp of natives—he called them enemies!—hidden out of sight somewhere. (p. 230)

It seems as objectless as the activities at the Outer Station, where rotting boilers, railway trucks, and "more pieces of decaying machinery" (p. 231) attest to the intentions of the Europeans. "Objectless blasting" (p. 231) on the face of a cliff that remains unchanged is all the work that is going on. Here the chain gangs of blacks are not enemies, but criminals. Marlow pauses near the grove of trees to collect his thoughts and realizes what the intentions of the men he is to meet will be.

As I stood on this hillside, I foresaw that in the blinding sunshine of that land I would become acquainted with a flabby, pretending, weak-eyed devil of a rapacious and pitiless folly. (p. 232)

When, in the grove of death, he gives a ship's biscuit to a dying Negro, we sense in him Right Intention—"to want that which has true value and which everyone may share" (Fitch, p. 114). Only the iridescent black canoemen and the immaculate and conscientious accountant, by parallel and contrast, can give Marlow the feeling that "I belonged still to a world of straightforward facts" (p. 229).

RIGHT SPEECH

At the Central Station Marlow's "first glance at the place was enough to let you see the flabby devil was running that show" (p. 238), and the place is a matrix of verbal duplicity, backbiting, plotting, calumny. "They beguiled the time by backbiting and intriguing against each other in a foolish kind of way" (p. 242). The manager, the brickmaker, the pilgrims all have the "wrong" speech and their actions prompt Marlow into his verbal duplicity, his "lie." He lets them think that he is aligned with the "new gang—the gang of virtue" (p. 244), as the manager calls it. But Marlow is not altogether lost; he realizes what he is doing. "I became in an instant as much of a pretense as the rest of the bewitched pilgrims," he says (p. 246). This sort of self-awareness contributes to his salvation. It is in this section also that the jungle first becomes a "dumb thing" (p. 245), that Kurtz becomes "just a word" (p. 246), and that the envelope narrator emerges for the first of three times to tell us that Marlow on the deck of the *Nellie* was "no more than a voice" (p. 246). And, of course, the word *Ivory* rings in the air. Only the boiler-maker with his expansive talk about pigeon flying (p. 248) gives Marlow the sense of saying "that which is true and kind" (Fitch, p. 114).

RIGHT ACTION

The matrix of *Action, Conduct,* and *Behavior* begins when Marlow finds the book by Towson.

Towson or Towser was inquiring earnestly into the breaking strain of ships' chains and tackle, and other such matters. Not a very enthralling book; but at the first glance you could see there a singleness of intention, an honest concern for the right way of going to work, which made these humble pages, thought out so many years ago, luminous with another than a professional light. The simple old sailor, with his talk of chains and purchases, made me forget the jungle and the pilgrims in a delicious sensation of having come upon something unmistakably real. (pp. 258–59)

Towson's *Inquiry* represents the "right action," for it proceeds from the right motives. It is a disinterested, non-craving inquiry, and contrasts with the actions of the men on the little steam-boat. When Marlow begins to fret and worry about what he will do when he meets Kurtz, he realizes that "any action of mine would be a mere futility" (p. 260). The remarkable restraint of the cannibal crew-men comes up here. The attack by Kurtz's savages, or the action,

what we afterwards alluded to as an attack was really an attempt at repulse. The action was very far from being aggressive—it was not even defensive, in the usual sense: it was undertaken under the stress of desperation, and in its essence was purely protective. (p. 265)

During the attack, the pilgrims and the Manager are shown in comic and ineffectual actions; they squirt bullets into the tops of trees and make a "deuce of a lot of smoke" (p. 267). Marlow performs the "right action" when he pulls the line of the steam whistle and stops the comedy of blood, but his best self is not in control when, because he is flustered by the death of the helmsman, he throws his shoes overboard. The people who can do something from such disinterested motives as Towson come off well in this section. The bewitched fireman ("he could fire up a vertical boiler." p. 257) and the "second-rate" helmsman ("Well, don't you see, he had done something, he had steered." p. 274) get our approval for their behavior, although they, like Kurtz, lacked restraint in their actions. We get here Kurtz's dissertation on action, the seventeen pages of recommendations, from 'by the simple exercise of our will we can exert a power for good practically unbounded' (p. 273) to 'Exterminate all the brutes!' (p. 274). The Russian clown is depicted as the opposite of Kurtz; his motives are completely unselfish—he survives because "he surely wanted nothing from the wilderness but space to breathe in and to push on through" (p. 279). "The absolutely pure, un-calculating, unpractical spirit of adventure . . . seemed to have consumed all thought of self so completely . . ." (p. 279).

Right Livelihood

Livelihood and ways of Earning a Living become the matrix of concern in the next section. Marlow and the Russian clown discuss Kurtz's methods of earning his living:

> To speak plainly, he [Kurtz] raided the country . . .
> They adored him. . . .
> There was nothing on earth to prevent him from killing whom
> he jolly well pleased. . . .
> He hated all this, and somehow he couldn't get away. . . .
> (pp. 280–81)

The skulls on the posts around Kurtz's hut "only showed that Mr. Kurtz lacked restraint in the gratification of his various lusts" (p. 283), lacked restraint in his means of livelihood. Kurtz had succumbed to savagery because he was morally hollow:

The wilderness had found him out early, and had taken on him a terrible vengeance for the fantastic invasion. I think it had whispered to him things about himself which he did not know, things of which he had no conception till he took counsel with this great solitude—and the whisper had proved irresistibly fascinating. It echoed loudly within him because he was hollow at the core. . . ." (p. 283)

Marlow reacts emotionally against such methods. When the Russian clown begins to describe the relations of the savages to Kurtz ("They would crawl . . ."), Marlow cuts him off, preferring the actual savagery of the heads on the stakes to the moral savagery of Kurtz's ceremonies:

"I don't want to know anything of the ceremonies used when approaching Mr. Kurtz," I shouted. Courious, this feeling that came over me that such details would be more intolerable than those heads drying on the stakes under Mr. Kurtz's windows. After all, that was only a savage sight, while I seemed at one bound to have been transported into some lightless region of subtle horrors, where, pure, uncomplicated savagery was a positive relief. (pp. 283–84)

But the Russian clown does not share Marlow's horror, for he has heard many of Kurtz's "splendid monologues on, what was it? On love, justice, *conduct of life*—" (p. 284—italics supplied). He is a loyal and forgiving disciple to the end.

A little later the manager and Marlow have a conversation about Kurtz's methods:

'the method is unsound,' [said the Manager]. 'Do you,' said I [Marlow], looking at the shore, 'call it "unsound method?" ' 'Without doubt,' he exclaimed hotly. 'Don't you?'
'No method at all,' I murmured after a while. 'Exactly,' he exulted. 'I anticipated this. Shows a complete want of judgment.' (p. 288)

Marlow condemns Kurtz's methods because of the moral savagery. But the manager condemns them because they have ruined the district for the ivory "robbery." Marlow is more repelled by the manager than by Kurtz, because the methods of imperialism are a greater moral savagery.

I had never breathed an atmosphere so vile, and I turned mentally to Kurtz for relief—positively for relief. 'Nevertheless I think Mr. Kurtz is a remarkable man,' I said with emphasis. He [the manager] started, dropped on me a cold heavy glance, said very quietly, 'he *was!*' and turned his back on me. My hour of favor was over; I found myself lumped along with Kurtz as a partisan of methods for which the time was not ripe: I was unsound! Ah! but it was something to have at least a choice of nightmares. (p. 288)

It is a complicated system of parallels and contrasts in alliances, but we know that Marlow is not choosing the moral savagery of Kurtz. His way of earning a living is near the ideal—"to work in a way that will do no harm to any person or animal" (Fitch, p. 114). He is aligned with the Russian clown in a spirit of pure adventure and non-self-seeking. When the clown goes back into the wilderness with a few Martini-Henry cartridges, a handful of Marlow's tobacco, and Towson's *Inquiry*—"He seemed to think himself excellently well equipped for a renewed encounter with the wilderness" (p. 290)—we, like Marlow, give him our approval, qualified only by the comedy of this innocent fool-or-saint. His livelihood, in contrast to Kurtz's and to the manager's, is the "Right Livelihood" with which to meet, and survive in, the wilderness of life.

RIGHT EFFORTS

These concerns are over as Kurtz is brought to the steamboat, and the concern shifts to *Efforts* to enact earlier concerns. Activities are called for, now, to "prevent and uproot evil; to cause and cultivate good; to endeavor always to overcome ignorance and selfish cravings" (Fitch, p. 114). Kurtz himself performs ideally in his gesture to the rioting natives. Later, Marlow goes after Kurtz, stalking him as one animal might stalk another, "I actually left the track and ran in a wide semicircle" (p. 292). There is effort in the actual physical wrestling, but Marlow rejects the possibility of completely physical means; he knows that he could club Kurtz with a rock, but that it would solve nothing. Then, since Kurtz had removed himself from all public controls, Marlow appeals to him—even as the worshipping savages had; as a God—in the name of himself: " 'You will be lost,' I said—'utterly lost' " (p. 292). And Kurtz

struggled with himself, too. I saw it, I heard it. I saw the inconceivable mystery of a soul that knew no restraint, no faith, and no fear, yet struggling blindly with itself. (p. 294) ... Both the diabolic love and the unearthly hate of the mysteries it had penetrated fought for the possession of that soul satiated with primitive emotions, avid of lying fame, of sham distinction, of all the appearances of success and power. (p. 296)

The struggle finally culminates in an effort of Kurtz's will and his judgment on his own life: "The horror! The horror!" (p. 297).

Marlow has to struggle with the awareness of these same elements of good and evil. He is sick with fever, has to "wrestle with death" also (p. 298). But his big struggle is with the same questions as Kurtz had. "I was within a hair's-breadth of the last opportunity for pronouncement, and I found with humiliation that probably I would have nothing to say" (p. 298). This is Marlow's horror, the realization that he was still incapable of judging his own life. (He does learn; his last act with the Intended shows an awareness of the forces in life that surpasses even Kurtz's judgment.) What saves him from the onslaught that would have been destructive on the river is simply work, physical *effort;* he has no time to let his mind run over Kurtz's issues because he has to tend his little steamer down the river, and when they break down, he tends the little forge during the repairs.

RIGHT MINDFULNESS

Marlow enters the episode of *Right Mindfulness* in a surly mood:

Back in the sepulchral city resenting the sight of people hurrying through the streets to filch a little money from each other, ... They were intruders whose knowledge of life was to me an irritating pretense, because I felt so sure they could not possibly know the things I knew.... (p. 299)

Still, "I had no particular desire to enlighten them" (p. 299). Here the matrix of "right mindfulness" is appearing. Marlow objects mildly to

My dear aunt's endeavor to 'nurse up my strength' ... It was not my strength that wanted nursing, it was my imagination that wanted soothing. (p. 300)

In the scene with the Intended, we see more clearly Marlow's new ability to "keep one's mind alert and watchful; to do no evil because of thoughtlessness" (Fitch, p. 114). This is precisely Marlow's motive for not telling the Intended the truth about Kurtz, for the truth would have caused more evil, more horror, than the lie. He deliberately does not destroy

that great and saving illusion that shone with an unearthly glow in the darkness, in the triumphant darkness from which I could not have defended her—from which I could not even defend myself. (p. 305)

because, "It would have been too dark—too dark altogether" (p. 307). Because he is "right mindful" of the consequences, he lies to avoid the evil that would come of thoughtlessness.

This theme of the saving illusion of women has been working in a minor way almost from the beginning. Marlow's aunt had lived in a beautiful world of her own, through which illusion she manages to exert a steadying influence on men. The saving quality of the illusion is more explicit in connection with the first mention of the Intended:

They—the women I mean—are out of it—should be out of it. We must help them to stay in that beautiful world of their own, lest ours gets worse. (p. 271)

"*Lest ours gets worse.*" The moral savagery that men develop when they are loose from all public controls is a worse moral horror to Marlow than the perpetuation of the illusion that keeps civilization solid.

RIGHT CONCENTRATION—MEDITATION

At the end of the story, Marlow returns to the pose of a *Meditating* Buddha, recalling his first pose, and suggesting that *the whole narrative* is the eighth stage of the process. It is not only that he "sits long and quietly, withdrawn from all external objects, with thoughts turned inward until there comes enlightenment" (Fitch, p. 114), as Buddha did, for his mind is not really withdrawn. External objects do not intrude, it is true, but experience does. His story is a compulsive and meditative retelling of the experiences that have taken him this far along the way to wisdom; it is the meditation and concentration that will remove the last veil of illusion. Just after his first mention of "the poor chap" (Kurtz) in the opening pages, he says that the whole trip to "the farthest point of navigation and the culminating point of my experience . . . seemed somehow to *throw a kind of light on everything about me—and into my thoughts*" (p. 222—italics supplied). Marlow is struggling throughout to make the men on the *Nellie understand,* to make them see this "kind of light"; he is indeed a teacher of moral notions, even as Buddha was.

Not only are there numerous fumblings for words throughout, the function of the three times when the narrative emerges from the African trip to the scene on the *Nellie* is precisely to bring the lesson to modern Englishmen.

Do you see him? [says Marlow in the first of the three shifts] Do you see the story? Do you see anything? It seems to me I am trying to tell you a dream—making a vain attempt, because no relation of a dream can convey the dream-sensation, that commingling of absurdity, surprise, and bewilderment in a tremor of struggling revolt, that notion of being captured by the incredible which is the very essence of dreams. . . .
He was silent for a while.
. . . No, it is impossible; it is impossible to convey the life-sensation of any

given epoch of one's existence—that which makes its truth, its meaning—its subtle and penetrating essence. It is impossible. We live, as we dream—alone. . . .
  He paused again as if reflecting, then added:
  Of course in this you fellows see more than I could, then. You see me, whom you know. . . . (p. 246)

This last paragraph gains virtually all its meaning in a context of Marlow's "sermon."

In the second of the shifts back to the deck of the *Nellie,* Marlow specifically compares the African experiences with "you fellows performing on your respective tightropes" (p. 254). In the third he is described as having "an aspect of concentrated attention" (p. 270), and his attempt is again to make his lesson comprehensible to his audience.

  "Absurd!" he cried. "This is the worst of trying to tell. . . . Here you all are, each moored with two good addresses, like a hulk with two anchors, a butcher round one corner, a policeman round another, excellent appetites, and temperature normal—you hear—normal from year's end to year's end. And you say, Absurd! Absurd be—exploded! Absurd! (pp. 270-71)

But even more importantly, the narrative is a new experience for Marlow, as repeated contemplation is, in the Buddhistic frame of wisdom. Marlow says,

  Mind, I am not trying to excuse or even explain—I am trying to account to myself for—for—Mr. Kurtz—for the shade of Mr. Kurtz. (p. 273)

  I've done enough for [the memory of Kurtz] to give me the indisputable right to lay it, if I choose, for an everlasting rest in the dust bin of progress, amongst all the sweepings, and figuratively speaking, all the dead cats of civilization. But then, you see, I can't choose. He won't be forgotten. (p. 274)

It is not Kurtz as a man that will not be forgotten; it is Kurtz as a "dead cat of civilization," as a species of humanity that failed to preserve his civil morality when all civil restraint had been removed. It is the meditation and the sermon on what happens to morality in society-and-solitude that is Marlow's purpose in telling the story. It is this that makes the envelope narrator and the scene on the *Nellie* not only valid, but necessary.

  Marlow's lie to the Intended, too, in spite of its being from the best of right-mindful motives, necessitates the envelope narrative. That "saving illusion" is still illusion and is shared by the men on the *Nellie.* Such illusion cannot be tolerated in any final idea of enlightenment. Marlow's telling of the story is an attempt at exorcising illusion, not so that he or the others can withdraw into Nirvana, but so that he can contribute to the moral structure of his own and others' experience. In a sense, Conrad has given us in *Heart of Darkness* a concrete, practical, even worldly example of applied Buddhistic method.

Thus, Conrad, no careless writer at that time, used a very careful pattern, a matrix of concerns, images, and terms, which are parallel to the Eight-Fold Path, and which help to specify Conrad's meaning. Far too numerous to be accidental, these details unify our perception of the whole and create a structure that lifts the story beyond the realm of initiation literature to make it the philosophical maneuver it is.

Unfortunately, we have tended to be content with discussions of the initiation story and its several manifestations in the mythic river journey and the night journey to the psychic interior, but these, after all, are Plot, not Thought, as Aristotle would have been quick to recognize. There is a change from innocence to knowing, certainly; but to knowing *what?* The initiation story, as story, cannot specify the lesson which is its prize and object. That information must come from some other source. (Structure, symbol, and cultural setting are the most common sources.) Conrad uses parallels to the Wheel of the Law of Buddhism—without the lotus and in European clothes—to specify his message in *Heart of Darkness.*

On the other hand, the initiation story has seemed meaningful to Western readers in a way that Buddha's ideal path has not. To Western minds, especially, Buddha's advice has seemed abstract, ideal, even unworldly, while Conrad's seems embroiled in the practicalities of empire in Africa and the realism of immersion in psychological experience. But the two are not mutually exclusive. The general meaning of Marlow's journey can be described with the general definition of the Noble Eight-Fold Path—*"the means to wisdom, to peace, to insight; the means of the Middle Way between the extremes of pleasure and pain, of surfeit and hardship."* [10] It remains, however, for Marlow's experiences before, during, and after the trip to specify, like exemplars, the structures of The Path.

[10] "The Sermon at Benares."

9

Theme:
Sources, Styles, Uses

It should be obvious by now that the uses of writing technique lead to ever sharper and sharper delineation of meaning. Techniques exist in order for the writer to say exactly what he means and to eliminate what he does not mean. Or, more precisely, technique determines the theme of the writer's work.

But what is theme? Meaning, in the broadest sense; the evocation of subject matter and some evaluation of it; the message the writer wishes, consciously or unconsciously, to communicate, whether it is "inspirational," polemic, nostalgic, objectively analytical, or agnostic in a total-experience sense; the tone, mood, feelings, value judgments that are perceived in the work; the mental image of characters acting and reacting with other characters in a time and a place, which—overtly or covertly—advocates a philosophy of life; in short, anything in the writer's work that *means*.

All such meanings that the reader perceives are derived from the general life and become a part of his life. Every idea, every imagined scene, becomes a part of his mind. It is quite possible for a person to have more conscious and real experiences in a few hours of reading than at a dozen cocktail parties, though cocktail parties, by lowering the censor, tend to permit a great deal of unconscious experience. Thought and contemplation have the power of making unconscious experience conscious; and literature, which has the power to inject thought into a reader's mind, can introduce him to a wide array of new experience, an array and a variety that would be otherwise unavailable to him. Such experience, too, must be reckoned as part of the theme of a literary work.

In our time, we have tended to say that the reader may neither prescribe nor proscribe meanings. The writer is at liberty to write about the subject matter he chooses, without pandering to the taste of readers who are ignorant of the particular experiences he wishes to include in his work; he can neither be told what to write nor what not to write (except, possibly, in the case of obscenity, and there is considerable dispute about that). The corollaries to this intellectual freedom are the responsibility of the writer to depict experiences that will be worthwhile for the reader to perceive, and the responsibility of the reader to suspend his judgment of the depicted experience until he has understood it. Whenever a reader opens a book, he makes a moral promise to the writer that he is interested in what the writer has to say; he morally obligates himself to listen. Once he has understood, he is at liberty to like or dislike the book, to advertise it or curse it or praise it or refute it or whatever he likes. But if he refuses to understand, by closing his mind before reading, he might as well not have picked up the book and have done the writer and himself such an injustice. Similarly, the writer makes moral promises when he offers a book; neither he nor the reader should waste the other's time.

The teacher's responsibility is to make the student aware of the ways in which theme can operate in a literary work. He can survey the sources of theme, the philosophical styles themes have taken in modern times, and the potential uses of meaning.

Sources of Meaning

"Meaning" supposes communication; communication involves a communicator, a thing to be communicated, and a recipient of the communication. These three—the author, the work itself, and the reader—have been forwarded at various times as the source of the aesthetic object and, thus, of meaning. Each, no matter how much we may disparage it, makes its contribution.

The Author as Source

Much in our experience of literature leads us to know that every work is an expression of a writer's particular mind, that it is indeed the author whose creative faculty is the source of the work and its meanings, that somehow he produced out of the wells of his Self and his Soul a distinct and unique entity. How he did it has bothered us; so has the difference of his product from what the ordinary man is capable of; but, as we read more and more literature, we become more and more convinced that this man whose work we are reading is responsible, through genius or madness, for what we perceive. Many men are capable of the experience he describes—if he has been sufficiently true to the potential to interest us—but only *he* has had that combination of perception and craft that allows him to make literary meaning of it.

The author, then, contributes perception and craft to each of his literary communications. We have had a tendency to ignore the effect of craft, partly because it is always visible in the finished work and seems to be more a part of the work itself than a contribution of the artist, and partly because craft is ancillary to perception. Craft without perception produces literary puzzles, whose pleasures are merely intellectual. But perception, even without craft, can stir the emotions and impress the memory. Thus young writers have often been advised to go out and live fiercely, for then, presumably, they could not write badly. They can, of course, but great perceptions have tended to excuse only partially adequate craft and to make it look as if perception were the author's all. This primacy of perception stirs up two persistent problems: that of art vs. madness, and that of the author's intention vs. the intentional fallacy.

Since ancient times, the artist's perceptions have been connected with insanity. Poets compose in irrational fits, said Socrates to Ion; it requires either genius or madness, said Aristotle; it takes more than cool reason ever comprehends, said Shakespeare. And when we look at a powerful emotional work, say one of Strindberg's plays, or a Dostoevski novel, we can hardly help thinking that the man must have been mad, or at least neurotic, to have written thus. D. H. Lawrence endorses the impulse: "One sheds one's sicknesses in books, repeats and presents again one's emotions to be master of them." [1] The emotions and experiences in literature, when they are powerful, tend to be the sort that the ordinary man comes close to only in feverish hallucinations and nightmares, that is, in states most like insanity.

That authors have to be insane, or at least neurotic, to write has been a popular attitude, especially since the development of psychology. Enemies of art and partisans alike have argued that the insanity is the source of the artist's perceptions, that the sickness opens perceptions to him that are not open to the ordinary man, and that these perceptions deal with real emotional material of a most meaningful and intense kind. Edmund Wilson has given us the metaphor that most nearly sums up this attitude.[2] He tells again the story of Philoctetes, the Greek warrior who had a magic bow which could not miss its mark and which only he could draw, but who also had a terrible, festered wound which gave off such a disgusting odor that his countrymen could not remain in his presence. En route to the Trojan War, the Greeks marooned Philoctetes on an island and stole his bow. They soon discovered, however, that none could draw the bow, that its magic was lost. Reluctantly, they returned to the island and retrieved Philoctetes: if you want the power in the bow, you must tolerate the sickness in the wound. If you want the power of imagination, you must tolerate, even nurture, the wound of the insanity.

---

[1] *The Letters of D. H. Lawrence,* Aldous Huxley, ed. (New York, 1923), p. 152.
[2] In *The Wound and the Bow* (New York: Oxford U. Press, 1947). The book is seven studies of the psychic wounds of writers with powerful literary bows.

Lionel Trilling brings this attitude into question. A man may have a psychic wound, as hundreds of men in mental institutions do, and yet not have literary power. That a man is neurotic does not make him a writer; there is no causal connection between the wound and the bow. What distinguishes the neurotic who writes well from the ordinary neurotic is his craft, "his faculties of perception, representation, and realization." [3] Trilling further suggests that the exercise of craft upon the materials of a neurosis is a profound sign of health, not sickness. The wound and the bow represent independent gifts.

We must also raise the case of the great writer who had no wound. Granted that the traumas of Dickens's childhood—being apprenticed at age nine to a sweatshop in the slums while his father was in debtor's prison—gave rise to the trenchant social criticisms in his best works, what gave rise to Shakespeare's great thoughts? Or Friedrich Schiller's? Or Thomas Mann's? Or what gave rise to all those themes in Henry James's work that cannot be accounted for by the theory of a wound? In these and many other cases, we must finally admit that a man brought his intelligence to bear on a problem of his *choice* and allowed the power in his craft to make the theme great. This process comes close to accounting for such different works as Flaubert's *Madame Bovary,* Joyce's *Ulysses,* and Forster's *A Passage to India.* And it explains otherwise inexplicable facets of *The Brothers Karamazov* and *War and Peace.* The bow, not the wound, is the source of the power.

The possibility of conscious intention brings up the problem of the intentional fallacy. Can we use the author's intentions in determining the theme of his work? Yes, says one group of critics.[4] To know what Flaubert intended is a legitimate and useful first step in determining how well he achieved his purposes. We can know such information from the writer's notes, correspondence, or his biography, and, even when he was himself possibly unaware of what he really intended—as Dickens may have been unconscious that his childhood traumas were shaping and choosing his materials—the intention is a part of the theme and its success.

No, says another group of critics, we may not use the author's intentions in understanding or judging a literary work, for those intentions are external to the work itself. It may be very interesting to know, as Edmund Wilson's study shows, that Dickens's childhood experience predisposed him to his subject matter and attitudes, but the study of it is literary biography, not literature. In

[3] Lionel Trilling, "Art and Neurosis," *The Liberal Imagination* (New York: Doubleday, Anchor, 1957), p. 174. Mr. Trilling is here using "perception" in a somewhat different sense from that of this discussion—as, approximately, the ability to understand experience.

[4] See, for example, J. E. Spingarn, "The New Criticism," in Irving Babbitt *et al.,* *Criticism in America* (New York: Harcourt, 1924), pp. 9–45.

understanding and judging a literary work, we are limited to what is internal to the work and resides in the nature of the language itself. If Dickens writes about a child with a trauma, it is irrelevant that Dickens himself was such a child. What is relevant is that the trauma be

discovered through the semantics and syntax of [the work], through our habitual knowledge of the language, through grammars, dictionaries, and all the literature ... through all that makes a language and culture.[5]

This critical debate still goes on in a region between the two points of view. The poetry of Emily Dickinson, for example, often uses a fairly private vocabulary, as in the special meanings she attaches to abstractions like circumference, eternity, and such. This is legitimate, says the Wimsatt-Beardsley point of view, for her poems are a part of the history of words and the language; if we have to read, say, twenty of her poems to discover her lexical meanings of a few words, that does not mean that the lexical meanings are not there. But this also looks a lot like determining the poet's intention, determining what she meant by particular words. We all know that study of an author's life, as well as criticism of his works, can sensitize us to themes that we might otherwise have overlooked. The danger is in discovering these themes where the work itself does not support them. For both groups, the index of legitimacy is finally one of craft:

... Only one *caveat* must be borne in mind ... ; the poet's aim must be judged at the moment of the creative act, that is to say, by the art of the poem itself, and not by the vague ambitions which he imagines to be his real intention.[6]

And craft involves intention. A writer sits down to write and intends, say, to write about an old couple sitting at home on a warm summer evening, or intends to write about a scene that follows a last, total war, or whatever. His choice of subject matter, style, people, scene, action—whether he is fully aware of them or not—are his choices and get involved in his meanings. Indeed, our perceptions of his conscious and unconscious intentions, embodied in the work, are the only way we can perceive his meanings at all. The work itself tells us what these intentions are.

The Work as Source

Whenever a writer puts words on a page, those words begin to take on a life of their own. From that moment on, they have an objective existence; they

[5] W. K. Wimsatt and M. C. Beardsley, "The Intentional Fallacy," *Sewanee Review,* 54 (Summer, 1946): 475.

[6] Spingarn, "The New Criticism," p. 25.

are quite distinct from the author himself. They can be shown to millions of people who can respond to the denotations and connotations without knowledge of who wrote the words or under what circumstances. Especially when the words are arranged into the principles and techniques that we perceive as a literary work, the work begins to have a personality. It takes on, quite independently of the writer or the reader, a capability for meaning. The work, the objective product of the author, then, is also a source of theme.

In the object that is the literary work, there are three principal sources of meaning: the referent of the imitation—that is, the cluster of objects and ideas referred to, the techniques that lead to aesthetic arousal, and the accidental suggestions that have crept in with or without the author's awareness. We must extend the words "object" and "objective" here to include the imagined referents of language. When reading a literary work, what we look at is ink on a page; but what we *see* is people acting in a time and a place. A tremendous amount of this imagined sight can be said to be objective, in that all people who understand the language would agree on most of the qualities—people, actions, scenes—that the language refers to. Imagined perceptions are aesthetically objective.

The referent of the literary imitation is the first and most important source of theme in a work. It answers the "five W's and H" of journalism—who is doing what, where, when, why, and how? That a given novel, say, is about a midwest girl whose petulance and small mindedness progressively destroy all the people she meets, and eventually herself, is a source of the meaning in that novel. Perception of the real subject matter of a work can be easy, as in the imagined example, or difficult, as in Glenway Wescott's *The Pilgrim Hawk*. Many readers are hard put to say just what Wescott's story is about, since it apparently does not follow a particular set of characters, is not consistent in action, and shifts scenes freely. In such a case, point-of-view controls and answers the questions of who, what, and so on. In the syntax of the images we perceive that the subject referred to in the novella is the narrator's mind in the process of reacting with others.

Within this imitated referent, the techniques of aesthetic arousal help us perceive meaning. The very perception of a beginning, middle, and end determines and limits the extent and poise of the imitated subject. The anticipation in the beginning, however, can whet our appetites for a particular evaluation within the subject; the complications and crises can (and inevitably do) determine which of the possible alternatives of meanings are functioning at what level; the ending imposes judgment by the very fact that it ends, and, thus, theme emerges. Plot is a way of determining and controlling theme.

All the techniques play similar roles in theme. The operations of style in tone, mood, evaluation, metaphor, image, have the power of focusing our attention, intensifying it, and securing response to selected elements of meaning.

What is said about a character, and how, give the reader the minds and the value systems that are the subject of the imitated experience. Setting not only describes, but narrates, explains, and argues as well, through the images it evokes and the symbolic suggestions that style can attach to it. Point-of-view tells us whom to focus on for meaning; focus upon a minor character could lead the reader into suggestions that are irrelevant and even destructive to the general tendencies of a work. Structure at once complicates and unifies a total perception of a work and, thus, can control the efficiency of the effects. Narrative, summary, dramatization, direct statement, allusion—all influence the subject that is imitated and the themes that are attached to it.

All these techniques, like the words they are made of, take on an objective existence, once they are on the page. The objectivity of them is much more difficult to evaluate and understand, however, than the objectivity of words. Words are what they are by convention and use. Literary techniques are still the subject of much literary and aesthetic discussion, but there is a certain amount of agreement and common sense that tell us how they operate.

Every technique inevitably arouses some response when we see it, whether we are aware that it is a technique or not. Every technique suggests subject matter; every suggestion of subject matter makes certain kinds of mental promises to us, which we expect to be filled. The filling of the promises establishes meaning by satisfying expectation. In this process, the nature of the promises of the techniques determines our reception of the subject as real or fantastic or impossible or whatever and, thus, determines the theme that actually comes through.

Words and techniques can be in the work quite "accidentally." It makes no difference if the writer is aware of them, or intended them, or not, if the words and the techniques are objectively there, they function in the theme. It is thus possible for works to mean things which the writers were ignorant of, or which later ages have discovered.

All writers very likely depend upon accidental meanings creeping into their work. E. M. Forster, in suggesting that the writer should have a plan toward which he moves, but that that plan had better change when he gets there or the work will go tight and dead, is assuming (and asserting) that the accidental meanings, the changes that come, will do the actual determining of subject and create its vividness (an integral part of it). It is probable that all writers experience the subject for the first time in the process of creation and begin to see potential that they had not seen before. The potential finds appropriate images before the author is aware of it. Most writers welcome such happy accidents and incorporate them into the general fabric of their creation. A good deal of most good writing is happy accident which the writer let stand, once it had an objective existence of its own. Happy accident is a very important force in creativity and makes self-criticism necessary.

Daniel Defoe is a famous example of a writer unaware, or at least pretending to be unaware, of his real subject. He said he was writing puritan moralism when he depicted Moll Flanders leading a life of sin that was not supposed to pay. And he does come in to preach a few times. But the real subject that emerges from *Moll Flanders* is that sin does pay and pay handsomely; Defoe's real subject was the glorification of middle-class mercantilism—the getting and keeping of money and materials. His *Robinson Crusoe* purports to be an adventure of a man on a desert island, but what it really tells is the value of industry, thrift, work, busy-ness—all the things that make up business.

Works sometimes acquire meanings with the passage of time. Words change and acquire new meanings. Techniques, too, change and grow; attitudes toward birth, food, sex, what-have-you, change and grow. If an age, equipped with the language of its time, discovers new meanings in a work, there is no way for us to say that the meanings are not legitimate. They are objectively in the work for that age.

This raises the problem of critical relativism: since an age can discover its own meanings in a work, each person, applying his own vocabulary and value system, can say that the work means what it says to him. This position is untenable for reasons that will be explained later. Suffice it here to say that the fact that a child does not understand an adult's language does not change the meaning and objectivity of that language. If the critical relativist can establish the *objectivity* of his subjective perception, he establishes his perceptions as real themes. Critical relativism also brings up the role of the reader in determining theme.

The Reader as Source

A reader always brings certain qualities to his reading of a literary work—his capacity for and level of language, his values and taboos, his own psychological problems, and, most importantly, a varying ability to project himself into the imagined world of the work. Since all these qualities obviously influence what a particular reader perceives, they function for that reader as a source of meaning. The problem is to determine how much of what the reader brings to theme is permissible and admissible as a part of the meaning of the work.

There is a tradition that says that exploitation of the reader is a legitimate and purposeful source of meaning. Gothic literature emerged expressly to do so. The Neo-Classical demands for propriety and reason, said young Gothicists, had shackled the capacity of man to feel, to experience sensations, to have emotions. They were seeking to reinstate that capacity by writing works that focused on stimulating and prolonging thrills in the reader. The strongest thrill they could imagine—and thus the most suitable starting point, they thought—was terror. It was unfortunate for sensational literature that most sensational writers never got beyond terror, though a few of the later Romantics discovered love and the tender emotions of the sentimental novel. Edgar Allan Poe capitalized on both strains in "The Raven," a terrifying poem about the loss of a sentimental object.

Longfellow exploited reader values in a rather a different way. He seems to have sought out the themes that most people in his day wanted to hear—which turned out to be approval of the status quo—and gave them out in forms that were acceptable (most people in his day wanted sermons, not poetry, so he wrote inspirational verses with moral tags).[7] Longfellow's poetry, then, was a mirror for reflecting back as theme exactly what the reader brought to it. It is a poetry of platitudes and vague expressions that are aesthetic blanks, which the reader fills with his own affective states of the moment. Popular weekly magazines are still full of this kind of literature.

There are two very serious problems with allowing the reader to project what he wants into the literary work. First, it makes literature an instrument of auto-eroticism. It allows the reader, as it were (and even encourages him), to fondle his own attitudes, to titillate his own affections, and to justify it all to his own conscience. Second, it fixates the general reader at the Freudian level of Oceanic Omnipotence, the condition of a six months baby who cannot distinguish between himself and his environment—when he is wet, hungry, and feeling miserable, the ceiling or the crib, too, is wet, hungry, and feeling miserable. He projects his subjective state upon the world and mistakes it for what it is not. Self-stimulation and Oceanic Omnipotence are standard components of escape literature. They may have legitimate uses in therapy, but they are inadmissible as influences on theme in serious literature.

Yet, it is essential that a reader project himself into the work. He has to bring to his reading a capacity to image the contents of the work; else he sees nothing; all books are dull to dull readers. He has to be able to perceive intelligently the characters, scene, and action that make up the work. His abilities to image and perceive depend upon his projecting his own language, values, problems onto the work, for it is only by comparing his own with the other that he can understand either. The extent of the reader's abilities influences the theme of a work for him.

Readers grow. Each reading can increase understanding, and the reader brings his increased capacity to his next reading. Each increase in a reader's capacity increases the potential themes that he can perceive.

Mature readers bring a great deal more than themselves to a work of litera-

---

[7] For an interesting discussion of Longfellow's career, see Odell Shepard's "The New England Triumvirate," Chapter 35, in R. E. Spiller *et al.*, eds., *Literary History of the United States* (New York: Macmillan, 1960), especially pp. 587–96.

ture. Ideally, they would bring a knowledge of the social history which permeates a particular book, an ability to objectify imaginatively the dynamic images of the book, and a willingness to respond to the ideas and values of the book. Ideally, they would be able to perceive everything that is there and nothing that is not.

The aesthetic object in a work of literary art comes of a cooperation of author, work, and reader. None of these alone can be said to create the theme of a particular literary experience; all of them contribute necessary elements. No work ever escapes its author's touch, not even when the authorship is communal or anonymous; yet, every work has an objective life of its own; and every reader perceives only what he is capable of. The result of the compromises among these three is the aesthetic object. The aesthetic object, while it is alive in the reader's mind, is the final, total, and only source of theme.

Philosophical Styles of Meaning

Aesthetic objects change from age to age. Every style is realistic to those who practice it; it contains and presents that which is REAL. But that which is REAL has been variously defined. The pragmatic compromises of authors, works, and readers in several ages have established distinctive styles, which are actually philosophical systems that define that age's reality. In modern times, the most important of these philosophical styles of meaning are Realism, Naturalism, Impressionism, Symbolism, Expressionism, Surrealism, Existentialism, and Mythism.

Realism

As a literary style, Realism is the direct and objective presentation of the literal facts of ordinary and familiar experience, without the author's or the reader's projection of morals or values onto the imitated experience. It focuses upon and renders details of time and place as they reflect common sense and materiality. It stresses the logic of the possible and the probable and is thus allied with the philosophy of pragmatism, which concerns itself with everyday, common sense *use* of material. It is strongly involved with the discovery and explanation of cause in experience; it therefore relies heavily on such literary techniques as plot and form. Its loyalty to materiality, logic, and causality makes Realism a prime expression of the philosophy of Mechanism—the cluster of beliefs that assays the universe as a huge machine in which the laws of matter, like cogs in mechanics, regulate the smooth function of existence.

Mechanism and Realism grew out of the scientific discoveries in mathematics and physics in the late eighteenth and early nineteenth centuries. They are conspicuously and incessantly concerned with *fact*-ness.

Literary Realism, then, is the imaginative depiction of quasi-facts. It has had some use in literature from the earliest beginnings, but its great period of emphasis is the middle and late nineteenth century, in the works of Balzac, Flaubert, Trollope, Thackeray, Henry James, Mark Twain, and others. William Dean Howells is generally said to be the father of American Realism, though the Puritans had been realists in their way—they readily admitted the facts of their existence but interpreted the facts according to their theology. In general, the realist's aesthetic task is to present enough detail to create in his readers the illusion of reality. The imagined product is to be responded to on the same basis as reality itself.

Factuality allies the realistic novel with traditional history and biography, and even the essay. From the time of Scott, many writers have tried to write fiction as if it were history or biography, and biography or history as if they were fiction. This movement culminates in the "documentary fiction" of our own time: works rendered in the techniques of the imagination, but presenting only verified fact. Such works aim at the re-creation of literal fact through material details, logic, and causality. Motivation and characterization are more matters of psychological research and court reporting than of invention, and form is a matter of selecting and emphasizing from the welter of detail those facts which establish logical cause and effect. The writer of documentary fiction sacrifices a great deal by straight-jacketing himself to "what did, in fact, happen," but he gains a great deal, in that the *illusion* of reality is no longer necessary; aesthetic assent is based on the documentary part, not the novelistic part. How strong this assent can be is illustrated by such books as Truman Capote's *In Cold Blood* and Meyer Levin's *Compulsion*.

Naturalism

Literary Naturalism is both a method and a philosophy in which the writer tries to be as scientific in literature as the scientist is in his laboratory. The method was first outlined by Emile Zola in *The Experimental Novel*. Zola meant the word "experimental" in the same sense as the scientist; life is a test tube or a laboratory in which scientific method—objective observation and recording of phenomena—will lead to the formulation of Natural Law. The laboratory scientist is seeking the Natural Laws of matter; the literary scientist is seeking the Natural Laws of man; hence the name. Rigorous application of scientific objectivity results in focus on superficial externals and limitation to them, for to record internals is to judge subjectively. Externality has been the method's most serious weakness.

Literary Naturalism got its philosophy primarily from the biological and social, not the physical, sciences. Toward the end of the nineteenth century, the prevailing belief in scientific thought was mechanistic determinism, the theory of the universe that holds the whole to be an organism regulated in its functions by such principles as gravity, inertia, genetics, and so on. Man is only a part of this organism, and his actions, including thought, are determined and controlled by the principles of the whole, which are completely outside himself. The methods of physics, applied to psychology, society, history, and such, had produced a belief that forces in the social sciences were as mechanistic as they were in physics. Psychologists looked upon the mind as a kind of telephone switchboard which connected all the stimuli of experience with appropriate responses. Sociologists looked upon man as a result of forces in his environment; historians, as a result of traditions. In all, man's actions, thoughts, emotions were determined. He had no free will. He was caught in a web of cause and effect, from which he could not escape. Scientific determinism became the dominant philosophy in Literary Naturalism, because the Naturalists believed it was part of the Natural Laws of man.

The rigor of its method and the insistence upon its theme distinguish Naturalism from Realism. The Realist would say that more than externals are knowable and real; and he would say that Determinism is a projection of opinion upon the materials.

Literary Naturalism flourished in the last decades of the nineteenth century and the beginning of the twentieth, in the works of Zola, Thomas Hardy, Stephen Crane, Frank Norris, Theodore Dreiser, and others. In general, Naturalistic writers chose settings of seamy realism and characters of animalistic or primitive tendencies. It happens, perhaps by accident, that such situations and characters are easiest to describe and illustrate Determinism most readily. In America, however, Naturalism was connected with a humanistic protest against social ills; indeed, social criticism and protest play a dominant and characterizing role in American Naturalism.

Impressionism

Impressionism deals also with superficial reality, but in contrast to Naturalism, it emphasizes sensory *impressions* as the primary component of reality, hence the name. Rather than objectivity, it stresses subjective responses as the source of meaning. It has affinities with the sensational philosophy of Locke, and others, and with the elevation of the individual and the Self, as in the work of Wordsworth and other Romantics. It was one form of late nineteenth-century reaction to the rigors of scientism.

As a technique in art, it is the selection of details of sensory experience and the rendering of them in such way as to create the impression of the whole.

In painting, one can easily see the influence of photography—in action suddenly stopped, forms cut by the border, and such; the literary counterpart of this quality is the "slice of life," depictions in which complicated and fleeting experience is suddenly made radiantly understandable. The careful selection of details of light, color, form, and so on, depends upon one of the Gestalt principles of perception—that certain forms move toward closure in such a way as to imply (and effectively communicate) completion.

Impressionism flourished in the last decade of the nineteenth century, but was more important in painting than in literature. Some painters emphasized movement; some emphasized light and color, even breaking down the surface of the perceived object into a technique called "pointillism." Isolated counterparts to most impressionistic techniques are fairly easy to find in literature; Stephen Crane's style is sometimes said to be "prose pointillism," for example; Henry James's "illusion of reality" depends a great deal on gesture; Chekhov's descriptive techniques are a kind of shorthand that extends impression into totality. Generally speaking, however, literary impressionism was immediately absorbed into Realism, Naturalism, Symbolism, and even Expressionism.

Symbolism

Symbolism (from Greek *symballein* "to throw together") is the use of images of ordinary, factual reality to communicate qualities that are not ordinary and factual, but are usually abstract. In a sense, it is a throwing together of two worlds, one visible and the other invisible, so that the one *becomes* the other. This is not to say that the factual world *represents* the world of thought (which is allegory), nor that the factual world *means* the other (which is the use of a sign and which merely communicates information), nor that the factual world is *compared* with the other (which is metaphor and simile). The description of the technique as two worlds may suggest philosophical dualism, but the symbolist insists upon the identity of the two. He also insists, however, on the ultimate reality of the invented world that is symbolized. Symbols are the factual images that the invented world takes on for expression; they at once reveal and conceal the ultimate reality. If everything is revealed, we have no more than mere scientific factuality; if everything is concealed, we have only obscurity. "A symbol is a sort of middle ground between what we know and what we do not know," said Harry Levin. "A reasoned derangement of the senses," said Rimbaud. "The illogical impingements of words on the consciousness," said Hart Crane.

In general, there are four kinds of symbols: (1) the natural, in which an object symbolizes the abstract quality that is naturally associated with it, as the rose is a natural symbol of beauty, or as light and dark by metaphorical extension are natural symbols of knowledge and ignorance; (2) the private, in which an image suggests something particular to an individual, as herons symbolized subjectivity to W. B. Yeats, or as a chair may symbolize a particular person's fear of his father's authority; (3) the public, or conventional, in which certain images come to communicate certain common, public ideas, as the Cross symbolizes the redeeming qualities of Christ, or the national flag, patriotism (such symbols can be used successfully in literature only with great difficulty, for they depend upon stock situations and uniform response in the audience); and (4) the literary, in which certain images are made, through use, to arouse certain ideas in a literary work, as in a story of a boy's struggles with his father's authoritarianism, a chair that is involved in physical or emotional punishment can come to symbolize the child's fear, or falling rain can be made to suggest the sense of impending disaster.

One should also note that symbols are usually more involved than our examples here. In Melville's *Moby Dick,* for example, the white whale is described as having many qualities—he is indestructible, so that he seems immortal; he is credited with wondrous feats, so that he seems omnipotent and omniscient; he is rumored to be in several places at the same time, so that he seems ubiquitous. For many people, the whale is therefore a symbol of God. For Starbuck, he is a dumb brute; for Stubb, a whale steak; for Flask, a species of magnified mouse. For Ahab, in Chapter XXXVI, Moby Dick is a mask that is held between man and knowledge of ultimate reality, therefore is a kind of God or a key to the universe. But what the whale symbolizes is finally inexplicable; he remains a symbol, not a sign, because he has the power to reveal, to evoke, to *be,* but continues to conceal ultimate reality. He has the power of mediating between what we know and what we do not know. It may take many images to create a symbol, but an ambitious symbol can stir up much thought.

Expressionism

Expressionism deals with reality, not as it appears to be on the surface, but as it is felt to be in the passions. It is an attempt to depict how reality *feels.* Emotions establish what is worthwhile and convey all that is important. Superficial reality is subordinated to this inner, expressionistic reality and, rather than described, is translated into abstractions or representations of affective states. Images are important only insofar as they can be made to convey the emotional values of the writer, who consciously distorts surface reality to make the image take on the evaluative emotions. Thus enlarged or caricatured scenery, action, and character can represent the affective states of characters and author.

Literary expressionism has been most notable in the drama, and especially in German drama. Some of the early plays of Eugene O'Neill are the standard examples in American literature. In *The Hairy Ape,* for example, when Yank greets the ape as brother and is crushed in the ape's arms, we recognize that Yank is not performing a realistic act, but one which shows, almost symbolically, how he feels. In *The Emporer Jones,* the Little Formless Fears of Brutus Jones's mind are actually represented on stage, as well as are his memories of Jeff, the Negro Convicts, the Prison Guard, the Slaves, the Congo Witch-Doctor, and others. We are shown, not objective reality, but the interior of a man's mind in the act of feelings. Arthur Miller's depiction of the states of Willy Loman's mind is perhaps the best recent example.

In prose fiction, expressionism has tended to take the form of stylistic tricks. The primary problem with the technique is the privacy of the evaluative emotion, which is made public only with difficulty. In drama, the setting can be used to objectify the emotion, but, in fiction, the whole burden is in the aesthetic conviction with which the emotion is described. The common tendency has been to try to represent the emotion with rhetoric, to stir up the passions with passionate expressions. But it is very difficult to motivate the intensity in such rhetoric when the evaluating motivation is private. Expressionism in prose has been limited to relatively short passages and to rather non-rational images; because of this, it was rather easily absorbed into the rather broader technique of symbolism.

Surrealism

Surrealism (literally, *super-realism*) is a psychological, aesthetic, and philosophical concept that had its roots in the Freudian theory of the unconscious. Its chief spokesman was André Breton, a disciple of Freudian psychiatry, who, beginning in 1924, issued a number of *Surrealistic Manifestos.* Breton believed that dream and reality, which are so apparently contradictory, would someday be resolved into a kind of absolute reality, a *surreality,* as Guillaume Apollinaire suggested he call it. His notion of the unconscious was based on Freud's *The Interpretation of Dreams* (1900).

Literary Surrealism is the attempt to render reality in the images and definitions that the unconscious fixes; it stresses three points—the identity of the products of the unconscious and reality, the rejection of middle-class values, and the rejection of artistic conventions. Unconscious material, of which dream is the most common conscious form, is the only source of beauty, truth, and value, said the surrealists, or, as Breton put it in the first *Manifesto,* "Only the marvelous is beautiful." The writer, then, must attempt to exploit the marvelous in its own language, the images and sequences of the unconscious. Thus, he writes non-logically, atemporally, accidentally, non-sequentially, and seeks to render the excitement and intensity of dreamlike reality in his characters, scenes, and actions. He attempts to define reality as a "stream-of-*un*consciousness." Middle-class values, because they hamper the free use of the unconscious and reject the psychic materials of it, must be rejected and destroyed if possible. The writer has to become completely amoral, allowing whatever images that come to him to create their own existence. (This sometimes resulted in experiments in automatic writing). Artistic conventions, too, constrained the free flow of unconscious material, so had to be ignored. Instead of conventions, the surrealists valued inspiration, sincerity, feeling, truth-to-self, experimentation.

Surrealism has three rather obvious affinities with other literary movements. The emotion-defined intensity and excitement in character, scene, and action are very like those of Expressionism, at least on the surface. The concern with the marvelous and with stimulation derives from Gothicism. And the emphasis upon spontaneity, feeling, sincerity, self-expression, and so on, is a latter-day manifestation of Romanticism.

Existentialism

Existentialism is a loose philosophy that stresses the subjective definition of existence and protests against a cluster of contemporary problems—the inevitability of death in a world made meaningless by the decay of metaphysics, the pressures toward loss of identity through conformity in a society geared to the duplications of mass production techniques, views of the world that hold that experience is rational (as, for example, Hegel's: "The real is the rational, and the rational is the real"), or views that hold that man is the plaything of historical or environmental or theological forces (as in all forms of Determinism). Against all these problems, the existentialist pits the subjective human consciousness, which has the freedom and the responsibility to define the reality of its own existence.

Jean-Paul Sartre is the foremost contemporary spokesman for Existentialism, though Kierkegaard (who invented the name), Jaspers, and Heidegger were important forerunners. Sartre's paradigm of the problem goes something like this: Man is condemned to be alone, since he can never be sure that he is communicating with others or, indeed, be sure of their existence. What he can be sure of is his own subjective existence. This loneliness makes him insecure. The irrevocability of experience adds to the insecurity, for man can never know what effect his acts will have and must act in dread of mistake. These threaten all a man has, his subjective consciousness, with constant peril. In spite of the anxiety, the serious man involves himself in striving to face the situation, in trying to work out his personal meaning and morality. There are no guide lines, no fixed values he can use, for what is right for one man may not be right for another. He is condemned to be free. The free choices he makes create the definition of his values and of his view of reality. Sartre stresses again and again that man exists first ("existence precedes essence") and that he creates his own values ("man makes himself"). Every choice a man makes imposes a moral structure upon that segment of his experience and affirms his existence; therefore man should make every choice as if it were his last one, as if death were imminent. Then his whole life will be affirmed by his subjective definitions of himself. In choosing for himself, a man is choosing for all men, for his choice is "the image of man as he ought to be."

Literature of the absurd has been the aesthetic vehicle of existential philosophy. There man is depicted amid his alienations and estrangements, his anxieties, faced with the absurdity of existence. In some cases, the writers attempt to get beyond the absurdity of experience and clarify reality, but all too often, writers have been content with the theme that life is absurd.

Mythism

Mythism is a fairly recent philosophical style of meaning which holds that myth is the key to reality. Myths are ideas or collections of ideas or clusters of images which determine and control action through people's belief in them. If the belief in them is sufficiently strong, if the subscription to them is intense enough, if deep emotion is invested in them, the belief, the intensity, and the emotion define the important and the real. Belief can even transform everyday normality into myth, as in the "myth of Shakespeare" or the "myth of democracy." More commonly, myth is a representation of supra-normal images, such as supra-mortal heroes, which explain normal and natural phenomena. In this, myths are akin to dreams and other productions of the unconscious; they express deep truth. Erich Fromm, in *The Forgotten Language,*[8] looks upon myths as a way of expressing inner psychic materials as sensory experience; thus they externalize unconscious material, make it understandable, make it meaningful without rationality. They tame the nightmare. Because myths are productions and representations of the deepest recesses of our being, they evoke deep emotion. When deep emotion is evoked, belief is aroused. Belief then defines reality.

This subjective process has a wide, objective application, say such people as Carl Jung. His theory of the archetype is that when myths engage the inner depths of man, they are repeating patterns of unconscious memories of the experiences of the race and of Man. To experience the symbols of the unconscious is to experience part of the ultimate reality.

[8] New York: Holt, 1951; Grove Evergreen, 1957.

Literary mythism has had two forms. In one form, parallels between a represented action and a known myth are pursued, as in Joyce's *Ulysses*. In lesser examples of this form, the story and the myth often go dead, because the writer neglects to supply anything more than the parallels. To arouse the emotion and belief that is in myth, the representation must itself become mythic, quite apart from the myth that is alluded to. The second form is an indirect depiction of mythic action with no specific reference to a myth or an archetype. Such a story is Twain's *Huckleberry Finn,* which deals so importantly with escape and flight that it becomes itself a mythic journey. It acquires the ability to evoke deep emotion and intense belief in millions of readers.

The Use of Theme

The next question is: although literature can communicate meanings in several versions of reality, what are such meanings good for? What are literature and theme good for? What are their uses? In the twenty-five hundred years or so that literature has been seriously discussed, there have been many answers. As apparently varied as they are, they can be subsumed to four theories of literature, says Yvor Winters [9]—didacticism, hedonism, romanticism, and what he calls (for want of a better term, he says) moralism. Three other theories—determinism, relativism, and absolutism—have, under different conditions, modified the four into particular historical styles. Winters's discussion is a good beginning to a description of what the uses of theme are, but it is finally inadequate because of its limited epistemology.

The didactic theory of literature is simply that literature offers "useful precepts and explicit moral instruction." From the earliest times, there has been a body of literature intended to increase the knowledge of citizens in useful branches of art and observation. Heriod's *Works and Days* is such a work; so is Virgil's *Georgics,* a treatise on farming; so is Pope's *Essay on Man* and *Essay on Criticism* and Wordsworth's *The Excursion.* Even so modern a work as D. H. Lawrence's *Lady Chatterly's Lover* contains a strong didactic element; it is intended to instruct readers in what is good and truthful, if not useful. According to didactic theory, a work is good insofar as it teaches. One may wonder whether some other form of teaching or study—religion or ethics, for example—might not do the job more effectively and efficiently. The answer is usually that literature can make the lesson more pleasant. This, of course, is the Horatian aesthetic formula: sugarcoat the bitter pill of knowledge. Another

[9] "A Foreword," *In Defense of Reason* (Denver: Alan Swallow, 1947), pp. 3–14. Several parts of the following discussion borrow heavily from Mr. Winters's compendious foreword.

question arises, says Winters, in whether the lesson is the whole object of literature, or whether there is something else, something not paraphrasable yet valuable, that creeps into the work and our response to the work. Didacticism cannot deal with such questions, says Winters, or with the something extra that distinguishes most literature from most philosophy. Didacticism, fully applied, leads to thought control.

The hedonistic theory of literature holds that literature is the purveyor and heightener of pleasure, which is the end and purpose of life.

... The service of philosophy, of speculative culture, [of literature] towards the human spirit is to rouse, to startle it to a life of constant and eager observation. Every moment some form grows perfect in hand or face; some tone on the hills or the sea is choicer than the rest; some mood of passion or insight or intellectual excitement is irresistibly real and attractive to us—for that moment only. A counted number of pulses only is given to us of a variegated, dramatic life. How may we see in them all that is to be seen in them by the finest senses? How shall we pass most swiftly from point to point, and be present always at the focus where the greatest number of vital forces unite in their purest energy?

To burn always with this hard, gemlike flame, to maintain this ecstasy, is success in life. . . .[10]

In general, says Winters, there are two forms of hedonism: that like Walter Pater's, as in the citation above, in which hedonistic aesthetics and ethics are identified, and that like T. S. Eliot's, in which aesthetics and ethics are dissociated. The trouble with identifying aesthetics and ethics is that no index remains for distinguishing one intense pleasure from another intense pleasure —one cannot distinguish aesthetically between a good glass of wine and a good reading of *Hamlet*. This makes ethical relativism necessary (what's good for me is good for me, what's good for you is good for you) and makes comparison, evaluation, and criticism of literature and life impossible. This leads to a kind of autoerotic impressionism—"adventures of the soul among masterpieces"—and a continuous pursuit of degrees or nuances of emotion, in which art becomes a substitute for life, and leads finally to disillusionment with life and art, when they fail to titillate that one moment more. The second form of hedonism, which had its beginnings in Poe and was developed somewhat by the French Symbolists, separates art and life and introduces some criteria for evaluating pleasures. Experiences from life are transmuted by the aesthetic process into a new kind of experience. Contrary to appearance, literature is not a depiction of human experience, but a thing in itself, whose aim is pleasure

[10] Walter Pater, from the "Conclusion" to *The Renaissance*, third edition, 1888.

and intensity, but pleasure of a special sort, pleasure that must be evaluated quite outside the experience of literature.

... Literary criticism should be completed by criticism from a definite ethical and theological standpoint.... The "greatness" of literature cannot be determined solely by literary standards; though we must remember that whether it is literature or not can be determined only by literary standards.[11]

This attitude subordinates aesthetics to ethics and denies art its traditionally high position among human activities.

The Romantic theory of literature holds that literature is essentially emotional experience. This theory emerged at a time when the emotional faculty had been starved; its most characteristic theoretical form is perhaps Wordsworth's famous definition of poetry as "emotion recollected in tranquility." When combined with the theories of man's natural goodness, the trustworthiness of his impulses and the unreliability of his rational faculty, this theory of literature is "dangerous or possibly evil," says Winters. Man achieves the good life by relying on his impulses and achieves a mystic union with the Divinity when he combines this notion with a pantheistic philosophy, as in the doctrines of Emerson. For such a man, literature is primarily a form of self-expression, in the popular sense of that term. Since he is already good, there is no need to understand or improve himself, only a need to "let himself go." Literature is valuable to such a man because it allows him to perceive the experiences of others who have let go. Ultimately, emotion is private, and the theory leads logically to automatism—each man in his own little isolated mechanism of feelings. Nothing in the theory will prevent automatism, and most Romantics rely on some other half-formed, half-conscious idea as a check on the tendency.

The moralistic theory of literature, which Winters does not describe, but which permeates his whole work, holds something like this: Literature depicts experiences that are as real as experiences in life. We can learn from these experiences in literature, just as we can learn from experiences in life. Indeed, because of the limits to our experiences in life—none of us can have all, or even a very large number, of possible experiences—and because of the ambitions of literature, we can learn more from literature than we can from life. Every learning involves understanding and judgment, both of which are necessary for growth. But judgment is evaluation, according to a hierarchy of personal and public values; it is the affixing of *moral* attitude, and the exercise of it leads to moral growth, just as understanding allows improvement. Literature,

---

[11] T. S. Eliot, "Religion and Literature" (1935), first paragraph. The dissociation of sensibilities ought to be obvious.

by facilitating moral growth and making it possible, can be said to be moralistic. Such a theory, thinks Winters, has been implicit in the most durable judgments in the history of literature.

Various combinations of these theories are possible. Horatian aesthetics is a combination of didacticism and hedonism; art combines precept with pleasure.[12] The didactic and the Romantic combine easily, as in the theories of Emerson. The combination of the didactic and the moralistic is fairly common, not least in the theories of Winters himself, but also in early Renaissance and Neo-Classical theories. The hedonistic and the Romantic are sometimes hard to distinguish from one another, except in the logical results toward which they lead. They combine fairly easily, as in the theories of Walter Pater. The hedonistic and the moralistic can combine when the moral evaluation of experience is based upon emotional pleasure, as it is in Epicurean theory. The Romantic and moralistic combination has been a very common and very important one; it is the theory of the early Romantic poets, especially Wordsworth.

The first three theories have all been combined with determinism, says Winters. It is natural that Romanticism and determinism should combine, for Romanticism leads logically to automatism, and determinism establishes its inevitability. And hedonism is compatible with determinism; since the determinist can control nothing, he often takes solace by taking pleasure along the way, without contemplating that the deliberate seeking of pleasure is in itself "a willful activity involving at least limited consideration and choice." Determinism and didacticism are logically incompatible, for one teaches the inevitability of non-human determination, the other, the supremacy of human determinations. Yet the most rigorous, one might say religious, of determinists (for example, the Calvinists and Marxists) have been the most didactic of men. Even Winters's own moralism combines with determinism to the extent that he insists upon the singleness of possible response to a work. His rationality leads him to assert that a particular word in a particular context can have only one meaning, hence should stimulate the same response in all readers. The poem or story, being a complex of words in context, should also have only one meaning, though much more complicated; in a sense, meaning is determined by convention and context, and, in Winters's view, *should determine* a specific response in the reader.

Two theories of knowledge, absolutism and relativism, have also been im-

---

[12] Such a theory deals with the weaknesses of didacticism, says Winters, by giving it a rationale for the something else besides precept that makes up literature; but the didactic element is no more efficient than it would be in another form, and the pleasure element is left to be purely hedonistic. Pragmatically, they can be combined, but logically, it is like mixing apples and oranges: one does not get a new species.

portant in the several theories of literature. Absolutism is that epistemology which holds that absolute truths and values exist independently of man's mind. Man, by study, can apprehend these truths and endeavor to live his life in accord with them. Relativism is that epistemology which holds that the individual's perception of the world is the only thing that can be known and that an individual's perception is right for himself. The Romantic is usually a relativist, says Winters, for the variety of judgments and actions that result from individual impulse force recognition and tolerance of others. The hedonist, too, is usually a relativist, though he often flirts with some absolutist notions when he tries to classify his pleasures as to their value, not for himself only, but for man in general. The didactic is traditionally an absolutist, though unless he is foolish, he does not pretend that his lessons are the final and immutable ones; he usually says his ideas are only part of the whole truth. Didacticism, when viewed as a method, however, has also combined with Romanticism, as in Emerson's work, where didactic method is used to forward relativistic doctrine. Moralists are logically absolutists, though many of them profess to a measure of relativism. Ideas like Justice are based upon moral absolutism, but are often administered relative to the particular case. "Our universities," says Winters, "in which relativistic doctrines are widely taught, can justify their existence only in terms of a doctrine of absolute truth." Winters's theory can take him no further, finally, than to an unsatisfactory competition between relativism and absolutism.

These two epistemologies have competed with one another over the past two thousand five hundred years, and their alternation accounts partly for the Classic and Romantic rhythm of our intellectual history. Some people claim to have worked out compromises between the two theories of knowledge, but no compromise is possible, because they are logically incompatible. People who profess a compromise view, as many do in periods of transition, turn out to be simply muddle-headed.

Yet, who of us would profess that each of the theories of literature, each of the doctrines of thought, has not each contained some element of truth? Surely, each body of thought accounts for some phenomena of human experience better than other bodies of thought? The eclectic, aware of this, goes around collecting the better parts of several theories, puts them in the same bag, and ignores the contradictions, arguing now one way, now another, whichever way is pragmatic. The eclectic has been most often criticized because he seems to have no epistemology, because he subscribes to neither relativism nor absolutism. But he does have an epistemology, one which the relativists and the absolutists alike have refused to recognize, but which is the pragmatic result of all theories and methods from the Socratic discussion to the sermon, is implicit in our understanding of history, and is explicit in the notions of the improvement of knowledge and the successive approximation of truth. In the nineteenth century, this epistemology was called Objective Idealism.

Objective Idealism is the assertion that truth exists objectively and that it is the sum of all the potential perspectives upon it. The classic illustration is that of twelve men, sitting in a circle and looking at a four-colored box in the middle. Each man has only a single perspective and can describe accurately what he sees. The first man says the object is a blue rectangle. The second says it is two parallelograms, a smaller blue one on the left, a larger red one on the right. The third man agrees with the second that it is two parallelograms, but insists that the blue one on the left is the larger. The fourth man says the object is a red rectangle. And so on, around the circle. Who is right? They all are. All of them describe accurately a part of the truth; but each of them is limited by his perspective from knowing all of the truth. Each is capable of understanding the others' perceptions, however, and by pooling their individual perceptions, they can arrive at an objective description of a box with four, colored sides. The object is the sum of the perspectives upon it.

Objective Idealism is inconsistent with both absolutism and relativism. It does not hold that truth is absolutely there, but that man discovers and invents it as he goes along. Absolutism, by assuming immutability, would preclude change in the potential of man, but Objective Idealism would allow for such growth, as in the ritual transformation of a god of war into a god of love. The Objective Idealist would hold that here is an idea that man has discovered or invented, but was not there before and certainly not there absolutely. Nor is truth relative to the Objective Idealist. Relativism depends upon a Lockean theory of perception, which holds that sensations are all that man can know and comprise all that is knowable. But to assume this is to assume that every man's interpretation of his sensations is accurate and whole, which precludes the common experiences of ignorance and mistake. In practice, many relativists, spurred by their tolerance of other men's perspectives and the functions of their intelligence and memory, do in fact arrive at a notion that approximates Objective Idealism—that each man's perception can be improved and corrected, and that a community of men working together can approach truth through successive stages. Modern literature and the history of thought have been processes of assembling more and better perspectives upon the human condition.

Most modern men are Objective Idealists, even when they profess other notions. Objective Idealism, as a philosophy, was pretty much overshadowed in the nineteenth century by the absolutists on the one hand, who were amassing overwhelming evidence for scientific determinism, and by the relativists on the other, who were insisting upon personal autonomy and free will. The modern thinking man, who typically believes in both scientific determinism and personal autonomy, can hold both beliefs by saying that each approximates the truth in its sector and by patiently awaiting the new perspective that will reconcile the contradictions. A much more internally consistent example of contemporary Objective Idealism is Carl Jung's theory of archetypes and his study of myth and dreams.

Every writer, in his every theme, is contributing to the sum of perspectives. It is his responsibility in using theme to be as whole, and as accurate, and as multifarious, and as unified, as he can, without becoming so relative as to be meaningless or so absolutist as to insist that his view is all. Every communication that is understandable contributes to the improvement of our knowledge and to the successive approximation of truth. Greater use of theme is hardly conceivable.

DRAMA

DRAMA appeals to all our aesthetic senses. It incorporates the verbal arts of oratory and poetry, the imaginative arts of fiction and romance, the auditory art of music, the visual arts of painting, sculpture, and architecture. And, at its best, it fuses all these stimuli into a single aesthetic product. But drama is also a coöperative art; traditionally, it has been the joint production of the poet, the actor, the scene-maker, the director, and, sometimes, the musician; and, today when audiences can exercise some taste but little judgment, we must add the advertiser and the reviewer to the list of collaborators. Its multiplicity makes complexity of production necessary and this source of strength is its primary source of weakness.

We cannot deal here with the whole of drama, but only with those aspects that the playwright is immediately and directly concerned with. In one sense, this is everything—the genre he chooses to write in, the design and structure of stages and auditoriums, styles of acting and viewing, theories of directing and staging, and so on. The script influences all of these, and more, though they represent separate arts. What the playwright needs to be continuously aware of are (1) the theoretical mechanics of his influence—which is to say, he needs to be familiar with the aesthetic materials of dramatic production—, (2) the contemporary conventions of theater, and (3) an arsenal of practical writing techniques, with which he can control the final aesthetic product.

Much that is practical for the playwright has already been discussed in the section on fiction, for there are close affinities between the materials and objectives of the playwright and the fictionist. Any full treatment of drama would have to include a chapter on style, one on character, one on setting, on plot, on structure, similar to the chapters in the section on fiction, and, indeed, the discussion has often made specific reference to stage practices. Even point-of-view—or better: *especially* point-of-view—in drama is related to that of fiction. Nor is there a possible discussion of theme that does not borrow from and apply to both drama and fiction. The student, therefore, should consider almost everything in the section on fiction as a substantive part of this discussion of drama, and we will focus here on those few, special adaptations of approach and technique that distinguish drama as a unique literary form.

10

Some
Aesthetic Materials
of Drama

Drama as a Dynamic Mode of Thought

Drama, we can define as the presentation, on stage, in sound, scene, and action, of characters, places, and incidents, which represent an experience as happening before our eyes and ears. The stage is essential to the drama as a literary form, which is to be distinguished from the play as a literary form. If and when we *read* a play, we apprehend it on the same aesthetic basis as we apprehend fiction—we depend upon our imagination to re-create character, scene, and incident. But on the stage, this "vocabulary" of experience is *there,* palpable and immediate, in sight and sound. This palpable immediacy gives drama its peculiar and characteristic aesthetic power.

Performance is the key-note, and the writer's performance is one of the last the audience becomes aware of. The presence of the actors is first and most noticeable, and we are acutely aware of them as delivering, through voice and tone, gesture and action, a performance. We also become aware fairly early of the performance of the set-designer, lighting-engineer, wardrobe mistress, and, perhaps, of the musician. We even become aware of the director and the stage manager, as men who have designed and coached a group of actions and movements, before we become aware of the playwright. Of course, the play-wright's script is behind all the performances. He tells the actors which lines to utter and includes enough specific details to control to a large extent the characterization of the roles. He gives directions to the set-designer and the director, as well, so that the performers are not at liberty to do just anything they want. But, in every case of a performance, there is inevitably and necessarily interpretation—each performer contributes something to the created product; and it is quite possible and common for a particular role or scene to come off better or worse than the playwright conceived.

The process in the performance accounts for the immediacy and allows the impact of drama. In a performance, we see human beings like ourselves involved, *now* and here, in living out an experience. There is no peeking ahead to see how it will come out; no looking back to review and verify what happened. These are roughly the conditions of our own time-bound and place-bound experience. Further, each performance is a re-creation of the experience, not a reproduction of a past event, but a new happening, proceeding here and now. This immediacy allows us the illusion of participation in the experience, as if we were a part of it. If the events represented are important to us, or can be made important in the context of the happening, our participation is heightened far beyond our ordinary kind of experience; this heightening and moving of emotions is described as impact. It is ironic and paradoxical that, while the playwright speaks to us less directly than any other writer, depending upon performers to convey his language and gestures, his drama often speaks most directly.

The aesthetic distinction of drama from other literary forms is in the dynamics of process. Poetry invites us to meditate, fiction to imagine, the essay to know logically; but drama invites us to perceive experience in the process of happening. On a stage, we see people and ideas moving and shifting in relation to one another. This perception is of a different order from abstracting meanings from the experience, or imagining possibilities, or of reporting after the fact. Drama appeals, in other words, to the dynamic mode of our minds.

Realism, Delusion, and Illusion

Dynamic process, then, is the aesthetic base of drama. The potential impact of dynamic process, especially when the viewer's psychic and conceptual distance are diminished until he feels the action on stage happening to him, gives rise to one of the oldest problems of drama—what is the relationship between the viewer and the happening? Is the experience he sees and feels real or unreal? And in what senses? Is it a lie, a delusion that is morally damaging? Or a delusion that is morally edifying? Is it only illusion, or especially illusion, or desirably illusion, in which we can perceive happenings that are potential to our own lives? Is the drama a world we enter willingly, or willy-nilly?

In modern drama—that is, drama beginning with Ibsen—we have tended to say that the production is a representation and imitation of reality: that which could conceivably and logically happen. And the several genres of drama have survived or dwindled in relation to their Realism. We have tended to demand that characters in serious dramas (and in the comparable form, the musical play, as, for example, *Lost in the Stars* and *West Side Story*) behave on stage in familiar ways, with fidelity to common experience, according to the patterns and extremes made possible by the represented motivations. Traditional tragedy and grand opera, partly because they cannot retain their traditional nature and meet our demands for ordinary characters and actions at the same time, have been moribund—though some excellent non-traditional tragedies have been written and produced in a realistic mold. Comedy, farce, and musical comedy have shown a fantastic fidelity to the statistical average of reality, to the point that they deal largely in stereotypes and caricatures, but these forms have also offered the most common escape from reality, partly through the falsifications of reality that are inherent in type, stereotype, and caricature. The biographical play, which represents some well-known person, such as F. D. Roosevelt, Al Jolson, or Helen Keller, on stage, has been prevalent, especially in musical comedy and the movies, but its corollary comic form, the burlesque, as in the British *The Entertainer* and Off-Broadway's *MacBird*, has been unfortunately rare.

The philosophy of experience inherent in Realism is not hard to isolate. Realism in the drama emerged at the same time that Realism was emerging in other literary forms—along with the development of scientific Naturalism. The scientists' interest in objective reality, whether grimy or pretty, in history and sociology, in accurate catalogs and descriptions of possibilities, are all reflected in modern drama. Even Expressionism is realistic in this sense; it attempts to depict the kinds of inner experiences that Freud and others have shown the scientific existence of. The viewer becomes analogous to the scientist in his laboratory, watching, recording, collecting the minutiae of facts, causes, and effects.

The stage conventions of Realism reflect this relationship. Not only does the scientist-audience expect characters to be possible and probable, by which is usually meant, capable of being substituted for real ones, the characters must also dress realistically, make themselves up so that they appear ordinary, and speak in language that one could hear on the street, or at least in the "real" situation represented. And the characters have usually had to move in settings that were not only realistic, but *real;* with tables, chairs, lamps, cigarettes, guns, and such, not represented but actually *on* the stage; so that the audience could look at the stage as a real house with one wall removed. The viewer became the passive voyeur.

Modern stage and theater conventions have had the effect of isolating the audience from dramatic impact. The actor and the audience have developed a convention of pretended ignorance each of the other, so that there is seldom any direct communication between them. Separation of the theater into well-defined areas—stage *vs.* auditorium; each on its side of the proscenium arch and footlights; one dark, the other light—has emphasized the pretended ignorance. All these conventions have the effect of preventing the viewer from ever mistaking the action on stage for something he might be involved in.

Of course, this barrier between the actors and the audience has been resisted. The most important devices for breaking it down have been the diminishing of psychic and conceptual distance. Playwrights learn to write, compensating for the barrier to such an extent that if certain plays are performed in other kinds of theaters, they become altogether too close, too painful. Some playwrights have tried to break through the barrier with soliloquys (as in O'Neill's *Strange Interlude* and several of his late plays), with direct address to the audience (as in *Our Town, Teahouse of the August Moon, After the Fall,* and others), and occasionally with asides, which differ from direct address primarily in length. More importantly, however, acting and directing styles and the structure of theaters have changed in ways that attempt to eliminate the barrier. Some of these factors are discussed in chapter 11.

Modern theater, then, has solved the problem of the dynamic impact of drama by neutralizing its existence, as far as possible, with Naturalistic and Realistic techniques. This solution by insulation may account, in part, for the common contemporary pronouncement that American drama is dead. But drama as a possibility is not dead. Nor is the problem of its dynamic impact solved.

Dynamic impact tends to convince the spectator of the play's reality. The process insists that the happening on stage *is.* French Neo-Classical critics, hoping to strengthen and enhance the impact and the sense of reality, insisted that every device that helps delude the spectator into believing the experience on stage *is* his own experience would be desirable. Thus they insisted that the unities of time, place, and action be held strictly, lest a breach in logic and possibility should lessen the dramatic impact.

Dr. Samuel Johnson answered the French critics thus, in his *Preface to Shakespeare:*

> The necessity of observing the unities of time and place arises from the supposed necessity of making the drama credible. The critics hold it impossible, that an action of months or years can be possibly believed to pass in three hours; or that the spectator can suppose himself to sit in the theater, while ambassadors go and return between distant kings, while armies are levied and towns besieged, while an exile wanders and returns, or till he whom they saw courting his mistress, shall lament the untimely fall of his son. The mind revolts from evident falsehood, and fiction loses its force when it departs from the resemblance of reality.

From the narrow limitation of time necessarily arises the contraction of place. The spectator, who knows that he saw the first act at Alexandria, cannot suppose that he sees the next at Rome, at a distance to which not the dragons of Medea could, in so short a time, have transported him; he knows with certainty that he has not changed his place, and he knows that place cannot change itself; that what was a house cannot become a plain; that what was Thebes can never be Persepolis.

Such is the triumphant language with which a critic exults over the misery of an irregular poet, and exults commonly without resistance of reply. It is time therefore to tell him by the authority of Shakespeare, that he assumes, as an unquestionable principle, a position, which, while his breath is forming it into words, his understanding pronounces to be false. It is false, that any representation is mistaken for reality; that any dramatic fable in its materiality was ever credible, or, for a single moment, was ever credited.

The objection arising from the impossibility of passing the first hour at Alexandria, and the next at Rome, supposes, that when the play opens, the spectator really imagines himself at Alexandria, and believes that his walk to the theater has been a voyage to Egypt, and that he lives in the days of Antony and Cleopatra. Surely he that imagines this may imagine more. He that can take the stage at one time for the palace of the Ptolemies, may take it in half an hour for the promontory of Actium. Delusion, if delusion be admitted, has no certain limitation; if the spectator can be once persuaded, that his old acquaintance are Alexander and Caesar, that a room illuminated with candles is the plain of Pharsalia, or the bank of Granicus, he is in a state of elevation above the reach of reason, or of truth, and from the heights of empyrean poetry, may despise the circumscriptions of terrestrial nature. There is no reason why a mind thus wandering in ecstasy should count the clock, or why an hour should not be a century in that calenture of the brains that can make the stage a field.

The truth is, that the spectators are always in their senses, and know, from the first act to the last, that the stage is only a stage, and that the players are only players. They came to hear a certain number of lines recited with just gesture and elegant modulation. The lines relate to some action, and an action must be in some place; but the different actions that complete a story may be in places very remote from each other; and where is the absurdity of allowing that space to represent first Athens, and then Sicily, which was always known to be neither Sicily nor Athens, but a modern theater?

By supposition, as place is introduced, time may be extended; the time required by the fable elapses for the most part between the acts; for, of so much of the action as is represented, the real and poetical duration is the same. If, in the first act, preparations for war against Mithridates are represented to be made in Rome, the event of the war may, without absurdity, be represented, in the catastrophe, as happening in Pontus; we know that there is neither war, nor preparation for war; we know that we are neither in Rome nor Pontus; that neither Mithridates nor Lucullus are before us. The drama exhibits successive imitations of successive actions; and why may not the second imitation represent an action that happened years after the first, if it be so connected with it, that nothing but time can be supposed to intervene? Time is, of all modes of existence, most obsequious to the imagination; a lapse of years is as easily conceived as a passage of hours. In contemplation we easily contract the time of real actions, and therefore willingly permit it to be contracted when we only see their imitation.

It will be asked, how the drama moves, if it is not credited. It is credited with all the credit due to a drama. It is credited, whenever it moves, as a just picture of a real original; as representing to the auditor what he would himself feel, if he were to do or suffer what is there feigned to be suffered or to be done. The reflection that strikes the heart is not, that the evils before us are real evils, but that they are evils to which we ourselves may be exposed. If there be any fallacy, it is not that we fancy the players, but that we fancy ourselves unhappy for a moment; but we rather lament the possibility than suppose the presence of misery, as a mother weeps over her babe, when she remembers that death may take it from her. The delight of tragedy proceeds from our consciousness of fiction; if we thought murders and treasons real, they would please no more.

Imitations produce pain or pleasure, not because they are mistaken for realities, but because they bring realities to mind.

Dr. Johnson, then, denies that we as audience are deluded into thinking that the representation on stage is a real one. We do not mistake it for our own experience, but "as a just picture of a real original; as representing to the auditor what he would himself feel, if he were to do or suffer what is there feigned." Our pleasure is derived, then, intellectually; not by diminishing psychic distance, but by increasing it and making it conscious. The impact is on the mind, not on the viscera.

Samuel Taylor Coleridge's answer differed somewhat from Dr. Johnson's. In *Biographia Literaria,* chapter XIV, Coleridge held that the spectator to drama grants neither "denial [nor] affirmation" of its reality, that he, in fact, treats its reality as irrelevant, having voluntarily entered the world of the representation on its own terms—with "that willing suspension of disbelief for the moment, which constitutes poetic faith." Coleridge held that each piece of literature has its own nature, its own probability (this is related to organic form), which is not to be mistaken for reality. Aesthetically, it is not the *reality* of consistency with life and probability that is important, but the *appearance* of probability. Coleridge developed his position in some detail in his *Lectures on Shakespeare, 1818–1819:*

... There is one preliminary point to be first settled, as the indispensable condition not only of just and genial criticism, but of all consistency in our opinions. This point is contained in the words, probable, natural. ... Now what are we to understand by these words in their application to the drama? Assuredly not the ordinary meaning of them. Farquhar ... first exposed the ludicrous absurdities involved in the supposition, and demolished as with the single sweep of a careless hand, the whole edifice of French criticism respecting the so-called unities of time and place. But a moment's reflection suffices to make every man conscious of what every man must have before felt, that the drama is an *imitation* of reality, not a *copy*—and that imitation is contradistinguished from copy by this: that a certain quantum of difference [from reality] is essential to the former, and an indispensable condition and cause of the pleasure we derive from it; while in a copy it is a defect, controvening its name and purpose.... Not only that we ought, but that we actually do, all of us judge of the drama under this impression, we need no other proof than the impassive slumber of our sense of probability when we hear an actor announce himself as a Greek, Roman, Venetian, or Persian in good mother English....

Still, however, there is a sort of improbability with which we are shocked in dramatic representation no less than in the narrative of real life. Consequently, there must be rules respecting it; and as rules are nothing but means to an end previously ascertained (the inattention to which simple truth has been the occasion of all the pedantry of the French school), we must first ascertain what the immediate end or object of the drama is. Here I find two extremes in critical decision: the French, which evidently presupposes that a perfect delusion is to be aimed at—an opinion which now needs no fresh confutation; the opposite, supported by Dr. Johnson, supposes the auditors throughout as in the full and positive reflective knowledge of the contrary. In evincing the impossibility of delusion, he makes no sufficient allowance for an intermediate state, which we distinguish by the term illusion.

In what this consists I cannot better explain than by referring you to the highest degree of it; namely, dreaming. It is laxly said that during sleep we take our dreams for realities, but this is irreconcilable with the nature of sleep, which consists in a suspension of the voluntary and, therefore, of the comparative power. The fact is that we pass no judgment either way: we simply do not judge them to be unreal, in consequence of which the images act on our minds, as far as they act at all, by their own force as images. Our state while we are dreaming differs from that in which we are in the perusal of a deeply interesting novel in the degree rather than in the kind, and from three causes: First, from the exclusion of all outward impressions on our senses the images in sleep become proportionally more vivid than they can be when the organs of sense are in their active state. Secondly, in sleep the sensations, and with these the emotions and passions which they counterfeit, are the causes of our dream-images, while in our waking hours our emotions are the effects of the images presented to us.... Lastly, in sleep we pass at once by a sudden collapse into this suspension of will and the comparative power: whereas in an interesting play, read or represented, we are brought up to this point, as far as it is requisite or desirable, gradually, by the art of the poet and the actors; and with the consent and positive aidance of our own will. We *choose* to be deceived. The rule, therefore, may be easily inferred. Whatever tends to prevent the mind from placing itself or from being gradually placed in this state in which the images have a negative reality must be a defect, and consequently anything that must force itself on the auditors' mind as improbable, not because it *is* improbable (for that the whole play is foreknown to be) but because it cannot but *appear* as such.

In other words, Coleridge says that psychic distance is diminished to such a point that our wills experience the action on stage, though our bodies remain seated in the auditorium. For him, the play takes place in the mind, as it were, with the conscious censor, editor, and rememberer suspended for the moment.

Although the notions of Johnson and Coleridge appear contradictory, it is possible that both are true—and true simultaneously. Experimental evidence from psychology indicates that the mind can hold only one image or thought at a time. Though rapid fluctuation between competing thoughts can give the impression of thinking two things at once, such competitors both suffer from half-attention. But it is a different thing to think and feel at the same time. It is quite common for us to emote and know why we are emoting. The two are different orders of experience. It is possible for us to immerse ourselves in a drama, as Coleridge describes it, and know, like Johnson, that we are watching a drama.

Eugene M. Waith, of Yale University, points out that the audience sees a drama "as a continuous flow of present time, . . . a succession of transient impressions, . . . [which] are like what are often called 'dramatic moments' in actual life. These are the moments in which more is at stake than is immediately apparent." [1] Waith's "moments" turn out to be the peaks of waves that rise toward a crisis and climax. Our perception of their importance is of a different order from our perception of them as moments.

The dynamics of ordinary experience includes both kinds of perceptions. Not always, but frequently, we are able to abstract, to compare, to evaluate an experience, even while it is in process. The dynamics of a dramatic performance, if it is a good one, gives us the illusion of personal participation in the represented experience *and* the understanding of the causes and implications of the experience. Since both kinds of perceptions are possible in the dynamics of life, both must be included in the dynamics of drama.

[1] "Introduction," *The Dramatic Moment* (Englewood Cliffs, New Jersey: Prentice-Hall, 1967), p. 3.

11

Some Aspects of
Recent American Drama[1]

Some Recent Changes in American Theater Practice

A number of important changes have come to American theater since World War II. Most importantly, perhaps, the themes which playwrights have chosen to deal with and which audiences have wanted to see have changed considerably. There are exceptions, of course, but generally speaking, there has been a trend away from social and toward psychological concerns. This change has influenced certain trends in the techniques of writing, directing, staging, and even viewing drama. Indeed, it has helped to change the very structure of the theater. It has encouraged auditoriums to grow smaller; has helped stages to free themselves from traditional restrictions; has created new theater companies while allowing others to fail. When we speak of an American playwright of today, we need to know which part of the general trend he reflects, which part he rejects, and which kind of theater he is working in.

The thematic change has been thorough-going. Seldom do we have a social-problem play anymore. As Gerald Weales points out,

The average play of the fifties concerns itself with the problems of adjustment, of acceptance. The protagonist, often enough, is put into a family situation where his wife, his parent, his child becomes the antagonist and drives him to or saves him from alcoholism, homosexuality, mental breakdown, drug ad-

[1] The major portion of this chapter appeared as the essay, "Some Aspects of Contemporary American Drama," by Howard C. Brashers, in *Moderna Sprak*, The Journal of the Modern Language Teachers' Association of Sweden, 59 (September 1965), pp. 294–305, to which thanks and acknowledgement are hereby made.

diction or simple boredom. In the absence of family, a love affair or a courtship can serve. . . . Much of the dialogue in that average play . . . is likely to be in the clichés of psychological jargon, and the general tone is inevitably didactic.[2]

There was, of course, plenty of psychological drama in the 20's in America when the dramatists discovered Freud. One need only think of Eugene O'Neill to bring to mind a number of the best. *The Hairy Ape* fails to become a proletarian drama because O'Neill was most interested in Yank as a psychological problem. *The Emperor Jones* is a study of mental disintegration. And *Strange Interlude,* with its long monologues of self-analysis, is to drama what the psychological novel is to fiction.

And it is true that the so-called proletarian drama of the 20's and 30's had a tendency to deal with private rather than public problems, but there were still plenty of sociologically important plays. Elmer Rice's *Adding Machine* (1923), for instance, is a sharply expressionistic criticism of materialistic society. Mr. Zero, the central character, finds that he is simply a number in the world, and not even a real number at that! His problem in a cash-register world is simply that he can't add up to anything, even when he dies and is translated to heaven. Rice changed techniques completely for another social-problem play, *Street Scene* (1929). This play is a minutely realistic criticism of a society that produces slums and poverty. It makes its point by presenting the dirtiest and grimiest details of socioeconomic class differences.

In the 20's, in addition to the works already mentioned, social protest of one sort or another was involved in such plays as *What Price Glory?, Processional, Marco Millions, Gods of Lightning,* and others. After the depression, this note became even stronger, in such plays as *Of Thee I Sing, Men in White, Dead End, Waiting for Lefty, Awake and Sing, Winterset, The Petrified Forest, Idiot's Delight, The Ghost of Yankee Doodle, Our Town, Key Largo, The Little Foxes,* and others. During the war years, too, protest against world forces of social and political significance competed successfully with escapist farces.

But we can see a transition away from the social in the work of older playwrights who continued to write after the war. Consider, for instance, four plays by Sidney Kingsley. His *Men in White* (1933) grows out of a doctor's dilemma of whether to use his profession to benefit himself or society. The problem is obviously psychological, but Kingsley's focus is on the social implications of his decision, not the personal. His *Dead End* (1935), like Rice's *Street Scene,* used ash-can realism to protest against the existence of slums and is said to have influenced slum-clearance legislation. In both these plays, Kingsley's focus is on social concerns. But after the war, a shift took place. His

---

[2] In a broadcast overseas for Voice of America, "Theater Without Walls," which is distributed in pamphlet form by the US Information Agency.

Detective Story (1949) obviously has its roots in the social problems of the police state and its stimulant in the Hitler situation. But Kingsley turns the situation into a psychological study of the effect that police brutality has on the soul of an individual and his family. *Darkness at Noon* (1951), Kingsley's dramatization of Arthur Koestler's novel, is not so much a criticism of the Communist Revolution and all the purges that followed, as it is a study of Rubashov's mind, as he remembers and re-lives his betrayal, deceit, and vicious sacrifice of love and friendship. In both these plays, the psychological concern far outweighs the social.

Even contemporary sociological issues are, almost invariably, treated in private terms. Since the war, there have been a number of plays about Negro-white relations. But most of them are sociological only by second thought and by implication. Most of them are explicitly psychological studies of individuals involved in, about to enter, or produced by miscegenation. In the same lecture quoted earlier, Gerald Weales cited Arthur Laurents's *Home of the Brave* as a typical play of the early post-war period. "Produced in 1945, it came close enough to the thirties to be concerned with so societal a problem as anti-Semitism, but it looked to the fifties by treating the problem purely in psychological terms." It may well be that there are social situations too hot to handle (no one has yet treated the concommitants of nuclear radiation, except comically) and the psychological approach is a means of avoiding the public issues.

But it seems more likely that Americans simply have lost their taste for sociological plays. In the fifties, British filmmakers sent a large number of pictures to America, and it seeemed that every second one was a British labor movie. A typical working-class man was organizing a typical union in a typical shop to combat the typical injustices of an upper-middle-class manufacturer. Americans got very irritated with such characters. They didn't care what a fellow was a symbol of; they wanted to know how he felt. They had almost universally accepted the individual, which the Angry Young Men were to make popular in England.

This focus upon the individual brings about certain changes in the techniques of drama. Since writers of such drama must make their plots depend upon emotions rather than upon reason, they must offer different kinds of dramatic evidence. Characters appear in ever smaller groups, seldom greater than the family. Making a personal emotion convincing is an altogether different thing from making a sociological issue convincing. Directors must use corollary techniques to emphasize these concerns. Loud voices and stage movements are no longer adequate; pace and timing have become of the utmost importance. Actors have to learn a whole new method of expression, both physical and verbal. Indeed, everyone connected with the stage now must be preoccupied with things that he might have tried to conceal before the war.

The very physical structure of theaters has been affected. Many a large theater has failed financially. On the other hand, many a new theater with a small auditorium, so that audiences can sit close to the stage, has come into existence. Stages have come out from behind the proscenium arch to become wholly or partly surrounded by the small audience. Experimenters have tried ramps and runways into the audience area, stylized sets, everything that will break down the traditional physical and empathic distance between the audience and the individual on the stage.

Different kinds of plays demand different amounts of this audience-to-character distance. An intimate, intricate, personal play may fail in a huge theater, but be quite successful in a small one. On the other hand, a play with a large cast and a lot of action may be only confusion in a small theater, but a clear success in a large one. The type of theater most suitable for a given play depends upon both the theme and the stage techniques with which it is presented. The theater nowadays has a greater range of these technical and physical possibilities than ever before, although—ironically—this situation has not given us great plays or significant, new dramatists. Instead, these technical experiments in theater and contemporary thematic tendencies have left Americans with some eight types of theater. Each has its particular demands upon theater people, and each its peculiar appeals to the public. While there has been a great deal of interchange of actors, directors, and writers, so that there is some homogeneity, each type retains its singularity. Each leaves its stamp on the artist.

Eight Types of Contemporary American Theater

The "Broadway" Theater

In describing the types of contemporary American theater, let us begin with Broadway, the traditional center of show-business in the United States. When we say Broadway, we mean a group of large, commercial theaters in New York, not all of them on the street called Broadway. These theaters are primarily concerned with long runs of popular plays because of the profits involved, not the aesthetics. Although the notions of the "Broadway play" are in continual flux, audiences have preferred certain kinds of plays in recent years.

Among these is the musical comedy, which, because of its high volume of sound, large cast, and great amount of movement, including dancing, is well suited to a large auditorium. But more importantly, the musical comedy must deal with familiar types and situations, usually love, since it does not have the facilities for developing unique characters. Consequently, most musical plays are comic. The best examples include the Rogers and Hammerstein *Oklahoma!* and *Carousel,* and the Lerner and Loewe *My Fair Lady. West Side Story* is almost unique in modern times as a serious musical play, but even it takes characters and situations from the common storehouse of public familiarity.

Another type of play that is common on Broadway is the situation comedy. John Patrick's *The Teahouse of the August Moon,* hit of the 1953 season and winner of the Pulitzer Prize and the Drama Critics Circle Award, is an excellent example. It took a situation that audiences were almost too familiar with—the occupation forces, this time on Okinawa—and managed to enliven it with the ancient device of letting the oppressed deceive the oppressor, all in good fun, of course, and with the help of a kindly American officer. The antics delighted people from a distance so well that very few of them noticed that the actors could have worn masks without loss of effectiveness.

The situation, not comic, is also quite popular. The big success of the 1960 season, William Gibson's *The Miracle Worker,* is a good example. It took the story of Helen Keller, a story which virtually every American school-child for the past thirty years has been familiar with, and treated it from a new angle— from the point of view of Anne Sullivan, the tutor who struggled against almost insuperable odds to teach the blind and deaf little girl the rudiments of education. In addition to knowing the outcome of the plot in advance— Miss Keller eventually became a moderately accomplished writer—the audience was treated to a great deal of unmistakable, physical action on the stage, as for instance when Miss Sullivan bodily forced Miss Keller into certain experiences.

The most typical kind of play nowadays, however, is probably the psychological drama of the type that William Inge, perhaps the most typical playwright of the fifties, writes. In this kind of play, everything mental has to be represented by some *thing* in the play, though that thing does not have to appear. In *Come Back, Little Sheba,* Inge represented a lonely middle-aged woman's dreams of lost youth and vigor by a lost puppy. In *Picnic,* he represented a lonely midwestern girl's urge for adventure by an adventuring drummer who is passing through. Audiences have learned to understand the Freudian jargon that tells them every person reacts to other persons through the refraction of the things he loves or hates about himself. When a playwright tells them that one character is an aspect of another's personality, they nod their heads at something familiar. Since about 1955, the grand panacea for all psychological problems has been love, by which the playwrights usually mean sex. "Consider, for instance, the end of William Inge's *The Dark at the Top of the Stairs,"* says Weales. "After sprinkling the stage with every implication from infidelity to anti-Semitism, Inge smoothes away all difficulties by sending Rubin Flood and his wife up the stairs, hand in hand. Earlier in the play, Inge has given the audience an endlessly explicit object lesson in the figure of Mrs. Flood's sister, a comic-pathetic character who cannot quit talking about her frigidity and what it has done to her marriage and her life." When one thinks about it, there is an awful lot of visible underwear, especially slips, but also brassieres and panties, in the contemporary actress's wardrobe.

Aesthetically, the most successful broadway playwrights of recent years are Tennessee Williams and Arthur Miller. We all know that both these dramatists participate in many of the trends already mentioned. We all know, also, that both of them rise well above the typical.

Tennessee Williams has shown an especial interest in the psychological problems of the victims of the world. The crippled girl, Laura, in *The Glass Menagerie*, is unable to gain normal contact with the world and substitutes a table-top world, populated by glass animals. Laura's psychological withdrawal is not condemned; rather, Williams's sympathy for her is as fragile as her collection of glass animals. In *A Streetcar Named Desire*, Williams's ambiguous attitude toward both Stanley and Blanche saves the play from any black-white interpretation. Stanley's victory is not altogether satisfying, nor is Blanche's insanity contemptible. His later plays seem less satisfactory in the proportion that they depend upon the now-familiar Williams mannerisms: his victims have become more and more perverse; their moral corruption more decadent; his plots more melodramtic. His limitation of subject is surely a weakness, and his melodramatic exaggeration is sometimes closer to satire than to seriousness. Every new play that he writes demonstrates increasingly that he is certainly not a playwright of ideas, but of the viscera. But it is in that that his greatness lies, for, after his weaknesses are admitted and discounted, his attitude toward his characters is more akin to that of the great dramatists of the past than to that of his contemporaries.

Arthur Miller seems more durable than Williams, partly because he is most certainly a playwright of ideas. *All My Sons*, his first major success, is an Ibsenesque study of a family and, as such, focuses upon individual emotions. But the primacy of family that Miller presents is more related to the American myth of the family than it is to a case history, so that his play becomes a kind of essay on the American character in a context of history. The same thing can be said of Willy Loman's ideas of success in *Death of a Salesman*, in spite of the fact that the play focuses emphatically on an individual case. *Death of a Salesman* is so personal, in fact, that almost every scene is a dramatization of Willy's thoughts, while his mind is in the process of disintegrating. It is significant that Miller's original title for the play was "The Inside of His Head." Yet, the play is so involved with sociology that many people find it an excellent illustration of David Riesman's *The Lonely Crowd*, which was published shortly after the play appeared. *The Crucible*, Miller's third great play, focuses with historical completeness and accuracy on the Salem witch trials of 1692.

Yet, the play was offered as a metaphor of our times, when such activities as Joe McCarthy's Un-American investigations could reach hysterical, witch-hunting proportions. While participating fully in the shift to psychological treatment, Miller has determinedly preserved sociological significance. Such depth of meaning creates greatness of dramatic performance. Miller is likely to survive as the best dramatist of the period.

The "Legitimate" Theater

A second type of contemporary American theater is in the legitimate theaters in major cities across the country. These theaters are usually large and commercial, like Broadway theaters, but unlike Broadway, they cannot attract large audiences for long runs. The populations of these cities are much, much smaller than New York's, and no other city attracts travel and business the way New York does. Consequently, the kinds of plays these theaters can produce are severely limited. For the most part, they prefer low-budget productions of safe plays, which means a play or playwright that already has a reputation. The greater part of their offering is the musical or situation play of two, five, or ten years before. This situation is not altogether regrettable, for it keeps worthwhile plays alive long enough for them to be properly assessed. Another important function of these theaters is as an outlet for the touring companies of current Broadway hits. It is through these theaters that current plays are carried to the very corners of the country, if not the corners of the world. Thus, audiences in Chicago, Denver, Dallas, San Francisco, and so forth, are given a higher level of drama than they would otherwise have. Theaters in a number of cities, especially in the East—Boston, New Haven, Philadelphia, Washington—act as places for trying out plays and productions that are often Broadway-bound. These theaters seldom do anything that is very adventurous. Indeed, about the only way a local playwright can get a new play into these theaters is to interest a New York producer in it.

Motion Pictures and Television

Motion pictures and television are a third and a fourth type of contemporary theater, which draw the largest crowds by far. In fact, they draw far more people than have the mental and aesthetic equipment to respond to drama. Consequently, a great deal of their effort goes into extra-dramatic concerns. The star-performer system, for example, is designed to cater to the personal-image, wish-fulfillment needs of girls and boys in Hoboken and Sioux Falls (and Madrid and Gothenburg), not to dramatic art. For this audience, reputation of the performer has replaced quality of the performance as an index of excellence and "deep emotion" is expressed, as often as not, by a full-faced stare into a camera lens.

However, movies and television have considerable dramatic possibilities. They share enough of these that we can consider them together, although they differ enough that we must finally separate them as types. No doubt, they have influenced the shift in subject matter. But that shift would probably have occurred without their influence—as, indeed, we can say it *did,* for Hollywood has been a follower, not a creator, of fancy.

Films have had a large, but unwitting, influence upon dramatic structure. Film-makers have preferred very many, very short scenes, with rapid and unlimited shifts in time and place. This has caused the dramatic unities to become very flexible and fluid, and these notions have modified stage practice via an interchange of personnel; most contemporary writers, actors, and directors have worked in both media. One readily sees this fluidity in such a play as *The Miracle Worker,* in which several stages in a difficult and time-consuming process of education are represented on the stage in an evening. One also sees it in the readiness with which Hollywood makes films of current Broadway hits with relatively minor changes in structure. (The changes in *mores* are, however, interesting from a social historian's point of view.)

Movies and television have been doggedly photographic in their notions of reality, which may be one of the reasons for their general aesthetic failure. For example, while *Death of a Salesman* moves rather fluidly within some twenty years of Willy's life and in New York and Boston so that "the play was sometimes called cinematographic in its structure, it failed as a motion picture," said Arthur Miller in his Introduction to his *Collected Plays.* "I believe the basic reason—aside from the gross insensitivity permeating its film production —was that the dramatic tension of Willy's memories was destroyed by transferring him, literally, to the locales he had only imagined in the play. There is an inevitable horror in the spectacle of a man losing consciousness of his immediate surroundings to the point where he engages in conversations with unseen persons. The horror is lost—and drama becomes narrative—when the context actually becomes his imagined world. . . . The mere fact that a man forgets where he is does not mean that he has really moved."

The primary difference between motion pictures and television is in the conception of plot. The motion picture writer must plot for an aesthetically integrated series of events that lead to a single, large climax. But because of the commercial sponsorship of American television drama, the writer must, in a sense, plot for the interruption for commercial announcements, which means that each portion of the action must be supplied with a climax and the cliff-hanging question, "what will happen next?" This situation is not as regrettable as Europeans have tended to think, the crassness of the commercial announcements aside, for it has forced television playwrights into the plot structures in which most of the world's great drama has been written. This is indicated by the relative ease with which a first-rate television play can be expanded and produced on Broadway. One can hardly think of even the best, original movie doing the same thing.

Unlike motion pictures, television has produced some new playwrights of note—Paddy Chayevsky, Richard Nash, Gore Vidal, Simon Winchelberg. As a consequence, television drama is competing more and more successfully with Broadway with respect to quality. Motion pictures were never much more than Broadway's highly successful financial rival.

The "Little" Theater

The traditional, aesthetic rival of Broadway has been the little theaters. When we speak of a little theater group, we mean a small, often semi-professional, company, in which the writers, producers, and managers are also the actors. The group is usually held together by some aesthetic ideal, which may range from topical satire to verse drama. Performances are likely to be in a small place, often one which the group have remodelled themselves. As a type, little theaters have been so extremely experimental that it is virtually impossible to make any generalizations about their dramatic theory. As soon as their experimentation has evolved something worthwhile, Broadway has always been ready to take it over. The grand example, of course, is the Provincetown Players of Provincetown, Massachusetts, who introduced Eugene O'Neill's first plays to the world.

In recent years, continually rising costs of production and ever-increasing problems with actors' guilds, and the like, have caused many of the little theaters to close. And those that have survived have done so by finding an "angel"—a wealthy man who is willing to lose a certain amount of money each year for art, or tax-manipulation, or both—or by going commercial, which usually means moving to larger quarters and becoming more safe than experimental in their repertoire. Considering the number of new playwrights and new staging techniques that have come from little theaters in the past century, it is regrettable that they are disappearing from all our civilized countries.

The University Theater

Part of the experimental function of little theaters has been taken over by university theaters, a sixth type of contemporary American theater. These theaters are the nearest thing to subsidized drama found in America, for they are supported by colleges and universities as workshops for students in all phases of dramatic art. Most of these theaters are admittedly timid. More than mundane success seems to depend upon an inspired teacher or an especially well-equipped laboratory-theater. The grand example of the first, of course, is Professor George Baker, whose "47 Workshop" at Harvard from 1905 to 1925 produced a number of notable dramatists, including Eugene O'Neill. Contemporary examples are Paul Baker, who until recently was uncommonly successful in training actors at Baylor University, and Glenn Hughes, at the University of Washington, who developed theater-in-the-round in the thirties. Special equipment often gives direction and tone to a given university's productions. The Elizabethan Theater which the University of Southern Oregon and Stanford University have constructed from original plans in Ashland, Oregon, has helped to make the annual Oregon Shakespearean Festival one of the most exciting anywhere. The various facilities, including a theater, which Edward S. Harkness donated to Yale University in the twenties, has enabled the Yale Graduate School of Drama to be the leading dramatic school in the country for some years. A similar gift to the Carnegie Institute of Technology helps account for the excellence of its drama school. The University of California at Los Angeles and Pasadena Junior College have good reputations for producing actors, especially for Hollywood. There are signs of a current revival of playwriting at Harvard, where Arthur L. Kopit wrote his Ionesco-like *Oh Dad, Poor Dad, Mamma's Hung You in the Closet and I'm Feelin' So Bad*. The principal dangers facing university theaters are that they are likely to grow academic and conservative. When they do that, the best thing that can be said about them is that they keep alive the Greeks and the Elizabethans, which has its value.

The Regional Theater

The most significant type of contemporary American theater is, in many ways, a fusion of the best parts of the other types. This is the regional theater, or, as it is called in New York, simply Off-Broadway. This type is composed of theater companies in most of the major cities across the country, who are as much interested in economics as in aesthetics, since they must maintain economic solvency. For the most part, they play in medium-sized theaters which try to strike a medium between the possibilities of large theaters and those of movie cameras. Often they have centralized or partly centralized staging, such as that of the Circle in the Square in New York, where the audience sits on three sides of the stage, or the late Margo Jones's Theater in the Round in the Dallas Community Center. Sometimes, these companies do not have a theater of their own, as was the case with the Actors Workshop of San Francisco. Other important companies are The Alley Theatre in Houston, The Arena Stage in Washington, D.C., and The Phoenix Theatre in New York.

The artistic achievement of these theaters in the past ten or fifteen years is quite varied and of a high order. Like the university theaters, they have kept alive the best of classical drama, including such worthwhile playwrights as Ibsen, Strindberg, Chekhov, and O'Casey. Such dramas will not draw the huge audiences necessary for a Broadway production, but in smaller theaters they can be both profitably and sympathetically produced. These theaters have sometimes been daring enough to produce plays that were failures on Broadway. O'Neill's *The Iceman Cometh,* Tennessee Williams's *Orpheus Descending,* and Truman Capote's *The Grass Harp* are post-war examples of plays that failed uptown and had to be "discovered" Off-Broadway. On the other hand, some plays that were Off-Broadway successes have failed when they moved to the larger theaters. It was probably the recognition of the basic aesthetic differences that made Tennessee Williams offer *Summer and Smoke, Suddenly Last Summer,* and other plays in regional theaters. Like the little, "art" theaters, regional theaters have had the courage to introduce such important modern dramatists as Beckett, Brecht, Sartre, Ionesco, Genet, Pinter to the American public.

The high level of experimentation Off-Broadway has helped to produce the first new playwrights of note—except Williams, Miller, and a few television writers—since the war: Edward Albee, Jack Gelber, Jack Richardson. Gelber's *The Connection* is an expression of the rebellious, narcotics-taking generations of the fifties. It includes jazz, and the actors mingle with the audience. It was both a popular and critical success when it appeared Off-Broadway in 1959. Richardson's *The Prodigal* (1960) showed wit, intelligence, and objectivity, and it tackled a serious, if grim, theme: the conflict between idealism and political opportunism. Albee's one-act plays, *The Zoo Story* (1958), *The Sandbox* (1959), and *The American Dream* (1960), deal with American social phenomena—historical types, especially of the family, embodiments of ideals, attitudes toward money, material things, and people—and make statements so brutally honest and penetrating that they seem absurd. Albee, Gelber, and Richardson showed, in other words, good signs of reviving sociological drama, and their early successes probably stemmed from this. But their first urges seem now to have collapsed. Albee's first full-length play, *Who's Afraid of Virginia Woolf?,* which was done on Broadway, sounded like a psychological essay on O'Neill, and his *Tiny Alice* was so private and internal as to be essentially obscure.

The Repertory Theater

In the early sixties, an eighth kind of theater began developing—the repertory theater. There were two varieties of this kind of theater—the kind founded as a group of actors and directors who then rented theaters suitable to their performances; the other founded as a resident group at a particular theater, as the Lincoln Center in New York. A good example of the first kind is the APA, the Association of Producing Artists, who try each season to maintain a balance and a variety in the kinds of plays they do. One season, for instance, they did Ibsen's *The Wild Duck,* Kaufmann's *You Can't Take it With You,* a world premier of MacLeish's *Herakles,* and Beckett's *Krapp's Last Tape.* After a pre-season festival or tour in Ann Arbor, Michigan, they moved to the Phoenix Theater in New York and performed these plays in repertory sequence. A similar group associated with the drama school of Carnegie Institute of Technology in Pittsburgh did Richard Wilbur's translation of Molière's *Tartuffe* and Edward Albee's new play, *Tiny Alice,* then went on to New York's Lincoln Center to present the plays in repertory. This was a slight departure from the organizing idea of Lincoln Center, which was intended to have a resident company of actors, directors, and technicians who could present plays outside the exigencies of commercial survival or inept reviews. The original company consisted of only twenty-two actors, however— a thin number compared to the repertory companies in London, Berlin, Moscow, and other drama centers. And dissension over what the Center was to do —experiment with the new, give hearing to the uncommercial, focus upon the "artistic," or what—has crippled much of its effectiveness. Some people fear that the Center will gradually be reduced to the role of booking agent for other companies and that the values of repertory and subsidization will be lost.

Such, then, are some of the theatrical practices and conditions that the contemporary playwright has to contend with. He should be aware of the aesthetic differences between all his possibilities and, since he is not powerless in determining the kind of production he gets, should exert his influence toward giving his plays the best possible chance with an audience. For a national drama that is so often pronounced dead, American theater today has a rich variety—perhaps a richer variety than has ever existed—in staging, in acting, in directing, in lighting, in all the technical aspects of drama. That little which seems memorable is being written, may mean that playwrights are not using the variety that is available to them.

12

Some Notes on Practical Playwriting

The playwright, like the writer of fiction, deals in characters, scenes, and incidents; they are his "vocabulary," his carriers of meanings. Unlike the fiction writer, however, his "voice" is always filtered through others: actors, designers, directors. His practical task, then, is to discover those techniques within stage conventions which will communicate his meanings. Most of what is said in this text about the techniques of fiction and poetry applies to the playwright's task at one time or another, in one form or another, and should be reviewed. The playwright is as much concerned with style as the fictionist or poet, perhaps more concerned with such aspects of style as speech and verse rhythms. He uses the same concepts of character, setting, point-of-view, plot, and structure as the fictionist; he may use the poet's vocabulary and some of his patterns of organization; but in every case, he adapts the techniques to the process of production. What follows is a brief catalog of some of these adaptations.

The Plot

A good many playwriting instructors today agree with Aristotle that plot is the first principle of drama, and, consequently, more advice has been written about the techniques of plotting than about other techniques. The importance of plot seems to arise from two facts. First, the dramatist has no means of narration outside the action of the moment, no means of summarizing, in any dramatic way, the kinds of materials about his characters which the novelist deals with importantly. Secondly, the dramatist's characterizations are limited to speech and action—for the playwright has no way in realistic conventions of revealing his characters' thoughts to the audience, especially not in the direct way open to the novelist. The playwright, then, must rely most upon action for the depiction of his ideas.

This primacy of action forces certain aesthetic and practical necessities upon the playwright. There is, first, a strong need for sequence or some device by which sequence can be easily discovered in the play. Since the playwright is limited to focusing upon action, here and now, he has to pay special attention to the action's cause and effect, which can establish logical sequence in his audience's mind. This amounts, secondly, to a need for unity of action, not so much in the Classical sense, as in Dr. Johnson's sense. Even when the effect of a certain cause happens to be removed in time and space, causal sequence is more important as an organizing device than temporal or spatial unity. If such a causal sequence is not the unifying principle of a play, we need an aesthetic substitute for it—a preoccupation of the characters with some sort of dating system that will re-create the temporal sequence, or a detective-like approach that is devoted to discovering cause, or some such device. Third, the playwright has to have ways of varying the action, to make part of it preparatory, part of it dramatic. The variation upon a theme (or upon an action) is very important, because it is a means of repeating and recalling action and action-patterns without exact repetition.

Many playwriting instructors agree with Professor Kenneth T. Rowe at the University of Michigan that a fairly Classical approach to plot best satisfies these needs. Professor Rowe's analysis of plot [1] echoes closely the analysis we have already used in connection with fiction, but adds a few important concepts and terms. He speaks of the conflict, the problem, the question of the plot as the *major dramatic question*. This question posits the existence of a crisis and a resolution, and causal unity consists of the resolution's answer to the question. Some directors prefer to call this question the *central controlling idea* of the drama. Materials before this question are exposition and preparation—what we have already called the induction. The point at which the major dramatic question is clear to the audience, the end of the induction, Professor Rowe calls the *attack,* or point of attack. *Complications* follow the point of attack in wave-like rising action—each wave consisting of a minor dramatic question, its crisis, and resolution. The rising action culminates in the *major crisis* of the play, the *point of determination,* what Aristotle called the turning point. Then follow more complications, in a wave-like descent that culminates in the *resolution* of the major dramatic question, though Professor Rowe cau-

[1] See his *Write That Play* (New York: Funk & Wagnalls, 1939), pp. 53–89.

tions us not to think of this as falling action—certainly not falling in the sense that the audience is less interested in it than in the other action; on the contrary, this is often where the playwright has the audience most involved and, sometimes, literally on the edge of their seats. The disposition of the characters after the resolution is clear is the *conclusion*. Such an approach to plot ensures causal sequence and makes variety possible in the series of minor dramatic crises. Additional attention to such necessary devices as foreshadowing and undercutting ensures a dramatic curve in the action.

Professor Rowe also strongly urges the use of a scenario, a sequential outline of the major elements of the plot. The divisions of the scenario are the points where characters enter or leave in such a way as to leave a new grouping of people on stage. The scenario should list each of these scenes, the characters that are present, and the things that the scene will accomplish—what advancement of the action it represents, what preparation for future actions it contains, what details of exposition it reviews, what characterization it does, and so on. These details of intention can be set as a long heading to a summary of the scene's actions, or they can be set down in a wide margin to one side—whichever form best suits the individual writer.

There are several advantages to using a fairly detailed scenario. First and most importantly, it forces the writer to deal with questions of sequence, unity, and variety. The discipline of setting it all down on paper can tell the writer in advance whether he, in fact, has a plot or not. This leads into the second major advantage: that the writer can revise out the irrelevant, re-think the inadequate, reinforce the useful. It is much easier and much more useful to revise in scenario than in full draft, for the full draft usually imbeds the mistakes in too much obscuring detail; in scenario, mistakes can easily be seen and corrected. Another advantage is that the author's extensive thought about his characters in action makes those characters well known; very often this will enliven them to a point that they practically write the play. This is related to another advantage: a fully imagined scenario frees the writer and his imagination during the actual act of writing so that he can focus his mind upon detail; he does not have to be continually worrying about his structure or characterization. It is axiomatic that the more a writer knows about his subject, the better his product will be. The scenario is a means of acquiring knowledge and depth.

Another pragmatic scheme of plot analysis that has been current in the twentieth century is the five point analysis which follows. (1) A situation is disturbed. Harmony is disturbed. "The times are out of joint," or "something is rotten in the state of Denmark." (2) The generating circumstance is revealed; that is—the character or action that causes the problem or focuses the conflict for us, is presented. (3) Next follows the involvement or rising action, in which someone is trying a variety of ways to set things right. As Hamlet says,

> The times are out of joint; O cursed spite
> That ever I was born to set it right!
>   (I, v, 188–89)

(4) The climax occurs at the decisive confrontation of the forces for disruption and the forces of harmony, and (5) the close follows: in comedy, there is a reëstablishment of the original situation—harmony is restored, but with a difference, having now been tested by the disruptive force; in tragedy, there is a chaotic destruction of one or both sides of the struggle.[2] Many of our modern playwrights have used such a scheme. (And there are many expositions of it as a method.)

There is nothing inconsistent between this scheme and the classical scheme of plot. The two are merely different ways of looking at material. Both can be used, even simultaneously. Both have the effect of assuring an overall structure. Both familiarize the playwright with his problems. Both create plots. The primacy of action on the stage makes it necessary for the playwright to employ some such scheme, even if it is only in his head. But to depend upon the head and memory, instead of notations and plans, is to flirt with the principles of accident and disaster.

Character

That the playwright has to represent his characters through the actors' performances imposes certain limitations and necessities upon his techniques of characterization. He is as much concerned with the kinds and concepts of character as the fictionist, as much concerned with unity of characterization and with the techniques of revelation, but the presence of actors on stage modifies his practice.

The concepts in the whole gamut of characters, from pawn to hero, are important to the playwright. He must use pawns—to carry a spear, deliver a letter, move a chair, or whatever—but he must be more careful of the pawn than the fictionist. On stage, represented by a human being, the pawn can take on too much life, can actually be a detriment to the interests of the play. The playwright must be sure that he does not let his pawns do or say much, lest they draw too much of the audience's attention. The type offers quite a

---

[2] The choices of tragedy or comedy (or other forms, like burlesque) are, of course, important pragmatic concerns of the playwright, but they are not limited to him. The fictionist and the poet, too, can deal in tragedy and comedy. The characteristics of the genres are already well known (see, for example, the introductory section of T. W. Hatlin's *Drama: Principles and Plays,* Appleton-Century-Crofts, 1967) and are more philosophical than pragmatic; so we have not treated them at length in this book.

different problem: since the type, too, is represented by a human being on stage and thus tends toward roundness, the playwright has to add details that de-humanize the character. Very often this means creating what in fiction would be a stereotype or a caricature. Stereotype and caricature, likewise have to be overdone; in fact, the exaggerations that the actor's presence force the writer into make the type, stereotype, and caricature most useful in, and most common to, comedy and burlesque. The playwright has to work much less than the fictionist to achieve a profile, or a round or fragrant character. The actor's presence does visually and immediately what the fictionist has to recreate through the imagination. On the other hand, the playwright has more trouble with heroic characters: the fixed visual elements of the stage prevent any manipulation of visual analogies, so that the "larger than life" figure has to be represented as larger in conceptual and aesthetic ways. He must generate his stature through empathy and sympathy, without the advantage of any superhuman metaphors. All ways are open to the fictionist, since he has no immediately apprehensible contradiction before his audience. The actor's presence is both an advantage and a disadvantage.

Unity or consistency of characterization is also modified by the actor's presence. On stage, where gesture and word make such a strong and memorable impression upon the audience, the tolerance for inconsistency is diminished. The stage audience is much more likely to detect and deplore a small deviation from the curve of a character's actions than in a fiction, where small details are more likely to be in un-heightened positions. The playwright, then, must be stringently critical, not only in the large outlines and motivations of his characters, but particularly in the incidental and momentary flux. One of the values of a scenario is that it frees the playwright to pay close attention to the texture of the flux.

The practical techniques for revealing character are considerably diminished on stage. The fictionist has his nine generic ways: his main character, his supporting character, and the author, each of which has his speech, his actions, and his thoughts. But on stage, the author is effaced, though not eliminated, and the thoughts of everyone are reduced to inferences or stage conventions. The actor's presence, again, is the strongest single factor, and consequently the main character's speech and action are primary in characterization and reduce our tolerance for inconsistency. His motive and manner must both be made manifest; neither can be left to the imagination. There are, of course, the old stage conventions of the aside or direct address to the audience and the soliloquy or direct address to the self—conventions which have been used as means of announcing the main character's thoughts. But these ways are inherently undramatic, in the sense that they interrupt character, scene, and incident on stage and appeal to a different mode of our knowing. The material thus presented, of course, can be highly interesting it itself and can deepen the drama of moments before and after.

The use of other characters to characterize the main character is diminished in importance on the stage. We can have our gossips, of course, and they can give us valuable information. But generally speaking, the presence of the actor focuses our attention more upon the word and gesture of the actor himself than upon the detail about others which he conveys. The fictionist can, to some extent, hide the personalities of the supporting characters and focus upon what they say about others, but the human being on stage shifts the balance toward characterization of himself. Especially, if he uses any of the conventions for conveying his thoughts to the audience, we tend to see him as a primary character, not as a source of information about others.

The author's role in characterization is everything and nothing. He created the characters, of course, designed the curve of action through which they go, wrote their lines, selected their environment, and so on. But he subordinates, rigorously, his style as an evaluative device to his character's voices as revealing devices; he subordinates his acts of selectivity to the dramatic curve that his characters' motivations define; and he eliminates all direct analysis or conveyance of his thoughts to the audience. In word and action, especially, he effaces himself. He leaves his thoughts to the inferences of the audience, except when he writes prefaces, as George Bernard Shaw did, or commentaries, as Arthur Miller did in the printed version of *The Crucible*. These devices are inherently undramatic, however; the first appeals in the same ways as the essay, the second in the same way as fiction—the printed version of *Saint Joan* is, in fact, an essay with a supporting anecdote; the printed version of *The Crucible* is, in fact, a novel. The playwright is condemned to leave everything dramatic to the inference of the audience—which is not so bad as it sounds, for it forces the audience into participation and heightens the potential impact.

Point-of-View

The playwright's point-of-view is severely limited by the stage and the actors, but he still has fairly rich possibilities to choose from. The use of actors makes the objective, or external point-of-view necessary, for, although they speak for themselves in first-person grammar, they are always "out there," external, presented by an effaced narrator. The use of action condemns the playwright to dramatization; he cannot summarize, except when one of his dramatized characters summarizes. The use of a stage fixes the physical distance for every spectator in the audience. The impetus toward belief and realism usually limits manipulations of time to simple lapses and moderate summary— we jump any amount of time from one scene to another without problem; and we easily accept six hours of action when it is presented in sixty minutes, though there is a limit to our tolerance for compressed time representing actual time.

What the playwright manipulates as point-of-view are conceptual and empathic (or psychic) distance, and whatever inferences he can cause his objective, dramatized, physically and temporally limited representations to arouse. Conceptual distance is, of course, extremely important and differs under particular conditions. The playwright must make certain that the kinds of concepts he is representing in his characters and their actions are not outside the conceptual possibilities of his audience. Differences in audiences once led critics to assert that tragedy was the genre of the court, comedy the genre of the middle class, and burlesque the genre of the peasantry. The prevalence of travelling businessmen in Broadway audiences, as opposed to serious play-goers, may have had some effect on the shift in subject matter toward comic entertainment that has left Broadway so moribund as a national theater. The playwright has to be careful to pitch his concepts at the level of the audience if he wishes to avoid boring them with too simple an offering or avoid con fusing them with one too difficult.

Empathic or psychic distance is the most powerful factor of point-of-view that is at the playwright's disposal. Much has been written about it, since it is directly related to the impact and the working of impact upon the audience. Essentially, psychic distance involves presenting a character in a particular relation to the audience's value system, of showing him in actions that make him admirable or pitiable or noble or deserving or mean or whatever. A member of the audience, in exercising his own value system on the character on stage, comes to intuit a possible exchange of position and situation between himself and the character. This, of course, is psychological identification. It makes possible the powerful impact of drama. The manipulation of psychic distance can be done unconsciously and badly, as in the typical sentimental movie, or it can be done consciously and well, with all the care and knowledge of a sociologist, as in the major plays of Arthur Miller.

Of equivalent importance are the inferences that the playwright can make his imitations carry. He is limited to depicting objective characters, acting dramatically on stage, but he can sometimes make them represent—without violating their objective and dramatic presence—states of mind or modes of experience that cannot be depicted physically. We are all familiar, for example, with the boy who, while riding his bicycle to the grocery store, imagines himself horseback in Indian country. Or the beginning skier who fancies that his snowplow curves have all the dash and speed of the slalom. In *Death of a Salesman*, Arthur Miller managed to depict this kind of internal experience, by dramatizing within the very limits of stage conventions the contents of Willy Loman's fantasies. Characters, physically in a corner of the stage or appearing behind a scrim, acted out Willy's thoughts. In this way, the audience was made to infer what was going on in Willy's head. These inferences made a subjective point-of-view available to the audience.

Style

It is popularly supposed that the playwright subordinates his style completely to the styles of his characters—and so he does at the simplest, linguistic level —but there are many other choices in a play that affect the tone and mood of the product, such as the tone and relationship between styles of characters, the choices of focus and shaping of the dramatic curve, the use of artificial styles, and so on.

Each character must have his own voice, and it must be consistent in itself, but it is the playwright's choice whether a given character will set the tone of a whole scene, or whether a group of characters will set a pace, or whether a particular tone and pace will be allowed to set a mood, and so on. The characters, scenes, and incidents, in a sense, become the language that the playwright manipulates. He can make this language convey different qualities to his audience. His choices are a mark of style.

The arrangements he gives this "language," too, are of his choosing. He can make one scene slow, another fast, another staid, another light or heavy or whatever he chooses. The arrangement he gives a sequence of scenes has a strong influence upon what the audience perceives and remembers. The best example of this manipulation is, perhaps, the standard technique of undercutting before the scene of most dramatic intensity. The playwright, in such a case, would be making deliberate use of the principle of contrast and relying upon the quality that contrast can be made to heighten, or even communicate. Such a choice, too, would be a mark of style.

Style, too, can be used to manipulate other aspects of the drama. The choice to write a play in poetry instead of in ordinary conversation, for example, influences the conceptual distance that is necessarily involved in production. Seeing and hearing a poetic drama is a different experience from seeing and hearing a farce. The playwright can choose to write his particular materials in inflated rhetoric, in poetry, in parody, or whatever. What he chooses marks his style.

Other factors, not always of the playwright's choosing, sometimes influence the total style of a play. If there is music, for example, the playwright must depend upon the composer for a part of the play's total style. He surely would discuss such matters as tone and mood with the composer, but a good deal would necessarily have to be left to the musicians, both in creation and performance. Sometimes, period styles will influence the playwright's choice, as when a playwright adapts an older drama to modern purposes, as Jean Anouilh did *Antigone,* Arthur Miller did *An Enemy of the People,* and Eric Bentley did *The Caucasian Chalk Circle.*

It is true that the playwright's voice is effaced by the actor, director, and set-designer, but this is not to say that his *style* is effaced. The playwright's script is the greatest single determinant of the style of a play, for the playwright's choices in the script are the guide to the choices in a production.

Setting

Setting is the factor that the playwright has traditionally had least to do with. Aristotle disparaged it by remarking that the spectacle was more a result of the dressmaker's craft than of the poet's art. And it is a common happening that the set-designer exceeds the playwright's fondest expectations, by discovering just that combination of setting and lighting that will enhance the dramatic content. We have already discussed the ways in which setting communicates, and such need not be repeated here.

The playwright, of course, indicates in his stage directions, prefaces, and usually in direct conversation with the set-designer, the kinds of things he has in mind. He may indicate the use of scrims (thin drapes which are invisible when back-lighted, but appear as solid as stone when front-lighted), or revolving stages, or the positions of platforms or doors, or whatever. He may yield to the strong practical pressure nowadays toward the one-set play (but that is an economic, not an aesthetic consideration, and many playwrights ignore it). Whatever the playwright decides upon, however, the main act of set creation is the set-designer's, and the playwright's role is limited to suggestion and final approval. These, however, are significant contributions to the final production, and the playwright should be familiar with the effects his suggestions and approvals can have. The complications of set-designing may be sampled in Jo Mielziner's *Designing for the Theatre.*[3]

Structure

Structure, the arrangement for aesthetic purpose of character, scene, and incident, according to the principles of design and pattern, is very important to the playwright. Rather more conscious attention to structure, design, and

---

[3] New York: Atheneum, 1965.

pattern is needed nowadays than in earlier times. Play-goers in, say, the Elizabethan period were more in the habit of committing to memory things which they felt were valuable. Sitting at a play, they could probably remember, with little effort, and perhaps even repeat, important stages in the development of a play or telling detail in the characterization of a role. But since the widespread availability of printed texts, people have felt less need to memorize than their ancestors, and, consequently, the playwright must compensate for the changes in their habits and abilities of attention. It is probable, therefore, that a new play for a contemporary audience has to be better designed than the typical historical play was. The effect of such design, of course, becomes a part of the whole dynamic process.

We have already indicated the kind of effect that such a device as contrast in dramatic intensity can have. Similar effects occur in contrasts between characters, in contrasts within a given character, in individual actions, and in full scenes. Each presentation of a contrast inevitably focuses the audience's attention upon the content of the contrast and helps to make repetition of the ideas less necessary. If related but different contrasts are presented in a graded series, each new contrast can have the effect of "repeating," by calling to mind, the previous situation. The most effective "repetition," however, is the theme and variation. Each variation is recognized as a presentation, in different form, of the original idea, so that there is both the effect of literal repetition and of presenting new material. Restraint in the use of such things as dramatic intensity can give the effect of pause and of fore-knowledge, especially if and when the restraint creates a graded series that leads to a climax. All of these devices have the effect of making the material of the drama more knowable and more memorable to the audience, and, when coupled with the unifying effect of pattern, overcome the limitations of the dynamic process. The use of a scenario in the writing process can ensure effective structure.

Theme

Little need be said here about theme. It is the first and last principle of any literary form and is modified in its particulars by each of them. The general philosophical considerations of theme have already been discussed; and the discussion on the aesthetic materials of drama suggests some of the modifications that are inevitable in stage presentation. It is outside our scope, here, to pursue these issues further, and we must content ourselves with the reminder that, whatever the theme, whether it has been done in one of the other literary forms or not, the quality that marks it as drama is the dynamic mode of knowing.

PROJECTS FOR WRITING AND DISCUSSION

A. ANALYSIS

1. Analyze a well-made play, say one by Henrik Ibsen, by making a scenario of it. Reduce the play to a short summary in one column and analyze in a second column what each of the stages in the summary accomplishes. Apply the same technique to a poorly-made play and see if you can discover what revision would improve it.

2. Come to class prepared to summarize and explicate the primary elements of a Shakespearean play or a Greek drama or a Restoration comedy.

3. Write analytical character sketches of typical characters by such famous dramatists as Shaw, Kaufmann, Rice, Odets, Williams, Miller, and Albee. What kind of character—type, pawn, round, profile, or what?—is typical of each? Can you suggest why each playwright uses the kind of character he does?

B. COMPARISON

1. Compare the plot structures typical of a given playwright with the typical structures of a different one. For example, Chekhov and Ibsen can be profitably compared and contrasted; so can Strindberg and O'Neill, Ionesco and Miller or Tennessee Williams, and so on. What accounts for the dramatic effectiveness of a plot that does not come to a crisis and resolution, as some of Chekhov's do not? To what extent will a firm process of conflict—crisis—resolution serve a playwright in lieu of important material.

2. Compare and contrast different playwright's uses and choices of character, in a similar way. Profitable pairs might include Shaw and Albee, Odets and O'Neill, Brecht and Ibsen, Miller and Williams, and so on.

3. Compare the uses of character and plot in one-act plays with their use in three-act plays. One might even find it profitable to compare one-act plays and three-act plays by the same man; O'Neill and Albee, among others, both wrote successful one-act plays before turning to the full length.

C. IMITATION

1. Analyze some of the more important, historical styles of drama. Then write a scene in imitation of each. For example,
   a. Sophocles and Greek theater conventions
   b. Everyman and the Medieval theater
   c. Shakespeare and Elizabethan theater
   d. Jonson and Renaissance classicism

e. Moliere and the French classical theater
f. Ibsen and realistic theater
g. Chekhov and Stanislavskian method
h. Shaw and the play of ideas
i. Strindberg and expressionism
j. Brecht and epic theater
k. Pirandello and the problem of illusion and reality
l. Odets and proletarian drama
m. O'Neill and psychological drama
n. Genet or Ionesco and absurd drama

2. Analyze some of the more important, historical styles of comedy. Then write a scene in imitation of each. For example,
a. Aristophanes and Greek comedy
b. Plautus and Roman comedy
c. Elizabethan comedy
d. Moliere, as in *The Misanthrope*
e. Sheridan and Restoration comedy
f. Shaw
g. Thornton Wilder

D. *CREATION*

1. There are three stages of preparation in the writing of any drama—the preparation of character sketches or dossiers, the selection and description of the setting, and the writing of a scenario. Go through the preparations for writing some of the following:
a. a burlesque
b. a farce
c. a satire
d. an absurd drama
e. a realistic play
f. a heroic drama or tragedy
g. a national pageant

LYRIC
POETRY

A GREAT deal of very good critical and theoretical writing on poetry has appeared, especially since about 1920. The result is that we have a fairly accurate and widely accepted vocabulary for discussing poetry, especially in regard to prosody and the use of figurative language, less so in matters of strategy and organization. This brief introduction to lyric poetry will put a good deal of that vocabulary into the framework of choices that the writer has to make—will introduce, in other words, some of the patterns of pronunciation, vocabulary, grammar, strategy, and convergence that occur in verse and poetry.

It might be well here to repeat certain basic distinctions: to distinguish poetry from prose is irrelevant, since they are in different realms. Poetry can and should be distinguished from fiction; both are modes of knowing, but the one imitates meditation, the other imitates experience. And verse and prose can and should be distinguished from each other. They are both ways of using language, but verse is organized on the basis of abstract and rhythmic recurrence of audible elements, such as meter, rime, stanza; prose is organized on the basis of syntax. To distinguish a mode of knowing from a way of using language is simple nonsense, when the distinction is offered as if it were the basic dichotomy along a continuum. Both poetry and fiction can exist in either verse or prose.

Verse, then, is not the same as poetry. Most poetry in English has, in fact, been in verse—and this "accident" has brought about the attitudes that everything that is verse is also poetry, and that poetry must be in verse. But verse and poetry have so little in common that they will be discussed in separate chapters.

13

Verse

Verse is limited to the qualities of style that come under the heading of "Pronunciation"; it is made up of patterns of audible rhythm. But that, after all, is quite a lot! Rhythm is the regular recurrence of any element, and, in verse, it is the regular recurrence of any *audible* [1] feature of language—stress, tone, length, rime, and so forth. Carefully controlled and highly formalized patterns of rhythm make up the verse forms; the most important of these forms in English are Hebraic prosody, accentual verse, alliterative verse, alliterative-stress verse, syllabic verse, quantitative verse, accentual-syllabic verse, and the rhythmic patterns generally known as free verse.

Hebraic Prosody in English

Walt Whitman is, of course, the most prominent user of Hebraic prosody in English, but other poets have often made use of the same techniques; see, for example, E. A. Robinson's "Luke Havergal." * Hebraic prosody is not "free," as some critics have asserted; it does not abandon rhythm or control or effective manipulation; but it achieves rhythm in ways not usually discussed in connection with English poetry.

---

[1] The visual patterns of verse have their effect and this gets incorporated into the total response, but the aesthetics of visual patterns in verse are cultural, not literary. They belong more to the world of prejudice than to the world of perception. Cultural patterns in the reception and approval of what looks like verse have conditioned in many a pernicious and non-literary response, a special, false response when they see the "block" upon the page, when they see an even left margin, an uneven right margin, and perhaps a few stanza breaks, or such visual peculiarities as "altar" poems, Easter wings, and that sort of thing. The sense of "reading poetry" causes far too many people to accept and forgive (and pretend to understand) atrocities that they would not tolerate in prose. This problem is social, not literary.

327

Grammatical structures in English have characteristic intonation patterns. Linguists describe these patterns in relation to four levels of pitch—1. low, 2. normal, 3. high, 4. extra high—and three kinds of clause terminals—fading (↘), rising (↗), and sustained (→). The choice and distribution of these tonal features, along with features of stress and juncture (the amount of break or pause between words and clauses), distinguish for us the meaning of an utterance. They account for the differences in meaning between such sentences as:

I'm going home. (*a simple declaration*)
I'm going home? (*meaning, may I go home? and presuming assent*)
I'm going home? (*Did you say, "I'm going home"?*)
I'm going *home*. (*and no place else*)
I'm *going* home. (*all right, all right, I'm going*)
I'm going home. (*regardless of what you do*)

Introductory phrases and dependent clauses at the beginnings of sentences have pitch contours that end in a 2—3 rise, as well as a rising clause terminal (↗). This rise in intonation means that the sentence is not finished; we are left "hanging in the air," waiting for more.

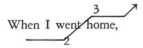

This is a kind of "pronunciation" of the comma that belongs at the ends of such phrases and clauses. Questions that can be answered "yes" or "no" and all but the last item in a series also normally end in such a rising intonation.

Declarative sentences and questions that begin with an interrogative word (*what, how, why*, etc.) characteristically end in a rising-falling intonation pattern—that is, the voice usually rises from normal pitch (level 2) to high pitch (level 3) on the last accent, then falls to low pitch (level 1) during the last syllable. This is the "dying fall" that marks the end of a sentence.

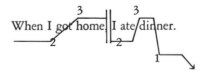

If, however, such an apparently complete utterance as "I ate dinner" ends in a level, sustained intonation (2—2→), the tone means that some coordinate material is following immediately.

                    3   3
      When I got home, I ate dinner and went to bed.
              2   2   2   2
                                                    1

   Clauses also have many other characteristic features. For example, the first
significant stress in a clause will normally have pitch 3. Any syllable singled
out for special emphasis will get pitch 4. Except for other significant syllables
in long clauses, the rest of the clause will usually have pitch 2. Certain kinds
of clauses (such as parenthetical insertions) also have characteristic patterns.
So much, for now, for the immensely complicated business of intonation.
   Intonation contours, thus described, give identity to a string of utterances,
or what in poetry we would call a line. In Hebraic prosody, these phrases or
lines are the units of rhythm, as G. W. Allen showed in *American Prosody*
(1935), which the following analysis essentially follows. When words, sounds,
grammatical structures, images, or certain kinds of images are repeated in successive phrases, we are forced to return to the intonation of the first appearances
of the word, sounds, and so on. Thus, repetition develops a rhythm based on
intonation, rather than on stress, syllable, or alliteration, which most English
poetry depends upon. Scansion—which usually means marking the stressed
and weak syllables and dividing the line into poetic feet—here would consist
of drawing intonation contours to mark pitch, pause, and juncture. The rhetoric
of repeated intonations can be consciously manipulated—can be made slow,
stately, fast, brutal, incantatory, almost anything—by the poet who is conscious
of the techniques at his disposal and who has the skill to use them well. More
specifically, these techniques with examples from Whitman are as follows:

Repetition of Sounds and/or Words Occur in Four Conditions

1. INITIAL REITERATION

> Out of the cradle endlessly rocking,
> Out of the mocking bird's throat, the musical shuttle,
> Out of the ninth-month midnight . . .
>   (from "Out of the Cradle Endlessly Rocking")

2. FINAL REITERATION

> I am the poet of the woman the same as the man,
> And I say it is as great to be a woman as to be a man,
> And I say there is nothing greater than the mother of men.
>   (from Sec. 20, "Song of Myself")

3. MEDIAL REITERATION

> I will know if I am to be less than they,
> I will see if I am not as majestic as they,
> I will see if I am not as subtle and real as they,
> I will see if I am to be less generous than they...
> (from Sec. 18, "By Blue Ontario's Shores")

4. DRIFTING REITERATION

Over the breast of the spring, the land, *amid* cities,
Amid lanes and through old woods, where lately the violets peep'd from the
    ground, spotting the gray debris,
Amid the grass in the fields each side of the lanes, *passing* the endless grass,
Passing the yellow spear'd wheat, every grain from its shroud in the dark-brown
    fields uprisen,
Passing the apple-tree blows...
           (from Sec. 5, "When Lilacs Last..." [italics supplied])

Repetition of Whole Lines

1. SIMPLE REPETITION, AS IN A "FRAME" AROUND A POEM

Joy, Shipmate, Joy

> Joy, shipmate, joy!
> (Pleased to my soul at death I cry.)
> Our life is closed, our life begins,
> The long, long anchorage we leave,
> The ship is clear at last, she leaps!
> She swiftly courses from the shore.
> Joy, shipmate, joy!

2. INCREMENTAL REPETITION

(See "Passage to India," in which cumulative emotion is developed at least partly through incremental repetition of a refrain-like line, each appearance of which is the keynote of its section of the long poem.)

> Passage O soul to India!... (Sec. 2)
> Passage to India!... (Sec. 3)
> Passage to India!... (Sec. 4)
> Passage to India!... (Sec. 6)
> Passage indeed O soul to primal thought,... (Sec. 7)
> Passage to more than India!... (Sec. 9)

Passage to more than India! O secret of the earth and sky!... (Sec. 9)
Passage, immediate passage! the blood burns in my veins! (Sec. 9)

This progression, presumably, could have been given a directly linear development, had Whitman chosen:

Passage to India!...
Passage O soul to India!...
Passage to more than India!...
Passage indeed O soul to primal thought!...
Passage to more than India; O secret of the earth and sky!...

Repetition of the Idea (Four Types of Parallelism from Old Testament Verse)

1. SYNONYMOUS

The last half of a line, or a second line, reinforces the first by repeating the thought:

I too am not a bit tamed, I too am untranslatable,
I sound my barbaric yawp over the roofs of the world.
(from Sec. 52, "Song of Myself")

2. ANTITHETICAL

The second statement contrasts with the first:

Our life is closed, our life begins,
(from "Joy, Shipmate, Joy!")

3. SYNTHETIC OR CUMULATIVE

The second line, or several consecutive lines, supplements or completes the first:

I celebrate myself, and sing myself,
And what I assume, you shall assume,
For every atom belonging to me as good belongs to you.
(from Sec. 1, "Song of Myself")

4. CLIMACTIC OR ASCENDING RHYTHM

Each succeeding line adds to its predecessor, usually taking up words from it and completing the thought:

When Lilacs last in the dooryard bloom'd,
And the great star early droop'd in the western sky in the night,
I mourned, and yet shall mourn with ever-returning spring.
Ever-returning spring, trinity sure to me you bring,
Lilac blooming perennial and drooping star in the west,
And thought of him I love.
                     (from Sec. 1, "When Lilacs last in the Dooryard Bloom'd")

Repetition of Grammatical Structures

1. PARALLEL GRAMMAR

Flow on, river! *flow* with the flood-tide and *ebb* with the ebb tide!
Frolic on, crested and scallop-edged waves!
                     (from Sec. 9, "Crossing Brooklyn Ferry" [italics supplied])

2. SERIES

See the series of sounds in Sec. 26, "Song of Myself": * note the series of nouns, of clauses, and even of sentences.

3. PARENTHETICAL INSERTIONS

Great are the myths—I too delight in them;
Great are Adam and Eve—I too look back and accept them.
                     (from "Great are the Myths")

Imagery and Figures

1. SUGGESTION

Concrete objects, rendered through metaphor and indirection, were involved in Whitman's ideals, as stated in the Preface to the 1855 edition of *Leaves of Grass,* which see.

2. CATALOG LINES

Lists of objects or activities which accumulate vivid emotion. See Sec. 26, "Song of Myself" * for a catalog of sounds.

3. RECITATIVES AND ARIAS

Verbal imitation of Italian opera, which Whitman claimed influenced his verse. See "Give me the Splendid Silent Sun."

Some other examples of Hebraic prosody:

Psalm 23

The Lord is my shepherd;
I shall not want.
He maketh me to lie down in green pastures:
He leadeth me by the still waters.
He restoreth my soul:
He leadeth me in the paths of righteousness for his name's sake.
Yea, though I walk through the valley of the shadow of death,
I will fear no evil:
For thou art with me;
Thy rod and thy staff they comfort me.
Thou preparest a table before me in the presence of mine enemies:
Thou anointest my head with oil;
My cup runneth over.
Surely goodness and mercy shall follow me all the days of my life:
And I will dwell in the house of the Lord for ever.

The Song of Solomon, 5:2–8

I sleep, but my heart waketh:
It is the voice of my beloved knocketh, saying,
Open to me, my sister, my love, my dove, my undefiled:
For my head is filled with dew,
And my locks with the drops of the night.
My beloved put in his hand by the hole of the door,
And my bowels were moved for him.
I rose up to open to my beloved;
And my hands dropped with myrrh,
And my fingers with sweet smelling myrrh,
Upon the handles of the lock.
I opened to my beloved;
But my beloved had withdrawn himself, and was gone;
My soul failed when he spake:
I sought him, but could not find him;
I called him, but he gave no answer.
The watchmen that went about the city found me,
They smote me,
They wounded me;
The keepers of the walls took away my veil from me.
I charge you, O ye daughters of Jerusalem,
If you find my beloved, that ye tell him,
That I am sick of love.

Charity (1 *Cor.* 13)

St. Paul

Though I speak with the tongues of men and of angels,
  and have not charity,
    I am become as sounding brass, or a tinkling cymbal.
And though I have the gift of prophecy,
and understand all mysteries, and all knowledge;
and though I have all faith, so that I could remove mountains,
  and have not charity,
    I am nothing.
And though I bestow all my goods to feed the poor,
and though I give my body to be burned,
  and have not charity,
    It profits me nothing.

Charity suffers long, and is kind;
Charity envies not;
Charity vaunts not itself, is not puffed up,
  Does not behave itself unseemly,
  Seeks not her own,
  Is not easily provoked,
  Thinks no evil,
  Rejoices not in iniquity, but rejoices in the truth;
Bears all things,
Believes all things,
hopes all things,
endures all things.

Charity never fails:
  But whether there be prophecies, they shall fail;
  Whether there be tongues, they shall cease;
  Whether there be knowledge, it shall vanish away.
For we know in part,
And we prophecy in part,
But when that which is perfect is come,
Then that which is in part shall be done away.

When I was a child, I spoke as a child,
      I understood as a child,
      I thought as a child;
But when I became a man, I put away childish things.

For now we see through a glass, darkly;
  But *then* face to face;

Now I know in part,
But *then* I shall know, even as also I am known.
And now abide three things: faith, hope, and charity,
But the greatest of these is charity.

Song of the Sky Loom

Anonymous, from the Tewa Pueblo, New Mexico [2]

O our Mother the Earth, O our Father, the Sky,
Your children are we, and with tired backs
We bring you the gifts that you love.
Then weave for us a garment of brightness;
May the warp be the white light of morning,
May the weft be the red light of evening,
May the fringes be the falling rain,
May the border be the standing rainbow.
Thus weave for us a garment of brightness
That we may walk fittingly where birds sing,
That we may walk fittingly where grass is green,
O our Mother the Earth, O our Father the Sky!

Section 26, "Song of Myself"

Walt Whitman

Now I will do nothing but listen,
To accrue what I hear into this song, to let sounds contribute toward it.
I hear bravuras of birds, bustle of growing wheat, gossip of flames, clack of
sticks cooking my meals,
I hear the sound I love, the sound of the human voice,
I hear all sounds running together, combined, fused, or following,
Sounds of the city and sounds out of the city, sounds of the day and night,
Talkative young ones to those that like them, the loud laugh of work people
at their meals,
The angry base of disjointed friendship, the faint tones of the sick,
The judge with hands tight to the desk, his pallid lips pronouncing a death
sentence,
The heave'e'yo of stevedores unloading ships by the wharves, the refrain of the
anchor lifters,
The ring of alarm bells, the cry of fire, the whirr of swift-streaking engines and
hose carts with premonitory tinkles and colored lights,

---

[2] Translated by Herbert J. Spinden, in *Songs of the Tewa,* 1933; reprinted in **A.**
Grove Day, *The Sky Clears, Poetry of the American Indians.*

The steam whistle, the solid roll of the train of approaching cars,
The slow march played at the head of the association marching two and two,
(They go to guard some corpse, the flag tops are draped with black muslin.)
I hear the violoncello ('tis the young man's heart's complaint),
I hear the keyed cornet, it glides quickly in through my ears,
It shakes mad-sweat pangs through my belly and breast.
I hear the chorus, it is a grand opera,
Ah this indeed is music—this suits me.
A tenor large and fresh as the creation fills me,
The orbic flex of his mouth is pouring and filling me full.
I hear the trained soprano (what work with hers is this?)
The orchestra whirls me wider than Uranus flies,
It wrenches such ardors from me I did not know I possessed them,
It sails me, I dab with bare feet, they are licked by indolent waves,
I am cut by bitter and angry hail, I lose my breath,
Steeped amid honeyed morphine, my windpipe throttled in fakes of death,
At length let up again to feel the puzzle of puzzles,
And that we call Being.

GETTYSBURG ADDRESS [3]

Fourscore and seven years ago our fathers brought forth on this continent a
new nation, conceived in liberty, and dedicated to the proposition that all men
are created equal. Now we are engaged in a great civil war, testing whether that
nation, or any nation so conceived and so dedicated, can long endure. We are
met on a great battlefield of that war. We have come to dedicate a portion of
that field, as a final resting place for those who here gave their lives that that
nation might live. It is altogether fitting and proper that we should do this. But,
in a larger sense, we cannot dedicate—we cannot consecrate—we cannot hallow
this ground. The brave men, living and dead, who struggled here, have consecrated it, far above our poor power to add or detract. The world will little
note, nor long remember, what we say here, but it can never forget what they
did here. It is for us the living, rather, to be dedicated here to the unfinished
work which they who fought here have thus far so nobly advanced. It is rather
for us to be here dedicated to the great task remaining before us,—that from these
honored dead we take increased devotion to that cause for which they gave the
last full measure of devotion—that we here highly resolve that these dead shall
not have died in vain—that this nation, under God, shall have a new birth of
freedom—and that government of the people, by the people, for the people, shall
not perish from the earth.

[3] By Abraham Lincoln.

EPIGRAPH TO *Look Homeward Angel* [4]

. . . a stone, a leaf, an unfound door; of a stone, a leaf, a door. And of all the forgotten faces.

Naked and alone we came into exile. In her dark womb we did not know our mother's face; from the prison of her flesh have we come into the unspeakable and incommunicable prison of this earth.

Which of us has known his brother? Which of us has looked into his father's heart? Which of us has not remained forever prison-pent? Which of us is not forever a stranger and alone?

O waste of loss, in the hot mazes, lost, among bright stars on this most weary unbright cinder, lost! Remembering speechlessly we seek the great forgotten language, the lost lane-end into heaven, a stone, a leaf, an unfound door. Where? When?

O lost, and by the wind grieved, ghost, come back again.

Accentual (and Alliterative) Verse

Accentual verse derives its rhythm from the number and distribution of stressed syllables—that is, the stresses in a phrase, but ignores the number and position of unstressed syllables. It is a common meter in English nursery rimes. Such verses as

> Mother, Mother, I am ill.
> Call the doctor from over the hill.

and

> Pat-a-cake, pat-a-cake; baker's man!
> Bake me a cake as fast as you can;
> Roll it and pat it and mark it with "B,"
> And put it in the oven for Baby and me.

derive their rhythm from phrases of paired stresses. And that rhythm is so strong that children often dance spontaneously to a recitation of such verses. It is interesting to note that the content of the verses is of little importance. Potentially or actually tragic subjects, such as

> Hipsy, hopsy, papa's got dropsy
> Run, run quick, hit him with a stick

[4] By Thomas Wolfe.

elicit the same delight in rhythm as tamer subjects. This may suggest what is possibly the only adult and serious use of the technique—the possibility for an ironic disparity between the rhetoric and the meaning, in which the irony becomes a part of the theme. (The rime in these verses is a more sophisticated matter and will come up later. For the present, one only needs to think of it as a second rhythm, based upon the recurrence of the same sound and laid over, or counterpointed to, the rhythm of stresses.)

Three-stress verse is also possible and occurs in some nursery rimes:

> Hickory, dickory, dock!
> The mouse ran up the clock.
> The clock struck one,
> And down he run;
> Hickory, dickory, dock!

It is a bit difficult to decide if lines 3 and 4 have two or three stresses in them. If three, the verse is quite regular; if two, it has the regular rhythmical pattern of a limerick, which involves a pattern of patterns.

Many ballads in English are also organized on the rhythmic principle of accentual verse. The following is an example from Middle English, but the student of contemporary lyrics should be able to think of some accentual verse in our time, too.

Lord Randall
Anonymous

> "Oh where hae ye been, Lord Randall my son?
> O where hae ye been, my handsome young man?"
> "I hae been to the wild wood: mother, make my bed soon,
> For I'm weary wi' hunting, and fain wald lie down."

> "Where gat ye your dinner, Lord Randall my son?
> Where gat ye your dinner, my handsome young man?"
> "I dined wi' my true love; mother, make my bed soon,
> For I'm weary wi' hunting, and fain wald lie down."

> "What gat ye to your dinner, Lord Randall my son?
> What gat ye to your dinner, my handsome young man?"
> "I gat eels boiled in broo: mother, make my bed soon,
> For I'm weary wi' hunting, and fain wald lie down."

> "What became of your bloodhounds, Lord Randall my son?
> What became of your bloodhounds, my handsome young man?"
> "O they swelled and they died: mother, make my bed soon,
> For I'm weary wi' hunting, and fain wald lie down."

"O I fear ye are poisoned, Lord Randall my son!
O I fear ye are poisoned, my handsome young man."
  "O yes, I am poisoned: mother, make my bed soon,
For I'm sick at the heart, and fain wald lie down."

Alliterative-stress verse is much the same thing, except that it imposes a pattern of alliteration upon the stress pattern. Alliteration is the recurrence of a consonant sound at the beginning of two or more stressed syllables; thus, it is often called beginning or initial rime. Most Anglo-Saxon verse was written in this rhythm. Here is the opening of *Beowulf* with the stresses marked and the alliterative pattern indicated:

Hwaet! we Gár-Déna ‖ in géardágum,	(a:b ‖ a:b)
þeódcýninga ‖ þrým gefrúnon,	(a:b ‖ a:c)
hu þa aéþelíngas ‖ éllen frémedon!	(a:b ‖ a:c)
Oft Scýld Scéfing ‖ scéaþena þréatum	(a:a ‖ a:b)

in which the mark ‖ stands for a caesura, a strong pause that divides the line into two rhythmic parts. Some Middle English verse also used alliteration, as the opening of *Piers Plowman* shows:

In a sómer séson ‖ whan sóft was the sónne,	(a:a ‖ a:a)
I shópe me in shróudes ‖ as I a shépe wére,	(a:a ‖ a:b)
In hábite as an héremite ‖ unhóly of wórkes,	(a:a ‖ a:b)
Went wýde in þis wórld ‖ wóndres to hére.	(a:a ‖ a:b)

This has seemed to many people, then and now, an excessive use of the technique. Alliteration as a structural principle fell out of widespread use by the time of the early modern period and survives today primarily as an occasional pattern that can be used to heighten the reader's attention, though sometimes it is used as mere decoration.

It is still possible to use the technique seriously, as well as for comic effects. Emily Dickinson, in "Safe in Their Alabaster Chambers," avoids overuse of alliteration by mixing accentual and alliterative-stress patterns. W. H. Auden, in "O Where Are You Going," capitalizes on a deliberate overuse of alliteration and, in "The Unknown Citizen," makes use of comic effects more typical of W. S. Gilbert and Ogden Nash than of himself. The technique bears serious experimentation by young poets, for it might offer them "new" patterns.

Safe in Their Alabaster Chambers (J. 216)

Safe in their Alabaster Chambers—
Untouched by Morning and Untouched by Noon—
Sleep the meek members of the Resurrection—
Rafter of satin, and Roof of stone.

Grand go the Years—in the Crescent—above them—
Worlds scoop their Arcs—And Firmaments—row—
Diadems—drop—and Doges—surrender—
Soundless as dots—on a Disc of Snow—

Springs—shake the Sills—But—the Echoes—stiffen—
Hoar—is the Window—and numb—the Door—
Tribes of Eclipse—in Tents of Marble—
Staples of Ages—have buckled there—

Light laughs the breeze in her Castle above them—
Babbles the Bee in a stolid ear,
Pip the Sweet Birds in ignorant cadence—
Ah, what sagacity perished here! [5]

O Where Are You Going

W. H. Auden

"O where are you going?" said reader to rider,
"That valley is fatal when furnaces burn,
Yonder's the midden whose odors will madden,
That gap is the grave where the tall return."

"O do you imagine," said fearer to farer,
"That dusk will delay on your path to the pass,
Your diligent looking discover the lacking
Your footsteps feel from granite to grass?"

"O what was that bird," said horror to hearer,
"Did you see that shape in the twisted trees?
Behind you swiftly the figure comes softly,
The spot on your skin is a shocking disease."

[5] The poem is here arranged as quatrains, as Emily once arranged it and as the verse rhythm demands. Emily seems never to have made a final version of this poem. She wrote stanzas 1 and 4 in 1859, but was unsatisfied with them. In 1861, she wrote stanzas 2 and 3 as possible substitutes for stanza 4, but made no fast decision as to which stanzas were to be used, which rejected. The poem has often been printed as two stanzas (1 and 4; 1 and 2) and as three (1, 2, and 4).

"Out of this house"—said rider to reader,
"Yours never will"—said farer to fearer,
"They're looking for you"—said hearer to horror,
As he left them there, as he left them there.[6]

The Unknown Citizen

W. H. Auden

To JS/07/M/378
This Marble Monument
Is Erected by the State

He was found by the Bureau of Statistics to be
One against whom there was no official complaint,
And all the reports on his conduct agree
That, in the modern sense of an old-fashioned word, he was a saint,
For in everything he did he served the Greater Community.
Except for the War till the day he retired
He worked in a factory and never got fired
But satisfied his employers, Fudge Motors Inc.
Yet he wasn't a scab or odd in his views,
For his Union reports that he paid his dues,
(Our report on his Union shows it was sound)
And our Social Psychology workers found
That he was popular with his mates and liked a drink.
The Press are convinced that he bought a paper every day
And that his reactions to advertisements were normal in every way.
Policies taken out in his name prove that he was fully insured,
And his Health-card shows he was once in hospital but left it cured.
Both Producers Research and High-Grade living declare
He was fully sensible to the advantages of the Installment Plan
And had everything necessary to the Modern Man,
A phonograph, a radio, a car and a frigidaire.
Our researchers into Public Opinion are content
That he held the proper opinions for the time of year;
When there was peace, he was for peace; when there was war, he went.
He was married and added five children to the population,
Which our Eugenist says was the right number for a parent of his generation.
And our teachers report that he never interfered with their education.

---

[6] Note that, except for a few lines, this poem can also be scanned as amphibrachic tetrameter (see p. 348), but the dominant caesuras and the alliteration give it a stronger flavor of accentual-alliterative verse. Note also the repetition of parallel grammatical forms, typical of Hebraic prosody, and the expostulation and reply structure, typical of ballads and Romantic lyrics.

Was he free? Was he happy? The question is absurd:
Had anything been wrong, we should certainly have heard.[7]

Exercise in Accentual Verse

Jerry Gretzinger

Born on a leaf in a forested hollow,
hung on a shadow, I strained to hear
the cricket incisions etched in the air,
scribbled absurdly, "no logic allowed."

Now carved from the summer, cast from the grain,
dust angels sing a redolent song;
my ear limply hanging gathers the tune,
and from furrows of silence, a bird calls my name.

Then brown apple autumn, its fruits at my feet,
counteracts death and supercedes fate;
the liquor that's wrung from caskets of peaches
broadcasts an odor, riming with spring.

Achilles Answers the Envoys
(*The Iliad,* Book IX)

set in accentual heroics by H. C. Brashers

Divine Laertes, Odysseus of many designs,
Openly I say, as say I must,
You're hateful as Hades to coax me like this!
To hide your heart and utter another's!
You'll not persuade me, No, nor other Danaans,
Since we went thankless, after trouble and trial,
After fearsome foes, much rage, and no respite.
He who waits at home shares with him that fights;
The cowardly and the brave both have their honor;
Death comes alike to the toiling and the untoiling;
Why, then, should I fight, that pools no profit
Though I suffer in soul, ever staking my life?
Even as the hovering hen nurtures her brood,
Passing on each morsel, herself going hard without,
So passed I to Agamemnon the spoils of deep-soiled Troy—

---

[7] Note what principles of rhythm make us accept, say, the last four lines of the long first section as four-stress accentual verse. Phrases that normally would have more than one stress are given only the space, "time," and emphasis of a single "musical phrase," as Pound put it, or of a single metrical beat.

And suffered his theft. I have no heart for it more.
Nor do I wish to watch thru many a sleepless night,
Nor pass thru many days, bloody in battle,
Warring with folk for their women's sakes:
Let him sleep with her and take his joy!

Syllabic Verse

Syllabic verse depends for its rhythm upon a fixed number of syllables per line, or a pattern of number of syllables per line, though it often uses, in addition, end-rimes. The system is not native to English and presents many difficulties in English verse.

When the English language reemerged after the Norman-French period, it showed considerable influence from the French of the invaders, and there was considerable debate whether poets ought to measure their verses by the number of stresses, as the Anglo-Saxons had, or by the number of syllables, as French poets did (and do). In languages with little or no regular stress, such as French, syllabic verse is easiest to construct, especially with the aid of rime. Since English stress-patterns solidified, it has been extremely difficult to write syllabic measures in English, though such lines as Milton's

Rocks, caves, lakes, fens, bogs, dens, and shades of death (*Paradise Lost*, II, 621)

and the last line in Tennyson's

> He is not here; but far away
> The noise of life begins again,
> And ghastly through the drizzling rain
> On the bald streets breaks the blank day.
> (*In Memoriam*, sec. 7)

which obviously have too many stresses to fit into the pentameter and tetrameter verse in which they appear, are probably tolerated because of their *syllabic* identity. Indeed, there has been a tendency to pay more attention to syllable count than to stress patterns in English verse, and ten-syllable lines with only three or four stresses are fairly common in pentameter poems.

In the twentieth century, there has been considerable experimentation with syllabic measures. Poets like Robert Bridges, Dylan Thomas, Marianne Moore, W. H. Auden, Kenneth Rexroth, and other have sometimes tried to use syllabics as the rhythmical base of their poems, often in complicated patterns. For example, here is the first stanza from Thomas's "Poem in October," with the syllable count indicated:

It was my thirtieth year to heaven   10
Woke to my hearing from harbor and neighbor wood   12
And the mussel pooled and the heron   9
Priested shore   3
The morning beckon   5
With water praying and call of seagull and rook   12
And the knock of sailing boats on the net webbed wall   12
Myself to set foot   5
That second   3
In the still sleeping town and set forth.   9

Marianne Moore, in "The Fish," experiments with varying line-length in conjunction with rime, and in "Critics and Connoisseurs," with variations upon the basic stanza pattern.

The Fish

wade
through black jade.
    Of the crow-blue mussel-shells, one keeps
    adjusting the ash-heaps;
        opening and shutting itself like

an
injured fan.
    The barnacles which encrust the side
    of the wave, cannot hide
        there for the submerged shafts of the

sun,
split like spun
    glass, move themselves with spotlight swiftness
    into the crevices—
        in and out, illuminating

the
turquoise sea
    of bodies. The water drives a wedge
    of iron through the iron edge
        of the cliff; whereupon the stars,

pink
rice-grains, ink-
    bespattered jelly-fish, crabs like green
    lilies, and submarine
        toadstools, slide each on the other.

All
external
    marks of abuse are present on this
    defiant edifice—
       all the physical features of

ac-
cident—lack
    of cornice, dynamite grooves, burns, and
    hatchet strokes, these things stand
       out on it; the chasm-side is

dead.
Repeated
    evidence has proved that it can live
    on what can not revive
       its youth. The sea grows old in it.

Critics and Connoisseurs

There is a great amount of poetry in unconscious
  fastidiousness. Certain Ming
    products, imperial floor-coverings of coach-
wheel yellow, are well enough in their way but I have seen something
      that I like better—a
         mere childish attempt to make an imperfectly ballasted animal stand up,
         similar determination to make a pup
           eat his meat from the plate.

I remember a swan under the willows in Oxford,
  with flamingo-coloured, maple-
    leaflike feet. It reconnoitered like a battle-
ship. Disbelief and conscious fastidiousness were the staple
    ingredients in its
      disinclination to move. Finally its hardihood was not proof against its
      proclivity to more fully appraise such bits
        of food as the stream

bore counter to it; it made away with what I gave it
  to eat. I have seen this swan and
    I have seen you; I have seen ambition without
understanding in a variety of forms. Happening to stand
    by an ant-hill, I have
      seen a fastidious ant carrying a stick north, south, east, west, till it
        turned on
      itself, struck out from the flower-bed into the lawn,
        and returned to the point

from which it had started. Then abandoning the stick as
  useless and overtaxing its
    jaws with a particle of whitewash—pill-like but
heavy, it again went through the same course of procedure.
        What is
     there in being able
        to say that one has dominated the stream in an attitude of self-defence;
  in proving that one has had the experience
    of carrying a stick

Much of the experimentation in syllabic verse has been severely criticized, because people can't tell it from prose. Indeed, the freedoms that the concept introduces, like those of free verse, invite the dilettante to chop up moderately colorful prose and try to pass it off as poetry. The poets who practice this branch of the art insist that this verse has rhythms of its own, but most people have considerable difficulty in hearing them. And unless these rhythms are supported by fairly ambitious use of other poetic devices, such as metaphor, or compression, or analogy (as above), they are generally failures.

Quantitative Verse

The rhythm in quantitative verse is based upon the duration of sound, not upon stress. Greek and Classical Latin verse are written in quantitative measures, and there have been—in addition to the general, accentual imitation of Greek patterns in accentual-syllabic verse—a few serious attempts to adapt Classical patterns to English.

One of the most notable experiments is Swinburne's imitation of Sapphics. The sapphic stanza is three lines of the pattern — ⌣ — — — ‖ ⌣ ⌣ — ⌣ — ≍ and a fourth in the pattern — ⌣ ⌣ — ≍ Long syllables are marked (—), short syllables (⌣), and deliberately ambiguous syllables (≍).

> All the night sleep came not upon my eyelids,
>   Shed not dew, nor shook nor unclosed a feather
> Yet with lips shut close and with eyes of iron
>   Stood and beheld me.
>
> Then to me so lying awake a vision
>   Came without sleep over the seas and touched me,
> Softly touched mine eyelids and lips; and I, too,
>   Full of the vision
>
> Saw the white implacable Aphrodite, . . .

Another good example is Tennyson's imitation of Alcaics m his "Milton." The Alcaic stanza is two lines of the pattern — — ‿ — — ‖ — ‿‿ — ‿ ⹊followed by — — ‿ — — — ‿ — — and — ‿ ‿ — ‿ ‿ — ‿ — ‿

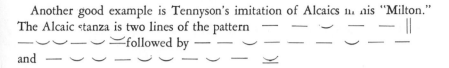

> O mighty-mouthed inventor of harmonies,
> O skilled to sing of Time or Eternity,
> God-gifted organ-voice of England,
> Milton, a name to resound for ages;

The most immediate and obvious problem with quantitative verse is, of course, our unfamiliarity with quantities as a basis for language; we simply do not hear (or pay attention to) duration. Even Robert Bridges, whose experiments in Classical prosodies are the most ambitious and generally thought the most successful in modern poetry, found quantities difficult. "Before writing quantitive verse it is necessary to learn to *think* in quantities. This is no light task, and a beginner requires fixed rules." [8] Bridges's own rules for determining the quantitative value of vowels are: "Vowel sounds are long not only by nature; many short vowels may be lengthened by position, the principle being that a short vowel followed by two or more consonants makes a long syllable, when one at least of the consonants is sounded with it."

Most people cannot hear this kind of verse accurately, and so must depend upon someone else's abilities and trust to their accuracy. Here is Albert J. Guérard's scansion of the first seven lines of "Wintry Delights," one of Bridges's most important "Poems in Classical Prosody" in the Oxford Edition:

```
 —  ‿  ‿    —  —    —   —   —   —    —  ‿  ‿    —  ‿
Now in win | try de | lights, and | long fire | side medi | tation,
 —   —    —  —    —  —   —  —    —    ‿  ‿    —  ‿
Twixt stud | ies and | routine | paying due | court to the | muses,
 —  ‿  ‿    —  ‿  ‿   —  —    —   —    —  ‿  ‿    —  ‿
My solace | in soli | tude, when | broken | roads barri | cade me
 —   —    —  ‿  ‿   —  ‿   —   —    —  ‿  ‿    —  ‿
Mudbound, | unvisit | ed for | months with | my merry | children
 —   —    —  ‿  ‿   —  ‿    —   —    —  ‿  ‿    —  ‿
Grateful | t'ward Provid | ence, and | heeding a | slander a | gainst me
 —  ‿  ‿    —   —    —  —    —   —    —‿‿   —  —
Less than a | rheum, think of | me to | day, dear | Lionel, | and take
 —  ‿  ‿   ‿   —   —    —   —    —  ‿  ‿    —  ‿
This letter | as some a | ccount of | Will Stone's | versifi | cation.[9]
```

[8] Robert Bridges, *Poetical Works* (Oxford Edition, 1953), p. 408.

[9] *paying* in line 2 is elided; said Bridges in a prefatory note in the Oxford edition: "I have used and advocate Miltonic elision," p. 408. Note also *t'ward* in line 5. *A/ccount* in line 7 is so divided because the geminated consonant here counts as a single letter. For more information, see Albert J. Guérard, *Robert Bridges: A Study of Traditionalism in Poetry*, Cambridge, Mass.: Harvard Univ. Press, 1942, 1965.

This should sufficiently indicate the strangeness of Classical prosodies in English and suggest the difficulty of hearing rhythm based upon duration or of scanning it accurately.

Accentual-Syllabic Verse

Accentual-syllabic verse derives its rhythm from the combination of accentual and syllabic patterns. It involves a series of fixed concepts, beginning with the poetic foot and progressing through the line, the stanza, and the set forms, such as the sonnet. The concepts and the names of the feet and the line come to us from Greek prosody, though relative presence and absence of stress in English have been substituted for length and shortness of sounds in Greek. The stanzas and the set forms come to us from a variety of sources, principally the Romance literatures.

The foot

The poetic foot is itself a pattern of un-stressed and stressed syllables, which we mark respectively (◡) and (╱). The feet usually mentioned are:

iamb	◡ ╱	spondee	╱ ╱
anapest	◡ ◡ ╱	amphimacer	╱ ◡ ╱
trochee	╱ ◡	pyrrhic	◡ ◡
dactyl	╱ ◡ ◡	amphibrach	◡ ╱

The iamb is by far the most common foot in English speech, and the anapest runs second. Indeed, it is rather difficult to get truly trochaic or dactyllic verse in English, for they have a habit of sounding iambic or anapestic. The four in the right column are often ignored by modern prosodists and some linguists think the spondee and pyrrhic actually impossible.

Each foot, of course, has its own characteristics and the writer must decide for himself which he thinks is abrupt in tone, which stately, which smooth, and so on. Here is Samuel Coleridge's idea of such tones:

Metrical Feet: Lesson for a Boy

Trochee trips from long to short.
From long to long in solemn sort
Slow spondee stalks; strong foot! yet ill able
Ever to come up with Dactyl trisyllable.

Iambics march from short to long;—
With a leap and a bound the swift Anapests throng.
One syllable long, with one short at each side,
Amphibrachys haste with a stately stride.

The line

The lines are named for the type of foot (which identifies the accentual pattern) and the number of feet (which identifies the number of syllables); thus the name of this kind of verse: accentual-syllabic. The most common lengths of lines are:

1 foot—monometer	4 feet—tetrameter
2 feet—dimeter	5 feet—pentameter
3 feet—trimeter	6 feet—hexameter

Thus a line of five iambs is called an iambic pentameter line; a line of two trochees, trochaic dimeter, and so on.

Each of these line lengths, like each of the feet, has its own quality of tone. Pentameter and hexameter have long been sanctioned as the "proper" voice of heroic and epic verse, though hexameter in English has a strong tendency to break into two trimeters or some other combination. Monometer and dimeter tend to be a bit awkward, but some people like them. Along with trimeter, they are typical of much comic verse. Alternating trimeter and tetrameter is typical of song. Oliver Wendell Holmes, Sr., who was a physician as well as a poet, thought that iambic tetrameter was the line most congenial to the human being, because, he thought, it most nearly approximated the normal rate of breathing. Holmes overlooked the fact that some of us breathe more slowly than others and that we breathe at different rates when we are afraid or angry or asleep—that is, during the normal affective states that poetry can produce. The young writer again must decide for himself which line best communicates the quality he wants.

Scansion

The act of putting the marks in a line of verse to indicate the unstressed and stressed syllables and to mark off the separate feet is called scansion. For example, the opening line of Longfellow's "Hymn to the Night" would be scanned as iambic pentameter, thus:

Ĭ heárd | thĕ tráil | ĭng gár | mĕnts óf | thĕ Níght

Or, the opening of his "Proem" to *Evangeline* is dactyllic hexameter, with the last foot short one syllable:

$$/ \smile \smile \quad / \smile \smile \quad / \smile \quad \smile \quad / \quad \smile \smile \quad / \quad \smile \smile \quad / \quad \smile$$

This is the | forest pri | meval. The | murmuring | pines and the | hem locks, |

Or, his opening to the "Introduction" to Hiawatha is trochaic tetrameter:

$$/ \quad \smile \quad / \smile \quad / \quad \smile \quad / \smile$$

Should you | ask me, | whence these | stories? |

(Longfellow was often a master of verse, seldom of poetry.)

There are real problems with such a system of scansion, because the system of marks does not correspond to the system of stresses in the English language. English scansion has always been defined as a simple contrast between unstressed and stressed syllables. But descriptive linguists, such as H. A. Gleason, Jr., from whom some of the following remarks are borrowed,[10] have shown that English phonology should be described as involving four stresses —from strongest to weakest: primary ($/$), secondary ($\wedge$), tertiary ($\diagdown$), and weak ($\smile$). Awareness and use of this four unit system helps us to understand some fairly complex elements of English rhythms that the traditional system cannot explain, and helps us also to scan accurately when marking with the two-unit system.

There are two general rules of scansion. First, every syllable is judged in the context of its foot and is assigned a relative, rather than an absolute, mark. Thus, any higher stress, preceded by a weaker stress, would be accented. Not only would a weak-primary progression ($\smile /$) be marked as an iamb; so would weak-tertiary ($\smile \diagdown$), weak-secondary ($\smile \wedge$), tertiary-secondary ($\diagdown \wedge$), tertiary-primary ($\diagdown /$), and secondary-primary ($\wedge /$). Second, according to descriptive linguists, the second of two identical stresses is accented, the first unaccented—which means that two *identical* stresses cannot occur together in English. This means that progressions which we evaluate as primary-primary ($//$), secondary-secondary ($\wedge\wedge$), tertiary-tertiary ($\diagdown\diagdown$), and weak-weak ($\smile \smile$), are also iambs. This makes the spondaic and pyrrhic feet impossible in English.

Thus there are at least ten kinds of iambs in English, not just one.[11] If we use these ten iambs in scanning some fairly complex verse, we discover some interesting things. Take the opening quatrain of Shakespeare's Sonnet 30, for instance:

---

[10] See his *Linguistics and English Grammar* (New York: Holt, 1965), pp. 426–428.
[11] If we consider such a linguistic element as juncture, as Edmund A. Epstein and Terence Hawkes do in their *Linguistics and English Prosody*, 1959, there are more than ten.

When to | the sess | ions of | sweet sil | ent thought |
I sum | mon up | remem | brance of | things past, |
I sigh | the lack | of man | y a thing | I sought, |
And with | old woe | new wail | my dear | time's waste. |

With the exception of the trochaic substitution in the first foot of the first line and the anapestic substitution in the fourth foot of the third line (both traditionally sanctioned means of securing variety), it is quite regular iambic pentameter, but iambic pentameter with a difference. One *can* read almost all of the feet with weak-primary stress, if one tries hard, but then one hears doggerel. Shakespeare avoids the doggerel quite nicely by using a variety of the ten kinds of iambic feet named above. In line one, for instance, he forces us to "accent" one of the weakest words in the language—"of"—by preceding it by an even weaker syllable. And in the foot following, he forces us to read a very strong word—"sweet"—as weak, by subordinating it to an even stronger syllable. Thus he achieves, in the two feet, a rising progression through the four varieties of stress. He achieves the same quality in the fourth and fifth feet of the second line, and again in the first two feet of the fourth line. Further, his use of three secondary-primary feet in the fourth line slows that line so much that it wails with the woe it carries. Such ambitious variety in verse-making is by no means accident among the great poets.

"With at least ten kinds of iambs to choose from in each foot," writes Gleason,

there would be some 100,000 differently scanning pentameter lines. No wonder there can be such a difference from one poem to another, even though both follow the same conventions!

Epstein and Hawkes makes a detailed examination of twenty-one lines of *Samson Agonistes.* In this passage every one of the ten types of iambs is used at least twice. The commonest one, (∪ ∕), averages only once per line. This diversity of feet is one of the features of the poem which can be said to characterize its style.

For comparison, *Trees,* an iambic tetrameter of very different quality, contains nineteen feet of the form (∪ ∕) out of forty-eight and uses in all only seven of the total possible types of iambs. Part of the difference in style which anyone will sense between these two poems is reflected in this very different patterning: one tends to concentrate very heavily on a few kinds of iambs—generally those with sharp difference between the stresses. The other tends toward full exploitation of the resources of the iambic meter.

In both there are places where different interpretations are possible, and another reading might give slightly different results. But no feasible reading could obscure the difference. Indeed, it is easy enough to exaggerate it *Trees* seems to present a constant temptation to recital in a style that approaches (ᴗʌ|ᴗʌ|ᴗʌ| ᴗ⁄).[12]

That is, with three iambs of secondary stress and a fourth of primary stress, or what amounts to sing-song or doggerel. Gleason points out on p. 434 that the tendency of major grammatical boundaries (clause ends) to coincide with major metrical boundaries (line ends) contributes to the doggerel quality of *Trees,* and that quite the opposite situation is true of *Samson Agonistes.*

Such [doggerel] recitation is perhaps possible with *Samson Agonistes* also, but rather than slipping into it, a reader must make a conscious effort to do so. Every verse is open to doggerel rendition, some only with great difficulty, some easily, and some permit no other.[13]

Doggerel, then, is excessive regularity. To avoid it, vary the differences in stress within the foot and from foot to foot, use occasional polysyllabic words which bridge more than one foot, vary the time lapse between feet, substitute other kinds of feet for the regular foot, and use some run-on and some mid-stop lines. In stanzas, slant rimes may help (as *haste/test* in the example below).

One might note, in passing, that most popular songs and church psalms also lend themselves easily to doggerel recitation. For example, one of Isaac Watt's hymns:

> That awful day will surely come,
> Th' appointed hour makes haste,
> When I must stand before my judge,
> And pass the solemn test.

is easy to recite in a wooden manner, but if the song is sung, one doesn't notice that quality at all. Indeed, it may be that lyrics which are meant to be sung have to be wooden so that they will contrast with the rich, varied, and artificial patterns that the music imposes upon the words. As with children's rimes, the meanings of the words in church and at teen-age dances are of very little import.

Other Audible Patterns

There are usually in poetry in English other audible patterns besides the pattern of stresses; the most important of these are rime, alliteration, assonance, consonance, and onomatopoeia.

[12] *Linguistics and English Grammar,* pp. 427–28.
[13] *Ibid.*

Rime is the recurrence of a vowel and a consonant sound at the end of a word, as in *rime-chime*. When such a sound recurs with regularity, it heightens attention and recalls to mind the first occurrence of the sound. It is often used as a kind of punctuation at the ends of lines and stanzas and, thus, helps us hear and identify those larger patterns. It has been tremendously important in English poetry, because of our aesthetic delight in perceiving it in patterns.

Rimes in English are variously described as strong rimes, in which a vowel and consonant group are repeated, as in *hate/gate;* exact rime, in which the same word, or more properly, the same sound is repeated, as in *beat/beat;* eye rime, in which the same letters are repeated but have different pronunciations, as in *come/home;* conventional rime, in which tradition sanctions the use of certain sounds as if they were something else, as in *eye/ditty;* weak rime, in which an accented syllable is rimed with a weak one, as in *wing/riding;* masculine rime, in which terminal accented syllables are rimed, as in *sent/occident;* feminine or double rime, in which a strong rimed syllable is followed by an identical weak syllable, as in *waiting/gyrating;* triple rime, in which a strong rimed syllable is followed by two identical syllables, as in *intensity/propensity.* Each of these kinds of rime is said to have its own qualities—some are definitely comic, others serious. Again, the student has to decide for himself the qualities each produces, for each one of them is always modified by context and by the general tone.

Alliteration is the recurrence of a sound or sounds at the beginning of stressed syllables, as in *summer season.* As has already been noted, it can serve, like rime, to help us identify patterns, and it heightens our attention when we hear it.

Assonance is the recurrence of a vowel sound in stressed syllables that have different consonant sounds, as in George Eliot's "*On* a stream of *ether* floating." The example is really two examples: one of the recurrence of "o's," the other, of "e's." As the example demonstrates, it is possible to organize such vowels into patterns. Further, these patterns are capable of very subtly reinforcing other elements in the sound patterns; they can be made to harmonize with the sense, contrast to it, imitate it (as the sequence e-i-o might be said to imitate an opening movement), or otherwise call the reader's attention to something of import.

Consonance is the recurrence of consonants in a series of syllables, as in Keats's "Much ha*v*e I trave*l*ed in the rea*l*ms of go*l*d." English consonants are said to be liquid (l, m, n, r), labial (b, f, p, v), dental (t, d, ch, st, th), gutteral (k, g), sibilant (s, z, j, sh), or aspirant (h). It is possible to arrange these consonants in patterns that are easy to pronounce or hard to pronounce, that move fast or slow, that enhance or detract from a subject. The recurrence of the same consonants in the example (but note that they are not alliterative) gives the line a round rhetoric, almost of the grand style, which gets incorporated into our reaction to the verse. *Dissonance* is the opposite quality and can be used also. Emily Dickinson, in the line "Requires sorest need," forces us with difficult combinations to pronounce each word separately, more clearly, and more slowly, than we would, had the sounds been consonant.

Onomatopoeia is a special use of alliteration, assonance, and consonance to imitate, through sound, the meaning in the words, as in Tennyson's "the moan of doves in immemorial elms,/and the murmuring of innumerable bees."

Stanzas

Often the lines of poetry are organized into patterns called *stanzas*. Beginning with the simplest, the most common stanza forms are:

the couplet	two lines of any length, riming *aa*
the triplet	three lines of any length, riming variously, most often in the form of *terza rima*
terza rima	a series of triplets with an interlocking rime-scheme—that is, a rime carried over from stanza to stanza: *aba, bcb, cdc,* etc.
the quatrain	four lines, riming variously, for example, *aabb, abcb, abab, abba;* special cases include the following:
ballad stanza	a special case of quatrain, in which the first and third lines are tetrameter, the second and fourth are trimeter, and the trimeter lines rime (as the tetrameter lines sometimes do)
elegaic stanza or heroic quatrain	four lines of iambic pentameter, riming *abab*
quintain	five lines
sextain or sextet	six lines
Chaucerian stanza	seven lines of iambic pentameter, riming *ababbcc;* also called rime royal

ottava rima	eight lines of iambic pentameter, riming *abababcc*
Spenserian stanza	nine lines, eight of iambic pentameter followed by an Alexandrine (iambic hexameter), and riming *ababbcbcc*

The Sonnet

These last three stanza forms, especially, border on the concept of the fixed form, a stanza or a number of stanzas in which the relationships are fixed. The most common example is the sonnet.

THE PETRARCHAN OR ITALIAN SONNET

The Petrarchan sonnet is made up of fourteen lines of iambic pentameter, organized into two parts: the Octave, riming *abba, abba,* and presenting a thought, concept, or emotion; and the Sextet, riming *cde, cde,* or *cdcdcd,* and containing an answer, a contrast, a reflection, or in some other way resolving the idea in the Octave.

Divina Commedia: I

Henry Wadsworth Longfellow

Oft have I seen at some cathedral door
  A laborer, pausing in the dust and heat,
  Lay down his burden, and with reverent feet
  Enter, and cross himself, and on the floor
Kneel to repeat his paternoster o'er;
  Far off the noises of the world retreat;
  The loud vociferations of the street
  Become an undistinguishable roar.
So, as I enter here from day to day,
  And leave my burden at his minister gate,
  Kneeling in prayer, and not ashamed to pray,
The tumult of the time disconsolate
  To inarticulate murmurs dies away,
  While the eternal ages watch and wait.

THE SHAKESPEAREAN OR ENGLISH SONNET

The Shakespearean sonnet is made up of fourteen lines of iambic pentameter, usually riming *abab, cdcd, efef, gg;* the organization of idea varies: sometimes the three stages of some growth are presented in the three quatrains and a quintessence or an epigram in the final couplet; sometimes the movement is thesis-antithesis-synthesis-epigram; sometimes it is a syllogism; sometimes the division is 8–6, sometimes 12–2.

Sonnet 30

William Shakespeare

When to the sessions of sweet silent thought
I summon up remembrance of things past,
I sigh the lack of many a thing I sought,
And with old woe new wail my dear time's waste:
Then can I drown an eye, unused to flow,
For precious friends hid in death's dateless night,
And weep afresh love's long since cancelled woe,
And moan the expense of many a vanished sight:
Then can I grieve at grievances foregone,
And heavily from woe to woe tell o'er
The sad account of fore-bemoaned moan,
Which I new pay as if not paid before.
    But if the while I think on thee, dear friend,
    All losses are restored and sorrows end.

Spenser and Milton have worked special variations of the sonnet form: Spenser used his intricate interlocking rime-schemes, of which he was so fond—for example, *abab, bcbc, cdcd, ee;* Milton often used the Petrarchan form, but sometimes wrote what is called a single-statement sonnet, in which there is no division of idea; see "On His Deceased Wife."

A number of other fixed forms have fascinated various poets in English —the villanelle, the triolet, the rondeau, the rondel, the ballade, the sestina, among others. These are fairly sophisticated matters and beyond our scope here. The interested student is referred to a good dictionary or to an appendix on prosody in some large anthology of poetry in English.

Nor will we here illustrate accentual-syllabic measures extensively, since most of the examples in the rest of the book are ample illustration.

The poet who chooses to write in accentual-syllabic meters assumes the advantages and the curses of tradition. The advantages are that the reader recognizes the forms in the poetry and comes to them with a certain burden of preconception and a certain readiness to react in established patterns. The poet can depend upon these preconceptions to aid his communication. The curses are that the reader recognizes the forms in the poetry and comes to them with a certain burden of preconception and a certain readiness to react in established patterns. These preconceptions can lead the reader astray, can cause him to expect things that are not there, and, consequently, can cause him to close his mind to new possibilities. Tradition makes possible some of the great poetry in English and makes possible also some of the worst. This paradox and the dissatisfaction it suggests were responsible for the searches for alternative rhythmical modes in the twentieth century,—Bridges's experiments with syllabic and quantitative verse on the one hand and the "free" verse movement on the other.

Free Verse

The free verse movement is best understood, perhaps, as a reaction to the trite use of accentual-syllabic measures. Centuries of accentual-syllabic usage had imposed upon poetic thinking a set of strictures, and many young poets began to think that all that could be said in those rhythms had been said. Walt Whitman reacted, in part, by introducing Hebraic measures in English. Gerard Manley Hopkins, in his time, tried to reintroduce sprung rhythm, a counterpointing of accentual rhythms with conventional measures, which he said had not been used in English since about 1600. Robert Bridges experimented with syllabics, especially in conjunction with Classical measures. And in the second and third decades of the twentieth century, there flourished a generation of experimental poets—Ezra Pound, T. S. Eliot, William Carlos Williams, Hilda Doolittle, Wallace Stevens, Marianne Moore, among others —whose successes and failures have come to be known as the free verse movement.

These experimenters began by trying to eliminate from poetry as many elements of conventional prosody as they could, and by modifying those they could not. They ignored the concepts of the poetic foot, of meter, of rime, of everything that tended to produce "jingling" regularity in traditional verse. They preserved the concept of the line, so that their poems appeared in blocks on the page, that is, with even left margins, uneven right margins, but they introduced compulsive and continual variations in line to counteract any tendency to create jingle. The ideal was, as Ezra Pound wrote, to compose in the musical phrase, with absolute precision and concision of thought compensating for the weak or non-existent rhythm. That is to say, Pound was working toward a conception of poetry without rhythm—which is a topic of *poetry*, not of verse, and which will be taken up in chapter 14.

However, Pound's concept of the "musical phrase" and William Carlos Williams's concept of the "spoken phrase" (which dates from about the same time, between 1909 and 1912) have important implications in the study and practice of free verse rhythms. Pound wrote about the "musical phrase" in quantitative or durational terms. Everyone knows, he said, that a musical phrase may consist of one whole note, or four quarter notes, or a combination of quarter and eighth notes and even smaller quantities; so, too, in poetry, one word may be "musically" as long as several other words. Its quantity, for Pound, was made up of its aesthetic weight, its descriptive precision, and certain phonological elements—assonance, consonance, dissonance. Thus, a line like Emily Dickinson's, quoted earlier:

Requires sorest need

is made longer than its redaction, which has more syllables:

Requires the sorest need

by the dissonance, which stops pronunciation, as opposed to the liquid regularity of the redaction, which speeds pronunciation.

Williams, too, thought of poetry as constructed in more or less equal-sized phrases, but he measured phrases by their relative accent, as well as their duration. Williams discovered that, in the normal patterns of spoken English, each phrase had only one primary accent and might have a varying number of secondary accents and unaccented syllables. The phrase became a kind of poetic foot for Williams. His discovery, incidentally, corresponds to the later discovery by descriptive linguists that only one primary accent can exist between two closed junctures, that is, in what is phonologically distinguishable as a phrase.

These early theories of Pound and Williams made it possible for Yvor Winters, an early practitioner of free verse, to describe it as a special subdivision of accentual verse.[14] Winters believed that free verse did not eliminate audible patterns of rhythm, but only modified them. He uses primary and "secondary" accents in scanning (his secondary accent is the tertiary accent of descriptive linguistics—see p. 350), but he pays little or no attention to the number and distribution of unaccented syllables. He also marks "irregular lines," lines that depart from the pattern. Thus he scans a poem by William Carlos Williams:

To Waken an Old Lady

Old áge is
a flìght of smáll
chèeping bírds
skímming
bare trées
abòve a snów glaze.

<hr>

[14] See "The Influence of Meter on Poetic Convention," *In Defense of Reason* (Denver: Alan Swallow, 1947), pp. 103–155.

*Gáining and fáiling
thèy are búffeted
by a dárk wind—
but whát?
Òn the hàrsh wéedstalks
the flóck has rèsted—
the snów
is cóvered with bròken
séed-husks,
and the wìnd témpered
with a shríll
*píping of plénty.[15]

The poets and critics of the movement have differed considerably on the issue of rhythm in free verse. Williams, especially in his early poems, preferred the single-stress or monometer line. A great many free verse poems, perhaps a majority of them, are written in two-stress lines, which suggests an added similarity to Anglo-Saxon verse. Some poets, notably Wallace Stevens, have composed very good verse in three-stress lines (see, for example, his "The Snow Man," *) and even in four-stress lines. Pound mixed all these, and more, in a rhythmic aesthetic that only he seems to have understood.

Some of the poets and critics deny the possibility of the other audible elements. Some say assonance and consonance are the only remaining audible patterns. Some admit alliteration in moderation. Others introduce syllabic concepts. Most use tertiary and primary accents in complicated patterns. All depend heavily upon their "ear" and taste. In the following poem, deliberate use is made of several of these devices.

Travelers

Kenneth Johnson

Inside my brain;
tangled in blankets
long since rubbed bald
of woolen down;
wearing bruised clothes:

[15] The scansion is from *In Defense of Reason,* pp. 117–18. Lines 7 and 18 are irregular, and are marked with an asterisk, because they contain two primary accents, although the metrical basis of the poem is one primary accent per line. One of the ideals was never to repeat, if possible, the accent pattern of any line in the poem; otherwise the poet was inviting the jingle of traditional rhythm. On the other hand, as Albert Guérard pointed out in his *Robert Bridges* (p. 246), "The principle of perpetual variety in meter usually leads to monotony."

the Don
     and Sancho
clumsily sleep . . .
Till the dawn-wind scuffs
their skin; and, slowly,

on legs the cold
stiffened to stilts,
they rise; teeter
in the bleary air;
scratch. Then saddle

and mount the remains
of their horse, their donkey,
and, still wordless,
resume
the usual pace.

While I, in my room,
no longer reading
the book, nor watching
the smoke from my cigarette
thaw into air,

I—not thin, not fat,
yet lean as the one,
paunchy as the other—
I doggedly follow
their bobbing backs.

The great contribution of free verse to our knowledge of rhythm is an awareness of the wide varieties of speed that language can be made to achieve. In the practice of Williams, the short, run-on lines, and the continual variation prevent a reader from ever being stopped by the rhythm, so that the poem approximates a breathless rush down the page. Dr. Williams recognized this quality and attributed it to his own nervous nature. On the other hand, Pound's short, truncated, dash-stopped lines, his dissonant progressions, and his dislocated syntax have the effect of stopping a reader and slowing the poem almost to a standstill, almost to the condition of observing a picture or an ideograph.

Free verse made two, very important contributions to our lore of poetry. For one thing, it freed the vocabulary that poets could use, by making available curiously accented or long words that had been eliminated before. This new vocabulary encouraged the second contribution: that of focusing the reader importantly upon the image as the basic element of the rhetoric. Both of these matters, however, are related to poetry, not verse, and will be treated in chapter 14.

The disadvantages of free verse are considerable. In the early work of Williams, the demands for variation and speed limit the poet to relatively short poems and to relatively minor, external subjects. Pound's ideographic method has the same effect. The form does not lend itself easily to philosophical speculation, except in the violation of its precepts. Williams, in his later poems, introduces repetitive patterns of intonations that are comparable to Hebraic prosody. Pound introduces the organizational principle of the anthology, which is larger but rhythmically very much like Stevens's use of fixed stanza and variant repetitions of images and expression in "Sunday Morning." Such reluctant returns to traditional elements were typical of the reaction to free verse that set in about 1930. The liberties of free verse had made it rhythmically indistinguishable from prose, and the writers were discovering—as writers today must, who wish to use the form—that they needed a source of poetic power other than audible rhythm, for free verse, as verse, can supply none.

PROJECTS FOR WRITING AND DISCUSSION

A. ANALYSIS

1. Analyze the prosodic base of each of the samples of Hebraic verse. Point out which repetitions create rhythm, which support it, and which are irrelevant to it.

2. Rearrange the two prose passages—Lincoln's Gettysburg Address * and Thomas Wolfe's epigraph to *Look Homeward, Angel*—* to be printed as verse. Do they gain or lose anything by the rearrangement?

3. Scan "Lord Randall." * Why can you not account for its rhythm using accentual-syllabic concepts? What is the effect of the very firm caesura in each line?

4. Scan W. H. Auden's "The Unknown Citizen," * according to the way it would be read aloud. Then scan it according to accentual-syllabic techniques. How do you account for the differences? For example, the line, "When there was peace, he was for peace; when there was war, he went," would have seven accents, seven iambic feet, if it were in an accentual-syllabic poem. Here it is read as having only four. Why? At what point in the poem can you say Auden has established his rhythmic base?

5. Devise a scheme for analyzing the prosody of "The Fish." * Does the poem have rhythm? How can you describe it? Try describing it, for instance, to a person whose native language is not English.

B. *COMPARISON*

1. Scan a selection of poems from the next chapter. Try to account for the rhythmic qualities of each. For example, why is much of Wordsworth's "I Wandered Lonely as a Cloud" * so wooden as to be doggerel to our ears? Why is Marvell's "A Dialogue between *The Resolved Soul* and *Created Pleasure"* * almost symphonic in its rhythmic organization?

2. Scan several of Emily Dickinson's poems from chapters 14 and 15. Is she consistent in each poem? If she is inconsistent, does her inconsistency add anything—that is, does the rhythmic inconsistency become a part of the theme?

3. Compare the rhythmic bases of "Charity" (1 *Cor.* 13) * and Lincoln's Gettysburg Address.* Both of them have if-then concepts in their themes. How does this affect the poems? What differences and similarities do you notice?

4. What differences can you see between one of the syllabic poems and the free verse poem? Are these differences audible? Are they effective as verse? What effect has the destruction of the sound of line-identity on the rhythmic natures of the poems?

5. Compare the narrative sections of "The Song of Solomon" * and "Critics and Connoisseurs." * What differences in rhythm do you notice? What are the effects of the differences? What similarities do you notice? What effect?

C. *IMITATION AND CREATION*

1. Here is what amounts to a prose paraphrase of a poem, the crude matter out of which a poem might be made:

> When I was young, my senses were sharper; and the smallest sound I heard—for example, the noise an insect might make—could cause me to stop and listen. Intense in my youth, I gazed into the forest, watching both the hunter and his prey.
> Was there meaning there? Or was it only a feeling, a state of mind that cast me in a kind of shadow, in which I simply existed without understanding?
> Now it is summer; and the heat browned grasses have released their fragrance into the air; even the dust beside the road seems sweet, and the earth, stark in the sunlight, lovely. The voice of the dove that is nesting caresses the silence; and that dove in its fluttering, uncertain flying, as close to the air as a hand is to a glove, caresses the brightness.

I stand in the orchard, amid the fruit that has fallen from the trees, that rots and ferments on the ground. And I know only this: the decay I see around me, like a liquor, enhances my apprehension of the gifts of nature, the life of my senses; and the awareness of the death of natural things gives a new sweetness to the life I know. (by John Williams)

If one could reconcile the contradictions, the incipient Romanticism, and the Renaissance conventions in this crude matter; then manage to select from it or add to it sufficient detail; and then manage to transmute those details into the statements or metaphors of poetry, one might come out with a poem. Try it—in fact, try it in several ways:

a. Make a poem in Hebraic prosody. You may, if you wish, imitate the Bible,* Whitman,* or E. A. Robinson (in "Luke Havergal" *), to name three quite various uses of Hebraic prosody.

b. Make an accentual poem with a three- or four-beat line. This poem may be loosely or regularly rimed, if you wish, or you may use alliteration in moderation, assonance, consonance, or any other auditory patterning device you feel is needed.

c. Make a metered poem of the matter: iambic tetrameter, rimed *abab* and using four-line stanzas; or make a poem of the matter in ballad measure.

d. Make an unrimed, blank verse version of the matter; or make a Shakespearean sonnet of it, using a partite logical structure.

e. Make an improved prose version of it—that is, make a prose-poem.

2. Write a poem in Hebraic prosody, paying at least as much attention to the tonal patterns as to the meaning. In fact, the meaning, at this stage, is relatively unimportant; you may write on almost any topic. Take a walk along a river, for instance, and write a lyric review of what you see—if it is a beautiful river, you can make it a sentimental poem; if it is polluted, you can make it ironic and critical. The principle of organization in such a poem would be narrative—united conceptually and connected in time.

3. Write a different kind of Hebraic poem—one in which the principle of organization is repetition in ever-changing and ever-widening contexts. Take, for example, such a beginning as:

> No thing is simple—
> No act, no word, no thought is simple—
> Drop a pebble in a pool and ripples travel far,

and write a poem from it. The pebble in the pool is a first metaphorical illustration of the core idea; a hundred others are possible; a careful selection among the possibilities would produce a poem.

4. Write an accentual poem that says the same thing as either of the Hebraic poems from the last two assignments. You will have to re-think the idea completely, for the rhythm and phrase patterns of one are quite different from the other approach to verse.

5. Write a poem in which three "voices" discuss a subject. For example, you might let a Whitmanian lyric voice praise the beauty of a river, an accent-jamming accentual-alliterative voice damn it as dirty slime and sludge, and an accentual-syllabic voice meditate on it as a metaphor for the road of life. Be sure to let each speaker have more than one speech, and make some attempt to let them answer or argue with each other.

14

Poetry

Poetry Without Rhythm

Poetry is many things. It has many attributes, but it does not necessarily or often have them all at once. Poetry usually employs metaphors or other figures of speech, but not always. Poems often use abstract rhythms of language: rime, meter, stanza; in fact, some people—especially those who are trying to distinguish poetry from prose—would even have us believe that poetry cannot exist without rime, meter, stanza. But it can. It has existed abundantly without these things, chiefly in so-called prose translations of poetry, in careful, concentrated prose (like James Agee's "Knoxville: Summer 1915"), and in rhythmless poems like "In the Desert," by Stephen Crane.

In the Desert

In the desert
I saw a creature, naked, bestial,
Who, squatting upon the ground,
Held his heart in his hands,
And ate of it.
I said, "Is it good, Friend?"
"It is bitter—bitter," he answered,
"But I like it
Because it is bitter,
And because it is my heart."

Ezra Pound taught us in his post-Symbolist way that poetry contains things that are far more important than mere sound, and, after a half-century of his influence, we have become quite used to hearing and accepting poetry without rhythm. (The recent increased availability and use of printed texts, which hastened the decline of oral recitation and of rhetorical habits in general, no doubt contributed to this acceptance.)

Patterns

Of the many things that poetry is, controlled and heightened patterns of language and meaning are perhaps most important. Poetry, it seems clear, cannot be without such patterns; at least, *poetry* without them hasn't yet been seen, though *verse* without them has. These patterns, like Kenneth Burke's Form, are the creation and satisfaction of expectation. But let's see how.

Pattern is mental connecting tissue: any principle of organization that enables, causes, forces the mind to perceive a series of items as a recognizable construct, as something other than the component series of items. A horizontal row of thin boards, set vertically, evenly spaced (and painted white?) is not a row of pickets, but a picket fence. The repetition, the spacing, the juxta-position are primary elements in the pattern that organizes this visual mate-rial. Relations to other patterns—this tree, that curb, the point where the house ends—help to define for our sense of expectation the proper stopping or turning point—that is, a picket fence creates and fulfills certain expecta-tions in our minds. (Try tampering with some of the pattern and the con-struct is disturbed; set the fence on end, for example, and it may well look like a ladder for Pygmy Siamese twins.) There can be, of course, patterns within patterns; the pickets can be arranged in groups of short, medium, and long pickets, in various combinations. Such a pattern would then influence other parts of the overall pattern, such as where an aesthetically permissible stopping or turning place is.

The human mind seems to have a terrific need for patterns. This need is so strong that people will impose pattern where none exists. For example, most English-speaking people will insist that a series of identical and evenly spaced sounds, such as the tick-tick-tick of a clock, is actually a pattern of pairs, with a qualitative difference: tick-tock, tick-tock, tick-tock. (This may well have been influenced by the stress pattern of the language.) Traditional poetry in English depends heavily upon such patterns of sounds, which have been discussed in some detail. The power of verse, the power of audible rhythm, is real, but it is separable from the other powers of poetry. Indeed, if it is out of phase, out of tone, with other patterns, rhythm can actually be detrimental to a poem.

Ideational patterns are more important to poetry than either visual or audible patterns. Ideas, as well as picket fences, have their high points, their series of elements, their turning points, their culminations—in other words, ideas too come in patterns, by which we recognize the ideational construct and its relation to its surroundings.

Ideational patterns fall into three phases (the word *categories* would be inaccurate because there are blended borders between them): the obligatory, the conventional, and the literary. Grammatical patterns, such as noun-verb, noun-verb-object, article-adjective-noun, and so on, are foremost among the obligatory patterns. The poet has least opportunity to tamper with these patterns, for, when he does, he destroys the language. The result is mere gibberish or word-salad, which possesses only the modicum of communicable content that is residual in bare words and random combinations. Some combinations may be manipulated without destroying sentence content, of course—"the dank mosses" can be changed (by convention) to "the mosses dank" without too much violence to our sense of grammar, but "the yellow birds" is less readily changed to "the birds yellow"; some conventions—"Went the giants, then, in to their women, and men-children they conceived"—have precedent in Biblical rhetoric and in other places. Such manipulations are part of the history and conventions of our language and are part of the poet's arsenal. They are conventional means with which he can heighten the reader's attention to the pattern of ideas. Thus, to use the earlier example, the poet can transform the pattern of a weak sentence, such as "You will not get one dollar from me!" (which begs for its exclamation marks), into something more effective—"Not one dollar will you get from me!" (in which the exclamation mark is actually gratuitous). By putting the key words at the heaviest part of the sentence, the poet can focus the reader's attention on the most important part of the message. Or the poet can force the reader to notice particular words (and their ideas) by using patterns of alliteration—or assonance, or consonance, or dissonance. Or he can shock the reader into consciousness with an unusually perceptive (and unusually placed) word, which would be, of course, participating in several patterns—grammatical, conventional, and literary. The same is said for simile. More so for metaphor. The aptness would be part of the literary patterns—those patterns not obligatory or conventional, but of the poet's choosing and invention—those strategies and structures with which he intends to convey his meanings to an ignorant audience (necessarily ignorant of the communication; otherwise there is no justification for attempting to convey it).

In the literary patterns, especially, and to a lesser extent in the conventional and obligatory phases, there are many ways the poet can heighten the reader's participation in theme and meaning. Some of these ways depend upon the tone of single words, or the texture of a line; other ways depend upon structural forms in the poem as a whole.

One of the simplest—and least satisfactory—of literary patterns is the abrupt change of tone or mood—the injecting, for example, of a colloquial word or phrase into otherwise formal language. Although this is a gimmick and thus calls attention to itself as mere device, it can be done effectively, as in the case of some of Wallace Stevens's poems. Some poets force notice of words by placing them erratically on the page, sometimes giving a whole line to an "important" word. More satisfactory in poetry are such uses of tone shift as ironic reversal, variations on a theme, and such.

Another means to invite the reader into the poem is to control the texture of the lines. The simplest form of texture is probably repetition of a phrase or more. Only when each repetition accrues more meaning than the last is the technique satisfactory, except perhaps as a species of dance music—as in the refrains of simple ballads. A more ambitious form of repetition is the allusion; the poet presumably invokes in the reader's mind an idea that is already familiar to him. The great pitfall here is that the poet may use the allusion to avoid phrasing the idea clearly and effectively himself.

Extreme clarity and accuracy (they are the same) is one of the best ways of demanding the reader's attention. In the presence of extreme clarity, one typically feels a dimension other than simple communication—a dimension of the universal, of multiplicity, of symbolic significance. Another "best" means is the deliberate use of symbolic overtones through metaphor or symbol. Here, however, the poet assumes some literary education in his audience. Less ambitious textures result from alliteration, consonance, and the like.

The poet can also manipulate the structural forms of the poem as a whole. He can, for example (this anticipates chapter 15), arrange the parts of his idea for logic, for focus on a particular element, for climax, for dramatic effect, even for diminishing attention (playing down a part). There are also a number of natural forms which he can use—the temporal sequence of narrative, for example, or the spatial sequence of a river, and the like. Then, too, our traditions have given us a number of standard molds for ideas—the pastoral elegy, the sonnet, and so on. If the poet's idea especially fits one of these molds, or if his idea needs a bit of artificial help, these molds are available. For example, among the sonnet's special strengths is the opportunity to use a four-part logical pattern—if-then-so-epigram, or a thesis-antithesis-synthesis-epigram structural movement of idea—along with Shakespearean rime scheme. And of course, the poet is always at liberty to invent structural patterns; the proportions and balance of the parts of a theme may be expressed in structures that contribute to the theme, as in organic form (see p. 423). This is essentially what the writer of an expository essay does when he invents the structure that will best communicate his ideas. In a real sense, this is the ultimate in pattern creating and fulfilling expectation. For example, if a writer aesthetically promises a tri-part division of idea in his opening statement, the reader will look for the three parts. The mind delights in discovering what it has been promised.

Now, each of these patterns has its high points and its low—identifiable by the heightening of the reader's attention or its relaxation. In ordinary language, one pattern will be high while another is low, a third approaching while a fourth is receding. The aesthetic result is that the effect of one pattern more or less cancels the effect of another. But it is possible to put the several patterns in phase, to make the high points coincide, to make several patterns converge on a single line, a single word, sometimes a single syllable. The poet can put his unusually perceptive verb (or adjective or noun) in an unusual grammatical position, can make it alliterate, or consonant, or dissonant, can make it metaphorical, can make it occur at the heavy part of a sentence or a line, can make it culminate a structural unit, can make it sing with the heft it heaves. Then, my friend, you are in the presence of poetry. Poetry is characterized by a high number of these intensifying convergences of patterns, while fiction contains relatively fewer. Poetry, most importantly—over and above whatever else it may be—is controlled and heightened patterns of language and meaning.

Meter, rime, stanza are conventional, audible patterns that can be superimposed on poetry. They each produce a rhythm, which can be made to converge with and intensify other patterns. And in the pens of uncompromising poets, such as Shakespeare and E. A. Robinson, and many between them, one can experience poetry that converges patterns of grammar, meaning, rhetoric, structure, and choice with patterns of conventional rhythm. Such poets can make meter, rime, and stanza sting.

But it is much more common for half-competent poets to fill the meter first and seek for meaning later, thereby probably forcing the rime, construing the stanza. Then you have verse, possibly competent verse, whose orbitings in poetry are only fitful and rare.

Rhythm is real, however, and can be used to supplement the subject. It is common for versifiers to take commonplace or popular sentiments (Longfellow, Tennyson) and to make them palatable to us through the excellence of the verse. Indeed, they occasionally make them into poetry. In such cases —where the subject limps—it is probably easier to write poetry with rhythm than poetry without rhythm, for the rhythmical patterns can emphasize ideas that are too weak to emphasize themselves. This is not a denial of the power of verse rhythms, but an urgent resistance to their tyranny.

It is probably harder to write first-rate *poetry* without rhythm than comparable poetry with rhythm, if only because the poet works with fewer tools. He throws away some of his artificial means of heightening patterns. Thus, any heightening he achieves will probably be closer to the poetry itself than to verse. This is to say that the demands upon the poet and the reader are greater and more pregnant in poetry without rhythm than in poetry with rhythm. Although much bad thought and language have been passed off as free verse, it remains that poetry without rhythm has very rich potential— perhaps the richest of all our possibilities. That few poets have exploited the potential does not alter its existence.

The Persona a Poem Makes

Many of the verbal elements of language cannot be represented in ordinary writing or print. We have seen, in the section on Hebraic prosody in chapter 13, that the same three words, given different intonation and emphasis, can be made to convey several different meanings, and we all know that such audible matters as attitude, stress, vocabulary, and speed, among others, are very important in our everyday conversation. The famous anecdote of the tourist screaming his anger in English at his African canoemen is not an example of non-verbal communication, as it has often been described, but merely a case of non-graphic communication. The screaming was certainly verbal. Because much of the most important meaning that language can convey is non-graphic, literature persists in remaining an audible art.

Poetry, more than any of the other literary forms, emphasizes the oral element of language, even amid the disappearance of oral uses of poetry. Perhaps this is because of the persona that the oral qualities of any poem make—because of the poses, the masks, the attitudes the poet takes in speaking his poem. It is no longer fashionable for the poet to take a declamatory attitude and expostulate his poem in all the artificial and orotund rhetoric that he can muster, but something of that quality remains, and remains perhaps for the same reasons that the artificiality existed in the first place. The artificiality is one of the things that distinguishes the poem from life; it helps the audience to establish aesthetic and conceptual distance. These distances are necessary and useful. "Poetry," as Chad Walsh notes, "by its very artifice and artificiality, makes it possible to express emotions that sound embarrassing in prose." [1] By "prose" Walsh apparently means "directly, in everyday communication." Language, whether in verse or prose, creates a persona, which can eliminate embarrassing egoism or subjective values or sentimentality or one-eyed didacticism or any other alienating, unsocial quality from the poet's actual production. The persona, then, is a mean of objectifying subject matter and feeling.

The adoption of a persona has been traditional with poets. We ought not

---

[1] *Doors into Poetry* (Englewood Cliffs, N.J.: Prentice-Hall, 1962) p. 4.

to take the "I" of Wordsworth's "I Wandered Lonely as a Cloud" as Wordsworth himself, but as a pose for saying what he wishes. We are not to take the "I" in Shelley's "To a Skylark" as Shelley, but as an imagined person who has no existence beyond the bounds of that poem. Emily Dickinson was careful to tell T. W. Higginson in a letter that she wanted no confusions between herself and her personae: "When I state myself as representative of the verse, it does not mean me but a supposed person."

Emily took a wide variety of poses in her poetry for a variety of purposes. She assumed the pose of a child in "I'm Nobody! Who are you?" and achieved a naïveté and freshness of detail that make her poetic statement outrageous in a way that an adult pose would not. She was wife in "I Got So I Could Take His Name" and mistress in "Wild Nights—Wild Nights!" These two poems thus contain a thematic dimension that a pose of child or man could not give them. In "The Soul Selects Her Own Society," she assumed a pose of royalty whose realms included weather, people, the sea, even God. Ranging across all these personae and across subjects from society to the Bible, she could take a pose of the satirist, as in "What Soft Cherubic Creatures" * and "I Heard a Fly Buzz When I Died." * She could be colloquial, hortatory, sing-songy, or natural.

The most common pose a poet takes, and the most common in Emily Dickinson's work, is that of a generalized perceiver—an eye and a mind are placed so that they perceive and understand the materials of the poem. The reader perceives the poem through this persona. For example,

I've Seen a Dying Eye (J. 547)

Emily Dickinson

I've seen a Dying Eye
Run round and round a Room—
In search of Something—as it seemed—
Then Cloudier become—
And then—obscure with Fog—
And then—be soldered down
Without disclosing what it be
'Twere blessed to have seen—

In this poem, the "I" of the first line is simply a generalized perceiver, external to the eye of the dying person. The persona stands in the position of a visitor in the typical nineteenth-century deathbed scene that so haunted and impressed Emily that she used it several times in poems. We, as readers, see what that persona sees—the progress of death as the eye becomes dizzy, clouds up, fogs over, and finally crystallizes. Aesthetically, the persona's eyes are our eyes; our identification with her makes it possible for us to perceive the poem. And the persona's consciousness makes, for us, the ironic comment on nineteenth-century religious expectations at the moment of death.

Here is a poem which clearly assumes a variety of poses:

Poetry of Departures
Philip Larkin

Sometimes you hear, fifth-hand,
As epitaph:
He chucked up everything
And just cleared off,
And always the voice will sound
Certain you approve
This audacious, purifying,
Elemental move.

And they are right, I think.
We all hate home
And having to be there:
I detest my room,
Its specially-chosen junk,
The good books, the good bed,
And my life, in perfect order,
So to hear it said

He walked out on the whole crowd
Leaves me flushed and stirred,
Like *Then she undid her dress*
Or *Take that you bastard;*
Surely I can, if he did?
And that helps me stay
Sober and industrious.
But I'd go today,

Yes, swagger the nut-strewn roads,
Crouch in the fo'c'sle
Stubbly with goodness, if
It weren't so artificial,
Such a deliberate step backwards
To create an object:
Books; china; a life
Reprehensibly perfect.

The speaker of the opening two lines quotes, as it were, an attitude not his own in the third and fourth lines. He envies the attitude a bit, but it is clearly not in his voice. A similar quotation occurs as the first line of the third stanza and the poet points up the effect this other attitude has upon him by using two further analogical poses—"Then she undid her dress," suggesting bus-terminal literature of erotic excitement and luxury; and "Take that, you bastard," suggesting the literature of luxurious violence. None of these poses is Larkin's own but are merely his ways of expressing several viewpoints that are relevant to the subject.

Here, as in virtually all lyric poetry, the characters are mere pawns. They exist only for the actions they perform, for the lines they speak, or for the attitudes they express. We do not ask them to be any more complicated as characters than this simplistic identification with role would indicate. This is why we are always wrong if we identify the personae of a poem with the poet. Philip Larkin may, in fact, want to opt out of society—he has been associated with the Angry-Young-Men generation in England—but such a fact would be irrelevant to his "Poetry of Departures." What is relevant is that a thinking mind within the limits of the poetry has expressed sentiments that may be yours, or mine, or Larkin's, or anyone's. The persona partly creates universality.

Each character, each persona in a poem, being limited to that poem, has his own characteristic rhetoric. He chooses a tone which is expressed in his pro-nunciation, his vocabulary, his grammar, his strategy, and he chooses a manner—belligerent, colloquial, friendly, satirical—which reveals his essential per-sonality. His rhetoric of tone and manner thus becomes directly involved in the possible meaning of the poem. Indeed, it may become the meaning.

This participation in meaning intimates that the persona participates also in form. The tone and manner of a persona in a poem create in a reader cer-tain expectations. When the poet gratifies these expectations, we feel that the subject of the poem has achieved a certain unity.

This unity, of course, must be consistent with the expectations which form creates in the reader; the expectation is that a single, aesthetically understand-able persona will exist. If there are shifts, as in "Poetry of Departures," we expect it to be made clear that these are in the nature of quotation and that the primary persona of the poem is aware of these ancillary personae. This is a need for aesthetic unity and operates similarly to point-of-view in fiction. The aesthetic unity of a theme is part of the theme. The persona of the poem results, as far as the reader is concerned, from all these qualities, hence the persona becomes a primary vehicle of meaning, a primary part of theme; it is the poem's persona which creates for the reader such evaluating data as the tone, the manner, the attitude toward a particular subject that the poet wants to communicate.

The Vocabulary of Poetry

Imagery

The human mind relies heavily upon images in the understanding of environment, so heavily that it will often impose spatial images upon things, like music, that do not have them—the tune went up, turned down, bounced along. In poetry, this demand for imagery is usually satisfied by figures of speech, a way of saying something so that the meaning is different from and richer than the literal meaning. To say "we fling our voice" means we project our voice, but moreover communicates those qualities of speed, distance, violence, playfulness perhaps, that we associate with the word "fling." Most poetry has such figures of speech, and there is a whole tradition that identifies and gives names to many varieties of them, from metaphor to oxymoron. However, poetry can exist quite nicely without such a vocabulary of lexical substitutes.

These substitutes exist because they communicate important things which ordinary denotative language cannot express. They are often a way of bringing to bear several ideas at once, rather than in sequence. And they have been so useful in the past that many of these *tropes*, as we call them, have fixed definitions. Here is a poem which, though not a good one, illustrates a dozen of the more important ones and their potentialities:

Tropes

H. C. Brashers

Thru the fresh salt smell and feel,
The sailboats drift, like clouds, on the bay;
The waves are pillows; the wind, a lay,
And the lotused crews let Chance choose their course,
With Cash on board and Sloth at the wheel.
Th' crews cry: "O Sun! Your light's a scorching curse!
"It shows our lives as vacant dreams,
"Which learning cannot right, nor the sword destroy.
"We've lost our way; we're not mere puling boys,
"But giants on the earth, swans on the streams."
Boats, crews, move and stay—changeless motion—
Desire, not work, the fatal potion.

Imagery: the representation in language of direct sensory experience, perceived through any of the five senses, as the light flashed (sight), the ground rumbled (feel and sound), the sweet odors of evening (taste?, smell, sight), and so on:

Thru the fresh salt smell and feel.

The term is usually extended to include any expression that evokes emotional experience. Indeed, the whole purpose of imagery and the reason the poet uses it is that it re-evokes for the reader the original experience of the poet. Thus the poet can show the reader, not tell him, what he means; he can re-create the experience for the reader. In this process, the image, not the word, is the carrier of meaning. Imagery is the primary vocabulary of poetic experience.[2]

Simile: a direct analogy or comparison between two things, expressly indicated by a connective word, "like" or "as":

The sailboats drift, like clouds, in the bay,

Both appearance and motion are involved in this comparison, but both things —sailboats and clouds—are kept distinct. One is merely *like* the other.

Metaphor: a comparison of two things, via direct identity:

The waves are pillows; the wind, a lay,

Metaphors can occur in several linguistic forms; in addition to the predicate-object of the above example, they can be verbs (the waves pillowed the sailboats), adjectives (the pillowed passengers), and among others, combinations of grammatical forms (the wind-swept waves—that is, a noun and verb made into one adjective—the wind is a broom that is sweeping the waves). In their most developed state, metaphors can actually be lexical substitutes, since they involve an identity between two things; oil on the waters now means any calming influence; the wolf at the door, adversity. During the time that such metaphors are dying, they are considered clichés. When dead, they become idioms: legs of a table, arms of a chair, head of a pin, eye of a needle, face of a clock, foot of a bed, neck of a bottle, tongue of a shoe, teeth of a comb, lip of a jar, mouth of a cave (thanks to Sheridan Blau for this list).

Symbol: an image used to mean something other than itself, usually some abstract concept:

And the lotused crews let Chance choose their course

A common use of symbols is as allusion. Since Homer's *Odyssey,* the lotus has symbolized a narcotic that causes men to withdraw from life and to sleep;

---

[2] About 1910, Ezra Pound and T. E. Hulme developed a theory of poetry that was based heavily upon the concept of the image. They called their theory *Imagism* and, among other things, wanted poetry to "render particulars exactly and not deal in vague generalities" and to "employ always the *exact* word, not the merely decorative word." They also borrowed concepts from Oriental ideographic poetry and from other sources, so that Imagistic poetry contains a great deal more than mere particular and **exact** images. It will be discussed further in connection with poetry of metaphor.

many poets have alluded to Homer's use of the flower in order to communicate those drugged attitudes that Ulysses' sailors possessed for a while. Ever since random activity was first called Chance, it has been possible to refer to the whole idea by using the single word. And it has become a matter of literary convention to let a journey or a ship's course symbolize the progress and direction of man's life.

Personification: the representation of an object or an idea as if it were a person, with human thoughts, powers, feelings:

> With Cash on board and Sloth at the wheel.

Apostrophe: a direct address to a personification:

> Th' crews cry: "O Sun! Your light's a scorching curse!"

Allegory: the use of one continuous action to represent another or to represent an extended idea, often using symbols and personifications; the following is not an example, but suggests the framework of an example:

> It shows our lives as vacant dreams,

Metonomy: the use of one thing to mean another with which it is closely associated, as "learning" substituted for the scholar:

> Which learning cannot right,

Synechdoche: the use of a part of something to signify the whole:

> nor the sword destroy,

Litotes: understatement; as for example, in the use of the negative to express the affirmative:

> We've lost our way; we're not mere puling boys,

Hyperbole: overstatement; exaggeration for serious or comic effect:

> But giants on earth, swans on the stream.

Oxymoron: the use of contradiction or incongruity to heighten effect:

> Boats, crews, move and stay—

Paradox: apparent contradiction, which is resolved in higher or richer meaning:

> —changeless motion—Desire, not work, the fatal potion.

Yet, in spite of the fact that "Tropes" has a respectable rime scheme, a metrical organization, and uses a dozen or more figures of speech, it is a dull, flat failure as a poem. Why? Trite allusions. Stock references in the figures of speech. Dead and dying thought is as dangerous and as easy to fall into as dead language.

The Vocabulary of Statement vs. the Vocabulary of Metaphor

A wide continuum of vocabulary—from pure statement to pure metaphor—is available to the poet. At the one end, he can describe experience directly, without ornament, with attention focused primarily on the intensity and truth of the experience. At the other end, he can describe experience by means of other experience, using these other experiences to throw new and valuable light on the first experience. Between these extremes, there are any number of mixtures of the two modes of vocabulary.

Emily Dickinson is one of our best poets of statement. For example:

Much Madness is Divinest Sense (J. 435)

Emily Dickinson

Much Madness is divinest Sense—
To a discerning Eye—
Much Sense—the starkest Madness—
'Tis the Majority
In this, as All, prevail—
Assent—and you are sane—
Demur—you're straightway dangerous—
And handled with a Chain—

With the exception of "divinest," which may be so conventional that it is no longer figurative, and the rhetoric of paradoxes, which deals only in lexical meanings—no figurative speech here—this poem is straightforward statement. Its effect comes from insight and concision. The poem means what it says and says what it means.

At the other extreme of the continuum is poetry like

In a Station of the Metro

Ezra Pound

The apparition of these faces in the crowd;
Petals on a wet, black bough.

The poem consists of a single comparison: people in subway stations are like petals on a wet, black bough; but the real meaning of the poem has little to do with subway stations or petals. This image, this metaphor, stands for something much more involved than itself. Pound evokes an image of a station of the metro (the Paris subway) at an hour when it is crowded, when people are either going to work or coming from work; the metro is not crowded at other hours. These people, then, are involved in metropolitan living, in the modern age—after the subway was constructed. The whole image is unmistakably a product of modern, industrial, urban society. The poet compares to this urban life a bough of petals—the contrast suggests that they are white; "wet, black" suggest that the branch is broken, for a branch with spring petals on it is black only when it is dead; otherwise the bark is brownish-green. These petals will never come to fruition; their potential is nipped in the blossom. Pound is saying that the modern, industrial, urban people in the metro station are like those petals; he calls the people "apparitions" and links the two images with a semicolon to stress their coordination, their identity. The metaphor, then, contains Pound's judgment that modern, industrial, urban society has suffered a spiritual death; his last word, "bough," is even an old word for gallows. This is poetry in which the metaphor, not the statements in it, is the primary carrier of the meaning. The metaphor is the vocabulary.

This extreme was the original ideal of Imagism, and, in fact, Pound's poem is an example of Imagism at its best. Pound and Hulme drew a great deal of their inspiration from Oriental ideographic poetry, especially the Japanese Haiku, in which the image presented must have far-reaching, metaphorical overtones. The strength of such an image compensates in our sense of poetry for the lack of traditional rhythms. After Pound had left the movement and Amy Lowell had become its chief spokesman, this metaphorical core tended to disappear. The verse—which Pound, in disgust, called "Amygism"—was indeed hard to tell from prose.

On a continuum between these extremes lies most poetry in English. One poem may come close to the statement extreme; another near the metaphor. Or the two modes may be mixed: Wallace Stevens's "The Glass of Water" begins with such pure statement that we call it a philosophical argument, then shifts to almost pure embodiment of idea in exotic metaphor. The subject of the poem appears to be poetry itself.

The Glass of Water

That the glass would melt in heat,
That the water would freeze in cold,
Shows that this object is merely a state,
One of many, between two poles. So,
In the metaphysical, there are these poles.

Here in the center stands the glass. Light
Is the lion that comes down to drink. There
And in that state, the glass is a pool.
Ruddy are his eyes and ruddy are his claws
When light comes down to wet his frothy jaws

And in the water winding weeds move round.
And there and in another state—the refractions,
The *metaphysica,* the plastic parts of poems
Crash in the mind—But, fat Jocundus, worrying
About what stands here in the center, not the glass,

But in the center of our lives, this time, this day,
It is a state, this spring among the politicians
Playing cards. In a village of the indigenes,
One would have still to discover. Among the dogs and dung,
One would continue to contend with one's ideas.

Some poets write sometimes in one mode, sometimes in another; Emily Dickinson and Stephen Crane, among others, often shift this way.

The most important mode between the two extremes is the one which uses metaphors and other figures of speech as substitutes in the statements of the poem. Most traditional poetry in English is in this mode. For example, Shakespeare's lines

> That time of year thou mayst in me behold
> When yellow leaves, or none, or few, do hang
> Upon those boughs which shake against the cold,
> Bare ruined choirs, where late the sweet birds sang.

can be roughly translated to

> That time of life you see in me
> When a few grey hairs, or none, are
> Upon my head, which shakes with the cold,
> Which is like empty choir benches, where recently
>   the spirit of youth was singing

Shakespeare also uses the ironic reversal of this mode, uses negative figures of speech to make his point, as in

Sonnet 130

> My mistress' eyes are nothing like the sun;
> Coral is far more red than her lips' red;
> If snow be white, why then her breasts are dun;
> If hairs be wires, black wires grow on her head.

I have seen roses damasked, red and white,
But no such roses see I in her cheeks;
And in some perfumes is there more delight
Than in the breath that from my mistress reeks.
I love to hear her speak, yet well I know
That music hath a far more pleasing sound;
I grant I never saw a goddess go;
My mistress, when she walks, treads on the ground.
   And yet, by heaven, I think my love as rare
   As any she belied with false compare.

In a sense, one can say that this mode uses figurative language primarily as ornament, but we must also admit that such ornament manages to say a great deal more than the usual bare statement would. To some extent, this achievement has to do with our response to assertion, as opposed to our response to proof.

Imagery of Assertion vs. Imagery of Proof

At any point in the statement-metaphor continuum, another dimension of vocabulary is always operating. This dimension can be described as a contrast between assertion and proof as devices of communication. This contrast can be described effectively by means of two poems: Longfellow's "The Cross of Snow" and Emily Dickinson's "After Great Pain." [3] Although Longfellow's subject is specific and Emily's is generalized, both poems treat the theme "after great pain," both suggest a sense of loss, both refer (at least briefly) to the conventional idea of vicarious suffering as a release from loss, and both discover in snow the final metaphor for the effect of pain. But what a difference in their use of imagery and form!

After Great Pain . . . (J. 341)

After great pain a formal feeling comes—
The nerves sit ceremonious like tombs;
The stiff Heart questions—was it He that bore?
And yesterday—or centuries before?

The feet, mechanical, go round
A wooden way
Of ground or air, or ought,
Regardless grown,
A quartz contentment, like a stone.

[3] Most of the material from here to the end of this section appeared in substantially this form in H. C. Brashers, "Teaching Poems in Pairs," *Exercise Exchange,* 13 (March, 1966): 3–5.

This is the hour of lead
Remembered if outlived,
As freezing persons recollect the snow—
First chill, then stupor, then the letting go.[4]

The Cross of Snow

In the long, sleepless watches of the night,
  A gentle face—the face of one [5] long dead—
  Looks at me from the wall, where round its head
  The night-lamp casts a halo of pale light.
Here in this room she died; and soul more white
  Never through martyrdom of fire was led
  To its repose; nor can in books be read
  The legend of a life more benedight.
There is a mountain in the distant West
  That, sun-defying, in its deep ravines
  Displays a cross of snow upon its side.
Such is the cross I wear upon my breast
  These eighteen years, through all the changing scenes
  And seasons, changeless since the day she died.

Longfellow's imagery is said to be deeply personal and Dante-esque,[6] but that is neither here nor there, for it remains that it is imagery of assertion. Moreover, his ideas are conventional, stock assertions. (Note, in this connection, the plethora of stock clichés of thought and word—long, sleepless nights, white soul, "nor can in books be read," the cross I bear (the myth of vicarious suffering), I'll never outlive it, and so on. Note, too, how distant they are from the horrible facts: his wife came running into the study, her dress in flames; Longfellow tried to smother the flames with a rug; she broke away, screaming, running to the door; came back; he tried to protect her face with his own embrace, but she was burned to death in spite of all he could do. What a poem that would make!) It is likely that if we are moved by the poem, our response is really a response to the biographical data that is usually printed as a note or gloss—that is, to the poem that could have been, not to what is on the printed page. Instead we are told: My wife, who died here, had a gentle

---

[4] The second stanza is here copied correctly. See Thomas H. Johnson (ed.) *The Poems of Emily Dickinson* (3 vols.; Cambridge, Mass.: Belknap, 1955), Vol. I, pp. 272–73. Subsequent reproductions of the poem are often in error.

[5] Longfellow's wife, who was burned to death in 1861. The poem bears the date, July 10, 1879, and was not printed until after the poet's death.

[6] See James M. Cox, "Longfellow and His Cross of Snow," *PMLA*, 75 (1960): 97–100.

face; she was a martyr. Such assertions, as any freshman student of rhetoric can tell you, evoke only the response "prove it" from the reader. Assertions without backing degenerate to mere opinion. An opinion, such as "my wife was a martyr," without any factual backing no more communicates the emotion or experience than a command, "Be sorry!," communicates sorrow. There is really only one valid image in the poem—snow on my breast.

Emily Dickinson, on the other hand, uses imagery of proof. After her opening assertion, "After great pain, a formal feeling comes," the poem consists entirely of examples that define, or prove, this formal feeling. Further, Emily's is the imagery of precise, "scientific" observation of experience. The personified nerves sit ceremonious(ly), but, after all, there are different kinds of ceremonies—happy, like birthdays; solemn, like weddings and funerals. In the interest of exactness, Emily eliminates all unwanted connotations with the simile, "like tombs." This cold, hard, heavy, dumb, "formal" image is the common denominator of all the imagery in the poem. It re-evokes (proves) its emotion in the reader's mind. The disorientation in time (she cannot remember whether the myth of vicarious suffering ever operated or not), the disorientation in space (compare Tennyson's "I cannot find my way"), the stupor of stone, the heaviness of lead, the chill of snow, all contribute to our emotional meaning of the formal feeling after great pain. Anyone who misses these images misses also the marvelous irony in "a quartz contentment" and the gratuitous simile (exactly fitting and meaningful *because* it is gratuitous) "like a stone." At the extremity of disorientation is stupor, where the mind can move only in the circular paths of gratuitous repetition.

Longfellow's form is superficially the conventional Petrarchan sonnet, but this seems to have very little to do with the poem. In Petrarchan strategy, the idea in the octave is related to the idea in the sestet by causality, implication, refutation, or some other logical way. In other words, the form of the sonnet encourages intellectual unity, but Longfellow's "sonnet" actually achieves a three-part division of thought and subject. The octave is a eulogy to his dead wife. The sestet breaks itself into two triplets, giving us the description of the distant mountain and the poet's feeling after the great pain of his wife's death. In a sense, these are three different subjects (for three different poems?) and tend to disintegrate the poem on the page. Longfellow can hardly be said to use form to enhance his theme. We see what he is doing, of course; he is using the first two subjects as preparation so that his one metaphor—the cross of snow—will work. All the meaning of the poem, as the title suggests, is concentrated in this snow, which, however, limps and has to borrow, from the stockpile of convention, the cross for a crutch.

Emily also uses a tripartite form, or at least three stanzas, which manage to produce unity out of apparent diversity. Indeed, her sources of imagery—the cemetery, the myth of vicarious suffering, personification of body organs, a kind of School-of-Education observation of stupor, "metallurgy," Arctic travel —are far more various than Longfellow's, yet they have a unity of connotation which Longfellow's imagery does not attain. All are cold, hard, and the like. This unity of imagery operates as a structural or formal device. Further, her superficial form comes to participate in our reaction to these images. If we accept the slant rime, *comes/tombs,* in the first two lines, a rhythmical norm of rimed pentameter couplets is quickly established. We may not want to dance to this rhythm, as we might to "Mother! Mother! I am ill!/Call the doctor from over the hill," but a change in it will give us the uneasy feeling of "missing a step." Emily's modulation of the couplet form manages to keep alive our expectations of the couplet rhythm while causing us to miss that step. (She did this too often for it to be an accident.) The second stanza on the page and in phraseology is five iambic lines of 4, 2, 3, 2, and 4 feet, but the chimed rimes, *round/ground* and *grown/stone,* continue the couplet structure, albeit at different lengths—the first is a tetrameter-trimeter couplet; the second is regular tetrameter. The irregularity of these short couplets and the competition in our response of the two structures—one of phrase and one of rime—enhance the subject of the stanza, physical disorientation, and make the gratuity of the simile work as stupor. It is the context of this stupor that makes the first line in the last stanza work, for, without this context, the line is somewhat innocuous and contains an "impossible" comparison. As it stands, however, the line has the heft and takes the time of a regular pentameter line. Indeed, this and the slant rime in this trimeter couplet and the run-on second line are part of the modulation back to the perfect pentameter couplet that ends the poem. In musical terms, this return to the tonic or major chord gives the tonal structure of the poem a definite sense of closing. It is because of the poem's structure, as well as its unified imagery, that we perceive it as such a single, unified, intense experience that it is difficult to decide which is the best line, which the best metaphor. Emily Dickinson has, at every image, proved her point; Longfellow could only assert his.

Dislocation of Language: E. E. Cummings's Diction

While it is true that the poet has least opportunity to manipulate the obligatory patterns of the language, E. E. Cummings tampered with these patterns considerably. Sometimes his poems look and sound like word-salad, but, when his dislocations of diction were successful, his linguistic shifts of function shocked readers into attention and shook commonplaces into significance. His techniques, then, might be of use to a young poet. Take, for example, one of his linguistically richest poems:

Anyone Lived in a Pretty How Town

anyone lived in a pretty how town
(with up so floating many bells down)
spring summer autumn winter
he sang his didn't he danced his did.

Women and men(both little and small)
cared for anyone not at all
they sowed their isn't they reaped their same
sun moon stars rain

children guessed(but only a few
and down they forgot as up they grew
autumn winter spring summer)
that noone loved him more by more

when by now and tree by leaf
she laughed his joy she cried his grief
bird by snow and stir by still
anyone's any was all to her

someones married their everyones
laughed their cryings and did their dance
(sleep wake hope and then)they
said their nevers they slept their dream

stars rain sun moon
(and only the snow can begin to explain
how children are apt to forget to remember
with up so floating many bells down)

one day anyone died i guess
(and noone stooped to kiss his face)
busy folk buried them side by side
little by little and was by was

all by all and deep by deep
and more by more they dream their sleep
noone and anyone earth by april
wish by spirit and if by yes.

Women and men(both dong and ding)
summer autumn winter spring
reaped their sowing and went their came
sun moon stars rain

A catalog of his linguistic function shifts in this poem would have to include:

Generalization used as a specification: "Anyone" does not refer here, as it does in usual language, to *any* person; it refers rather to a specific man and actor. In fact, the word takes on the linguistic function of a proper name. The same is true of Anyone's wife, Noone. Similarly, the townsfolk become "everyones." Cummings thus gains an ambiguity: the line "that noone loved him more by more" suggests both that no person has found him worthy of love and that this girl named Noone has. The irony of the first and the pathos of the second are central to the theme of the poem.

Shift in adverb placement: "pretty how town" contains a dislocated adverb, suggesting both the usual "oh, how pretty a town!" with all the attendant sentimentality and the slightly derogatory "pretty cow town," which is relevant to the theme of the poem. Cummings's discovery of the ability of language to thus convey multiple meanings was his greatest contribution to poetry. One of the richest cases of adverb shift is in the opening line of Cummings's poem called "I Thank You God for Most this Amazing." One of the principles of Gestalt psychology and a human empathic habit is that we try to correct dislocations in perceptual fields and figures. Cummings's dislocation allows several corrections:

I most thank You God for this amazing day
I thank most You, God, for this amazing day
I thank You most, God, for this amazing day
I thank you, God, most for this amazing day
I thank you, God, for this most amazing day

The effect is that Cummings has managed to suggest all of these with his dislocation; all of them become part of the poem.

Shift in adjective placement: "with up so floating many bells down" is a happy permutation of "with so many bells floating up and down," but it commands the reader's attention in a way that its prosaic parent does not. The change in adjective position aids the sense and the rhythm. All the parts of the idea having to do with the upward swing of a ringing bell come in the first part of the line, all parts relating to the downward swing in the last part. Consider, too, the intonation contour: "up so floating" has three rising syllables, as compared to two falling syllables in the more common phrasing, "floating up so." "Many bells down" has three falling intonations. The line's rhythm, thus, imitates the rise and fall of the bell. This effect is made possible, at least partly, by our traditional tolerance for rising and falling movement in lines of poetry; we demand this quality, for instance, in ballads. Cummings here makes good use of our predisposition to respond in a certain way.

Reduplication: "little by little and was by was / all by all and deep by deep / and more by more" is a string in which linguistic forms are simply repeated, as in the common idiom, "little by little." "Was by was" suggests "happening by happening"; and the reduplications of adjectives and adverbs in the rest of the string have similar effects. Again, the linguistic trick has a profound effect on rhythm. Here, it almost makes the verse doggerel, which Cummings seems to have been flirting with, deliberately, for thematic purposes.

Grammatical shift: adjective to noun: "anyone's any was all to her" contains two examples of adjectives used as nouns. This is the easiest of grammatical function shifts to grasp, because it is the most common in everyday speech. "Any" here means "any thing," just as "basic" means "basic training" to young men, or "basic dress" to style-conscious young women. "All," meaning "every thing," is so common in speech as to escape notice as a grammatical shift.

Grammatical shift: verb to noun: "he sang his didn't he danced his did" offers two examples of verbs used as nouns. "He sang his didn't" would not be so difficult, were it worded, "he sang his actions," or "he sang of his deeds." "Didn't" and "did" are here nouns, meaning "all those things he did and did not do." This is a very common device in the poem, going through several permutations, down to "reaped their sowing," which offers no problem because we are used to participials as nouns, and "went their came," which uses both verbs curiously—"came their went" would do the same service as "went their came": their comings were indistinguishable from their goings.

Transference of idiom: "down they forgot as up they grew" transmutes the usual idiom, "they grew up," and creates another "impossible" idiom in the same pattern, "they forgot down." The balance and contrast in the line, of course, help us to accept this new idiom, by offering us the analogy on which it is created. "bird by snow and stir by still" are harder idioms. Do they mean, "She laughed his joy she cried his grief / as birds do in snow, or whether things were stirring or were still"? The oxymoron in "stir by still" is easier to grasp than the other idiom; and Cummings's other uses of the same technique in this poem, "earth by april / wish by spirit and if by yes," have a quicker relationship to public meanings of words (April, for example, suggests spring, rebirth, fertility, cyclic seasons, and such) than does "bird by snow." Carried too far, Cummings's techniques do not multiply meaning, but prevent it.

Cummings's subject is commonplace enough. A little, anonymous man lives in a small town, marries, lives a life of quiet passions, dies, and is buried—but is never noticed by the townsfolk because of their busy cycles of meaningless activity. It is a subject that hardly evokes pathos or ire. It tends to be dead, because we have ceased, like the townsfolk, to notice such commonplaces.

Cummings's dislocation of language not only forces us to pay attention to the language itself, but also enlivens the meanings conveyed. He shocks us into noticing. Thus, he makes a subject work that we might have thought impossible. Once again, technique, treatment, is all.

Grammar in Poetry: Patterns of Predication

In grammar, "syntax" means "a joining together," specifically of words in an utterance, but the meaning here is extended, metaphorically, to mean the joining together of ideas or the parts of ideas. Similarly, "predication" is usually limited to the concepts of the sentence, but here it is used in the context of a total poem. In this extended sense, every poem is a maneuver in predication. It has its subject matter, its action or movement, its object—this amounts to a kind of "sentence" which communicates a mood, a feeling, an emotion, an attitude toward the subject matter or the world. Thus, every poem may be said to have a kind of larger grammar—not a matter of nouns, verbs, and prepositions, but a matter of the relationship of the parts of the idea to one another. Insofar as these relationships are satisfactory and knowable, they create a pattern of predication. A poem's success depends upon this total predication. If the pattern of predication is incomplete or disunified or unbalanced, the poem will be incomplete, disunified, or unbalanced.

Every successful poem, then, is grammatical—not in the sense meant by a school marm, who would take the poem to the blackboard and pronounce it grammatical only if it would parse. Ezra Pound did not have such a meaning in mind either when he wrote in a letter to Harriet Monroe in 1915 that "poetry must be [at least] *as well written as prose*," though he has often been understood school-marmishly. And yet, even the traditional meaning of the word *grammatical* applies, if one can accept that a thing exists by mere promise, that implying it is there actually puts it there. All the syntax must be there, at least by implication.

The poet may leave out some things if he wishes, for the ellipsis, whether indicated by three dots or not, is a proper grammatical device. That we are in fact leaving words out of the normal syntactical structure of the language does not mean that they are not aesthetically there, in the communication. Pound, in fact, leaves out the verb in "In a Station of the Metro," and allows a semicolon to do its work, but the omission does not mean that Pound's sentence is non-syntactical.

The larger grammar of a poem has a great deal to do with our aesthetic perception of completeness and unity in the poem. It involves what is predicated, or proclaimed, as the Latin root suggests. Historically, there have been four important patterns of predication: deduction, induction, comparison, and dialectic. Some discussion of each of these is in order.

Deduction: Poetry of Definition

The first method that comes to mind when one wants to say something is likely to be simple assertion. But assertion bare, without proof, is mere opinion and not the intended communication of the ideas. When the evidence is added —whether in the form of examples, anecdotes, arguments, or citation of authority—the resultant "grammar" is the strategy of the deduction. In poetics, this strategy produces poetry of definition.

Poetry of definition is poetry that begins with a generalization, in the form of an image or a concept, and continues and ends with explication or illustration of the opening. In a sense, the "whole meaning" of the poem is contained in the generalization, the notion the poet started with, and the rest of the poem is there only to define for the reader the extent and complexity of that generalization. The generalization may be contained in an image of the title, as in several of Herbert's poems, or in a first section or stanza, or in a first line, as in Emily Dickinson's "After Great Pain" and other poems.

Here is a poem which is wholly assertive, which leaves the proof for the reader to supply from the stockpile of the common catechism:

Prayer (I)
George Herbert

Prayer, the church's banquet, angel's age,
   God's breath in man returning to his birth,
   The soul in paraphrase, heart in pilgrimage,
The Christian plummet sounding heaven and earth;

Engine against th' Almighty, sinner's tower,
   Reverséd thunder, Christ-side-piercing spear,
   The six-day's world transposing in an hour,
A kind of tune, which all things hear and fear;

Softness, and peace, and joy, and love, and bliss,
   Exalted manna, gladness of the best,
   Heaven in ordinary, man well dressed,
The Milky Way, the bird of Paradise,

   Church bells beyond the stars heard, the soul's blood,
   The land of spices; something understood.

Compare this with Emily Dickinson's definition of prayer:

Prayer Is the Little Implement (J. 437)

Prayer is the little implement
Through which Men reach
Where Presence—is denied them.
They fling their Speech

By means of it—in God's Ear—
If then He hear—
This sums the Apparatus
Comprised in Prayer—

Both are poems of definition and both work on the principle of assertion. The "grammar" is barren and the idea unproven. We accept the communication or not, according to the way we already think.

The poem of definition built upon an image is a little more effective. George Herbert is usually cited for this kind of poem, too. His "Collar," for example, is about a man who is resisting the pull of the church, who wants to pound the communion table and quit. But in spite of all his raving, he has, at every moment, a "spiritual collar" on his soul; God has him collared, as the poems illustrates. So, too, Herbert's "The Pulley" illustrates, almost comically, a theological notion of how men are induced into heaven:

The Pulley

When God at first made man,
Having a glass of blessing standing by,
"Let us," said he, "pour on him all we can.
Let the world's riches, which disperséd lie,
Contract into a span."

So strength first made a way;
Then beauty flowed, then wisdom, honor, pleasure.
When almost all was out, God made a stay,
Perceiving that, alone of all his treasure,
Rest in the bottom lay.

"For if I should," said he,
"Bestow this jewel also on my creature,
He would adore my gifts instead of me,
And rest in Nature, not the God of Nature;
So both should losers be.

"Yet, let him keep the rest,
But keep them with repining restlessness.
Let him be rich and weary, that at least,
If goodness lead him not, yet weariness
May toss him to my breast."

A still more ambitious use of deductive strategy, one that begins in generalization and continues and ends in specification, is the kind of poem in which the first line or first section states the subject and theme of the poem, while the rest explicates that subject or theme. We have already seen a very good example of this, Emily Dickinson's "After Great Pain——." Everything after the first line simply repeats the theme in detail and, more specifically, defines for us the cold, hard, heavy quality of the word "formal." Or, to take another example:

I Heard a Fly Buzz—(J. 465)

Emily Dickinson

I heard a Fly buzz—when I died—
The Stillness in the Room
Was like the Stillness in the Air—
Between the Heaves of Storm—

The Eyes around—had wrung them dry—
And Breaths were gathering firm
For that last Onset—when the King
Be witnessed—in the Room—

I willed my Keepsakes—Signed away
What portion of me be
Assignable—and then it was
There interposed a Fly—

With Blue—uncertain stumbling Buzz—
Between the light—and me—
And then the Windows failed—and then
I could not see to see—

In this poem, the poet imagines a death-bed scene—"when I died"—and simply tells what happened—a fly buzzed. She explains in considerable detail what dying implies in her world. She has a feeling of being suspended between two storms, two kinds of life, that stillness we call this life, and that stillness we call eternity. The relatives who have gathered to watch have cried all they are going to and are waiting, as nineteenth-century relatives did, beside the bed to see if the dying person will reveal anything in this life about her first glimpses of the next, will reveal anything about that moment when, the tradition says, Christ the King will collect his little lamb. The poet goes on to say that she has prepared herself for this Onset (the worldly person does not get into the kingdom of heaven any more than a camel can pass through the eye of a needle); she has willed her keepsakes away, signed away materiality, and is spiritually prepared. All this evokes a total definition of the meaning of the moment of death.

But all these expectations are foiled. All that happens, in spite of what is anticipated, is that a fly buzzes against the window. Instead of Christ, one sees a fly; a most insignificant, putrifying, unHeavenly creature comes between the light (of Paradise? of enlightenment?) and her expectation. All this meaning is "contained" by implication in the first line, and the poem deductively defines that first line's full meaning.

Induction: Poetry of Discovery

Induction, in logic, is the method of reasoning that contrasts with deduction; it produces a contrasting kind of poetry. Poetry of discovery is poetry that begins in specific details, accrues as many as are needed, then leads the reader to make the inductive leap into the generalization. Whitman's Section 26 of "Song of Myself," * is a good example of this kind of poetry. He starts out merely to listen, to allow the sounds he hears to make a song for him. Each sound in the rather wide and varied catalog presumably accrues the lyric emotion that is appropriate to it, and the poem builds in intensity as an accretion of emotional significances. At last, these significances become strong enough to allow Whitman his mystic leap into the real subject and theme of the poem, "that puzzle of puzzles, / and that we call Being." He has discovered, inductively, a pantheistic vision.

Whitman's is generalized narrative, almost so far removed as to be meditation, and his outlook is religious. Contrast his discovery to this one of Emily Dickinson's, in which the narrative is specific and the outlook psychological:

I Had Been Hungry All the Years (J. 579)

> I had been hungry, all the Years—
> My Noon had Come—to dine—
> I trembling drew the Table near—
> I touched the Curious Wine—
>
> 'Twas this on Tables I had seen—
> When turning, hungry, Home
> I looked in Windows, for the Wealth
> I could not hope—for Mine—
>
> I did not know the ample Bread—
> 'Twas so unlike the Crumb
> The Birds and I, had often shared
> In Nature's—Dining Room—

The Plenty hurt me—'twas so new—
Myself felt ill—and odd—
As Berry—of a Mountain Bush—
Transplanted—to the Road—

Nor was I hungry—so I found
That Hunger—was a way
Of Persons outside Windows—
The Entering—takes away—

Here, the poet draws the induction explicitly, as she does on the same theme a number of times: it is the distance from a desired object that is savory; it is deprivation that defines sumptuousness.

It is also possible for the poet to give the reader only the series of specific instances and leave him to infer the generalization. This is not to say that the poet would ever let his reader draw his own conclusions; it is to say that the poet might let the reader draw the poet's carefully prepared conclusions. It can be a very effective device if the poet gives all the steps of the logic but the last, then allows the reader to "discover" the theme, the generalization, the subject of the poem. For an example:

Heaven

Rupert Brooke

Fish (fly-replete, in depth of June
Dawdling away their wat'ry noon)
Ponder deep wisdom, dark and clear,
Each secret fishy hope or fear.
Fish say, they have their Stream and Pond;
But is there anything Beyond?
This life cannot be All, they swear,
For how unpleasant, if it were!
One may not doubt that, somehow, Good
Shall come of Water and of Mud;
And, sure, the reverent eye must see
A Purpose in Liquidity.
We darkly know, by Faith we cry,
The future is not Wholly Dry.
Mud unto mud!—Death eddies near—
Not here the appointed End, not here!
But somewhere, beyond Space and Time,
In wetter water, slimier slime!
And there (they trust) there swimmeth One
Who swam ere rivers were begun,

Immense, of fishy form and mind,
Squamous, omnipotent, and kind;
And under that Almighty Fin,
The littlest fish may enter in.
Oh! never fly conceals a hook,
Fish say, in the Eternal Brook,
But more than mundane weeds are there,
And mud, celestially fair;
Fat caterpillars drift around,
And Paradisal grubs are found;
Unfading moths, immortal flies.
And the worm that never dies.
And in that Heaven of all their wish,
There shall be no more land, say fish.

This is parody, of course, of Victorian compacency in general and of Tennyson's *In Memoriam* in particular. The world of the poem consists of all the stages of inductive thought, except the last—the inductive leap—and the reader supplies that: how foolish and absurd fish are! The parody comes, of course, in the elaborate system of parallels that the reader is invited to make between the world of the poem and the world of fatuous thinking. This invitation to draw analogies is another sort of "grammar" from induction.

Comparison (and Contrast): Poetry of Analogy

A third way of getting the point across to a reader is to juxtapose one thing against another, in such a way that the juxtaposition makes your point for you. This can be done for comparison, as in the case of Pound's "In a Station of the Metro," or for contrast, as in "What Soft—Cherubic Creatures" (immediately below), or for an analogy of parallels, as in "I Started Early—Took My Dog," (also below). This strategy results in poetry of analogy.

What Soft—Cherubic Creatures (J. 401)

Emily Dickinson

What Soft—Cherubic Creatures—
These Gentlewomen are—
One would as soon assault a Plush—
Or violate a Star—

Such Dimity Convictions—
A Horror so refined
Of freckled Human Nature—
Of Deity—ashamed—

It's such a common—Glory—
A Fisherman's—Degree—
Redemption—Brittle Lady—
Be so—ashamed of Thee—

In this comparison between the kind of lady that Redemption would accept and the kind of vain clothes-horses these "cherubic" women are, the significant, evaluating intonation—satiric irony—emerges *because* of the juxtaposition, and not because of any deductive or inductive statement. Simple juxtaposition can create other tones as well—Pound's lugubrious criticism of western culture, for instance; or comic irrelevance, as in most of Ogden Nash, some of W. H. Auden, and others. But it is the mere juxtaposition, nothing else, that communicates the comparison or contrast to the reader.

At the level of vocabulary, this technique renders the simile and the metaphor; as a pattern of predication, it is often extended to become a matrix of simile or of metaphor, as in

I Started Early—Took my Dog (J. 520)

Emily Dickinson

I started Early—Took my Dog—
And visited the Sea—
The Mermaids in the Basement
Came out to look at me—

And Frigates—in the Upper Floor
Extended Hempen Hands—
Presuming Me to be a Mouse—
Aground—upon the Sands—

But no Man moved Me—till the Tide
Went past my simple Shoe—
And past my apron—and my Belt
And past my Bodice—too—

And made as He would eat me up—
As wholly as a Dew
Upon a Dandelion's Sleeve—
And then—I started—too—

And He—He followed—close behind—
I felt His Silver Heel
Upon my Ankle—Then my Shoes
Would overflow with Pearl—

Until We met the Solid Town—
No one He seemed to know—
And bowing—with a Mighty look—
At me—The Sea withdrew—

What happens here is that a village maiden goes down to the sea-shore, walks out into the water, up to about her neck, then turns around and comes back. But this, obviously, is not what the poem is about. This little narrative is juxtaposed against other possible narratives, so that it becomes an extended metaphor for a quite different experience. The first and most obvious of these possible other experiences is a flirtation with death. As Yvor Winters says, "The sea is here the traditional symbol of death; that is, of all the forces and qualities in nature and in human nature which tend toward the dissolution of human character and consciousness." [7]

Kate Flores suggests, on the other hand, that the poem is a "study in fear, fear of love, of which the sea is here the symbol." [8] The maiden starts early— early in life, as well as early in the day—takes her dog—watchdog? man's-best-friend-guide-and-protector?—and leaves her "solid town"—repressive and protective environment. The mermaids (enticing and taboo love objects, created by the libidinous imaginations of sailors long away from shore) offer a comparison with the maiden's enticements and taboos. The hempen hands invite the touch of the image of timidity, the mouse. But the maiden is out to flirt with erotic experience, which she finds in the sexually suggestive progression of images in the third and fourth stanzas, and which startles her and makes her turn back. Then the sea becomes, not a seducer, but a courtier and follows her back to the edge of that repressive environment where the young are safe, if inexperienced.

There is an interpretation in which these two above are reconciled. One finds it suggested elsewhere in Emily Dickinson's poems, as well as in some of her contemporaries (see Melville's "Masthead" in *Moby Dick,* for instance). It is the idea that the immersion of the Self in any kind of experience outside the self is dangerous, and, in cases of total immersion, fatal to the character and consciousness of the Self. It is psychological suicide. In our psychoanalytically oriented times, one finds this idea expressed as the notion that tough-minded people may not be capable of love at all and do not really want to "give" themselves to anyone.

At any rate, the comparisons the poem invites are the grammar of its statement. Here, these comparisons are couched in metaphors and the matrix of metaphor is given a sequential organization (see chapter 15 for more on

[7] *In Defense of Reason,* pp. 285–86.
[8] *The Explicator,* 9 (May, 1951): item 47.

organization)—which makes this poem an allegory, the ultimate, perhaps, in the analogical grammar of communication.

Dialectic: Poetry of Analysis

Dialectic, in poetry, is derived from the Medieval Scholastic tradition, which in turn was derived from Classical models. It is essentially a question and answer technique which tries to expose all the possible attitudes toward a topic. When the method is imitated in poetry, we usually get a dialog either between two people or between two aspects of a single person. In arguing, these two viewpoints introduce all the aspects, pro and con, of the subject. Thus, the technique produces a poetry of analysis.

The earliest and perhaps most common imitation of the technique was the dialog between the body and the soul, a recurrent problem in medieval philosophy, prompted by St. Paul's Epistle to the Romans, Chapter 8, which produced many and many a nineteenth-rate verse. Several Renaissance poets and many of the religious poets of the seventeenth century, as well as a few poets down to our own day, also practiced the form, with somewhat better results. Here is a poem by Andrew Marvell, in which worldly Pleasure tempts unworldly Soul, first, with delights of taste, feeling, smell, sight, and hearing, and then—these sensory temptations having failed—with Beauty, Wealth, Power, and Knowledge. After the first section, which sets the scene via battle and combat imagery, the poem takes the form of an argument, stanza by stanza, between the body and the soul.

A Dialogue Between

The Resolved Soul and Created Pleasure

> Courage my Soul, now learn to wield
> The weight of thine immortal Shield.
> Close to thy Head thy Helmet bright.
> Balance thy Sword against the Fight.
> See where an Army, strong as fair,
> With silken Banners spreads the air.
> Now, if thou bee'st that thing Divine,
> In this day's Combat let it shine:
> And shew that Nature wants an Art
> To conquer one resolved Heart.   10

PLEASURE: Welcome the Creation's Guest,
> Lord of Earth, and Heaven's Heir.
> Lay aside that Warlike Crest,

And of Nature's banquet share:
Where the Souls of fruits and flowers
Stand prepared to heighten yours.

SOUL: I sup above, and cannot stay
To bait so long upon the way.

PLEASURE: On these downy Pillows lie,
Whose soft Plumes will thither fly: 20
On these Roses strowed so plain
Lest one Leaf thy Side should strain.

SOUL: My gentler Rest is on a Thought,
Conscious of doing what I ought.

PLEASURE: If thou bee'st with Perfumes pleased,
Such as oft the Gods appeased,
Thou in fragrant Clouds shalt show
Like another God below.

SOUL: A Soul that knows not to presume
Is Heaven's and its own perfume.   30

PLEASURE: Every thing does seem to vie
Which should first attract thine Eye:
But since none deserves that grace,
In this Crystal view *thy* face.

SOUL: When the Creator's skill is prized,
The rest is all but Earth disguised.

PLEASURE: Hark, how Music then prepares
For thy Stay these charming Airs;
Which the posting Winds recall,
And suspend the Rivers Fall.   40

SOUL: Had I but any time to lose,
On this I would it all dispose.
Cease Tempter. None can chain a mind
Whom this sweet Chordage cannot bind.

CHORUS: *Earth cannot show so brave a Sight*
As when a single Soul does fence
The Batteries of alluring Sense,
And Heaven views it with delight.
Then persevere: for still new Charges sound:
And if thou overcom'st thou shalt be crowned.   50

PLEASURE: All this fair, and soft, and sweet,
Which scatteringly doth shine,

> Shall within one Beauty meet,
> And she be only thine.

SOUL: If things of Sight such Heavens be,
What Heavens are those we cannot see?

PLEASURE: Where so e're thy Foot shall go
The minted Gold shall lie;
Till thou purchase all below,
And want new Worlds to buy.   60

SOUL: Wer't not a price who'ld value Gold?
And that's worth nought that can be sold.

PLEASURE: Wilt thou all the Glory have
That War or Peace commend?
Half the World shall be thy Slave
The other half thy Friend.

SOUL: What Friends, if to my self untrue?
What Slave, unless I captive you?

PLEASURE: Thou shalt know each hidden Cause;
And see the future Time;   70
Try what depth the Centre draws;
And then to Heaven climb.

SOUL: None thither mounts by the degree
Of knowledge, but Humility.

CHORUS: *Triumph, triumph, victorious Soul;*
The World has not one Pleasure more:
The rest does lie beyond the Pole,
And is thine everlasting Store.

l. 18 bait: stop for refreshment
l. 27 show: appear
l. 39 posting: fast-travelling
l. 46 fence: ward off

l. 61 That is, the value of gold is established
by mere convention.
l. 77 beyond the Pole: in Heaven

Secular subjects have also been treated in this question-and-answer strategy. We have already looked at the medieval ballad, "Lord Randall"; * the narrative there is suggested by the questioning dialog and the answers, the tragedy and heartbreak by a comparison of the answers with what we might have expected. Another example, oriented toward satire, rather than tragedy, is:

The Ruined Maid

Thomas Hardy

"O 'Melia, my dear, this does everything crown!
Who could have supposed I should meet you in Town?
And whence such fair garments, such prosperi-ty?
"O didn't you know I'd been ruined?" said she.

—"You left us in tatters, without shoes or socks,
Tired of digging potatoes, and spudding up docks;
And now you've gay bracelets and bright feathers three!"—
"Yes: that's how we dress when we're ruined," said she.

—"At home in the barton you said 'thee' and 'thou,'
and 'thik oon' and 'theäs oon,' and 't'other'; but now
Your talking quite fits 'ee for high compa-ny!"—
"Some polish is gained with one's ruin," said she.

—"Your hands were like paws then, your face blue and bleak
But now I'm bewitched by your delicate cheek,
And your little gloves fit as on any la-dy!"—
"We never do work when we're ruined," said she.

—"You used to call home-life a hag-ridden dream,
And you'd sigh, and you'd sock; but at present you seem
To know not of megrims or melancho-ly!"—
"True. One's pretty lively when ruined," said she.

—"I wish I had feathers, a fine sweeping gown,
And a delicate face, and could strut about Town!"—
"My dear—a raw country girl, such as you be,
Cannot quite expect that. You ain't ruined," said she.

Dialectic technique also lends itself to purely internal subjects. In the follow-ing Emily Dickinson poem, for example, the "grammar" of each pair of lines in the first half of the poem is that of an answer to an implied question.

It Was Not Death—(J. 510)

It was not Death, for I stood up,
And all the Dead, lie down—
It was not Night, for all the Bells
Put out their Tongues, for Noon.

It was not Frost, for on my Flesh
I felt Siroccos—crawl—

Nor Fire—for just my Marble feet
Could keep a Chancel, cool—

And yet, it tasted, like them all,
The Figures I have seen
Set orderly, for Burial,
Reminded me, of mine—

As if my life were shaven,
And fitted to a frame,
And could not breathe without a key,
And 'twas like Midnight, some—

When everything that ticked—has stopped—
And Space stares all around—
Or Grisly frosts—first Autumn morns,
Repeal the Beating Ground—

But, most, like Chaos—Stopless—cool—
Without a Chance, or Spar—
Or even a Report of Land—
To justify—Despair.

This poem also suggests the possibility for mixing the various "grammars." It begins in dialectic, shifts to comparisons, and finally discovers its subject in the last word.

An Exercise in Originality

It is a paradox that the truly original would be impossible to conceive, so we typically explain newness as realignments of the old. Thus our Martians, moon-men, and other monsters all have some organ like eyes, since we cannot imagine a being without sensory perceptors; and they have feet, or wings, or move by levitation, since we cannot conceive of them moving except by means we are already familiar with. True, we may translate them, transmogrify them, transubstantiate them, trans-materialize them—but these methods, too, we are already familiar with, though we may not be able to explain them. Once enough familiar elements are combined, in ways they have never before been combined, we have novelty. Novelty generally passes for originality, in literature and in life.

Now, novelty is manipulable, and the writer, who must be "original" to be accepted, should learn how to manipulate it. The human mind seems to love and demand novelty. And the mind is in the habit of creating it by the deliberate combination of the unusual. "Wit," as Dr. Johnson wrote in his famous criticism of metaphysical poetry, ". . . may be more rigorously and philosophically considered as a kind of *discordia concors;* a combination of dissimilar images, or discovery of occult resemblances in things apparently unlike . . . the most heterogeneous ideas . . . yoked by violence together." The joining may be bizarre or bland, but the most important thing for the writer to realize is that it may be done, and done consciously. The conscious impulse toward novel wit produces both our literary works, those "discoveries" about ourselves, and our clichés, those prefabricated henhouses of unthinking minds.

Take, for example, a common cliché, "wind-swept waves." It may well have been consciously, deliberately created. It must have been originated by a housewife or husband who noticed that dust fogs out before a broom in waves, then went to the beach and noticed that the wind pushes the water into similar configurations. What a stroke of originality that must have been, when fresh! Of course, it is also quite easy, the kind of thing almost anyone would think of—like looking at the stars and thinking of man's insignificance. In literature, we usually demand that the writer look harder for his comparisons, and part of our aesthetic response is to the difficulty.

Lawrence Hart, the San Francisco mentor of the Activist poets, used to give his verse-writing classes an exercise in originality. He asked the student to go to some place, say the living room of his own home, and write down twenty-five nouns, verbs, or adjectives that the place produced in his mind. Second, the student was to go to some quite different place, say the beach, and write down twenty-five other nouns, verbs, adjectives. Then the student was to try to combine words or concepts from the two lists to make original images or metaphors. One comes up with a certain burden of *wind-swept waves,* people *as thick as flies* or *packed like sardines,* of course, but he may also come up with *a rug of sand, a curtain of rock,* a man *gasping like a grunion, tide-pools of sentimental souls,* or something even novel, witty, or original.

Now, the upshot of this exercise is that the writer can choose, for a particular purpose and theme, the sources of his images. He can deliberately produce a particular, preconceived effect. Let's say he wants to write a satire about a variety store. He goes to such a store and writes down the dozen or twenty-five words that will best evoke the image and type of the variety store. Then he goes to a source of negative, dirty, derogatory imagery, let's say a junk yard or a second-hand furniture store. He may get lists like these:

VARIETY STORE	JUNK SHOP
sleepy cashier	cobwebs
toothbrushes	crud
clocks	dust

nylon scarves	paint flecking off
manikins	out-dated furniture
keys	old-fashioned
toys	crystal glassware
gaudy colors, red, yellow, blue	silver, tarnished
cheap glasses	dog-eared books
thimbles and thread	spilled paint
polished wood	fly-specks
mirrors	"dust-kittens" on floor
brass lamps	

It is obvious that some of these words are unusable. Words like *crud, clocks, furniture* are too slangy, too nominal, or too general for use in any very novel perception. And it is also obvious that certain combinations of prior experience take place in the making of the lists: the transfer of the polished quality of manikins and wooden counters to customers; the dust-kittens on the floor. Such combinations themselves become material for further combinations.

Using the two lists above, a writer might come up with something like this:

The old-fashioned sofa of a girl behind the fly-speck of a cash register gazed with cobweb eyes at polished manikins; sold dog-eared scarves, tarnished toothbrushes, and spilled-paint mirrors to gaudy, polished, dust-kitten customers with thimble and thread minds.

The passage illustrates the variety of result that one can get via deliberate combination of two lists. "Old-fashioned sofa of a girl" is overly "cute," but it is also quite evocative. We've all known girls who, draped in chintz, would be comfortable to sit on. Still, it's "cute"—cute for the sake of the cuteness. "Fly-speck of a cash register" seems to be begging. It asks one to associate the negative qualities of the fly-speck, not the fly-speck itself, with the cash register. This is dangerous. It seems to beg for a response that is not entirely there on the page, but has to come out of a stock response to fly-specks. "Cobweb eyes" is quite good. Excellent. It evokes the dry, static, hazy quality one sees in the eyes of the benighted, and we even see the veins in an eye, crystallized like the radiating threads of a web. "Polished manikins" is dead. It evokes only what everyone would take to be a part of the definition of manikin. "Dog-eared scarves" is fair-to-good. It merely applies a clichéd perception to a new object. Such a figure will do to "swell a progress," undercut before an excellence, contribute to a scene—but it is not strong enough to carry the core of a poem or story. "Tarnished toothbrushes" is bad. In this day of plastics, it is impossible. The attempt to save the figure with alliteration only calls attention to the feebleness of the attempt. "Spilled-paint mirrors" comes off after a bit of thought.

First, turn it into a simile: mirrors like spilled paint. Then, enumerate the qualities: wavy surface, bubbles at the edges, irregular, accidental in design rather than precisely engineered, cheap, tawdry. It does its duty, but not so immediately as "cobweb eyes." "Gaudy, polished, dust-kitten customers" suffers from more than one fault: gaudy and dust contradict; so do polished and dust; dust-kitten is a bit private; there is begging all the way. But the most serious fault is the figure's adjectivitis. Piling up of adjectives is no way to evoke a clear image. "Thimble and thread minds" is somewhere between being cute and doing duty after thought. The writer who would deliberately combine lists must also exercise taste and critical ability. If he gets one excellent image out of a list, he is one image ahead.

The results may seem so meager as to make the device unusable, but don't blanch before you have considered some of the great literature that seems to have sprung from this very process. Our whole conception of the conceit and of the matrix of metaphor are nothing more nor less than deliberate combinations of lists. Shakespeare must have been quite conscious and calculating when he sat down to describe the Renaissance conventions of the rejected lover in the terminology of the bankruptcy court: "When to the sessions of sweet silent thought..." (see Sonnet 30 *). And he even tells us of his deliberation in "Shall I compare thee to a summer's day...."

Sonnet 18

Shall I compare thee to a summer's day?
Thou art more lovely and more temperate:
Rough winds do shake the darling buds of May,
And summer's lease hath all too short a date:
Sometime too hot the eye of heaven shines,
And often is his gold complexion dimmed;
And every fair from fair sometimes declines,
By chance or nature's changing course untrimmed;
But thy eternal summer shall not fade,
Nor lose possession of that fair thou ow'st
Nor shall death brag thou wander'st in his shade,
When in eternal lines to time thou grow'st:
   So long as men can breathe, or eyes can see,
   So long lives this, and this gives life to thee.

Shakespeare reverses the process, with negative, or false, comparisons in "My mistress' eyes are nothing like the sun" (see Sonnet 130 *). All through our literary history, we can find myriad examples where a conscious writer has not settled for the one or two images from a list, but has gone on to force combination after combination into novel insight.

Mark Schorer, in his essay, "Fiction and the 'Matrix of Analogy,' " * has pointed out the thematic implications of this kind of strategy. "Metaphorical language expresses, defines, and evaluates theme, and thereby demonstrates the limits and the special poise within those limits of a given imagination." The careful, conscious, and thoughtful writer—in other words, the serious writer— will be greatly concerned with the implications of this oversimplified mental gymnastic, for its mechanism is the same at the highest level of creative achievement. It is a means by which the poise, limits, and meanings of a writer's perceptions can be made manifest to his readers. It is a way in which writers eliminate accident and control communication.

PROJECTS FOR WRITING AND DISCUSSION

A. ANALYSIS

1. Analyze the matrix of analogy in Whitman's Section 26, "Song of Myself," * in "Song of the Sky Loom," * in Lincoln's Gettysburg Address,* in Wolfe's "A stone, a leaf, an unfound door," * and in any poem that strikes your fancy. Such analysis should be one of the first reactions to reading a poem.

2. Analyze and describe what is poetic in the following statements by Alexander Pope. Try, for example, rearranging the sequence of words so that the metric is spoiled: what remains? What is lost? Try to determine for yourself what characterizes poetry of statement, here and elsewhere.

> All Nature is but art, unknown to thee;
> All chance, direction, which thou canst not see;
> All discord, harmony not understood;
> All partial evil, universal good:
> And, spite of pride, in erring reason's spite,
> One truth is clear: Whatever IS, is RIGHT.
> (Conclusion to "An Essay on Man")

> Know then thyself, presume not God to scan;
> The proper study of mankind is Man
> (From *Epistle II*)

3. Analyze the persona in some of the poems you have examined in the exercises above. What tone, mood, evaluation, does each persona imply? What techniques of language or verse account for the implications? Try changing the persona of some poems: what does the trick do to the poetry?

B. *COMPARISON*

1. "Song of the Sky Loom" * is built upon a matrix of analogies to weaving. Imagine the same poem, built upon analogies to cooking (Oh, Father, cook us a pot of stew; lay our plates on available tables; and so on) or built upon analogies to brewing, or horse-racing, or something else. Write down several possible figures of speech for these imagined poems. Compare your imagined poems with the original. What have you gained? What lost? Can you suggest any reasons why one matrix is better than another?

2. Compare the persona in Whitman's Section 26, "Song of Myself," * with Pope's persona in the extracts above. The two men are concerned with the same subject, but leave quite different impressions. Why? What accounts for each tone? mood? Try to imagine Pope's poem written with Whitman's persona, and vice versa.

C. *IMITATION*

1. Using the materials of Whitman's Section 26, "Song of Myself," * or of some other poem, write a poem with the persona of an old man. Then write the same poem with the persona of a young girl who has been attacked on a dark street.

2. Write a poem that you think President John F. Kennedy would have approved of.

3. Experiment a bit with dislocation of language, in the ways E. E. Cummings did. See if you can put together a pastiche of such dislocations to make a "Cummings-esque" poem.

D. *CREATION*

1. Write a poetic satire on some institution, say a gasoline station. Choose your persona with care; use the "Exercise in Originality" to develop a matrix of figurative speech; pay some attention to the "grammar" you want.

2. Now write a eulogy on the same subject as above, using the same techniques.

3. Write poems from several points of view on some great man, say Henry Ford, or on your grandfather, or an uncle. By choosing tone, mood, diction, grammatical strategy, and such, you can write poems that are perfectly contradictory.

4. Write a poem in which several different voices, expressing several different points of view, as in the previous exercise, compete with one another. You will thus be working with dialectic and with the long poem; be sure that some point of view—presumably the one you really believe—"wins" in the resolution of the contrasts.

15

Shaping a Poem
in Verse or Prose

Organization and heightening are the qualities that most account for the aesthetic effect of a poem; they give it a kind of "shape." These also are the qualities most often lacking in student poetry. Students manage to achieve quality diction and have a real poetic intention of "grammar" long before they master the container or the shape of the container in which they communicate the poem to a reader. It's of use, therefore, to enumerate here a few of the possible patterns of organization and convergence.

Organization in Poetry: Patterns of Strategy

The materials of poetry thus far discussed lend themselves to differing methods of organization. An idea in dialectic "grammar," for example, expressed in metaphors and metrical language, with rime, can yet be organized in various ways—according to the sequence of the ideas, for example, or according to the logic, or in analogy to some spatial or conventional relationship, or in some other way. To use an analogy from house-building—we now have the paint (tone), the boards (vocabulary), and nails (grammar; way of joining the rest together); we now need the blueprint for organizing the whole. Or, in the terms of grammar and rhetoric—we have the three primary systems of language (sounds, words, and syntax); now we need the rhetorical principles for expressing them literarily. It is very useful to be aware of eight strategies by which poetry can be organized. These are narrative, spatial, situational, meditative, logical, conventional, concatenative, and created patterns of strategy.

Narrative Patterns

Temporal sequence is, perhaps, the first method that comes to mind. First things come first, then second things, and so on. This is the structure of experience and the structure of the narratives by which we usually tell each other of our experience. The poetry it produces is therefore experiential. However, the focus in narrative poetry has not been upon the imitation of experience for some centuries, but upon the lyric meaning that resides in the experience—which is to say that narrative, as such, has not seemed poetic to us for quite some time. The temporal pattern of narrative can still be used in organizing lyric poetry, however, if the poet modifies it in certain ways.

In fact, narrative pattern can be a great asset. Since it is wholly and immediately understandable, it can be used to offset matter that is not so lucid. Juxtaposed thus, it can be a source of poetic tension. Let me relate here my considerations of tension and modification while writing one of my narrative poems.

The genesis of the poem was the imagery before me on a summer vacation to northern Michigan. There was a world of redolent decay, several kinds of plant and tree diseases, roads ripping through the wilderness, spreading dust, and upsetting the balanced distribution of moisture, soil, sun, wind—and leaving pockets of debris and decay. At first, these details were perceived one at a time, in a sequence that was mere accident, and were not poetically suggestive at all. One night, however, they all swarmed back, simultaneously, in a dream, and this time there was a poem in them. The swarm of imagery was confusing, chaotic, bordering—if not entering—the surrealistic. If that imagery was to be used in a poem, it would have to be organized in some way that would give it apparent lucidity. I settled immediately on narrative, as a principle of organization. Happily, I thought, the plodding common-sense quality of the story would counteract, and create a tension with, the continual tendency of the material to become irrational. But narrative, as such, is not very poetic, not very lyrical, so I decided to prop it up with blank verse (thereby gaining from tradition an illusion of its being poetry) and to prop up the blank verse with a rather redolent movement of metaphorically suggestive but actually concrete imagery—which brought me back to my subject matter.

The Proverb

H. C. Brashers

The preparations for the proverb were
Elaborate as dreams: tho it was spring,
A fungus fogged; dry moss hung from dead trees;
A freeway passed to spread debris, decay,
And, in its clover-leaf, stale water stood.

Lake waves ground stones as smooth as slime. Beyond,
The trees were dying from some blight that crowned
Them gold, or red; the marsh unjoined a deer;
The fossil in the stone was withering.

And in this midst, there rose a derrick that bore
Four red-gold oriental characters;
Beside it stood a hot-bed box, in which
Grew onions—and delicate green herbs.
I raised the glass and fierce fertility
Moved in the onion's blades and roots of herbs.

Nearby, appeared a little Eastern man
With prophet's beard and hands in patient sleeves.
Then I began to see, to understand,
To translate symbols which none would explain;
For he was one who looked on dying trees,
Yet saw the immortality of trees—
Who saw persistent stone and lasting waves—
Who looked at alien me, but made no move.

I felt the need for pardoning ritual
And tested my translations of his signs:
"All these things will come to me in time?"
He spoke of beetles eating to the heart,
Of fungus bubbles on the withered bark,
And answered lovingly: "Say rather *gifts*—
All these gifts are yours and mine, in time."

Poets through all times have done what was done here, either consciously or
intuitively. The modifications of subject and strategy are especially typical of
Romantic poetry, which usually has as its subject individual lyric emotion that
is prompted by an experience. The poet, then, is obligated to let his reader
know what that experience was, so that he can append the lyric passage that
is his real subject. Such a poet, too, is faced with the poetically dead material
of the narrative and has to seek some means to prop it up and make it appear
to be poetry. Wordsworth most often uses a mediocre metric and a vocabulary
of similes or metaphors. For example:

I Wandered Lonely As a Cloud

I wandered lonely as a cloud
That floats on high o'er vales and hills,
When all at once I saw a crowd,
A host, of golden daffodils;
Beside the lake, beneath the trees,
Fluttering and dancing in the breeze.

Continuous as the stars that shine
And twinkle on the milky way,
They stretched in never-ending line
Along the margin of a bay:
Ten thousand saw I at a glance,
Tossing their heads in sprightly dance.

The waves beside them danced; but they
Outdid the sparkling waves in glee;
A poet could not but be gay,
In such a jocund company;
I gazed—and gazed—but little thought
What wealth the show to me had brought:

For oft, when on my couch I lie
In vacant or in pensive mood,
They flash upon that inward eye
Which is the bliss of solitude;
And then my heart with pleasure fills,
And dances with the daffodils.

If we can ignore the old fashioned inversions of grammar and the often wooden rhythm, the poem comes through as a particular kind of meditation upon experience. It is communicated to us through the narrative sequence of that experience and the assertion at the end.

Much more successful as lyric, as verse, and as poetry are Wordsworth's "Lines Composed a Few Miles Above Tintern Abbey. . . ." Here, again, the subject is the lyric emotion that results from experience, but he has allowed this emotion to gestate more fully than he did his emotional response to the sight of the daffodils. In fact, the lyric component of "Tintern Abbey" amounts to a philosophy of life. How very much that philosophy gains by being related in the context of a narrative from life!—by being imbedded, literally, in questions of where are we going, why are we going there, what is the value, and so forth.

The narrative can be firm but ancillary, as it is in Marianne Moore's "Critics and Connoisseurs," * which we have already seen. There, two small narratives stand in relation to the opening as the illustrations stand to a generalization. And the opening generalization and the ending question use the narratives as the means of making the statement of the poem.

The narrative can also be submerged, almost out of sight, as it is in E. A. Robinson's "Eros Turannos," * which we will look at later, and in Robert Frost's "Stopping by Woods on a Snowy Evening." Frost gives us only his thoughts while he is stopped, but the narratives that are implied—the trip this night, the trip through life—are what give those thoughts context and meaning. The poem can hardly be said to be narrative, yet it depends upon narrative for its organization.

The narrative can also be generalized; the passage of time can be treated conceptually, as it is in "seasons" poetry, poetry built upon the organizing principle of the passage from one season to another, or through all the seasons. See for example, E. E. Cummings's "Anyone Lived in a Pretty How Town." *

In Cummings's poem, time is conceptual, rather than experiential, and, because of this, the narrative has an aesthetic effect that borders on spatial organization. Large passages of time, as well as relationships between such passages, are most readily represented in some spatial way when we are talking about them.

Spatial Patterns

Space, like time, is an inevitable aspect of perception; so it is quite natural that it functions as a principle of conceptual organization. Joseph Frank has discussed the history and aesthetics of spatial perception in his long essay, "Spatial Form in Modern Literature," [1] and many of his insights apply specifically to poetry. The reader responds to images as static relationships, not developments, in the subject. "An image," Pound wrote, "is that which presents an intellectual and emotional complex in an instant of time." This is the opposite of discursive progression; it is illumination and understanding of analogies and contrasts—of all the parts of a complex—simultaneously, momentarily, and intuitively.

"In [Pound's] Cantos and [Eliot's] The Waste Land," writes Mr. Frank (p. 228), "it should have been clear that a radical transformation was taking place in esthetic structure; ... where syntactical sequence is given up for a structure depending on the perception of relationships between disconnected word-groups. To be properly understood, these word-groups must be juxtaposed with one another and perceived simultaneously; only when this is done can they be adequately understood; for while they follow one another in time, their meaning does not depend on this temporal relationship."

Among the simplest and easiest of spatial patterns are those which imitate some spatial configuration or contrast in our experience. The natural symbol of the first is the river,[2] and one of the finest illustrations of it comes from music:

[1] *Sewanee Review*, 53 (1945): 221–240, 433–456, 643–653.

[2] Rivers are definitely spatial, not temporal. All of time that is ever immediate is the present moment; the rest is memory and anticipation. But all of the river is always there; each point on the river exists in time, but more importantly each point has a spatial relationship to all the other points. It is spatial relation of the parts that constitute and define the image and concept of a river.

Smetana's *Die Moldau,* a tone poem on the Danube. One thinks also of the big, middle section of *Huckleberry Finn,* in which the sequence and flow of the river is the organizing principle that links together, as one big image, the various somewhat discrete segments of life on the river. Virtually all picaresque literature, whether in verse or prose, forces us to talk about its river or its road in spatial terms. On the other hand, it is also quite natural to proceed by contrasts, rather than flow. Each idea, as Hegel suggested, calls up not only its sequential position, but its opposite as well. To proceed from one idea to another for purposes of contrast and variation on a theme, as Aldous Huxley does in *Point Counterpoint,* as T. S. Eliot does in "The Love Song of J. Alfred Prufrock," is to give the material a spatial organization.

Perhaps the most important of spatial patterns, however, is the concentric pattern, in which the progress of the material revolves about a central symbol or idea. In fiction, the grand example is Nathaniel Hawthorne's *The Scarlet Letter,* in which the action and the themes center in, revolve around, and return to the scaffold in the town square. Walt Whitman used the same principle of organization in "Passage to India," in which he returns to the theme of the title again and again, especially in connection with the three "passages" that he is celebrating: the opening of the Suez Canal, the completion of the Trans-Atlantic Cable, and the completion of the Trans-Continental Railroad to San Francisco. The "23rd Psalm," * which we have already seen, revolves about the central concept of Divine protectiveness, and Emily Dickinson uses a similar principle of organization in this poem of definition:

Success is Counted Sweetest (J. 67)

Success is counted sweetest
By those who ne'er succeed.
To comprehend a nectar
Requires sorest need.

Not one of all the purple Host
Who took the Flag today
Can tell the definition
So clear of Victory—

As he defeated—dying—
On whose forbidden ear
The distant strains of triumph
Burst agonized and clear!

It is also possible to make the poem circular, as well as concentric, and let it return to its point of beginning:

Death Is What Makes Hunger Hurt

H. C. Brashers

Death is what makes hunger hurt:
Without death, starving
Could be a way of turning on.

Starvation, after all, *is* sensation—
Galvanometric stimulation—
Thrill—

What less is beauty?

Imagine some campus esthete,
Jaded with the pleasures
Of cops-and-acid-heads, tired

Of cars and clitori, filled
With the fix, buffered
With the buzz, seeking

One more-savory sensation,
Contemplating hunger. and cold.
And nights in the rain.

He forsakes starvation with a sigh—
Ah— He foregoes the intensity,
The mind-manifesting reality:

Death is what makes hunger hurt.

Situational Patterns

The invitation in the middle of the last poem to imagine a situation from one's experience suggests a third way to organize a poem by drawing upon ordinary perception. For to invoke a situation is to invoke a set of relationships—relationships which occur in time and space, but in which time and space are unimportant—and to focus upon the mere occurrence, the fact of existence, of those relationships as the organizing principle.

There is a certain harmony and interchange here with the usual concept of character that is characteristic of lyric poetry. Persons in poems are seldom more than pawns; we accept them for the action they perform or the thought they have and do not ask them to imitate reality. It is one of our conventions of reading poetry that we accept them so. Their importance as characters is limited to their immediate function in the poem; we need and want no more. Similarly, the situation projected in a poem is accepted in and for itself. We accept it, by convention, as the most efficient rendition of what is significant. That it has no surrounding referent in time or space is irrelevant. For example:

They Flee from Me

Sir Thomas Wyatt

They flee from me that sometime did me seek,
    With naked foot stalking in my chamber.
I have seen them gentle, tame, and meek,
    That now are wild and do not remember
    That sometime they put themselves in danger
        To take bread at my hand; and now they range
        Busily seeking with a continual change.

Thanked be fortune, it hath been otherwise
    Twenty times better; but once, in special,
In thin array, after a pleasant guise,
    When her loose gown from her shoulders did fall,
    And she caught me in her arms long and small,
        Therewith all sweetly did me kiss,
        And softly said: "Dear heart, how like you this?"

It was no dream; I lay broad waking:
    But all is turned through my gentleness
Into a strange fashion of forsaking;
    And I have leave to go of her goodness;
    And she also to use new-fangleness.
        But since that I so kindly am served,
        I fain would know what she hath deserved.

Wyatt's narrative is generalized and the space unspecified, except for "my chamber"; all is subordinated to the situation, which posits the central question of the poem—a question of man's relation to his surroundings. Wyatt gives us the impression that he started from a situation and, through thinking about it, arrived at the comment on relationships that he implies. Wordsworth can give us just the opposite feeling. In "Expostulation and Reply," for example, we feel that he had the idea of man's relation to nature and books first and then invented the situation that would reveal his ideas. This feeling persists through the companion poem, "The Tables Turned, an Evening Scene on the Same Subject."

The Tables Turned

Up! Up! my friend, and quit your books,
Or surely you'll grow double;
Up! Up! my friend, and clear your looks;
Why all this toil and trouble?

The sun, above the mountain's head,
A freshening luster mellow
Through all the long green fields has spread,
His first sweet evening yellow.

Books! 'tis a dull and endless strife;
Come, hear the woodland linnet,
How sweet his music! on my life,
There's more of wisdom in it.

And hark! how blithe the throstle sings!
He, too, is no mean preacher;
Come forth into the light of things,
Let Nature be your teacher.

She has a world of ready wealth,
Our minds and hearts to bless—
Spontaneous wisdom breathed by health,
Truth breathed by cheerfulness.

One impulse from a vernal wood
May teach you more of man,
Of moral evil and of good,
Than all the sages can.

Sweet is the lore which Nature brings;
Our meddling intellect
Misshapes the beauteous forms of things—
We murder to dissect.

Enough of Science and of Art;
Close up those barren leaves;
Come forth, and bring with you a heart
That watches and receives.

Meditative Patterns

Situations are evoked, of course, so that they will stimulate certain kinds of thoughts. There is a particular and separate pattern based upon this intention. It is the typical Romantic strategy and grows out of the Romantic's common

desire to discover meaning in individuals and the situations they create. Typically, in organizing a poem for the meditation it will stimulate, a good part of
the non-situational thought that follows from a situation is depicted along
with it.

This is the strategy of many poems. Wordsworth is walking along a lake,
sees a field of daffodils, has a certain rapturous feeling, recreates in verse exactly
the pattern that led to his meditation, then gives us the emotion of the meditation. Or, he sees a solitary reaper working in a field, hears her singing, and
goes through the same process:

> The music in my heart I bore,
> Long after it was heard no more.

William Cullen Bryant, in "To a Waterfowl," sees a duck flying overhead
and asserts

> There is a Power whose care
> Teaches thy way along that pathless coast—
> The desert and illimitable air—
> Lone wandering but not lost.

From this view of the duck, he draws an analogy to man's situation:

> He who, from zone to zone,
> Guides through the boundless sky thy certain flight,
> In the long way that I must tread alone,
> Will lead my steps aright.

The "grammar" of analogy is an integral part of this strategy of organization,
which focuses upon meditation and evaluation of experience.

This pattern is so common as to be a convention and, as such, perhaps
should be included in the next category.

Conventional Patterns

Through the history of literature, certain patterns have been used over and
over and have undergone standardization until they have become conventional.
Because of our familiarity with such conventions, whether we are conscious
of them or not, poetic material put into one of these ready-made frames
strikes us as organized. The deliberate use of one of these conventions then
is a possible pattern of organization. There are so many of these that I will
only mention and illustrate a few here.

Prayer is one of the most common conventions, and one that usually employs a grammar of analogy, similar to typical Romantic strategy. It is a request, couched in a command form. The poet is usually forced into talking of his unworldly subject by drawing analogies to common things. For example:

Housewifery

Edward Taylor

Make me, O Lord, thy spinning wheel complete;
   Thy holy word my distaff make for me.
Make mine affections thy swift fliers neat,
   And make my soul thy holy spool to be.
   My conversation make to be thy reel,
   And reel the yarn thereon spun of thy wheel.

Make me thy loom then, knit therein this twine:
   And make thy holy spirit, Lord, wind quills:
Then weave the web thyself. The yarn is fine.
   Thine ordinances make my fulling mills.
   Then dye the same in heavenly colors choice,
   All pinked with varnished flowers of paradise.

Then clothe therewith mine understanding, will,
   Affections, judgment, conscience, memory;
My words and actions, that their shine may fill
   My ways with glory and thee glorify.
   Then mine apparel shall display before ye
   That I am clothed in holy robes for glory.

Epic convention should already be fairly well known. It uses a special arrangement of time—begins *in medias res,* then flashbacks—and dwells upon certain aspects of space and certain situations, such as the preparations for a battle, the detailed, heroic, often fulsome description of the heroes, the depiction in detail of the battle itself, and so on. Alexander Pope fulfills and parodies the convention in "The Rape of the Lock," which is much too long to include here. Belinda's vanity table becomes the scene of the preparation; the courtiers become the epic list of participants; a card-game becomes the battle itself. The complete convention produces necessarily a long poem, but it is possible to use various parts of the convention for purposes of organization.

The pastoral elegy is another such convention. In its formula, the opening is an announcement of a death, usually done in vocabulary that suggests or describes shepherds and country folk. Then follows an invocation to the Muse, a request to help sing the worth of the deceased in a funeral ceremony. Then follows the speech, sometimes at grave-side, of the principal mourner. Then follow speeches by various other mourners. Sometimes, this section takes on the form of a dialectic discussion from several angles. Finally, Nature itself—the whole universe—sings its praise of the deceased; and this permits the final scene: the apotheosis, the acceptance of the deceased into the "heaven" of afterlife, where the deceased takes on a different kind of life. This transformation consoles the poet and mourners and reconciles them to death, in general and in particular. Milton's "Lycidas" is an excellent example of the conventional pastoral elegy.

The Renaissance sonnet is often involved in such conventions and often with conventional situations, such as that of the unrequited lover. Take, for example, "Sonnet C," from *Astrophel and Stella,* by Sir Philip Sidney:

> O tears! no tears, but rain, from Beauty's skies,
> Making those lilies and those roses grow,
> Which are most fair, now more than most fair show,
> While graceful Pity beauty beautifies.
>
> O honey'd sighs! which from that breast do rise,
> Whose pants do make unspilling cream to flow:
> Wing'd with whose breath, so pleasing zephyrs blow,
> As can refresh the hell where my soul fries.
>
> O plaints! conserv'd in such a sugar'd phrase,
> That eloquence itself envies your praise;
> While sobb'd out words a perfect music give.
> Such tears, sighs, plaints, no sorrow is, but joy;
> Or, if such heavn'ly sighs must prove alloy,
> All mirth fairwell, let me in sorrow live.

According to Maurice Evans,[3] decorum, which was very important to the poets of the sixteenth century, dictated that the sonnet not be considered a serious verse form; therefore, the poet could use as many rhetorical devices as he desired and was free to experiment with figures and tropes of complexity and exaggeration. In the sonnet above, Sidney uses a favorite Renaissance trope, the rhetorical figure *merismus,* presenting the idea piece by piece, the purpose being to make an analysis into parts of an idea which might otherwise be expressed in a single statement. Note here the four formal and sharp divisions, hingeing upon the uses of the words, *tears, sighs, plaints.*

---

[3] In *English Poetry in the Sixteenth Century* (Hillary), pp. 93–94, 102.

Note also the gathering in summary fashion at the end of the words used earlier. Elementary—but still form.

Many of these conventions are out of date now, but they are still available to the poet who has a good purpose and the courage to use them well.

Logical Patterns

The human mind has rather consistently searched for logical relationships among ideas and between the parts of complex ideas. Although the Sensationalist philosophers and psychologists would insist upon the mere accidence of one event following another, the mind has always sought to define some causal relationship between ideas. This is one way of imposing order or organization upon experience. And although it is highly conceptual and a bit abstract (or perhaps, *because* of these qualities), logic has always been an important principle of organization in poetry. Usually the logical patterns of poetry are some form of truncated syllogism or some other form of Classical reasoning.

A poem that depends almost entirely upon the logical pattern of the syllogism for its effect is Emily Dickinson's "Much Madness is Divinest Sense," * which we have already seen in another connection. The paradoxes in the opening line and in line three are resolved by syllogisms, and that resolution is then used as the first premise in the two syllogisms that make up the poem: *If* madness is sense, according to the majority, *and if* you assent, *then* you are sane; if madness is sense, and if you demure, then you are insane. The logical pattern, of course, leads us to an absurdity, but the very absurdity of the process and the ironic comment that such absurdities *do* happen in life and majorities—these *are* the thematic concerns of the poem.

A similar kind of logic lies behind the when-but-so progress of the following:

Sonnet: The Power To Enter

H. C. Brashers

When we were young and puppets still were tragic,
Before we learned behavior, so to speak,
Imagination filled, swelled, burst in magic
Our puppet hearts, our summer nights, our meek
Imagery. But up we grew and learned to pose,
Became the public man, and acted age,
Adopted masks, learned shame, and chose
Containment and contempt for our young rage.

So we are known by names and adjectives
Like level-headed, grown-up, objective,
Intelligent, perhaps, but O! the cost!
For it's the power to enter we have lost:
We stand alone outside the bordered parks,
Afraid to walk where children race with larks.

Consider the logical pattern of this poem:

To His Coy Mistress

Andrew Marvell

Had we but world enough, and time,
This coyness, lady, were no crime.
We would sit down, and think which way
To walk, and pass our long love's day.
Thou by the Indian Ganges' side
Shouldst rubies find; I by the tide
Of Humber would complain. I would
Love you ten years before the flood,
And you should, if you please, refuse
Till the conversion of the Jews.
My vegetable love should grow
Vaster than empires and more slow;
An hundred years should go to praise
Thine eyes, and on thy forehead gaze;
Two hundred to adore each breast,
But thirty thousand to the rest;
An age at least to every part,
And the last age should show your heart.
For, lady, you deserve this state,
Nor would I love at lower rate.
But at my back I always hear
Time's wingèd chariot hurrying near;
And yonder all before us lie
Deserts of vast eternity.
Thy beauty shall no more be found,
Nor, in thy marble vault shall sound
My echoing song; then worms shall try
That long-preserved virginity,
And your quaint honor turn to dust,
And into ashes all my lust:
The grave's a fine and private place,

But none, I think, do there embrace.
Now therefore, while the youthful hue
Sits on thy skin like morning dew,
And while thy willing soul transpires
At every pore with instant fires,
Now let us sport us while we may,
And now, like amorous birds of prey,
Rather at once our time devour
Than languish in his slow-chapped power.
Let us roll all our strength and all
Our sweetness up into one ball,
And tear our pleasures with rough strife
Through the iron gates of life:
Thus, though we cannot make our sun
Stand still, yet we will make him run.

There are many other possibilities of adapting patterns of logic to organizing specific poems, but this should be sufficient to introduce the subject and stimulate some thought.

Concatenative Patterns

In the twentieth century, many poets have tried to organize their poems on the principle of concatenation—a simple linking of one ideal to another, like the rings of a chain. T. S. Eliot, perhaps, has been the most successful of these poets. Most of his poems are concatenations of objective correlatives, associative progressions of highly emotive lines, apparently accidental linkages from one feeling to the next. These progressions, in Eliot's work, are usually irrational on the surface; they are often obscure. All this derives ultimately from John Locke and the Sensationalists, who believed that ideas are associated with one another this way in the mind; for them, the structure of the mind was an associative progression. Thus, the principle has a long and respectable history, but use of it by half-conscious poets usually produces the worst sort of verse. Indeed, his making this principle popular once again is the most pernicious aspect of T. S. Eliot's influence. It produces unorganized verse.

Eliot's own verse was far from unorganized. His method of composition depended upon the "objective correlative," which he defined in his essay, "Hamlet and His Problems." In order to express an emotion, explained Eliot, the poet had to find "a set of objects, a situation, a chain of events which shall be the formula of that *particular* emotion," that is, which shall recreate that emotion in the reader. Thus, the objective thing in the poem is correlative with the subjective emotion behind it. There is a kind of one-to-one relationship between the objects in the poem and the meaning attached to those objects. Now, Eliot organized his poems on the *subjective* level and let the objective level fall into irrationality or obscurity. Thus, "The Love Song of J. Alfred Prufrock" progresses, superficially, from an invitation to tour the town, to cocktail party talk, to a description of a winter evening, to a discussion of our daily personae, back to the cocktail party, to Prufrock's self-conscious description of himself and the questions that plague him, to a several part dialectic analysis of his past, to ragged claws on the floors of the sea, and so on. There is no causal relationship between these objects and they have baffled many. But if we translate each of them into its subjective component, its emotional meaning, we get a highly organized rhetoric of comparisons and contrasts, with irony and value judgments emerging.

Unfortunately, most of Eliot's young imitators (for the young learn poetry, as they learn language, by imitation) have not perceived the "grammar" that makes his concatenative organization possible. Instead, they imitate only the superficial obscurity. They produce verses that are associational progressions of highly emotive lines, which are so unorganized that they can often be read backwards as well as forwards without doing appreciable violence to the meaning or feeling.

Take this student lyric, for example:

> Two flickering flames burn side by side
> Reaching toward the skies.
> One is a tall flame burning bright,
> The other small and dim.
> The two flames meet in sweet caress,
> Then part and meet again.
> The small shaft bows, oh so low,
> And touches the other with love.
> Two flickering flames burn down fast
> Two souls meet again at the last.

Transpose its lines into reverse order:

> Two souls meet again at the last.
> Two flickering flames burn down fast
> And touches the other with love.
> The small shaft bows, oh so low,
> Then part and meet again.
> The two flames meet in sweet caress,
> The other small and dim.
> One is a tall flame burning bright,
> Reaching toward the skies.
> Two flickering flames burn side by side.

The sentiment, and even the sentimentality, are unchanged by the trick; the grammar, though dislocated, is not destroyed. There is something wrong with a poem that can be read backwards. And there is something seriously wrong with the notions of organization that allow such verse to be written.

This problem can plague poets of far more talent than the author of the above lyric. Here is a poem, for instance, in which the order of the stanzas can be reversed, with some improvement in effectiveness:

Cricket Monotony

Andrea Yunker

cricket monotony
wound like a rope
through the night

padded-paw-foot cat
treading on stealth

moon-mute silence—
a sullen silence—
and shadowed etchings . . .

yet a breeze
full of the hope of morning,
waiting for dawn

but there is no light . . .
only the sodden stench
of a nacreous half-light,
blurred by the idiot ramblings
of uncomprehending tongues,
of brains in which senses are mingled,
indistinguishable.

why are those faces,
sunlight-pelted full faces,
awaiting?

A number of poets—among them Eliot, Hart Crane, Wallace Stevens, and others—have also worked consciously with a second form of concatenation, which "Cricket Monotony" illustrates. This is the image-shift, a technique of making the descriptive component of an image the basis of shift and the conceptual link between two images. In "'Cricket Monotony," the general and specific tone of the first stanza is "night." The mood thus engendered is consonant with the second stanza stealth of the cat, which is generally associated with night, and both are explicitly repeated in stanza three, with "moon-mute," "silence," and "shadowed etchings." Stanza four offers contrast, which—in its Hegelian way—advances the first mood. The moods of night, light, and half-light compete in stanza (or is it section) five, but everything dissolves in the question and dawn in the last stanza. There is, in other words, a certain continuity in the lyric, a continuity that knits together—but does not lead anywhere. To read the poem in reverse, to pose the question first and then the competition of moods, with one emerging as dominant and thematic, maintains the image concatenation and gives the lyric a structure.

Created Patterns

The most important and most effective patterns of organization are those created by the material itself or by the poet's treatment of it. The first of these may be called organic form; the second, aesthetic form. Both of these can be either embracing or skeletal pattern, though skeletal pattern is perhaps more common—this seems to derive from the sequential nature of language and from the logical habits of the Western world, which are most often based on division and sub-division, through the several branches of a subject.

There are hundreds, perhaps thousands, of possibilities in organic or aesthetic organization, far too many (and as yet uncreated) to be described here. All the principles of "grammar" and organization suggest ways of looking at material; the principles of structure, design, and pattern should suggest, too, ways of shaping poetic material. With experience, the young poet learns to create and impose the patterns he needs.

The young poet should begin by asking if his subject has an inherent "shape," and end by asking if he wants to give it a particular one. In between, there may be thousands of questions: is there a contrast that is basic to the idea that could be used as the basis for form in the poem? Is there a motif that can be used as the basis for variations? What is the unifying principle, the pattern, of the material? Is it fragmented, so that the form should be fragmented? Is it sequential? Is there a fixed spatial relationship?

When the several divisions of a poem grow out of the several divisions of the subject, the form of the poem is said to be organic. The image most often used to describe this analogically is the tree. The trunk branches out, the branches limb out, the limbs leaf out, and we get, finally, a picture of the whole, integrated by the organic relationships. In the following poem the trunk, the subject, is man's historical concern with faith and fear; in Western tradition, there have been three main answers of faith to the problem of fear

—"Greek truths or God or Nature's/green sagacity"; each of these branches are brought into focus momentarily and are finally considered collectively, as they impress the observer today. The nature of the subject determines the nature of the poem.

Remedies

Kenneth Johnson

When will those men who see
the rusted faiths, clogged hopes,
the fears that leak from cracks
throughout this house our lives,
and promptly offer us
Greek truths or God or Nature's
green sagacity
as tools sure to rebuild
each room better than new:
once doubt their remedies?
once pause to wonder if
their timeless tools do still
possess the power to mend?
Once also see: Greek truths
now equal maps of roads
long since submerged in sand;
Christ's God—a redwood tree
pruned down to stump; Nature—
a wise friend turned dumb brute.
Once realize: it is
the very loss of these—
of all—past remedies
that rusts and clogs and cracks
our daily crumbling lives.

Nearly the opposite strategy of organization is also possible. One can impose a division and sub-division structure on a subject that has none, by the aesthetic promises that the presentation makes. In the poem below, there is no inherent form to the core idea; it has a three-part elaboration (it could have been two or four, though many more might have been aesthetically confusing); the choice of a three-part development then made it necessary to let the reader in on the secret of the organization very early, which is done in general terms in the opening stanza. Each of the parts, then, became the controlling idea and image for its stanza in the body of the poem. The general metaphor that runs through them then informs the general restatement of the core idea at the end.

A Point, Beyond Which

H. C. Brashers

There is a point, they say, beyond which
The brain refuses to register pain:
Beached, wrecked ends of heart,
Slacked breath, razed nerves
          No longer connect.

For the hurt heart surges surf-like,
Pumping in ebb and flow, pounding
The jaws of his trap, unable to resign
To quiet terror, even when pain closes,
          As fingers, on him,

And the breath blows fast and fish-like,
Fluttering in catches and gasps, held
Beach-wreck still, unable to go on,
While pain pumps, like a fish left ashore
          When the tide goes out.

The nerves just stop. Derelict. Too much
Attack leaves a numb network—
These remains may be viewed: the skeleton of nerves,
Tense, crisp, stretched across
          The corners of pain.

After one cries for a long time, the tears
Refuse to ebb or flow: the point,
Harbored in torture, anchored in pain,
Where you or I implode to void,
          Collapse in vacuum.

Heightening in Poetry: Patterns of Convergence

Such, then, are the materials of audible and ideational rhythms in poetry—meter, persona, diction, grammar, and strategy of revelation. It remains to discuss the combinations of these elements as they heighten our response to an image, a line, or a poem. As we have noted before, the use of these elements fall into patterns. Each use has its beginning, its high-point, and its attenuation. In the usual run of language, some of these patterns will be quiescent, others demanding. In good poetry, the poet arranges these patterns so that their high-points converge upon a particular image, line, or effect. Good poets consciously employ these patterns for the deliberate heightening of the aesthetic content of their poems.

Although these convergences of two or more patterns seldom occur in any simplistic isolation, we must try at a stage like this to separate them. The effect of meter should be considered separately with the effect of diction, the effect of diction with the effect of grammar, the effect of grammar with the effect of organization, and so on. Thus, we get a number of simple combinations from the matrix of meter, diction, grammar, and organization. A brief illustration of some six of these possible combinations should be enough to illustrate the point.

Meter and Diction

It is already clear that meter alone has a certain aesthetic effect. One sees this in such verses as "Hickory Dickory Dock" and other nursery rimes, where the lexical content is irrelevant. In a similar way, such rhythmical patterns as ballad measure can be used to combine with and enhance lexical meaning. Wordsworth's stanza,

> One impulse from a vernal wood
> May teach you more of man
> Of moral evil and of good
> Than all the sages can

uses meter, rime, and stanza to increase the aesthetic effect of the idea. This rhythm is less exciting than a nursery rime, but, nevertheless, has some effect. Try rephrasing the idea in rhythmless prose and you will see the difference.

The other elements of audible rhythm also affect aesthetic content. Emily Dickinson uses alliteration in

> I've seen a Dying Eye
> Run round and round a room.

The alliteration of the *r*'s here does not create the sensation of vertigo. It merely intensifies the lexical meaning already there. This is always true of alliteration; it has no inherent meaning but has the power to intensify elements already present. Poe's "silken, sad, uncertain rustling of each purple curtain," is said to be sinister, but *s*'s can also be used to intensify the "sweet songs of the summer sycamores." The *r*'s in Emily Dickinson's line merely focus our aesthetic attention upon the meaning "round and round." Alliteration can do no more, but how very much that is, after all!

Another kind of audible rhythm can be illustrated by E. E. Cummings's "anyone lived in a pretty how town." * His use of variations upon the lines "summer autumn winter spring" and "sun moon stars rain" return at strategic moments to heighten and intensify our sense of the cycles of his narrative. At the end, these lines play almost as a musical coda and point up the irony of his rime.

Meter and Predication

In the Cummings poem, the repetition of diction comes close to altering the total statement of the poem. Meter and predication working together have the power actually to change the aesthetic content the reader receives. The American Indian poem, "Song of the Sky Loom," * has a different aesthetic meaning, predicates a slightly different content, if we read it without its last line, that is, if we end it with "that we may walk fittingly where birds sing,/ that we may walk fittingly where grass is green." If the verse is read without the final line for a re-orientation, when the last rhythmic line returns and puts the frame around the poem, the aesthetic orientation of the poem becomes that of a prayer, rather than that of a pantheistic celebration of existence.

The accentual ballad "Lord Randall" * uses rhythm to heighten its arrangement for climax. Each of the questions and answers is relatively unimportant in itself. What they do rhythmically is signify to us that something important is being foreshadowed. The rhythm focuses our expectations upon the very predication of the poem, heightening our response. At the same time the poet further strengthened that response with the incremental repetition, the variation upon the key rhythmic line.

Andrew Marvell uses still another rhythmic device to heighten our attention to predication in "A Dialogue Between the *Resolved Soul* and *Created Pleasure*." * The rhythm of alternation between the speakers focuses our attention upon the dialectic predication. Marvell further heightens our attention with the alternation of quatrains for Pleasure's voice and couplets for the Soul's voice. The punctual, brief epigrammatic answers of the Soul have a different effect from what they would if they were longer. Imagine Pleasure speaking in pithy couplets and Soul answering in rimed quatrains and you will hear Soul snivelling, trying desperately to find an argument. The rhythmic punctuation of each section with the celestial chorus in praise of the Soul further heightens the aesthetic predication of the poem.

Meter, Diction, and Predication

We can combine the effects of the paired patterns we have already seen in a kind of three-way effect of rhythm, image, and grammar. In Emily Dickinson's poem "The Snake" (J. 986), one finds all three of these elements operating simultaneously. The final stanza, and especially the last line,

> But never met this Fellow
> Attended, or alone
> Without a tighter breathing
> And Zero at the Bone—,

obviously works in the rhythmic pattern and with exact rime. The diction of "Zero at the Bone" is heightened by the rhythm and the strong rime. Further, the feeling involved is the point and climax of the predication. Here Emily has caused the last three patterns to converge and create the aesthetic heft of the line.

In "Much Madness is Divinest Sense," * she adds a fourth pattern. In addition to the regular metric, the effect of the rime "sane/chain," the happy diction of "handled with a chain," and the completion of the predication with the last line, she uses a pattern of syllogistic logic. The third syllogism of the poem coincides with and heightens the effect of this last line and the point of the poem.

Diction and Grammar

The combinations of pattern we have been looking at produce rhythmed poetry, but a combination of such elements as diction, grammar, and organization would produce a poetry without rhythm. In such poetry, the convergence of patterns other than those of verse create the aesthetic effect. Few poets have practiced this kind of poetry, perhaps, because of the prejudice for verse, but it is, nevertheless, rich in potential. We have already seen an excellent example of poetry without rhythm, namely Pound's "In a Station of the Metro." * The total poetic effect in that poem depends upon the accuracy and penetration of his diction, along with his "grammar" of analogy.

Stephen Crane was, perhaps, the first of the moderns to practice poetry without rhythm. His poems are rhythmically indistinguishable from prose, yet they have considerable poetic value; for example:

The Wayfarer

The wayfarer
Perceiving the pathway to truth,
Was struck with astonishment.
It was thickly grown with weeds.
"Ha," he said,
"I see that none has passed here
In a long time."
Later he saw that each weed
Was a singular knife.
"Well," he mumbled at last,
"Doubtless there are other roads."

This poem gains its effect from the ironic use of the traditional metaphor, "path of life," along with other fairly easy metaphors, such as "the blades of grass," and organizes the whole on a fairly simple narrative. The pattern of diction, the "grammar" of the stock analogy, and the abandonment of the quest of the road, all coincide at the end of the poem. Another Crane poem, "In the Desert," * uses a more original diction, a "grammar" of dialectic, and a pattern of situation to focus our attention upon an ironic psychological perception.

Diction, Grammar, and Organization

In both "The Wayfarer" and "In the Desert" the pattern of organization is relatively unimportant. But the pattern of organization can be the difference between a successful poem and a set of notes for a poem. Consider the following:

Lucinda Matlock

Edgar Lee Masters

I went to the dances at Chandlerville,
And played snap-out at Winchester.
One time we changed partners,
Driving home in the moonlight of middle June,
And then I found Davis.
We were married and lived together for seventy years,
Enjoying, working, raising the twelve children,

Eight of whom we lost
Ere I had reached the age of sixty.
I spun, I wove, I kept the house, I nursed the sick,
I made the garden, and for holiday
Rambled over the fields where sang the larks,
And by Spoon River gathering many a shell,
And many a flower and medicinal weed—
Shouting to the wooded hills, singing to the green valleys.
At ninety-six I had lived enough, that is all,
And passed to a sweet repose.
What is this I hear of sorrow and weariness,
Anger, discontent and drooping hopes?
Degenerate sons and daughters,
Life is too strong for you—
It takes life to love Life.

The diction and "grammar" of this poem are based upon the contrasts of what occurs before "passed to a sweet repose" with what follows. The lyric quality in the diction of the first part is counteracted and balanced by the extreme irritation in the apostrophe to "degenerate sons and daughters." And clearly this simple break in tone exists to evoke the comparisons and contrasts between generations that is the point. But both of these patterns would be insufficient to carry the poem; it is their combination with the narrative organization that accounts for the aesthetic effect. The compressed survey of biographical details creates in us a certain expectation by its mere weight; the sequential progression of those details through ninety-six years focuses our attention powerfully on whatever is to follow. The contrast comes after long and careful narrative preparation. The epigrammatic ending, "It takes life to love Life," completes and focuses both the narrative pattern and the contrast between generations. It is a summation of the poem, referring narratively to the details of Lucinda's life and contrasting with the implied details of the lives of her "degenerate sons and daughters."

In Wallace Stevens's "The Snow Man," the pattern of organization becomes more important in its convergence of patterns of diction and grammar. (It is true that many people would scan this poem with the "rhythms of free verse," but it is true, too, that here and elsewhere these rhythms are no stronger than the ordinary rhythms of prose.)

The Snow Man

One must have a mind of winter
To regard the frost and the boughs
Of the pine-trees crusted with snow;

And have been cold a long time
To behold the junipers shagged with ice,
The spruces rough in the distant glitter

Of the January sun; and not to think
Of any misery in the sound of the wind,
In the sound of a few leaves,

Which is the sound of the land
Full of the same wind
That is blowing in the same bare place

For the listener, who listens in the snow,
And, nothing himself, beholds
Nothing that is not there and the nothing that is.

The diction here is at once the diction of philosophical statement and metaphorical reference to metaphysical ideas. The statements of the poem force the reader into abstraction, into the processes of thought, while the metaphors and imagery force him into sensory perception. The tension and contention between these two qualities of diction are resolved in the last line, with the listener in the snow perceiving life just as it is, perceiving what Stevens thinks is the only sensible relationship between the two qualities of mind and experience represented by the abstract and the sensory. This perception is neither wholly abstract nor wholly concrete, but both at once; it neither imposes meaning on experience nor misses any that is there, but sees life just exactly as it is; it "beholds/Nothing that is not there and the nothing that is."

The "grammar" of the poem is based upon logic. The opening line is a statement of condition; this condition becomes the first premise of one line of reasoning, which continues through the third stanza, especially the middle line of the poem, and to the conclusion. The opposite line of logic is suggested by the very concern Stevens shows for rejecting it. There have been people—there are people—who are unable to separate their subjective, sensory responses from their environment; there are people who hear misery in the mere sound of the wind, people who "perceive" their sensory subjective states in the scientifically objective, abstract world. Stevens especially disliked this Romantic habit of projecting self upon symptoms. Thus, one can find both premise and conclusion to two logical notions: if man is x, then y follows. The tension and contrast between the two are resolved only in the last line, with the resolution of the abstract-metaphorical movement of diction.

The organization of the poem is thus built upon two situations, each of which is harmonious within itself, but contrasts with the other. The first part of the poem constitutes the preparation for each of these situations or lines of thought; the contention between them whets our anticipation for what is to come, as preparation ought to. From the middle to the end of the poem, the conflict is resolved, first by putting each idea through antithesis, and then by the synthesis in the last line. The contrast between such lines as "and not to think/Of any misery in the sound of the wind," and "beholds/Nothing that is not there and the nothing that is" actually creates the situation of the poem. Each half of the contrast creates appetite for the other. When the contrast is resolved, we feel that the meaning is complete, unity has been achieved, and our aesthetic expectations have been satisfied. All this happens in the last stanza, and especially in the last line. Thus, Stevens causes patterns of diction, grammar, and organization to converge for aesthetic effect.

Rhythm, Diction, Predication, and Organization

Most of the great poetry of the world can be profitably analyzed in the context of all the converging patterns: rhythm, diction, predication, and organization. Shakespeare's "Sonnet 130" * is a case where patterns of meter, rime, statement, metaphor, analogy, contrast, anticipation, and climax all converge to give the poem its particular effect.

You should now be able to point out important convergences in these two highly patterned poems:

Luke Havergal

Edwin Arlington Robinson

Go to the western gate, Luke Havergal,
There where the vines cling crimson on the wall,
And in the twilight wait for what will come.
The leaves will whisper there of her, and some,
Like flying words, will strike you as they fall;
But go, and if you listen, she will call.
Go to the western gate, Luke Havergal—
Luke Havergal.

No, there is not a dawn in eastern skies
To rift the fiery night that's in your eyes;
But there, where western glooms are gathering,
The dark will end the dark, if anything:
God slays himself with every leaf that flies,
And hell is more than half of paradise.
No; there is not a dawn in eastern skies—
In eastern skies.

Out of a grave I come to tell you this,
Out of a grave I come to quench the kiss
That flames upon your forehead with a glow
That blinds you to the way that you must go.
Yes, there is yet one way to where she is,
Bitter, but one that faith may never miss.
Out of a grave I come to tell you this—
To tell you this.

There is the western gate, Luke Havergal,
There are the crimson leaves upon the wall.
Go, for the winds are tearing them away,—
Nor think to riddle the dead words they say,
Nor any more to feel them as they fall;
But go, and if you trust her she will call.
There is the western gate, Luke Havergal—
Luke Havergal.

Eros Turannos

Edwin Arlington Robinson

She fears him, and will always ask
    What fated her to choose him;
She meets in his engaging mask
    All reasons to refuse him;
But what she meets and what she fears
Are less than are the downward years,
Drawn slowly to the foamless weirs
    Of age, were she to lose him.

Between a blurred sagacity
    That once had power to sound him,
And love, that will not let him be
    The Judas that she found him,
Her pride assuages her almost,
As if it were alone the cost.
He sees that he will not be lost,
    And waits and looks around him.

A sense of ocean and old trees
    Envelops and allures him;
Tradition, touching all he sees,
    Beguiles and reassures him;
And all her doubts of what he says
Are dimmed with what she knows of days—
Till even prejudice delays
    And fades, and she secures him.

The falling leaf inaugurates
  The reign of her confusion;
The pounding wave reverberates
  The dirge of her illusion;
And home, where passion lived and died,
Becomes a place where she can hide,
While all the town and harborside
  Vibrate with her seclusion.

We tell you, tapping on our brows,
  The story as it should be,
As if the story of a house
  Were told, or ever could be;
We'll have no kindly veil between
Her visions and those we have seen,—
As if we guessed what hers have been,
  Or what they are or would be.

Meanwhile we do no harm; for they
  That with a god have striven,
Not hearing much of what we say,
  Take what the god has given;
Though like waves breaking it may be,
Or like a changed familiar tree,
Or like a stairway to the sea
  Where down the blind are driven.

PROJECTS FOR WRITING AND DISCUSSION

A. ANALYSIS

1. Analyze the principles of organization in Robinson's "Luke Havergal" * and "Eros Turannos." * How would you describe each? What comparisons and contrasts between the two are possible?

2. Analyze Robinson's strategy of heightening in each of the poems. Any differences? Similarities? Which do you think more effective?

3. Analyze the favorite organizational and heightening strategy of your favorite poet. Then, for balance, analyze the same strategies in a poet you do not especially care for.

B. COMPARISON

1. Try to imagine Emily Dickinson's "Success is Counted Sweetest" * with the strategy of Wordsworth's "I Wandered Lonely as a Cloud," * and vice versa —that is, imagine Emily telling a short narrative about a fallen soldier and drawing an emotional conclusion from the narrative, and imagine Wordsworth stating his theme and working concentric variations upon it. You might even write out new versions. Compare the imagined version of each poem with the real version. What reasons can you suggest for each poet settling on the strategy he or she used? Do you think either or both poems could be improved by a change in strategy?

2. Experiment with rearrangement of some short poems, say Shakespeare's Sonnet 130 * and Longfellow's "The Cross of Snow." * Compare your rearrangements with the poets' versions. What harm were you able to do to the poems? What help were you able to give them?

C. IMITATION

1. Using material of your own invention, say from the exercises in chapter 14, write a poem in which you imitate the strategies of your favorite poet. Then write the same poem in the strategies of a contrasting method.

2. Using your own materials, try to imitate Pound's ideographic method, as described on pp. 374 and 378.

3. Using your own materials, imitate the speed of language that William Carlos Williams often achieved, but do not use the free verse tricks of Williams. Set yourself the task of achieving the speed in various forms: short metrical lines, short rhythmless lines, heroic couplets, and so on. Discover for yourself what role caesuras, phrases, assonance, and so on, play in the tone and mood that you can produce.

D. CREATION

1. Write a pastoral elegy to your grandfather, if he is dead, or to some friend or relative you have lost, or to Death in general. Vary the techniques of verse and poetry with the varying speakers in the poem, and be careful to structure each part, as well as the whole. Try to distinguish sharply, by the techniques of persona, between the different parts of the poem, but be sure that you resolve the differences to some harmony by the end.

2. Write a sonnet, proving a point of your beliefs.

3. Write whatever kind of poem you wish, but write it with consciousness. If these chapters on poetry have been of any use to you at all, you should have less need of a teacher than you once did. You should be able to set yourself your own exercises. Those you set yourself are best and most valuable.

THE
ESSAY
AS ART

THE essay is that literary form which has as its aesthetic base the communication of fact. No one, apparently, has yet been able to explain satisfactorily why we human beings so delight in perceiving fact; yet there is no doubt that we do. From that time in childhood when we begin to separate fantasy from fact, we develop a never-slaked thirst for knowing. Elementary school children cannot seem to get enough of books that tell all about everything; teen-agers, when they read books rather than one another, prefer biography and diluted histories; adults *will* have their how-to books and their newspapers. From youth to old age, we have a passion for facts, and "It's the truth!" are magic words. The essay is the literary form that most caters, and most directly, to this passion for knowing.

Yet, hold two essays up side by side, say a student essay called "Pastoral Elements in Milton's *Lycidas*" and James Agee's "Knoxville: Summer of 1915," and we ought to perceive (or at least intuit) considerable difference between the two. Although the subject of both is pastoralism, their organization, their language, their procedures are so different that they have almost nothing in common. And hold up a third essay beside these, one which a historian of ideas might say completes a triad of essays on the subject, say John F. Kennedy's "Inaugural Address, January 20, 1961," and we can perceive another dimension of difference—a dimension that Kennedy's modification in subject matter does not begin to account for. If you want to remove some of the conscious attempt at being literary from the three types, pick up a newspaper and you will see affinities between the first and the news story, affinities between the second and the feature article, affinities between the third and the editorial.

All three still deal in facts. They do not appeal, either primarily or necessarily, to our experiential mode of knowing, or our dynamic mode, or our meditative. They appeal to our logical mode of thinking, which can separate truth from untruth. "Even a fire-breathing political sermon?" you ask. Yes, even that; for, while it appeals to our passions, our passions are integral to our logical mode of thinking. Knowing must always consist of both knowledge

439

and belief; either quality without the other leaves us inoperative. And, in this, we must hold with Aristotle that good sense will eventually prevail against the demogogue. You cannot fool forty million Freshmen forever.

"And what about the familiar essay?" says someone else; "Does it, too, deal in the logical mode of thought?" Yes, but it assumes its subject matter, rather than asserts or proves it. It is also true, however, that the familiar essay has more affinities with the lyric poem than with, say, the drama. Indeed, at one time, it was widely held that the familiar essay was the province of the poet, and so such people as Walter Pater, John Ruskin, and others, wrote long, marvelous, lyric poems in prose. Make no mistake about it; they are poems. "To burn always with this hard, gemlike flame, to maintain this ecstasy, is success in life," says Pater in his "Conclusion" to *The Renaissance,* and he is inviting us to think upon a relation between ourselves and life, between the individual and the universe; and this particular kind of meditation we habitually perceive as poetic. The familiar essay often dips over into lyric poetry, especially in its style, but its strategy of communication is directed toward the factual modes of our minds.

These three kinds of essays exemplify Quintilian's plain, middle, and grand styles.[1] The plain style, says Quintilian, is best suited to instructing and explaining, and, therefore, its primary virtue is clarity. The grand style is best suited to moving and persuading, and, therefore, its virtues are force of expression and argument. The middle style is best suited to pleasing (to charming, as Quintilian says), or arousing an aesthetic response, and its virtues are attractiveness, gentleness, and conciliation.

The rhetoric of the plain style we know quite well as the rhetoric of exposition. It deals in defining and describing, in asserting and proving, in comparing and contrasting, and in other ways partitioning the subject into those factual fragments that will fit into the pigeon-holes our abstracting, analyzing, and summarizing minds create. The typical strategy of the expository essay is to assert that there are three (or five, or fifteen) aspects to a subject, to define and describe each of them in turn, to compare them with something, contrast them with something else, and, perhaps, conduct a logical demonstration, either inductive or deductive, of their factuality. This is the rhetoric generally taught in freshman composition courses.

The rhetoric of the grand style is also fairly well known. In addition to political and pulpit oratory as examples, we have editorials, advertising copy,

---

[1] Quintilian uses the word "style" much more broadly than we do. He includes both what we would call style and what we would call rhetoric. And he defines it with regard to its aims, not the choices that make it up.

national and international propaganda, and adulation of heroes in Hollywood and elsewhere. Further, the principles of persuasion are taught in courses in formal debate, of which most of us have had a taste. In its classic form, the strategy has six stages: (1) the exordium, which interests the audience and disposes them favorably toward the speaker—what the slick writer would call a "narrative hook"; (2) the narrative, which introduces the subject matter, the problem, and its background; (3) the partition, which offers an argument and a method for proceeding through and examining the problem—what police officers on television would call a *modus operandi;* (4) the confirmation, which argues the case in the sequence promised in the partition, demonstrating the argument's truth and virtue by induction, deduction, analogy, anecdote, appeal to the audience's prejudices (this last one is naughty but common), or whatever; (5) the refutation, in which the conceivable opposition's arguments are presented and refuted, by the same methods as are used in the confirmation; and (6) the peroration, which sums up the argument, excites indignation at the opposition, and invites pity and sympathy for the argument. This compendium of the rhetoric of persuasion is drawn from Cicero's *De Inventione,* which is still one of the best short discussions of persuasion.

No corresponding rhetoric of the middle style exists. When we hold up the aesthetic essay between the other two, we have no set of principles to help us distinguish the one from the others. There are differences. The notes in the next chapter are offered as a beginning toward the discovery of a way to describe these differences. The major clues are these: the middle style emphasizes wit rather than clarity or force, and the rhetoric of charm depends upon aesthetic, not logical, arrangement.

One more objection: cannot the plain and grand styles be aesthetic, too? Yes, of course, they can. Thomas Huxley's "Chess and Life" combines the virtues of the plain and middle styles, and Lincoln's "Gettysburg Address" is both a model in miniature of a classical oration and a well-formed aesthetic product. But our aesthetic response to either combination depends not upon exposition or persuasion, but upon the wit and charm that exist in spite of the rest. Exposition and persuasion are both "useful," but they are not primary components of charm and wit. Those aspects of the plain and grand styles that are *merely* plain and grand are irrelevant in a discussion of the essay as art.

16

Notes on
The Familiar Essay

Suppose you have completed an essay in the middle style and you think that, being artistic, it is worth publishing. The next thing you do is send it to an editor of a magazine, for magazines are the primary outlet for this literary form—indeed, magazines developed historically with the literary essay. After an interval, you get the essay back, with a little note from the editor, or one of his assistants, which says that they have read your essay with care and interest, but that it does not meet their editorial needs at the moment; thank you for submitting. Then you have a small rage about editors who don't recognize quality when they see it, or who can't tell what's good from what's bad, or who use "what will sell," not "what is good," as their index of selection, or who don't know what they want or what would be best for their readers, or whatever. Maybe, after your rage has subsided, you ask yourself what goes into a good essay? And that gives you the idea that you ought to analyze some. So you get an anthology of the best essays of the past (for it's the best, those that have been considered worth reprinting, that you want to analyze and imitate), and you begin making notes on the qualities of the essay.

First Note: It's Got to Be Familiar

Tone

Most good artistic essays are familiar in both tone and subject. Tone, of course, results from the language, from the persona that the language creates, and from the author's attitude toward both the persona and the language. The most common tone is chatty and familiar, but it had better not be gratuitously loquacious. There's a good deal of direct address to the reader, a lot of projecting of hypothetical situations upon the reader ("Suppose that you . . ."), and some taking into confidence. Most writers strive for the qualities of coffee-table or cocktail-hour conversation in pronunciation, word choice, and grammar— conversation that readers will readily recognize; conversation that is relaxed, congenial, conciliatory; conversation that contains enough puns and figures of speech to be, at once, entertaining and perceptive, what an earlier age would have called witty.

But, an essay is *not* a conversation; it's a maneuver in formal communication. And the tone has to reflect that, too. The progression of idea may appear accidental, may appear associational, drifting from one subject to another as it does in conversation, but the drift in the essay has to be controlled; it has to come to a point some time, preferably soon. And grammar in the essay has to be more fully formed and more "correct" than in conversation, where nods, monosyllables, and grunts of assent and dissent link casual and often fragmentary utterances into some familiar and knowable pattern.

Some fragments, or, more accurately, what Martin Joos calls extracts, are permissible in the essay—"a minimum pattern from some conceivable casual sentence." [1] which stands for and communicates that sentence. A good example comes from E. M. Forster's "My Wood." Forster is meditating on, not to say gloating over, a piece of property that he has just bought. He hears a snap and suspects poachers. "On coming nearer, I saw it was not a man who had trodden on the twig and snapped it, but a bird, and I felt pleased. My bird." [2] The extract, "my bird," stands for some sentence like: My gloating, satisfied feeling of ownership extended and made the bird my bird, for he was in my wood. But the conversational extract carries the meaning very much better than a full formal sentence would. And probably carries more.

Northrop Frye points out [3] that an associative rhythm dominated by such short and irregular phrases as extracts is the real basis of conversational speech and distinguishes speech from prose, with its subject-predicate rhythm, and from verse, with its regular recurrence of a beat. (And I would add, regular recurrence of any audible element.) This rhythm influences the tone of the familiar essay not only in free-standing extracts, but also in elliptical sentences, discontinued sentences, and sentences that agglomerate a mass of clauses or phrases through parallelism.

Tone derives, too, from such incidental elements of language as usage—

[1] *The Five Clocks* (Bloomington, 1962), p. 23.
[2] *Abinger Harvest* (New York, Meridian, 1955), p. 22.
[3] In *The Well-Tempered Critic* (Bloomington: Indiana U. Press, 1963).

formal, informal, colloquial, dialectal, sub-standard, and so on. Regional or esoteric words and expressions tend to destroy the familiar tone and make it private; so they must be used with caution, if at all. Sub-standard or dialectal pronunciations, indicated through spelling or grammar, tend to make the tone vulgar; so a writer who uses them has to invest the language with hints that tell his readers that he is posing for a moment, even as we often pose for moments at the coffee table or cocktail party. In this, as in all elements of tone, the persona is poised on a tight-rope; he must be conversational without becoming colloquial and formal without becoming stilted.

The persona's manners help him most in bringing off this act. He must be polite and gentle. If he is forceful, it must be a different kind of force from that of pulpit or political oratory. He inevitably has to explain things, but should never adopt the manner of the teacher. In short, he must pretend to a point of view, not a revelation.

It all sounds pretty neutral, yet the familiar conciliating, personal voice of the writer is his primary tool of communication. The writer attempts to convince the reader in the same way as does the lyric poet. "The essay, as a literary form," wrote Alexander Smith, "resembles the lyric, in so far as it is molded by some central mood—whimsical, serious, or satirical. . . . It is not the essayist's duty to inform, to build pathways through metaphysical morasses, to cancel abuses, any more than it is the duty of the poet to do these things. . . . The essayist is a kind of poet in prose."[4] And he convinces in the same way. He says, in effect, that here is an experience or a thought which has seemed sensible or illuminating to me; I want to share it with you. It is this spirit of sharing information—facts about the world and experience—that most marks the tone of the familiar essay.

Subject

The spirit of sharing affects the subject matter of the art essay, too. Almost all essayists of the middle style assume that their readers are familiar with their subject matter, which is usually so big and so common to life that the essayists are usually right. When Charles Lamb set out to write his "Dissertation on Roast Pig," for example, he assumed—however unconsciously—that his readers would see that he was really talking about gourmet delights, which freed him to talk about a specific delight, roast pig. When E. B. White wrote his "Death of a Pig," he assumed, quite rightly, that his readers would see that the essay was not about a pig, but about our cultural attitudes toward death

---

[4] In his *On the Writing of Essays* (1863). Quoted in *Eight Modern Essayists,* William Smart, ed. (New York: St. Martin's Press, 1965), pp. 369–70.

and dying. Both essayists were able to use metaphors for their real subjects, precisely because their subjects were already familiar to their audiences.

This assumption of subject matter is peculiar to the essayist of the middle style. The orator or debater has to announce his subject, tell what is controversial about it, then argue his case—though often some of these stages are assumed through the operation of such forces as a national or religious mythos. The explainer, or teacher usually is careful to establish his subject, define and refine it, before partitioning it for our understanding. Not so with the familiar essayist. Since his essay is intended to charm or entertain, he uses the same kinds of subjects used in urbane conversation—current topics, recent experiences, common issues, all of which his readers readily recognize.

It follows that he deals a great deal in the evocation of memories. His essays abound in anecdotes, which, when they are nostalgic, deal directly with sentiment for the past, and which, when they are original, are offered as an illustration of concept. It is also common for this essayist to allude to past national events or well-known works of literature, to quote from prominent persons or famous poetry, to use or adapt the proverbs that are as old as the folk. To the extent that the essayist deals in memory and memory-connected concepts, his real subject is the past. And the basis of our interest is a shared historicity.

Some essayists, even some of the best, evoke the past for its own sake. And for ours! Remember the delights of E. B. White's "Farewell, My Lovely," and James Thurber's "Here Lies Miss Groby"? But more often, the past is evoked to make a comment on, to give us a new insight into, the present. Remember here Edmund Wilson's "The Old Stone House" and, most poignantly, James Baldwin's "Notes of a Native Son," one of the most insightful pieces of prose since World War II.

The essay that uses the past to illuminate the present deals in the same techniques—anecdote, allusion, quotation, proverb, and such—but usually injects some contemporary wrinkle into the reference to the past. An excellent example is E. B. White's anecdotal allusions in his essay "Walden" [5] to some of Thoreau's proverb-like passages in *Walden*. White is disturbed by the asphalt improvements of our time and quips that motorists today can, if they wish, "live deliberately, fronting only the essential facts of life on Number 126." Or, he sees a woman, gamely wrestling with a lawn mower, and alludes to Thoreau by saying it looked as if "the lawn was mowing the lady." For those who don't catch the allusion, White adds, "Concord hasn't changed much, Henry; the farm implements and the animals still have the upper hand."

---

[5] In *One Man's Meat* (New York: Harper & Row, 1939), and widely reprinted in anthologies.

Which recalls not only Thoreau's lines in *Walden,* but Emerson's lines in his "Ode to W. H. Channing," as well: *"Things* are in the saddle and ride mankind."

It follows that this essayist's real subject is the present. He manipulates the past primarily because he can depend upon it to be familiar to his audience. He alludes to that which is familiar in order to evoke and illuminate that which is not. He applies old quotations to new thoughts. He modifies our proverbs and impresses them into the service of intellectual discovery. To the extent that the essayist deals in these and similar techniques, his subject is a process of thought. And the basis of our interest is wit.

Second Note: It's Got to Be Perceptive and Entertaining

Perceptive and entertaining. Which are the same thing. Perception, discovery, learning—all delight the mind for some unclear reason. Perception inevitably *entertains* the mind, in all the senses of the word; it demands and holds the attention and it amuses, delights. Nor is there any entertainment, which must secure the attention before it can delight, that is not perceptive. Together, perception and entertainment make up wit.

The Style of Wit

In our time, the word *wit* has generally been limited in meaning to "witticism, amusement, that which excites laughter," but this is only one side of it. *Wit* properly refers to all those intellectual and mental faculties which allow us to perceive new meanings and relationships through the juxtaposition of one thing against another. When the juxtaposition is incongruous and the expression of it epigrammatic, the result is irony, satire, or, if merely verbal, a pun. When the juxtaposition is penetrating or illuminating and the expression economical, if not epigrammatic, the result, being serious and important, is acumen: a new, abrupt, and revelatory glimpse into the nature of the subject at hand. Both the comic and serious forms of wit, and typically both at once, are the index of choice in the style of the familiar essay. We can, therefore, call this style the style of wit.

Style, being the quality that results from the choices among the sounds of the language, among its words, its grammar, its organizational patterns, and so on, can be described with respect to the techniques that produce characteristic effects. Some of the effects of the choices among certain pronunciation, vocabulary, and grammatical devices upon tone and subject have already been hinted at and need not be repeated here. But there are several other techniques, whose primary effect is perceptive or entertaining or both, that ought to be looked at.

RHETORICAL FIGURES

A very common and effective figure of speech whose effect is derived largely from its sound is *paronomasia*. In today's dictionaries, paranomasia is identified with the pun, but, unlike the pun, it is always serious in its discoveries, however small. One invents it in the same way as one invents a pun—by modifying one letter, one sound, one syllable or the meaning of a word and juxtaposing the modification against the original. Examples are the Miltonic "To begird the Almighty's throne, beseeching and besieging," Hamlet's "A little more than kin, and less than kind," and Frederick Lewis Allen's title, "Alcohol and Al Capone." Such arrangements of sound make comfortable mouthfuls and sometimes startle the attention, which is what they are supposed to do. Like alliteration, which is also common in a "witty" style (as Forster's "one permanent victory of our queer race over cruelty and chaos" in "What I Believe"), this manipulating of the audible element of the language heightens and focuses our attention, and thus reinforces the discoveries in such lines as Forster's "I do not believe in Belief," the opening line of "What I Believe," and James Baldwin's "now that my father was irrecoverable, I wished that he had been beside me so that I could have searched his face for the answers only the future would give me now," the closing lines of "Notes of a Native Son."

There are at least three, somewhat related figures, which also emphasize the sound, though perhaps the balance has begun to shift toward meaning. The first is what Lewis Carroll's linguistic expert, Humpty Dumpty, called *portmanteau words*—two words crammed into the same package, the same portmanteau, as it were. For example, that aspect of our universities that is both academic and anaemic might be called *acadenaemic*. Or, the wish-fulfilment adventures of confession literature might be called *romanterotic*.[6] Again, the attention-startler intensifies.

The second related figure is the *reversal,* in which ordinary elements of sentences are reversed—object and subject trade places, or the terms of familiar expressions get mixed. Good examples are the line from E. B. White above, "the lawn was mowing the lady," and George Orwell's opening to his "Reflections on Gandhi": "Saints should always be judged guilty until they are proved innocent."

A third figure so rhetorically charged that it must be used only rarely is called *crossing.* It can occur only in balanced structures, so that the linguistic

---

[6] The young writer should use this device with extreme caution, for it often results in the cute, false linguistic "wit" of a Walter Winchell or a slick magazine.

elements in the first can be "crossed over" in the second, as when the object of the first clause becomes the subject of the second, and the subject of the first becomes the object of the second. James Baldwin's "People are trapped in history and history is trapped in them" from "Stranger in the Village" is an example, but the most famous example of our time, though not from a familiar essay, is President Kennedy's inaugural demand, "ask not what your country can do for you; ask what you can do for your country."

Such verbal figures (and this catalog is surely incomplete) delight and illuminate. They are palpable evidence that the writer "has his wits about him." In reading his works, we share that wit and, thus, forward that spirit of sharing which is the index of tone in the familiar essay.

LEXICAL FIGURES

There are several other common figures of speech which, while still strongly rhetorical, emphasize lexical meaning rather than sound. They, too, participate in the discoveries of wit, through perception and entertainment.

Apostrophe is perhaps the most verbal of these figures. It typically occurs in three forms. The first is the classical, direct address to an entity outside the matter proper of the discussion, as in "Pacification in Viet-Nam means napalm for bamboo villages, fire or mold for grain harvests, grotesque wounds for old women and children; blush, America, for such pacification!" (Here, incidentally, are some of the parallel structures that derive from the associative flow of conversation.) The second form is what is commonly known as the rhetorical question to the audience, when neither the audience nor the writer is expected to answer. An example from Susanne K. Langer's "Man and Animal: The City and the Hive": "Yet we need the emotional security of the greater, continuous life—the awareness of our involvement with all mankind. How can we eat that cake, and have it too?" (And, incidentally, there's an example of a reversal trying to prop up a sickly cliché.) The third form is the public letter, or essay, that is addressed to a person, but is sent only publicly. Examples can be found in the letters to the editor column, the open letter to a prominent or historical person, and in such essays as E. B. White's "Walden" and Virginia Woolf's "Middlebrow."

The appeal of the apostrophe is in the direct invitation to the reader to share in the formation of the perception. Its strategy is based on the inductive process. The writer is willing to give you the reader all the examples you need (and a final direction-giving question) to allow you to draw his conclusion for yourself.

At least three figures that emphasize lexical meaning depend upon irony. *Hyperbole,* the exaggeration for effect, and *litotes,* the use of the negative to affirm the opposite, are the weakest. An example of the first is James Baldwin's use of the word *palace* to describe the incredibly decrepit hotel in "Equal in Paris." An example of the second is the use of "not bad" to mean "pretty good," or "little she cared" to mean "she care not at all." (This one, of course, falls dangerously and easily into what George Orwell called the *not-un-* disease, which can produce such pompous ludicrosity as "a not un-white house on a not un-paved street.") In both these figures, the irony is easy.

A third figure, *zeugma*, requires more of the reader and, thus, has considerably more effect. Zeugma is the use of two words after a given construction, usually a verb, with one word apparently fitting and the other apparently not fitting. Examples: "Waging war and peace," "an advantage they enjoyed and feared," and "a person he loved and avoided." F. L. Lucas combines this device effectively with a question in "On the Fascination of Style": "How many women would dream of polishing not only their nails but also their tongues?" With a little thought, such zeugmas turn into ironic insights, for both words ultimately must fit their positions. And when they do, two thoughts that had never been combined before are suddenly combined satisfactorily. Irony always involves such a sudden juxtaposition.

Another figure that achieves this kind of sudden insight, although it is not usually or necessarily ironic, is the proverb-like quip. A *proverb* is a distillation of a large idea into a quintessential expression of it. *Aphorism, apothegm* and others are related to, and often hard to distinguish from, proverb, the simplest difference being that proverbs are usually of unknown authorship, the others of known. Because it always takes much more space and many more words than itself to explicate a proverb or an aphorism or an apothegm, they are often thought of as essays in little. Thoreau's line "The mass of men lead lives of quiet desperation" is such a figure. Had Thoreau's last word been "satisfaction," as the word "quiet" leads one to expect, or had it been "happiness," which the middle words, "men lead lives of," usually evokes, the line would have been flat and clichéd. The word "desperation" contradicts both those expectations and, since it is a private emotion, introduces a tension against the word "mass," which it takes Thoreau a good part of "Where I Lived and What I Lived for" to explain. But to those familiar with the subject matter, all the insight is there, in that epigrammatic juxtaposition.

JUXTAPOSITION AND THE STRATEGY OF COMMUNICATION

Juxtaposing one thing against another can be done in a number of ways, which, without escaping being rhetorical or lexical, function primarily as the strategy of communication. Among these are *metaphor, simile, irony,* and *parody.* Metaphor and simile are commonly "vocabulary," of course; they limit and define particular meanings through the comparisons and contrasts they evoke. Irony occurs sometimes in individual words, too, but even then, like parody, it is rather a way of joining, not a way of expressing, ideas. Here, metaphor and simile are used in this larger sense—as a strategy of joining the parts of what a writer wants to say. The difference is precisely the difference between a textural and a structural metaphor. Again, the governing index in the familiar essay is wit.

There are, of course, other strategies of communication, which are not without their effect. One often sees, for example, straight expository essays in the general magazines, side by side with familiar essays. But the objectivity necessary in an expository essay precludes the familiar tone we expect of a familiar essay. Which is not to say that expository essays are not good; many of them are expressed with insight and grace and are both instructive and entertaining. But, generally speaking, we ask the familiar essayist to bring to bear considerably more of the personal and familiar—as we have already discussed—than the expository essayist can logically do. This means bringing in personal experience, a personal system of perception and evaluation, a point of view. With the personal note comes the anecdote. Familiar essays abound with anecdote, either supposed and projected, or real and reported. Even the essayist's personal tone tends to make the whole essay feel like one big anecdote. The anecdote, then, becomes one of the first and most important objects of juxtaposition through strategies like metaphor, simile, irony, and parody.

Anecdotes in familiar essays are typically structural metaphors. We have already suggested that E. B. White's "Death of a Pig" is not about a pig; yet the entire essay consists of the anecdotes of worry, consultation, attempted medication, suffering, and eventually death, during the three days (or was it four?) that the pig was dying. The real subject is the worry, consultation, and so on, which the pig's dying evokes. The anecdotes, which make up the entire essay, are a structural metaphor for the subject.

Similarly, George Orwell's "Shooting an Elephant" is neither about elephants nor shooting, though an elephant is, in fact, shot. The shooting of the elephant is an anecdote which Orwell can make to carry all sorts of other meanings—analyses of the imperial personality, of the humanist's response to that personality, of the Burmese people's hatred and personality, of racial attitudes, and so on. His subject is the destructive influence of the British Empire's presence in colonial territory; but instead of using his anecdotes to substantiate assertions, as the expository essayist would have done with what he calls a "support paragraph," Orwell uses the anecdote to evoke the whole subject. His strategy is to use a structural metaphor as his basic mode of communication.

The most important effect of using the metaphor as strategy is in the width of implication the writer can evoke from his reader's familiarity with the real subject. The strategy of exposition identifies the assertion with its proof, identifies the idea with its anecdote; but the strategy of the structural metaphor maintains a separation between the two—a separation which allows and prompts discovery of a resonant and expanding subject. It is often said that it is virtually impossible to exhaust the implications and comparisons in a good metaphor; just so, the structural metaphor builds upon the reader's common knowledge to expand an anecdote into a subject much larger than the anecdote. Such a larger subject always resists and defies an economical, expository expression of it. The juxtaposition of the anecdote against the larger subject allows the perception and entertainment of the larger subject to come through.

The simile as a structural principle operates in a similar way, but less ambitiously. Again, I do not mean the textural example, the simile that is complete in a single sentence, but the strategy of an expanded likeness. It is possible for the simile, like the metaphor, to furnish the structural principle of the whole essay, but it is more common for it to become a paragraph or a series of paragraphs—a smaller part of the whole. An example is Winston Churchill's simile on relations with Russia (relations, the coldness of which were influenced by just such similes!): "Trying to maintain good relations with a Communist is like wooing a crocodile. You do not know whether to tickle it under the chin or beat it over the head. When it opens its mouth, you cannot tell whether it is trying to smile or preparing to eat you up." [7]

Irony is more clearly a method of juxtaposing one idea against another. It always involves an evocation of the situation as it is and a comment upon that situation, either through a direct or implied comparison. This is true even of verbal, that is, textural, irony, but more true of structural irony. In his review-essay of the movie "Carmen Jones," James Baldwin demonstrated with all-pervasive irony that, as his title proclaimed, "The Dark is Light Enough," that the attitudes and myths projected upon the condition of being black were so disparate with possibility or reality that the black man could not know, from his myths, who he was. There is hardly a line in the essay that can be said to be ironic; yet the entire essay is.

In Baldwin's "Equal in Paris," ideas of justice and fairness are juxtaposed against realities of inefficient, rattle-brained bureaucracy; ideas of Christmas compassion against realities of cold, isolated jail-cells; ideas of escape from the self against the reality that the mind carries self with it. The account of

[7] Quoted in F. L. Lucas's "On the Fascination of Style."

personal experience is expanded by philosophical and psychological data until the anecdote evokes the juxtapositions that are the subject.

In "Good Manners," Jonathan Swift criticizes the legislature's and society's manners by comparing without anecdote what they implicitly ought to have done, with the situation as it is. "I should be exceedingly sorry to find the legislature make any new laws against the practice of dueling, because the methods are easy and many for a wise man to avoid a quarrel with honor, or engage in it with innocence. And I can discover no political evil in suffering bullies, sharpers, and rakes, to rid the world of each other by a method of their own, where the law hath not been able to find an expedient." Swift is even more explicit in his comparisons in "A Modest Proposal": "I grant this food will be somewhat dear, and therefore very proper for landlords, who, as they have already devoured most of the parents, seem to have the best title to the children." And, later in the same essay, "this kind of commodity will not bear exportation, the flesh being of too tender a consistence to admit a long continuance in salt, although perhaps I could name a country which would be glad to eat up our whole nation without it." The best modern examples of this technique, and examples in which the strategy of irony is pervasive, include C. Northcote Parkinson's "Parkinson's Law or the Rising Pyramid," and Jacques Barzun's "Myths for Materialists."

The last three essays are all parodies, imitations of the style of something we are already familiar with. Swift's "Modest Proposal" follows fairly closely the Ciceronian formula for a persuasive oration. Parkinson and Barzun both parody learned, expository prose of the sort too prevalent in our textbooks and in the bureaus of our society. All three juxtapose the parodied situation against the familiar one. All three benefit from a disparity between subject and style.

Parodies come in three varieties, which result from the three possible relationships between style and subject. Low burlesque or travesty results when the style is "lower" than would be appropriate to the subject; here the examples are the incredulous slapstick treatments of everyday experiences like getting a tooth pulled or going to an astronomy class. Such treatment is typical of Robert Benchley, S. J. Perelman, and James Thurber at his worst. High burlesque or mock-epic results when the style exceeds the subject; the most famous example is an anecdote in verse, Pope's "Rape of the Lock." Modern examples are hard to find, though perhaps Frederick Crews in some of the articles in his *Pooh Perplex* and James Thurber in some of the sketches in *My Life and Hard Times* come close. Parody proper (for want of a better name) results when the style and the subject are suitably matched, but the arguments lead to a ludicrous, ironic or macabre description of life as it is.

The Swift, Parkinson, and Barzun essays mentioned above are examples; so is Max Beerbohm's "The Mote in the Middle Distance," perhaps the finest parody of Henry James's style and subject matter. Parody proper is the only variety that can successfully spoof the style and the content simultaneously. Again, the perceptions and entertainment emerge from the juxtaposition, but now effect depends not only upon insight, but increasingly upon grace.

Third Note: It's Got to Be Graceful

As with the weather, everybody has a notion of what grace is, but few are able to give any accurate description of it. In the seventeenth and eighteenth centuries, French critics, after what seemed an endless argument, threw over the attempt to define it and said *un je ne sais quoi,* an I-don't-know-what, which actually became the aesthetic term for that inexplicable and apparently ineffable quality of beauty that some writing had and other writing lacked.

Part of the problem, of course, is that what is graceful for one person is not necessarily graceful for another: a graceful way to say one thing may not be a graceful way to say another; a graceful thing in one context may not be graceful in another. Grace, then, is a function not only of what is said, but also of how it is said and by whom. It is also related to the thought, to the persona in the language, to the wit and strategy of expression. Obviously, then, we have already been talking about some of the components of grace in talking about tone, persona, perception, entertainment; and, in a sense, everything that we can say about writing has a bearing on grace. Without hoping to come to any definitive notions of grace, we can still make a few generalizations and talk about some of the linguistic structures that are present in most graceful writing.

Grace is a quality of the texture, not of the structure, of a work. There is writing which one would call graceful, yet which has no overall structure and arrives nowhere in aggregate. This sort of writing is sometimes parodied as the graceful and profitable art of saying nothing at all, and one finds it in our magazines, as well as on the floor of the Senate. And there is writing which is well-structured and highly insightful, yet which is anything but graceful. Grace seems to occur in individual phrases, in sentences, in small places. It is of single thoughts and junctures of thoughts that we can say, "That was expressed with grace."

Impressionistically, we may describe grace as the smooth flow of language and idea, as the happy turn of phrase that melts into meaning rather than calling attention to itself, as moderation and good sense, as the variety and effectiveness of individual sentences and groups of sentences. These impressions nudge at one of the simplest of aesthetic formulas for beauty: "unity in variety, variety in unity." We can describe some of the grammatical and textural qualities of language that give rise to the impression of unity, and others that keep alive the impression of variety. If we describe some of these structures, would we be describing some of the techniques by which grace is recognized?

Coherence

Before everything else, we can safely assume that graceful writing is grammatically coherent—that pronouns have their clear referents, that no real fragments (not the same as ellipses or extracts) are present, that no participials or modifiers are left dangling, that split constructions which may cause the reader to stop and hunt for the parts have been fused, that point-of-view is reasonably consistent in tense and person, and so on. Without such coherence, grace cannot possibly exist.

But graceful writing is much more than good, correct grammar. Indeed, it is possible to have a sentence that is both correct and confused, a sentence that follows the rules of grammar accurately, but fails to communicate its message. Given grammatical coherence, what we are looking for are the felicities of grammar and idea that create the impression of flow, turn, moderation, variety, and effectiveness of phrase and sentence.

Articulation and Flow

Flow of language is enhanced by the use of connectives, by clarity of transitions, by continuity in both sound and idea, and by rhythm. Connectives are the easiest and most disparaged means of creating flow. Such words as *when, if, therefore, nevertheless, firstly, secondly, and so forth* act as signboards to keep the reader on the track of thought. They establish relationships between the parts of sentences, between sentences, between paragraphs. They are disparaged because they are a bit mechanical; one can go back after he has finished and put them in—at least to some extent. Critics of connectives think it would be better if the relationships could be expressed as part of the idea itself, and so it would, but ideas and the words they are couched in are not always cooperative in making the necessary connections between themselves that will keep the reader from getting lost. When such means fail, and this is often, the writer has to supply the connectives to keep the thought flowing from one element to the next. This aspect of graceful flow resides in expression and tone.

Transitions without connectives are perhaps more important in keeping up the flow. These, too, are signposts in the sentence, but now we are concerned with the ideas themselves, not the mechanics of connecting them. If one uses the words or ideas that are the object of one sentence as the subject of the following sentence, he creates a kind of flow from one sentence to the next, which can be effective and efficient, if naturalness, moderation, and good sense are not violated. If one uses the same or similar words or ideas as the subject of several successive sentences, he also creates continuity of thought and unity of expression. References back to earlier ideas can keep the subject in mind and make new predications about it possible. This aspect resides in vocabulary.

Transitions quite outside the grammar are also possible and valuable. These transitions are those which derive from the texture and structure of thought. If one promises a discussion of five specific items, he needs only remind the reader of the structure of his thought when he takes up a new item for discussion. The structure of the thought creates certain expectations which the discussion fulfills. The thought then becomes the basis of transition from one facet to the next. The most common structures of thought include the movement from generalization to specific instance, deductive arrangement, inductive arrangement, associative analogy, and pro and con arguments. By creating unity of thought, these techniques encourage flow of idea. This aspect resides in strategy of communication.

The impression of continuity of idea emerges from just such techniques of thinking, which keep one sticking to the point. Continuity of sound is quite a different matter and depends upon mechanics that can be manipulated—such poetic devices as assonance, consonance, dissonance, and alliteration. Alexander Pope long ago demonstrated in a verse essay how these devices can be made to slow or speed the flow, or to load it with appropriate echoes:

> 'Tis not enough no harshness gives offense,
> The sound must seem an echo of the sense.
> Soft is the strain when Zephyr gently blows,
> And the smooth stream in smoother numbers flows;
> But when loud surges lash the sounding shore,
> The hoarse, rough verse should like the torrent roar.
> When Ajax strives some rock's vast weight to throw,
> The line too labors, and the words move slow;
> Not so when swift Camilla scours the plain,
> Flies o'er the unbending corn and skims along the main.

Assonance, consonance, and dissonance account for a good deal of the effective flow of Pope's lines. Consider the ease of pronunciation and flow in the line "Soft is the strain. . . ." There's not a combination in the line that stops the tongue. Then contrast the line "When Ajax. . . ." The contiguity of *s*'s between *Ajax* and *strives,* between *strives* and *some,* the dissonance between *rock's* and *vast,* the contiguity of *t*'s between *weight, to,* and *throw,* and other features make us stop after almost every word with a tongue-worker. Consider how much smoother and easier it would have been to pronounce "rock's paltry weight" than to pronounce the dissonant "rock's vast weight." And, of course, if one wants, he can boom it out big with a bit of bally-hoo. The manipulation of these devices influences the impression the language gives. This aspect of grace resides in intonation patterns.

Rhythm operates best in the flow of prose when it, in effect, disappears. Verse is an artificial use of language which uses regular rhythm as one of the devices that distinguish it from conversation. But prose is organized on the subject-verb-object pattern and its variations, and the dominant "rhythm" of prose is an irregular movement through subject, verb, and object. When rhythm becomes regular in prose, as it does in a string of prepositional phrases or other grammatical structures tacked one after the other (through a series like this), the prose becomes graceless. The same is true when sentence or phrase length, say a series of sentences of nine words each, is repeated until it produces a regular rhythm. Whatever the length, such sentences become choppy. Rhythm in such a case hinders, rather than helps, the flow; it is probably best when absent.

Naturalness

The turn of phrase is a part of grace, too, and is probably best when it "melts into meaning," as Hawthorne once phrased it. Some of the qualities with which one can describe the turn of phrase are naturalness, position, word-order, arrangements such as the series, repetition, and grammatical voice. Naturalness is the most elusive of these qualities and the key to all the others. It derives from what is common in a culture, and therefore sounds "natural." Natural writing would be writing that is derived from, refined from, speech— writing that uses the current idioms of language, that allows no particular structure to develop into a mannerism or artificial manipulation for its own sake, that avoids what is recognized as a mannerism of a past age, that chooses words and phrases that are ordinary, not those that the dictionary contains or those that are borrowed from a foreign language or a jargon (except when usage makes those natural). Something unnatural sounds when a person uses a word in such a way that its connotations don't fit—a most common fault of people who have "expanded their vocabularies." Yet, the same word in another's writing may be altogether convincing; we may *hear* the quality that tells us he would use that word in this place, naturally. Naturalness, then, consists of first adhering to the patterns of the language, and then adhering to the choices of a particular speaker of that language. And a usage seems most natural when the turn of phrase melts into the meaning, that is, when the expressing and the expression are matched. The quality of fitting is uppermost in naturalness and grace.

But within naturalness of language, there are still some manipulable elements, such as position of an idea in a sentence, word-order, arrangement for series, and the like. We have all been told that a particular idea, say the idea in a dependent clause, can be placed at the beginning, middle, or the end of a sentence with different effect. All three positions can be made to sound natural, depending for naturalness upon the insight or wit and upon the logic of the expression. If the idea in the dependent clause comes before the idea of the main clause in logical thought, it would be most natural to place the dependent clause before the main clause in the sentence. But a rephrasing of the two clauses might make it possible for the ideas to be reversed in position.

Normal word order in English and for most speakers of English is subject-verb-object, but it is possible to write inverted sentences and still sound natural. In fact, inversion is one of the sanctioned means of injecting variety into our writing. Overdone, it can become a graceless mannerism, such as is parodied in "If backward too much run the sentences, will reel the mind like hawks and handsaws." Such inversion for the sake of inversion seems unnatural to most people. But inversion to emphasize and heighten meaning, if meaning is there, is natural and acceptable.

The arrangement of sentences, clauses, and phrases into series is a natural maneuver in English, too. But a series will sound vacuous and graceless when it is empty of meaning or wit. To fill a triad for the habit of filling triads sounds as bad as to use two words where one would do, as in much legal terminology and some slang—for example, "cease and desist." A phrase like "cease, desist, and go away" is surely less graceful than "cease and go away." In each of these manipulable extra-grammatical structures, the index of grace is the contained meaning.

Two "errors" that diminish the grace of a piece of writing are redundancy and the passive voice. Redundancy is not merely repetition, for one can repeat the subject matter of an idea, and even the same words, as often as he has something new to say about it, and not become redundant. The impression of redundancy comes when a writer says the same thing about a subject, either in the same or in different words. We have been conditioned against such redundancy, just as we have been conditioned against the passive voice. The evils of redundancy may be real, but we all know that some things are more gracefully said in the passive voice than in the active. Forcing some ideas into the active voice makes them awkward and unnatural.

Moderation

Moderation and good sense are qualities of personality and of mind, which emerge, too, from the texture of writing. One may liken the first to decorum. It appears in such maneuvers as avoiding quarrels, in being conciliatory rather than overbearing, in admitting and hearing contrary opinions, in avoiding dogma, and so on. These maneuvers of mind have their linguistic expression in such devices as saying "some, not all" and the like. "Fish are scaly beasts" is an overbearing, dogmatic statement that is demonstrably untrue and immoderate and would break the familiar, sharing tone of a good essay. "Some fish are scaly" is a statement that can raise no quarrel. To qualify what one has to say, to bring it ever closer to the truth as a temperate person would know it, injects moderation and grace into expression.

The impression of good sense arises from fairness and judiciousness in expression. This means that ideas that are of the same importance are put in coordinate structures; ideas of different importance are made non-coordinate. Parallelism and the economy it makes possible through ellipsis, balance and the insight it makes possible through comparison, antithesis and the definition it makes possible through contrast, are all important devices in establishing and maintaining good sense. Failures at moderation and good sense contribute to gracelessness.

Variety

Variety and effectiveness of sentences should already be fairly familiar to most people, for style manuals and high-school textbooks usually remind us that there are simple, compound, complex, and compound-complex sentences and recommend that we not use the same kind too much. It's a difficult bit of advice to think of as a "rule of style," for we all know that there are very complex simple sentences and very simple complex ones. And there can be a great deal of variety in any of the kinds—inversions, left-branching, right-branching, or imbedded phrases and clauses, multiple predicates and subjects, and what have you. Still, it is a good idea to avoid using the same kind of structure too often; it tends to become monotonous and to reduce grace.

The same kind of variety is desirable in sentences when we look at them from other points of view. For instance, most sentences in essays are declarative, but it is often effective and enhancing to salt and pepper one's prose with a few interrogative, imperative, and exclamatory sentences. Then, too, sentences are classified as loose, run-on, periodic, or balanced. Too many loose or run-on sentences, while each has its use and effect, will give an impression of intellectual laxness. Too many periodic or balanced sentences will give an impression of artificiality. The choices of how many and what combinations of each are to be used are important devices in variety. Sentences are also long, short, and of medium length; have appositive insertions or pre- or postnominal modifiers; lend themselves to arrangement in series or arrangement for climax. In bundling them up into the structures we call paragraphs and essays, a pleasing variety that causes most sentences to disappear into the texture is more graceful than the use of structures that call attention to themselves. Harsh or dramatic structures that call attention to their ideas are a different matter.

For the ideas expressed are the key to any instance of grace. In a particular instance, grace consists of the best way to say the particular thought; it is the judicious fitting of language to idea. The *fiat* of grace is importance of idea.

Fourth Note: It's Got to Be Effective

We're talking now about total effect, not textural—which means we're talking about structure or "form." Form for the familiar essayist is quite different from form for the expository essayist. The explainer partitions his subject, discusses each of the parts, and stops. If he leaves out something—if he discusses three parts and overlooks a very obvious fourth one that ought to have been central—not only his concept, but his form will seem incomplete. We will be left waiting for more. The familiar essayist, on the other hand, usually has such a huge topic that neither he nor his reader hopes or expects to exhaust it; instead, he works an "angle" or a "gimmick" on the subject, manipulates it to the verge of boredom or silliness, and stops. In other words, form is recognized in the expository essay by the completion of the subject; it is recognized in the familiar essay by the completion of a strategy.

The Structure of Strategy

The typical strategy of the familiar essay has some three to five parts—one has to be indefinite here, because it is part of the relaxed quality of the familiar essay that the writer can often leave out some parts of his strategy. The beginning, middle and end are pretty well set by practice and the necessities of some vestige of logic, but beyond this the parts of strategy are optional.

The most common strategy in the best essays consists of a lead-in, a statement of the thesis, a body of discussion, a climax, and a concluding clincher.

A lead-in is obligatory—at least in magazine practice and probably in good manners. This is what the slick writer calls the "hook"—a maneuver intended to get the reader interested, to secure his attention, to dispose him to listen. The lead-in is most often narrative, which is to say that it is commonly an anecdote. It begins by entertaining, just as an anecdote would at a party or an ordinary conversation, and leads to some kind of point. The personal quality of the familiar essay often gets established in this beginning, because writers tend to select personal anecdotes. The lead-in, however, can have a variety of qualities. It can be history, that is, narrative of a quite different sort; it can be descriptive; it can even be expository or argumentative—whatever form is most economical and interesting for the particular subject. The lead-in should not be long. It must deal directly and efficiently with the background or the situation or the thoughts that lead into the thesis of the essay.

Every essay worth calling an essay has a thesis, but a *statement* of the thesis in the familiar essay is optional. In fact, it is often missing. The writer, in dealing with his familiar subject, apparently assumes that his readers will be able to divine his point, as well as his subject. And when the thesis grows out of the subject, as it does in White's "Death of a Pig," he is safe. The expository essayist fails miserably, of course, if he neglects to tell his readers what he is saying about what—but the familiar essayist can tell or not, as he wishes, or as his subject demands. The expository essayist also has to follow his thesis, usually, with a statement of partition, which becomes the road map through the morass of the thought he is explaining. But a statement of partition is poison to the familiar essay. Editors and writers apparently feel that such a maneuver has so little charm that they simply cut it out.

The lead-in and the thesis (sometimes implied) together make up the introduction, or beginning part, of an essay and often come in the same paragraph. E. M. Forster's first paragraph to "My Wood" is a good example. Forster begins by telling us that one of his books sold well in America and that the resulting income has allowed him to buy a bit of property for the first time in his life. This experience of buying leads him and us to the statement (or, in this case, the question) of his thesis: "What is the effect of property upon character?" This question then controls everything that goes into the body and conclusion of the essay.

The body, of course, is the part that follows the introduction. Here the several points that the essay is to make are developed to whatever extent the writer wants or the material needs. Again, the familiar essay abounds in anecdotes, for an anecdote has the effect of making a point—it is definable as a story that illustrates a particular point of view. Familiar essays also typically include a great many allusions in the body and often deal in deliberately sought and illuminating analogies. Seldom, if ever, does the familiar essay deal with the kinds of definition, assertion, proof, logic, and authoritative opinion that the expository essay lives on.

The arrangement of the points in the body of a familiar essay is often very lax. In the expository essay, the partition gives us the arrangement, which usually follows some logical pattern—natural order, spatial relationship, order of importance, and so on. The familiar essay can use these methods of arrangement—if it can make the fact of the arrangement unnoticeable. Since so many familiar essays contain a great deal of narrative material, their bodies are often ordered as narrative. But it is also common for the series of anecdotes to have no apparent connection in time, space, or logic. This laxness sometimes makes the familiar essay look like a concatenation of trivialities.

The best and aesthetically most durable essays, however, arrange the points in order of climax, which means that dramatic effect, not logic, becomes the ordering principle. Edmund Wilson is one of the most conscientious of familiar essayists about arrangement for climax. In his "Books of Etiquette and Emily Post," for example, he introduces us to the background of etiquette books in America, suggests a dichotomy that marked post-Civil War guides, focuses upon the two most successful etiquette guides in our time, examines Emily Post's book closely. So far, he is leading us into ever more detailed refinements of his subject, but the body of the essay is also arranged for climax. In discussing Emily Post's book, he gives us a general quality of the book, introduces us to some of its most typical characters, recounts anecdotes of some of the more important ones, and finally comes to a detailed account of Mrs. Post's *pièce de résistance,* The Oldnames, whose etiquette controls the conduct of all the others. Wilson then draws the major point of his essay: the connection of Mrs. Post's etiquette with post-Civil War attitudes and the implications of these attitudes upon our lives today. This point also ends his essay, for anything else would be anticlimactic.

The climax and the concluding clincher often coincide, but where they do not, the clincher is mandatory in magazine practice. The clincher is usually a dramatically packed and rhetorically eloquent statement that leaves us with the illusion that something has been said and concluded. It often employs some device from classical oratory that balances, summarizes, and looks forward. Patrick Henry's "I know not what course others may take, but as for me, give me liberty or give me death" is an excellent clincher.

The clincher is, in fact, a textural climax and is often substituted for a structural climax. In Forster's "My Wood," for example, there is no apparent connection or order between the four points of the body, that property makes one stout, avaricious, falsely creative, and selfish. But he manages to wind up the essay and give it a dramatic conclusion with a summarizing, clinching passage: ". . . until I really taste the sweets of property. Enormously stout, endlessly avaricious, pseudo-creative, intensely selfish, I shall weave upon my forehead the quadruple crown of possession until those nasty Bolshies come. . . ."

E. B. White's clincher in "Once More to the Lake" is even more telling in the uses and necessity of the concluding, dramatic gesture. The essay consists of a series of anecdotes about himself and his son, going back to a lake where White had spent many a summer in his youth. The series of anecdotes have no order, other than that of time, and that's not very firm; and they seem to have no point, other than White's nostalgia. The essay is a concatenation of anecdotes that could go on and on. But he brings the last of the anecdotes to the point for them all: as his son is buckling on a wet bathing suit to go swimming again, as White had often done when a boy, he tells us (it is his last line), "my groin felt the chill of death." Without his clincher, his essay would have no illusion of either ending or saying anything. The clincher keeps the essay from just stopping.

Arrangement for Aesthetic Effect

It should be clear by now that the principle of organization in the familiar essay is the arrangement for aesthetic effect, not the arrangement for clarity of expression or force of argument. The principles of aesthetic design are contrast, gradation, theme and variation, and restraint. Conscious or unconscious use of these principles gives the successful familiar essay its impression of unity, its impression of organized variety.

Theme and variation is probably the most important of these structural principles, or at least, the most common. It appears omnipresently in the familiar anecdote. The anecdote that leads in to a subject, the one that evokes that subject, the one that offers a related view, the one that summarizes or epitomizes are all variations on a theme or motif. The principle that knits them together is their common subject matter, which means that their relationship is conceptual. Being conceptually related, they need not be mechanically related.

Some unstated conceptual relationship ordinarily replaces the partition of the thesis in a familiar essay. One can, if he wishes, outline E. M. Forster's essay "What I Believe" and discover that it has a structure of idea that would make a fairly good expository essay. But Forster has left out his thesis and the partition of his thesis, on the grounds, presumably, that such a pose of the teacher would be boorish and would alienate readers from the aesthetic purposes of his essay. There is also logical relationship between the stages of his beliefs, but he has not made these relationships explicit; rather he leaves them to the inference of his readers. His strategy assumes that his readers will be able to perceive his subject, his thesis, without his making it explicit, and that arranging his ideas as variations upon a theme will replace the logical partition we expect in exposition. And it does, of course. Arrangement as theme and variation communicates both conceptually and aesthetically.

The allusion, the quotation, the modified proverb, the choice of common words, the building of metaphors and other figures of speech that seem familiar as soon as they are expressed—all are textural variations upon a theme. In each case, we as readers recognize the theme in our culture—that is what makes it all familiar to us—and are delighted by this writer's being able to put a new wrinkle in that familiarity. Such a textural use of the principle keeps the surface of the writing alive and active.

The principle of contrast operates primarily in texture, though it is sometimes used structurally. It consists simply in a writer noting what he does not mean. This can be done by simple statement, contrasted to the implied statement of an anecdote, for example. Or it can be the use of a contrasting anecdote to fix more clearly what the first is intended to fix; one defines by delimiting. Contrast operates, too, in many of our rhetorical figures—balance, antithesis, crossing, zeugma, and others—and operates in such attitudes toward experience as irony and parody. It is seldom used as a full structural principle, though such use is possible, as is shown by Edmund Wilson's structural contrast of Lillian Eichler's *Etiquette* with Emily Post's in "Books of Etiquette and Emily Post," or his contrast of A. E. Housman as he was with A. E. Housman as many of his critics wish he were in the essay called "A. E. Housman."

Gradation as a principle has not been very important to the familiar essayist, though it would certainly be possible to use it as an organizing conception. Simply, it is the use of a series, either static or dynamic, the members of which share some quality and differ on some other. Riverbank society in *Huck Finn* is such a gradation. So are the repeated glimpses of several levels of society in Proust. Perhaps the ambition of this form of comparison demands more space (and more thought?) than most familiar essayists want to use. It might well be that the principle of gradation would work best in a very long composition, but James Thurber used it successfully at least once in smaller scope: in his "Ivorytown, Rinsoville, Anacinburg, and Crisco Corners," which discusses the social and moral stratification of radio soap operas.

The principle of restraint functions in two ways, which are two sides of the same effect. First, the writer has to avoid blurting out all he has to say right at the beginning. He might alienate the reader with his blurting manner; he might not communicate the effect or the concept he wants because his reader is unprepared to notice it; he might have nothing but anticlimax to follow. Restraint means avoiding oversaying a thing, as in bombast, or avoiding saying a thing until the time is right for it. This, of course, brings in the other side of the effect—the arrangement for climax, or for order of importance, or for logical demonstration, or whatever. Such arrangements involve a strategy of conserving the reader's responses until those responses can be maximized. Restraining yourself from saying all you have to say on a point can whet the reader's anticipation for what you finally say. This is both structural and aesthetic preparation. It allows you to put your best words in the best places.

The style and rhetoric of the aesthetic essay, then, are characterized by familiarity, by wit, by grace, and by structural effect. Editors to whom we submit our supposed and real essays look for these qualities, consciously or unconsciously, and they reject the essay that does not have all of them.

None of these qualities is necessary to either the persuasive or the expository essay, though those persuasions and expositions are best that are also aesthetically sound. There is no reason why the partitioning and body of either an oration or an explanation should not be expressed with grace and wit, no reason that they should not be familiar and effective. Our politics, churches, and classrooms could benefit from a bit of enjoyable expression.

In our time, there has been a strong impetus toward the essay as a primary form of literary expression. It is sometimes said that the essay has been the dominant creative form in the United States since World War II. Perhaps so. Certainly, several of our literary figures have had their most succesful expression in the essay; one thinks of Norman Mailer, James Baldwin, Ralph Ellison, among others. In fact, our impetus toward the essay has been so strong that the monthly, popular magazines nowadays often include straight expository essays, which, however clear, are not always well expressed. With a good deal of conscious study and effort, we might yet make this the age of the essay as a literary form.

PROJECTS FOR WRITING AND DISCUSSION

A. ANALYSIS

1. There are several kinds of familiar essays, not discussed or defined here. Analyze a number of them and see if you can isolate a set of principles for each. For instance, you might read a number of character sketches or profiles such as appear in the *New Yorker, Atlantic, Harper's,* and elsewhere. What characteristics do they share? How do they differ from obituaries in the New York *Times* or in *Time* magazine?

2. Analyze a number of "letter" essays, such as E. B. White's "Walden" and Virginia Woolf's "Middlebrow." What do they share? What do they share with ordinary letters? With expository essays? With political or church oratory?

3. Analyze a number of essays that are primarily descriptive rather than narrative or anecdotal. You might look for some in travel magazines, though travel articles have a tendency to be personal narratives. Again, what characteristics identify this sort of essay?

4. Analyze a number of philosophical or reflective essays, such as E. M. Forster's "What I Believe." What rhetorical devices do people taking and defending a "stand" favor, if any?

5. Analyze a number of "informative articles" in the monthly magazines—that is, the articles that are admittedly expository. What elements of aesthetic felicity do they tend to use, if any?

B. COMPARISON

1. Analyze some of the historical essayists—Charles Lamb, Walter Pater, John Ruskin—and compare your results with contemporary practice in the essay.

2. Both Edmund Wilson, in such an essay as "The Old Stone House," and E. B. White, in such a piece as "Once More to the Lake," use personal narrative and nostalgia as basic elements of communication, but with quite different effects. Analyze and compare these two, or two similar essays. Can you arrive at any statement of principle about the use of nostalgia?

3. Compare some of James Baldwin's narratives in such essays as "Equal in Paris," "Notes of a Native Son," and "Stranger in the Village" with fictional narratives. What makes one kind of narrative fictional and another kind essayistic?

4. Compare Edmund Wilson's "A. E. Housman" with a scholarly essay on Housman. Are there significant differences in the insight in the two kinds of writing? What makes one familiar and the other scholarly?

5. What are the differences between a book review and a familiar essay? Can the two be combined? How? Formulate a set of principles about what a book review ought to do and the best way of achieving those ends.

C. *IMITATION*

1. Our memories are made up of significant dramatic moments, which are remembered because they seem more meaningful, more exemplary, than ordinary experience. Write a personal narrative of a dramatic moment in your life in the style of say, James Baldwin.

2. Write a more objective account of the same moment, focused on the general rather than the personal, so that the essay becomes what might happen to one of your readers.

3. Write a nostalgic account of the same event, in the manner of, say, Max Beerbohm.

4. Write a satiric account in the manner of James Thurber.

5. John Gunther has developed a formula in his "Inside—" literature. Analyze, criticize, imitate, and improve his formula if you can. Be careful in such imitations, for the danger is that you will fall unwittingly into parody. If you intend parody, that is another matter and not dangerous at all.

D. *CREATION*

1. Choose an expository essay from a magazine that you have found insightful, but not especially graceful, and rewrite it as a familiar essay.

2. Benjamin Franklin claimed in his *Autobiography* that he developed his style by rewriting some of the *Spectator* papers of Addison and Steele, and he even suggested whimsically that he improved some of them. Set yourself the same exercise.

3. Make a news account of some dimension into an artistic essay. Many examples of extended reportage, as reports of race riots and major events like elections, verge on the techniques of the familiar essay. Choose a subject that lends itself to treatment in an essay, use the newspaper as your research source, and write a good essay.

4. Write a parody of an expository style that you are familiar with. Or write one of a style you have to analyze first. Such imitative creation can help you to avoid undesirable "influences" on your own style.

5. Ask yourself what goes into a good travel article; then write an account of a trip that you took. Choose a trip to a place that is inherently *un*interesting, is very familiar to the audience, or has some other disadvantage to it, so that you will have to find a new angle or gimmick to enliven recalcitrant material.

Index

Author Index to Reprinted Matter

Below is an alphabetical index, by author, of all anthologized material in this text. It will provide quick location for all cross references, which appear particularly in Projects for Writing and Discussion. Asterisks after such cross references indicate inclusion of the author and title in this index.